drama and **desire**

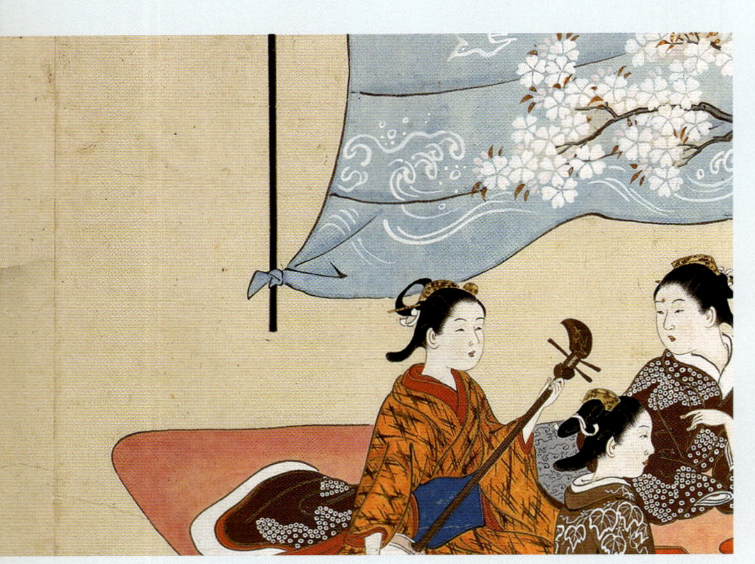

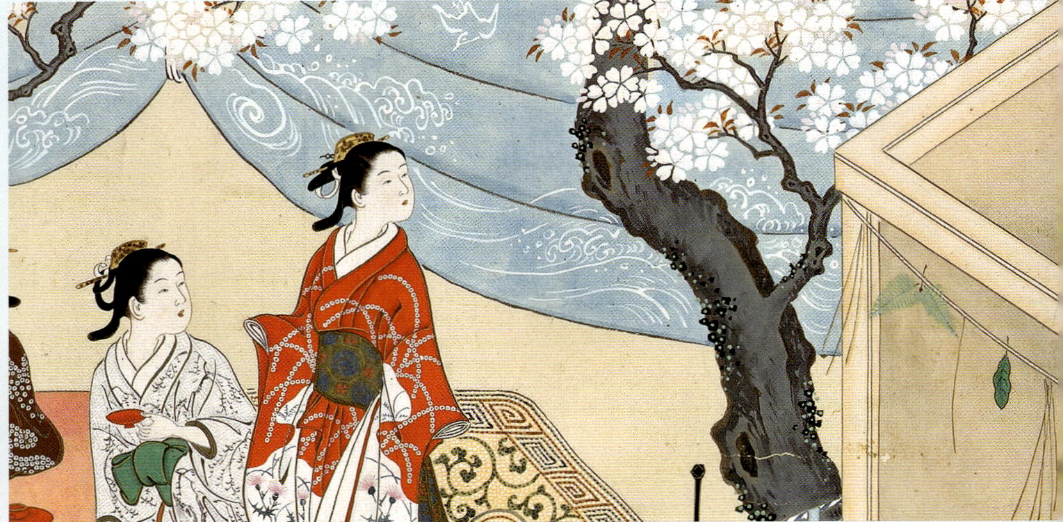

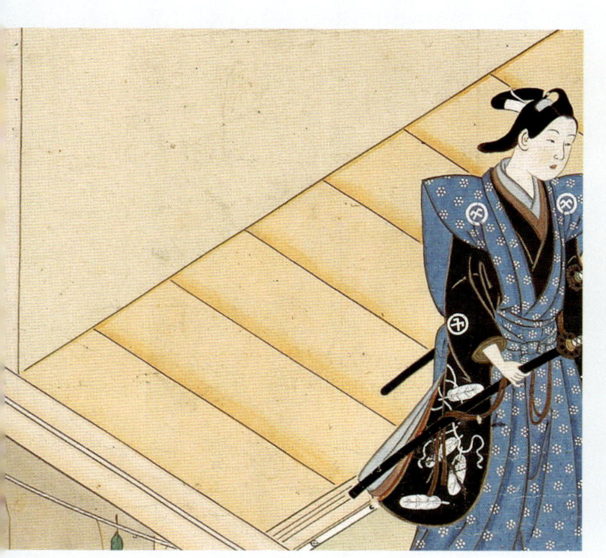

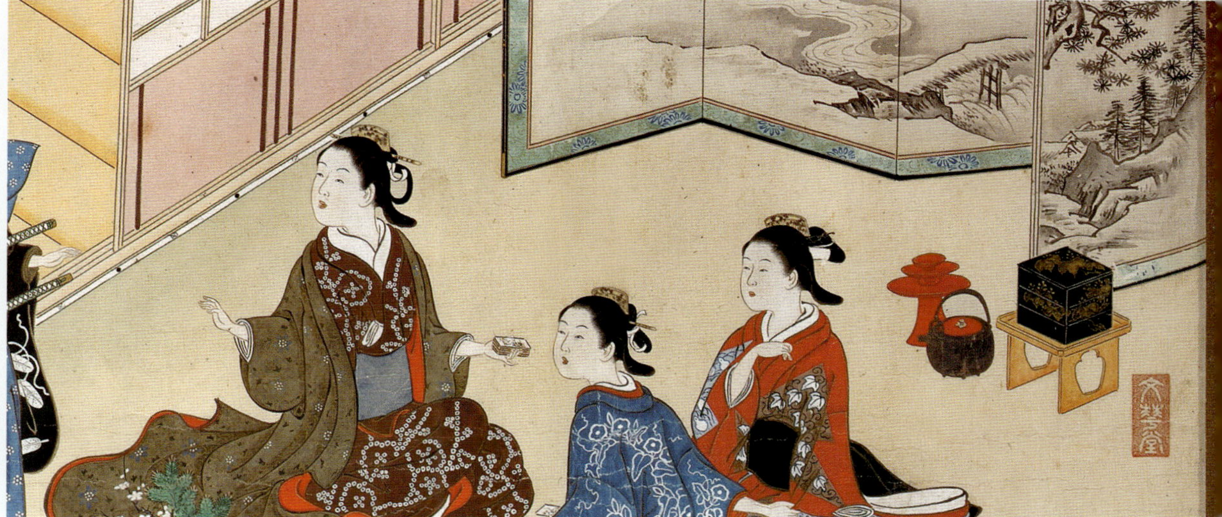

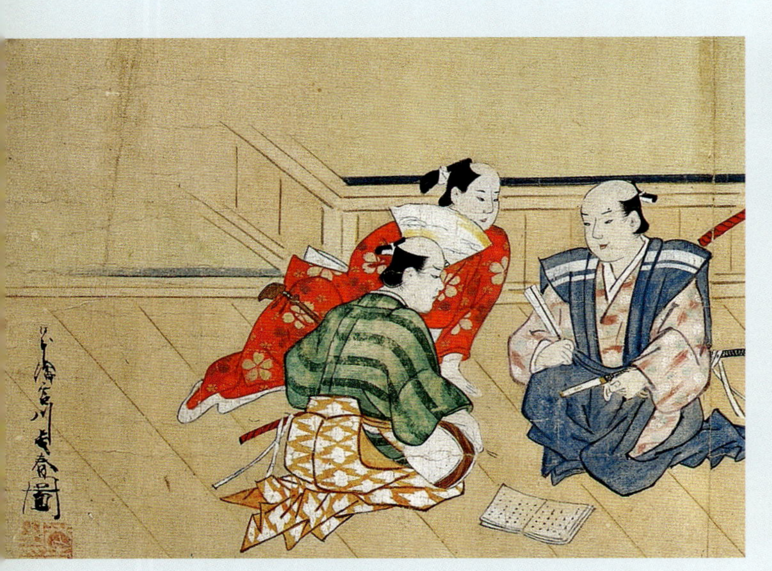

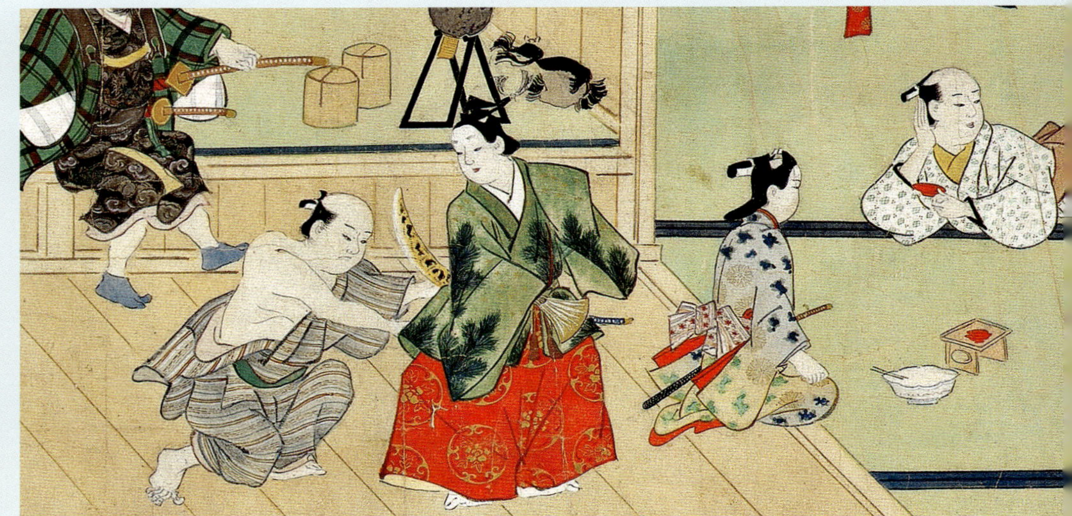

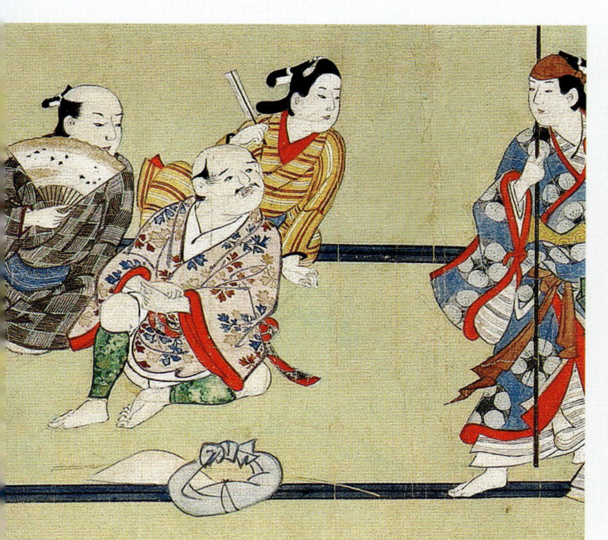
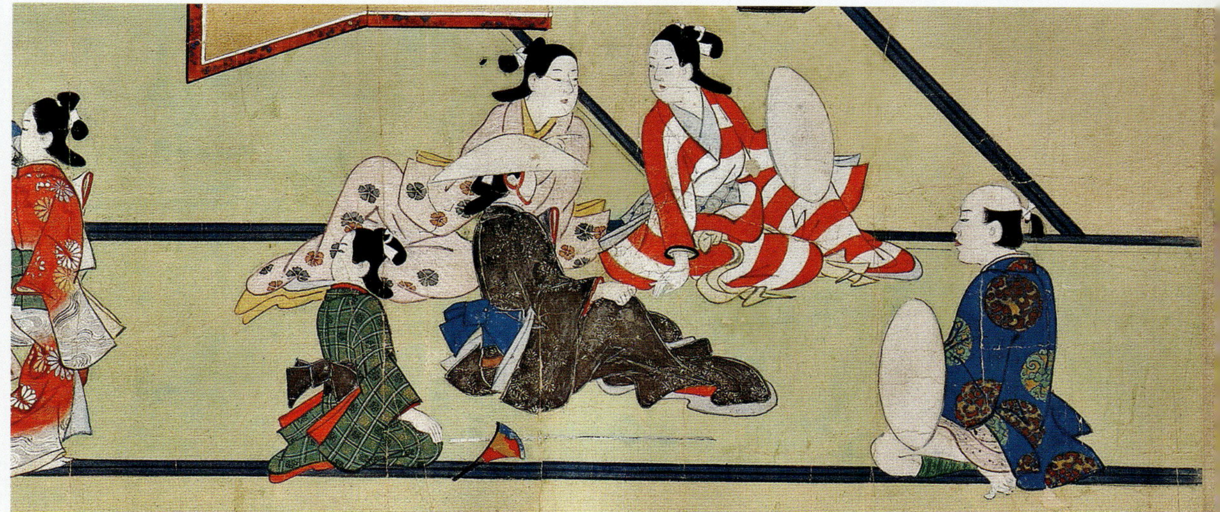

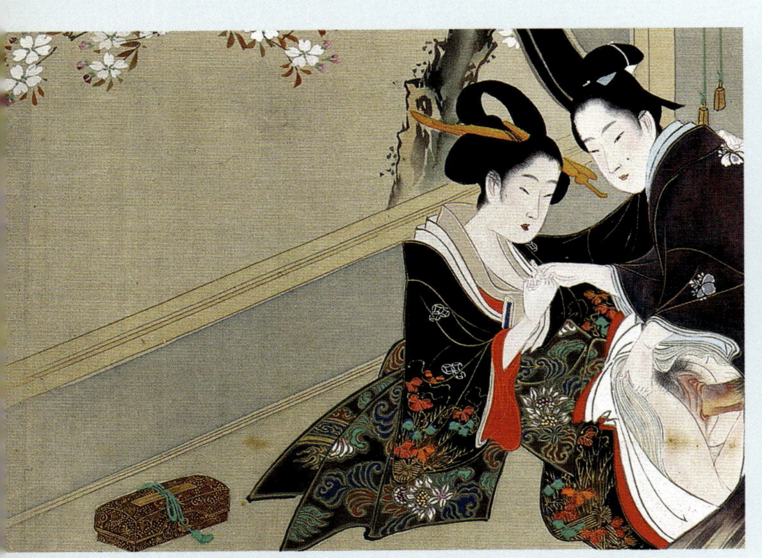

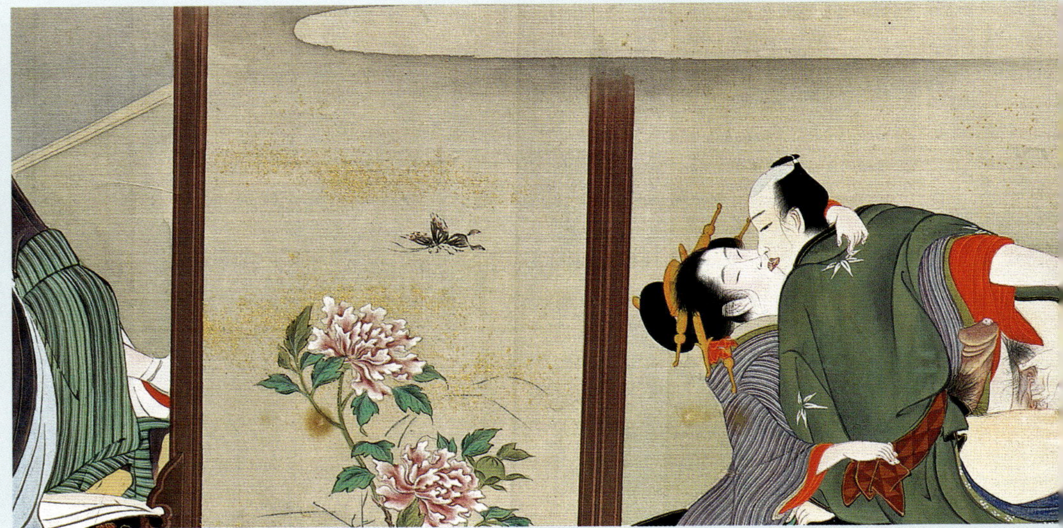

. . . Living only for the moment,

turning our full attention to the pleasures of the moon,

the snow, the cherry blossoms and the maple leaves;

singing songs, drinking wine, diverting ourselves

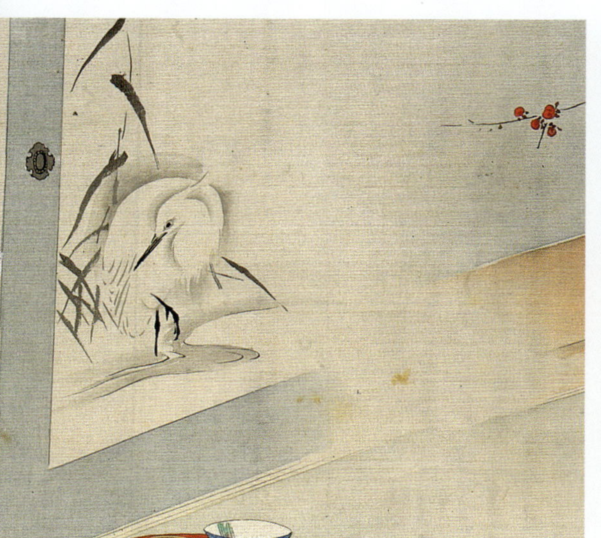

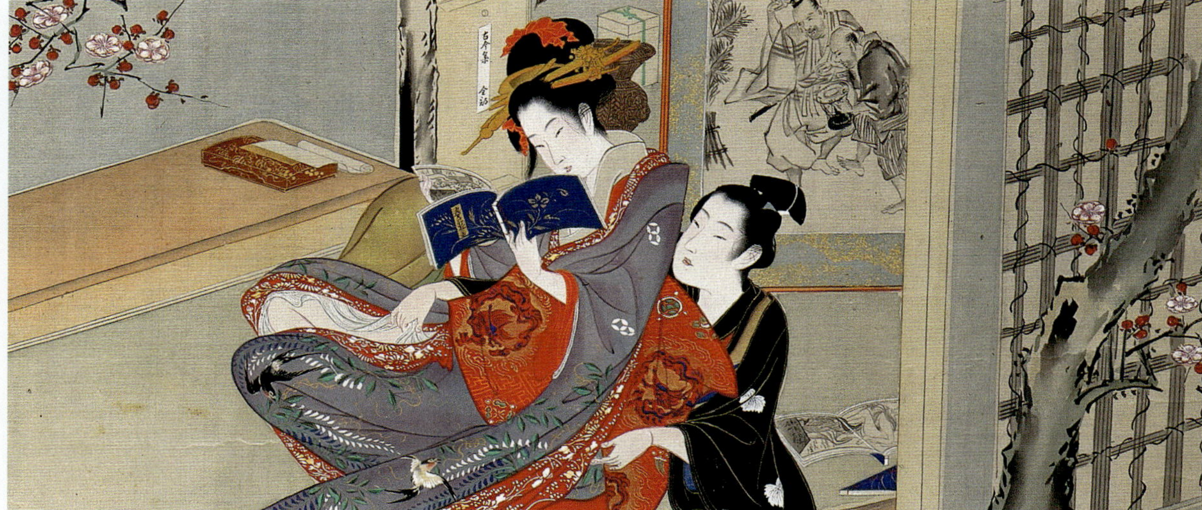

in just floating, floating;

caring not a whit for the pauperism

staring us in the face,

refusing to be disheartened,

like a gourd floating along with the river current:

this is what we call the floating world . . .

ASAI RYŌI Tale of the Floating World

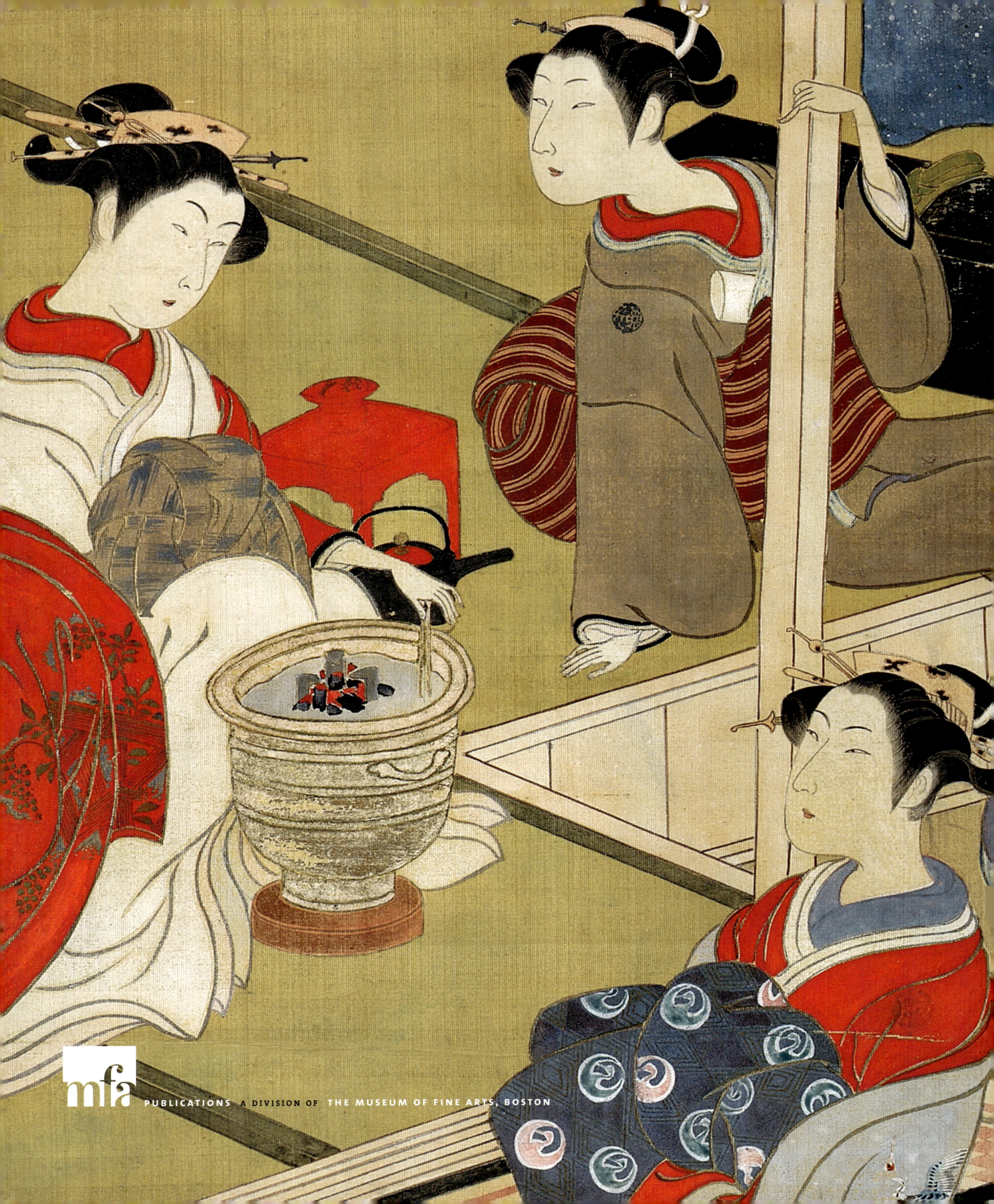

mfa PUBLICATIONS A DIVISION OF THE MUSEUM OF FINE ARTS, BOSTON

drama and **desire**

JAPANESE PAINTINGS FROM THE FLOATING WORLD, 1690–1850

EDITED BY **ANNE NISHIMURA MORSE**

WITH CONTRIBUTIONS BY ASANO SHŪGŌ, HOWARD HIBBETT, KOBAYASHI TADASHI, NAITŌ MASATO, TSUJI NOBUO

MFA PUBLICATIONS
a division of the Museum of Fine Arts, Boston
465 Huntington Avenue, Boston, Massachusetts 02115
www.mfa-publications.org

Published in conjunction with the exhibition in Japan **"Edo no yūwaku: Bosuton bijutsukan shozō nikuhitsu ukiyo-e ten" (The Allure of Edo: Ukiyo-e Painting from the Museum of Fine Arts, Boston),** and in North America **"Drama and Desire: Japanese Paintings from the Floating World, 1690–1850,"** organized by the Museum of Fine Arts, Boston, and made possible by Fidelity Investments and Fidelity International through the Fidelity Foundation.

Kobe City Museum
April 15–May 28, 2006
Nagoya/Boston Museum of Fine Arts
June 17–August 27, 2006
Edo-Tokyo Museum
October 21–December 10, 2006
Kimbell Art Museum
February 11–April 29, 2007
Royal Ontario Museum
May 18–August 12, 2007
Museum of Fine Arts, Boston
August 28–December 16, 2007
Asian Art Museum of San Francisco
February–April, 2008

Generous support for this publication was provided by the Andrew W. Mellon Publications Fund.

For a complete listing of MFA Publications, please contact the publisher at the above address, or call 617-369-3438.

ISBN 0-978-0-87846-710-5 (hardcover)
ISBN 0-978-0-87846-711-2 (softcover)
Library of Congress Control Number: 2006934965

All photographs are by Kodansha Ltd.
unless noted otherwise.

Manuscript edited by Emiko K. Usui
Copyedited by Dalia Geffen
Produced by Terry McAweeney
Designed by Lucinda Hitchcock
Typesetting by Matt Mayerchak

Available through D.A.P. / Distributed Art Publishers
155 Sixth Avenue, 2nd floor, New York, New York 10013
Tel.: 212 627 1999 · Fax: 212 627 9484

FIRST EDITION
Printed on acid-free paper
Printed and bound in Italy
Cover art: Katsushika Hokusai, *Woman Looking at Herself in a Mirror* (detail from page 200)

Translation and adaptation from Japanese-language manuscripts unless noted otherwise: Kobayashi Tadashi's essay and Naitō Masato's essay by Emiko K. Usui; Asano Shūgō's essay by Anne Nishimura Morse; catalogue entries by Anne Nishimura Morse with the assistance of Akiko Walley; and inscriptions by Joe Earle and Sarah E. Thompson.

Some texts in this catalogue were adapted from *Edo no yūwaku: Bosuton bijutsukan shozō nikuhitsu ukiyo-e ten* (Tokyo: Asahi shinbunsha, 2006). Naitō Masato's essay was partially adapted from Naitō Masato, *Ukiyo-e saihakken: Daimyō-tachi ga medeta ippin, zeppin* (Tokyo: Shōgak-kan, 2005), with permission of the publisher.

Catalogue entries 1, 5, 8, and 13 are adapted from *The Dawn of the Floating World, 1650–1765: Early Ukiyo-e Treasures from the Museum of Fine Arts, Boston* (London: Royal Academy of Arts, 2001), with permission of the publisher.

Poem on page 7 by Asai Ryōi, *Tale of the Floating World*, translation by Richard Lane, *Images from the Floating World* (Secaucus, NJ; Chartwell Books 1978), 11.

CONTENTS

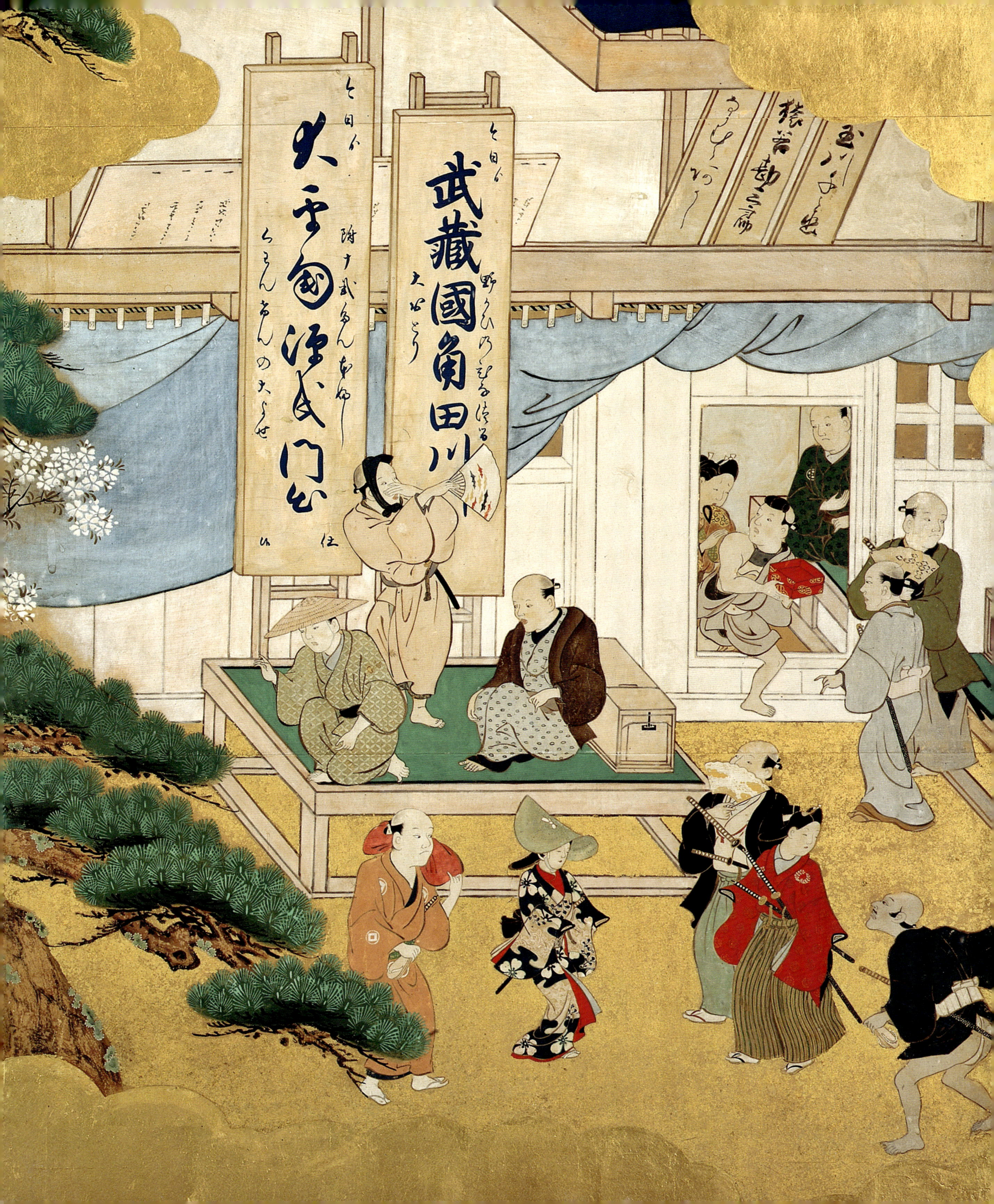
武蔵國角田川

DIRECTOR'S FOREWORD

Westerners have been fascinated by depictions of Japan's "floating world," the world of the theaters and brothel districts, since the mid-nineteenth century. Under the influence of such images, called ukiyo-e, the Impressionist painter Claude Monet even portrayed his wife as a Japanese dancing girl in *La Japonaise* (1876), now in the collection of the Museum of Fine Arts, Boston. Contemporary European and American connoisseurs were eager to form extensive collections of ukiyo-e, but their access was primarily limited to woodblock prints. The costly, individualized paintings of the type displayed in this exhibition were relatively rare outside Japan.

In light of this, the MFA is particularly fortunate to have amassed one of the largest and most comprehensive collections of these important paintings. Largely acquired through the efforts of Boston physician William Sturgis Bigelow (1850–1926) during his residence in Japan in the late nineteenth century, the Museum's holdings of ukiyo-e paintings number over seven hundred works. Included are exquisite paintings by all of the major masters from the seventeenth through the mid-nineteenth centuries. "Drama and Desire" represents the first exhibition to highlight this collection.

We would like to express our appreciation to the team of Japanese scholars led by Professor Tsuji Nobuo who, through a grant from the Kajima Foundation for the Arts, first participated ten years ago with members of the Museum's curatorial staff in a collaborative study of our ukiyo-e painting collection. They have been most supportive of the Museum's efforts to make these works accessible via publication and exhibition. We are also thankful for the generous funding provided by Fidelity Investments through the Fidelity Foundation, which made it possible for the Museum's Asian Conservation Studio to undertake the extensive conservation work many of the paintings required.

The Museum of Fine Arts, Boston, is pleased to be able to offer Japanese art lovers the opportunity to view more than eighty of the finest and most intriguing masterpieces of ukiyo-e painting. We hope that this exhibition will greatly enrich an understanding of this highly sophisticated art of the floating world.

Malcolm Rogers
Ann and Graham Gund Director
MUSEUM OF FINE ARTS, BOSTON

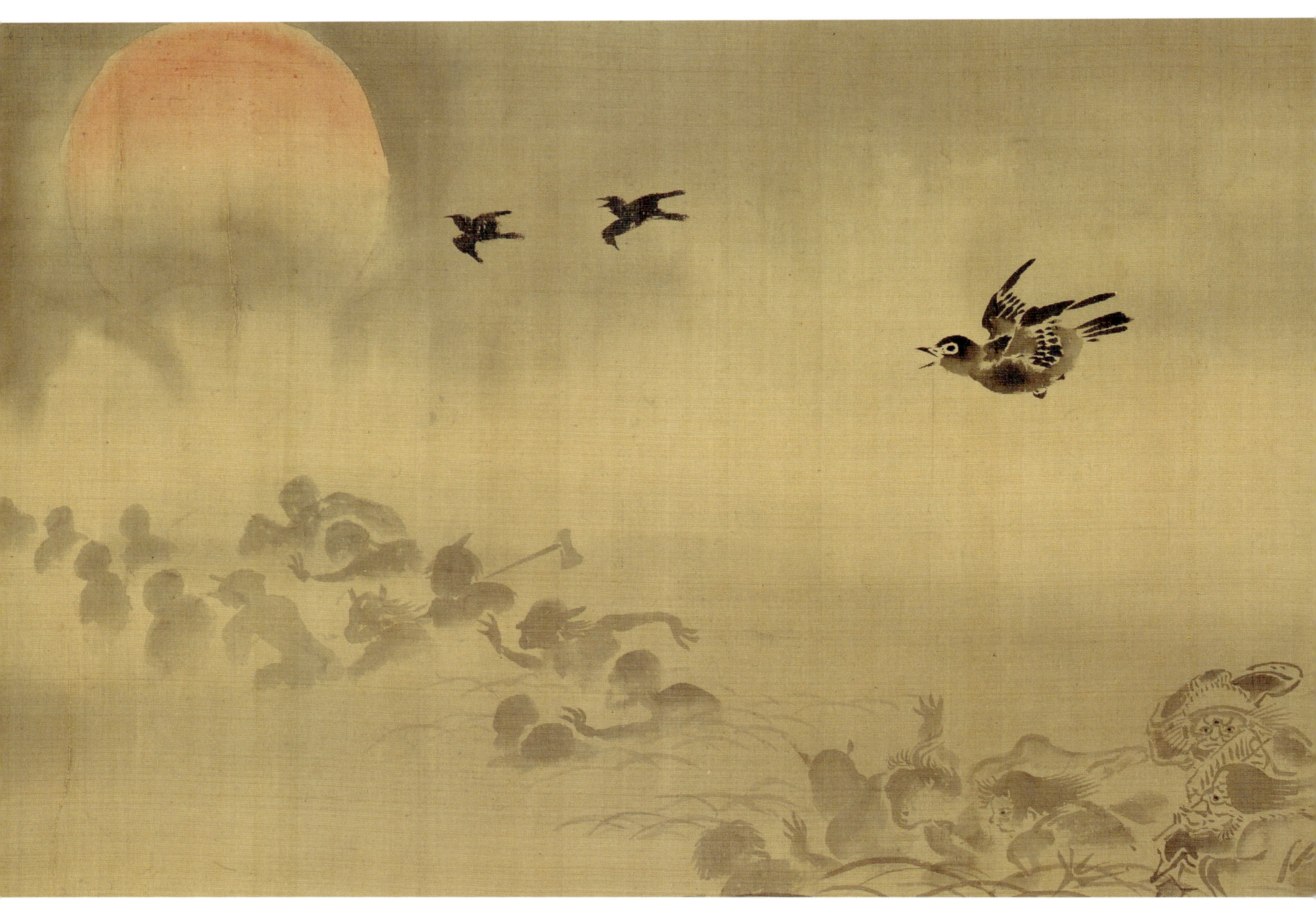

ACKNOWLEDGMENTS

The genesis for "Drama and Desire" took place over fifteen years ago, when Tsuji Nobuo, Professor Emeritus at the University of Tokyo and now Director of the Miho Museum, first encouraged the Museum of Fine Arts to make an application to the Kajima Foundation for the Arts for a collaborative study of the Japanese painting and decorative art collections. From 1991 to 2005, through the sustained generosity and support of Dr. Kajima Shōichi and the Foundation, twenty-eight scholars traveled to Boston to study more than four thousand paintings, sculptures, textiles, masks, and lacquer works—works that had not been systematically reviewed since the early twentieth-century tenure of Okakura Kakuzō. Photographs were taken of each object and bilingual catalogues published to make the Museum's Japanese holdings available both to scholars and interested members of the general public.

During the summers of 1996 and 1997 Professor Tsuji was joined by Kobayashi Tadashi, Professor at Gakushūin University and Director of the Chiba City Museum; Asano Shūgō, Chief Curator of the Chiba City Museum; and Naitō Masato, Chief Curator at the Idemitsu Museum of Arts. Timothy Clark, now Head of the Japanese Section at the British Museum, also came from London for several weeks to take part in the cataloging of the ukiyo-e painting collection. Almost immediately the depth and breadth of the Museum's astonishing holdings became apparent; they truly form the best collection of their type anywhere in the world.

We would like to express our heartfelt appreciation to this team of scholars, who have always been immensely supportive throughout the years of preparation for publications in scholarly journals, a multivolume illustrated series of books, and now this exhibition and catalogue. Deep gratitude is also offered to the many individuals at the Museum of Fine Arts who have helped launch "Drama and Desire": Danielle Berger, Helen Connor, Jennifer Cooper, Karen Gausch, Katie Getchell, Claudia Iannuccilli, Tomomi Itakura, Sonia Janks, Jill Kennedy-Kernohan, Debra Lakind, David Matthews, Terry McAweeney, Meredith Montague, Jessica Nemczuk, Richard Newman, Pamela Parmal, Mark Polizzotti, Jennifer Riley, Malcolm Rogers, Rachel Saunders, Joseph Scheier-Dolberg, Hao Sheng, Angie Simonds, Jodi Simpson, David Sturtevant, Ben Weiss, and John Woolf.

Particular thanks are given to Joe Earle and Sarah E. Thompson, who enthusiastically offered to translate the painting inscriptions, and to Travis Seifman, who assisted with the glossary. We are very grateful to past and present members of the Asian Painting Conservation Studio—Jacki Elgar, Jo-fan Huang, Philip Meredith, Kim Nichols, John Robbe, Tanya Uyeda, and Joan Wright—who with the support of the Fidelity Foundation ably and patiently prepared the works of art so that they could be seen to their best advantage.

In addition we would like to acknowledge the tremendous contributions by Lucy Hitchcock, Inoue Hitomi, Komiya Keiko, Kurohashi Masae, Marumoto Shin'ichi, Mino Mamoru, Morita Miki, Samuel C. Morse, Midori Oka, Shima Masaru, Akiko Walley, Yamauchi Keisuke, and Yamauchi Tatsuya. Finally a personal expression of sincere appreciation to Emiko K. Usui, who, first as my research assistant, participated in the original survey of the ukiyo-e paintings and, now as translator and manuscript editor, has helped bring this project to completion.

Anne Nishimura Morse
Curator of Japanese Art: Art of Asia, Oceania, and Africa
MUSEUM OF FINE ARTS, BOSTON

NOTE TO THE READER

EDO-PERIOD ERAS

The Japanese followed a lunar calendar throughout the Edo period. Therefore, era years may overlap when noted according to the Gregorian calendar as follows:

GENNA	1615–24
KAN'EI	1624–44
SHŌHŌ	1644–48
KEIAN	1648–52
JŌŌ	1652–55
MEIREKI	1655–58
MANJI	1658–61
KANBUN	1661–73
ENPŌ	1673–81
TENNA	1681–84
JŌKYŌ	1684–88
GENROKU	1688–1704
HŌEI	1704–11
SHŌTOKU	1711–16
KYŌHŌ	1716–36
GENBUN	1736–41
KANPŌ	1741–44
ENKYŌ	1744–48
KAN'EN	1748–51
HŌREKI	1751–64
MEIWA	1764–72
AN'EI	1772–81
TENMEI	1781–89
KANSEI	1789–1801
KYŌWA	1801–04
BUNKA	1804–18
BUNSEI	1818–30
TENPŌ	1830–44
KŌKA	1844–48
KAEI	1848–54
ANSEI	1854–60
MAN'EN	1860–61
BUNKYŪ	1861–64
GENJI	1864–65
KEIŌ	1865–68

NAMES

All Japanese and Chinese names appear in traditional style, with surnames preceding the given names, or in some cases the artistic names. Subsequent mentions use the artistic name if the person referred to is an artist; otherwise they use the surname.

PERIODS AND ERAS

Heian period (794–1185)
Kamakura period (1185–1333)
Nanbokuchō period (1333–1392)
Muromachi period (1392–1568)
Momoyama period (1568–1615)
Edo or Tokugawa period (1615–1868)
Meiji era (1868–1912)

CATALOGUE

artist Works are arranged by artist, generally following the chronological sequence of their careers.

title The titles of the paintings in this catalogue were assigned not by the artists but by participants in the survey of the MFA collection sponsored by the Kajima Foundation for the Arts.

date When a specific date can be assigned to a work of art, the Japanese-era name and year are provided with the Gregorian date in parentheses. When only a broad date range can be assigned to a painting, this catalogue follows Japanese scholarly practice by identifying the era in which it was created.

media The current format of the painting (which in some cases differs from the original format) is followed by a description of the materials used in the work.

dimensions Height precedes width. The dimensions refer to the size of the painted image (without its mounting).

signature Transcriptions of the signature and seal(s) are given with translations in parentheses.

collection All works in the catalogue are from the holdings of the Museum of Fine Arts, Boston. The collection name refers to the donor(s) or the manner in which the Museum acquired the painting. The accession number that follows is used by the Museum for inventory and identification.

references Footnote citations of translations and illustrations were added by the editor.

authors

ANM	Anne Nishimura Morse
AS	Asano Shūgō
KT	Kobayashi Tadashi
NM	Naitō Masato
TN	Tsuji Nobuo

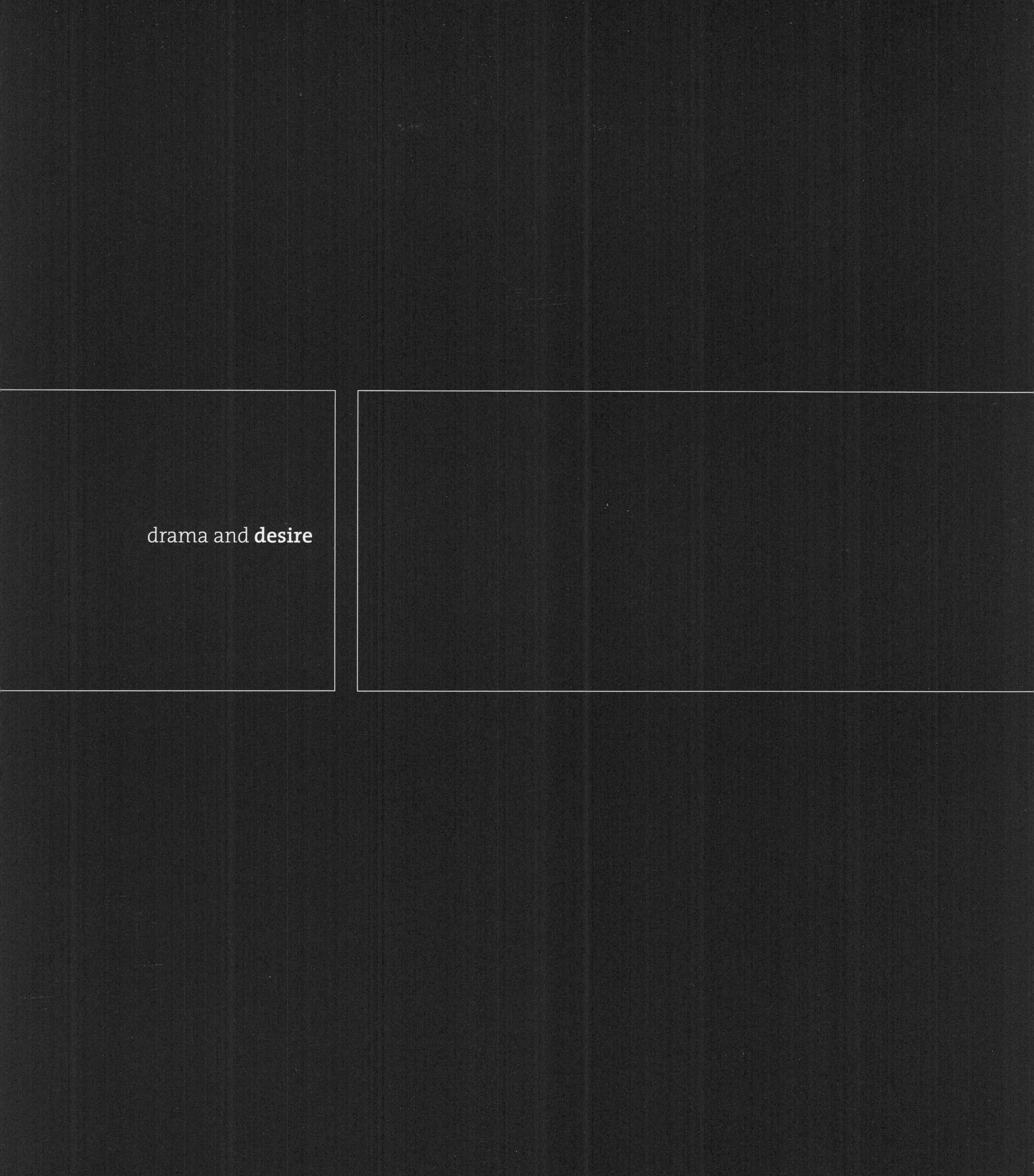

drama and **desire**

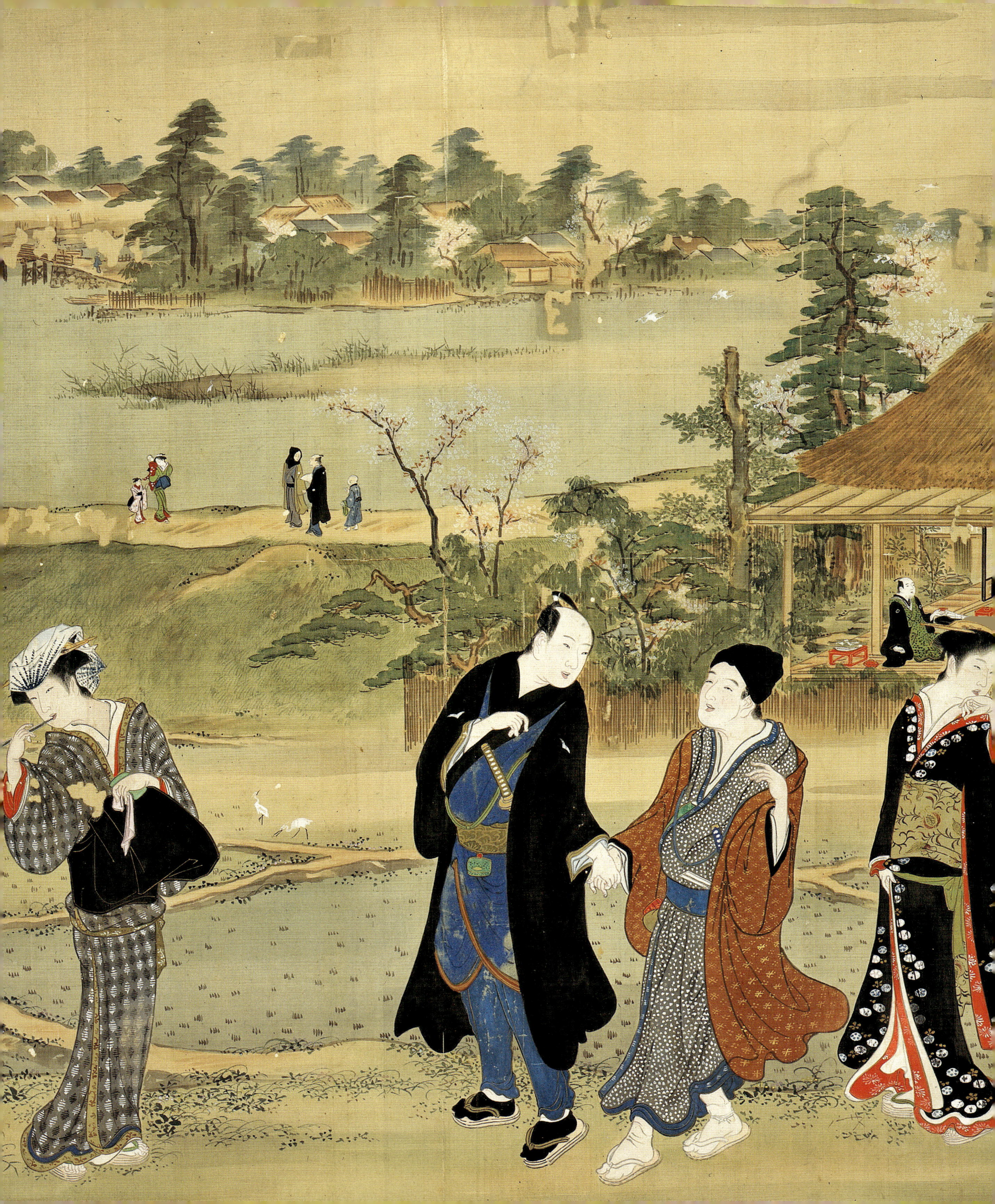

EDO SOCIETY AND CULTURE: UKIYO-E'S SETTING *Kobayashi Tadashi*

Edo (modern-day Tokyo), the city that gave rise to and nourished ukiyo-e, was the real capital of Japan during the period 1615–1868. The emperor and his court lived in the nominal capital of Kyoto, but all their political influence was usurped when Tokugawa Ieyasu, the leader of Japan's most powerful samurai clan, placed the imperial court "under the supervision" of his government based in Edo and forced the emperor to appoint him shogun in 1603. Lying three hundred miles east of Kyoto, Edo came to be called Tōto, the "Eastern Capital."

Edo-period Japan was a feudal society ruled by the warrior class headed by the Tokugawa family. Because they relied on taxes paid in the form of rice, members of this elite group respected the peasants, at least formally. However, they despised the so-called townspeople (*chōnin*) class, slighting the contributions it made to society in commerce, manual labor, and handicraft industries. The townspeople were frequently subjected to ill-treatment as a result of the samurais' contempt. As time went on, however, the simplistic distinctions between the classes began to break down. Relations became more complicated as merchants in particular grew increasingly wealthy, and many families with samurai origins became impoverished.

Edo was celebrated as a "castle town under heaven," and indeed its character was strongly influenced by the military government that ruled it. Over time the population burgeoned, with more than half a million samurai, including the shogun and his direct vassals, as well as the provincial lords, who were required to spend half their time in Edo and to leave behind their families whenever they returned to their home regions. An equally large number of townspeople, confirmed by the 1733 census with a count of 536,380, came to live in Edo to support the many samurai. By 1750 Edo was one of the largest cities in the world, with more than a million inhabitants.

The ratio of men to women in the 1733 census was highly disproportionate: 63.4 percent (340,277) male versus only 36.6 percent (196,103) female. This discrepancy was due to the many temporary sojourns of farmhands looking for extra work, clerks dispatched to do business from stores in other cities such as Kyoto and Osaka, and other itinerant male laborers not native to Edo. Further, the Edo estates belonging to more than two hundred provincial lords (each of whom might have owned a major residence near the shogun's castle, plus a number of smaller ones in the city) housed legions of samurai retainers stationed without their families, and as a result Edo was an unnaturally male-dominated, brutish sort of town.

From birth, samurai and townspeople were raised to think and act differently. As the ruling class, the samurai stood for a conservative, genteel culture that upheld tradition, whereas the townspeople, forced to carve out and sustain a livelihood using their own resources, gauged life in practical terms and sought a more worldly culture that favored change. These attitudes extended to the arts: the samurai class is closely associated with the long-standing, officially recognized Kano and Tosa schools of painting and their traditional Confucian and aristocratic subjects; by contrast, the townspeople were interested in the more contemporary themes and bold new forms of ukiyo-e.

There was also quite a gap between the sexes, at least in theory. A woman's life was generally devoted to the "three obediences": "In childhood, obey one's father; in marriage, obey one's husband; and in widowhood, obey one's (eldest) son." Under such rules, women could hardly exert their own will, let alone choose the path their lives might take. Although men were similarly restricted to the social class into which they were born, they enjoyed considerably greater freedom in controlling their lives.

Both the men and women of the town needed special places and amusements that would let them forget their humble circumstances or temporarily leave behind the bitterness of their day-to-day existence. As a result, certain *akusho,* "bad places," prospered. Essentially theater and red-light districts, these *akusho* gave rise in turn to such entertainments as Kabuki and music in the performing arts; *gesaku, kyōka,* haiku, and *senryū* in the literary arts; and ukiyo-e in the visual arts. Town culture thus flowered and matured over the course of the Edo period, supplanting a stagnating warrior culture.

Edo Geography and Topography

When Rutherford Alcock, British minister to Japan, arrived at his post in 1859 (Ansei 6), he admired the splendor of Edo and described it in *The Capital of the Tycoon: A Narrative of a Three Years' Residence in Japan* (1863). Though it is almost impossible to imagine when compared with the concrete desert that is Tokyo today, old Edo is described by Alcock as a beautiful garden metropolis, with green open spaces spreading out before him.

> Yeddo [Edo] . . . might be one of the pleasantest places of residence in the far East [*sic*]. The climate is superior to that of any other country east of the Cape. The capital itself . . . can boast what no capital in Europe can—the most charming rides, beginning even in its centre, and extending in every direction over wooded hills, through smiling valleys and shady lanes, fringed with evergreens and magnificent timber. Even in the city, especially along the ramparts of the official quarter, and in many roads and avenues leading thence to the country, broad green slopes, and temple gardens, or well-timbered parks gladden the eye, as it is nowhere else gladdened within the circle of a city.[1]

This lush green world was limited, however, to the samurai mansions and temples in the Yamanote district. By comparison, the *shitamachi* area, where the townspeople lived, was so densely populated that people were nearly on top of one another, and for the most part open space blessed with greenery was not to be found. In fact, the area allotted to Edo's townspeople was limited to a meager 15.8 percent of city space despite the fact that they made up about half of the entire population. Roughly the same percentage was allotted to temples and shrines, and the remaining 68.8 percent of the region was taken up by the ruling class.

Unlike the hilly places of the samurai ("Yamanote" is made up of the characters for "mountain" and "hand"), the land assigned to the townspeople was mostly reclaimed from Edo Bay and nearby waterways and was therefore low and damp. To relieve the stifling conditions of daily life in such places, commoners sought out distractions with quite literally broader horizons. Plucking wild greens or viewing flowers along the banks of the Sumida River in spring, boating or watching fireworks near the Ryōgoku Bridge in summer, going to famous foliage spots in autumn, and viewing snowscapes in winter—their diversions changed locales with the seasons. Ukiyo-e treated such outdoor pleasures frequently because they were what the commoners enjoyed.

To Be an *Edokko*

Edo pride developed to the point where its citizens came to refer to themselves as *Edokko,* or children of Edo. To a certain extent *Edokko* consciousness and its accompanying mores differed from ours today, particularly when it came to attitudes toward sex. In ukiyo-e, this consciousness is reflected in the subgenre called *shunga.* Translated literally as "spring pictures," these images explicitly depict boudoir activities between members of the opposite sex (or sometimes of the same sex).

Today *shunga* is frequently distinguished from the rest of ukiyo-e and at times even branded as pornography. However, the people of Edo did not consider the depiction of sex pornographic; in fact, they do not seem to have been overly ashamed or embarrassed by it. At least in sexual terms, theirs was a much more liberal society than ours, and, accordingly, *shunga* was simply a natural part of the ukiyo-e artist's repertoire.

Prostitution was also not considered immoral. Like everything else in Edo Japan, however, it was carefully monitored by the Tokugawa shogunal government. In 1617 a large-scale red-light district called the Yoshiwara was established near Nihonbashi as an officially licensed area for men's amusement and diversion. It was rebuilt in the northern outskirts of Edo as the Shin ("New") Yoshiwara after a fire devastated much of the city in 1657. There, even the most reliable, serious-minded family man luxuriated shamelessly in all manner of musical entertainment and dance performance by geisha or in witty conversation and other intimacies with a courtesan. Under the strictest rules of red-light-district etiquette, the courtesans, essentially prostitutes, were treated as provisional wives; a man could not consort with one while having an affair with another. Even so, the Yoshiwara was a realm in which a man separated himself completely from his daily reality and freely enjoyed another existence — the *ukiyo,* or, as it is commonly known in English, the "floating world."

In another dreamlike floating world consisting of Kabuki theaters and teahouses, a person could be transported to the space and time of the fictions enacted on stage or immersed in the pleasures of entertaining a star performer in a teahouse. In such places, not only men but also women could savor the joys of the floating world to their hearts' content.

Ukiyo-e art captured the brilliant manners and customs of the "bad places" and made recognizable subjects out of the beautiful people who populated them. Kabuki actors were heroes, the pride of Edo; courtesans were heroines, the objects of desire. When making sets of three hanging scrolls or three-sheet compositions of multicolored prints (*nishiki-e*, literally "brocade pictures"), ukiyo-e artists always gave a high-ranking Yoshiwara courtesan the place of honor in the middle and flanked her with women from the town on the left and right. From our perspective, a strange consciousness seems to have been at work: courtesans were held in higher esteem than were wholesome married women and their daughters.

Edokko Education

Edo parents were keen to have their daughters, from infancy, study such arts as playing the samisen, singing, and dancing. They hoped that by mastering these polite accomplishments, their girls might find better employment in a samurai household, make good matches in marriage, and generally secure their future happiness. As for the daughters, they carefully studied ukiyo-e "beauty" and actor pictures (*bijinga* and *yakusha-e*) so that, much like today's young girls who study fashion or pop-culture magazines, they might copy the fashions, hairstyles, and manner of wearing makeup or keep up with those who had made the latest celebrity A-list.

The truly education-obsessed parents of Edo also sent their children — boys and girls — for primary schooling at local temples and at teachers' private residences. Aside from the basics of "reading, writing, and abacus," boys might receive instruction in ballad drama and girls might be taught piecework sewing or etiquette, depending on the instructor or the institution. It is amazing to think that there were more than a thousand such places of instruction in Edo, any one of which would have been the equivalent of a private elementary school today. Because the commoners received instruction in Chinese and Japanese characters and in how to read books, write letters, and do sums from early childhood on, their education level was remarkably high. Furthermore, they gained a wealth of culture and knowledge from the native Japanese narrative and historical traditions, No chanting, ballad drama, and the richly developed poetic forms of *waka,* haiku, *senryū,* and *kyōka.* Thus, understanding ukiyo-e frequently requires a familiarity with classical subject matter. For example, most Edo people understood the parodies presented in the subcategory of ukiyo-e called *mitate-e* and enjoyed those adaptations for the clever twists they gave to original stories. Particularly appreciated was an artist's flair for satire and a sense of play, whether with words or images, historical or mythical subjects, or even contemporary social or political conditions when they could evade the government censors. The depth of *Edokko* culture should not be underestimated.

Ukiyo-e Prints and Paintings

Most ukiyo-e art took the form of cheap, mass-produced prints created for distribution to as many people as possible. Nevertheless, it is important to remember that ukiyo-e was also enjoyed as paintings, which were made individually, brushstroke by brushstroke, on paper or silk. From the beginning, ukiyo-e developed through both prints and paintings, each genre indispensable to its history.

Ukiyo-e paintings (*nikuhitsuga*) conformed to traditional Japanese formats such as sliding-door panels and folding screens that adorn room interiors, hanging scrolls for the *tokonoma* alcove (fig. 1), and handscrolls that are unrolled or picture albums that are unfolded directly in front of the viewer. These flexible, decorative formats are often a surprise to uninitiated Western viewers, who are more familiar with pictures placed in rigid frames.

Even ready-made paintings, produced in advance as standard merchandise for sale in picture shops rather than as special commissions, were more expensive than prints. Therefore only those townspeople who enjoyed some financial flexibility could afford them. Daimyo and other high-ranking samurai or wealthy merchants had the means to commission original, one-of-a-kind works from famous artists. Such patrons encouraged greater refinement in the choice of subject matter and manner of painting, and as a result they helped to raise the quality and dignity of ukiyo-e to new levels.

Among the ukiyo-e artists who tried their hand at painting, some did so as a sideline to making prints, and others dedicated themselves to the brush alone. A good example of the former is the founder of ukiyo-e, Hishikawa Moronobu; another is the self-styled "Old Man Mad about Painting," Katsushika Hokusai. The artists who specialized in ukiyo-e paintings, such as the eighteenth-century Kaigetsudō Ando and Miyagawa Chōshun, stand out as superior early Edo-period artists when color printing was still in its infancy. In either case, those artistic expressions that have the fine, full flavor peculiar to ukiyo-e painting offer a beauty that differs from that of prints. Paintings and prints conjointly widened the axis of ukiyo-e and heightened its appeal.

1. Sir Rutherford Alcock, *The Capital of the Tycoon: A Narrative of a Three-Years' Residence in Japan*, vol. 1 (London: Longman, Green, Longman, Roberts, & Green, 1863), 128.

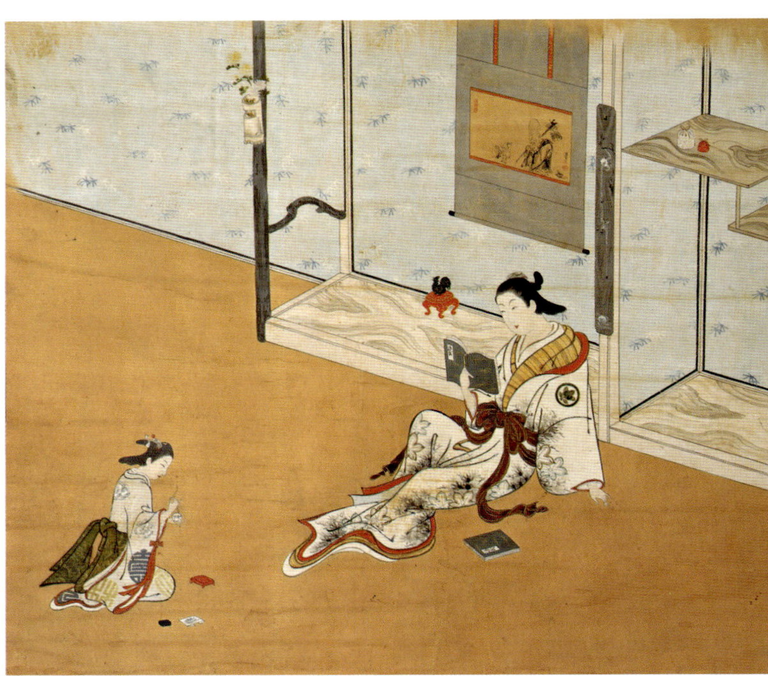

fig. 1. Kondō Katsunobu
Courtesan Reading a Book, about 1716–36

THE FLOWERING OF LOW AND HIGH ARTS IN EDO JAPAN

Howard Hibbett

Low and high arts have had a long, sometimes contentious, and fruitful history in Japan. The multifarious distinctions between the "elegant" (*ga*) and "vulgar" (*zoku*) and their complex interplay have often served to characterize the numerous genres practiced by Edo artists. For persons who favored certain elegant arts — Chinese poetry and painting, prose and poetry in the courtly Japanese tradition, No plays, the Tosa and Kano schools of painting — vulgarity on its many levels was worthy of contempt. Yet they were often tempted by its charms, even by those of the theater and pleasure quarters.

The great seventeenth-century poet Matsuo Bashō instructed his followers to "seek the high and then return to the low." Both levels were accommodated even within a seventeen-syllable haiku, as well as in *haikai,* the linked-verse sequences usually composed by a group of poets. Bashō's spiritual "high" was indeed lofty, far above the mere elegance of most of the refined arts, and his "low" by no means descended beneath the chance experiences of ordinary life. These moments inspired him to compose such verses as

Michinobe no	The roadside flower
mukuge wa uma ni	Of a mallow tree —
kuwarekeri.	Gulped down by my horse.[1]

Images may have a faintly vulgar fate — cherry blossoms drift down into the soup — and yet, like Bashō's famous frog, may yield a glimpse of Zen enlightenment: "An old pond . . . / A frog jumps in / The sound of water."

The descendant of a provincial samurai family, a family slipping below the lowest fringe of that exalted class, Bashō came to Edo in 1672 and was able to support himself for a few years as a superintendent of canals and waterworks in the service of the fourth Tokugawa shogun, Ietsuna. After that, living frugally as an increasingly esteemed poet on the riverside edge of the city, he enjoyed the patronage of his wealthy pupil Sanpū, a lowly merchant but a purveyor of fish to the shogun. Nature was the quintessential source of Bashō's poetry, but Edo was a source of livelihood. Even after the longest of his poetic journeys, when he was sustained by worshipful disciples, he returned for his last years to a newly rebuilt urban hermitage in Edo.

Two centuries before Edo became Tokyo, it had grown into a great city — the nexus of power to which people of many kinds were drawn. In 1600, after more than a century of civil wars, Japan had been reunified under a military regime that established a long age of stability and peace ruled by samurai — hereditary warriors who, from the shogun down to the lowest, unemployed, and impoverished foot soldier, belonged in theory to the highest social class. As time went on, samurai turned to intellectual and artistic pursuits, especially in the realm of an imported Chinese culture, and to service in bureaucratic duties. Their swords and often neglected martial skills helped them maintain a strong sense of superiority over the lower classes. These were, in declining order: farmers, considered essential to the rice-based economy; craftsmen of all kinds; and at the bottom rung merchants and shopkeepers, rich or poor, seen as a parasitical lot devoted to making money. Actors and courtesans ranked entirely below the official Confucian-derived class system. Still, these entertainers were often lionized by the rapidly growing Edo populace, with its influx of men from Kyoto, Osaka, and elsewhere.

Historians see Edo as the heart of early modern Japan, the seat of the dominant Tokugawa clan, for which the period from 1615 to 1868 has been named. But Edo was also a late traditional metropolis, grown from a small fortress town to an ever expanding city centered on the Tokugawa shogun's enormous castle, ringed with spiraling concentric moats and immense stone walls. (Within this defensive circle lies the oasis of greenery surrounding the Imperial Palace at the center of modern Tokyo.) The high, hilly western and southern regions and the parts of the city near the castle were occupied by more than 250 daimyo, subordinate lords required to come to Edo from all parts of Japan to spend half their lives in attendance on their ruler. Alternate periods of residence in Edo forced the vassal lords to demonstrate loyalty, and their sheer expense helped to weaken them. Second only to the shogun, with his vast army of samurai retainers and bureaucrats, lords of the major domains maintained huge estates: the lord of Kaga had eight thousand samurai to serve him when in Edo, and half of that force had to remain there permanently, along with his family. One of his estates, still marked by its imposing red gate, is now the main campus of Tokyo University. Smaller domains had smaller holdings, but important daimyo required lavish surroundings. The spacious Kōrakuen landscape garden of modern Tokyo once belonged to the Mito daimyo; now, however, it is one-sixth of its former size, having been reallocated to military purposes in the Meiji era (1868–1912) — as a guide leaflet explains, "due to city planning."

The "low city" (*shitamachi*), downtown flatlands east of the castle and along the broad Sumida River, was filled with the shops and houses of craftsmen, merchants, performers, and other commoners, both the proud native sons (*Edokko*) and the men who had come from other regions to work in Edo. Commerce and commoners played a critical role in stimulating the cultural era in which both old and new arts thrived.

Outings along the banks of the Sumida, and in the spring the spectacular cherry blossoms at Mukōjima, attracted Edo people of every sort (see cat. no. 50). But the low city was also the site of temples, shrines, and, notoriously, the downtown Kabuki theaters and Yoshiwara pleasure quarters. Kabuki had had its somewhat disreputable origins in Kyoto but had evolved into a complex theatrical art of dance and highly stylized acting performed by men trained from childhood and enhanced by elaborate costuming and makeup. In Edo theaters the predominant taste was for a style of vigorous panache, whether in history plays or those featuring spirited townsmen, but no playbill was complete without actors in romantic female roles. Women, banned from the stage in 1629, were later to find that they had something to learn from the dress and performance skills of these male role models.

Military control over prostitution led to the establishment in 1617 of a licensed quarter called the Yoshiwara, and later on to a "New Yoshiwara," in the northern outskirts, after the earlier site burned to the ground in the great fire of 1657, one of the many fires that were nonchalantly called "flowers of Edo." Paradoxically, the teahouses, luxurious bordellos, and more modest brothels of this large walled and moated pleasure quarter developed a strict etiquette as the pinnacle of demimonde society. In just one of its highly stylized rituals, a famous courtesan, bearing the name of an illustrious predecessor, would proceed through the quarter attended by a male servant, a matron, one or two women of lower rank, and a pair of young girls not yet initiated into prostitution. Though dependent, like many actors, on an affluent patron who might eventually pay a large sum of money to release her from her service to a Yoshiwara house, the courtesan's pride in rejecting unwanted clients, even the rich or wellborn, was a significant part of her appeal. Samurai as well as townsmen found all this irresistible.

The proximity of Buddhist and Shinto worship, fairs, festivals, and the most sought-after — and expensive — entertainment heightened awareness of the transitory joys of *ukiyo,* the "floating world" of all-too-fleeting pleasures. Fads, fashions, Yoshiwara grand courtesans, dashing actors such as Ichikawa Danjūrō I and his successors, willowy beauties of both sexes, and other lesser celebrities of the licensed quarter or the Kabuki stage — all had roles to play in the flourishing arts of Edo.

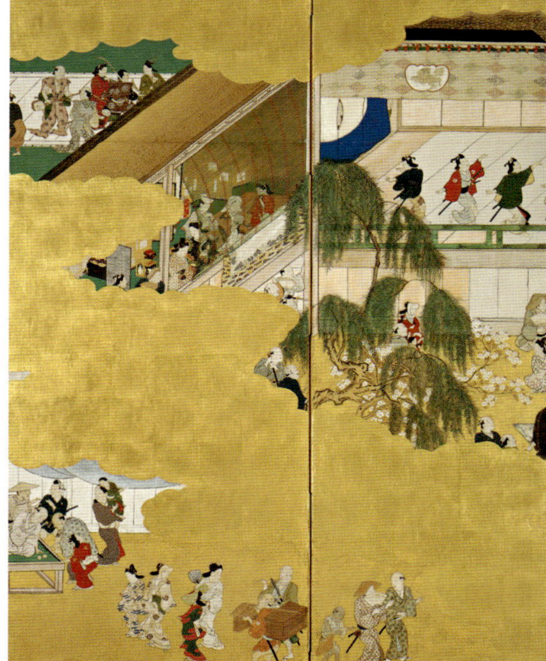

Meanwhile, Kyoto, the home of the faded imperial court and of many arts and crafts, and Osaka, the bustling center for merchants of rice and a growing wealth of commodities and services, remained important cities, with their own rival cultures. Their pleasure quarters, like the Yoshiwara, were already well established in the early seventeenth century, as were their shops and theaters. In Osaka another former samurai, the dramatist Chikamatsu Monzaemon, wrote historical plays and poetic tragedies about the latest love suicides for the virtuoso chanters of the puppet theater. Both his puppet plays and the plays written for the star Kabuki actor Sakata Tōjūrō in Kyoto were freely adapted for performance in Edo and elsewhere.

Osaka was also the home of the flamboyant poet Ihara Saikaku, Bashō's disdained contemporary, a well-to-do merchant who retired early to travel, practice his art, and, in his forties, write his best-selling stories of the floating world. The first of his witty "amorous tales" (*kōshokubon*), a parodic satire of a man engaged in a lifelong pursuit of sexual conquest, soon became popular in Edo and was republished there in 1684, without permission but with Saikaku's own jaunty illustrations reinterpreted by Hishikawa Moronobu, the founder of the leading Edo school of ukiyo-e painters and printmakers. Later Moronobu issued a new picture-book edition, in which Saikaku's drastically cut text is relegated to a slim panel running along the top of the handsome double-page illustrations.

Book illustration of Saikaku's first work of *ukiyo* fiction was a natural assignment for the equally pathbreaking ukiyo-e artist, who had already produced many books, prints, and paintings of Edo pleasure-seeking, from bold erotica to idyllic scenes along the Sumida River. Yoshiwara courtesans on promenade with their attendants and Kabuki actors onstage or with their admirers in a theater district teahouse were other essential subjects for his ukiyo-e. A pair of Moronobu's screen paintings—scenes at the Nakamura Theater and at the Yoshiwara—give a broad, richly detailed, and balanced view of these two principal Edo attractions (see cat. no. 1, fig. 2 details). Actors and courtesans were the object of intense adulation. Audiences might be variously distracted during a day-long Kabuki performance, but there was no question of their fascination with actors, whether in male or female roles. Townspeople sightseeing on the main Yoshiwara avenue would be thrilled to see a noted courtesan pass by with her entourage, even if few could join one of the parties where a rich client, with his own entourage, would be elaborately entertained by music and dance performed by male or female geisha.

A related pair of images, on a much smaller scale, illustrates one of Saikaku's last works, a solo hundred-verse linked *haikai* sequence derived, like his floating-world stories, from his wide observation of city life. An opening set of its verses was published only later, but Saikaku composed the entire poem in the autumn of 1692 (the year before his death) and added comments to each verse in his distinctive calligraphy. The work was mounted in a sixty-foot handscroll, perhaps for presentation to a temple or an important patron, and includes almost a dozen ukiyo-e paintings, also attributed to Saikaku.

The two largest paintings show a canal-bordered street at the entrance of a theater in the Osaka Dōtonbori district and the gateway to the Shimabara, a Kyoto pleasure quarter almost as renowned as the Yoshiwara; both are subjects of the longest "comments," descriptive passages in the style of *ukiyo* fiction.

fig. 2.
Hishikawa Moronobu
Scenes from the Nakamura Kabuki Theater and the Yoshiwara Pleasure Quarter (details), about 1684–1704

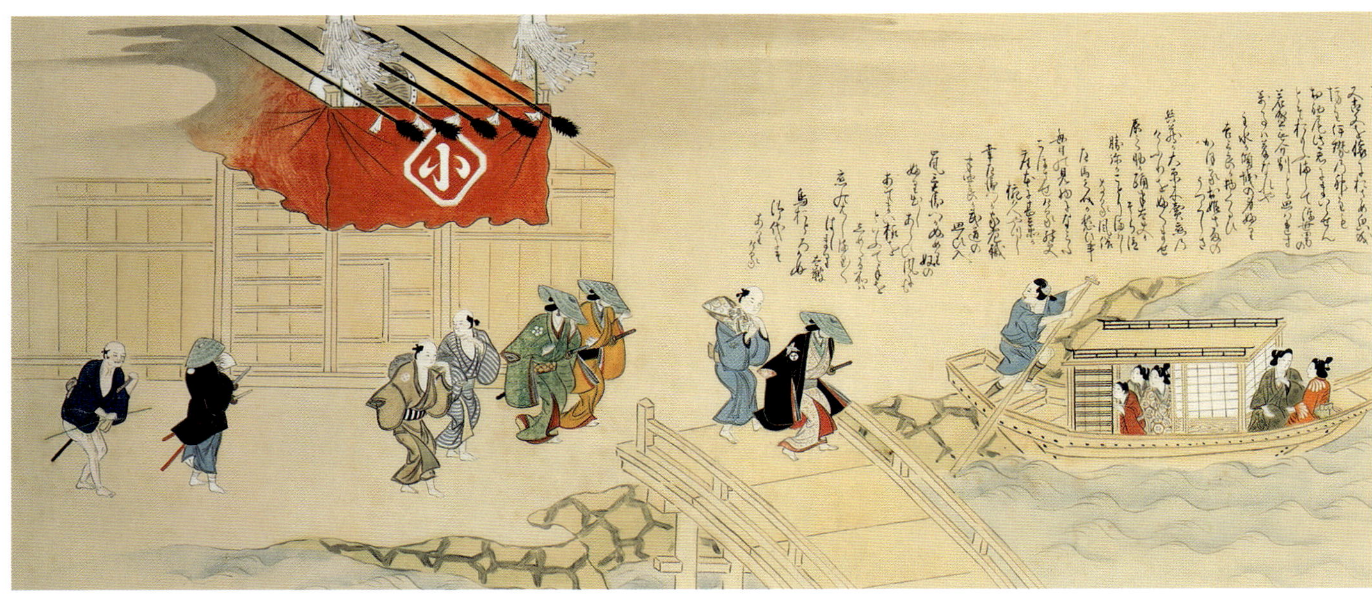

Fig. 3.
Ihara Saikaku, Suzuki Heishichi depicted in *Self-annotated Solo One Hundred Linked Verse Scroll* (*Dokugin hyakuin jichūemaki*, detail), 1692
Tenri University Library

In the former, a samurai and his servant stare from one side, while from the other a group of proper bourgeois ladies, leaving by boat, are transfixed (like the boatman) by the sight of actors emerging from the theater. One of them is the youthful matinee idol Suzuki Heishichi, a splash of his underkimono revealing the brilliant crimson of the wide theater banner (fig. 3).

Yakusha-gasa	Actors under their sedge hats—
aki no yūbe ni	Stared at endlessly
mitsukushite.	In the autumn evening.

Saikaku's prose comment is a lively homage to the objects of their gaze:

This verse shifts to show business . . . not one of the young actors of the four theaters could fail to charm. Some of them stir up deep pools of love. That fellow crossing the bridge wears a crest of oak leaves and triple commas—There he is! Suzuki Heishichi, famed for his art, turned out in all his finery. Who could compare with him? Wanton city women set their passions loose, and their spirits leap up his sleeves. Poor priests from temples and monasteries hide their faces with their black robes and forget their vows—"If only I had the Buddha's money!"—and long to share a pillow with him in a brothel till dawn on each of the Ten Holy Nights! Again, prim-looking pedants with the Ancient Writings engraved in their hearts are smitten; even priests of the Great Shrine at Ise want to present the first rice of the season to this entrancing youth. How much the more natural for worldly men still in their prime! All dreams!

Then there are the actors who play female roles: Shusui miming a courtesan . . . Kichisaburō playing a madwoman . . . the beauty of Kaoru's Princess . . . Hyōzō's Ōhara woodseller feeding the fires of love . . . Tatsunosuke's dancing . . . Handayū's pretended weeping . . . Katsuya's seductive manner . . . Samanosuke's sad scenes drenching the audience's eyes in tears day after day . . . The drum beats for the play to begin, but birds remain undisturbed in this peaceful realm.

In the early eighteenth century the realm was peaceful but faced economic and social problems that had accumulated in the course of the exuberant Genroku era (1688–1704) of Saikaku and Moronobu. In 1716 the eighth Tokugawa shogun, Yoshimune, initiated a period of reform that lasted for most of the Kyōhō era (1716–36). In those years of frequent exhortations to the samurai, as well as innumerable edicts demanding thrift, hard work, and moral elevation from the lower orders, there was a lapse in publication of some of the most popular kinds of floating-world arts. Erotic books and prints were banned but continued to circulate privately. Albums and handscrolls of these "spring pictures" (*shunga*), always a lucrative sideline for ukiyo-e painters, customarily opened modestly, but proceeded at once to more daring images of predictable appeal (see cat. no. 6, fig. 4, detail). In Edo, a city with a disproportionate male population, the market for erotica was especially strong.

The same years, among other changes, saw the rise of scholar-amateur poets and painters who emulated Chinese literati of the Ming and Qing dynasties. Yosa Buson, born to a prosperous farmer family near Osaka in 1716, studied poetry in Edo in his twenties and went on to become a *haikai* master. Venerated as a poet, next to Bashō, he was also a master painter in the elegant literati style. In old age he recalled telling one of his followers that *haikai* should use the vulgar (*zoku*) while remaining detached from it. "This," he acknowledged, "is extremely difficult." An art of high refinement (*ga*) was to be cultivated by withdrawing to observe, from a certain distance, a *zoku* world. Detachment would have been even more difficult in Edo, where the bond between commerce and vulgarity was strongest. Most of Buson's later years were spent in Kyoto, where he often visited the entertainment district.

By then, long after Yoshimune's Kyōhō reforms had given way to a more relaxed policy, business and pleasure were pursued more ardently than ever in Edo. Tsutaya Jūzaburō, who had begun his career selling Yoshiwara guidebooks in a convenient little shop at the main gate of the quarter, went on to publish books, some of which sold more than ten thousand copies, and also issued ukiyo-e color prints of the highest technical excellence.

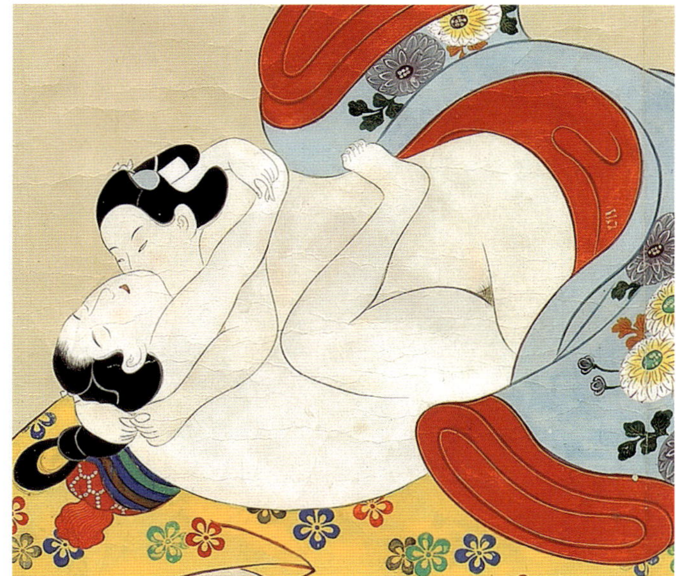

Fig. 4.
Torii Kiyonobu
Erotic Contest of Flowers
(detail), about 1704–11

As a major publisher, Tsutaya was notable for the many ukiyo-e artists — Kitao Shigemasa, Katsukawa Shunshō, Kitagawa Utamaro, among others — who supplied illustrations for his books and for the albums and single-sheet polychrome "brocade pictures" (*nishiki-e*) of actors and courtesans, which commanded a higher price. The sophisticated cartoonish yellowbacks (*kibyōshi*), which combined picture and text in a mode often seen as a forerunner of modern comic books and graphic novels, were also illustrated by gifted ukiyo-e artists. These little books were wildly popular (and profitable to Tsutaya) during their heyday in the An'ei and Tenmei eras of the 1770s and 1780s.

Tsutaya was familiar not only with the Yoshiwara quarter — he grew up there, his grandfather was a teahouse owner, and his parents were in a related business — but also with artists, with poets, and, as a backer of Kabuki plays, with actors. The career of Santō Kyōden, Tsutaya's most popular writer, epitomizes the intermingling of the Edo arts in those years.

The son of a downtown pawnbroker, Kyōden was born in Edo in 1761 and studied calligraphy, Chinese, and music, along with calculation (with or without an abacus) and other necessary merchant skills. In his early teens he was apprenticed to ukiyo-e artist Shigemasa; at seventeen he published his first yellowbacked *kibyōshi,* combining text and illustrations to satirize the manners and morals of the day; in his twenties he was much in demand as a writer and, under the name Kitao Masanobu, as an illustrator and print designer. By that time he was also a well-known connoisseur of the theater and pleasure quarters. In 1784 he produced a striking album of large color prints of Yoshiwara courtesans, showing each of the celebrated beauties together with a pair of attendants and the inscription of one of her poems in what appeared to be her own calligraphy (fig. 5).

The following year, however, Kyōden became even more successful as the author and illustrator of a yellowback (signed Kyōden/Masanobu) about a would-be playboy who goes to extravagant lengths to make himself the talk of the town. (He succeeds at last, by means of a fiasco in trying to stage an aborted love suicide.) After that, Kyōden applied most of his energy to writing, though he continued to illustrate a large number of his own yellowbacks. His playful humor extended to the grotesqueries prominent in Edo wit, such as a struggle between the forces of yin and yang embodied in a two-headed child, half-male and half-female, who grows up to become a pleasure-quarter entertainer. Each half wears the latest masculine or feminine style of dress and coiffure, and each is seen being tugged aside by (or in bed with) a lover. The plot revolves around the conjoined twins, Onatsu and Hanbei, and their lovers, the rakish Seijūrō and the passionate Ochiyo, characters realigned from two of Chikamatsu's tragic dramas. The dialogue and slender thread of narrative (translated by Adam Kern in his illuminating new study of the *kibyōshi* genre) fill the blank spaces in the book's black-and-white illustrated pages (fig. 6):

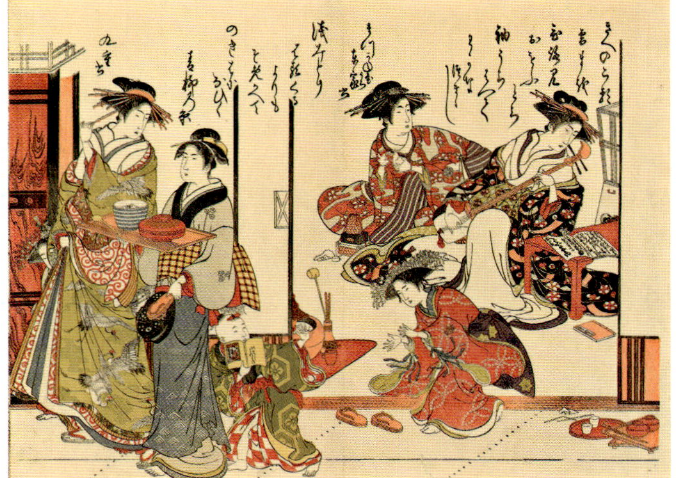

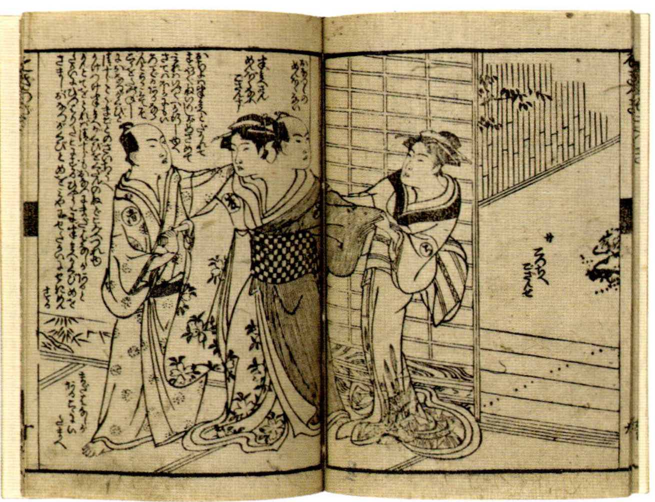

fig. 5
Kitao Masanobu
New Beauties of the Yoshiwara in the Mirror of Their Own Script (Shin bijin awase jihitsu no kagami), 1784
fig. 6
Kitao Masanobu
The Unseamly Silverpiped Swingers (Sogitsugi gingiseru), 1788

In a world full of debauchery, no place is as scandalous as Edo, where even the malformed do not get by unscathed. Thus did Ochiyo, the daughter of the greengrocer next door, fall for Hanbei's handsome visage, plying him with love letters. . . . That is until late one night, when after noticing Onatsu sound asleep, Hanbei indulges in some secret love-making. . . . No sooner has Hanbei fortuitously dozed off, though, than Onatsu sneaks out of the bedroom, ever so daintily, to meet Seijūrō for a little hanky-panky. . . . Ochiyo [had] collapsed softly in Hanbei's embrace, though when she came to, he was nowhere to be found. Incensed that he might be two-timing her, she searches high and low, only to gallop into the midst of Onatsu and Seijūrō horsing around. Ochiyo grabs Hanbei's arm to drag him back to her boudoir, Seijūrō informs Onatsu *they* have some things that need discussing too, and as the ever-so-popular Onatsu and Hanbei are practically tugged apart like so much dried octopus, Hanbei wakes up, eyes meeting Onatsu's, embarrassment flushing both faces red.[2]

The octopus in question is a slang term for a Kabuki star being tugged from all sides by overzealous fans.

Kyōden's comic brothel-fictions (*sharebon*) are decidedly unflattering to the profession. One of them provides a broader than usual view: its title, *Kokei sanshō*, puns on the classical Chinese literary and painting theme "Three Laughers at Tiger Ravine"—three talkative sages laugh at a lapse of memory—but here refers to a trio of jaded alumnae of three Edo pleasure quarters, who remember everything. The book (translated by Robert Campbell as *Three Madames and Their Dirty Tale*) begins with a drawing of a Yoshiwara beauty and an inscribed Chinese verse.

In the fledgling town of Edo
Brothels brim with beauties,
Pillows are carved from coral and jade,
Bedclothes stitched with lovebirds in brocade.
One girl hitches her saddle to a guy from Musashi;
Another sews "love" to a sash in Hitachi.
Clouds burst into rain each dawn,
And at night, they switch men just like pawns.[3]

Two more drawings (with brief verses in Japanese) show prostitutes of Fukagawa and Shinagawa, the two busiest unlicensed quarters, and the text itself opens with a verse about the prosperity of Edo.

Kane hitotsu	Not a day unfolds
urenu hi wa	With a temple bell left unsold
Edo no haru.	Edo in springtime.

After a panoramic tour of the low city, Kyōden focuses on its seamier side and launches into a salty, gossipy dialogue between retired veterans of the three districts. Their reminiscences dwell on the rivalries and realities of Edo teahouse and brothel life. Even the carefully cultivated elegance of high-ranking courtesans and their rich patrons is satirized as comic vulgarity.

In the low Edo arts, bawdy jokes, fiction of consummate vulgarity, and startlingly explicit *shunga* flourished along with works of exquisite taste. Indeed, language and images of pornographic intent were often as fastidious, in their way, as those of quite unworldly poet-painters. The erotic prints and albums of Moronobu, Utamaro, and Katsushika Hokusai were notable for the textile patterns of clothing in disarray, as well as for suavely drawn (usually partial) nudity and stylishly contorted poses; there were also *shunga* as delicate as those of Suzuki Harunobu: scenes observed by the tiny voyeur Maneemon, for example, or a set titled Eight Modern Parlor Views (Fūryū zashiki hakkei), erotic variations on the theme of women engaged in more mundane activities in his earlier series Eight Parlor Views (Zashiki hakkei). (The picture titles in both sets allude to those of the Chinese landscape series Eight Views of Xiaoxiang.) Witty transmogrification was hardly new, to be sure, but by the later eighteenth century it had become one of the hallmarks of Edo ukiyo-e arts and literature.

The affinity of low and high arts in those years is exemplified by Ōta Nanpo, a scholarly samurai of humble rank but precocious accomplishment. In 1766, at the age of seventeen, he published a work on Ming poetry, and the next year, a book of parodic verse and prose in Chinese. His learning might have led to a career of unalloyed prestige, except that he also had a special talent for parodying classical poetic forms in "wild poetry," whether Chinese (*kyōshi*) or Japanese (*kyōka*). The high regard for Chinese arts and letters made China's poetry a tempting parodic target, but there was also much to invite irreverence in the thousand-year native tradition of thirty-one-syllable verse known as *waka* ("Japanese poetry," par excellence). Nanpo became so famous for his *kyōka*, the most contagious fad of eighteenth-century Edo, that his influence among the literati was unparalleled. He relieved the tedium of his bureaucratic post at Edo Castle by joining or organizing groups of like-minded friends — Kyōden, Utamaro, Tsutaya, actors, courtesans, teahouse or bathhouse owners, samurai or shopkeeper poets and scholars — for gatherings devoted to poetry, wit, and conviviality held in Yoshiwara and other congenial settings. Everyday identities were masked by outrageous pseudonyms as Nanpo and his friends indulged in their fanciful play of imagination.

Like ukiyo-e parodies of fashionable beauties posed as figures in a No drama, visual allusions through which a familiar theme or image was transformed into one of up-to-date wit and charm, Nanpo's verses often draw on time-honored themes from high culture and are given a provocative change of gender, setting, era, or cultural status. His *kyōka* exploit the rich possibilities for wordplay and playful reference — not without a parodic edge — to Chinese and Japanese history and legend. Knowledgeable in both the elegant native traditions and those of Chinese poetry, Nanpo was also adept at providing inscriptions for ukiyo-e artists such as Chōbunsai Eishi. A verse about the Three Vinegar Tasters — "When they try a nip / The connoisseurs can tell you / Whether it's sweet or sour" — harks back to three proponents of Confucianism, Daoism, and Buddhism and the somewhat acrimonious debates about their essential unity. In Eishi's painting, they are personified by three superlatively beautiful women grouped around a large vinegar jar: Yang Guifei, the fabled consort of the Tang emperor Xuanzong; Ono no Komachi, a legendary Japanese beauty; and their peer, a Yoshiwara courtesan (see cat. no. 48).

Another *kyōka* by Nanpo typically deflates the high-minded hedonism of the group of third-century Chinese philosopher-poets known as the Seven Sages of the Bamboo Grove.

Chikurin wa	Serene in the Bamboo Grove
yabuka no ōki	And perfectly oblivious
tokoro to mo	Of the mosquitoes' whine
shirade ukauka	Are all those blissful sages,
asobu namayoi.	Sodden with all that wine.

Artists sometimes depicted the sages as demure courtesans studying a long scroll; others, like the authors of comic fiction, brought such revered historical and religious figures as Confucius, Laozi, the Japanese Sun Goddess, and the bodhisattva Kannon into a brothel setting.

The careers of Nanpo, Kyōden, Tsutaya, Eishi, and many others were sharply diverted for a time by a second wave of reform beginning in 1787 under a fourteen-year-old Tokugawa shogun (the eleventh) and his senior councillor (soon-to-be regent), the energetic young daimyo Matsudaira Sadanobu. Famine, floods, a volcanic eruption, and the excesses of the previous regime were more than enough to warrant a reformist's zeal, but Sadanobu, himself highly cultivated in the literature and arts suitable to his rank, also wanted a cultural revolution. He found it deplorable that certain daimyo were not only fond of the vulgar samisen music and song of theater and pleasure-quarter performers, but were spending a great deal of money ransoming courtesans, patronizing actors, and commissioning ukiyo-e paintings. All the worse that Eishi, a samurai of impressive rank, unlike painters and printmakers of an artisan class only in theory superior to the money-grubbing merchants who employed them, should have left the official Kano painting school to become one of the premier ukiyo-e artists of his era.

Samurai in general were sternly warned to confine themselves to "the double path of learning and martial arts," but on the eve of the reforms Nanpo had produced a yellowback satirizing just such slogans. His dramatically illustrated tale (set in the thirteenth century) depicts a society turned upside down by a new law requiring total honesty. In this society, unpleasant truths have replaced politeness, lottery vendors explain their fraudulent details, courtesans insult their clients, and a Kabuki theater, now dedicated to realism, replaces the docile two-man prop horse with a live animal, resulting in chaos onstage. By the time of Sadanobu's more severe edicts, Nanpo had discreetly withdrawn from satirical writing.

The new censorship edicts of 1790, reiterating the opinion that books had in fact existed since times long past and so "no more are necessary," told publishers to confine themselves to serious works. None of this deterred Tsutaya Jūzaburō from publishing three more of Kyōden's Yoshiwara sketches the following year. The books were banned, Tsutaya was fined half of his assets, and Kyōden himself was given the standard punishment to fit the writer's crime: being placed in manacles under a fifty-day house arrest. Not long after, Kyōden opened a downtown pipe shop, which he took care to advertise in his yellowbacks. Later he turned to writing illustrated revenge tales and antiquarian accounts of Edo manners and customs, with special concern for the history of the pleasure quarters that he (and his two successive wives from the Yoshiwara) knew so well.

By 1800 Sadanobu himself had retired from the shogun's direct service to an Edo bayside villa (now the site of Tokyo's fish market), still advocating his outmoded vision of an orderly Confucian society devoted to the aesthetic ideals and aristocratic traditions of Japan from ages long past. But by the mid-nineteenth century ukiyo-e vividly reflected a wider world that included, in Hokusai's prodigious oeuvre alone, expansive landscapes, ghosts, demons, and every aspect of the human comedy from the gargantuan sumo wrestlers that the historian Harold Bolitho has aptly called "Leviathans of the Floating World" to acrobats, contortionists, and street entertainers. Utagawa Hiroshige became immensely popular in the 1830s for landscape prints, especially his series Fifty-three Stages of the Tōkaidō, consisting of scenes of the heavily traveled winding coastal highway, with all its official checkpoints, from Edo to Kyoto. In his last years, beginning in 1856, he produced One Hundred Famous Views of Edo, a culminating series on his native city, its shrines, temples, shopping streets, scenic vistas from Edo Bay to the farthest outskirts, and its many waterways and bridges, particularly those along the Sumida River.

Popular Edo writers, always subject to commercial pressures, had already embarked on works of similarly large scale. Jippensha Ikku, according to the prolific historical novelist Takizawa Bakin, became the first author to live entirely on income garnered from his writings—and to admit that he wrote for money. Ikku, the son of a low-ranking samurai, was born in 1765, grew up in an Edo mansion, went to Osaka as a minor official in his midtwenties, married into a lumber merchant's family, and engaged in such diversions as painting, poetry, calligraphy, and incense connoisseurship. But he also began theatergoing and playwriting, quit his job, divorced his wife, and went back to Edo to seek a literary career. By then almost thirty, he was taken in by Tsutaya and encouraged to write and illustrate yellowbacks, which he did successfully, soon at the rate of about twenty a year. (Bakin said that Ikku's work was published only because he provided his own illustrations.) Ikku was an accomplished draftsman and had begun his Edo career by illustrating one of Kyōden's yellowbacks.

In 1802 Ikku published *A Floating World Journey on Foot (Ukiyo dōchū hizakurige)*, the first of a series of installments that appeared regularly over the next two decades. This mock-guidebook picaresque tale relates the comic misadventures of Yaji and Kita, two irrepressible Edo traveling companions as they saunter up and down the high roads of Japan, satisfying the robust Edo appetite for low humor. Each edition sold between twenty and thirty thousand copies and was widely read through the hundreds of Edo lending libraries. It is no wonder that a disgruntled Bakin, an ex-samurai with considerable Chinese learning, wrote to a friend in 1818 that a work that was 70 percent vulgar and 30 percent elegant would always sell, but one that was 30 percent vulgar and 70 percent elegant would not sell very well—and a work that was 100 percent elegant would not sell at all.

Early in the 1840s the last and by far the least of the rallies intended to reinvigorate the Tokugawa system was beginning yet another assault on the Edo dilettanti; as usual, books were banned, authors clapped into manacles, ukiyo-e artists chastised for images deemed excessively vulgar, and theaters and pleasure quarters curtailed in their operations. Censorship and the suppression of low morals and high spirits were among the measures taken to strengthen the shogun's shaky grip on the powerful domain lords and their restless underlings in the face of danger from abroad.

The arrival of U.S. Naval Commodore Matthew Perry's ominous black ships in Edo Bay in 1853, and again a few more ships early the next year, confirmed the fears of the severely weakened government. After two and a half centuries of peaceful, quasi-feudal equilibrium, the Tokugawa shogunate was on the verge of a tsunami of political, economic, military, and cultural change, bringing with it Shakespeare, Ibsen, and other great names of Western arts and letters, along with now-forgotten nineteenth-century authors and a flotsam of ephemera, all helping to widen the horizon in the brilliant new dawn of Meiji. Cultural change was swiftest and most profound in the metropolis of Tokyo, formerly named Edo, where on January 3, 1868, the victorious rebel government established Emperor Meiji as the ruler of Japan.

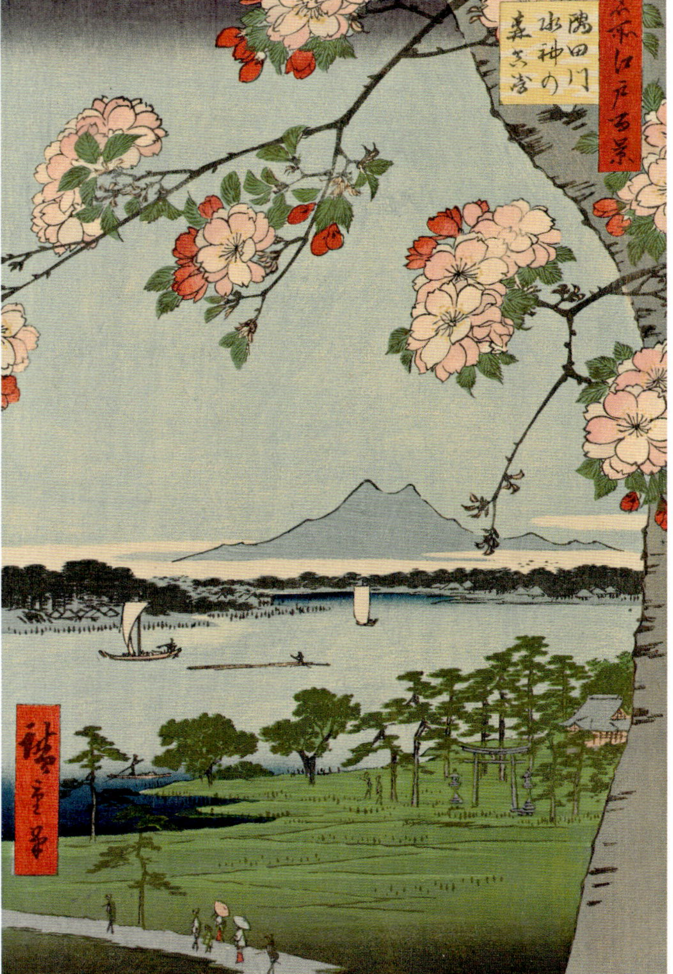

fig. 7
Utagawa Hiroshige
Suijin Shrine and Massaki on the Sumida River,
from the series One Hundred Famous Views of Edo (Meisho Edo hyakkei), 1856

"Civilization and enlightenment" (*bunmei kaika*) was the new slogan justifying every innovation in public life as well as the most exotic fashions. The low and high arts of the past also changed, often in combination or conflict with the flood of imports from the West. Low humor made fun of the high-collared Victorian style of the Meiji gentleman; print artists were quick to record these revolutionary changes; practitioners of the traditional high arts had to guard their prestige more jealously than ever—and for years their work was grossly undervalued. Much that had become the new high culture of the Edo theater and pleasure quarters managed to adapt to the new circumstances. Kabuki actors were urged to modernize and to provide more edifying dramas, especially in wartime, but preserved their forms and their panache. Yoshiwara traditions and festivals survived long after the emergence of the modern geisha, still an adornment at parties supported by unlimited expense accounts but now free to travel, perhaps for a weekend at a hot-spring resort with a favored patron. For the Yoshiwara, though, artistic parity with Kabuki had been lost by the time the quarter was rebuilt at the end of Meiji after another one of its devastating fires. Meanwhile the guiltless pleasures of excursions along the banks of the Sumida, in spite of noisier forms of transport, retained much of the atmosphere of times past.

Writing in late Meiji after two victorious wars had established Japan as a world power, the young novelist Tanizaki Junichirō, a son of Edo's deep-rooted merchant class, opened a story set in the pleasure quarters with a boating scene on the great river that Hiroshige had shown in so many of his Views of Edo (fig. 7).

Just then the cherries along the bank of the Sumida River at Mukōjima were in full bloom. From early Sunday morning under a glorious blue sky the trolleys to Asakusa and the little steamboats coming up the river were crowded with passengers. Beyond the Azuma Bridge, where throngs of people were streaming across like ants, a warm mist had settled. . . . The opposite bank drowsed in the hazy indigo light, with the Twelve-Story Tower in the park looming dimly in the background against the stiflingly moist deep blue sky. Emerging out of a dense fog in Senjū, the Sumida wound its way around the tip of Komatsu Island and broadened into a languid expanse of tepid water, as if spellbound by the springtime along its banks, and then, glittering in the sunlight, flowed on under the Azuma Bridge. On the river's surface gently billowing waves, soft as a downy quilt, lapped lazily against the many boats, some of them especially for flower viewing.

One of these boats is a roofed barge draped with gaudy red and white striped curtains, sheltering a party enlivened by a number of Fukagawa geisha who, except for the attire of the nouveau riche stockbroker who is their patron, would have been at home in an Edo pleasure quarter. In the springtime of modern Japan, the allure of Edo, with its network of canals and waterways, its long-standing customs and old-fashioned entertainments, had taken on an appealing patina of nostalgia. Elegance and vulgarity, ambiguous as ever, were being redefined in contemporary terms.

---

1. *Editor's note:* The translations in this essay are by the author unless noted otherwise.
2. Adam L. Kern, *Manga from the Floating World: Comicbook Culture and the Kibyōshi* of Edo Japan (Cambridge, MA: Harvard University Asia Center, forthcoming).
3. From Robert Campbell, trans., *Three Madames and Their Dirty Tale*, vol. 10 of *An episodic festschrift for Howard Hibbett* (Hollywood, CA: highmoonnoon, 2002).

THE ORIGINS OF UKIYO-E *Naitō Masato*

It is a common misconception that ukiyo-e is limited to prints. That has been the case only from as recently as the early Shōwa era (1926–89), when the auction of the forged "Shunpōan collection" caused ukiyo-e paintings to all but disappear from public view.[1] Evidence for how heavily this history has weighed may be found by comparing ukiyo-e journals before and after the scandal, which was perpetrated in 1934. Most ukiyo-e journals published after that date contain only prints, whereas it was customary in those published until about 1933 to separate a few pages in the front matter to introduce masterpieces of painting. The earlier treatment was more consistent with a real understanding of ukiyo-e in the Edo period.

Another idea that many embrace as a historical truth is that ukiyo-e belonged to the commoners of old Edo. This theory, which contends that, for the most part, city-dwelling commoners purchased ukiyo-e and that popular taste dictated how an ukiyo-e artist fared, is by now well established around the world. Under this rubric, printed ukiyo-e—particularly woodblock prints—were fundamentally commercial publications produced and sold according to consumer demand. Similarly, popular novels, picture books (*ehon*), and picture albums (*gafu*) illustrated by the same artists were directed toward as broad an audience as possible, whether they were sold as subscription series or circulated through popular lending libraries. General trends, therefore, rather than individual taste, were the driving forces behind ukiyo-e production.

To be sure, most famous ukiyo-e artists and popular fiction writers came from the *chōnin,* or townspeople, class, and it is easy to understand a situation in which things born of *chōnin* were enjoyed by *chōnin*. Although some artists had once been shogunal vassals or retainers of provincial daimyo, they were not, for the most part, from high-ranking families. It stands to reason then that commoner art and culture in the Edo period was basically borne along by the *chōnin* and a small portion of lower-ranking samurai.

However, even this modified view assumes that such elite members of society as the emperor and his imperial retinue living in Kyoto, or the shogun and leading daimyo living in Edo, were completely disconnected over the course of their lives from ukiyo-e. Significantly, the existence of a number of documents and artworks directly disputes that contention and provides concrete evidence that some among the top ranks of Edo society kept ukiyo-e within their grasp.[2] Paintings, which tended to be more costly to produce and procure, formed some of the direct links between the classes. Hence they must be studied along with prints and books if we are to have a complete understanding of ukiyo-e and the realities, rather than just the theory, of class relations during the period that gave birth to it.

Precedents for Ukiyo-e

Ukiyo-e were in fact born of a painting tradition developed for high-ranking patrons. Known today as *fūzokuga,* genre paint-

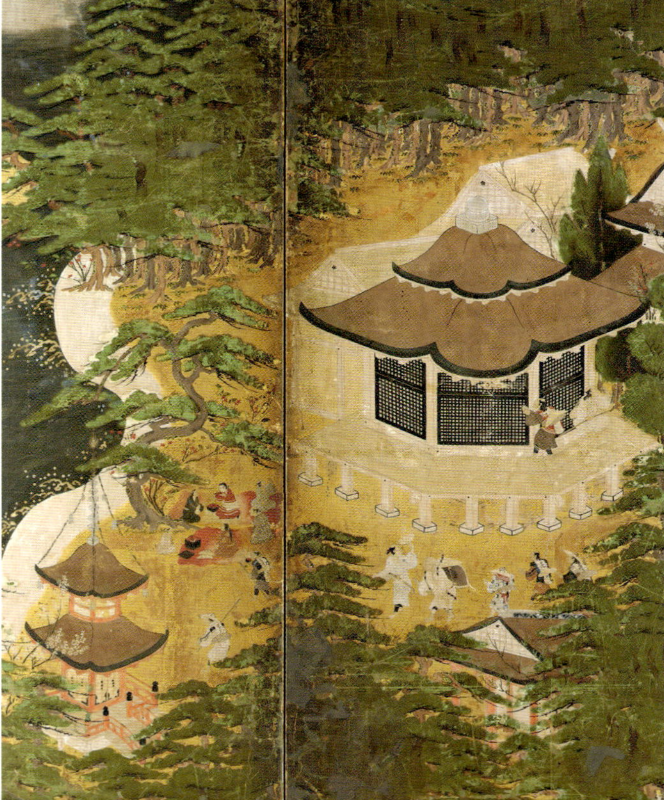

fig. 8
Amanohashidate (detail of screen). First quarter of the 17th century
John C. Weber Collection

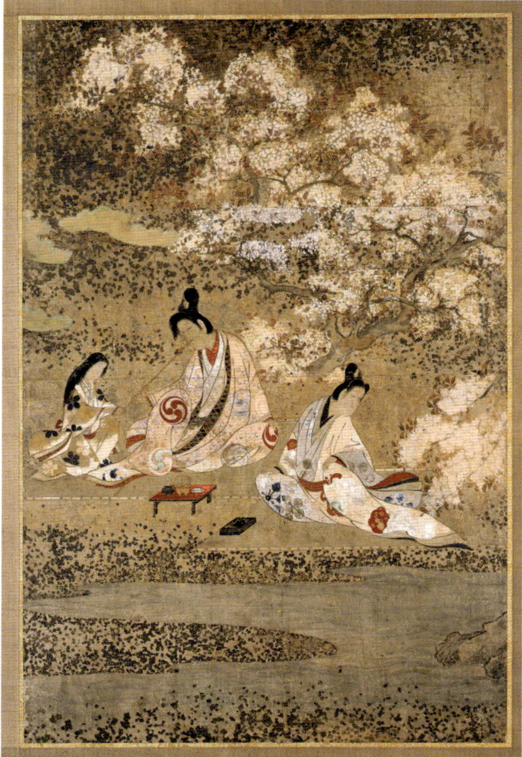

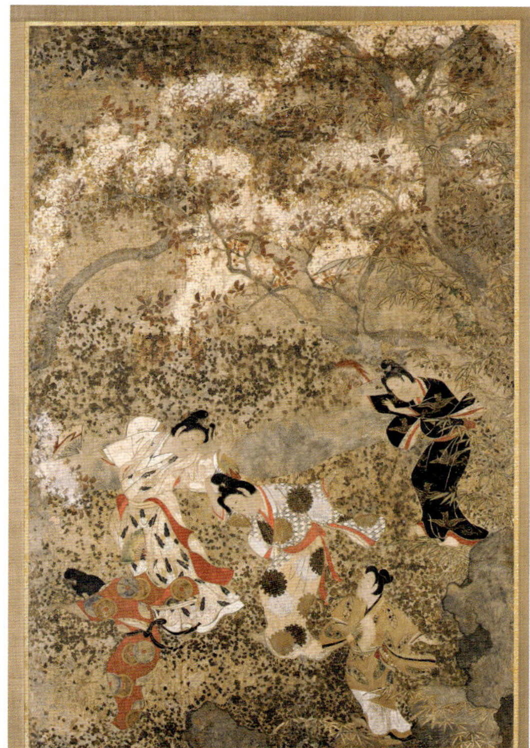

fig. 9
Partying Beneath Blossoming Cherry Trees, about 1624–44.

ing, that tradition takes as its subjects the manners and customs of people's day-to-day lives. There are examples of *fūzokuga* in Japanese painting from ancient times, but the immediate precedent for ukiyo-e comes from the early modern period at the beginning of the seventeenth century. In fact, it was from as early as the end of Japan's middle ages, during the sixteenth century, that *fūzokuga* slowly began to develop on its own. Painters of the Kano and Hasegawa schools who were patronized by powerful members of the military aristocracy, for example, depicted lively scenes of commoners in famous places such as Higashiyama and Arashiyama (the eastern and western hills of Kyoto) or Amanohashidate on the surfaces of folding screens, sliding doors, and other large formats that depended on grand architecture (fig. 8). Because such works were commissioned for castles and temples, they were essentially paintings of commoners for exclusive delectation by the elite.

Kano artists worked primarily in Chinese painting styles of the Song and Yuan dynasties. From the end of Japan's Muromachi period (1392–1568) to the Edo period, they exerted tremendous influence as official painters to the leading samurai families. The school founded by Hasegawa Tōhaku in the Momoyama period (1568–1615) also worked mostly in Chinese-derived styles and served a similar clientele, including the abbots of major Buddhist temples in Kyoto. At the beginning of the Edo period, however, painters more closely associated with parties out of power took up genre painting. Simultaneously, artists began to make smaller-format works of art, such as hanging scrolls, in greater numbers.

Among the artists who appeared just as *fūzokuga* began to undergo great change was Iwasa Matabei. Matabei independently studied the traditional Japanese style that had been revived by Tosa Mitsunobu, an official painter to the imperial court during the Muromachi period, as well as those of other schools. Working in both Kyoto and Fukui, Matabei excelled in many types of painting—portraits of poets, narrative subjects, and genre. Once considered the founder of ukiyo-e, Matabei is known for his depiction of opulent, full-cheeked, long-jawed figures with a worldly air, and surely the essential elements of ukiyo-e may be traced back to them (fig. 9). Genre painting was only one part of his rich repertoire, however, and it is important to note that he did not make it a specialty.

In the early Edo period, the Japanese figural tradition also gave rise to *Kanbun bijinzu,* "beauty pictures" that depicted young courtesans or young men (*yūjo* and *wakashu*) standing alone against a blank background (fig. 12). Such images were made in large numbers from the end of the Kan'ei through the Kanbun eras (hence the name) and, despite being prized by a part of the nobility, were affordable to commoners because of their smaller, less expensive hanging-scroll format. Both figure types were based on early Kabuki performers, so they may be viewed as the prototypes from which ukiyo-e courtesan and Kabuki actor pictures developed later in the Edo period.[3]

The genre paintings of the early modern period discussed so far were all made in Kyoto, the imperial capital and Japan's cultural center at the time. If we consider that the evolution of ukiyo-e was realized primarily in Edo, and that "ukiyo-e" and "Edo souvenirs" (*Edo meibutsu,* literally "Edo's famous goods") were essentially synonyms, it becomes critical that we find the seeds of ukiyo-e in Edo soil.

The *Scenes of Famous Places in Edo* (*Edo meishozu byōbu*) dating from the Kan'ei era, which has been convincingly argued as having been painted by someone under the influence of the

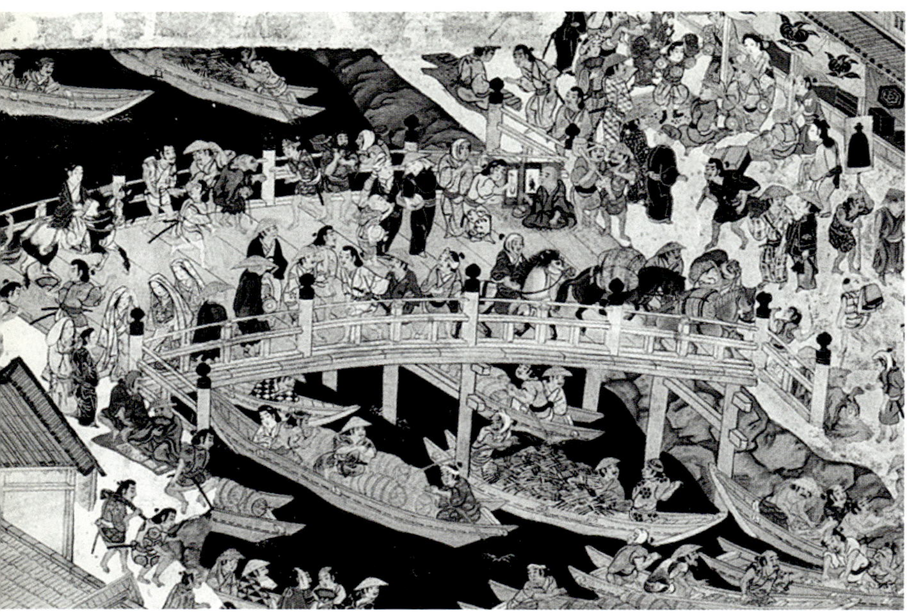

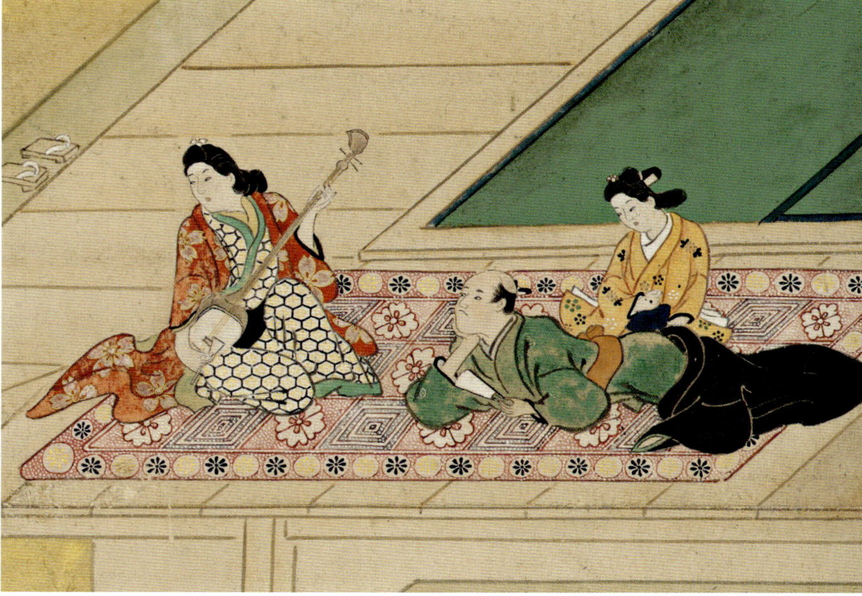

fig. 10
Scenes of Famous Places in Edo (detail), about 1624–1644

fig. 11
Genre Scenes at Famous Places in Edo (detail), about 1684–1704

Matabei style, is therefore an extremely important work of art (fig. 10). It is the oldest extant example of an Edo *keikanzu,* a scenic view describing the relationship between the city and its inhabitants. From a bird's-eye perspective, we see a bustling scene of commoners in a broad sweep of early Edo from Ueno to the bay. Its primary subject is the newfound, radiant energy of this class in the growing shogunal capital, with a particular focus on the *wakashu kabuki* (an older form of Kabuki featuring teenage male performers) in the Kobikichō section of town.[4] Among the more than 2,200 figures that appear on this screen, many connect directly to later ukiyo-e; some could even be *Kanbun bijinzu* just as they are, if only enlarged and isolated. One might view this work, therefore, as ukiyo-e in its original form.[5]

Hishikawa Moronobu and the Development of Ukiyo-e Thereafter

Ukiyo-e could not have earned a popular following among the people of Edo if it had remained an art form limited to painting; its artists also had to produce a great many designs for prints and printed books. As commodities that could be reproduced in large quantities at low prices, prints were more conveniently sized and far more affordable than painted works that drew directly on the genre tradition.

Hishikawa Moronobu was the primary link between ukiyo-e's painted and printed origins. As a young man from a family of fabric decorators and embroiderers in Awa Province, Moronobu went to Edo around 1670 to launch a career in printed book illustration. His manner of drawing figures, which he based on *Kanbun bijinzu* and an enhancement of Matabei's refined urbanity, became the first truly individual ukiyo-e style. Moreover, perhaps due to the influence of the Hishikawa family profession, he paid particular attention to the colors and patterns of clothing, especially in his painted works (fig. 11). Indeed, the fine colors and elaborate detail of clothing patterns in later ukiyo-e can be traced to Moronobu.

Ukiyo-e subsequently developed along a dual axis of "beauty" and actor pictures (*bijinga* and *yakusha-e*), into a rich genre of printed and painted works rarely seen in the art history of the world. At first, monochrome prints called *sumizuri* were hand colored with a brush; later, about a century after the birth of ukiyo-e, full-color images were made with separate woodblocks printed in stages, giving rise to the brilliant "brocade picture," *nishiki-e*. This landmark invention of the mid-eighteenth century changed the history of ukiyo-e prints, but before then, many ukiyo-e artists specialized in painting. It seems that some were able to offer premade pictures at low prices and in large volume, thus providing the early printmakers with some competition. However, because of the basic cost differential between handmade paintings and commercially published prints, the phenomenon of both types of artists vying for a single consumer group occurred less and less frequently after the Kaigetsudō school of the early eighteenth century. After the mid-Edo period, around the time that *nishiki-e* were invented, the two types became increasingly differentiated so that the divide between low-priced, generally popular commodities — prints — and high-priced, specially commissioned commodities — paintings — widened even further.

Sale Prices of Ukiyo-e

Unfortunately, there are no surviving records that satisfactorily inform us about ukiyo-e painting fees, and the evidence regarding the price of prints is fragmentary. What monochrome and hand-colored prints of the early period cost is unclear, but we have fairly concrete figures from the mid-eighteenth century, around the time that *nishiki-e* were invented, and after. For example, a record from that period states that the manager of Echigoya-Mitsui (which would become today's Mitsukoshi Department Store) paid 160 mon for *chūban*-size *nishiki-e* by Suzuki Harunobu to give to female patrons of the main store in Kyoto. Apparently, matched sets of superior-quality prints made with multiple color blocks were fairly expensive.

Prices were down by the Tenmei era, and *nishiki-e* could be purchased for 16 mon; *hosoban* actor prints were even cheaper, at just 8 mon. There is also evidence that round fan pictures of the Kansei era cost between 12 and 16 mon, and *ōban nishiki-e* of that era appear to have been about 24 mon, but toward the end of the Edo period, all of these prices rose gradually with inflation. In today's currency, these figures translate into approximately four hundred yen, about what one would pay for chocolate at a Tokyo train station. Except when *nishiki-e* were invented, prints in the Edo period were exceedingly affordable. The contemporary pulp fiction novelist who claimed that even small children with pocket change could buy the latest portrait prints of their favorite Kabuki actor must have been telling the truth. Paintings, of course, could not be acquired so readily. Also, it is commonly argued that *shunga,* erotic pictures, were made more expensive by their prohibition in the Kyōhō reforms. There is, however, only one documented case of a selling price for *shunga,* an entry by a contemporary purchaser of Hokusai's *Patterns of Loving Couples* (*Tsui no hinagata*) from the Bunsei era stating that it cost 100 hiki, which equaled 1,000 mon.[6]

For ukiyo-e to become a truly popular art form, certain conditions were necessary — people needed to get their hands on them, see them, and generate a "buzz" about them and the artists who created them. A system began in the early Edo period at the time of Moronobu by which ukiyo-e prints and books were published and sold at stores specializing in male tastes. Yet, there were still many studios in bustling town areas that produced and sold their own paintings. For example, picture makers specializing in paintings up to the mid-Edo period, such as the members of the Kaigetsudō, Miyagawa, or Kawamata schools, appear to have dealt in ready-made paintings sold "as is" in standard formats. Retail operations that formed the direct point of contact with customers fronted both the *ezōshiya,* which produced printed materials of all kinds and consisted of artists, block carvers, and printers, and the *eya,* which produced paintings and were run by the artists themselves. By carefully monitoring the latest trends, both types of producer-retailers were able to create a continuous, stable supply of images that kept up with demand.

If the prints were reasonably priced, some consumers enjoyed their new purchases right away by sticking them on walls and shoji doors. Those with more finicky personalities probably stored them away carefully in wicker trunks and delighted in taking them out for viewing only from time to time. Whether or not prints were collected was a matter of the times, as well as of personal taste. There is a theory that theatergoers wore *hosoban* actor prints on their backs when taking in a show. In most cases, prints were quickly consumed at whim, and more were lost than those that we know of today.

There is a high probability that ready-made paintings too, much like prints before the advent of *nishiki-e,* were not taken care of all that well. However, after full-color prints appeared and paintings essentially became carefully produced works by individual masters (aside from loose, offhand paintings made on the spot, such as those on folding fans), it appears that by and large painted hanging scrolls and handscrolls came to be treasured.

A Take-No-Prisoners Fight to the Death

The world of ukiyo-e—whether painted or printed—was an extremely volatile, harshly competitive one at the mercy of popular taste. Although the art form overall captured fashions and the latest trends in real time, the fate of its artists depended on the consumer, who often proved to be quite fickle. Even successful, well-known studios could never rest on their laurels, for every day was a continuing battle between popularity and oblivion. Indeed, contemporary artists' biographies make nonchalant mention of numerous ukiyo-e schools that ended within a single generation of a brilliant master, of the limited number of artists who could last ten years in the business, or of others who lost popularity and were forced to close up shop and switch to other trades. To answer the calling of ukiyo-e and continually keep up with the times, like artists working for popular *manga* houses today, was extremely difficult. It was not unusual for even the few who managed to acquire fame and glory to be deeply in debt by the end of their lives.

Be that as it may, the artists who learned to market themselves as brand names were fortunate. Their prosperity was due not only to designs for prints and printed books but also to the occasional order for a painting that would come their way because of their popularity in the other media. Although there are no surviving documents to tell us exactly how much ukiyo-e paintings cost during the Edo period, we do know that they were usually not so expensive that an artist could easily get rich in that arena. The fees earned by those who made pictures, divided into the categories of craftsmen (*shokunin*) and picture makers (*gakō*), were considered wages for manual labor, quite unlike the fees earned by those one rank above, known as "original artists" (*hon'eshi*). There was certainly a big difference between what a typical ukiyo-e artist was paid and the countless ryō (1 ryō equaled about 5,000 mon) given to an artist of an officially sponsored Kano-school studio. Therefore, devoting the time, materials, and energy necessary to making a single ukiyo-e painting must have had other benefits. Aside from the pride of the craftsman, there must have been times when patrons were generous in their payments. More important, the most talented artists who made names for themselves, using their fame as a foothold, gained access to people of higher status. In circular fashion, access to patrons with greater resources at their disposal must have led to more special commissions. Unique, exquisitely executed paintings must have been the ultimate acquisition.

1. *Editor's note:* For a detailed discussion of the Shunpōan forgery scandal in English, see Timothy Clark, *Ukiyo-e Paintings in the British Museum* (London: British Museum Press, 1992), 38–43. According to Clark, the scandal made scholars unwilling to pass judgment on the authenticity of paintings, a situation that lasted until at least the 1960s.
2. *Editor's note:* Ukiyo-e patronage by the upper levels of Edo society is the primary theme of the author's book *Ukiyo-e saihakken: Daimyō-tachi ga medeta ippin, zeppin* (Tokyo: Shōgakkan, 2005), from which this essay has been adapted; see pp. 4–20.
3. These paintings have recently led me to question the involvement of the Hasegawa school in the early development of ukiyo-e. There is a high probability that both the Matabei and the Hasegawa schools were deeply involved in developing such early precedents for ukiyo-e. According to the Iwasa lineage, Matabei's son became the adopted son of Hasegawa Tōhaku and took the name Tōtetsu, thus connecting the families by marriage. Such a connection has implications for genre painting and ukiyo-e: Both Tōhaku, who is known today primarily as having been an ink painter to high-ranking samurai and priests, and Matabei, whose followers carved out a market niche among the commoners, must have played important roles in the formation of ukiyo-e. *Editor's note*: See the author's *Ukiyo-e saihakken*, p. 12.
4. Male performers young enough to still have their forelocks unshorn are shown. Such boy actors were popular after females were banned from the stage, but they too were banned after 1652.
5. Naitō Masato, "Edo meishō zu byōbu," in *Aato serekushon* (Tokyo: Shōgakkan, 2003).
6. Introduced in Shibui Kiyoshi, *Ukiyo-e naishi* vol. 2 (Tokyo: Taihōkaku shobō, 1933), 26. Editor's note: Also published in Richard Lane, ed., *Katsushika Hokusai Tsui no hinagata*, vol. 13 of *Tehon ukiyo-e shunga meihin shūsei* (Tokyo: Kawade shuppan kenkyūjo, 1997).

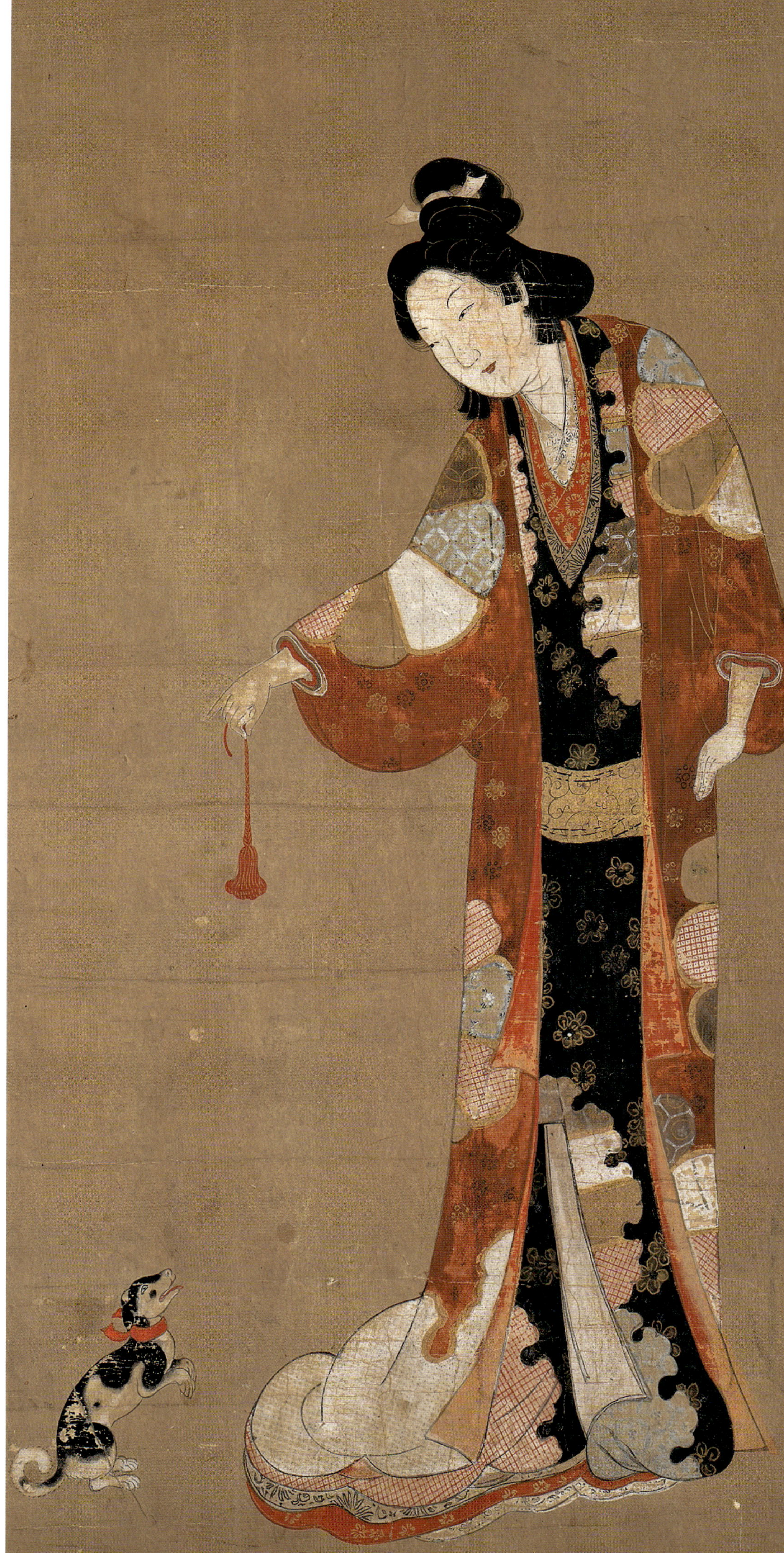

fig. 12
Courtesan Playing with a Dog, about 1661–73

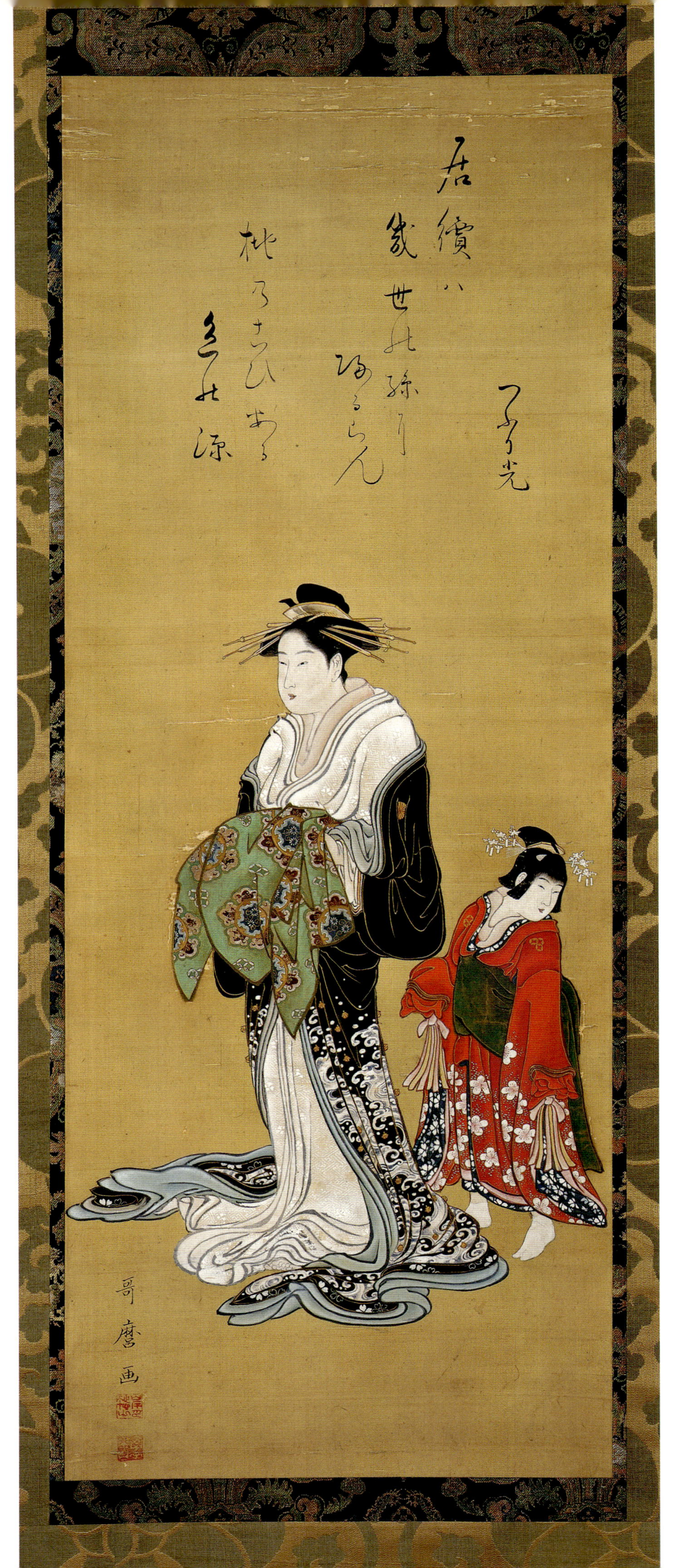
哥麿画

"Ten years in a world of suffering" was the harsh reality of courtesans in Edo's pleasure districts, despite their image as elegant and cultured trendsetters adorned in the latest fashions and hairstyles. Forced into prostitution at a young age, these women were bound by a ten-year contract that could be redeemed only by a wealthy patron or by death. Although the term *yūjo* was applied to all women who made their living in that trade, in its narrow sense it designated a courtesan in one of the quarters licensed by the shogunal government. In Edo the officially sanctioned brothel district was the Yoshiwara, which was established in 1617 near Nihonbashi, in the center of the city, and then rebuilt in 1657 on the outskirts to the northeast. Similar areas were demarcated in Kyoto and Osaka, respectively called the Shimabara and Shinmachi. However, because most ukiyo-e paintings and prints were produced in Edo, the image of the courtesan is largely associated with the Yoshiwara.

The Yoshiwara was immense. It employed countless individuals to support the business of pleasure in all of its many guises and generated approximately 1,000 ryō (about ¥100,000,000, or $877,200 in today's currency) every day.[1] Throughout the Edo period the number of courtesans remained relatively stable, averaging three thousand women at any given time, but the system of ranking them underwent significant changes.[2]

During the 1670s and 1680s, when the pioneer ukiyo-e artist Hishikawa Moronobu was active, the brothels were divided into three levels: *kōshi mise* (latticework shops), *sancha mise* (powdered tea shops), and *tsubone mise* (compartment shops). *Kōshi mise* were high-end establishments that specialized in the most elevated courtesans of the *tayū* or *kōshi* rank, whereas *sancha mise* featured *sancha* or *umecha* courtesans, and *tsubone* had *tsubone jorō*. Although the modern reader might confuse the reference to latticework in the name of the highest-ranking shops with the latticed viewing areas visible in some ukiyo-e paintings, neither *tayū* nor *kōshi* engaged in such public displays (*harimise*) of a brothel's "wares" in the manner of courtesans at other levels. Instead, these Yoshiwara celebrities were summoned by clients to houses of assignation, called *ageya*, where the clients were wined, dined, and entertained while they waited. Admirers with limited means were permitted only glimpses of these women as they paraded with their entourages from their brothels, down the main avenues, and finally to the *ageya*.

The *tayū* and *kōshi* designations were abandoned by the 1790s, when Kitagawa Utamaro was creating his images of the Yoshiwara. Instead, high-level courtesans belonged to the *yobidashi sanbu* class. Women of this standing were accompanied by an apprentice courtesan and commanded a fee of 1 ryō, 1 bu (approximately ¥120,000–130,000, or $1,050–1,140). However, on top of this fee, the expected tip — euphemistically called "flower money" — increased the cost of a night of pleasure to a staggering 10 ryō (approximately ¥1,000,000, or $8,772) or more.

fig. 13
Kitagawa Utamaro
Moatside Prostitute (*Kashi*), from the series Five Shades of Ink in the Licensed Quarter (Hokkoku goshiki-zumi), about 1794–95

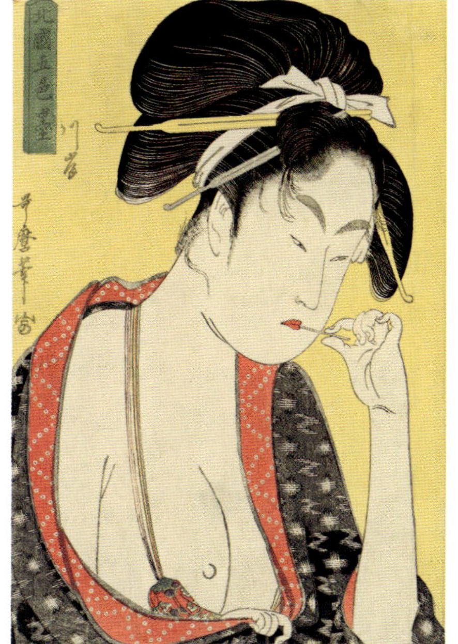

Below the *yobidashi sanbu* were a number of other ranks; those immediately below the *yobidashi sanbu* were the *zashiki-mochi* courtesans (literally, women who "had their own suites"). Their fee was 2 bu (approximately ¥50,000, or $440) during the day, and only 1 bu at night. The next level included the *heyamochi* courtesans (courtesans with "their own rooms"), who charged 1 bu during the day and one half of that, 2 shu, during the evening; there were others who earned only 2 shu and 1 shu (approximately ¥6,000, or $53). The lowest-ranking prostitutes worked out of narrow compartments known as *tsubone mise* and *kiri mise* and received a meager 1 sen, 100 mon (¥2,000, or $18). Yet despite

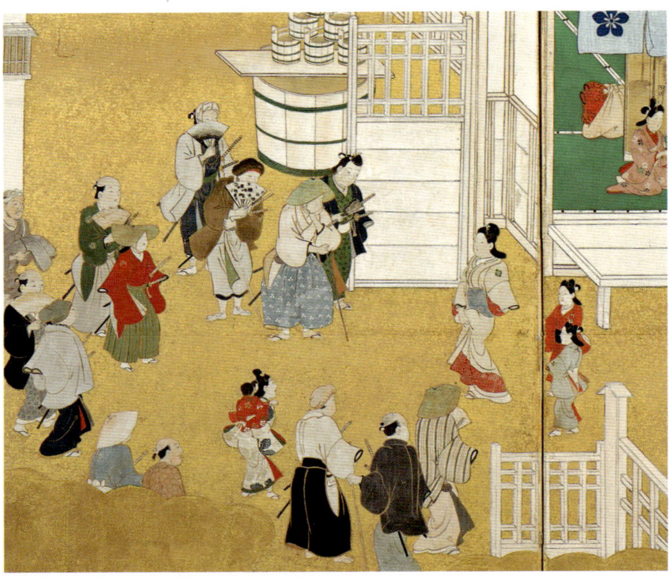

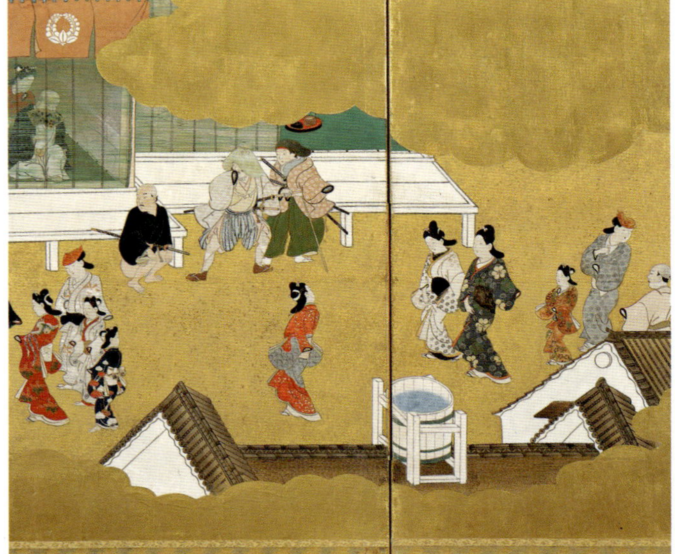

fig. 14
Hishikawa Moronobu (died 1694)
Scenes from the Yoshiwara Pleasure Quarter (details from panel 4 and panel 2), about 1684–1704

the number of ranks during the late eighteenth century, aside from the *kashi* (moat-side prostitutes), the *kiri mise no musume* (young women from low-class brothels), and the *teppō* (gun prostitutes), whom Utamaro included in his Five Shades of Ink in the Licensed Quarter (Hokkoku goshiki-zumi) print series (fig. 13), all the courtesans depicted in ukiyo-e were of the *zashi-kimochi* rank or higher.[3]

Courtesans in the Yoshiwara: The Late Seventeenth Century

Scenes from the Yoshiwara Pleasure Quarter, the left-hand composition from a pair of screens attributed to Hishikawa Moronobu (see cat. no. 1), provides a panoramic view of Nakano-chō, the broad main avenue of the brothel district. In the lower section of the fourth panel from the right, a group of people stands at the entrance to Ageya-chō, the street named for the well-appointed houses of assignation that lined it. They partake in the spectacle of the courtesan's stately promenade (*dōchū*) with her entourage from their living quarters to the *ageya,* where she will meet her client.[4] With her right hand lifting her skirts and her left hand tucked in her extended sleeve, a high-ranking *tayū* or *kōshi* is walking (fig.14, left). A comparison with other contemporary illustrations makes it possible to determine that this distinctive positioning of the hands (which is sometimes reversed) was part of the standard posture assumed by processing courtesans. In fact, in this screen a woman wearing a dark blue outer garment patterned with trefoil roundels repeats the pose in the lower section of the first panel from the right, as does a woman looking over her shoulder and wearing a black outer garment with a plum motif in the lower section of the second panel.

Although the positioning of the hands permits an identification of the woman in the fourth panel as a courtesan, her hairstyle and apparel do not distinguish her much from other women of the period. She does wear a fine-quality robe emblazoned with her crest, but her coiffure, in the knotted *Hyōgo* style, is secured only with a paper cord. Furthermore, she does not wear the unbelted outer robe with a padded hem (*uchikake*), or the elevated lacquered sandals typically worn by later courtesans of the eighteenth century; her footwear consists simply of straw sandals (*zōri*).

Other late seventeenth-century images reveal that contemporary high-ranking courtesans also wore their hair in the *tama-musubi* style, in which the tresses were pulled back into a low ponytail, then looped around and secured with a tie. Another popular coiffure was the upswept *Shimada* style, in which the

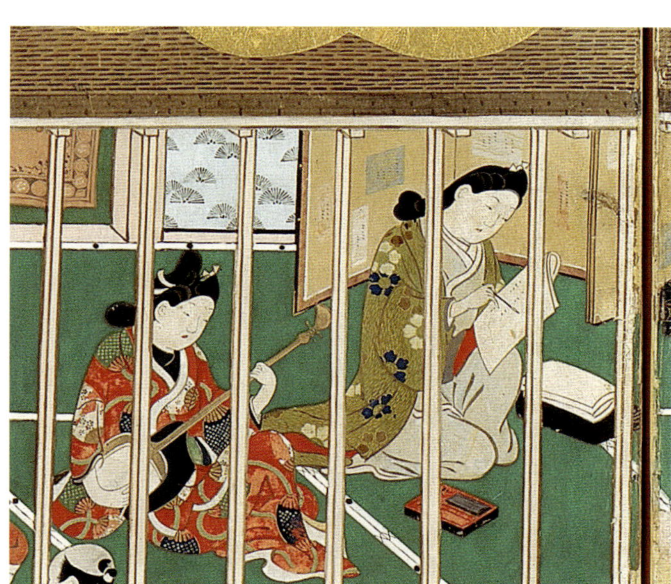

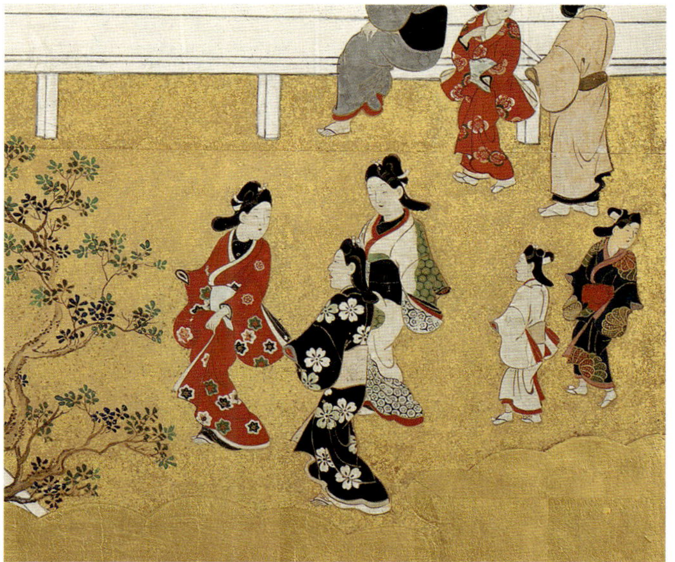

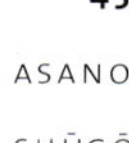

hair was pulled into a high ponytail and then pinned under, with the stiffened side locks fanning on either side of the face. Typically courtesans donned short-sleeved robes (*tomesode*) of fine materials and sported wide obi. Few wore *uchikake* during this period. However, in the lower sections of the fifth and sixth panels of the Moronobu screen, which depict the latticed front parlor of a brothel where courtesans were displayed to prospective clients, a woman writing a letter wears this type of unbelted outer robe (fig.15, left).[5] Young courtesans sometimes also dressed in robes with long, pendant sleeves (*furisode*), a type of garment typically worn by unmarried women, as another painting by Moronobu, *Procession of a Courtesan,* demonstrates (see cat. no. 2).

SHINZŌ: **"NEWLY LAUNCHED" COURTESANS** During the seventeenth century, *shinzō* were the attendants to the high-ranking *tayū* and *kōshi*, and later, during the eighteenth century, they were the teenage entourage members of an *oiran*, as elevated courtesans were called by then. In the lower section of the second panel of the Moronobu *Yoshiwara* screen, the woman, garbed in a red *furisode* with phoenix motifs and standing just behind the courtesan who looks over her shoulder, is without a doubt a *shinzō*. Other figures that can be identified in the screen as *shinzō* include the woman wearing a *furisode* with her sleeves extended and turning back at the right edge of the second panel toward her *tayū* in the first panel, and the white-robed woman walking directly in front of the courtesan in the first panel.

Aside from the fact that many *shinzō* wore their hair in the *Shimada* style and arrayed themselves in brightly colored *furisode*, there was not much difference in the appearance of these teenagers and the courtesans to whom they were in service. Often one can determine their identity only by considering their overall form and placement within a composition.

KAMURO: **CHILD ATTENDANTS** *Kamuro,* the children who were brought to the brothel districts at the age of seven or eight, tended to the needs of the courtesans. As one can see in the two girls who follow behind the *yūjo* in the fourth panel and the right edge of the third panel, *kamuro* are relatively easy to identify (fig. 15, right): Their hair is arranged in a variant *Shimada* style (*yakko Shimada*), their robes are of the *furisode* type, and their stature is necessarily smaller. During the seventeenth century courtesans were accompanied by one or two *kamuro*. When two girls were in attendance, they did not have the matching robes that one typically finds in images of the eighteenth century and later.

fig. 15
Scenes from the Yoshiwara Pleasure Quarter
(details from panels 5–6 and 3–4)

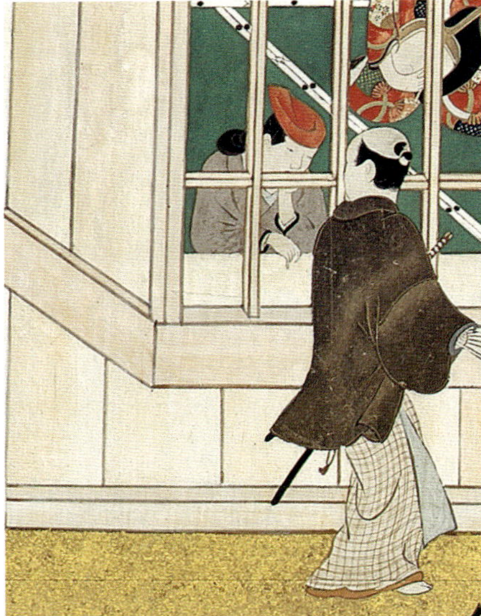

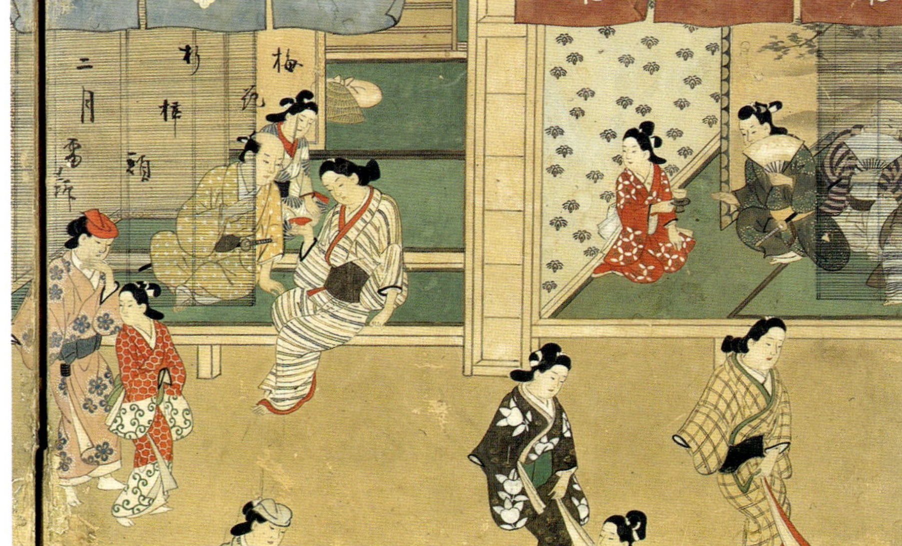

fig. 16
Scenes from the Yoshiwara Pleasure Quarter (detail of panel 6)

fig. 17
Attributed to Miyagawa Chōshun
Scenes in the Yoshiwara Pleasure Quarter (detail of panel 5), about 1704–36

***YARITE:* FEMALE CHAPERONES** *Yarite,* the middle-aged women who served as the supervisors of courtesans, can often be identified by their flat cotton caps (*wataboshi*). The Moronobu *Yoshiwara* screen includes several women of this position: one wearing a red cap in the lower section of the first panel, one inside the latticed brothel conversing with a client strolling by in the lower section of the sixth panel (fig. 16), and two others in the lower sections of the second and third panels. Although in the Moronobu hanging scroll *Procession of a Courtesan* the *yarite* also wears a red cap, the color was not prescribed; some *yarite* wore white ones, and others wore none at all. However, *yarite* generally wore robes in somber colors, with short sleeves and a narrow obi.

Determining the status of the various women of the Yoshiwara through their hairstyle and clothing alone is extremely difficult. Waitresses and servants often assume appearances similar to those of *yarite*. Sometimes aprons are the only markers of a woman's position as a servant.

Courtesans at the End of the Seventeenth Century

Representations of courtesans dating to the end of the seventeenth and early eighteenth centuries reflect minor changes in contemporary dress. As is evident in *Standing Courtesan* by Matsuno Chikanobu (see cat. no. 9), *yūjo* (and later, other women) began to wear decorative combs in their hair.[6] With the advent of the eighteenth century, it also became popular among courtesans to tie their sashes in front.

The two hanging scrolls entitled *Courtesan Seated on a Bench* by Kaigetsudō Anchi (see cat. nos. 8, 13) depict high-ranking Yoshiwara courtesans from the early eighteenth century. As many as thirty works dating to this time have a similar iconography of women seated on a bench, but in these latter works the surroundings—often willow trees or streams—do not necessarily suggest the Yoshiwara.

Genre paintings of the Yoshiwara from the late seventeenth to the early eighteenth centuries rarely include scenes like those found in the Anchi and the Chōshun hanging scrolls. Instead there are images of courtesans seated on teahouse verandas, looking out on the passersby on the street, as in the fifth panel from the right in Chōshun's screen *Scenes in the Yoshiwara Pleasure Quarter* (see cat. no 11). Others include the Yoshiwara sections of the screens *Genre Scenes of Famous Places in Edo* (about 1700), in the Seikadō Art Museum, Tokyo; the screens in the Idemitsu Museum of Arts, Tokyo (which were copied from the Seikadō paintings); and the handscroll *Genre Scenes in the Yoshiwara* by Hanabusa Itchō (about 1703), in the Suntory Museum, Tokyo.[7] In these the courtesan sits on a bench placed in front of a brothel or on the dirt floor of the entrance and flirts with the passersby. Furthermore, in the hanging scroll *Courtesan Waiting for a Client* by Okumura Masanobu (about 1711–16), in the Ōta Memorial Museum, Tokyo, the scene is definitely set in front of a brothel—a courtesan reposes on a bench with her pair of *kamuro*.

In the upper section of an illustration of two courtesans seated on a bench, from Moronobu's woodblock-printed book *Compendium of Fan Designs* (*Uchiwa-e zukushi*, 1682), the following passage is inscribed:

> If you pay a visit to the Yoshiwara on a cool summer's evening, you will see the sexiest girls, after they've taken their baths and made their other preparations, sitting on long, narrow benches trying to catch the attention of men passing by. If one of them spots a client or acquaintance, she'll beckon to him and call out his name.[8]

From this passage it is clear that sitting on a bench was one way in which courtesans attracted clients.

Examples of similarly posed women can also be found in representations of theatrical performances. In a perspective print by the early eighteenth-century artist Nishimura Shigenaga entitled *Illustration of a Kyōgen Play,* which depicts the interior of the Ichimura Theater in Edo on New Year's Day 1746,

fig. 18
Utagawa Toyokuni
Procession of Courtesans inside the Main Gate of the Yoshiwara (detail), about 1795

a female figure is seated on a bench on the stage.[9] The play being performed is *Sukeroku,* in which the title character, wishing to avenge the death of his father, assumes the disguise of a swaggering townsman. Sukeroku frequents the Yoshiwara in order to be closer to his beloved, the courtesan Agemaki, the character in the print portrayed by the actor Arashi Wakano II.

How should one interpret scenes in which the Yoshiwara is not definitively the location portrayed? Examples include *Landscape: A Yūjo Sitting on a Bench* by Chōshun, in the Freer/Sackler Gallery of Art, in which a woman cools off under the willows near a stream, and *Enjoying the Water beside Willow Trees* by the same artist, in the MOA Museum, in which a man and a woman repose on a bench while watching others play in the water.[10] The seated woman in the MOA scroll does look like a courtesan. However, even a close scrutiny of the iconography of the paintings may not necessarily illuminate the status of the women depicted. These scenes are part of a fictional world presented by the artist. Chōshun, who produced a number of compositions of beautiful women seated on a bench, transformed the form that originated in the courtesans' real pose.

Courtesans during the Eighteenth and Early Nineteenth Centuries

Utagawa Toyokuni's hanging scroll *Procession of Courtesans inside the Main Gate of the Yoshiwara,* of about 1795 (see cat. no. 53), provides a detailed portrait of courtesans at the end of the eighteenth century. The Great Gate (Ōmon), which served as the only entrance to the Yoshiwara, frames the composition on the left. Immediately to the right a male geisha (*hōkan*) holding a fan approaches a client. The high-ranking courtesan (*ane jorō* or *oiran*) in the center of the painting is surrounded by her retinue: an older *shinzō* called a *bantō shinzō,* who serves as her personal manager, and two child attendants. At the far right another courtesan promenades with her young *shinzō* (*furisode shinzō*) and two *kamuro*.

Several markers help identify the high-ranking courtesans of this period: the elaborate coiffure, the hair ornaments, a wide obi tied in front, a luxurious outer robe with a padded hem, and the elevated sandals. In the Toyokuni painting, the *oiran* in the center wears her hair in a variation of the *Hyōgo* style; the courtesan to the right, in the *Ōkatsuyama* style, a coiffure with an extravagant topknot named after a particularly stylish mid-seventeenth-century *tayū* (fig. 18). Each woman wears approximately eight hair ornaments, including pins and combs, and sports a costly *uchikake,* which she allows to drag on the ground as she promenades along the main avenue of the pleasure quarters.[11] Although the courtesans are outfitted with expensive lacquer sandals, they and the *bantō shinzō* do not wear the white toed-socks (*tabi*) that are worn by the younger female figures.

The appearance of *shinzō* did not undergo significant changes from its counterparts in the seventeenth century. The teenage attendants continued to wear their hair in the *Shimada* style. Furthermore, they did not wear *uchikake.* However, the paired child attendants began to wear matching costumes.

Geisha

The appellation *geisha* or *geiko* for professional female entertainers is not particularly old. In fact, from the late seventeenth to the early eighteenth centuries, the term *odoriko,* "dancing girl," was more widely adopted.[12] However, it has always been difficult to make a rigid distinction between courtesans and geisha. During the seventeenth century courtesans in the Yoshiwara certainly possessed some artistic accomplishments, and presiding over performances was an important duty.

To find portrayals of these seventeenth-century entertainers, let us turn again to Moronobu's *Yoshiwara* screen, in which there is a drinking party in one of the houses of assignation in the upper section of the second panel. There it is possible to find two courtesans who are skilled in performance — one in a

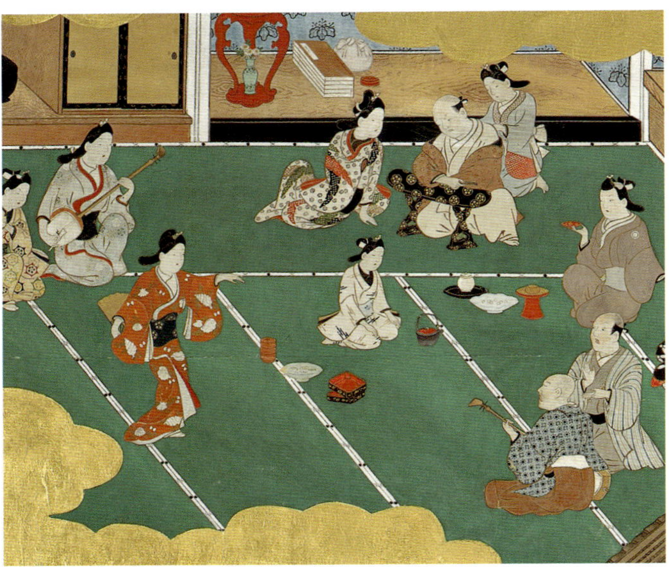

fig. 19
Scenes from the Yoshiwara Pleasure Quarter
(detail of panel 2)

furisode dancing, the other plucking the three-stringed samisen (fig. 19). A young man tapping a drum and a blind musician playing the samisen with his back to the viewer complete the ensemble. In contrast, the women playing samisens in the latticed brothels in both the upper and lower sections of the fifth and sixth panels are probably not high-ranking courtesans; they are most likely *shinzō*.

Over time distinctions were made among those who truly excelled at performance, and by the mid-eighteenth century the vocation of female geisha had been established. With this designation came a prohibition against these women's engaging in prostitution. Outside of the Yoshiwara, though, this proscription was not strictly enforced. In the unlicensed brothel district of Fukagawa in southeast Edo, for example, there was not a clear distinction between the area's Tatsumi geisha and its courtesans, who were called "children" (*kodomo*).

From the third quarter of the eighteenth century, geisha became one of the primary subjects of ukiyo-e prints and paintings. Later in the century there were two types of geisha — the Yoshiwara geisha and the town geisha. The talents of these latter geisha varied greatly. Some performed while in attendance at banquets, and others taught female puppet-drama chanters, comic dramatists (*kyōgen*), and amateurs in the performing arts.

GEISHA IN THE LATE EIGHTEENTH CENTURY Distinguishing the different types of women employed in the pleasure quarters, both as courtesans and geisha, remains a challenge. Approximately one hundred years after Moronobu produced his visions of the floating world, Utagawa Toyoharu took a traditional poetic grouping of natural elements and likened them to contemporary women in his *Courtesans with Snow, Moon, and Flowers* (see cat. no. 52). The subject of the center *Flowers* hanging scroll is immediately identifiable as a Yoshiwara courtesan. Holding a fan decorated with blossoms in her left hand, the commanding figure wears an elegant black *uchikake* patterned with peacock feathers and a wide damask obi tied in front. Her hair is arranged in a *Hyōgo* coiffure secured with multiple pins and combs.

Through a careful examination of the *Moon* scroll on the left it is possible to determine that the willowy courtesan is a high-ranking *yūjo* from the unlicensed Shinagawa pleasure quarters, which were located at the southern edge of Edo. The grass patterns on the outer robe of the woman and the selection of flowers in the arrangement are indicative of autumn — a season traditionally associated with the full moon — and Shinagawa, located on Edo Bay, was a favored location for moon viewing.

The subject of the *Snow* scroll on the right must be associated with Fukagawa, since this area in southeast Edo was the city's other major pleasure district. The snow on the tray next to the charcoal brazier supports this conclusion. However, it is almost impossible to determine whether the woman huddled in her black robe patterned with cherry blossoms and secured with a wide white obi with a feather motif is a Fukagawa geisha or a courtesan (*kodomo*). If there were a samisen by her side identify-

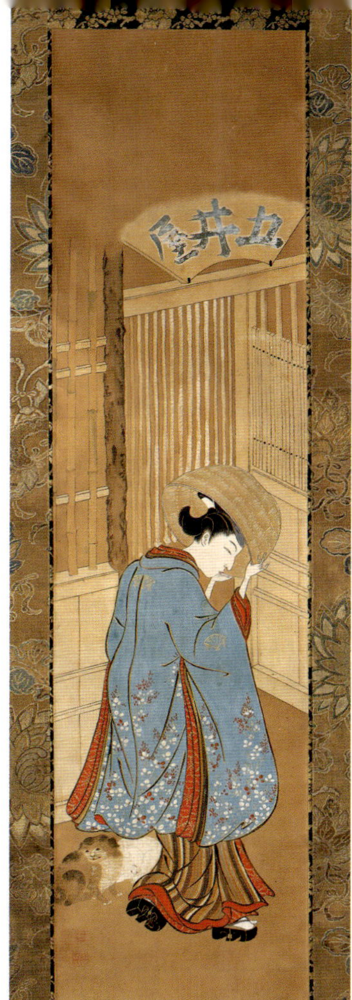

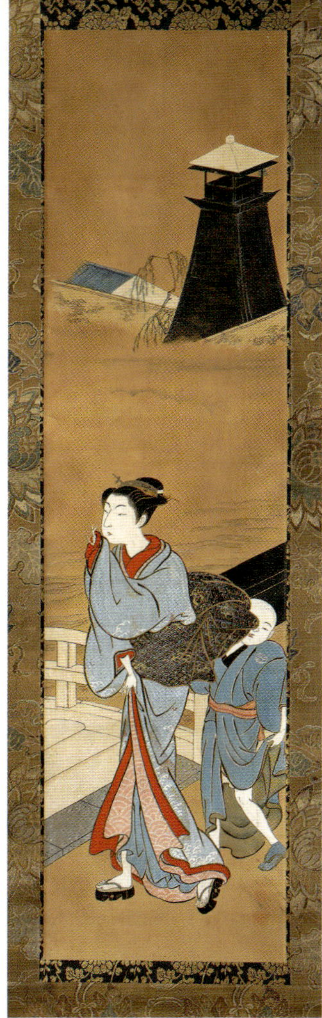

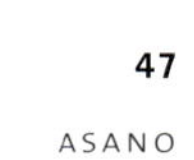

ing her as a performer, then the identification would be simple, but there is none.

Even during the late Edo period, geisha, unlike high-ranking Yoshiwara courtesans, were difficult to distinguish from other women. As the title of Utagawa Toyokuni's *Geisha and Waitress* (see cat. no. 54) suggests, scholars have determined the status of the two women in this MFA painting, but the identification is only tentative. The woman perched on a cloth-covered *kotatsu* heater and eagerly reading a love letter has been labeled a geisha. Strictly speaking, however, there are no clear indications of her profession; there is only the balance and the overall mood conveyed by the painting. In the case of Kitagawa Utamaro's *Young Woman Playing the Samisen* (see cat. no. 44) and Keisai Eisen's *Geisha* (see cat. no. 58), though, the clues are relatively easy to decipher. In the first work the three-stringed instrument is certainly central to a geisha's profession. In Eisen's scroll the wooden samisen box decorated with ivy leaves in the background is an irrefutable marker of the subject's position as a geisha — one who specifically performed at banquets.

Male Prostitutes: *Iroko* and *Kagema*

During the seventeenth and early eighteenth centuries, homosexual relationships among men were accepted at all levels of society. In the male-dominated world of Edo, where marriage with women was a contractual rather than an emotional bond, many members of the military aristocracy retained young men not only as loyal servants but also as bed partners. Others patronized young actors who were open to sexual liaisons (*iroko*) and who by their profession cultivated particularly alluring feminine appearances, or they sought out boy prostitutes (*kagema*) in the city's brothel districts of Yoshi-chō, Yushima, and Fukiya-chō.

In a pair of hanging scrolls in the Museum's collection dating to around 1772–73 (fig. 20), Isoda Koryūsai depicts a geisha passing by the watchtower at Fukagawa and a *kagema* walking in front of (or perhaps entering) the Itsusui, which was probably a teahouse for male prostitutes (*kagemajaya*). The young man in the left scroll holds a sedge hat in both of his hands over his head. Underneath we catch a glimmer of his topknot pulled over the purple silk cap (*yarōboshi*) that conceals his shorn forelock — the tresses that were thought to make boys particularly attractive sexually but that were cut upon their coming of age. The *kagema* is dressed in a light blue pendant-sleeved outer jacket (*furisode haori*) and elevated sandals.

Although the attire of the *kagema* closely resembles that of young females, three of its elements would not have been adopted by contemporary women: the sedge hat, the purple silk cap, and the *haori*. While the jackets with their front panels secured by silk cords are now standard in a kimono ensemble, during the eighteenth century only certain geisha (women who performed *gidayū*, samisen chanting for puppet dramas, or those who hailed from Fukagawa) would don *haori*.

Several other compositions confirm these three traits as identifying features of *kagema*. In the Chiba City Museum collection, there is a pair of hanging scrolls by Hishikawa Morotane, presumably dating to 1716, titled *The Actor Nakamura Takesaburō and the Courtesan Komurasaki of the Miuraya*.[13] In the left-hand composition, Takesaburō, who was a Kabuki actor specializing in young female roles, largely assumes the prescribed appearance; however, he wears a short-sleeved *haori* and straw sandals. Another painting of a *kagema*, by the early eighteenth-century

fig. 20
Isoda Koryūsai
Geisha and Male Prostitute, about 1764–81

artist Kawamata Tsuneyuki (formerly in the collection of the Azabu Museum), shares the same traits as the figure in the Morotane painting, with the exception of the elevated sandals, which can be found in the MFA's Koryūsai scroll.[14]

Woodblock prints dating to the second half of the 1760s, such as *Iroko Ascending the Stairs and Woman Carrying a Samisen*, document the manners of the *kagema* in their houses of assignation.[15] Although in this work the young man does not wear the sedge hat, the sandals, or the purple silk cap, his appearance otherwise resembles that found in the Koryūsai painting. One additional point of interest is that a woman hands a samisen to the *kagema,* who carries bedding at his side. From this image we can determine that *kagema* were able to play the samisen. Furthermore, like "appointment only" Fukagawa courtesans (Fukagawa *yobidashi*), *kagema* would come to the teahouses carrying (or having someone else carry) their bedding from their quarters.

The same scene is reproduced in Kitao Shigemasa's woodblock-printed book *The Tucking Up of Garments by Eastern Men* (*Ehon Azuma karage*, 1786). A *kagema* ascends the staircase in a teahouse in Yoshi-chō; below him a man carries a samisen and bedding (fig. 21). Further research is required to determine whether all the *kagema* of that period went back and forth between their quarters to the teahouses; however, based on the extant works, such an assumption seems justified.

Historical Record or Painted Convention?

Despite the specificity of the manners and elaborate clothing and hairstyles in the images of the denizens of the brothel districts, ukiyo-e paintings were never portraits in the strictest sense of the term. In fact, although the names of celebrated geisha and *kagema* were occasionally inscribed on printed images during the early eighteenth century, by the late eighteenth century the military government strictly forbade this practice; only the high-ranking courtesans from the licensed Yoshiwara pleasure quarters were exempt from this prohibition. Rather than celebrating the features of a particular person, contemporary artists were primarily concerned with the status of their subjects and coordinated their appearances accordingly. Thus, as images, ukiyo-e paintings project an ideal that was subject to individual interpretation by different artists, rather than a recording of reality. However, today, when little remains of historic Edo, these images have come to shape our understanding of the vibrant environment of the floating world.

---

1. The dollar equivalent is based on an exchange rate of $1 = ¥114.
2. The oldest extant guide to the Yoshiwara, the *Yoshiwara saikenzu* of 1680, notes that in that year there were 2,868 courtesans; in the *Shocho no itomaki* of 1787, the man of letters Santō Kyōden (also known as Kitao Masanobu) comments that the number of courtesans and their child attendants was 2,500; and records of the nineteenth century indicate that there were 3,000 courtesans then.
3. See Asano Shūgō and Timothy Clark, *The Passionate Art of Kitagawa Utamaro* (London: British Museum Press, 1995), 145–46.
4. During the late Edo period a client would come to call at a teahouse (*hikitejaya*), where the high-level courtesan would process to meet him. She would then escort him back to the brothel, where they would have their assignation.
5. This *kōshi* is probably from the famed Miuraya managed by Shirōemon, which was located in the Kyōmachi 1 section of the Yoshiwara.
6. The adoption of the comb is documented by the hanging scroll of Hishikawa Moronobu's later years, *Woman Looking over Her Shoulder* (*Mikaeri bijin*), in the collection of the Tokyo National Museum.
7. Published in Idemitsu Museum of Arts, *Idemitsu bijutsukan zōhin zuroku: Fūzokuga* (Tokyo: Heibonsha, 1987), illustration 8.
8. English translation by Joe Earle.
9. Nishimura Shigenaga, *Illustration of a Kyōgen Play*, 1746, *yoko ōban* woodblock print with hand coloring, Ōta Memorial Museum, Tokyo.
10. Miyagawa Chōshun, *Landscape: A Yūjo Sitting on a Bench*, 18th century, hanging scroll, ink and color on silk, 37 x 58.1 cm, Gift of Charles Lang Freer, F1898.429, Freer/Sackler Museum of Art, published on www.asia.si.edu/collections, accessed May 28, 2006. Miyagawa Chōshun, *Enjoying the Water beside Willow Trees*, Kyōhō era (1716–36), hanging scroll, ink and color on silk, 61.8 x 91.2 cm, MOA Museum, published in *MOA bijutsukan*, vol. 4 of *Nikuhitsu ukiyo-e taikan* (Tokyo: Kōdansha, 1994), illustration 31.
11. The luxuriousness of the robes worn by the *oiran* is evident in *Courtesan with Child Attendant*, a hanging scroll in the MFA's collection by Kitagawa Utamaro, which is dated just a few years earlier than the Toyokuni work (see cat. no. 43). By looking closely at the black *uchikake* decorated with wave patterns, one can see many small bells that have been sewn onto the garment. They would have tinkled as the courtesan walked.

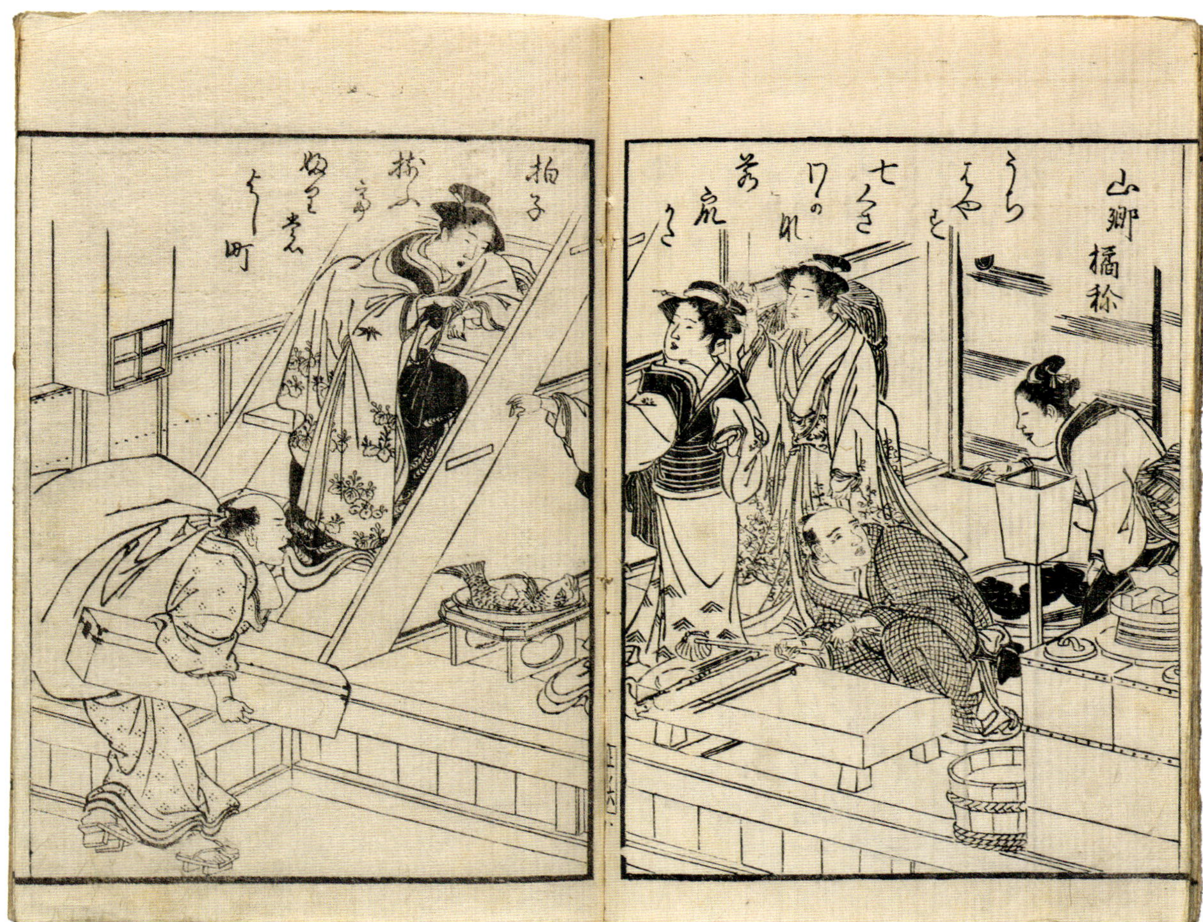

fig. 21
Kitao Shigemasa
The Tucking Up of Garments by Eastern Men (*Ehon Azuma karage*), Vol 1, 1797 edition

12. Even when the terms *geisha* and *geiko* were more widely used, the *furisode geisha* of Nihonbashi Tachibana-chō in Edo continued to be called *odoriko.*
13. Hishikawa Morotane, *The Actor Nakamura Takesaburō and the Courtesan Komurasaki of the Miuraya,* 1716, pair of hanging scrolls, ink and color on silk, each 69.9 x 32.6 cm, Chiba City Museum of Art, published in *Chiba-shi bijutsukan,* vol. 10 of *Nikuhitsu ukiyo-e taikan* (Tokyo: Kōdansha, 1994), illustrations 13–14.
14. Kawamata Tsuneyuki, *Kagema in Front of a Teahouse,* about Kyōhō (1716–36) through Kanpō (1741–44) era, hanging scroll; ink and color on paper, 87.6 x 26.2 cm, formerly collection of Azabu Museum, published in *Azabu bijutsu kogeikan,* vol. 6 of *Nikuhitsu ukiyo-e taikan* (Tokyo: Kōdansha, 1994), illustration 31.
15. Artist unknown, *Iroko Ascending the Stairs and Woman Carring a Samisen*, Meiwa era (1746–72), woodblock print; ink and color on paper. Published in *Fūzoku*, vol. 5 of *Genshoku ukiyo-e daihyakka jiten* (Tokyo: Taishūkan shoten, 1980), p. 47.

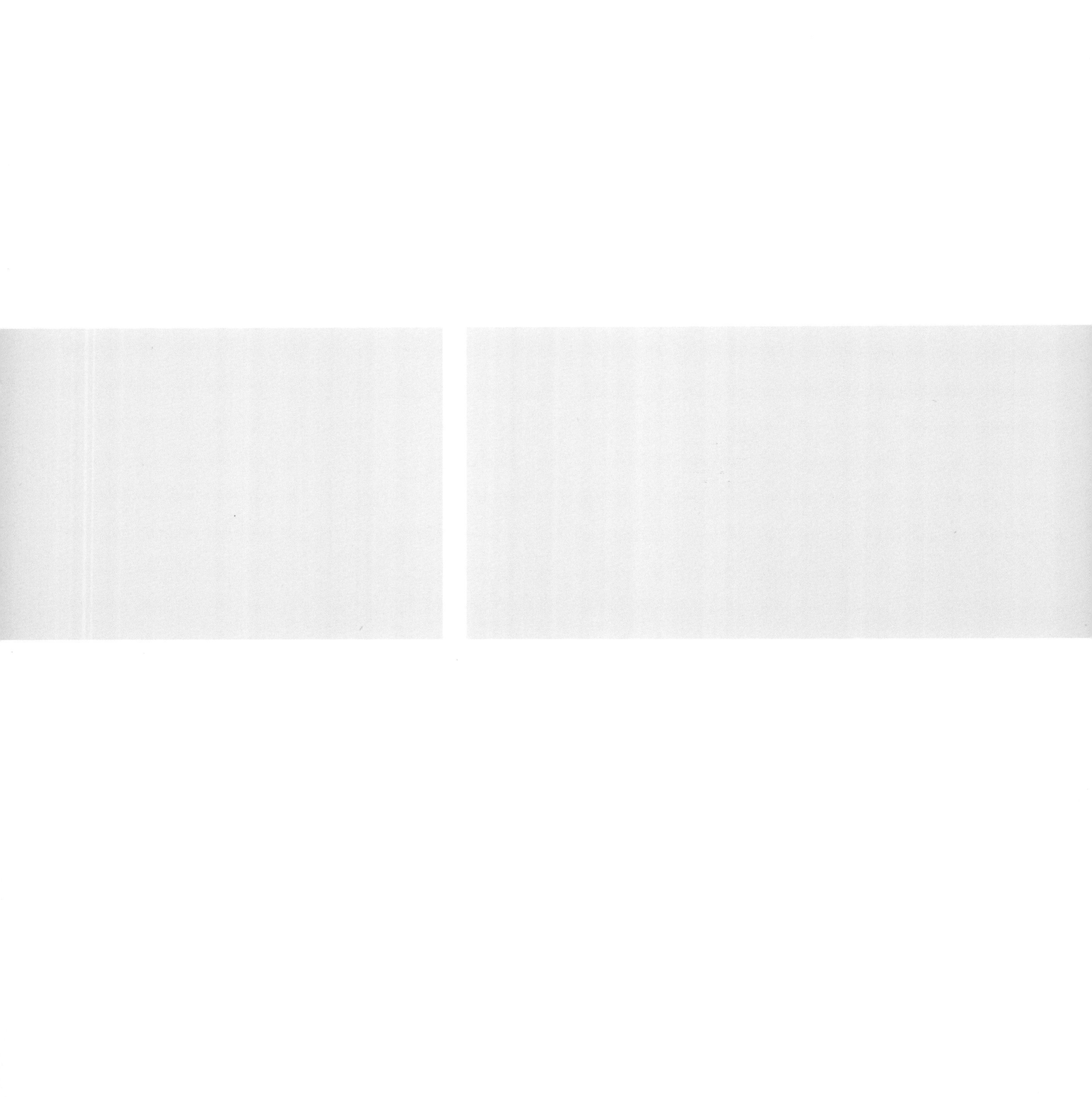

WITH AN EYE TO STYLE, 1690–1765 **EARLY UKIYO-E**

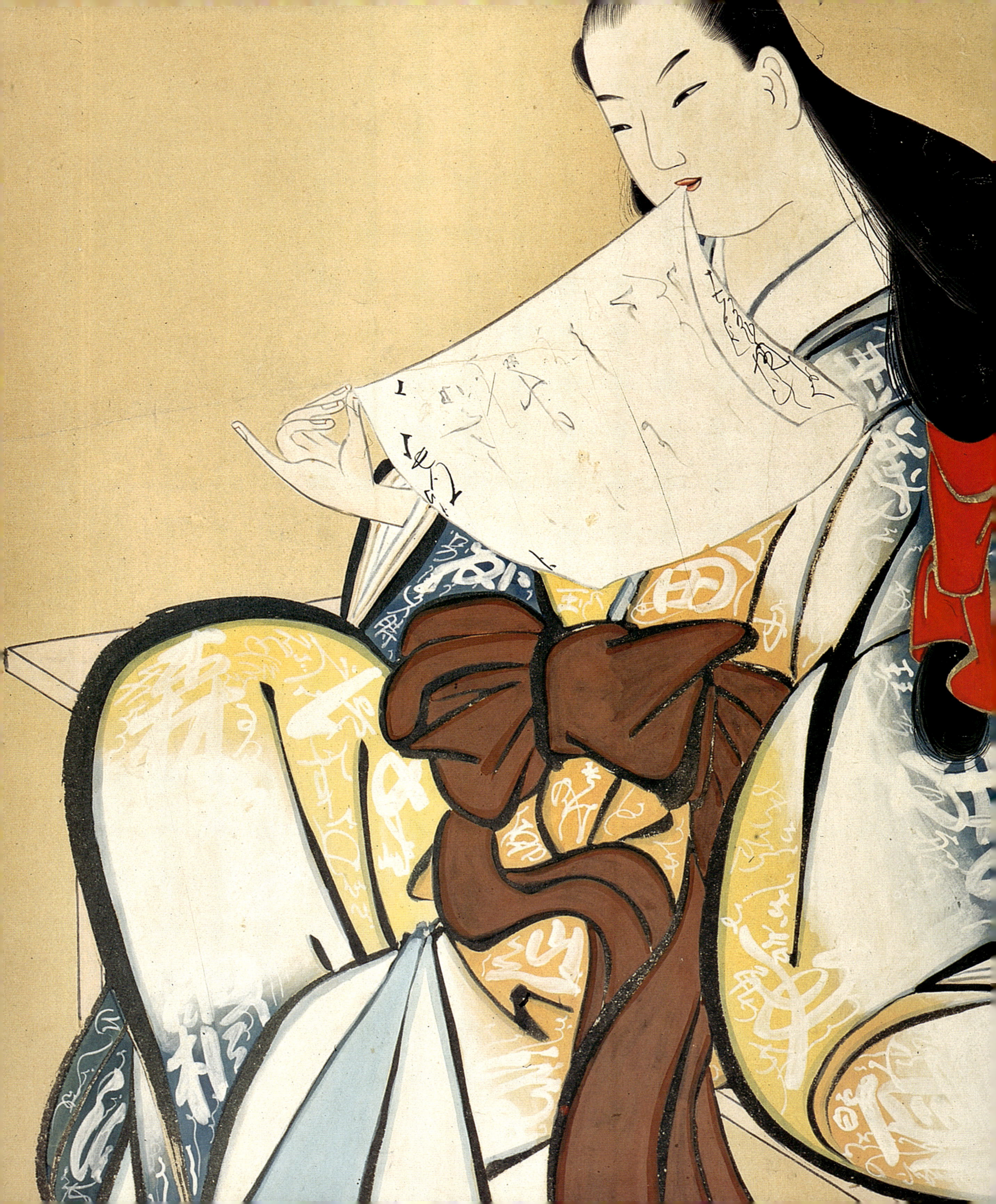

Hishikawa Moronobu was the first artist to be described as an ukiyo-eshi, *a painter of the floating world. When the term* ukiyo-e *itself initially came into use is unclear, but by Moronobu's time it had come to refer to paintings, prints, and printed books depicting the pleasures found in the theaters, brothels, and annual festivals of Japan's leading urban centers. Moronobu described these subjects with a self-assured, independent style, and his works reveal a fascination with the chic fashions that preoccupied the residents of Edo.*

Scholars today designate images of the floating world generated during the one hundred-year period from the time of the appearance of Moronobu in the 1670s to the introduction of full-color printing in 1765 as "early ukiyo-e." Aside from the Hishikawa school centered around Moronobu, schools that dominated ukiyo-e production in Edo during this period were led by Torii Kiyonobu I and Kiyomasu I, Okumura Masanobu, Kaigetsudō Ando, and Miyagawa Chōshun. The Torii were celebrated for their portrayals of dynamic actors, with billowing sleeves and bulging muscles, and stately courtesans. Kaigetsudō artists composed standard-setting, iconic images of courtesans with boldly patterned voluminous robes, described in striking calligraphic lines. In Kyoto, Nishikawa Sukenobu produced more refined, gentle images of beautiful women in a pastel palette that had a profound impact upon other artists in the military capital during the mid-eighteenth century.

From its inception ukiyo-e developed through the interrelated media of painting (nikuhitsuga) *and prints — single sheets as well as illustrated books. Many early ukiyo-e artists, such as Moronobu, established their reputations through their designs for widely circulated prints and then devoted themselves almost exclusively to painting. Others, such as Torii Kiyonobu I, created images in both genres throughout their careers. In contrast, members of the Kaigetsudō and Miyagawa schools worked almost exclusively as painters. The artists in these two groups produced compositions that ranged from special commissions with costly pigments and elaborate techniques for wealthy patrons to almost identical designs with limited palettes for purchase by members of the general populace. Early ukiyo-e artists thus established the pictorial conventions of images of the floating world which would be carried into later periods.* AS

1. **HISHIKAWA MORONOBU** (DIED 1694)
Scenes from the Nakamura Kabuki Theater and the Yoshiwara Pleasure Quarter

Jōkyō (1684–88) or Genroku (1688–1704) era
Pair of six-panel folding screens; ink, color, and gold on paper
Seals: Hishikawa; Moronobu
139.8 x 355.2 cm (55 1/16 x 139 13/16 in.) each
Gift of Oliver Peabody 79.468, 79.469

In the decades after the Tokugawa shogunate moved the seat of Japan's political authority to Edo from Kyoto in 1615, Edo was physically transformed by the construction of vast housing complexes for the military clans in enforced attendance on the shogun, and the growth of a large urban infrastructure to service them. The Meireki Fire of 1657 precipitated that transformation when it reduced more than two-thirds of the city to ashes. Rebuilding began almost immediately, but government supervision enforced some strict rezoning of the theaters and the pleasure quarters previously scattered around Edo. The theaters were kept to a single district in the adjoining neighborhoods of Sakai-chō and Kobiki-chō, and the Shin Yoshiwara (New Yoshiwara), as the rebuilt brothel district came to be known, was given an officially sanctioned area in the marshy plains in the north of the city.

Hishikawa Moronobu was a native of Awa province, modern-day Chiba prefecture. It is not clear when he moved to Edo, but after mastering the traditional painting styles of the Kano and Tosa schools then favored by the military, Moronobu developed a new dynamic mode of figural depiction that captured the increasingly confident spirit and sophistication of the thriving metropolis.[1] He was one of the first artists to develop an iconography for the rebuilt city. Moronobu borrowed some elements, such as the arrangement of the structures at the Tokugawa tutelary temple Kan'ei-ji in Ueno, from earlier pre-conflagration screen paintings with panoramic visions of Edo.[2] However, in *Sparrow of Edo* (*Edo suzume*, 1677) the artist provided fresh vignettes of daimyō processions outside Edo Castle, the fish market at Nihonbashi, the bamboo yards at Yotsuya, and the fireworks at Ryōgoku Bridge. He also explored the two *akusho*, the "bad places" of the theater and the brothels. In this and his other woodblock-printed books dating to the 1670s, we can see his gradual development of a visual vocabulary to describe different types of establishments and the people of all social classes who frequented them.[3]

In *Genre Scenes of the Yoshiwara (Yoshiwara fūzoku zukan)*, a handscroll now in the collection of John Weber, New York, and dated by Asano Shūgō to the Enpō (1673–81) or Tenna (1681–84) era, the artist combined the different elements in a composition that moves from right to left to provide a view of the Yoshiwara from its outskirts, through its main gate, Ōmon-guchi, along the chief thoroughfare, Nakano-chō, and into the luxurious interior of a high-class *ageya*, a house of assignation where courtesans entertained their clients.[4] *Scenes from the Nakamura Kabuki Theater and the Yoshiwara Pleasure Quarter* illustrated here, two screens which probably date from before 1690, are attempts at an even more ambitious composition in a larger format.

The New Yoshiwara's main avenue dominates the expanse of the left screen, but additional areas of interest—the interior of a house of assignation and lower-level brothels—are arranged in the upper sections set off by bands of gold clouds. Several details contribute a strong narrative element to the composition: the highest-ranked courtesans promenading with their attendants along the main street in the early evening on their way to the *ageya*; the men gathering to gawk at these almost unattainable visions of feminine charm; and the inhabitants of the latticed

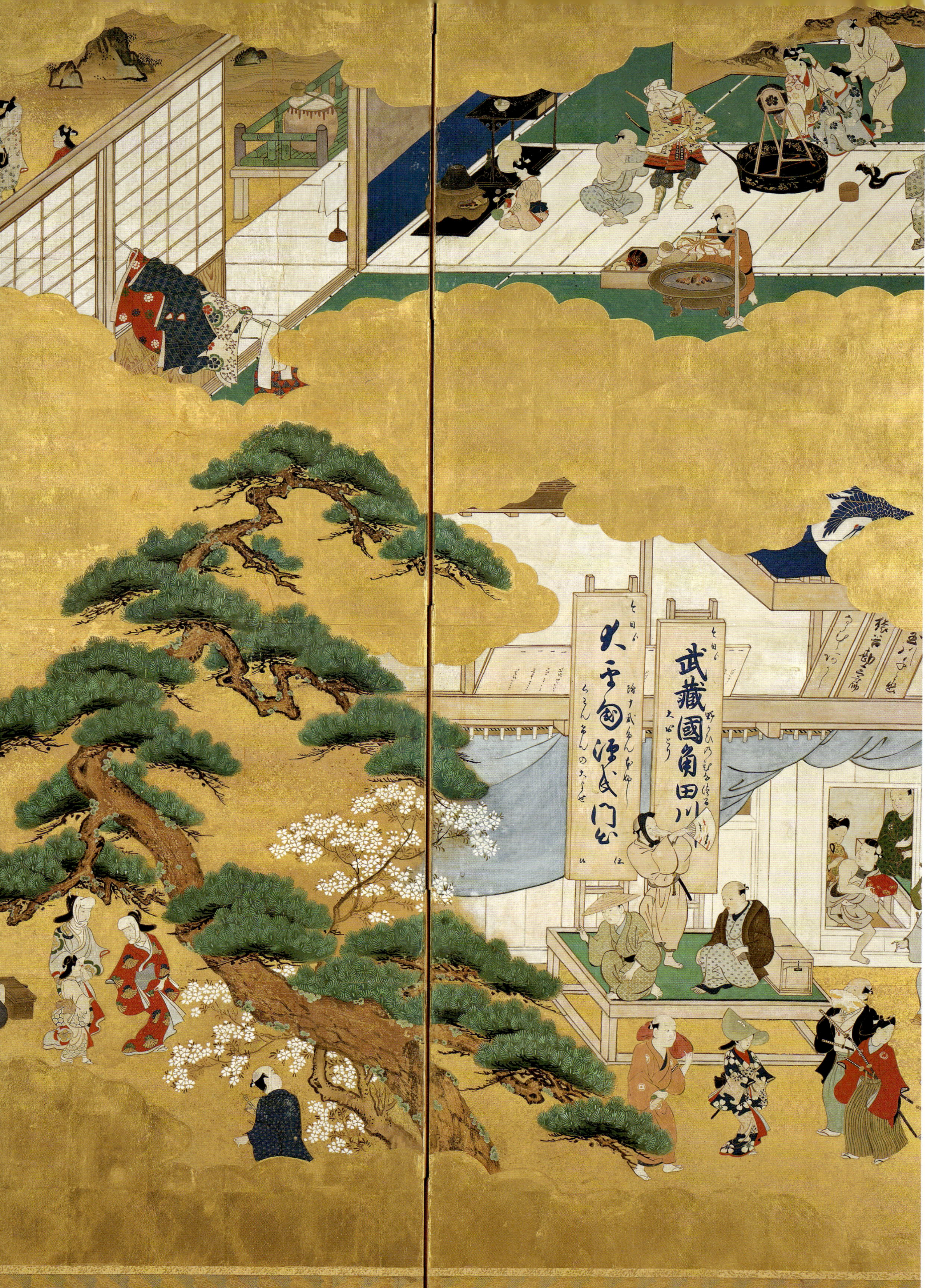
武蔵國角田川

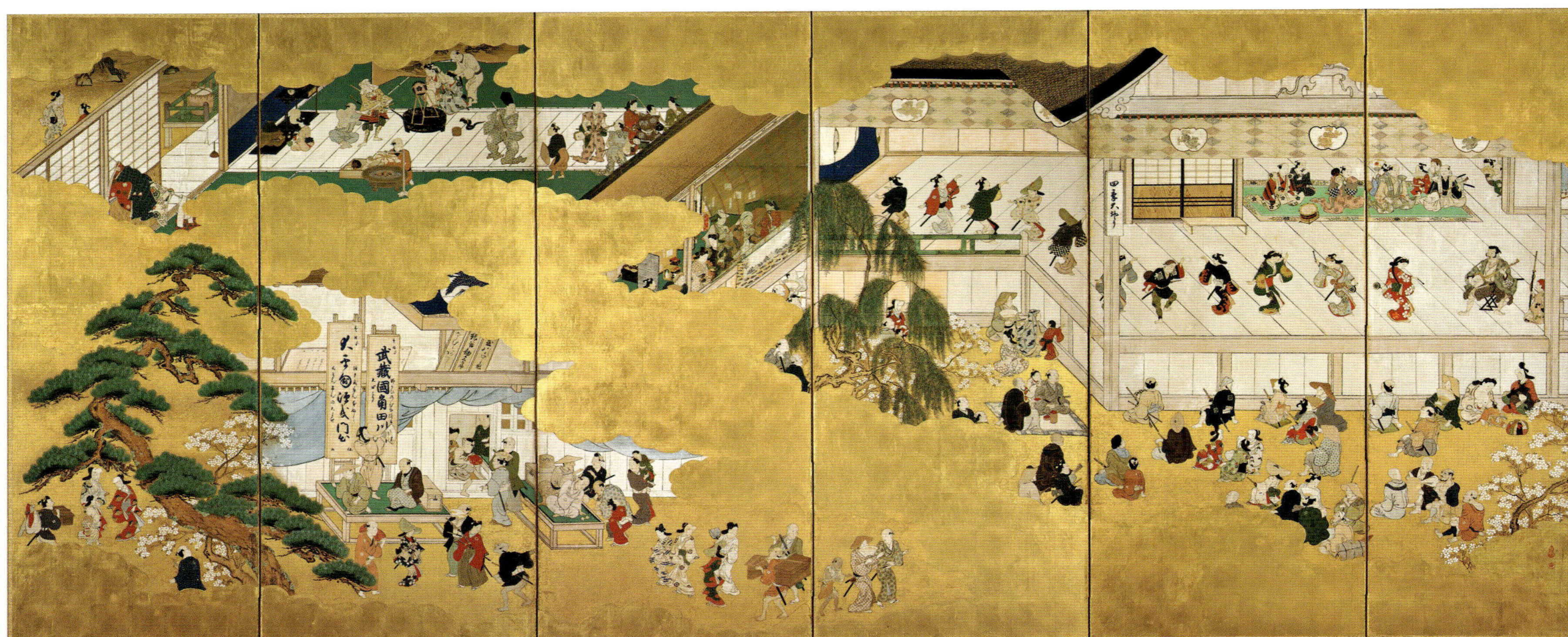

brothels displayed to those in search of entertainment as well as sexual adventure.

In the right-hand screen Moronobu presents three views of the Nakamura Theater. The lower-left corner, framed by a massive pine tree, depicts the bustle of activity at the theater's entrance, with a barker standing on a raised platform and motioning to the passersby to attend the day's performances of group dances and war epics detailed on the vertical signs behind him.[5] The three panels farthest to the right are dominated by the wooden stage, on which a festive procession of actors in male and female roles wends its way rhythmically toward a seated samisen player. Shaded from view by bamboo blinds, upper-class women watch the performance from their well-appointed box, while less privileged members of the audience sit on the ground. In the upper-left corner Moronobu illustrates the activities backstage, with one actor preparing to don a wig for a female role and another receiving assistance with lacing his armor.

Moronobu must have adapted the representation of the Nakamura stage from earlier woodblock illustrations, such as *Kyoto Child* (*Kyō warabe*) of 1658, which includes a scene in a Kabuki theater in the Shijōgawara area of Kyoto.[6] The unknown artist of that Kyoto guidebook offered a similar view, with a retinue of four dancers parading across the wooden floor. Moronobu further developed the juxtaposition of stage and entrance in at least two later works — the *Genre Scenes of the Nakamura Theater* (*Kabuki zu byōbu*), in the Tokyo National Museum, which has been dated to 1692 or 1693, and *Cherry Blossom Viewing and Kabuki Theater* (*Ueno hanami kabuki zu byōbu*), in the Suntory Museum, Tokyo, which dates to 1693 or 1694.[7]

During the late seventeenth and early eighteenth centuries Moronobu's vision of theaters and brothels had a profound influence upon members of the Hishikawa school. Morohira, for example, in *Pastimes in Spring and Autumn* (*Shunjū yūraku zu byōbu,* Idemitsu Museum of Arts, Tokyo), which dates to the Genroku

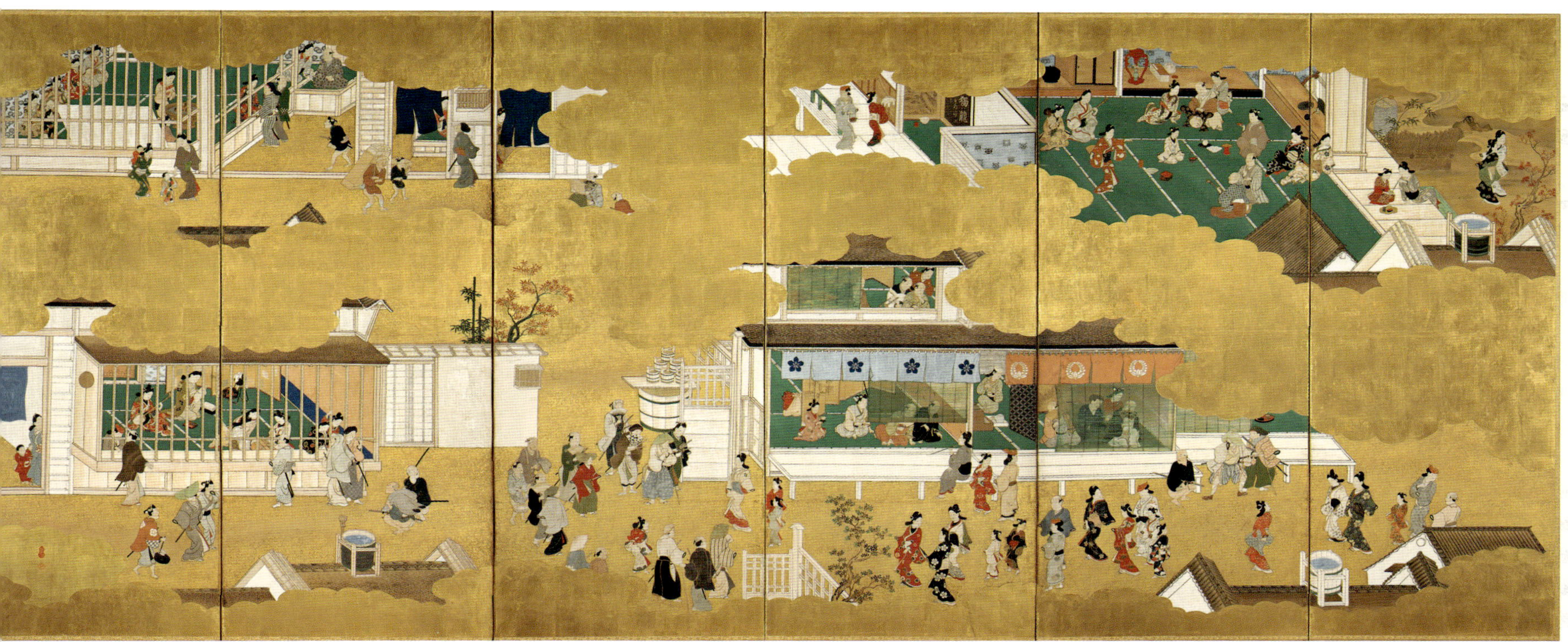

era (1688–1704), borrows freely from Moronobu's descriptions of the Yoshiwara. Okumura Masanobu and Miyagawa Chōshun also turned to Moronobu's works for inspiration during the early stages of their careers, in such paintings as the pair of hanging scrolls, *Scenes in the Yoshiwara* (*Yoshiwara fūzoku;* private collection), dating to the first half of the Kyōhō era (1716–36) and the six-panel screen *Scenes in the Yoshiwara Pleasure Quarter* (*Yoshiwara fūzokuzu byōbu*) dating to the Hōei (1704–11) or the early Kyōhō era, (1716–36) (see cat.no. 11).[8] ANM

1. Moronobu's facility with the painting themes of the Kano and Tosa schools is evident in *Birds, Flowers, and Scenes from Classical Tales,* about 1684–94, album of fourteen paintings, ink and color on silk, 30.1 x 25.8 cm (each), Joe and Etsuko Price Collection, published in Chiba City Museum of Art, *Hishikawa Moronobu* (Chiba: Chiba City Museum of Art, 2000), 77–79.
2. Examples of the pre-conflagration works include *Famous Scenic Places and Amusements in Edo (Edo meisho yūraku zu byōbu,* Hosomi Museum, Kyoto) and *Famous Scenic Places in Edo* (*Edo meisho zu byōbu,* Idemitsu Museum of Arts, Tokyo); see Okano Tomoko, "Edo meisho zu no tanjō: Hosomi bijutsukan bon Edo meisho yūraku zu byōbu o chūshin ni," *Bijutsushi* 48, no. 2 (March 1999): 268–83.
3. Other examples include *Great Miscellany of the Yoshiwara* (*Yoshiwara ō-zassho*) of 1675, *A Guide to Love in the Yoshiwara* (*Yoshiwara koi no michibiki*) of 1678, and *Actors, Past and Present* (*Kokon yakusha monogatari*) of the same year.
4. Chiba City Museum of Art, *Hishikawa Moronobu*, 50.
5. Kobayashi Tadashi in *Bosuton bijitsukan nikuhitsu ukiyoe*, vol. 1 (Tokyo: Museum of Fine Arts, Boston, and Kōdansha, 2000), nos. 38–39, transcribes the program named on these signs as "Nogai no Hinazuru," "Musashi no Kuni, Sumidagawa," and "Ō-odori" on one, "Jūni-dan no Honbushi," "Taiheikoku Genji no Kado-ide," and Kangen no Ō-yose" on the other.
6. Reproduced in Kyoto bunka hakubutsukan, *Kyō no kabuki ten* (Kyoto: Kyoto bunka hakubutsukan, 1991), no. 60.
7. Dating by Asano Shūgō in Chiba City Museum of Art, *Hishikawa Moronobu*, 38.
8. *Bosuton bijutsukan nikuhitsu ukiyo-e,* vol. 2 (Tokyo: Museum of Fine Arts, Boston, and Kōdansha, 2000), no. 10; and Anne Nishimura Morse, "Miyagawa Chōshun hitsu Yoshiwara fūzoku zu byōbu," *Kokka*, no. 1261 (November 2000): 19–23.

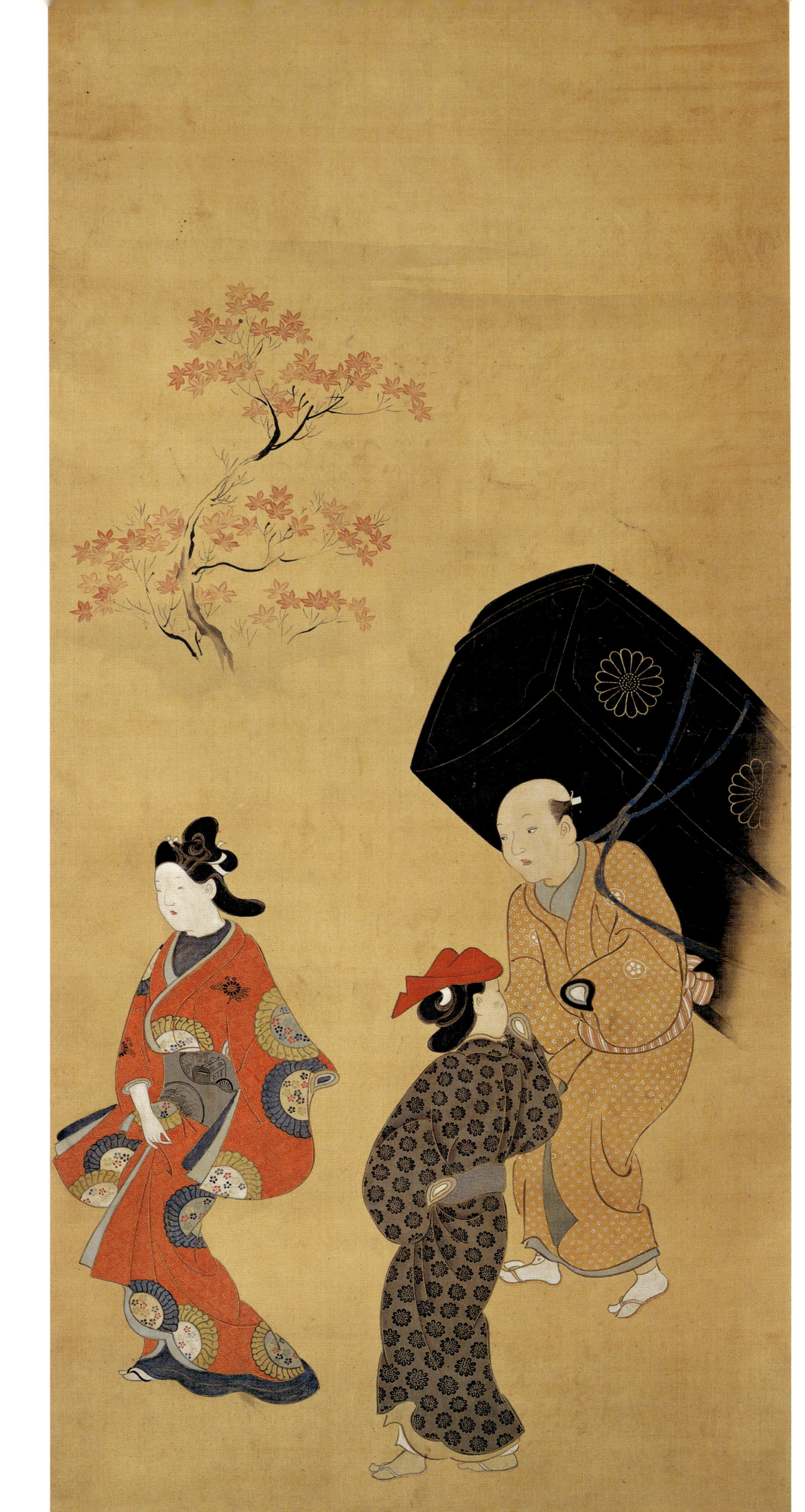

2. **HISHIKAWA MORONOBU** (DIED 1694)

Procession of a Courtesan

About the Tenna era (1681–84)
Hanging scroll; ink, color, gold, and silver on silk
80 x 39.3 cm (31 ½ x 15 ½ in.)
Fenollosa-Weld Collection 11.4618

When summoned for an evening's entertainment at the house of assignation (*ageya*), high-ranking courtesans (such as *tayū* and *kōshi*) paraded there along with their attendants (*shinzō* and *kamuro*), a female chaperone, and a young man who carried their bedding. This procession is known as the *ageya* procession. In this painting, set against the red maple leaves of late autumn, an elegant courtesan assumes the distinctive posture of a woman on parade. She holds the skirt of her robe with her right hand and places her left inside her sleeve. The older female supervisor of the brothel (*yarite*), in her customary red cap, speaks to the man transporting the clothes. The chrysanthemum motif on the chest matches the ones on the unidentified courtesan's robe, which suggests that this floral symbol was her crest.

Depictions of young men bearing clothing chests are rare. An inscription in gold next to a similar attendant in the handscroll *Genre Scenes in the Yoshiwara*, now in the collection of John C. Weber, reads, "The bedding-chest carrier arrives."[1] This notation suggests that the man in the handscroll did not accompany the courtesan to the house of assignation, but rather (as must have occurred in real life) brought her articles later. The male attendants in both paintings carry the chests without putting their arms through the shoulder straps. It is unclear whether boxes were actually transported in this way or if the cords were used.

The postures and the facial features of the figures are typical of Moronobu's style — not of his later works but of those produced at the height of his career, around the Tenna era. Except in special cases, Moronobu did not add his signature or seal to his paintings until after the Jōkyō era (1684–88).[2] Therefore, it is natural that this work is unsigned. In fact, Moronobu's best works can be found among his unsigned pieces. AS

1. The figure appears in the fourteenth scene of the Weber scroll.
2. Asano Shūgō, "Hishikawa Moronobu hitsu 'Hokurō oyobi engeki zukan' no kentō,'" *Kokka*, no. 1295 (September 2003): 5–21.

3. ATTRIBUTED TO HISHIKAWA MORONOBU (DIED 1694)

Genre Scenes in Edo in the Four Seasons

Jōkyō era (1684–88)

Handscroll; ink, color, gold, and silver on silk

34.4 x 859.5 cm (13 9/16 x 338 3/8 in.)

William Sturgis Bigelow Collection 11.7619

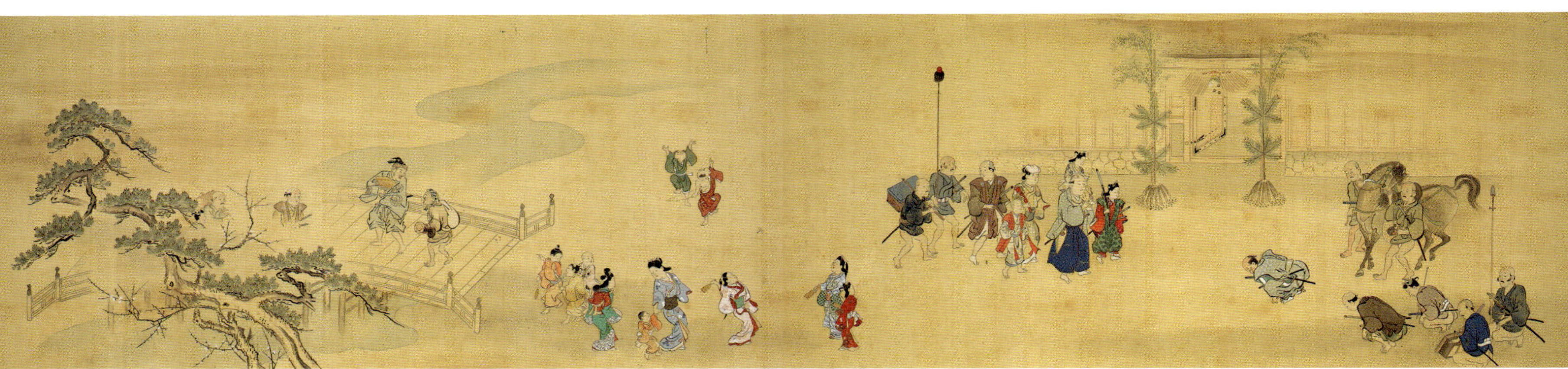

One of the primary endeavors of Hishikawa Moronobu and his studio was the production of handscrolls with genre scenes of the four seasons in Edo. Today there are more than ten extant examples, and all are thought to have been produced in the latter part of the master's career or after his death. None of them are thought to predate 1682–83.

Moronobu and his studio created two types of four seasons scrolls — one provided scenes of the Yoshiwara pleasure quarter, and the other did not. The work illustrated here is a standard piece of the latter type. Composed of multiple rectangular sheets of paper, the scroll depicts approximately two scenes per sheet as follows:

1. New Year's customs with two samurai households exchanging greetings as they encounter each other on the road, followed by a scene of children playing in the street and people performing a semicomical *manzai* dance on a bridge.
2. Scene of cherry-blossom viewing.
3. Enjoying the cool of a summer evening on the *Azumamaru* and the *Kawatakemaru*, two covered pleasure boats on the Sumida River.
4. Dance celebrating the Festival of the Dead (*obon*), which takes place during the thirteenth through the sixteenth days of the seventh lunar month. An aristocratic woman and her entourage watch the proceedings from afar.
5. Preparations in the kitchen and a banquet at an unidentified location during the autumn or winter months.
6. Bathhouse with female attendants (institutions that were banned in 1657) and a thatched outbuilding with men relaxing during a snowy winter.

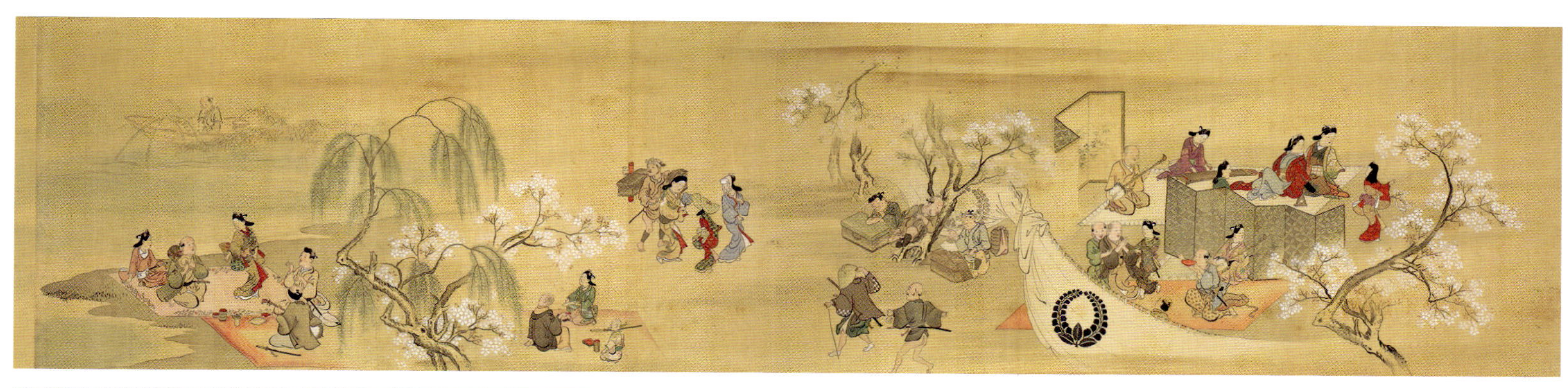
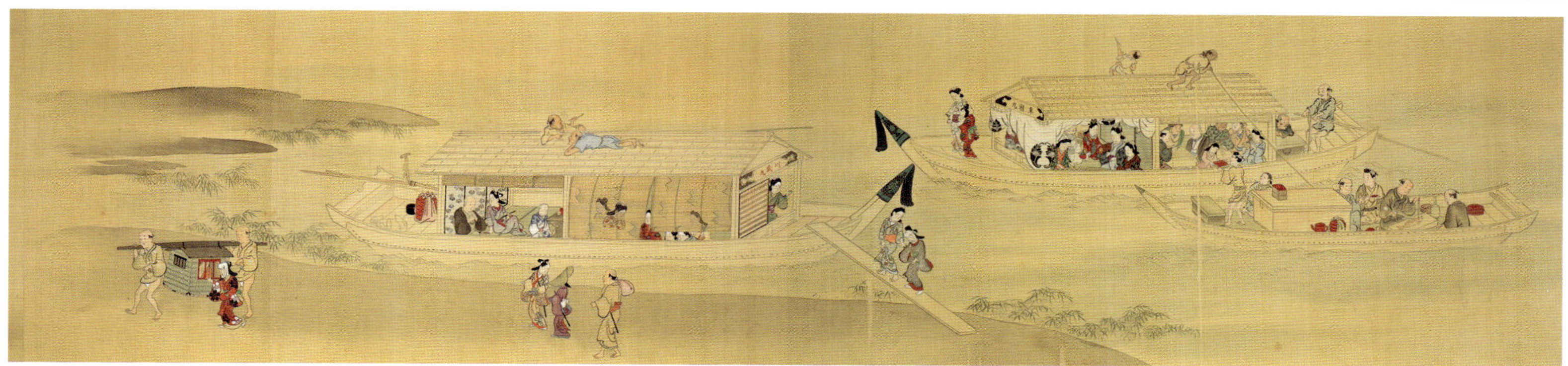
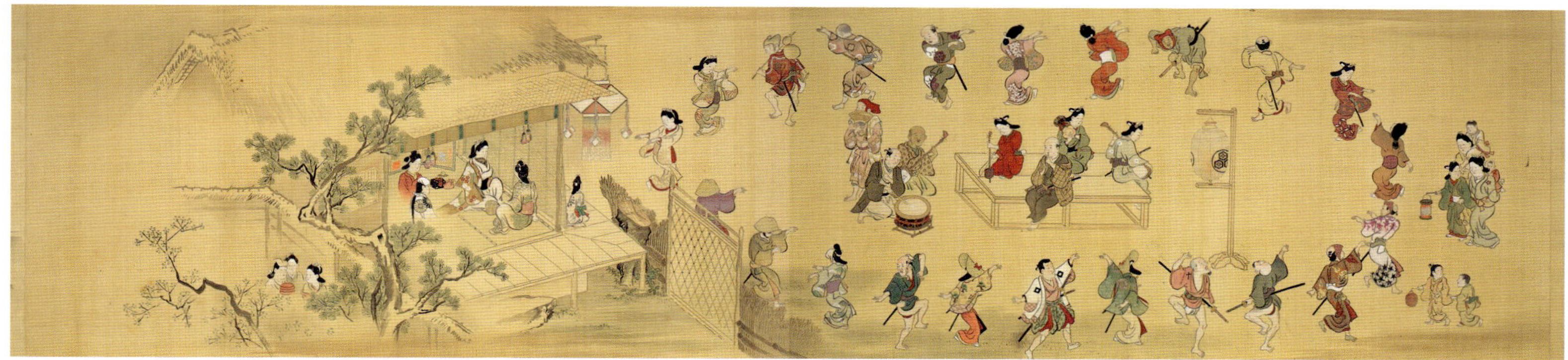
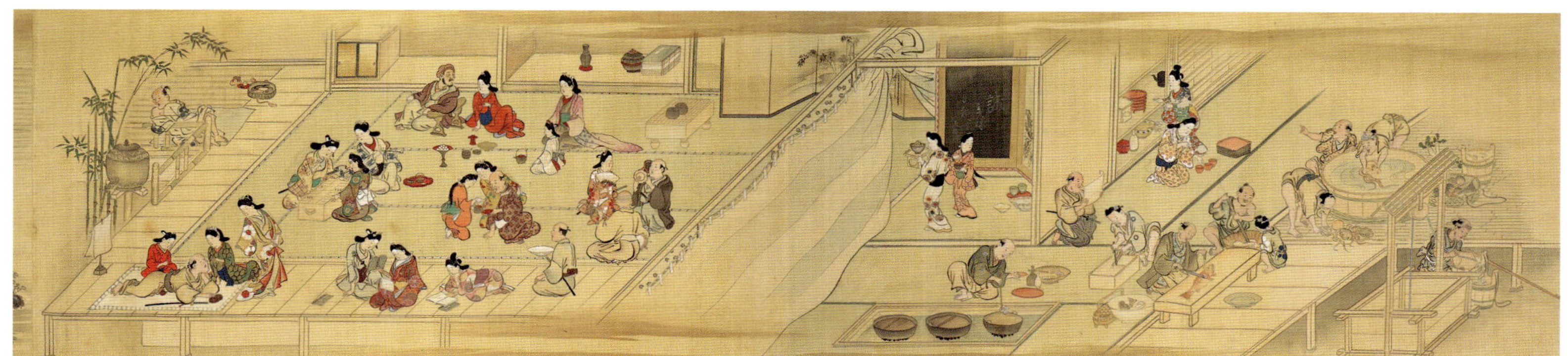
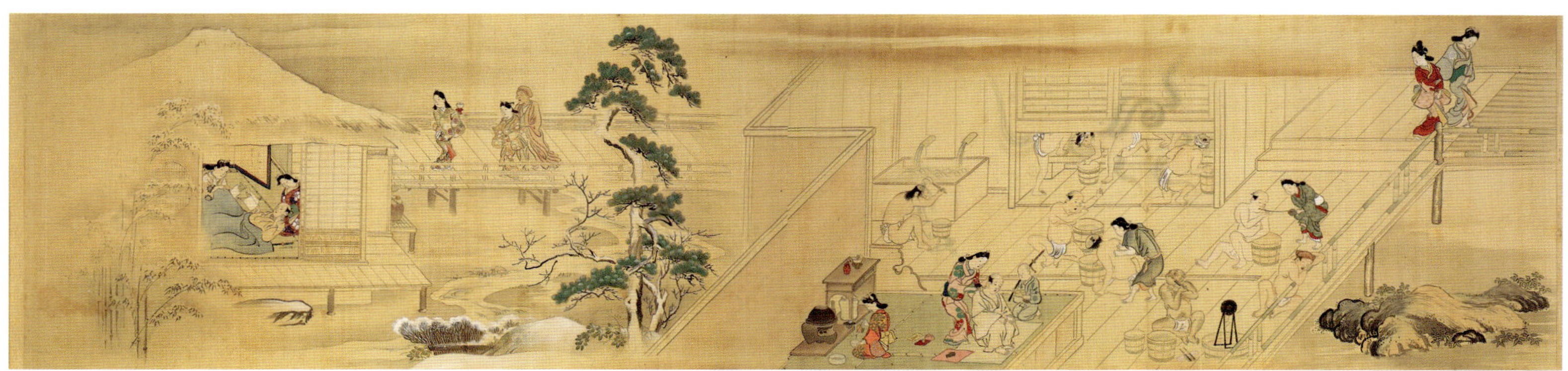

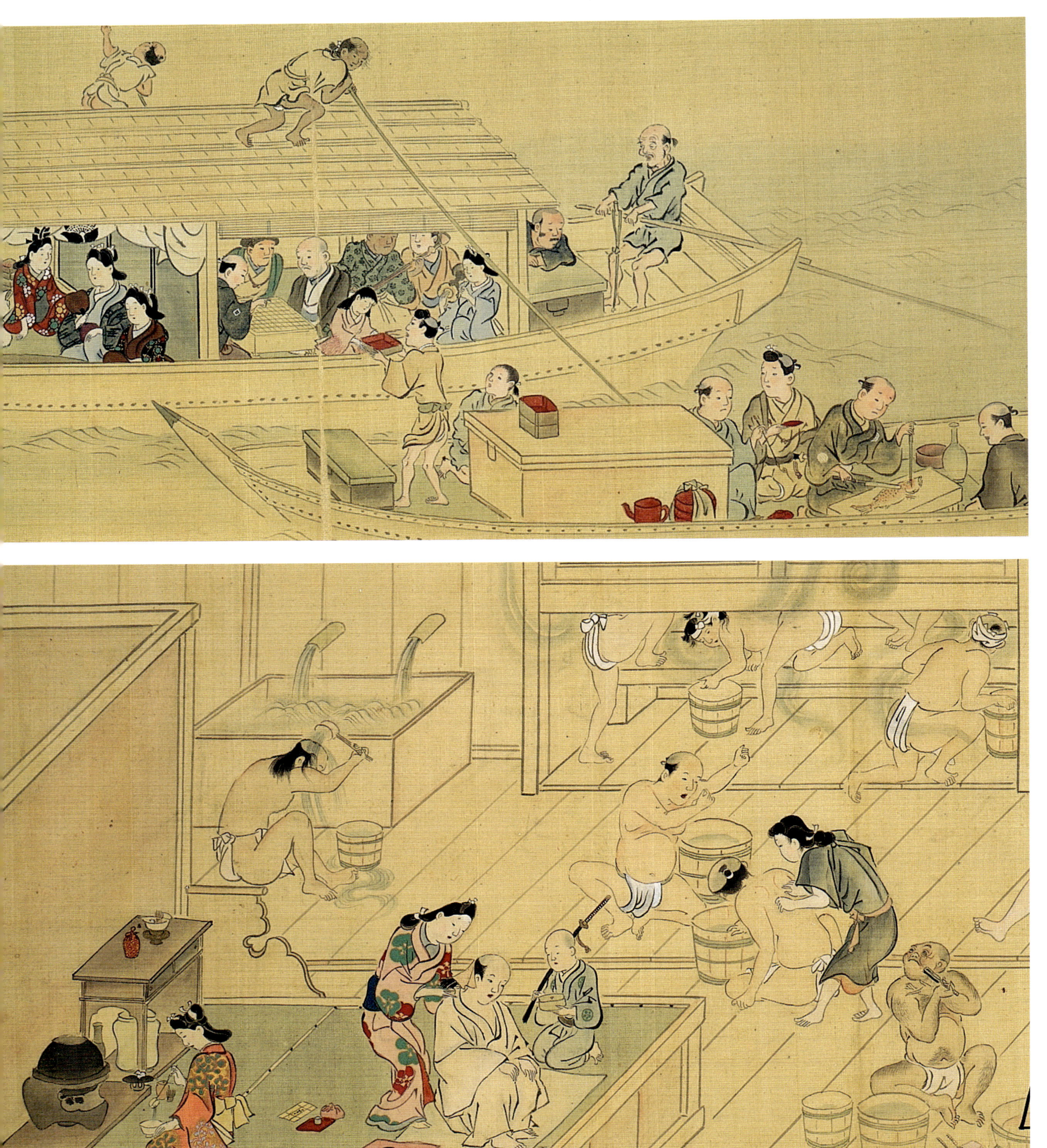

This scroll does not bear a signature, but Moronobu did not usually add his name to his work until very late in life (except on special occasions). As for the dating, the figures here do not display the voluptuousness of those in Moronobu's paintings from the last years of the Genroku era, and their postures and expressions seem to be individualized. Yet the stylized manner of grouping the figures in clusters of two or more suggests that the theme of the four seasons was already part of Moronobu's studio's standard repertoire by the time that this composition was produced. The party scene in the second half of the fifth sheet is somewhat awkward with its inclusion of six clusters of seemingly unrelated people, and bathhouses of the type depicted in the last sheet no longer existed by the 1680s, but nevertheless this scroll should be seen as an authentic work by Moronobu himself.

Scenes of Daily Life in the Four Seasons, which belongs to the Tokyo National Museum, is also unsigned and presumably dates from the same period.[1] Unfortunately it is missing the winter scenes, thereby making this scroll in the Boston collection, which has been preserved in its entirety, much more important for considering Moronobu's career. Further study of this painting, including a comparison with Moronobu's woodblock-printed book *Monthly Entertainments* (*Tsukinami no asobi*, published in 1680), is needed.[2] AS

1. Hishikawa Moronobu, *Scenes of Daily Life in the Four Seasons*, handscroll, ink and color on silk, 29.1 x 471.4 cm, Tokyo National Museum, published in *Tōkyō kokuritsu hakubutsukan*, vol. 1 of *Nikuhitsu ukiyo-e taikan* (Tokyo: Kōdansha, 1994), entry 13.
2. Hishikawa Moronobu, *Customs and Festivals of the Year* (*Nenjū gyōji no zu*), woodblock-printed book, 25.7 x 17.7 cm, Tokyo University Library, published in Chiba City Museum of Art, *Hishikawa Moronobu* (Chiba: Chiba City Museum of Art, 2000), 133. The title *Nenjū gyōji no zu* differs from the one that is given in this entry, for the former is not the original title of the book. A reprint of the book dating to 1691 was issued with the title *Tsukinami no asobi*.

4. HISHIKAWA MORONOBU (DIED 1694) AND THE HISHIKAWA SCHOOL

Fantastical Scenes

Jōkyō 2 (1685)
Pair of handscrolls; ink and light color on paper
Scroll 1: 45 x 1,372.9 cm (17 11/16 x 540 1/2 in.)
Scroll 2: 45 x 1,514.5 cm (17 11/16 x 596 1/4 in.)
Signatures: Hishikawa Moronobu zu
(Drawn by Hishikawa Moronobu)
Seals: Moronobu
William Sturgis Bigelow Collection 21.262, 21.263

Thirty-seven illustrations depicted in ink and light color are divided between two scrolls, one composed of eighteen sheets and the other of twenty-one sheets. No text accompanies these images except for an inscription at the end of the second scroll:

> "Illustrations of Transfigurations," two scrolls done by Hishikawa Kichibei Moronobu's own hand. They were copied by various individuals in the summer of the year corresponding to Jōkyō 2 (1685) in Kōfu (Edo). The copiers: Kondō Kaku no jō; Saitō Hanzaemon; Hishikawa Kichizaemon (Moronobu's son [Morofusa]); Yamaoka Jiemon (Moronobu's student); Terada Hanbei (*machieshi*). Out of these two scrolls, however, two sections are by Moronobu's own hand.

Despite the identifying title provided by the inscription, the lack of narrative makes it difficult to decipher the plot of the story. However, recent studies have revealed that it is based on a text dating to the Kan'ei era (1624–44) entitled *The Tale of Transfigurations in Tango* (*Tango henge monogatari*), a later copy of which is preserved in the National Diet Library, Tokyo.[1] According to that story, a group of foxes moved into the house of the warrior Tsuda Tōjurō from Tango province (modern-day Kyoto) and harassed the family by transforming themselves into various monstrous shapes. Finally a certain Toshinobu stood up to them and drove them away.

As the inscription relates, the scrolls were created in 1685 when Kondō Kaku no jō, Saitō Hanzaemon (thought to be a samurai), Moronobu's son Morofusa, his student Yamaoka Jiemon, and the *machieshi* Terada Hanbei got together and copied Moronobu's original scrolls, but two sections were done by Moronobu himself. The twelfth and sixteenth sheets of the first scroll not only bear Moronobu's signature and seal but are also executed in a freer and more expressive style compared with the other illustrations. These scenes are of interest from an artistic standpoint because they show Moronobu, who is usually thought of as the originator of images of the floating world, trying his hand at ghost imagery. Furthermore, the story, with its various permutations, is an important one in the history of Japanese fantastical literature. TN

1. Preserved in eight volumes, with the text accompanied by illustrations; see Suwa Haruo, "'Henka monogatari' no keisei to tenkai," *Kokka*, no. 1280 (June 2000): 5–15; and Tsuji Nobuo, "Moronobu oyobi Hishikawa ha no 'Henka no e' (Bosuton bijutsukan zō) ni tsuite," *Kokka*, no. 1280 (June 2000): 16–19.

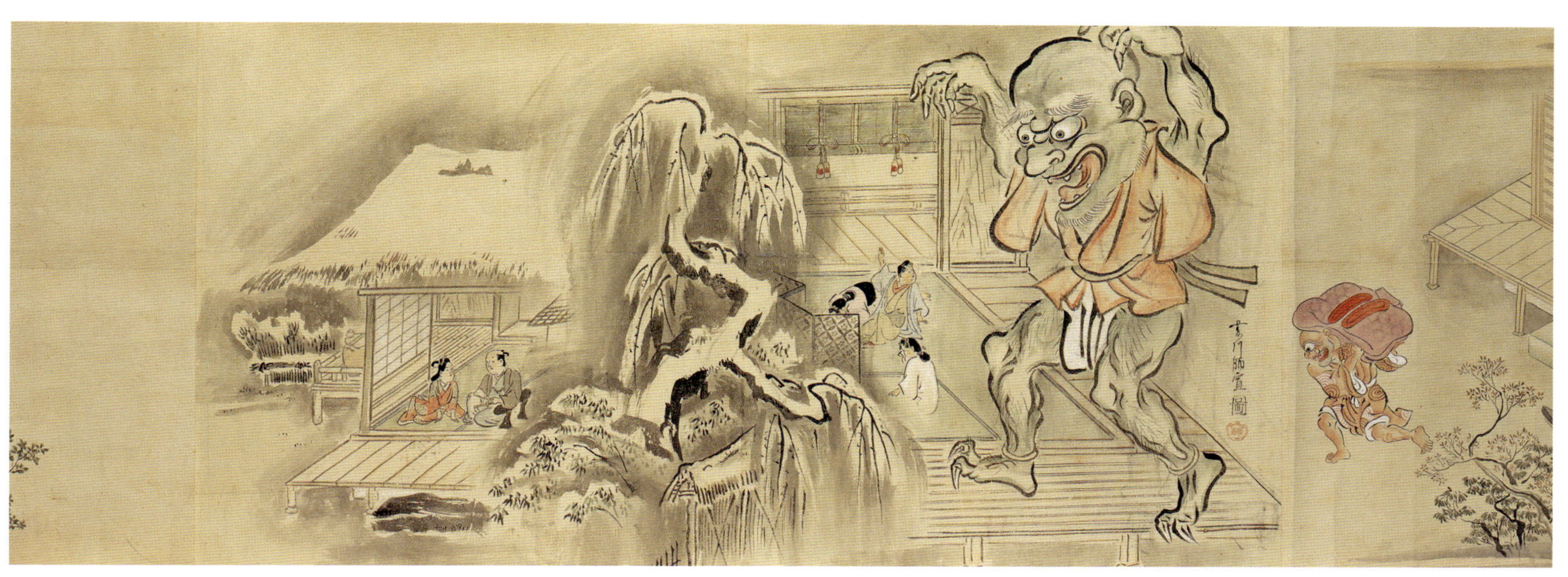
菱川師宣圖

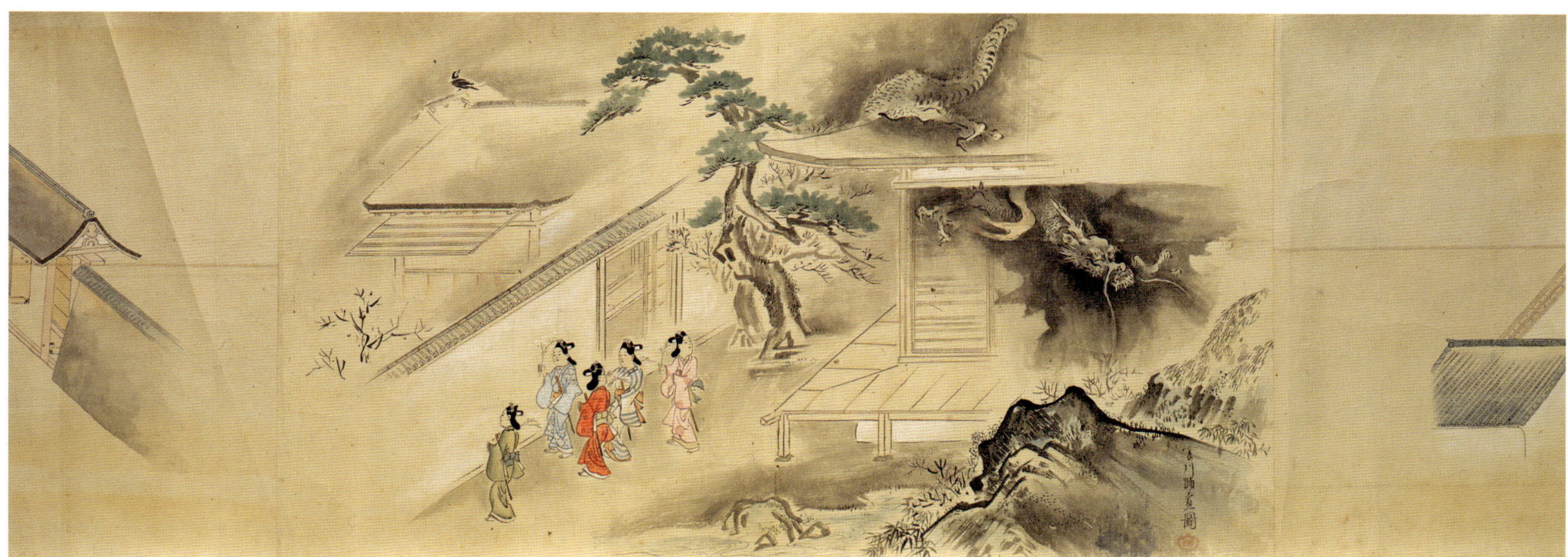
菱川師宣圖

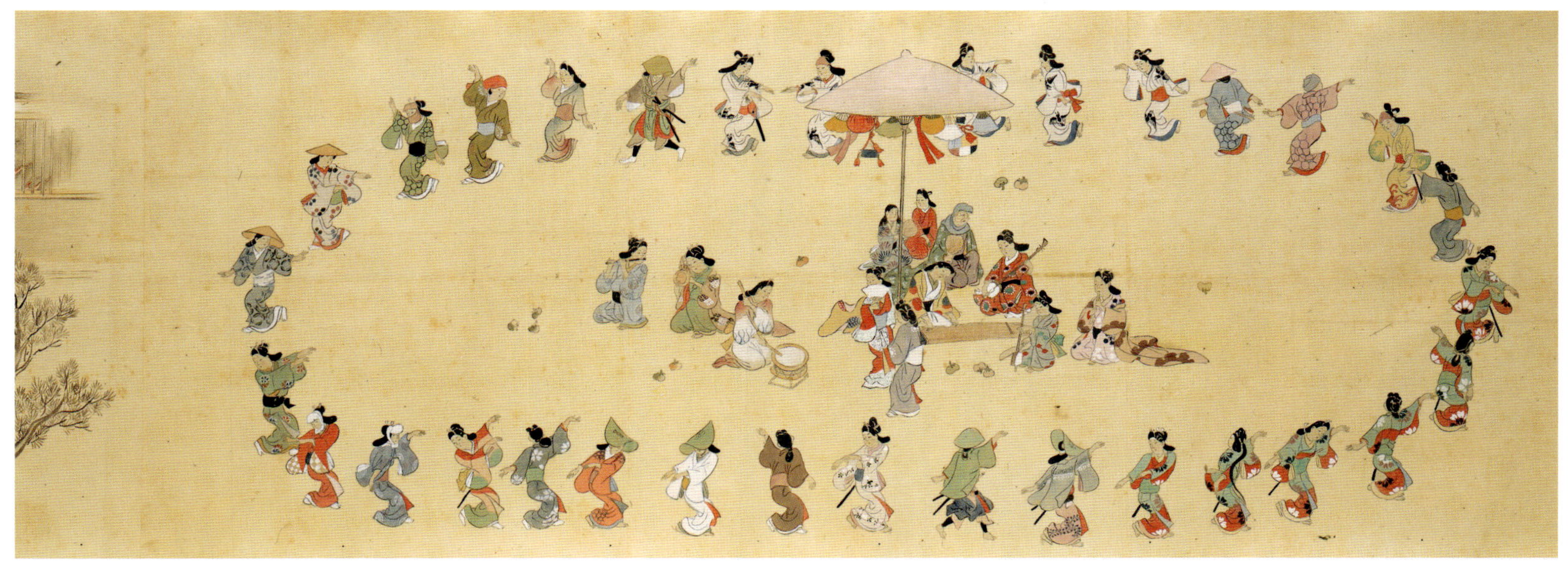

5. **TORII KIYONOBU I** (1664–1729)
Armor-Tugging Scene

About the Kyōhō era (1716–36)
Hanging scroll; ink, color, and gold on paper
80.1 x 34.3 cm (31 9/16 x 13 1/2 in.)
Seal: Kiyonobu
William Sturgis Bigelow Collection 11.7538

The historic vendetta of the Soga brothers against Kudō Suketsune, a principal adviser to the powerful shogun Minamoto Yoritomo, inspired numerous No and Kabuki plays beginning in the early fifteenth century. During the Edo period, the determination of the youths in avenging the death of their father appealed to a society that was ruled by military leaders and that valued the Confucian ideal of filial devotion.[1] The events of 1193, when the brothers burst in on a shogunal hunting party at the foot of Mount Fuji and murdered Kudō, became embellished over time with fictional exploits of the brothers and their companions.

The subject of this painting was the dramatic highlight of many Soga plays, which were traditionally performed at New Year's in Edo. Gorō, dressed in armor with an inverted water plantain crest (*saka omodaka*) and his characteristic butterfly-ornamented underrobes, charges to the rescue of his elder brother while Kobayashi Asahina, a sympathetic warrior noted for his tremendous strength, attempts to restrain the impetuous youth by grabbing his protective skirt (*kusazuri*). Asahina wears an underrobe decorated with a design of stripped roundels and an upper outer robe (*hitatare*) with five large wheeling cranes.

The actor Ichikawa Danjūrō was closely identified with the "Armour-Tugging Scene" and the *aragoto* style of Kabuki, which developed in Edo at the end of the seventeenth and the beginning of the eighteenth centuries, and which emphasized expressive movement and loud foot-stamping. Danjūrō was thought to be the flamboyant style's quintessential expression. Artists from the Torii school, such as Kiyonobu I and Kiyomasu I, were the primary producers of compositions with the scene. Most of their images, however, celebrated specific actors with individual crests. With no such identifiable crests, this hanging scroll must not have been designed with any particular actor in mind.

The painting is executed with the signature stylistic conventions of the Torii school, which were developed by Kiyonobu I for describing the *aragoto* genre: the gourd-shaped legs (*hyōtan ashi*) and the wriggling worm-lines of the drapery (*mimizugaki*). However, the work lacks a sense of epic thrust, suggesting that it was produced in the last years of Kiyonobu's career. In fact, this painting bears similarities to a much later image — the votive tablet (*ema*) dedicated in 1763 at Yamaguchi Kannon in Tokorozawa, Saitama prefecture.[2] AS

1. The brothers were Jurō Sukenari (1172–1193) and Gorō Tokimune (1174–1193).
2. Torii Kiyonobu, *Armour-Tugging Contest*, ink and color on wood, 60 x 90 cm, Yamaguchi Kannon in Tokorozawa, Saitama prefecture, published in Yomiuri shinbunsha and the Nihon ukiyo-e kyōkai, *Torii ha sanbyaku nen to kyūdaime Kiyomitsu ten* (Tokyo: Yomiuri shinbunsha and the Nihon ukiyo-e kyōkai, 1990), illustration 3.

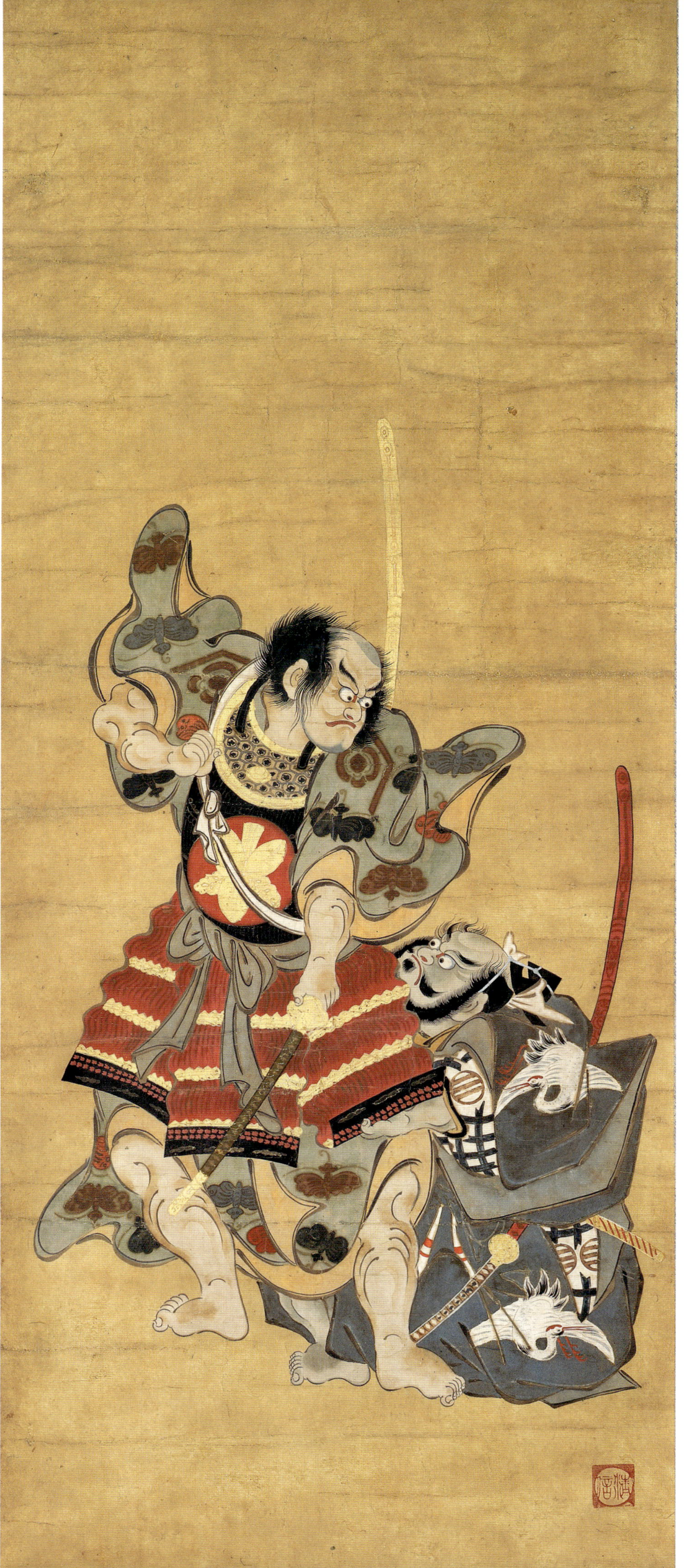

6. **TORII KIYONOBU** (1664–1729)
Erotic Contest of Flowers

Hōei era (1704–11)
Handscroll; ink, color, gold, and silver on paper
34.8 x 507.8 cm (13 11/16 x 199 15/16 in.)
Signature: Eshi Torii Kiyonobu zu
(Drawn by the picture master Torii Kiyonobu)
Seal: Kiyonobu
William Sturgis Bigelow Collection Res. 09.234

Although it has long been recognized that most of the leading artists of ukiyo-e produced erotic paintings and prints (*shunga*), such images have been frequently omitted from exhibitions due to prudish sensibilities in the West and censorship laws in Japan. The Museum of Fine Arts was no exception, and in fact, until only recently, its *shunga* were stored and catalogued separately from the rest of the Japanese art collection. Research conducted in preparation for the publication of the Museum's holdings of ukiyo-e, however, revealed the significance of some of these long-closeted works.[1] *Erotic Contest of Flowers* by Torii Kiyonobu has been acclaimed not only as one of the most important erotic scrolls by the founder of the Torii school, but also as one of the finest examples of the entire genre.[2]

In creating *shunga*, artists favored formats that invited private rather than public viewing: handscrolls, albums, and woodblock-printed books. Although there has been much academic debate as to their audience and purpose, these works could not have failed to be great sources of fantasy in the tightly controlled society of Edo Japan.[3]

From the 1680s on, the pioneer ukiyo-e artists Hishikawa Moronobu and Sugimura Jihei produced many series of album prints of this kind; the art historian Richard Lane estimated that these works comprised at least two-thirds of Jihei's oeuvre.[4] Japanese novels of the seventeenth century suggest that Moronobu, too, was well known for his erotica. The central character of *The Life of an Amorous Woman* (*Kōshoku ichidai onna*) remarks:

> For a warrior's household is bound by the strictest rules, and the women who dwell there never so much as set their eyes on a man, not to speak of enjoying the scent of a loincloth. One day, as I was examining a fascinating depiction by Hishikawa of an erotic scene, I was stirred despite myself to the most intense excitement. I sought, then, to quench my amorous flames.[5]

Asano Shūgō has determined that Kiyonobu must have designed approximately one hundred erotic images, which were originally sold in sets of eight to twelve prints. All are executed in the *yoko ōban* or *yoko chūban* format in ink; some have had later hand coloring applied. The most celebrated of the complete series is the *Scenes of the Bedchamber* (*Neya byōbu*), which was published by Takeda Chō'emon in 1711. These prints include humorous parodies of certain festival rituals and incidents in Kabuki plays. For example, the well-known "armor-tugging incident" from the tale of the Soga Brothers (see cat. no. 5) has been transformed into a "valorous penis-pulling incident."[6]

Erotic Contest of Flowers provides eleven spirited visions of lovemaking from what was originally a scroll of twelve images.[7]

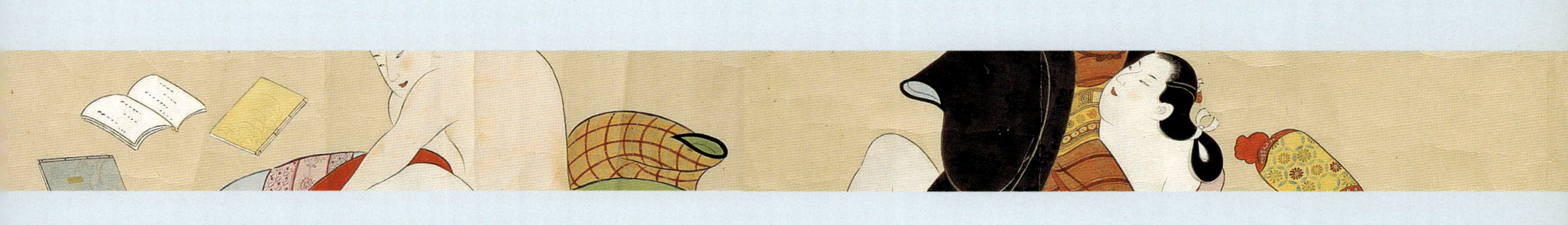

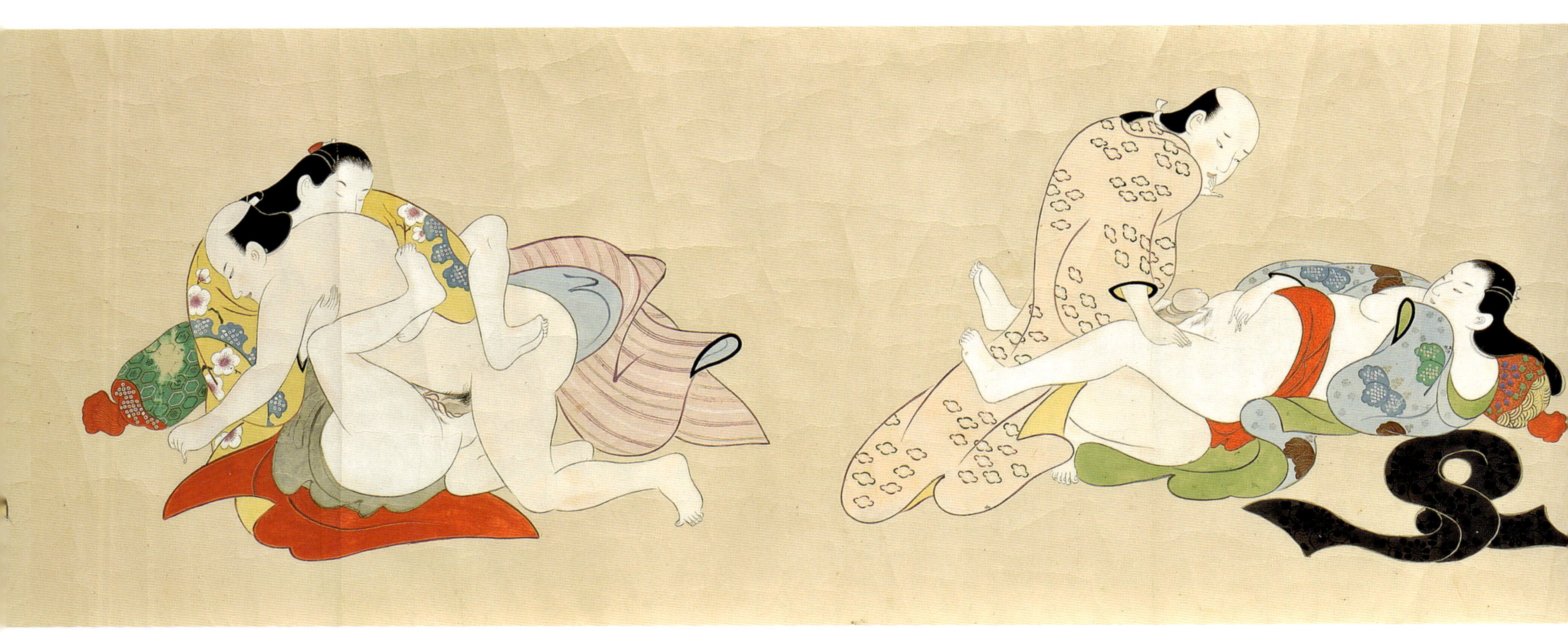

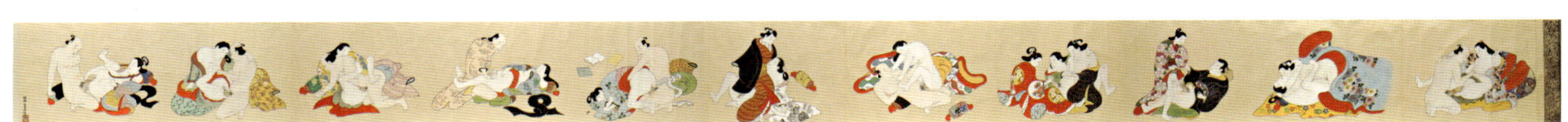

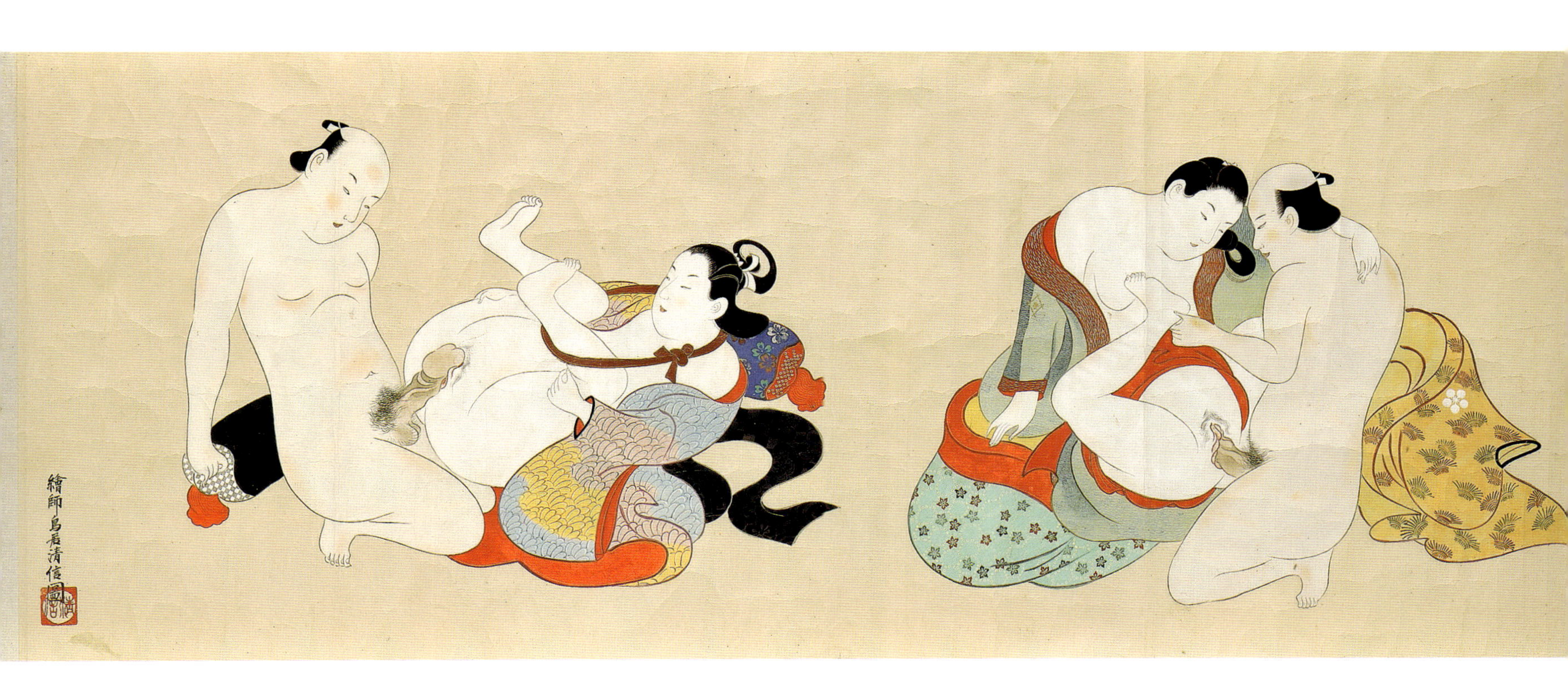
繪師鳥居清信圖

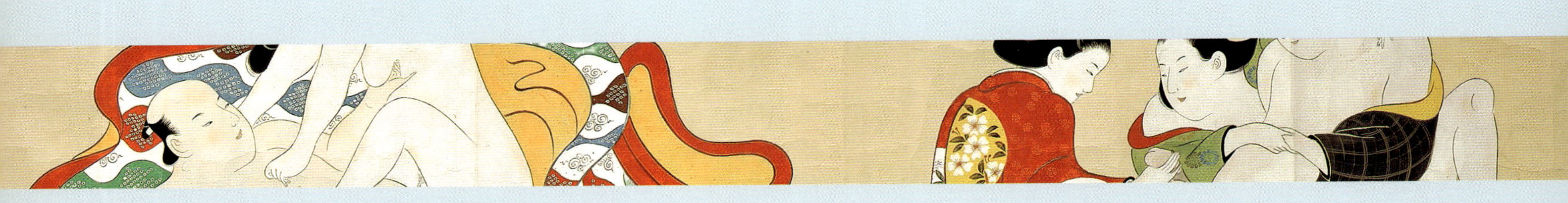

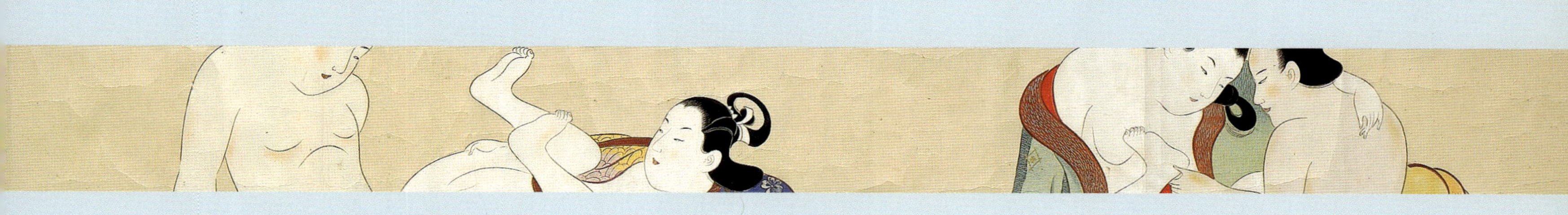

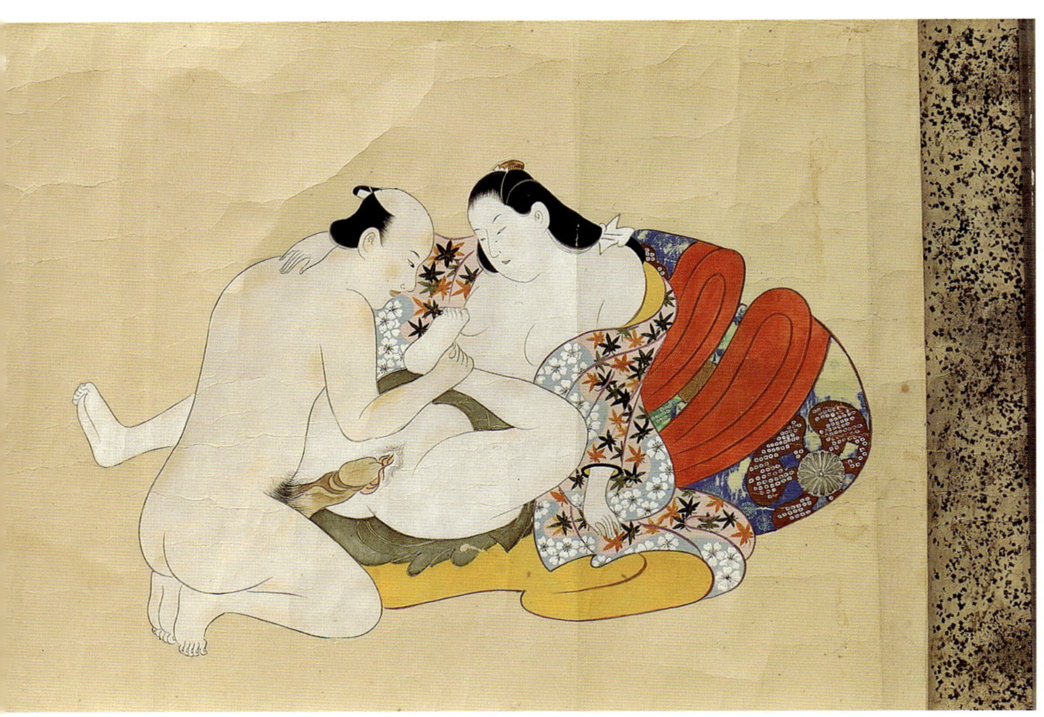

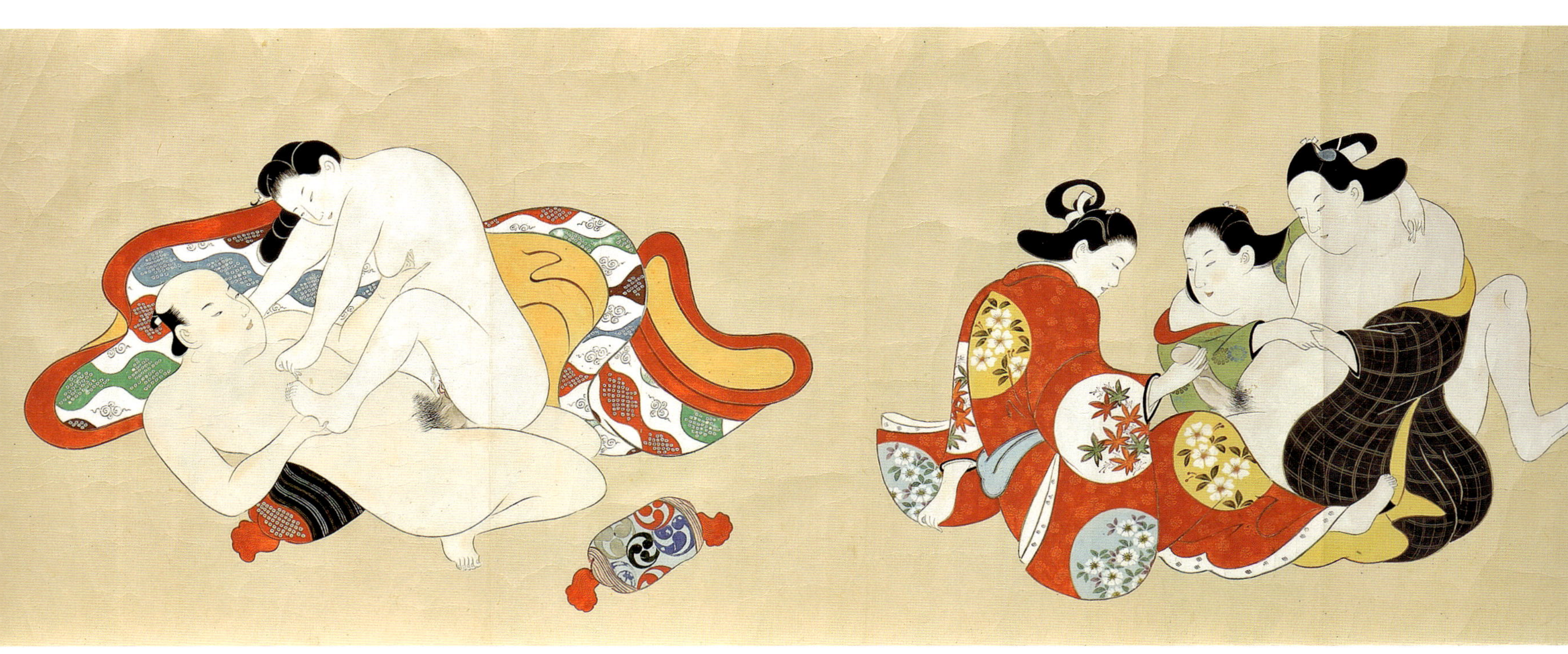

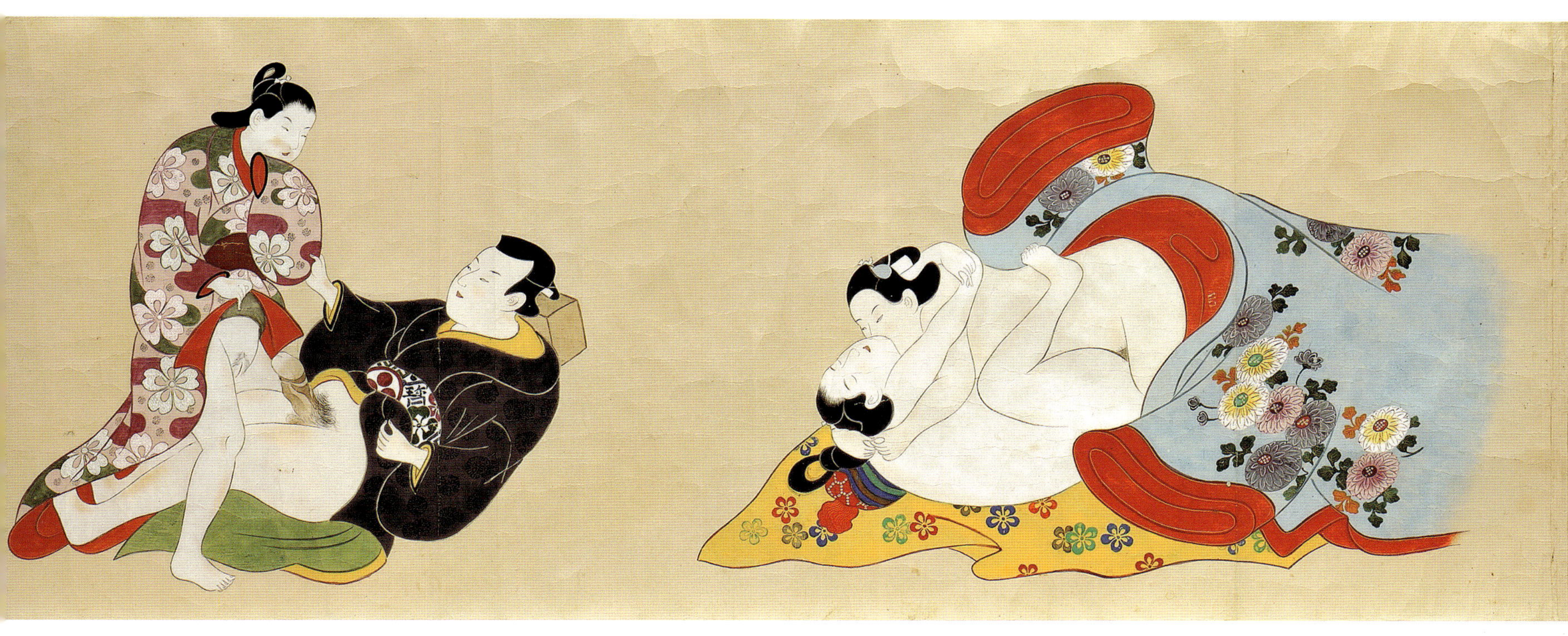

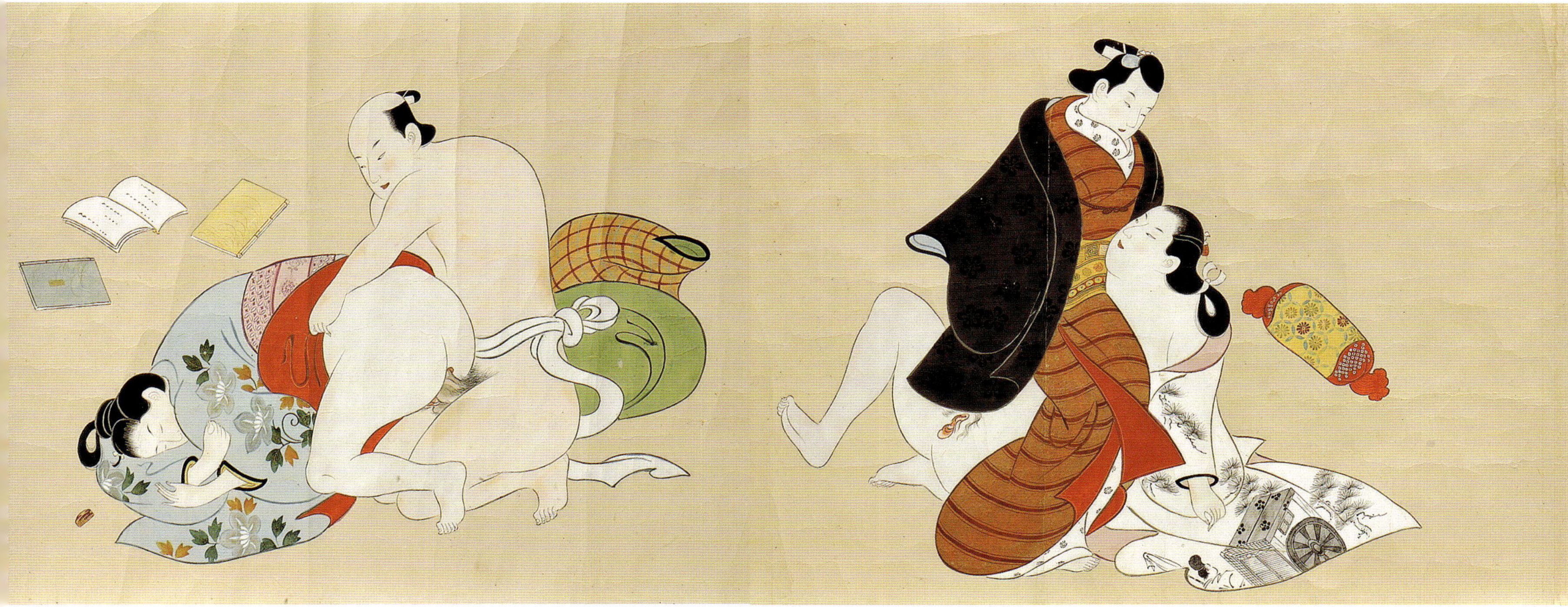

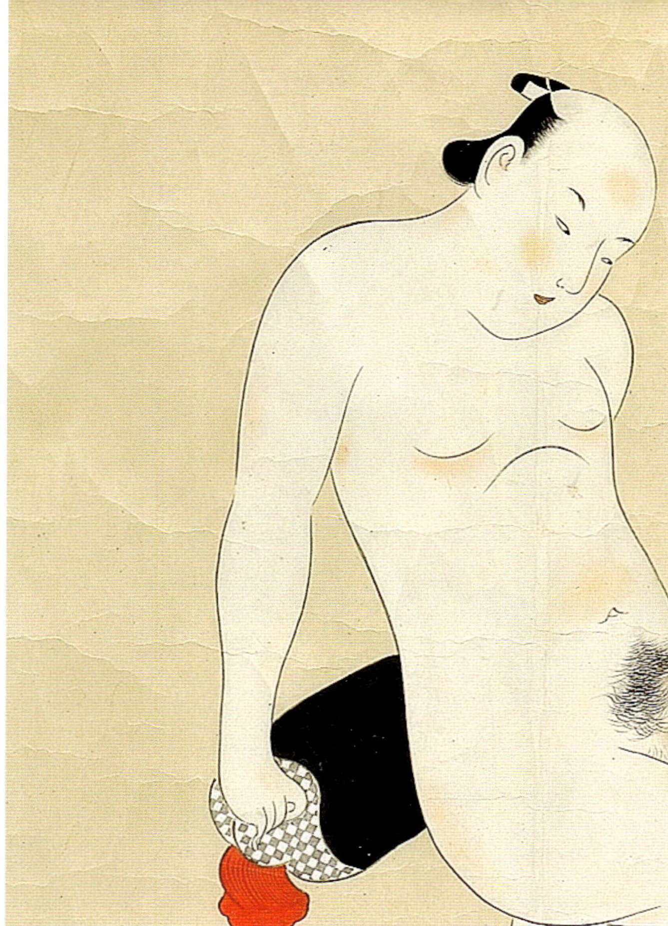

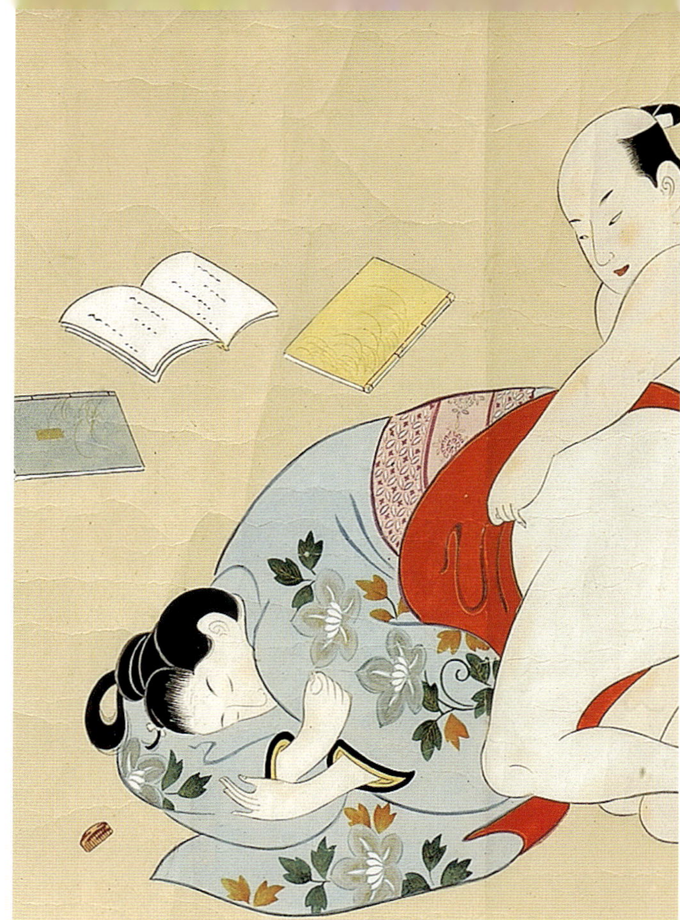

In each scene the individual couples, with their attendants and bedding, are isolated against the undecorated paper; their horizontal positions and the rhythm of the colors lead the viewer through the handscroll. Comparison with Kiyonobu's printed *shunga* suggests that the artist adopted the same compositional arrangements in that medium, allotting one couple to each sheet. The young samurai shown in union with a woman lost in ecstasy in the second section of the scroll, for example, is virtually a simplified mirror image of the couple in a print dated by Lane to the early 1710s.[8] Or again, in the last section of the scroll, the man supporting his hips on a pillow in order to gain easier access to the exposed charms of the recumbent woman closely resembles a couple in an unsigned print published as the work of Kiyonobu.[9] The latter differs from the scroll image only in the man's hairstyle, the detailing of the textiles, and the absence of a cord binding the woman's neck and leg.

Despite the similarities between painted and printed compositions, the works themselves are quite different. With the limited palette of the prints, Kiyonobu had to exploit strong contrasts of lights and darks to evoke moods. The handscroll, on the other hand, provides a veritable explosion of color, which seems to energize the lovemaking. The juxtaposition of clear, warm reds with the whites of the exposed bodies and the touches of red for the genitals contribute to the eroticism of the images. The lustrous black of the hair and the silver in areas of the clothing heighten the vibrancy of the painting, and the use of a flat white pigment for the bodies of the women and of a flesh tone for those of the men adds an element of contrast. ANM

---

1. *Bosuton bijutsukan nikuhitsu ukiyo-e*, supplementary volume (Tokyo: Museum of Fine Arts, Boston, and Kōdansha, 2001).
2. For this entry, I am indebted to Asano Shūgō's "Torii Kiyonobu gakan 'Koshoku hana awase,'" in *Bosuton bijutsukan nikuhitsu ukiyo-e*, supplementary volume, and personal conversations, May 2001.
3. Timon Screech has declared that *shunga* functioned as autoerotic stimuli for a predominantly male population. *Sex and the Floating World: Erotic Images in Japan, 1700–1820* (Honolulu: University of Hawai'i Press, 1999). Allen Hockley, questioning whether that was their sole purpose, believed that they may also have been viewed communally. "Shunga: Function, Context, Methodology," *Monumenta Nipponica* 55, no. 2 (Spring 2000): 257–69.
4. Richard Lane, *Images from the Floating World* (Secaucus, NJ: Chartwell Books, 1978), 52.
5. Ihara Saikaku, *The Life of an Amorous Man*, trans. Kengi Hamada (Rutland, VT: Charles E. Tuttle, 1984), 135.
6. Asano Shūgō, ed., *Ukiyo-e soroimono makura-e (ge)* (Tokyo: Gakken, 1995), 123.
7. Asano has determined that the opening scene is missing, since the original scroll consisted of six sheets of paper with two scenes distributed on each. Asano, "Torii Kiyonobu."
8. Lane, *Images*, 59.
9. *Ryōashi kakae*, reproduced in *Ukiyo-e*, no. 95 (October 1983): n.p. The cover of this issue of *Ukiyo-e* features a detail of a painting nearly identical to the fifth section of the Boston scroll, in which a woman with disheveled hair engages energetically with her reclining partner.

Kaigetsudō Ando
Miscellaneous Subjects

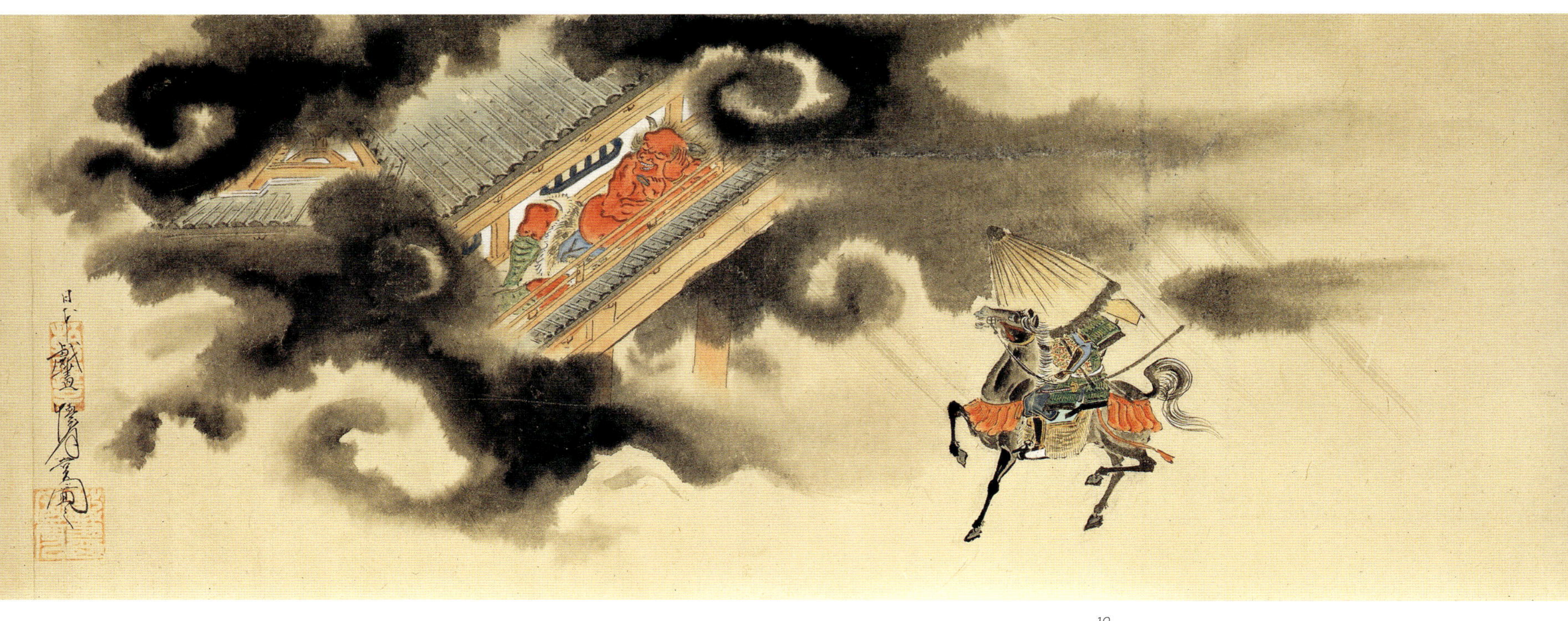

10

7. **KAIGETSUDŌ ANDO** (ACTIVE ABOUT 1704–1736)

Miscellaneous Subjects

9

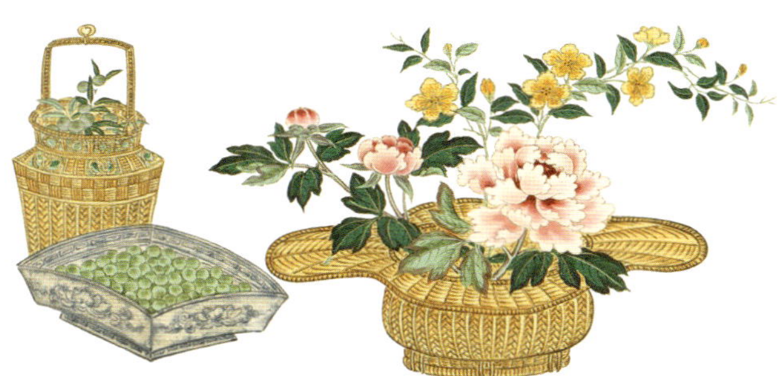

About the Hōei (1704–11) or Shōtoku (1711–16) era
Handscroll; ink, color, gold, and silver on paper
28.1 x 660.8 cm (11 1/16 x 260 3/16 in.)
Signature: Nihon giga Kaigetsudo kore [o] zusu (Lighthearted painting in Japanese style; this picture was done by Kaigetsudō)
Seals: Kan'unshi; Giga Ando (Lighthearted painting by Ando)
William Sturgis Bigelow Collection 11.7498

The relatively short period from the late seventeenth to the early eighteenth centuries witnessed the sudden popularity in Edo of images of beautiful women (*bijinga*) by members of the Kaigetsudō school. Although the six painters associated with the group — Ando, Dohan, Doshin, Doshu, Doshū, and Anchi — are celebrated for their stylized presentations of women against a neutral background in hanging-scroll format, Ando and Anchi also produced handscrolls, some of which included military subjects.[1]

This handscroll by Ando includes the following scenes:

1. Amusements (lottery) in a brothel
2. Courtesan at her toilette
3. Zhong Kui (Shōki), the Demon Queller, splitting a watermelon
4. Sumo match between the twelfth-century warriors Matano Gorō Kagehisa and Kawazu Saburō Sukeyasu
5. Kabuki performance of the *aragoto* ("rough-style") type; the play is unidentified, but the protagonist may be wearing the crest of the actor Nakamura Denkurō.
6. Farming in China
7. (not shown) Asahina no Saburō tugging the armor of Soga no Gorō (see cat. no. 5)
8. (not shown) A lacquer craftsman
9. Flower basket and fruit containers
10. The warrior Watanabe no Tsuna battling the demon that had been haunting the Rashōmon Gate at the entrance to Kyoto (see cat. no. 16)

According to the *Ukiyo-e ruiko*, Ando began his career as a painter of votive tablets (*ema*) in the Asakusa district of Edo; he was not affiliated with any particular artistic school before founding his own. In fact, this handscroll displays many styles not generally associated with Ando's work: the Chinese farming scene is reminiscent of Kano-school paintings influenced by Chinese Song- and Yuan-dynasty prototypes; the lacquer craftsman recalls a visual tradition depicting medieval craftsmen engaged in poetry contests (*shokunin zukushi uta awase-e*) as interpreted by early Edo-period painters such as Iwasa Matabei (1578–1650); and finally, the flower basket draws upon refined Chinese Ming- or Qing-dynasty renditions. The number of varying motifs might make the work appear to be a painting model were it not for the exceptional quality of the pigments used (unlike those usually found in Ando's paintings) and the signature and seals of the artist prominently placed at the end. This scroll may therefore have been Ando's response to a specific request by a wealthy patron. NM

1. *Editor's note:* Ando is also known to have worked in other genres. Included among his works are images of the bloody tale of Ōeyama, a portrait of the warrior Takeda Shingen, still lifes, and a youthful image of the Japanese Buddhist patriarch Shōtoku taishi. For illustrations, see *Moronobu*, vol. 2 of *Nikuhitsu ukiyo-e* (Tokyo: Shūeisha, 1982).

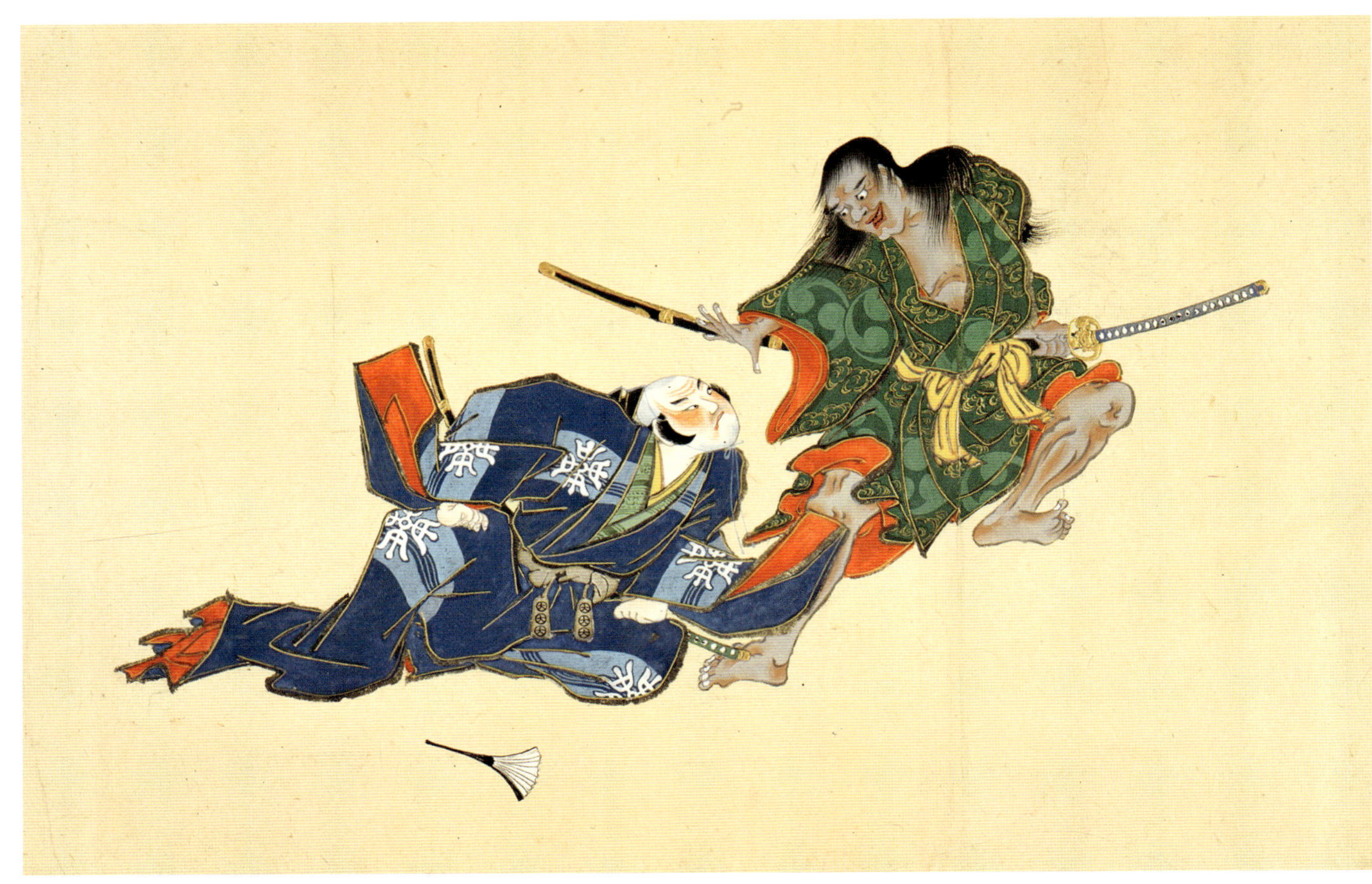

5

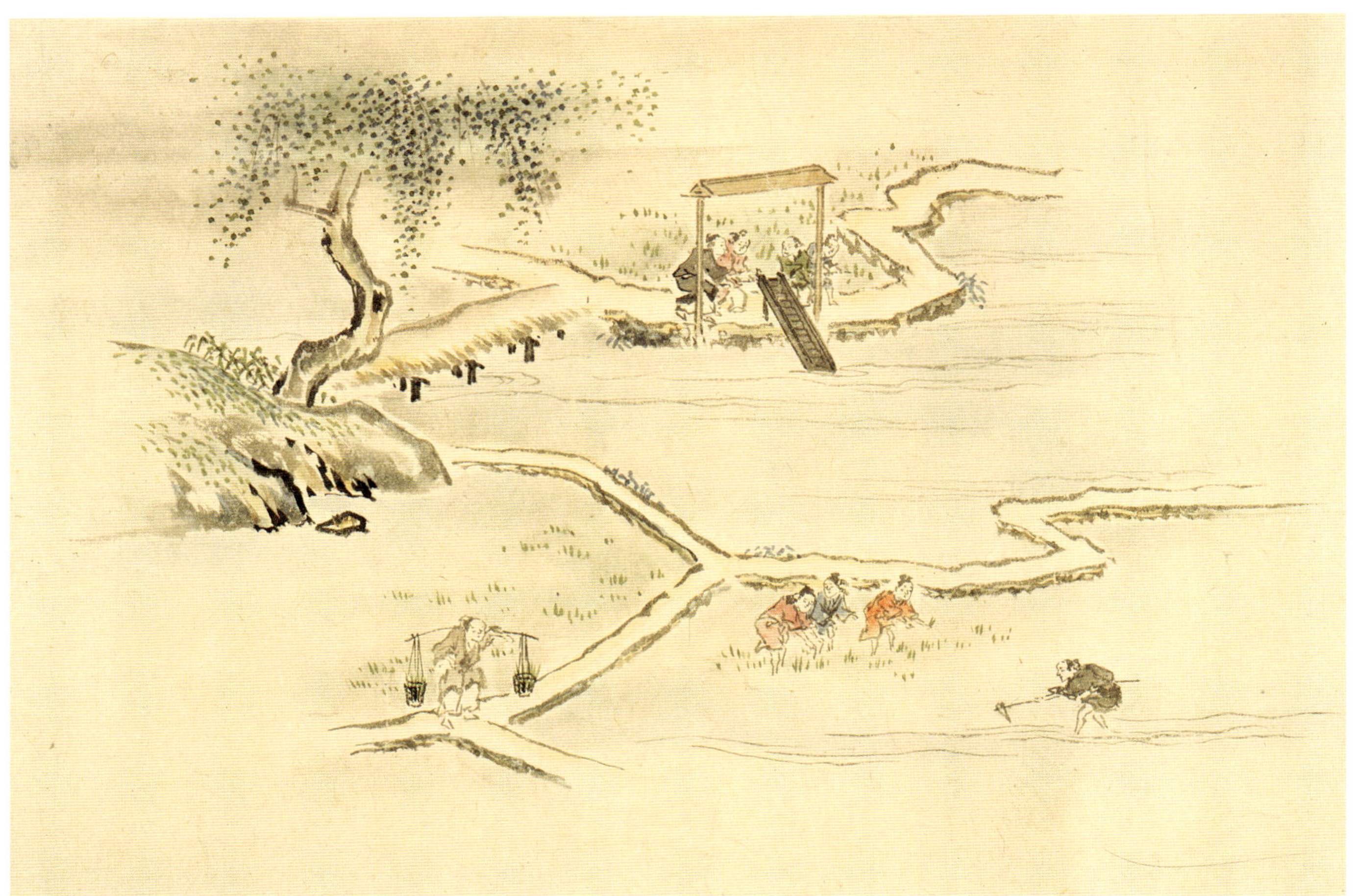

6

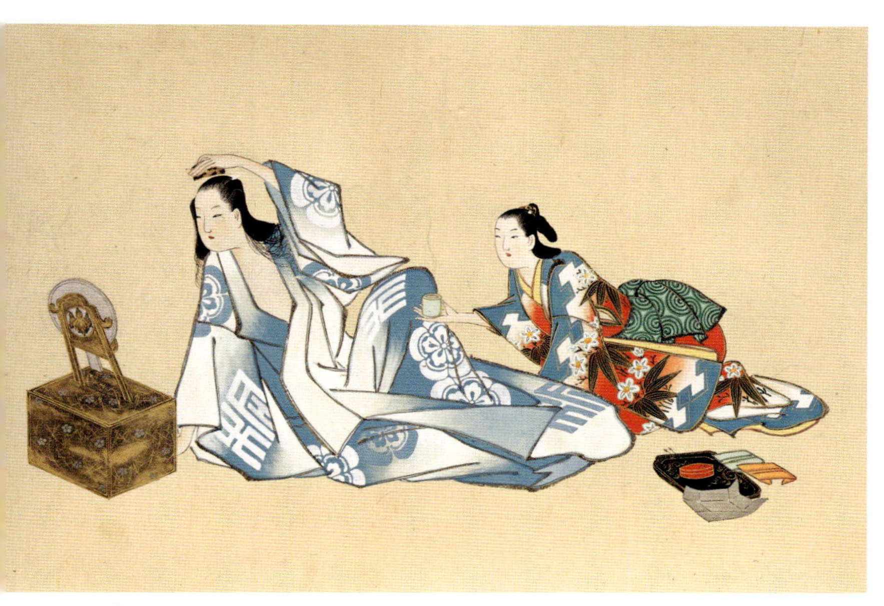

2

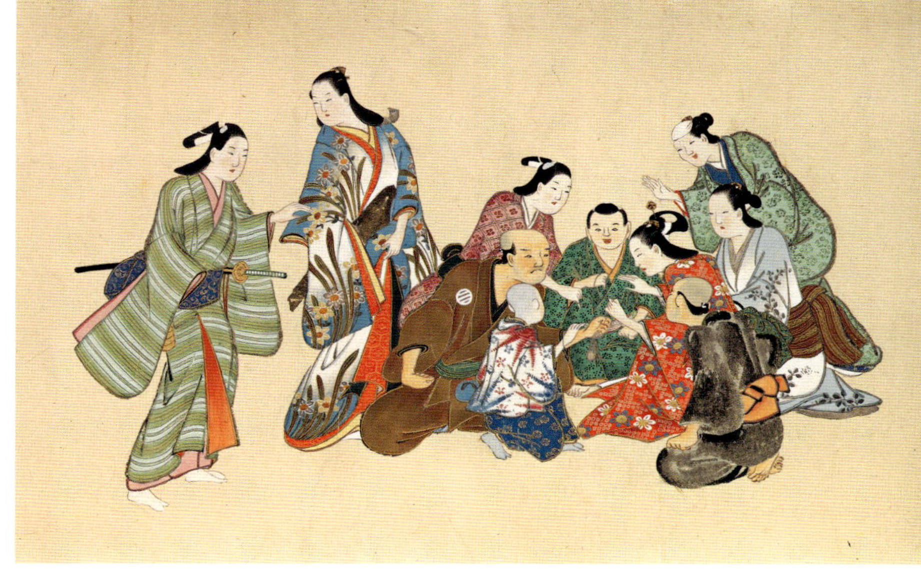

1

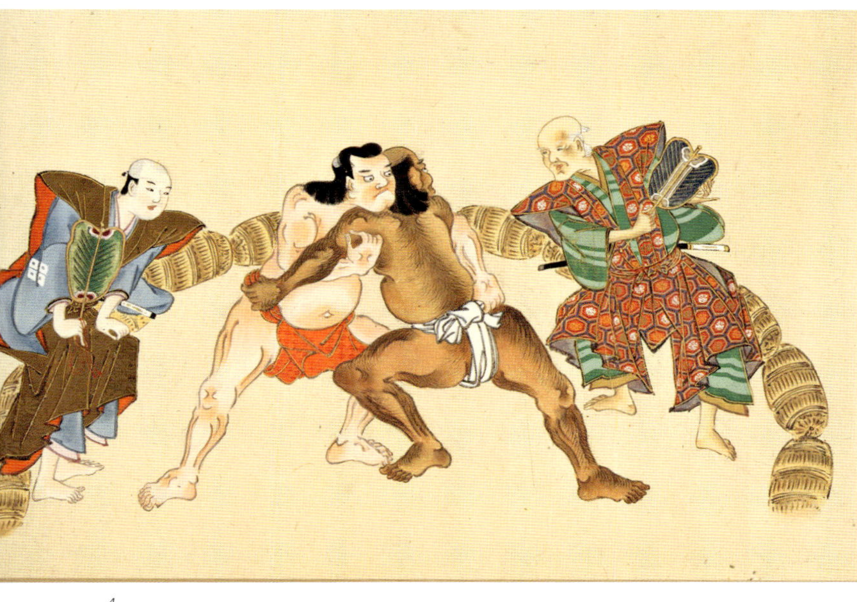

4

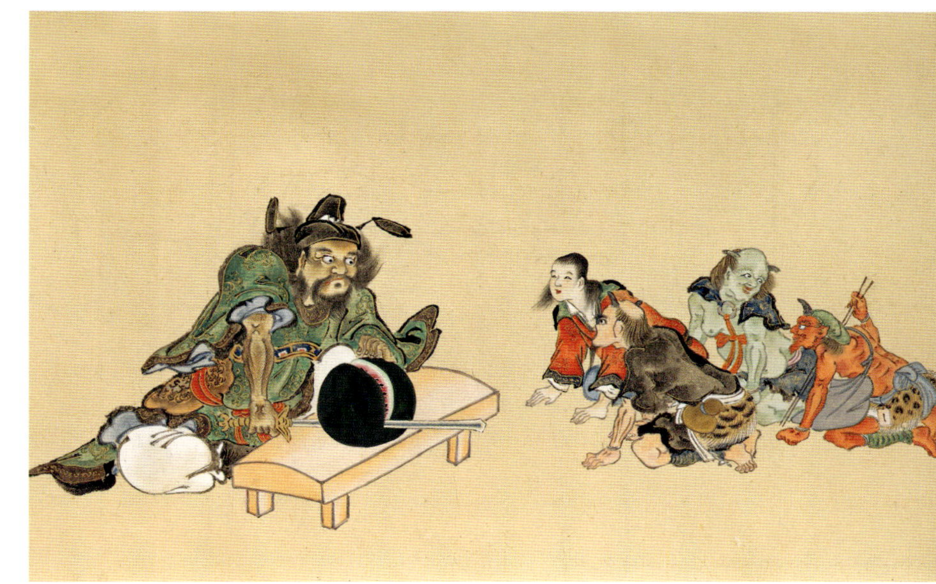

3

8. **KAIGETSUDŌ ANCHI** (ACTIVE ABOUT 1704–16)
Courtesan Seated on a Bench

About the Hōei (1704–11) or Shōtoku (1711–16) era
Hanging scroll; ink and color on paper
96.8 x 51 cm (38 1/8 x 20 1/16 in.)
Signature: Yamato giga Kaigetsudō matsuyō Anchi kore [o] zu [su] (Lighthearted Yamato painting; this picture was done by the Kaigetsudō follower Anchi)
Seals: illegible. William Sturgis Bigelow Collection 11.7495

A pupil of Kaigetsudō Ando, Anchi largely confined himself to producing images of beautiful women according to models popularized by his teacher. Contemporary scholars have been able to identify eight print designs and more than seventeen paintings by the artist.[1] The painting shown here is unusual in that the courtesan is portrayed seated on a wooden bench rather than standing. She holds a letter in her mouth, a gesture that generally signifies emotional turmoil but that the courtesan here makes almost seductive. She teasingly offers glimpses of the text along the edges and through the back of the paper. Her long, slender left hand helps to support her body, which is enveloped in voluminous robes enlivened with bold characters written in white against bands of deep blue, white, and yellow. Discernible among the Chinese characters are those for *Asabune* (the name of a boat that transported passengers across Lake Biwa) and *Azuma tsuma* (Wife of the Eastern Provinces).[2]

Several Kaigetsudō-influenced artists active in the Hōei and Shōtoku eras, particularly Baiyūken Katsunobu, delighted in dressing their female subjects in these robes ornamented with scattered writing.[3] The textile design, suggestive of paste-resist dyeing, is distinctive, but art historians know of no extant *kosode* robes of this type from the early eighteenth century. This absence has led the scholar Sharon Takeda to question whether the Kaigetsudō painters were recording actual textiles or creating designs from their own imaginations.[4] ANM

1. The number of prints is provided by Naitō Masato in *Bosuton bijutsukan nikuhitsu ukiyo-e*, vol. 1 (Tokyo: Museum of Fine Arts, Boston, and Kōdansha, 2000), 185. A catalogue raisonné of Kaigetsudō's paintings has not been published. Richard Lane gave the number of attributable works as "around seventeen" more than forty years ago in *Kaigetsudo (circa 1700–1750)*, ed. Takahashi Seiichirō (Rutland, VT, and Tokyo: Charles E. Tuttle, 1959), 74.
2. Conversation with Asano Shūgō, May 21, 2001. Asano believes that the characters do not have any specific poetic reference.
3. Examples include *Courtesan Seated on a Bench*, hanging scroll, ink and color on silk, 119.8 x 44.4 cm, British Museum, published in Timothy Clark, *Ukiyo-e Paintings in the British Museum* (London: British Museum Press, 1992), 77; and *Standing Woman*, hanging scroll, ink and color on paper, 88.6 x 41.9 cm, Asian Art Museum of San Francisco, Avery Brundage Collection, published in Sharon Takeda, "Clothed in Words: Calligraphic Designs on Kosode," in *When Art Became Fashion: Kosode in Edo-Period Japan*, ed. Dale Carolyn Gluckman and Sharon Sadako Takeda (Los Angeles: Los Angeles County Museum, 1992), 169.
4. Takeda, "Clothed in Words," 168–69.

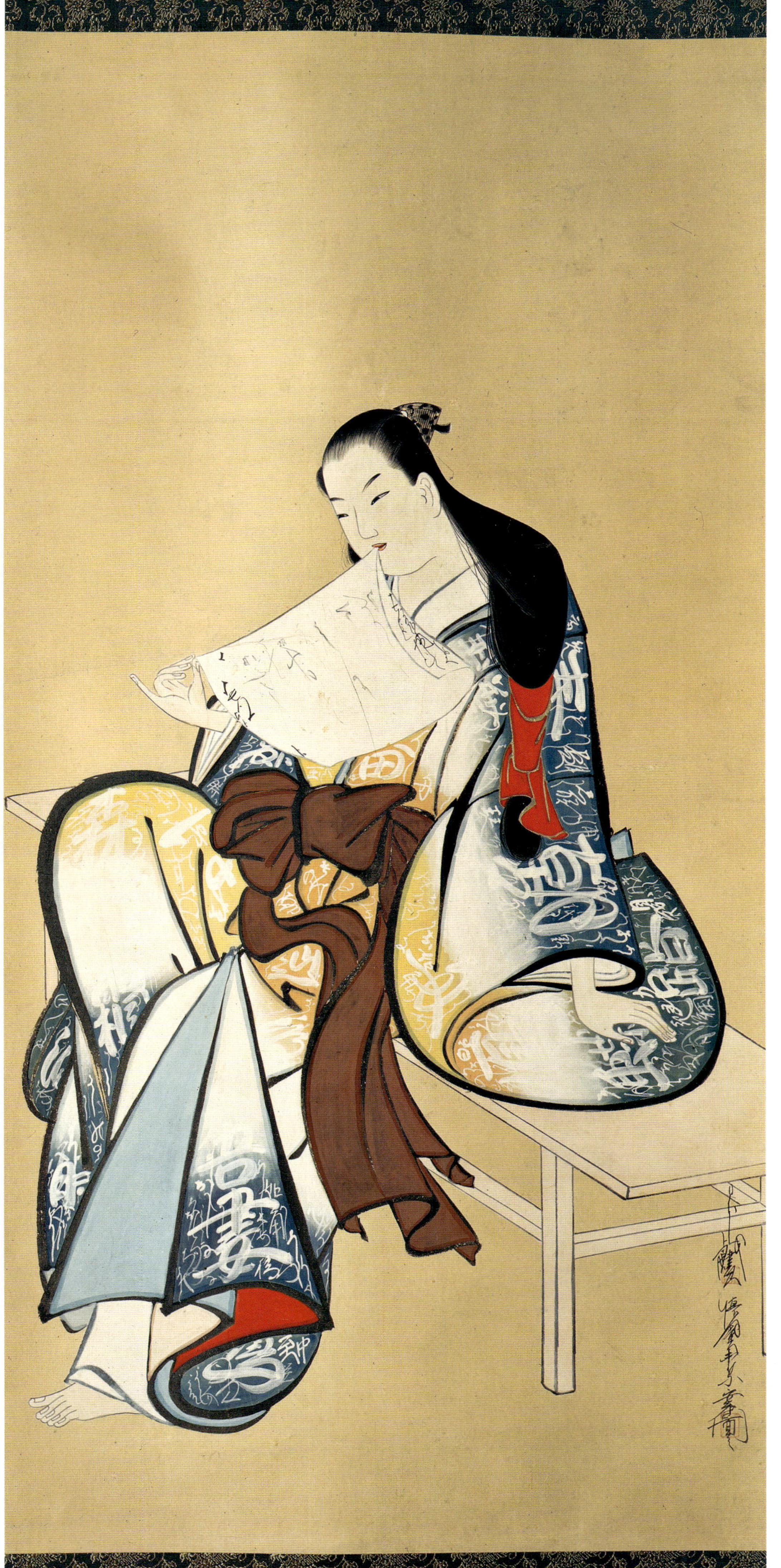

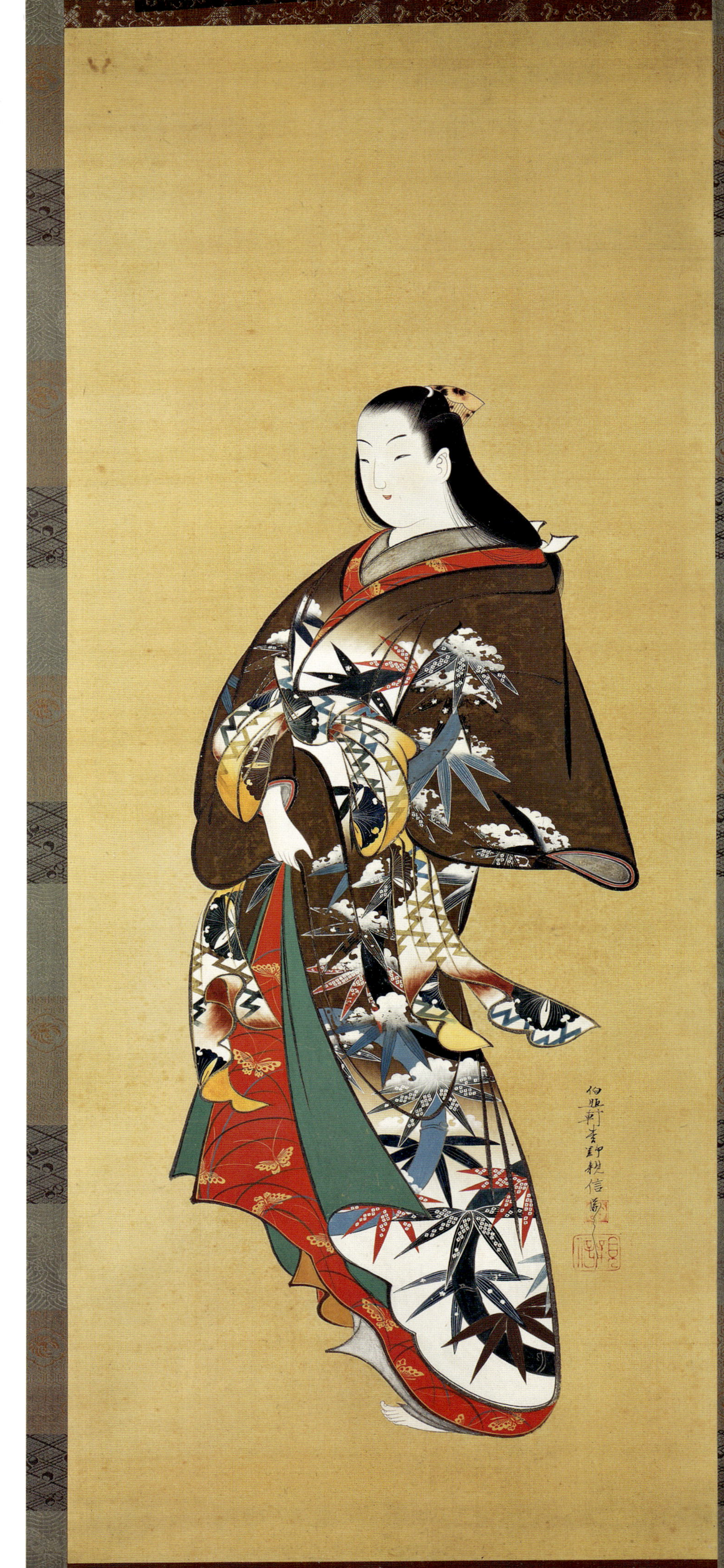

9. **MATSUNO CHIKANOBU** (ACTIVE ABOUT 1704–1736)
Standing Courtesan

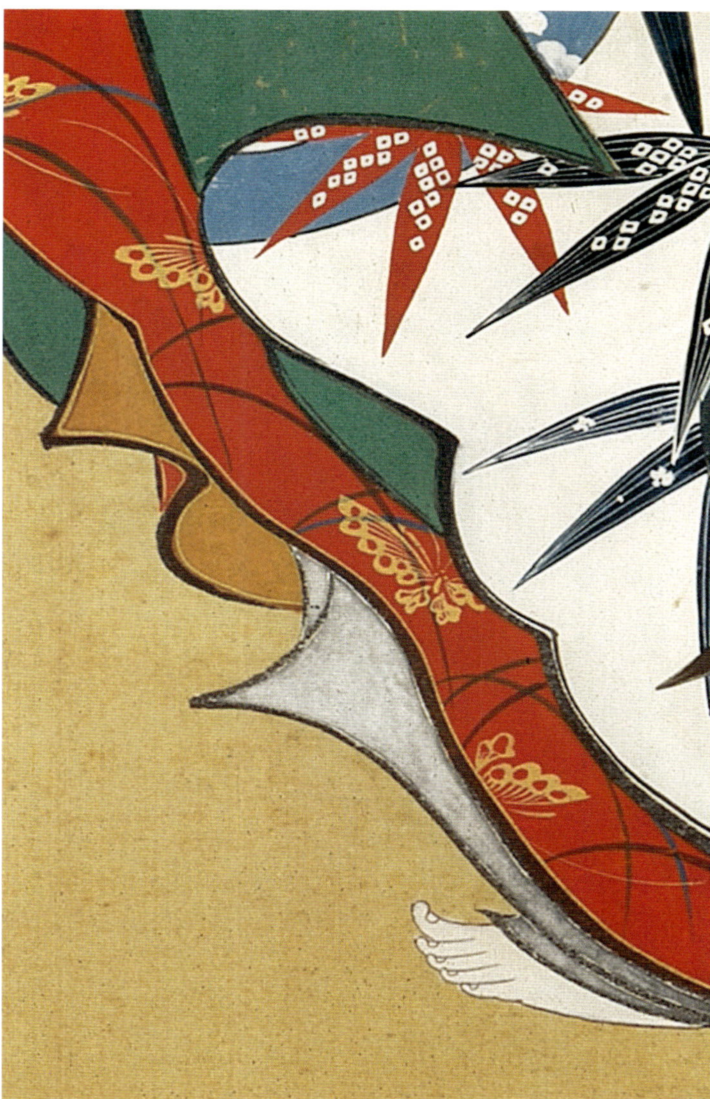

About the Hōei (1704–11) or Shōtoku (1711–16) era
Hanging scroll; ink, color, gold, and silver on silk
100.1 x 42.2 cm (39 7/16 x 16 5/8 in.)
Signature: Hakushōken Matsuno Chikanobu kore [o] zu [su] (This was drawn by Hakushōken Matsuno Chikanobu)
Seals: Sen; Chikanobu
William Sturgis Bigelow Collection 11.7330

A courtesan lifts the skirt of her kimono; the end of her tied sash flutters as she walks. Her robe is patterned with striking motifs of snow-covered bamboo leaves and bamboo circles in primary colors over a graded brown ground. In the stylized lines of her robe's drapery folds and the stateliness of her body, this courtesan resembles the beautiful women painted by the Kaigetsudō school, which had flourished for little more than ten years at the end of the Genroku era (1688–1704). However, unlike the female figures by the Kaigetsudō painters, this one by Chikanobu has a slightly rounded face. Furthermore, her faintly laughing eyes and smiling lips produce a somewhat sweet feminine expression.[1]

The Kaigetsudō school established their new, distinctive mode of depicting *bijin* in the early eighteenth century and attracted many imitators; Chikanobu was probably the artist who followed their style most carefully. Because the members of the school specialized in painting, their contemporaries likewise produced most of their images of beautiful women in hanging-scroll rather than print format. In fact, all of the dozen or more extant works attributed to Chikanobu are paintings. NM

1. *Editor's note:* Chikanobu created a composition of a courtesan with an almost identical pose and dress that is now in the collection of the Musée Guimet, Paris. *Processing Courtesan* (Courtisane paradant), Hōei (1704–11) or Shōtoku (1711–16) era, hanging scroll; ink and color on silk, 93.2 x 36.1 cm. Published in: *Images du Monde flottant: Peintures et estampes japonaises XVIIe–XVIIIe siècles* (Paris: Galeries national du Grand Palais, 2004), 186–187.

10. **TAKEDA HARUNOBU** (ACTIVE ABOUT 1710–1736)
Parody of Shakkyō and Eguchi

Kyōhō era (1716–36)
Pair of hanging scrolls; ink, color, and gold on silk
Each 85.8 x 35.2 cm (33 3/4 x 13 7/8 in.)
Signature: Nihon ga Takeda Harunobu zu
(Japanese painting, drawn by Takeda Harunobu)
Seals: illegible
William Sturgis Bigelow Collection 11.7359, 11.7360

This pair of scrolls parodies the two deities who attend the Historical Buddha—Monju, the Bodhisattva of Wisdom, and Fugen, the Bodhisattva of Universal Virtue—by replacing them with figures of contemporary Kyōhō-era women. They include the standard mounts of the bodhisattvas: Monju's *karashishi* (Chinese lion) in the right-hand scroll, and Fugen's elephant in the left.

This imagery developed from separate Buddhist tales; that on the left from the legend *The Lady of Eguchi* (*Eguchi no kimi*), popularized in the fourteenth-century No play *Eguchi*, which in turn had taken inspiration from a story in *The Tale of Saigyō* (*Saigyō monogatari*), written earlier in the thirteenth century. According to *Saigyō monogatari*, the twelfth-century monk-poet for whom the narrative is named met a prostitute living in the village of Eguchi, located at the mouth of the Yodo River. She refused to let him take lodging for the night lest he be tempted to break his vows. This story is referenced in the inscription at the top of the scroll:

PRIEST SAIGYŌ:

Yo no naka o	Although it is hard
itou made koso	to renounce this world of ours
katakarame	as a transient home,
kari no yadori o	surely you would not begrudge
oshimu kimi ka na.	this temporary lodging![1]

THE PROSTITUTE'S REPLY:

Yo o itou	Just because I knew
hito to shikikeba	you renounced the world, I thought
kari no ya ni	that I should warn you
kokoro tomuna to	not to let your heart linger
omou bakari zo.	in temporary lodgings.

The No play provided the details for this illustration: An itinerant monk of a much later time also meets a courtesan, who later reveals that she is a manifestation of the bodhisattva Fugen. The boat she is riding is transformed into a white elephant.

The scroll on the right is drawn from the story *Stone Bridge* (*Shakkyō*), which was celebrated in both No and Kabuki performances. The Heian-period monk Jakushō (lay name Ōe no Sadamoto) made a pilgrimage to Mount Tiantai in southeastern China. There, at the celebrated narrow stone bridge, he had a vision of a Chinese lion (*karashishi*) frolicking with a peony. In this painting a beautiful woman holds a branch of peony and

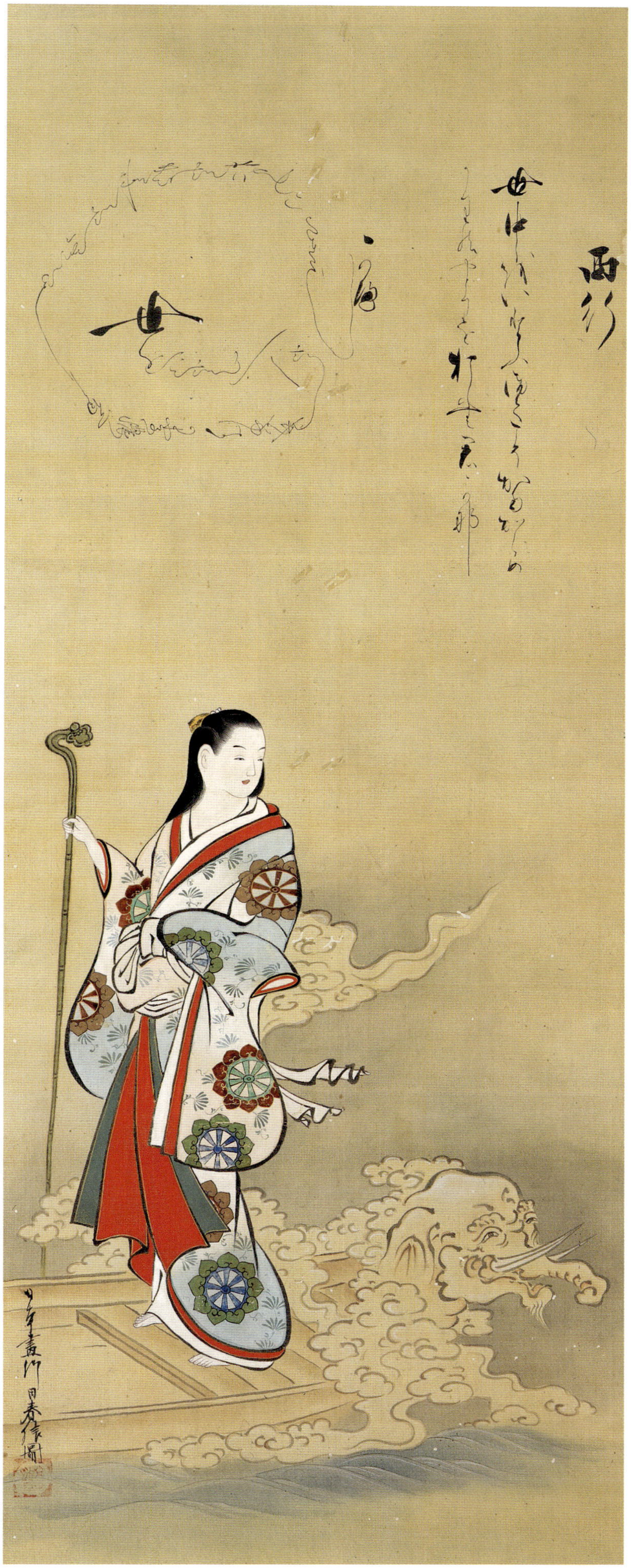

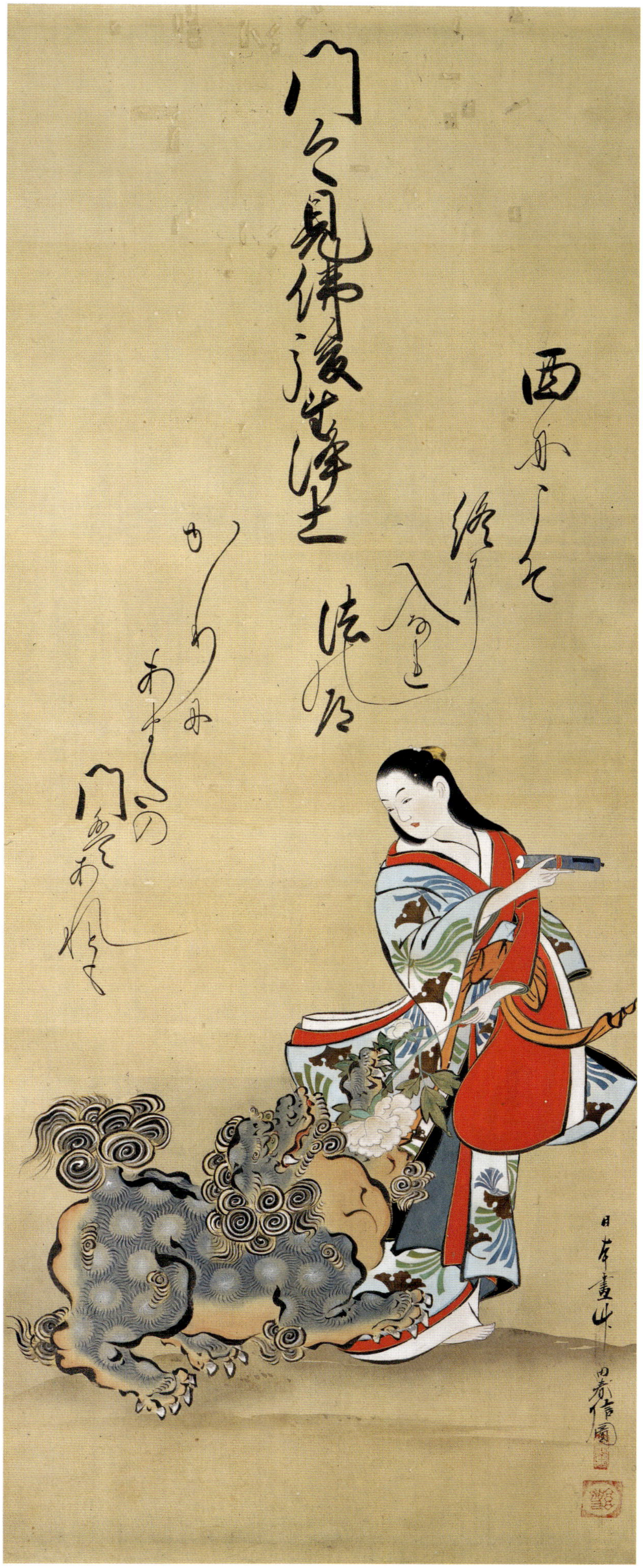

a scroll, another emblem of the bodhisattva Monju, and toys with the *karashishi*. The accompanying inscription reads:

Monmon kenbutsu go	Seek the Buddha at gate after gate [2]
Jōdo ni umu	and ye shall be reborn in the Pure Land

Nishi ni koso	At the very end
tsui ni irenare	Buddha's road will lead us west
hō no michi	into Paradise
kari ni amata no	even though for now it seems
mon wa aredomo.	its gates are all too many.

The artist of these paintings, Takeda Harunobu (distinct from the later Suzuki Harunobu), first called himself Baiōken Eishun. He created another independent painting of the Lady of Eguchi with an almost identical composition, now in the Idemitsu Museum of Arts, Tokyo.[3] In these works the roundness of the faces, the stateliness of the figures, and the scale of the motifs on the robes are stylistic traits that developed under the influence of paintings by Kaigetsudō Ando. NM

---

1. The Saigyō poem, which was included in the *New Anthology of Ancient and Modern Waka* (*Shin kokinshū*), was prefaced with "Once, on my way to Tennō-ji, there was a sudden downpour. I asked for lodging at Eguchi but was refused, so I wrote the following poem." (Translation by Joe Earle.)
2. *Editor's note:* According to Joe Earle, the sentence "Seek the Buddha at gate after gate and ye shall be reborn in the Pure Land" has been paraphrased from the Sutra on the Meditation on the Buddha of Infinite Life (*Kanmuryōju-kyō*). The poem was included in the fourteenth-century *Anthology of Poems from a Grass Hut* (*Sōan wakashū*), compiled by Ton'a.
3. Takeda Harunobu, *Representation (Mitate) of the Courtesan from Eguchi*, hanging scroll, ink and color on silk, 80.6 x 35 cm, Idemitsu Museum of Arts, published in *Idemitsu bijutsukan*, vol. 3 of *Nikuhitsu ukiyo-e taikan* (Tokyo: Kōdansha, 1994), illustration 27.

11. **ATTRIBUTED TO MIYAGAWA CHŌSHUN** (1682–1752?)

Scenes in the Yoshiwara Pleasure Quarter

About Hōei (1704–11) to early Kyōhō (1716–36) eras
Six-panel folding screen; ink, color, gold, and silver on paper
83.2 x 266.6 cm (32 ¾ x 104 15/16 in.)
Fenollosa-Weld Collection 11.4624

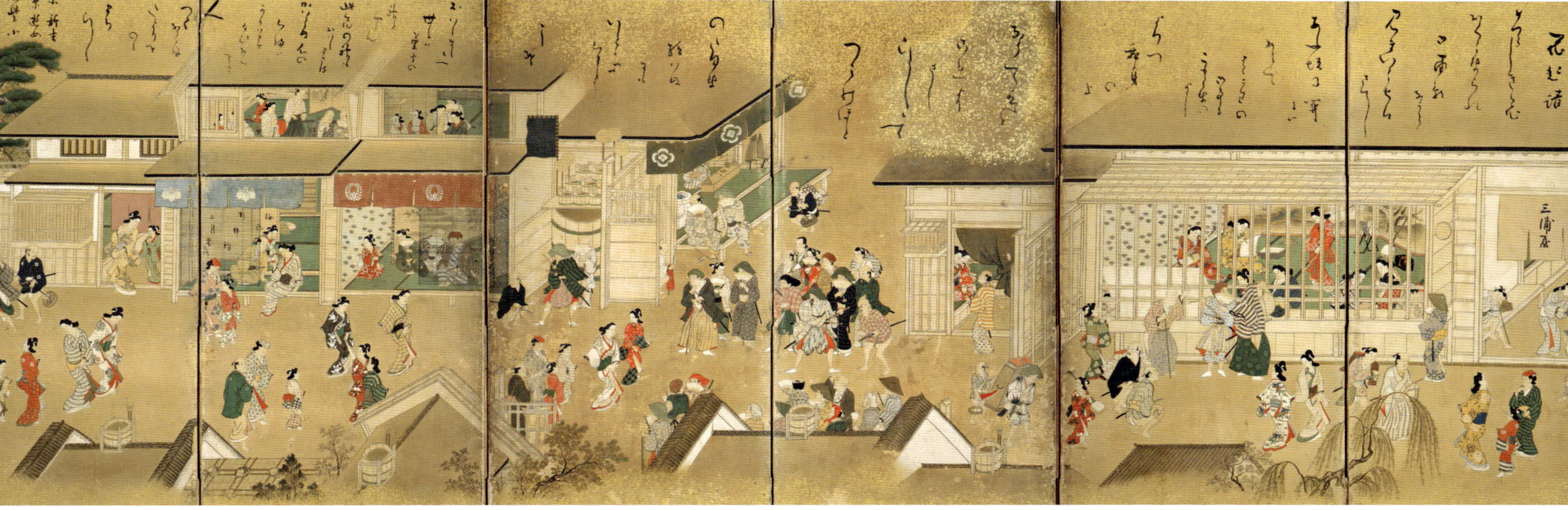

Organized across the entire horizontal expanse of a six-panel, midsize screen, this painting vividly describes the varied activities of social commerce along Nakano-chō, the main boulevard of the Shin ("New") Yoshiwara, Edo's officially sanctioned pleasure quarters (constructed in 1657 after the Meiriki Fire; see cat. no. 1). On the right is the latticed parlor of the grand Miuraya, a high-class brothel where the courtesans demonstrate their refinement through samisen playing, letter writing, and *suguroku* gaming against a background of elaborate landscape screens. Juxtaposed with this enterprise is a lower-class brothel (*tsubone mise*) just to the left; a customer arranges for an assignation with two women seated in the entranceway. On the last three panels, teahouses outfitted with their own landscape and calligraphic screens shelter male clients, who peer through the bamboo blinds at a slow-moving parade of the highest-level *tayū* courtesans and their retinues. Although the focus of the composition is this evening procession of the *tayū* making their way along the boulevard lined with gawking admirers, the painting includes a wealth of detail about the other commercial activities in the quarter — itinerant book lending, egg vending, and money changing.[1]

Along the lower edge of the screen the roofs on the opposite side of the street, with buckets of water placed on ridges as protection from much-feared fires, form a band that emerges from the gold mist. Across the upper reaches of the screen is another band of atomized gold on which is brushed an excerpt from a letter by Komurasaki, a famed courtesan of the Miuraya from the second

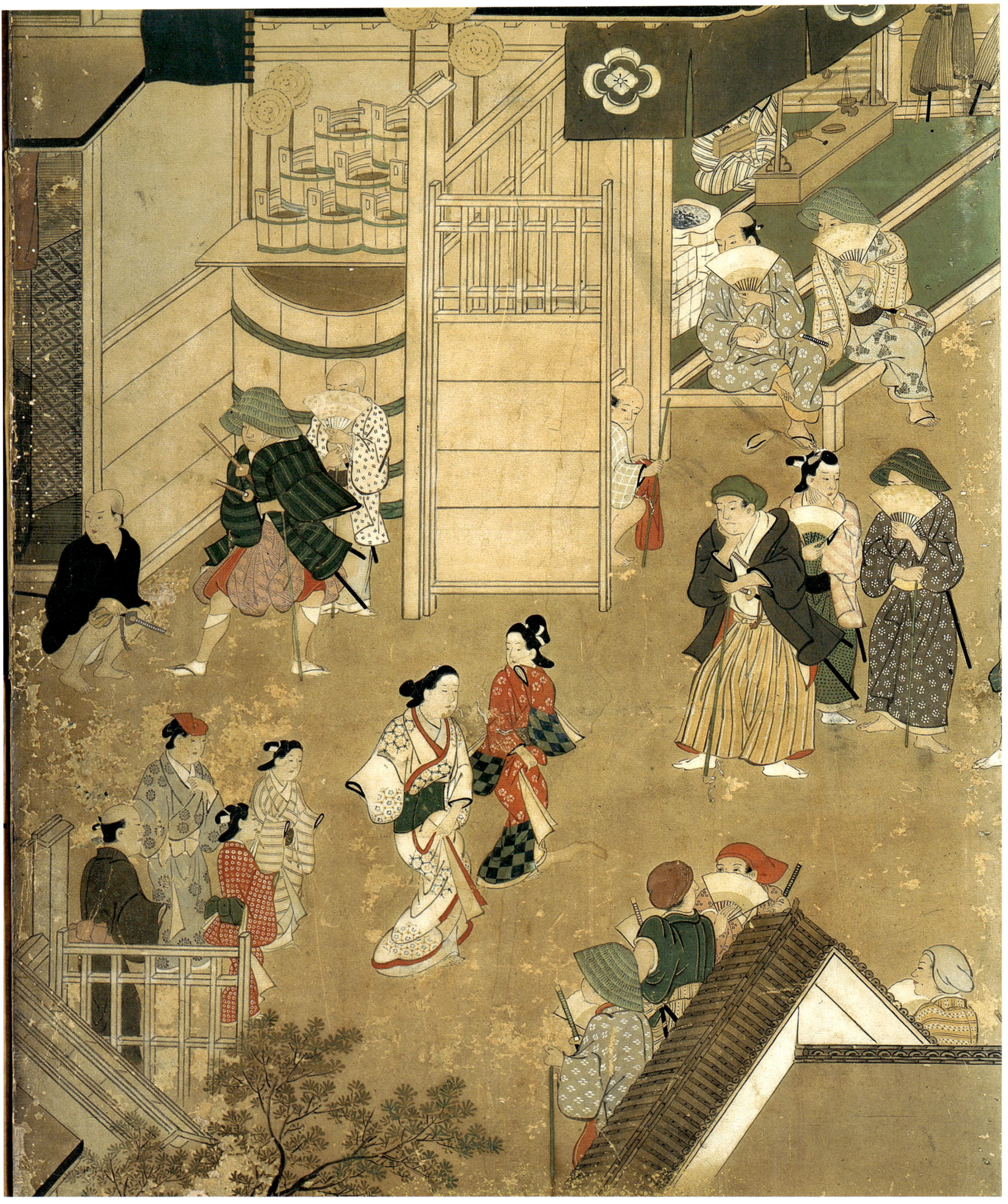

half of the seventeenth century. The inscription is followed by the signature of the celebrated *kyōka* poet and Yoshiwara habitué Ōta Nanpo (Shokusanjin, 1749–1823).

The painting does not bear any artist's signature or seals. However, since it was acquired by the Bostonian Ernest Francisco Fenollosa in the late nineteenth century, the MFA has attributed the work to Miyagawa Chōshun, the preeminent ukiyo-e painter of the first half of the eighteenth century. According to some scholars, the absence of Chōshun's signature and the high quality of the screen suggest that the work was commissioned by an individual of high social standing.[2]

Chōshun's organization of the composition, with the various brothels and teahouses lining the main avenue of the Yoshiwara and the selection of figural groupings, comes from a vision of the Pleasure Quarters already made popular by a previous generation of artists under Hishikawa Moronobu and members of his atelier.[3] For example, the courtesans displayed in the interior of the Miuraya — the samisen player, the letter writer, and the *suguroku* players — bear strong similarities to the denizens of the Miuraya as depicted by Moronobu in the left screen of *Scenes from the Nakamura Kabuki Theater and the Yoshiwara Pleasure Quarter* (see cat. no. 1). Only slight changes have been made to the patterns of the robes and the treatment of the hair. The older, bald man pausing to lean on the lattice with a staff in his right hand has his precedent in *Street Scene in the Yoshiwara* from the woodblock series Scenes of the Yoshiwara (Yoshiwara no tei).

By presenting the Yoshiwara with the iconography created by Moronobu, Chōshun allied himself with the prestige and authority of the Hishikawa school.[4] His individual artistic innovation lies in the attention to the subtleties of dress — important in a world where displays of clothing were statements of rank — and the nuances of the relationship between figures. ANM

1. Kobayashi Tadashi, "Yoshiwara fūzokuzu byōbu," *Bosuton bijutsukan nikuhitsu ukiyo-e*, vol. 2 (Tokyo: Museum of Fine Arts, Boston, and Kōdansha, 2000), 145–46.
2. Kobayashi Tadashi, for example, is of that opinion; he makes the same assumption for other paintings including the Hishikawa Moronobu handscroll *Scenes in Yoshiwara*, now in the collection of John Weber, New York. "Hishikawa Moronobu no Yoshiwara fūzokuzu ni tsuite," *Manno bijutsukan*, vol. 7 of *Nikuhitsu ukiyo-e taikan* (Tokyo: Kōdansha, 1996), 214–17.
3. For example, Hishikawa Morohira adopted Moronobu's scheme for the Yoshiwara in *Pastimes in Spring and Autumn*, early Genroku era, pair of six-panel folding screens, ink and color on paper, in the Idemitsu Museum of Arts. Okumura Masanobu would do the same in *Scenes in Yoshiwara*, around first half of the Kyōhō era, pair of hanging scrolls, ink and color on paper, in the Manno Museum. See *Idemitsu bijutsukan*, vol. 3 of *Nikuhitsu ukiyo-e taikan* (Tokyo: Kōdansha, 1996), illustrations 14–15; and *Manno bijutsukan*, vol. 7 of *Nikuhitsu ukiyo-e taikan*, illustrations 34–35.
4. Kobayashi has indicated that Chōshun borrowed elements from Moronobu works for other paintings as well; see *Chōshun*, vol. 3 of *Nikuhitsu ukiyo-e taikan*, 39. Naitō Masato notes that Chōshun signed a *shunga* handscroll "Hishikawa Chōshun," which he views as an indication of the artist's admiration for the Hishikawa school; see Naitō Masato, "Ryushi bijin zu," *Idemitsu bijutsukan*, vol. 3 of *Nikuhitsu ukiyo-e taikan*, 210.

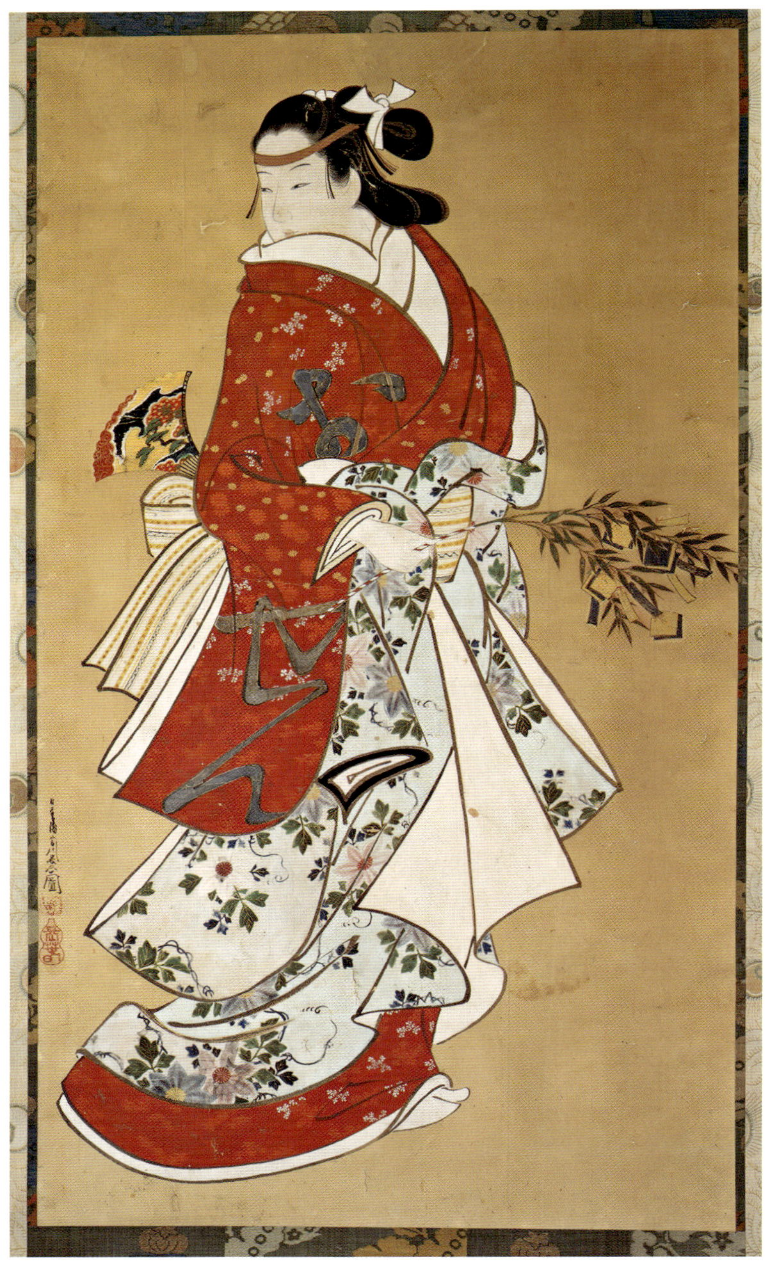

12. **MIYAGAWA CHŌSHUN** (1682–1752?)
Female Dancer

About the Hōei (1704–11) or early Kyōhō (1716–36) era
Hanging scroll; ink, color, gold, and silver on paper
94.5 x 55.4 cm (37 3/16 x 21 13/16 in.)
Signature: Yamato-e Miyagawa Chōshun zu (Yamato picture drawn by Miyagawa Chōshun)
Seals: Chōshun no in (Seal of Chōshun); Chōshun
William Sturgis Bigelow Collection 11.7662

Performing a dance that belongs to the "crazed" genre (*kyōranmono*), the subject of this painting wears a *yamai hachimaki* (a headband worn by actors portraying sick characters in Kabuki and No plays) and turns around, exposing her red underrobe at both shoulders. She holds a branch of bamboo decorated with square and oblong poem cards and tucks a fan into the back of her sash.

Silver characters for the name "Osen" are scattered across her chrysanthemum-decorated underrobe. These may indicate the name of the dancer, but it is difficult to determine what type of woman she was. She may have been a member of a *kōwaka-mai* troupe, dancers who performed by invitation in the private quarters of a regional lord's home.[1] Such women appear in Chōshun's masterpiece handscroll *Scenes of Daily Life*, in the Tokyo National Museum.[2] However, by the early eighteenth century, women dancers (who later came to be called female geisha) also existed in Edo. If this Osen was an actual dancer, it is possible to imagine that her patron had Chōshun paint her portrait as part of a special commission. AS

1. Specifically, *onna-mai* dancers who had branched off the Daigashira line.
2. Suwa Haruo, ed., *Kinsei fūzoku zulcan*, vol. 3 (Tokyo: Mainichi shinbunsha, 1974).

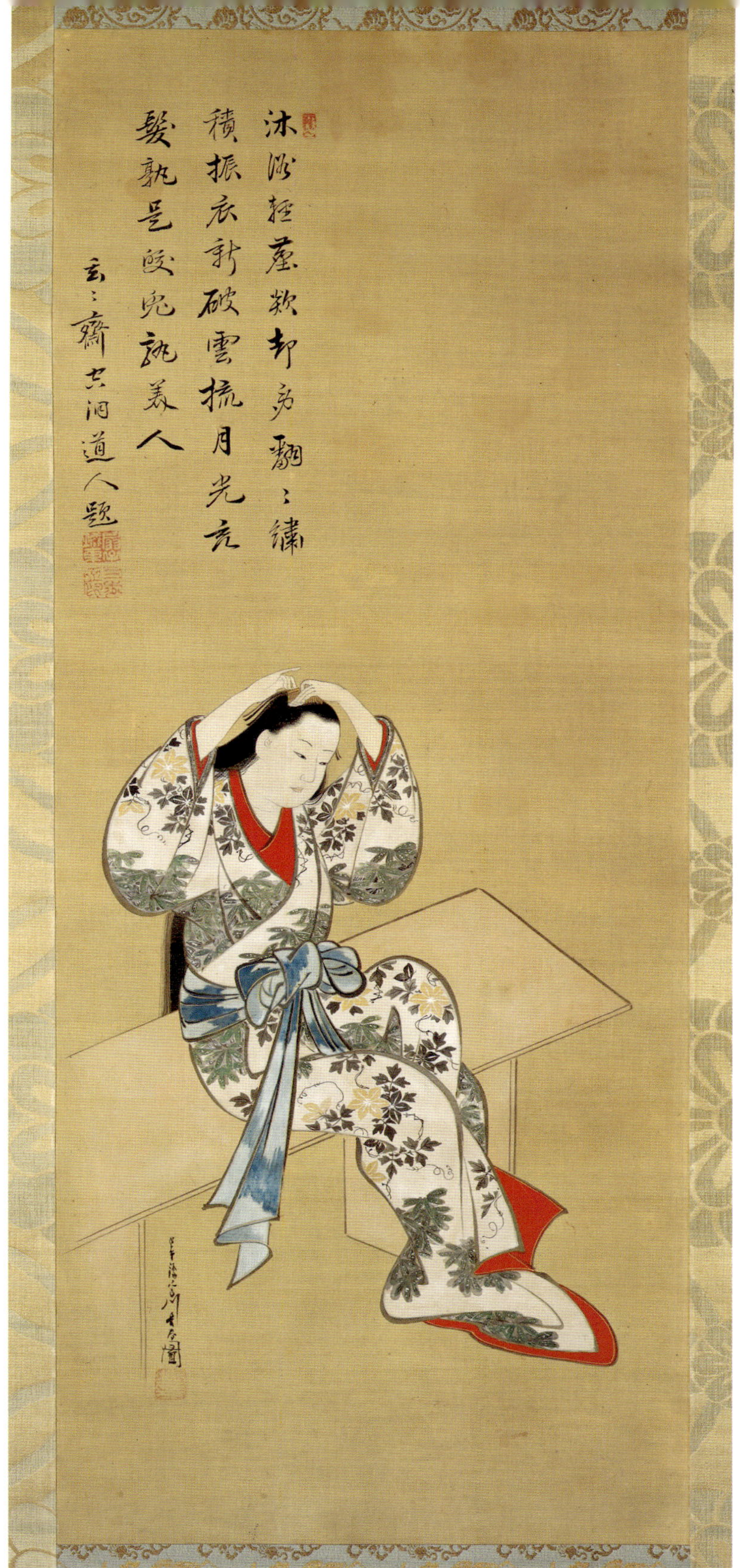

13. **MIYAGAWA CHŌSHUN** (1682–1752?)
Courtesan Seated on a Bench

Kyōhō era (1716–36)
Hanging scroll; ink, color, gold, and silver on silk
85 x 35.8 cm (33 7/16 x 14 1/8 in.)
Signature: Yamato-e Miyagawa Chōshun zu
(Yamato picture drawn by Miyagawa Chōshun)
Seal: Chōshun no in (Seal of Chōshun)
William Sturgis Bigelow Collection 11.7659

Arranging a tortoiseshell comb in her luxurious, long black hair, a courtesan is seated on a wooden bench that extends in a diagonal across the lower middle of the painting. She is dressed in an elegant, yet understated outer robe with motifs of snow-covered bamboo (*sasa*) juxtaposed with climbing clematis in gold leaf and oxidized silver. The lines of the ikat-woven sash, loosely secured in the front, and the bright red underrobe are reinforced in gold.

In the upper left of the composition is a poem signed by Gengensai Kūdō Dōjin, about whom nothing is known. Writing a Chinese verse in a quatrain of seven-syllable lines, the poet describes his response to the painting.

She washes the fine dust away,
leaving her old body behind;
embroidered silks flutter in the wind,
making a whole new garment.

Moonlight combs through the broken clouds,
shining brightly on her tresses;
Is this really a fair maiden,
or the White Rabbit in the Moon?

As Asano Shūgō has pointed out in his essay for this catalogue (see pp. 44–5), the pose of a courtesan seated on a bench can be found in a number of

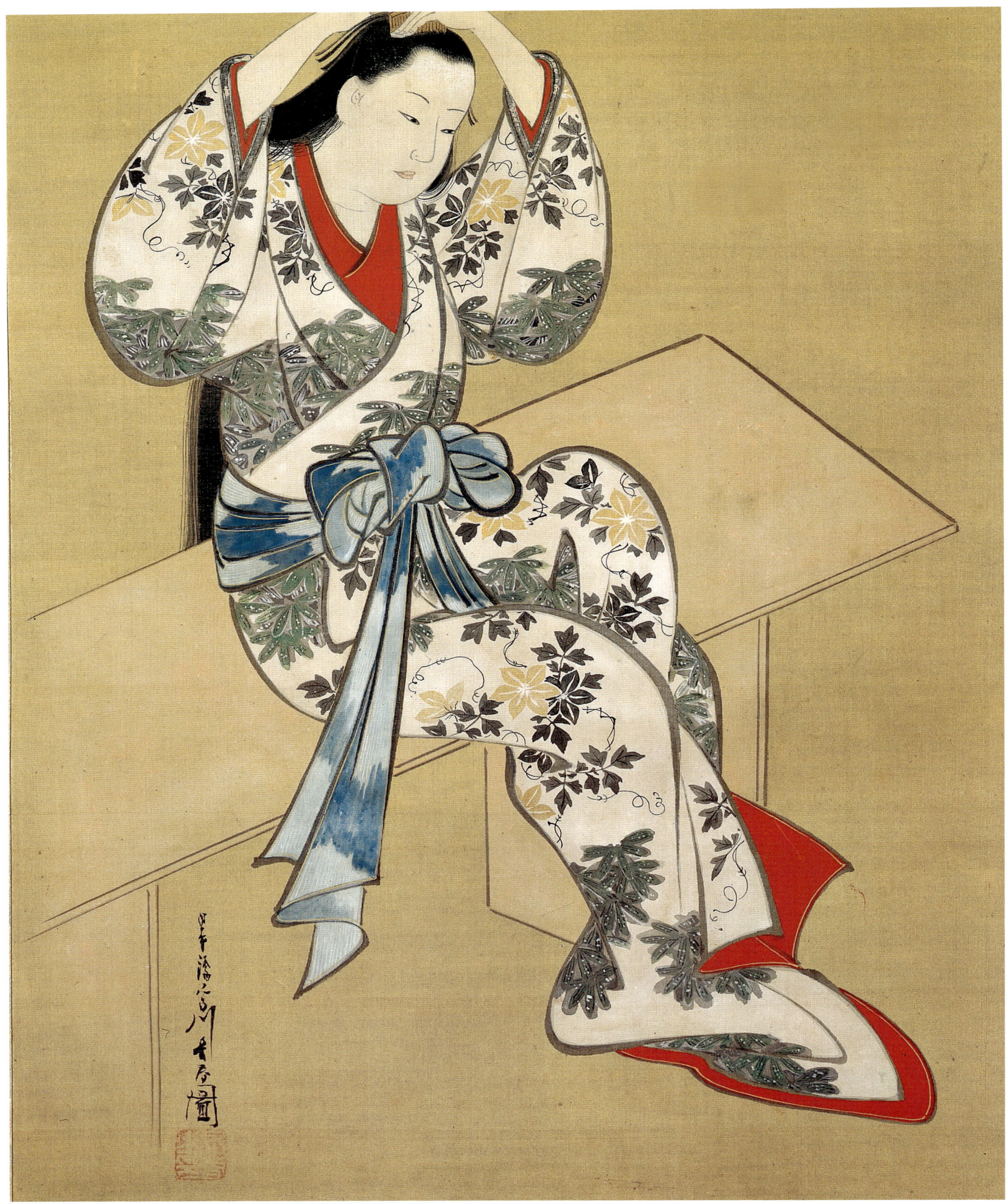

images from the early eighteenth century, including works by Baiyūken Katsunobu (active 1704–16) in the British Museum and by Takizawa Shigenobu (active 1716–36) in the Idemitsu Museum of Arts.[1] Despite the congruences with other works, Chōshun has created an entirely different feeling in his painting — one of intimacy. He achieves this effect through the delicate handling of the courtesan's facial features and the subtle selection of the textile patterns. The inscription with its moon imagery highlights the mood that Chōshun was able to achieve with his use of silver on the clematis-leaf motif in the robes. ANM

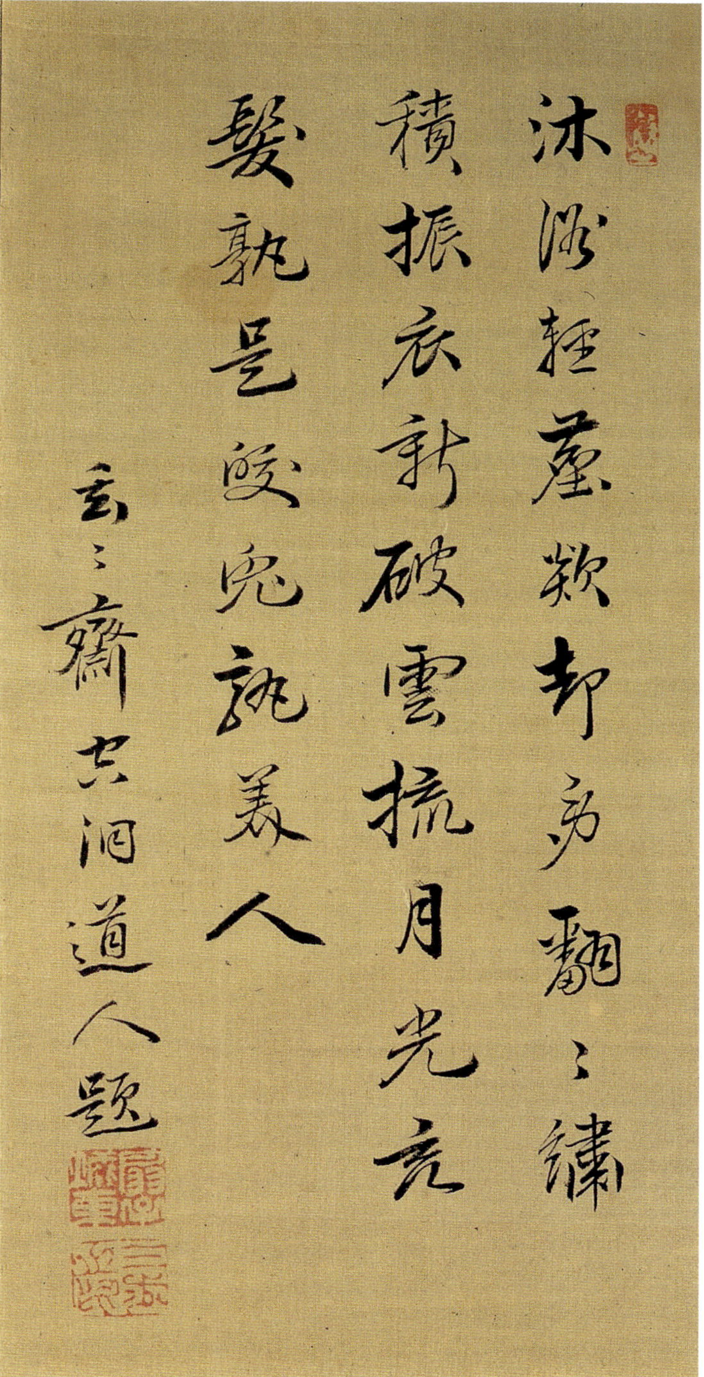

---

1. Baiyūken Katsunobu, *Courtesan Seated on a Bench*, 1704–16, hanging scroll, ink and color on silk, 119.8 x 44.4 cm, British Museum, published in Timothy Clark, *Ukiyo-e Paintings in the British Museum* (London: British Museum Press, 1992), pl. 26. Takizawa Shigenobu, *Beauty on a Bench*, 1716–36, hanging scroll, ink and color on paper, 103.9 x 48.9 cm, Idemitsu Museum of Arts, published in *Idemitsu Museum*, vol. 3 of *Nikuhitsu ukiyo-e taikan* (Tokyo: Kōdansha, 1994), monochrome illustration 32.

14. **MIYAGAWA CHŌSHUN** (1682–1752?)
Scenes of Pleasurable Pastimes

Before the Kyōhō era (1716–36)
Handscroll; ink, color, gold, and silver on paper
27.5 x 385.5 cm (10 13/16 x 151 3/4 in.)
Signature: Nihon-e Miyagawa Chōshun zu
(Japanese picture drawn by Miyagawa Chōshun)
Seal: Chōshun no in (Seal of Chōshun)
Fenollosa-Weld Collection 11.4619

With the advent of the New Year, a member of the military aristocracy has summoned a troupe of actors and musicians for a private performance in his home. Led by a blind man, the group wends its way to the mansion, passing street players who are performing the traditional lion dance. In the central section, the troupe makes its theatrical presentation for the master of the house (who reclines leaning against an armrest) and for a small group of his retainers; his wife and her female attendants watch from behind bamboo blinds (*sudare*). The last section of the scroll shows members of the delegation waiting behind the scenes while another young actor is readied for his appearance.

In creating the narrative of his handscrolls, Miyagawa Chōshun often wove together visual elements adopted from other works — some that he composed himself and others that he borrowed from his "spiritual teacher" Hishikawa Moronobu. For example, quotations from the dressing room sections of Moronobu's paired screens *Genre Scenes at a Kabuki Theater* (*Kabuki zu byōbu*) in the Tokyo National Museum are readily evident in the last scene of this Chōshun handscroll.[1] The bearded man seated at the edge of the elevated side room and the group of three men conversing at the end of the scroll have their counterparts in the second panel of the left-hand screen in Tokyo. Similarities can also be found in the opening sections of this handscroll and others by Chōshun in the Tokyo National Museum and the Idemitsu Museum of Arts which chronicle daily life.[2] However, Chōshun's oeuvre never appears repetitious, for the artist carefully details the individual expressions and clothing of his figures as well as the fabulous furnishings of his interiors, particularly the delicately rendered landscapes on the screens (here in the Kano-school style). ANM

1. Hishikawa Moronobu, *Genre Scenes at a Kabuki Theater*, about 1692–93, pair of six-panel folding screens, ink, color, and gold on paper, each 170 x 396.7 cm, Tokyo National Museum, published in *Tōkyō kokuritsu hakubutsukan*, vol. 1 of *Nikuhitsu ukiyo-e taikan* (Tokyo: Kōdansha, 1994), illustrations 9–10.
2. Miyagawa Chōshun, *Scenes of Daily Life*, about 1716–36, handscroll, ink and color on paper, 36.9 x 391 cm, Tokyo National Museum, published in *Tōkyō kokuritsu hakubutsukan*, illustration 45; and Miyagawa Chōshun, *Scenes of Daily Life in Edo through the Four Seasons*, about 1716–36, handscroll, ink and color on silk, 34.4 x 782.7 cm, Idemitsu Museum of Arts, published in *Idemitsu bijutsukan*, vol. 3 of *Nikuhitsu ukiyo-e taikan* (Tokyo: Kōdansha, 1994), illustration 37.

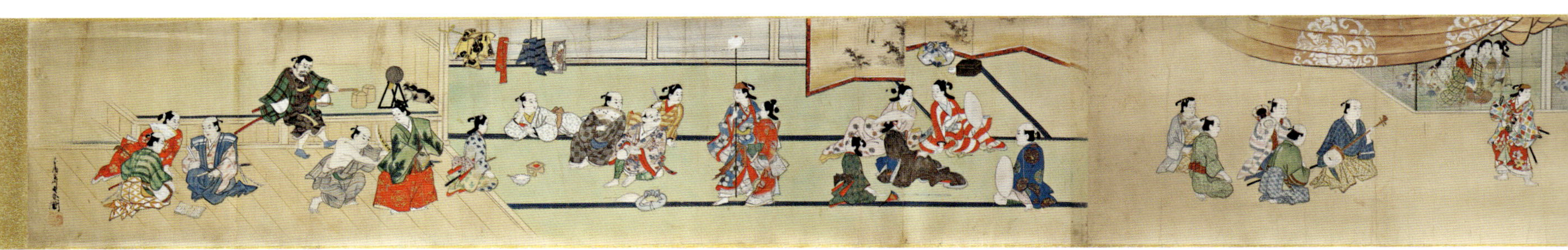

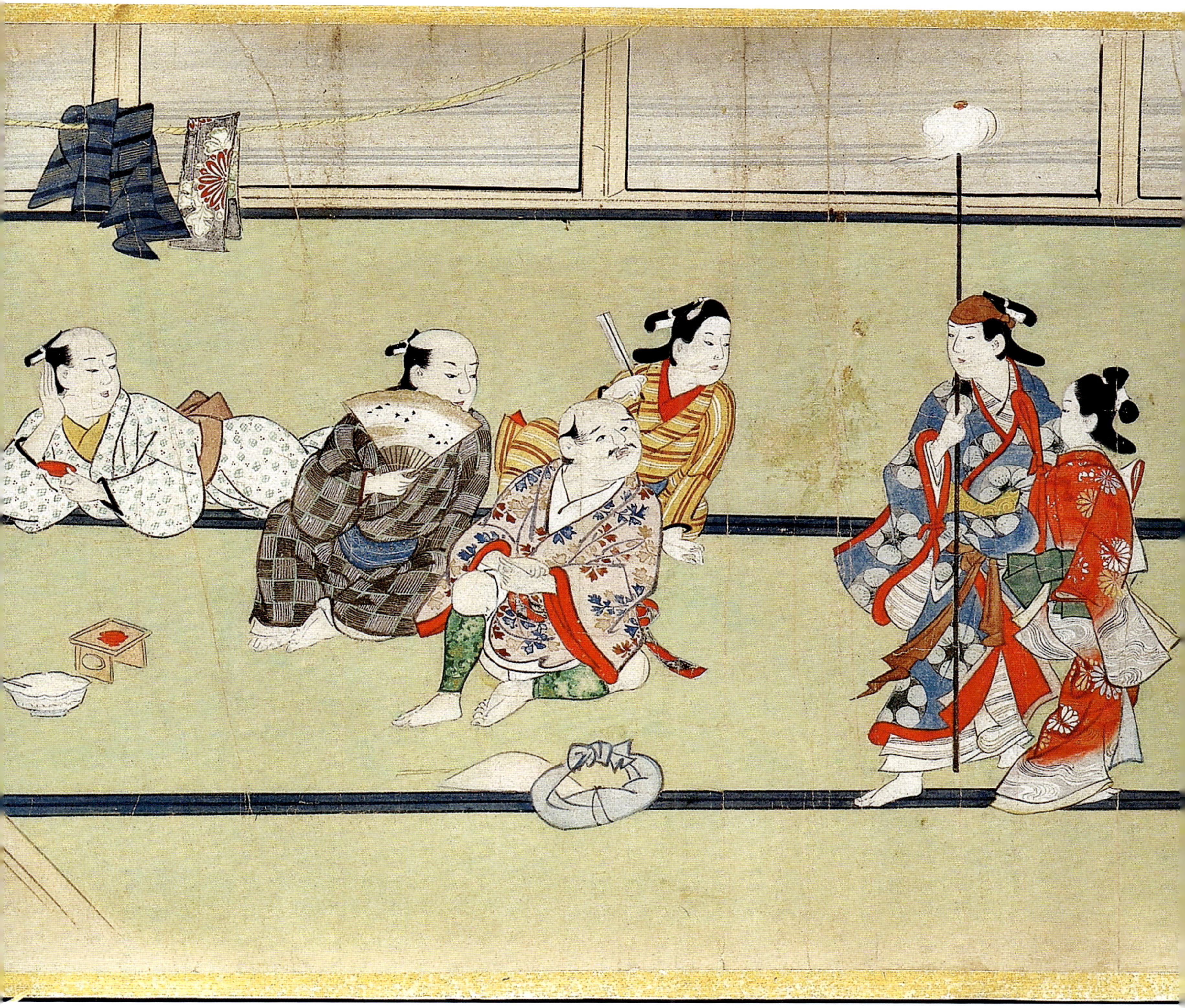

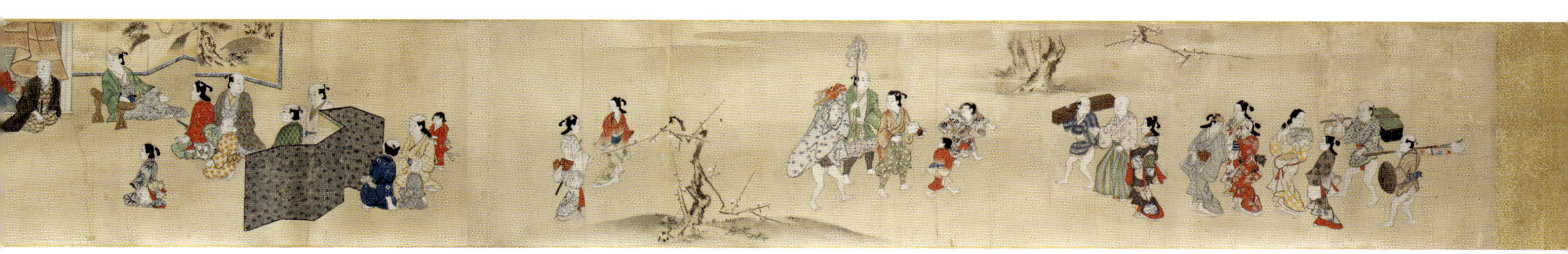

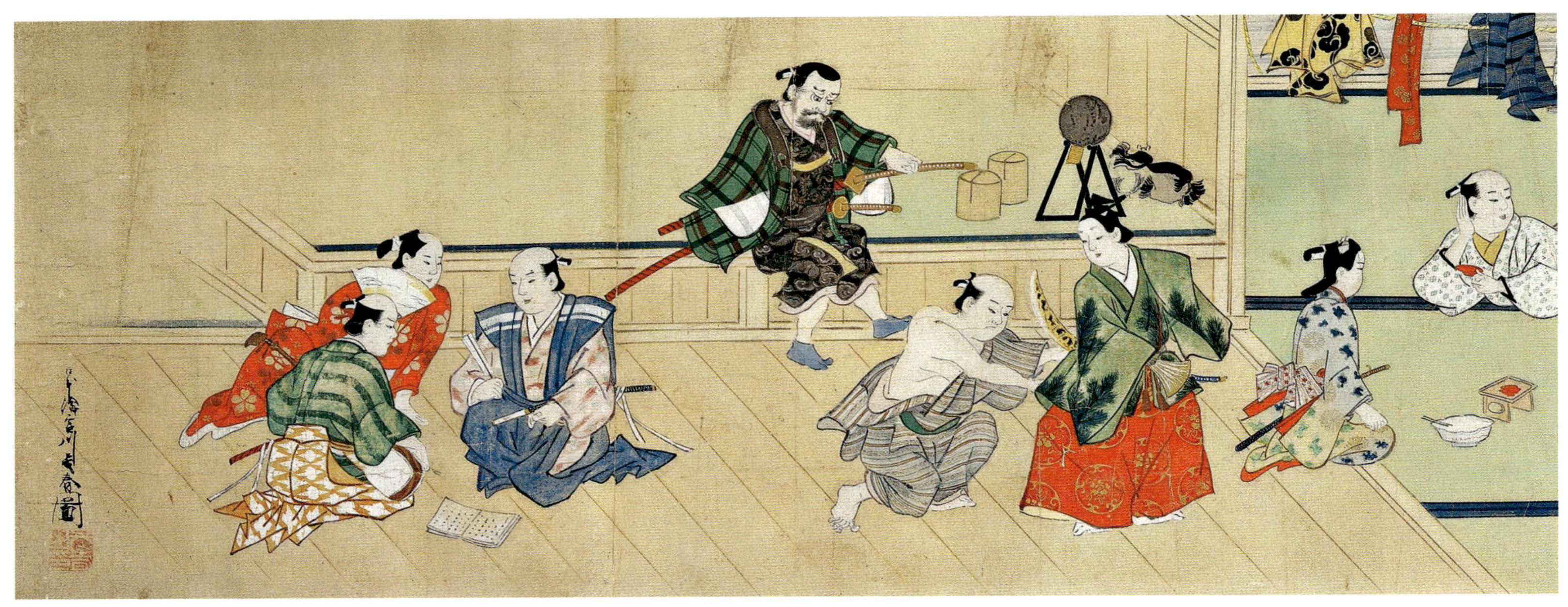
宮川長春圖

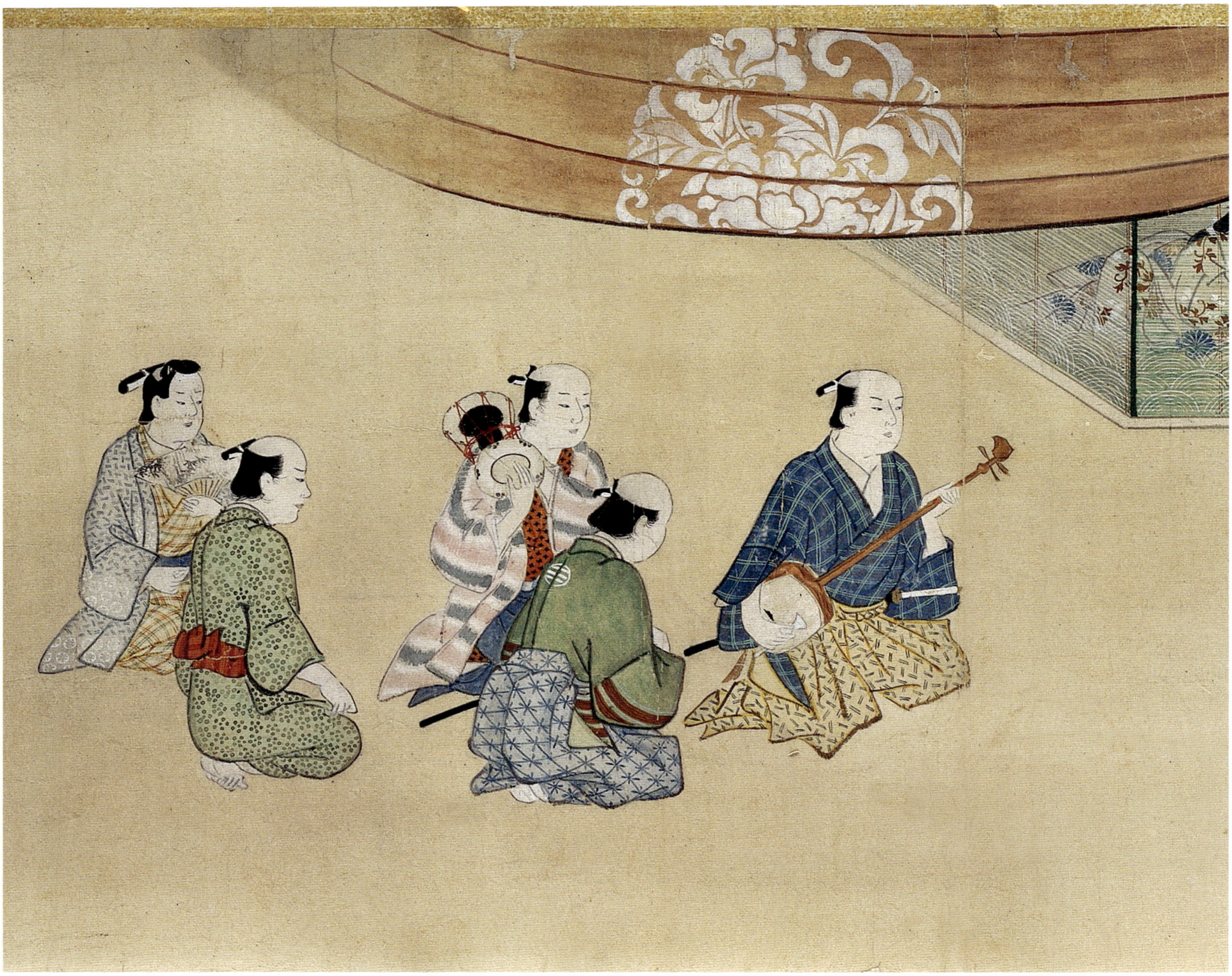

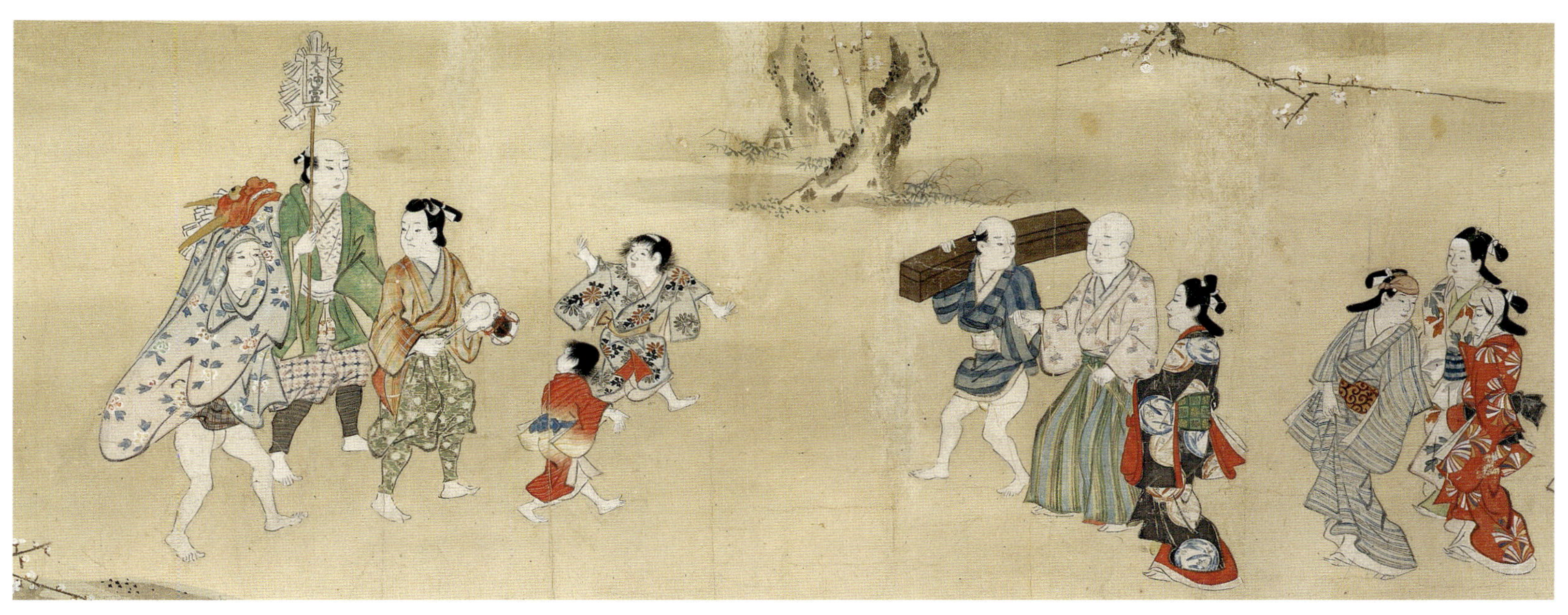

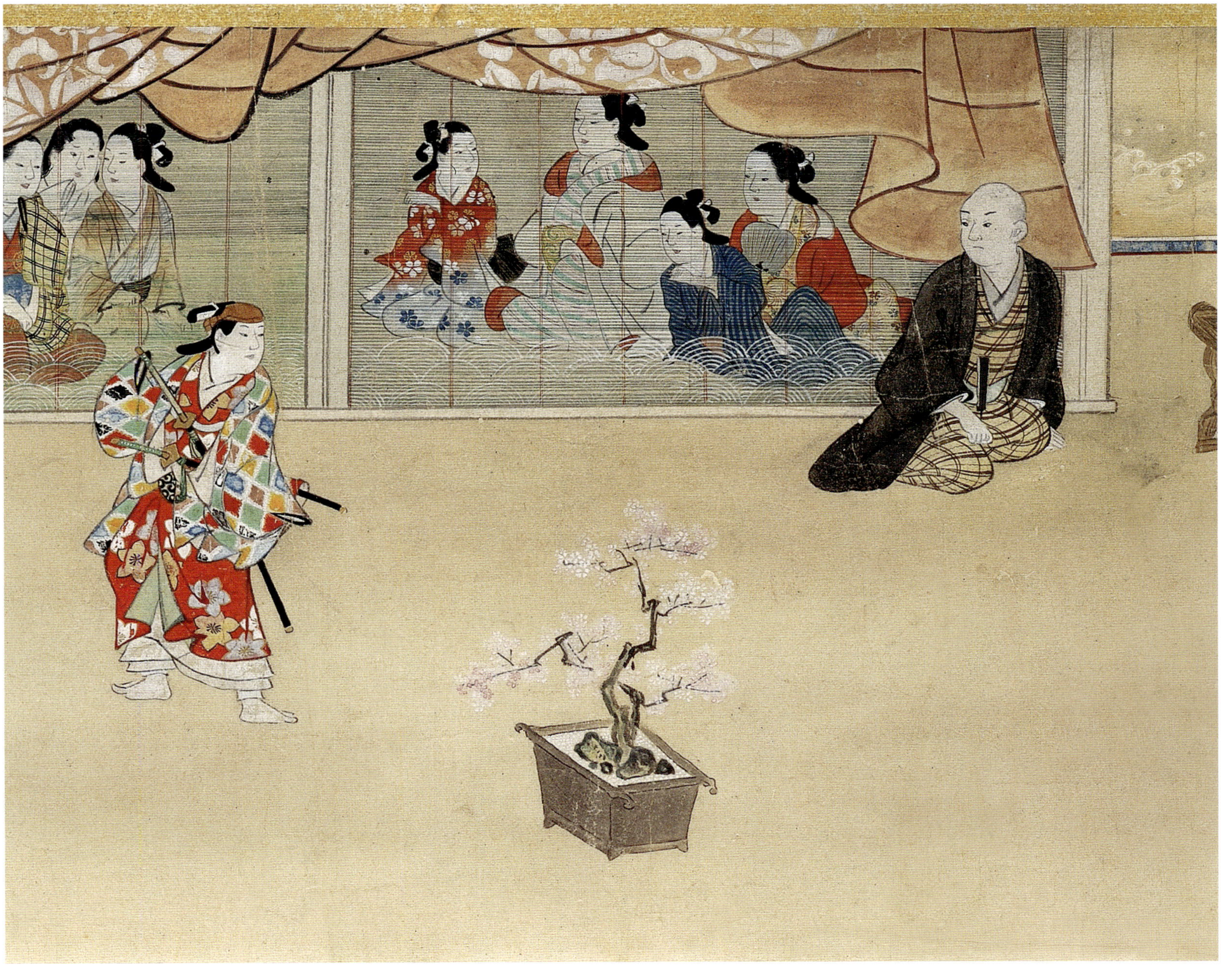

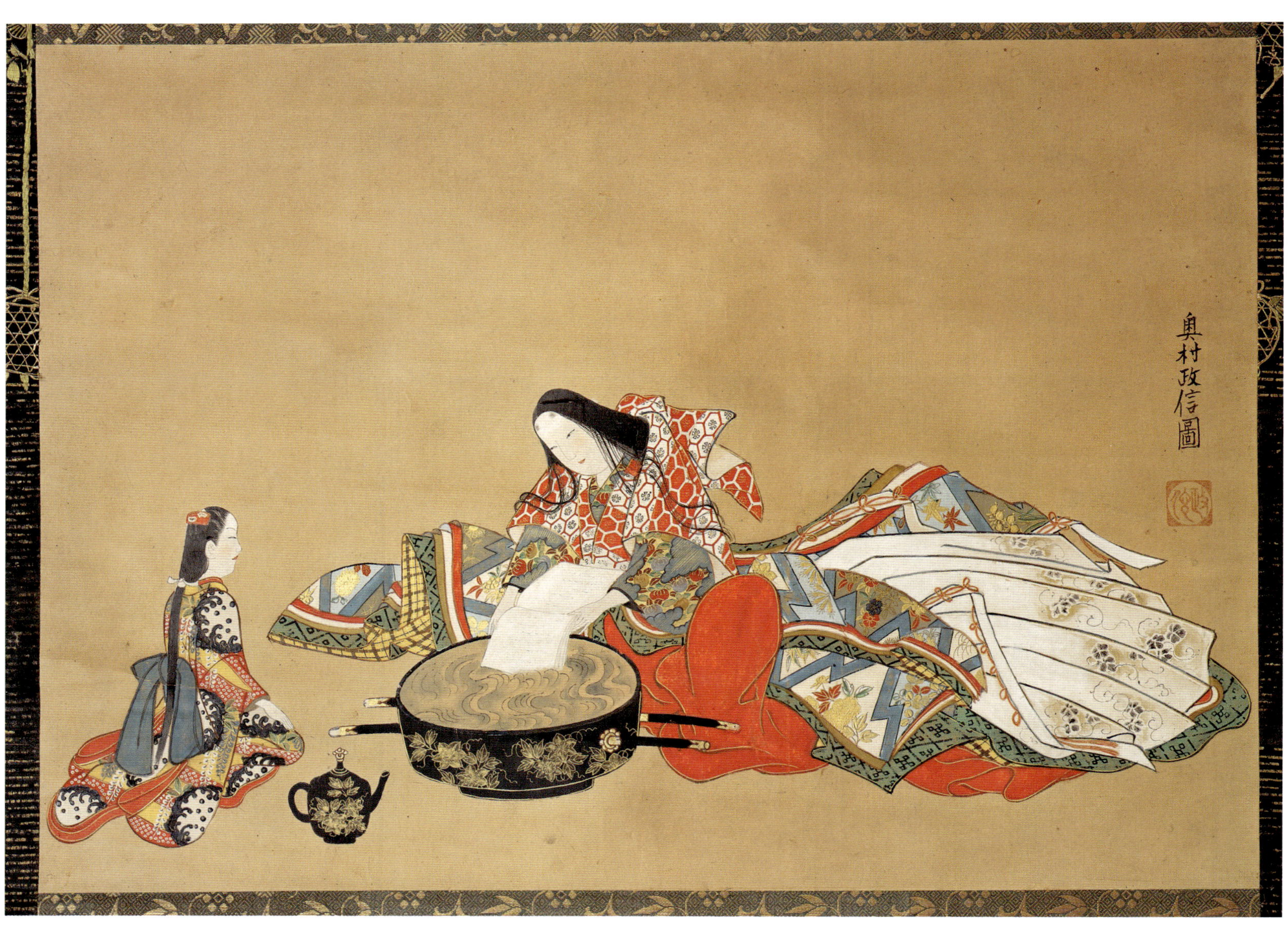
奥村政信圖

15. **OKUMURA MASANOBU** (1686–1764)
Ono no Komachi Washing a Manuscript

About the Shōtoku (1711–16) or early Kyōhō (1716–36) era
Hanging scroll; ink, color, gold, and silver on paper
38 x 55.8 cm (14 15/16 x 21 15/16 in.)
Signature: Okumura Masanobu zu (Drawn by Okumura Masanobu)
Seal: Masanobu
William Sturgis Bigelow Collection 11.7604

The celebrated ninth-century poet Ono no Komachi was the subject of many legends; this painting recounts one of these, widely known through the fourteenth-century No play *Ono no Komachi Washing a Manuscript* (*Sōshi-arai Komachi*) by Kan'ami and his son Zeami. According to the fictional account, the courtier Ōtomi no Kuronushi, Komachi's opponent in an imperial poetry contest, sneaked into her residence and eavesdropped as she prepared her poem. He then inscribed the verse into a copy of the *Collection of Ten Thousand Leaves* (*Manyōshū*), a revered eighth-century poetry anthology. Later during the match, Kuronushi accused Komachi of plagiarism, asserting that the poem she had composed was actually an ancient one. Suspicious of the charge, Komachi took the copy of the anthology and immersed it in water. The contested verse washed away, and Komachi was ultimately able to clear her name.

The Komachi theme was extremely popular in ukiyo-e of the eighteenth century. Sometimes it was presented in a straightforward manner, as one finds here with the poet dressed in aristocratic garments, washing the anthology in a handled basin. Other times it parodied the No drama, which was part of a series of seven plays that took the legendary life of the poet as their subject. Komachi's appearance in this hanging scroll closely resembles that of another painting, by Matsuno Chikanobu, in the Ōta Memorial Museum, Tokyo.[1] The latter painting may be contemporary with this one, in which case the two were probably based on similar models.

During the 1740s Okumura Masanobu produced other versions of the theme in woodblock prints, including a horizontal *ōban beni-e* in the Bremen Art Museum (a design that was later reused in a *benizuri-e* edition) and a monochrome illustration for *Illustrated Picture Book of the Four Accomplishments of the Elegant Seven Komachis* (*Ehon fūga Nana Komachi kingo shoga*, 2 vols.). These works and a few others depict Ono no Komachi in contemporary rather than ancient dress. However, in the composition of this painting, the poet wears Heian-period garb whereas her attendant, who sits to the left with a ewer at her side, wears an Edo-period *furisode* robe. Thus, this hanging scroll can be seen as the prototype for Masanobu's later prints. AS

1. Matsuno Chikanobu, *Ono no Komachi Washing a Manuscript*, Hōei (1704–11)–Shōtoku (1711–16) eras, hanging scroll, ink and color on silk, 36 x 47 cm, Ōta Memorial Museum, published in *Ōta kinen bijutsukan/Hokusaikan/Itabashi kuritsu bijutsukan*, vol. 5 of *Nikuhitsu ukiyo-e taikan* (Tokyo: Kōdansha, 1996), illustration 3.

16. **OKUMURA MASANOBU** (1686–1764)
Parodies of Rashōmon and Ogurayama

Kyōhō era (1716–36)
Two-panel folding screen; ink and color on paper
Each 131.4 x 57.7 cm (52 3/4 x 22 11/16 in.)
Signature: Okumura Masanobu hitsu (Brush of Okumura Masanobu)
Seal: Masanobu
William Sturgis Bigelow Collection 11.7607

This two-panel screen is representative of one of Okumura Masanobu's great achievements—his development of the parody genre known as *mitate-e* or *yatsushi*. The right panel takes as its subject a contemporary adaptation of the Rashōmon legend. According to the original account, one rainy night the eleventh-century warrior Watanabe no Tsuna, one of the four guards in attendance to Minamoto no Yorimitsu, did battle with the ogre Ibaraki dōji at the Rashōmon Gate at the entrance to the Heian capital and cut off one of its arms.

In Masanobu's parody a fashionable young Edo-period warrior wearing the Watanabe star crest (three circles with a bar) takes the place of Watanabe no Tsuna, while a courtesan in the center of a spiderweb holding on to the warrior's umbrella stands in for the ogre Ibaraki. The maple-leaf motif on the courtesan's robe suggests that she may have been modeled after the famed *tayū* Takao, who used the maple leaf as her crest. In the original story, Ibaraki attacked Watanabe no Tsuna from a dark cloud, but here the courtesan seduces the young warrior from a spiderweb, thereby playing on the homonymic relationship between the Japanese words for cloud and spider.

During the first years of the 1710s, Masanobu produced another parody on the theme of Rashōmon, a series of twelve monochrome woodblock prints entitled *The Hair Ornament Rashōmon* (Sashigushi Rashōmon). In that version a youth, who stands inside a braided curtain, extends his right arm and tries to pull out a young woman's hair ornament as she walks along. She responds by biting him. The artist also provided the design for the last piece in a set of twelve horizontal *ōban* monochrome woodblock prints accompanied by miscellaneous playful poems in which a man dreams of a courtesan sitting in the center of a spiderweb. The right panel of the MFA screen appears to have combined these two earlier works.

The other panel presents a parody of a 1708 *jōruri* puppet play from the Tosa region (present-day Kōchi prefecture) entitled *Teika*. According to the story, Princess Shokushi, disguised as a handsome young man, visited her lover, the renowned thirteenth-century poet Fujiwara no Teika, who was living as a hermit in a retreat called the Autumn Rain Hut (Shigure no chin) on Mount Ogura in western Kyoto. She was accompanied by her attendant Nowake, who held an umbrella as the two walked along the mountain road covered with autumn leaves. This play also became a popular Kabuki subject; for instance, the opening all-star performance at the Ichimura Theater during the eleventh month of 1719 was *Tategami Teika kazura*. In this painting the inclusion of the purple caps worn by male actors in female roles relates to the Kabuki presentation.

Masanobu painted the hanging scroll *Representation of the Legend of the Villa at Mount Ogura*, now in the Tokyo National Museum, and designed a *yoko ōban* monochrome print entitled *Ukiyo-e Version of Teika's Autumn Rain Hut* (*Ukiyo-e Teika Shigure no chin*) prior to producing the images for the MFA's screen.[1] The two earlier works, particularly the Tokyo National Museum painting, must have provided models for the left panel here. AS

1. Okumura Masanobu, *Representation of the Legend of the Villa at Mount Ogura*, hanging scroll, ink and color on silk, 32.3 x 48.3 cm, published in *Tōkyō kokuritsu hakubutsukan*, vol. 1 of *Nikuhitsu ukiyo-e taikan* (Tokyo: Kōdansha, 1994), entry 61.

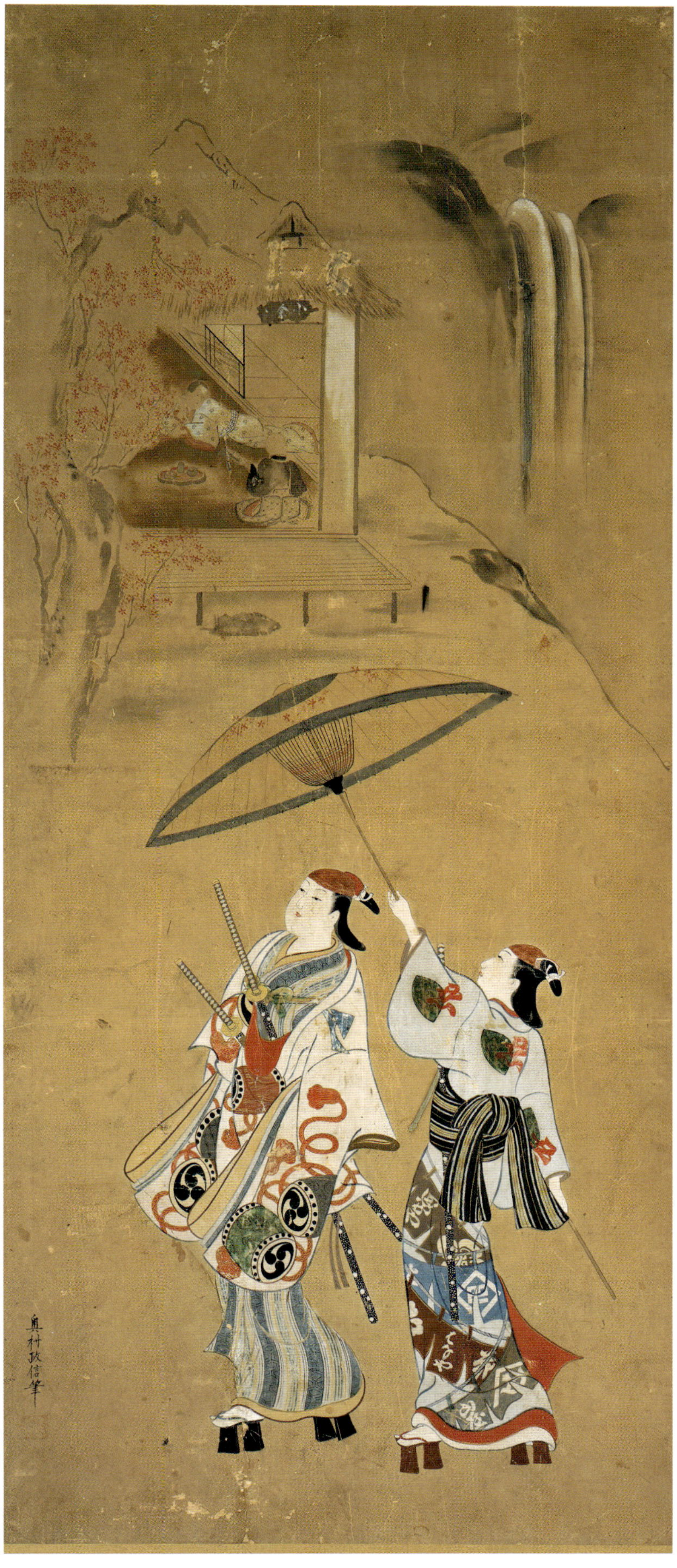

奥村政信筆

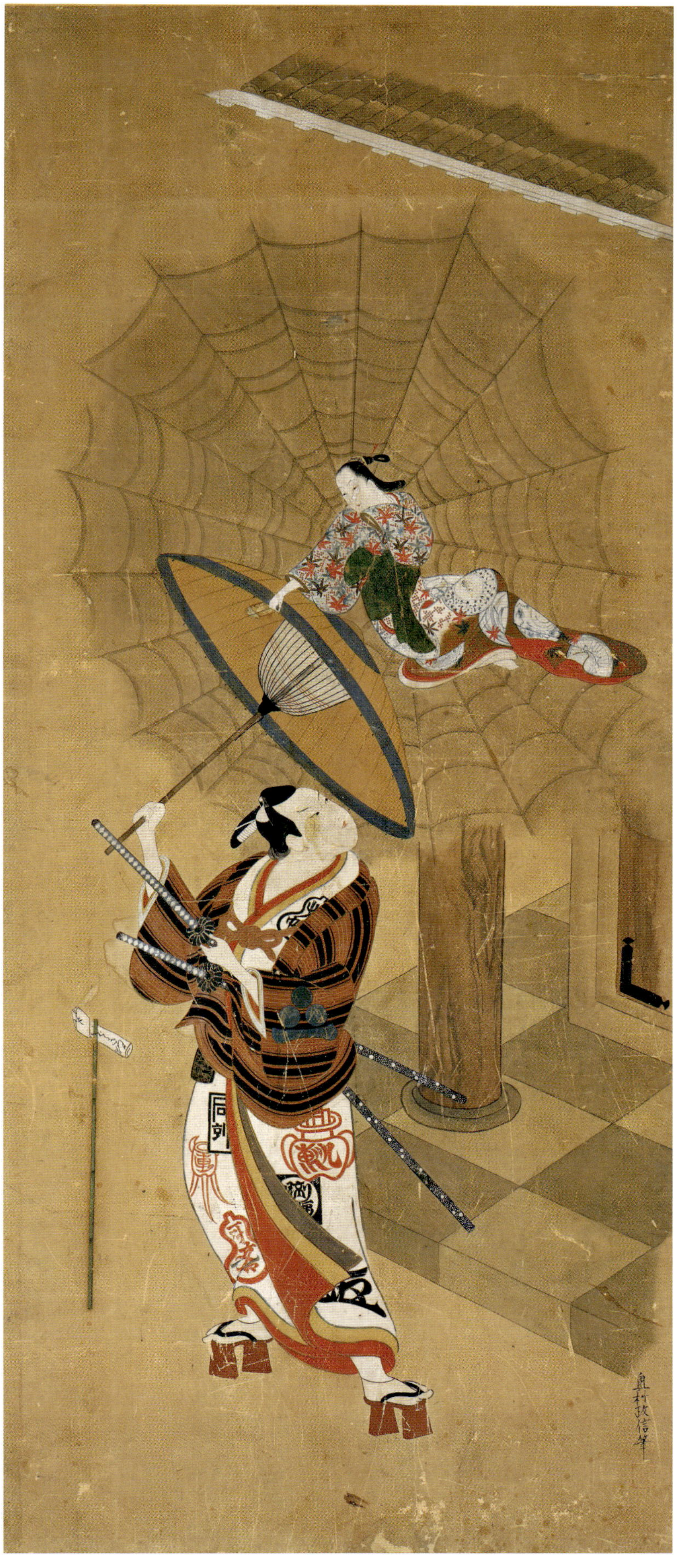

奥村政信筆

17. **OKUMURA MASANOBU** (1686–1764)

Townswoman and Courtesan with a Puppet

About Shōtoku 6 (1716)–Kyōhō 2 (1717)
Hanging scroll; ink, color, gold, and silver on silk
36.7 x 54.1 cm (14 7/16 x 21 5/16 in.)
Seals: Yamato gakō (Yamato painting artisan);
Okumura; Masanobu
William Sturgis Bigelow Collection 11.7605

Dressed in her New Year's best, a long-sleeved robe (*furisode*) embellished with luxurious embroidery and gold, a young woman holds a battledore and shuttlecock. She looks gracefully toward her left, to a woman wearing her overrobe with the right sleeve slipped down to reveal her underrobe. The latter woman holds a puppet of Sukeroku, the dandy who frequented the pleasure districts in order to see his beloved, the courtesan Agemaki. Judging from her hairstyle (a low-knot *Hyōgo* chignon) and her connection with the Sukeroku Kabuki plays set in the Yoshiwara, this woman is probably a Yoshiwara courtesan. Thus, one of the aims of the artist here was to juxtapose the New Year's fashion sense of a young townswoman with that of a courtesan. The scroll also presents a complicated double play on the theme of love. Agemaki (here represented by the courtesan), who was enamored with Sukeroku, manipulates a puppet of Sukeroku. In turn this puppet gazes toward the young townswoman, who is placed there as an allusion to the Agemaki of the original Kabuki story.

The inclusion on the puppet's black robes of the peony motif, the alternate crest used by Ichikawa Danjūrō II, alludes to the famed actor and his performance of Sukeroku.[1] Danjūrō II appeared three times in the role. The first was during the fourth month of 1713, but at that time he assumed the bravura *aragoto* style; he had yet to make his entrance with the "bull's-eye umbrella" that would later become his signature. In 1716 Danjūrō made his second appearance in the role, during the second act of *Shikirei yawaragi Soga* at the Nakamura Theater. Several prints produced by artists such as Torii Kiyomasu I provide us with a good image of this particular performance. Compared with the previous rendition, this version seems to have centered more on the love affair of Sukeroku and Agemaki. Danjūrō's third appearance in the role did not take place until thirty-three years later, in 1749.

Since the style of the painting conforms to that of Masanobu during the second decade of the eighteenth century, we can assume that it was produced either in 1716 or in the following year. That the piece was not signed suggests that it was made at the special request of a wealthy patron. AS

1. The peony motif appears as two peony leaves that confront each other, and at the center a bud and a blossom respectively emerge from the top and bottom.

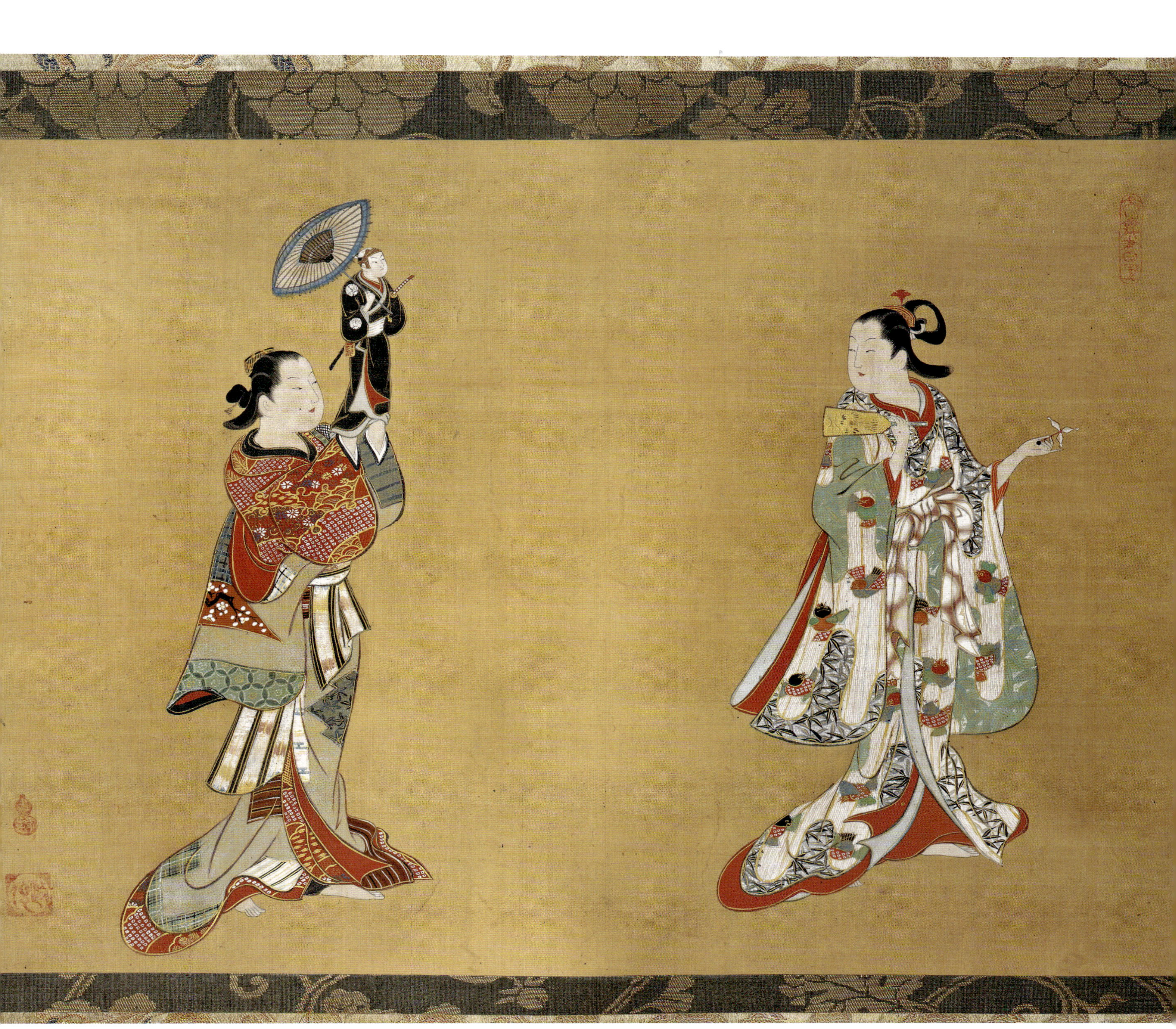

18. **NISHIKAWA SUKENOBU** (1671–1750)
Genre Scenes in the Four Seasons

About the Kyōhō era (1716–36)
Handscroll; ink, color, and silver on paper
32.6 x 545.2 cm (12 13/16 x 214 5/8 in.)
Signature: Nishikawa Ukyō Sukenobu kore [o] egaku
(This was painted by Nishikawa Ukyō Sukenobu)
Seals: Bunkadō; Nishikawa-uji;
Sukenobu kore [o] zu[su]
(This was painted by Sukenobu)
William Sturgis Bigelow Collection 11.7794

Nishikawa Sukenobu skillfully presents two unrelated scenes for each of the four seasons on similarly sized papers in a composition that at first glance appears to be continuous. The eight scenes depict the following:

SPRING:

1. New Year's celebrations in a samurai household. A young samurai (his forelock has yet to be shorn) in a long-sleeved kimono has just entered the room where three women play with *karuta* cards.
2. Cherry-blossom viewing party within a curtained enclosure.

SUMMER:

3. Four women walking along a path past a flowering deutzia bush. A young girl in a red *furisode* robe walks ahead. She points to a cuckoo while another woman in the center, wearing a headdress (*kazuki*) typically donned by upper-class women to shade their faces, looks up.
4. Two women seated on a bench covered with a felt carpet enjoy the evening breeze underneath a willow tree by a stream. They are playing with sparklers, which burn in the brazier of their smoking set.

AUTUMN:

5. An ensemble plays koto and samisen music in front of offerings made for the Tanabata Festival, which is celebrated on the seventh night of the seventh month. Above them hangs a *kiriko* lantern that was used for the Festival of the Dead (*obon*), which takes place during the thirteenth through the sixteenth days of the seventh lunar month.
6. Moon viewing. On the floor next to the figures is a writing kit, presumably used to write poems, and in front of the screen a ewer with sake and some finger foods.

WINTER:

7. A group of people congregates at night to take part in the telling of "One Hundred Scary Tales." As each story is related, a candle is blown out. Supposedly ghosts and monsters of various types appear after the hundredth candle is extinguished. In this scene a woman pulls on the ear of a young man, who has just put out a candle; the others laugh at the sight.
8. Two women watch a young man play in the snow.

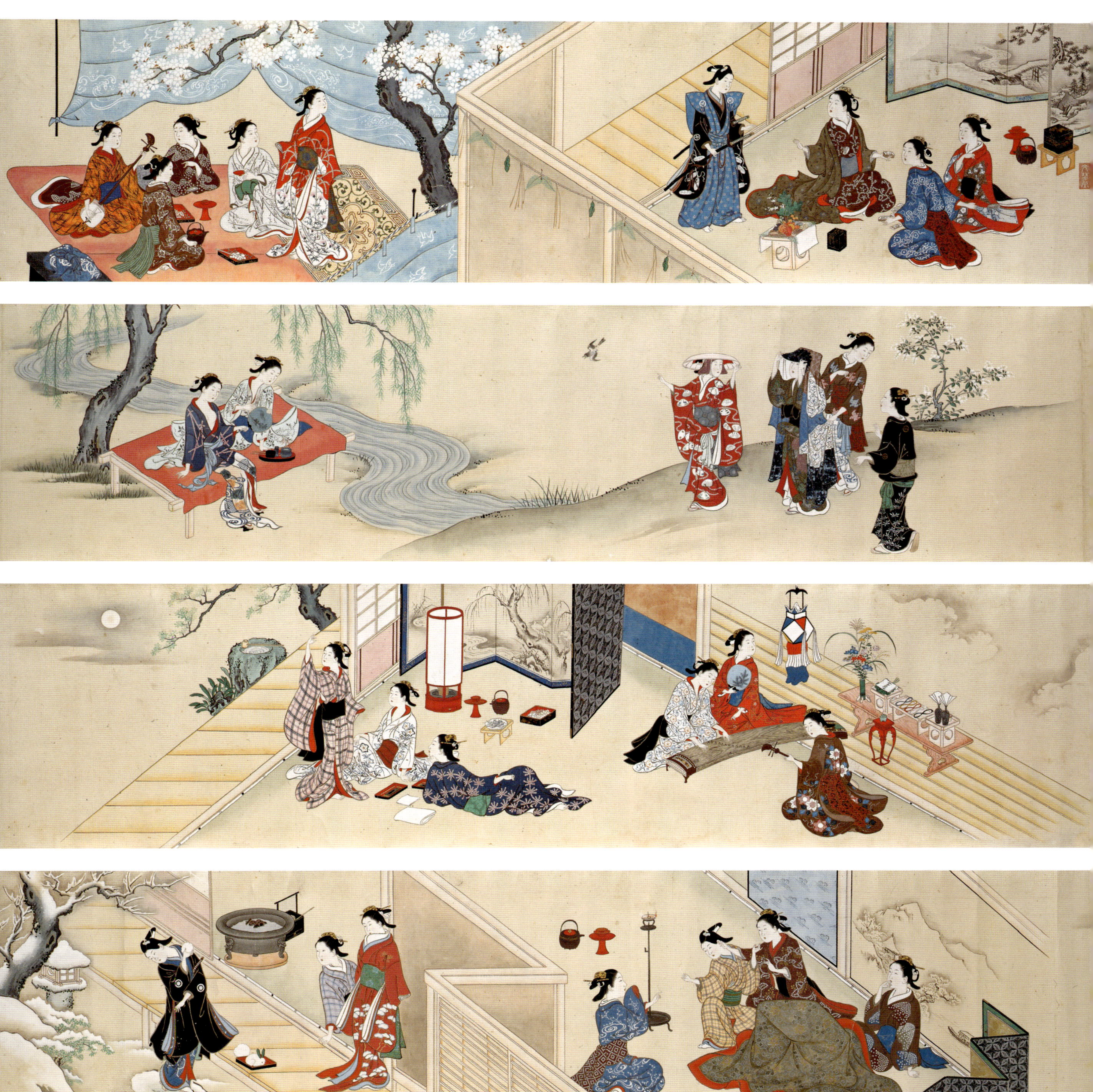

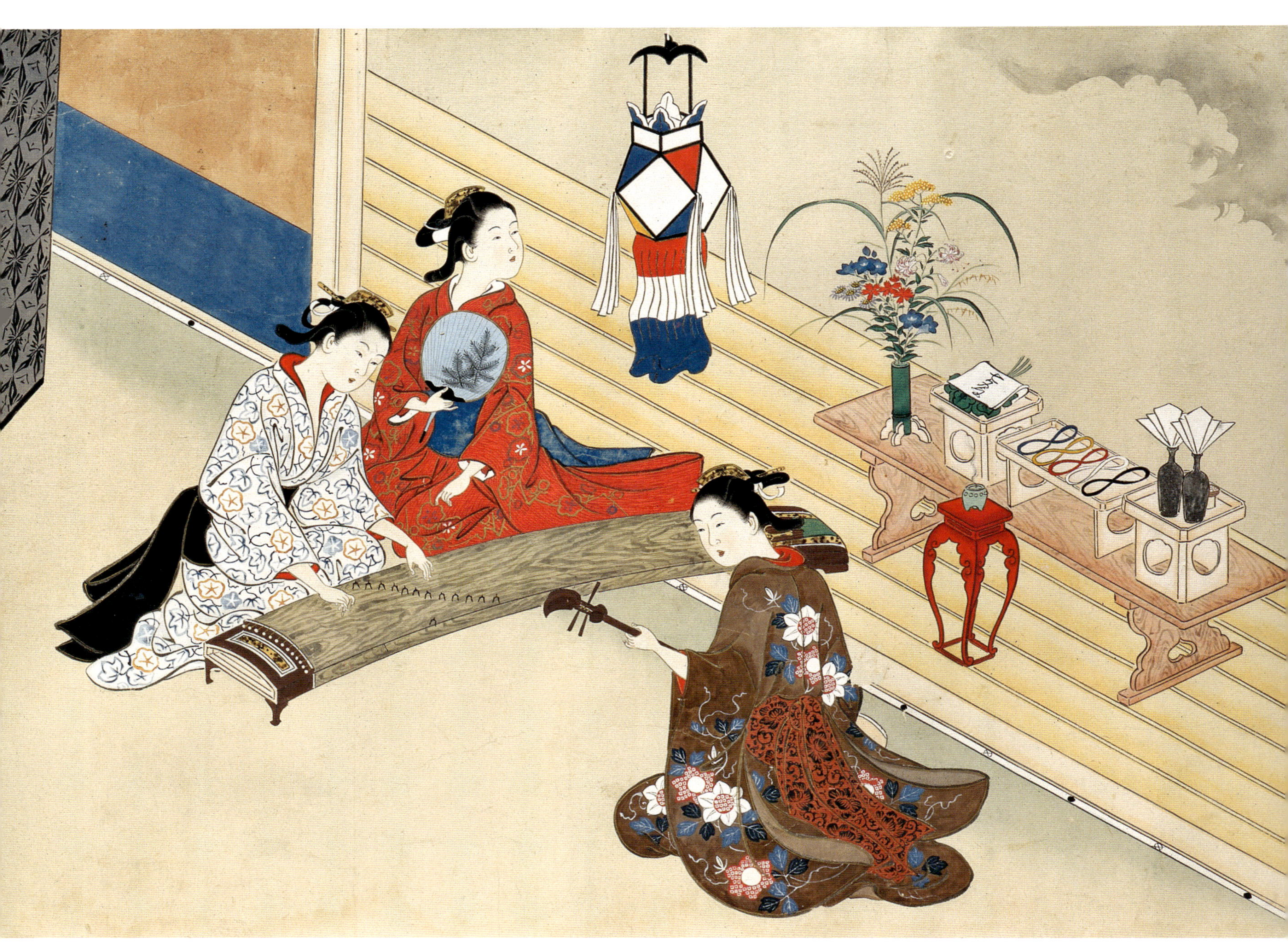

As the scholar Timothy Clark has pointed out, similar compositions are included in Sukenobu's woodblock-printed book *Ehon Tokiwagusa*, which was published in 1730. Due to the similarity of their styles, this scroll was probably painted around that time.[1]

Although several of Sukenobu's paintings have survived, this painting and one in the Chiba City Museum of Art with the same title are the only known handscrolls by the artist that do not have erotic subjects.[2] The two paintings deal with the same theme of daily scenes in the four seasons and share similar motifs. The women playing instruments during the Tanabata Festival here, for example, closely resemble the musical ensemble performing in the evening cool in the Chiba scroll. Both scrolls also include scenes in which a woman pulls someone's ear. However, the works do differ in their modes of depiction. The Chiba scroll includes many more male figures and presents the scenes from the different seasons much as they would have taken place in daily life. On the other hand, the MFA scroll focuses primarily on women (there are only three men in the entire scroll) and depicts the figures on a larger scale. In addition, it divides the composition among the four seasons equally, whereas the autumn scene in the Chiba scroll is twice as long as the other seasons. AS

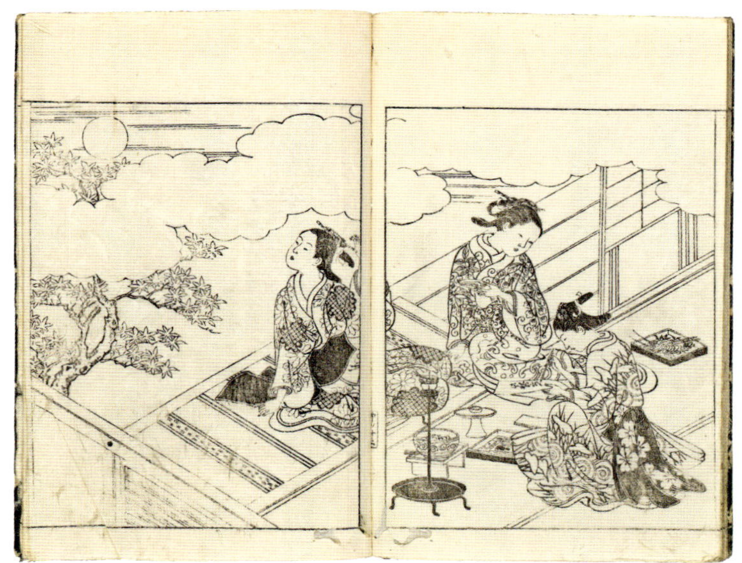

fig. 22
Nishikawa Sukenobu (1671–1750)
The Picture Book of Evergreens (Ehon tokiwagusa), vol. 2, 1731

1. Timothy Clark, "Shiki fūzoku zukan," in *Bosuton bijutsukan nikuhitsu ukiyo-e*, vol. 2 (Tokyo: Museum of Fine Arts, Boston, and Kōdansha, 2000), 150–52.
2. Tanabe Masako, "Shiki fūzoku zukan," *Siren*, no. 7 (March 2004), 42–46

19. **NISHIKAWA SUKENOBU** (1671–1750)
Yu Zhi Playing Her Qin

About the Kyōhō era (1716–36)
Hanging scroll; ink, color, and gold on paper
88 x 39 cm (34 5/8 x 15 3/8 in.)
Signature: Nishikawa Sukenobu kore [o] egaku
(This was painted by Nishikawa Sukenobu)
Seals: Nishikawa uji; Sukenobu kore [o] zu[su]
(This was drawn by Sukenobu)
William Sturgis Bigelow Collection 11.7795

Yu Zhi (Japanese: Gyokushi) was the daughter of the mythical Queen Mother of the West (Xiwangmu) and upon her marriage became known as Lady Taizhen Wang. In this painting the sensual Chinese Daoist divinity rides a dragon. Her phoenix crown and white and blue robes with touches of red contrast with her mount, done primarily in ink. The iconography of the immortal became widely known in Japan with the reprint of the sixteenth-century Chinese *Complete Legends of All Immortals with Illustrations* (*Youxiang liexian quanzhuan*) in 1650. In this book there is a depiction of Yu Zhi holding a single-stringed *qin* with an inscription that states, "This is Yu Zhi, Lady Taizhen Wang and daughter of the Queen Mother. With each pluck of her single-stringed *qin* hundreds of birds and beasts immediately come flying. Sometimes she rides a white dragon and journeys the Four Seas."

The seventeenth-century ukiyo-e artist Hishikawa Moronobu included a picture of Yu Zhi in his illustrated book *Collection of Unusual Figures of Daoist Immortals* (*Igyō sennin tsukushi*, 1689), with an inscription reading, "Lady Taizhen Wang is Yu Zhi, the daughter of the Queen Mother of the West. When she plays her single-stringed *qin*, a hundred animals gather to listen to its tune. Then she rides on a white dragon and departs to the Four Seas."[1] Although Moronobu clearly consulted either the *Youxiang liexian quanzhuan* or its Japanese reprint, it is unknown whether Sukenobu based his portrayal on either of these works or on some other source. However, judging from the treatment of Yu Zhi's sleeves in the Sukenobu painting, it is highly likely that the eighteenth-century artist did refer to Moronobu's illustration.[2] AS

1. Hishikawa Moronobu, *Igyō sennin tsukushi* (Collection of Unusual Figures of Daoist Immortals), 3 vols., woodblock-printed books, ink on paper, 26.9 x 18.8 cm, private collection, published in Chiba City Museum of Art, *Hishikawa Moronobu* (Chiba: Chiba City Museum of Art, 2000), 192.
2. In this painting the single-stringed *qin* has been replaced with a seven-stringed one. Perhaps Sukenobu wanted to accentuate its lavishness.

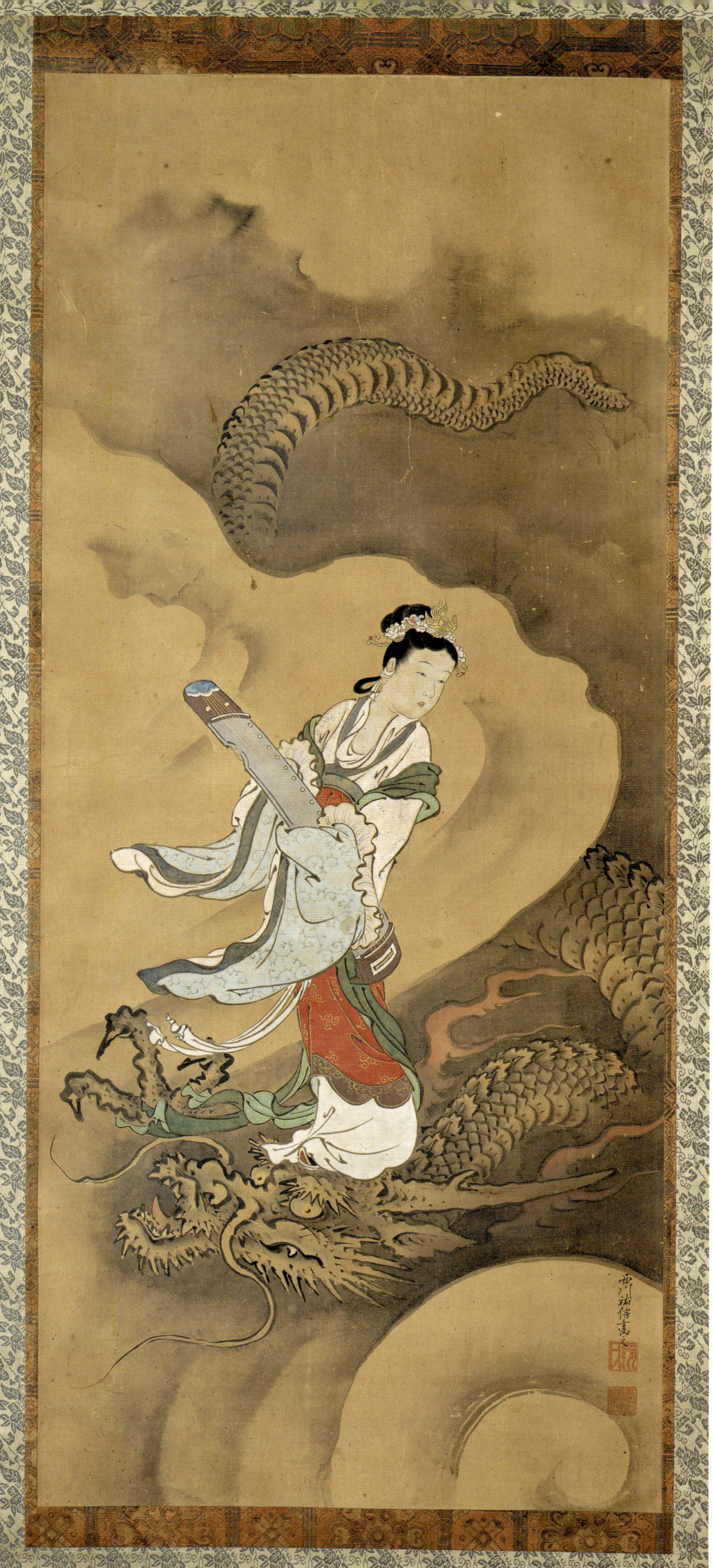

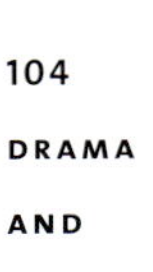

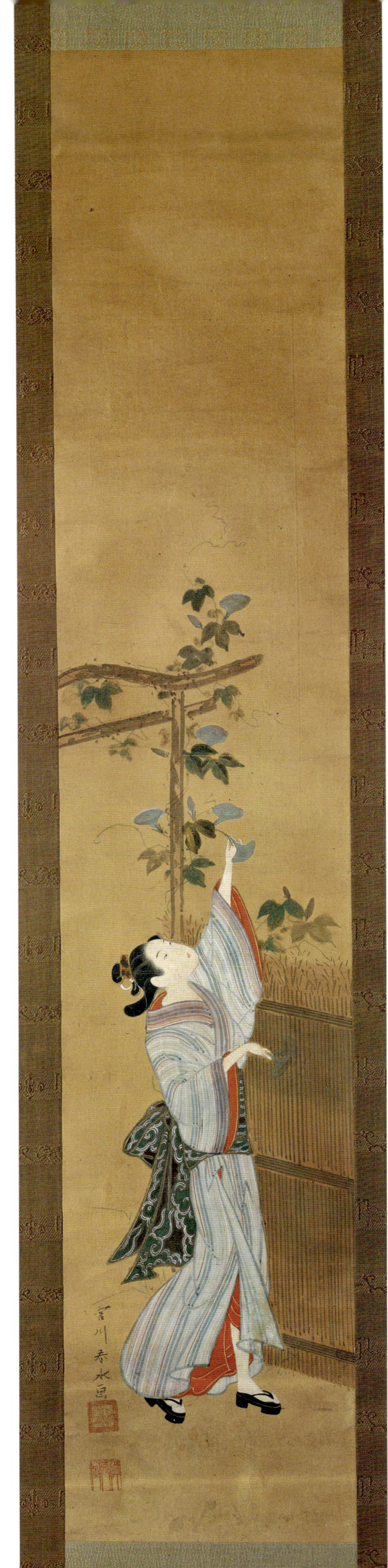
宮川春水画

20. **MIYAGAWA SHUNSUI** (ACTIVE ABOUT EARLY 1740S–EARLY 1760S)
Woman Picking Morning Glories

About the Genbun (1736–41)–Enkyō (1744–48) eras
Hanging scroll; ink, color, and gold on paper
84.3 x 16.5 cm (33 3/16 x 6 1/2 in.)
Signature: Miyagawa Shunsui
Seals: Shunsui no in (Seal of Shunsui); Mankōdō
William Sturgis Bigelow Collection 11.7779

Dressed in a summer robe, a woman ventures out to pick morning glory blossoms from a vine entwined around a slender gatepost. The transparency of her thin underrobe, through which one can see her arms, and the slight opening of the front hem add a certain sensuality to the work.

The relative dimensions of this painting make it similar in shape to so-called pillar-size woodblock prints. Okumura Masanobu claimed to have invented the pillar-print (*hashira-e*) format, and such works began to be produced around 1740. However, it is possible that Masanobu was actually inspired by painted pillar images, which were already popular among contemporary Edoites, and created printed works as a more affordable alternative.

More than twenty of Shunsui's paintings have survived.[1] Works such as this one that are signed "Miyagawa Shunsui" and accompanied by a square intaglio seal reading "Shunsui no in" and a square relief seal reading "Mankōdō" were probably produced early in Shunsui's career. AS

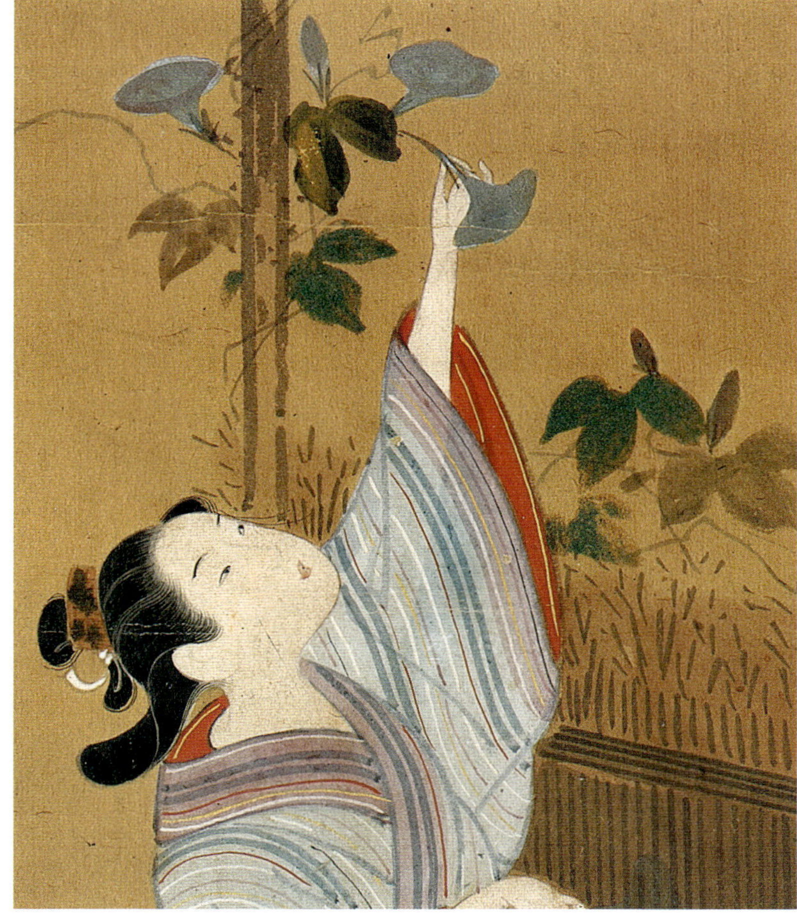

1. Asano Shūgō, "Hatsune," in *MOA bijutsukan*, vol. 4 of *Nikuhitsu ukiyo-e taikan* (Tokyo: Kōdansha, 1997), 224–25. Aside from this scroll, there are four others in the MFA collection, including *Perspective Picture: Gidayū Performance in a Reception Room*, hanging scroll, ink and color on paper, 51.3 x 67.5 cm; *Courtesan and Attendant*, hanging scroll, ink and color on paper, 56.1 x 26.4 cm; *Two Women under a Cherry Tree*, hanging scroll, ink and color on paper, 65.9 x 27.5 cm; and *Parody of Bodhidharma (Daruma) by a Courtesan*, hanging scroll, ink and color on silk, 41 x 39.9 cm.

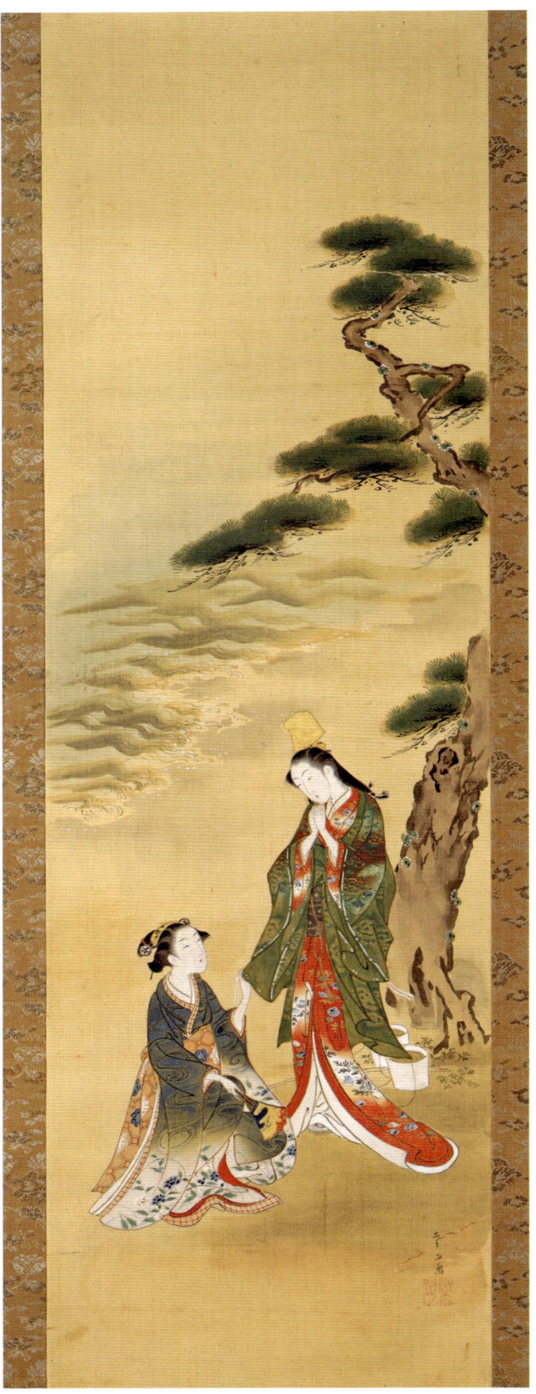

center

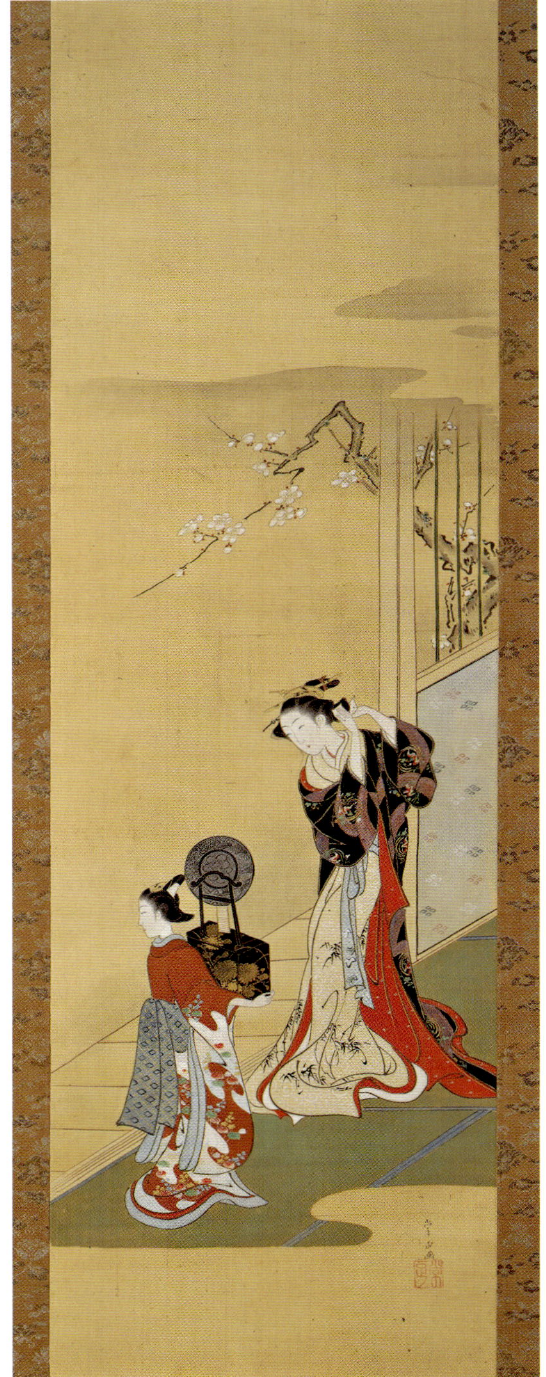

right

21. **KAWAMATA TSUNEMASA** (ACTIVE ABOUT 1716–1764)
Parodies of Historical Figure Subjects of China and Japan

About the Enkyō (1744–48) or Kan'en (1748–51) era
Set of three hanging scrolls; ink, color, and gold on silk
Each 85.1 x 27.2 cm (33 ½ x 10 ¹¹⁄₁₆ in.)
Signature: Tsunemasa ga (Painted by Tsunemasa)
Seal: Tsunemasa
William Sturgis Bigelow Collection 11.7896, 11.7897, 11.7898

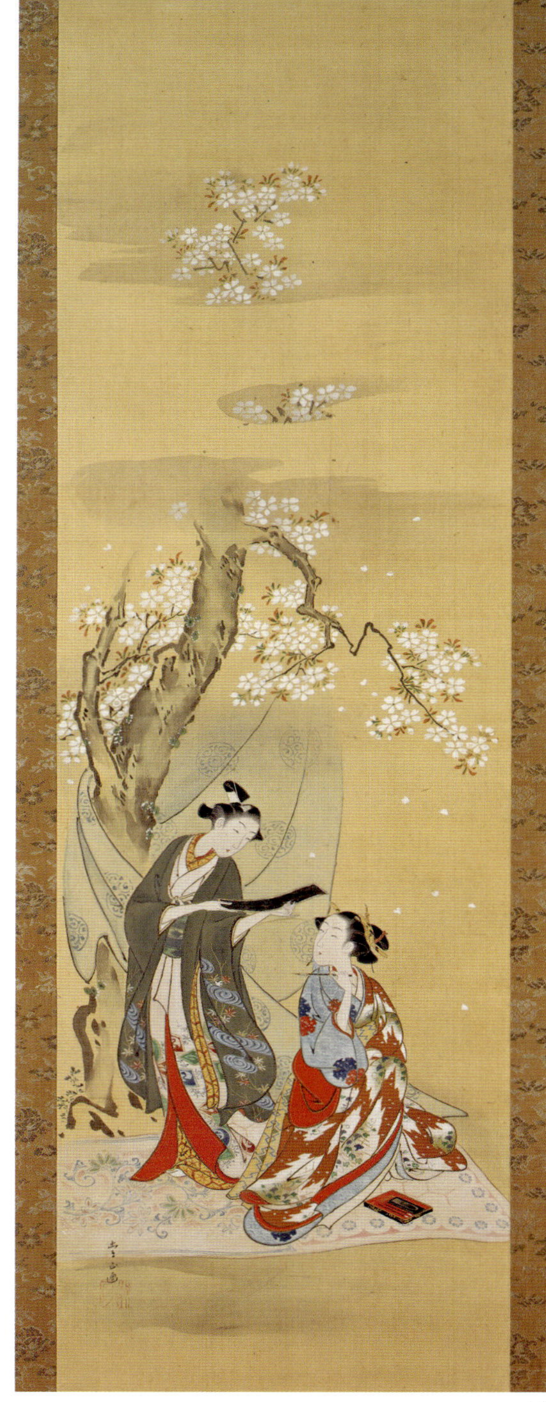
left

In these three paintings Kawamata Tsunemasa presents elegant contemporary interpretations (*mitate-e*) of well-known themes from Chinese and Japanese legend and literature. The center scroll depicts Matsukaze and Murasame, two celebrated sisters who appear in the No play *Wind in the Pines* (*Matsukaze*) and the Kabuki play *Gathering Seawater for Salt* (*Shio kumi*). According to the plot of the two theatrical works, the Heian-period courtier Ariwara no Yukihira was exiled to Suma, where he befriended the two sisters. When he returned to the capital, he gave them his gauze jacket (*kariginu*) and court hat as emblems of his affection. In the painting the beautiful women rest their brine buckets under a pine tree and, longing for their beloved, don his garments.

In the left scroll a young man and a beautiful woman rest on a mat, composing poetry under a blossoming cherry tree. Their appearance is reminiscent of images of classical literary figures, such as the poet Ono no Komachi or the fictional Prince Genji. Renditions of classical themes in contemporary guise already existed by this time, and this painting must have followed that tradition. Finally, in the right scroll a courtesan arranges her hair in front of a mirror held by a child attendant. The scene is set in early spring, with a white plum tree blooming in the garden. Although the subject cannot be identified with any certainty, many works since ancient times have pictured a beautiful woman gazing into a mirror — one notable example being Wang Zhaojun (Japanese Ōshōkun), a concubine of the Han-dynasty emperor Yuandi who was later sent to marry a "barbarian" Xiongnu king.

The *bijin*, or "beauties," in all three paintings of the set are presented as innocent young women. Their slender, willowy figure style was favored by Kawamata Tsunemasa, who specialized in compositions of *bijin*, and was later adopted by Suzuki Harunobu during the Meiwa era (1764–72). Furthermore, Tsunemasa's interest in *mitate* provided an important precedent for Harunobu. NM

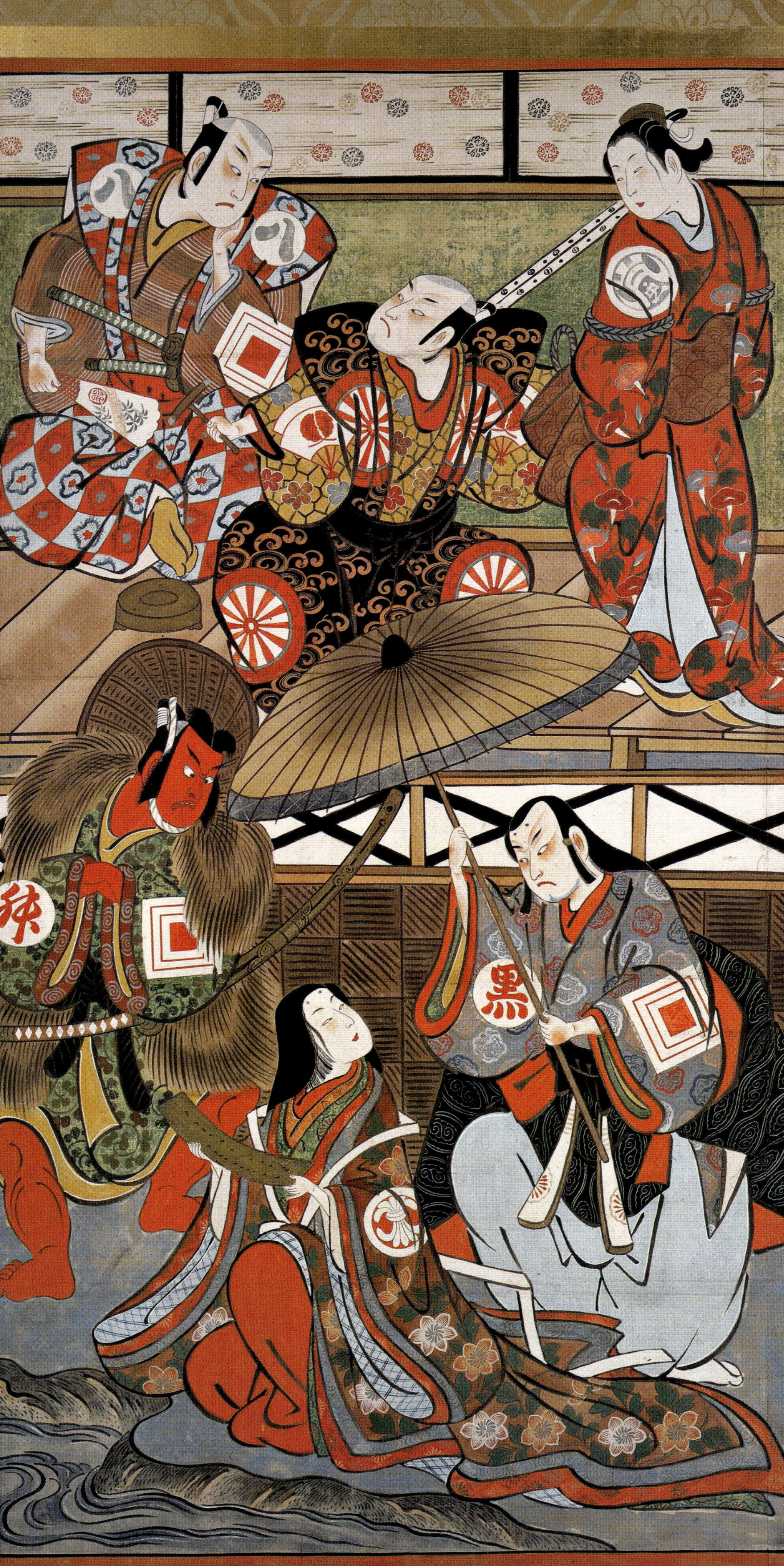
黒

22. **TORII SCHOOL**

Theater Signboard Depicting Scenes from the Play Nishikigi sakae Komachi

Hōreki 8 (1758)
Panel; ink, color, and gold on paper
177.6 x 97.2 cm (69 5/16 x 38 1/4 in.)
William Sturgis Bigelow Collection 11.7529

Much like the movie posters of today, signboards (*kanban*) served as an effective means of drawing in passersby to attend a Kabuki performance. These framed paper advertisements were installed at the eaves of the theaters so as to project at an angle and thereby be visible to pedestrians in the narrow streets below. The signboards featured the lead actors—their crests prominently displayed—in selected dramatic moments. Considered ephemera rather than art in their own time, most of these paintings have been lost. This work is the oldest known extant example.

The signboard was produced for the performance of *Nishikigi sakae Komachi*, which premiered on the first day of the eighth month of 1758 at the Nakamura Theater. According to the program, the actors and their roles were as follows:

UPPER RIGHT	Arashi Tominosuke in the role of Gion no Kaji
UPPER CENTER	Onoe Kikugorō in the role of Godai Saburō
UPPER LEFT	Ichikawa Yaozō in the role of Kanja no Tarō Sadakage
LOWER RIGHT	Ichikawa Danjūrō IV in the role of Ōtomo no Kuronushi
LOWER CENTER	Segawa Kikunojō II in the role of Ono no Komachi
LOWER LEFT	Ichikawa Masuzō in the role of Hannya no Gorō Terukage

The play belonged to the *ōchōmono* genre (stories that related to the Heian period), and the plot revolved around the unfairly maligned poet Ono no Komachi and the villainous Ōtomo no Kuronushi (see also cat. no. 15). Unfortunately the details of the performance have been lost, but because the actor Kikunojō, kneeling at the bottom center, holds an oblong poem-card, the play may have incorporated scenes from such popular Komachi legends as those of the ninth-century poet washing a manuscript (*Sōshi-arai Komachi*) or praying for rain (*Amagoi Komachi*).

Until recently it was believed that the oldest extant Kabuki signboard was *Embellished Greengrocer Oshichi* (*Junshoku yaoya Oshichi*), now in the Waseda University Theater Museum, Tokyo, produced by Torii Kiyonaga in 1793.[1] However, research has demonstrated that this and three other signboards at the MFA (out of a total of five in the collection) predate the Kiyonaga work.[2] Since the production process for signboards by members of the Torii school is not known, identifying the artist of this advertisement for *Nishikigi sakae Komachi* is difficult. However, for now it is possible to conclude that the signboard was done by someone from the Torii school—possibly Kiyonobu II, Kiyomasu II, or Kiyomitsu I. AS

1. Published in *Kiyonaga Shigemasa*, vol. 5 of *Nikuhitsu ukiyo-e* (Tokyo: Shūeisha, 1983), illustration 21.
2. The relationship between the Boston signboard for *Nishikigi sakae Komachi* and another work, *Genpei kasen zu* (The Genpei Wars), attributed to Torii Kiyonobu (illustrated in *Nihonga taisei*, vol. 40 [Tokyo: Tōhō shoin, 1933], plate 108), is significant. The *Genpei* signboard is executed in the same style as catalogue number 22 here, suggesting that it was produced around the same time. Unfortunately the title of the play being promoted by the *Genpei* signboard has not been identified, but a young actor, perhaps Sanogawa Ichimatsu, appears to be depicted as the Kamakura-period warrior Nasu no Yoichi.

23. **ATTRIBUTED TO TORII KIYOMITSU** (1735–1785)
Theater Signboard for Nue shigedō sakiwake yūsha

Meiwa 4 (1767)
Pair of panels; ink and color on paper
Each panel: 179 x 82.7 cm (70 ½ x 32 ⁹⁄₁₆ in.)
William Sturgis Bigelow Collection 11.7523, 11.7524

These two panels are sections of a signboard advertising the opening (*kaomise*, "face-showing") performance of the new theatrical year by the Ichimura troupe of the play *Nue shigedō sakiwake yūsha* in the eleventh month of 1767. A third panel, which would have been between the others and of the same size, is now missing. A pair of stone guardian dogs (*komainu*) appears in the bottom-left and bottom-right corners. In the background are bamboo blinds, indicating that the play takes place in a palace or shrine. Thick black lines in front of the architectural structure suggest a dark cloud or eerie wind.

The different roles in the play can be reconstructed from the program and the *Yakusha tōshisen*, contemporary critiques of performances.[1] The actor Ichimura Uzaemon IX, depicted in the upper section of the right panel, is described in the program as "Sahei, the farmer from Miyagino in Ōshū who is actually a manifestation of a chimera [*nue*] from Higashi Sanjō," and in the review as "the jocular dance by a country bumpkin." Below him is Azuma Tōzō II, who possibly assumed the role listed in the program as "Ofuji, the humble woman from Mount Kiso in Shinshū," and in the critique as "a *jōruri*-style imitation of a peasant."

On the left panel Uzaemon appears again, this time in the role of "Sainenbō, the mendicant bowl beater who is actually a manifestation of a chimera from Higashi Sanjō," and as "banging on a bowl in the eight-bell striking rhythm." However, the depiction of the actor differs substantially from the description and illustration of this role included in the *Yakusha tōshisen* review. In the signboard Uzaemon appears as a tea seller beating on a gourd, whereas in the review he is portrayed as a monk striking on a cluster of eight bells. Such discrepancies may have occurred because the signboard was painted in advance of the opening of the show, and the critique was written following the performance.

Tōzō is shown again in the upper left of the left panel, disguised as "the ghost of the femme-fatale Ayame." According to the review, the narration stated that "the one Tanatsuna encounters is the spirit of Lady Ayame." If one uses one's imagination, the dark cloud in the upper section represents the chimera. The figure holding a bow, barely visible at the bottom left of the right panel, could be Sawamura Sōjūrō II in the role of Gen Sanmi Yorimasa, and the one partly appearing at the bottom right of the left panel may be Bandō Sanpachi in the role of Ino Hayata.

In 1767, when this signboard was created, Torii Kiyomitsu was the head of the Torii school. He quite likely supervised the production of this work. AS

---

1. Critiques of the *kaomise* performances were issued in the third month of each year.

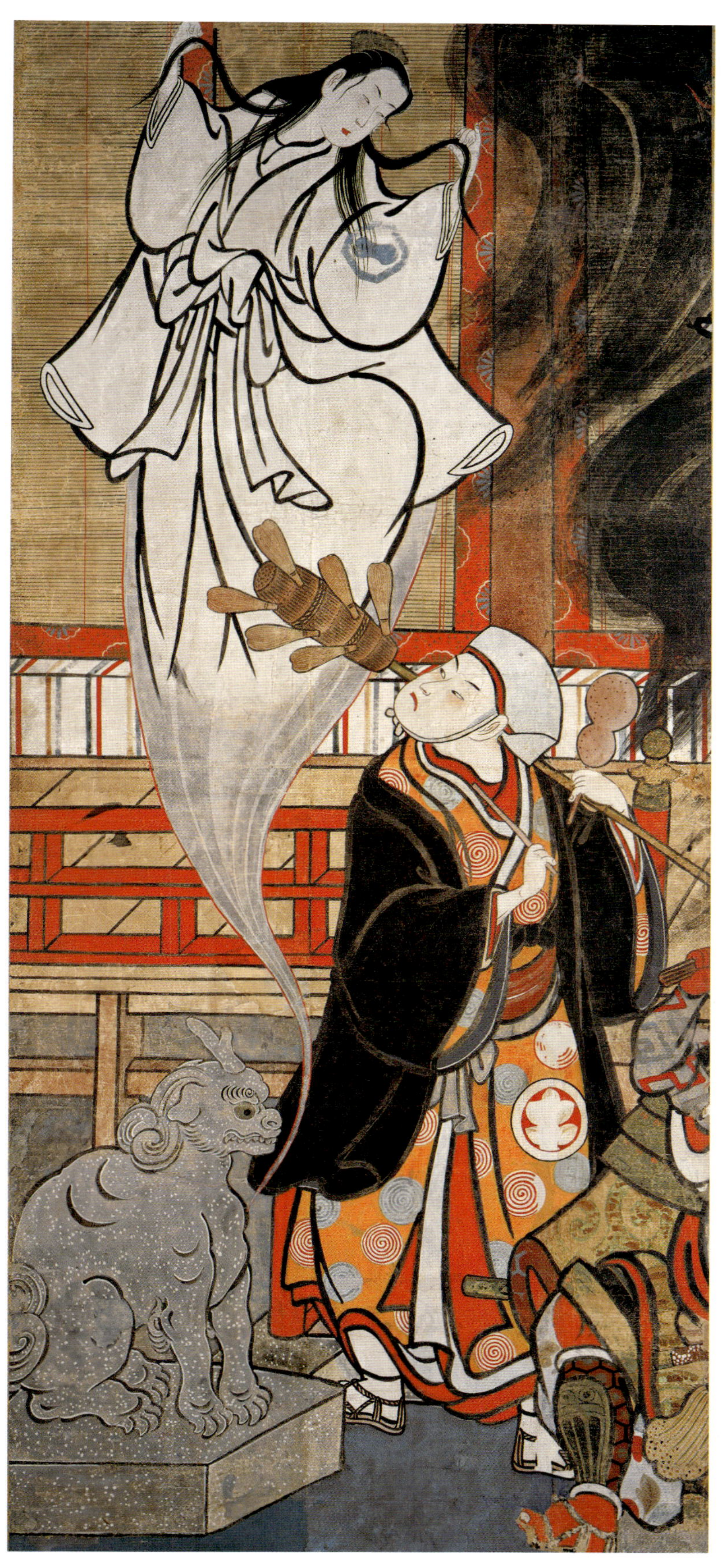

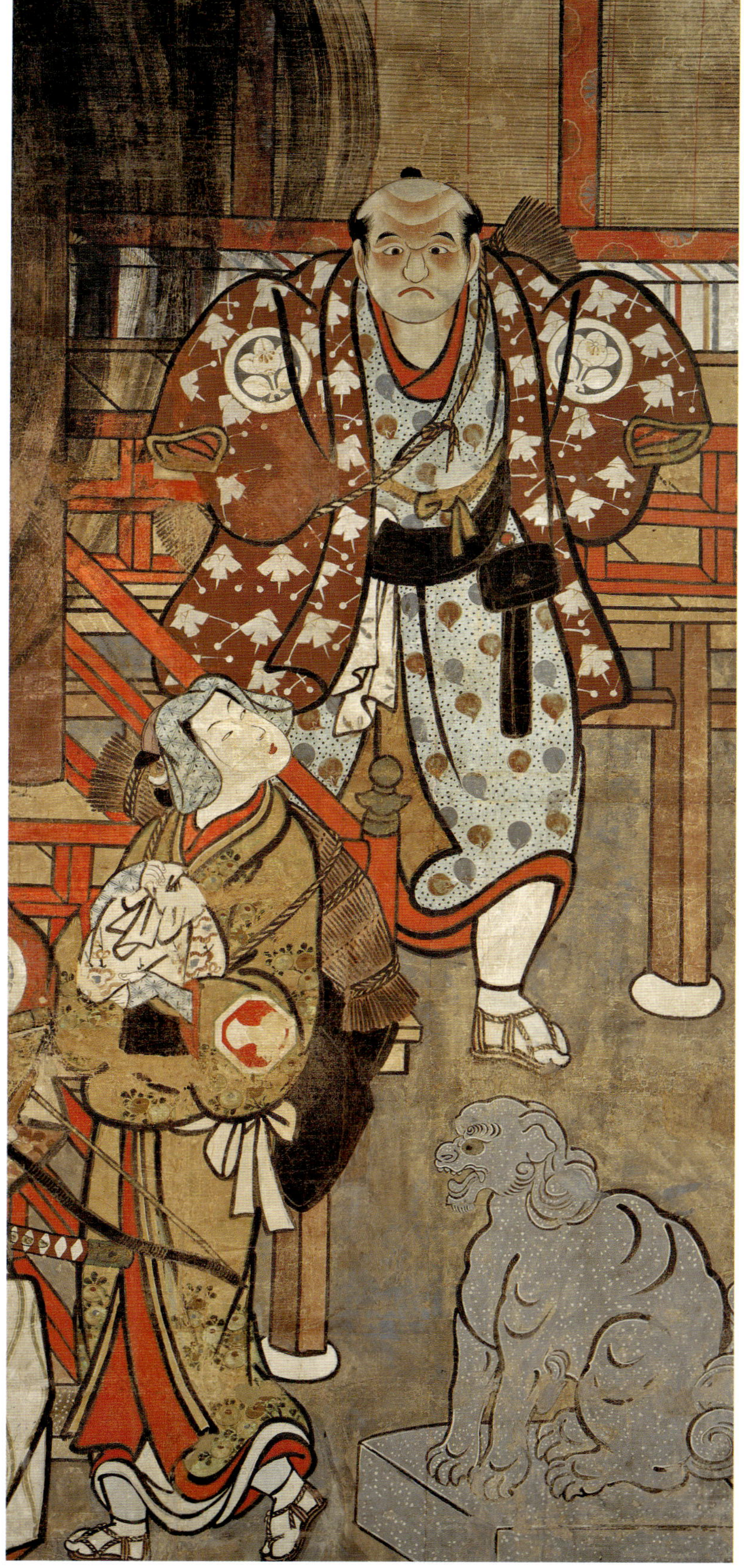

24. **ATTRIBUTED TO TORII KIYOMITSU** (1735–1785)
Theater Signboard Depicting Scenes from Shusse Taiheiki

An'ei 4 (1775)
Panel; ink, color, and brass on paper
163.9 x 127.5 cm (64 ½ x 50 3/16 in.)
William Sturgis Bigelow Collection 11.7530

This signboard was produced to advertise the performance of *Shusse Taiheiki*, at the Nakamura Theater on the seventeenth day of the eighth month of 1775; the crests on the actors' costumes correspond to those found on the street posters (*banzuke*) for the eighth and ninth acts of the play. *Shusse Taiheiki* was a Kabuki play of the *taikōkimono* genre, which took as its subjects the life of the sixteenth-century military warlord Toyotomi Hideyoshi, sometimes called Hashiba. This particular play chronicled the revenge of Hideyoshi against his rival Akechi Mitsuhide, who had assassinated their mutual lord Oda Nobunaga in 1582. However, in accordance with the prescription by the military government against political commentary, the names of the individual characters in the drama were slightly modified.

In this signboard the artist selected several dramatic moments from the play and combined them in one composition. By correlating the images in this painting with descriptions in theatrical archives, it is possible to identify the actors and their particular roles in the *Shusse Taiheiki* performance:

UPPER RIGHT: *Ichikawa Monnosuke II* playing Konishi Yajūrō, who thrusts a bamboo spear from a bamboo grove and ultimately kills Mitsuhide. *Nakamura Nakazō* as Takechi Jūbei Mitsuhide (modeled after Akechi Mitsuhide), who fights back.

UPPER LEFT: *Nakajima Mihoemon II* as Matsushita Kaheiji, who holds a fishing pole and a basket. *Nakamura Rikō* as Satsuki, the wife of Takechi Mitsuhide, who wears a white, short-sleeved robe (*kosode*) and holds her hands in prayer.[1]

MIDDLE RIGHT: *Iwai Shigehachi* as Omaki, the food vendor, who has a hand towel over her shoulder.

LOWER RIGHT: *Arashi Otohachi II* as Shōya Mosaku (or Yamakuma Tarō), who carries the container for holding his enemy's head.

LOWER MIDDLE: *Nakamura Nakazō* again as Mitsuhide, who thrusts his sword into the tatami mat. The female figure next to him is his wife, Satsuki. *Nakamura Shichizaburō III* as Takechi Jūjirō, who stands inside the armor box. *Ōtani Hiroji III* as Mashiba Hisayoshi (modeled after [Hashiba] Toyotomi Hideyoshi) stands next to the box with his arms folded in front of him. *Nakajima Mihoemon II* again as Kaheji, who holds out a letter. *Ichikawa Raizō II*, as Sakurai Koshingo, kneels below them. *Matsumoto Daigorō, Nakamura Otozō, Onoe Kanōsuke,* and *Ichikawa Takizō* (or *Ichikawa Matsuzō*) as the four foot soldiers (right to left) with their backs to the viewer.

That there was a close relationship between signboards and street posters is not surprising, since both were produced by members of the Torii school prior to the opening of individual plays. However, it is significant that the signboards in the MFA make it possible to document this connection at such an early date. Torii Kiyomitsu was the head of the Torii school in the third quarter of the eighteenth century, when this piece was created, and there can be no doubt that the signboard was executed in his studio. AS

1. Her depiction here suggests that the scene represents the rescue by Kaheiji of Satsuki, who is about to throw herself into the river.

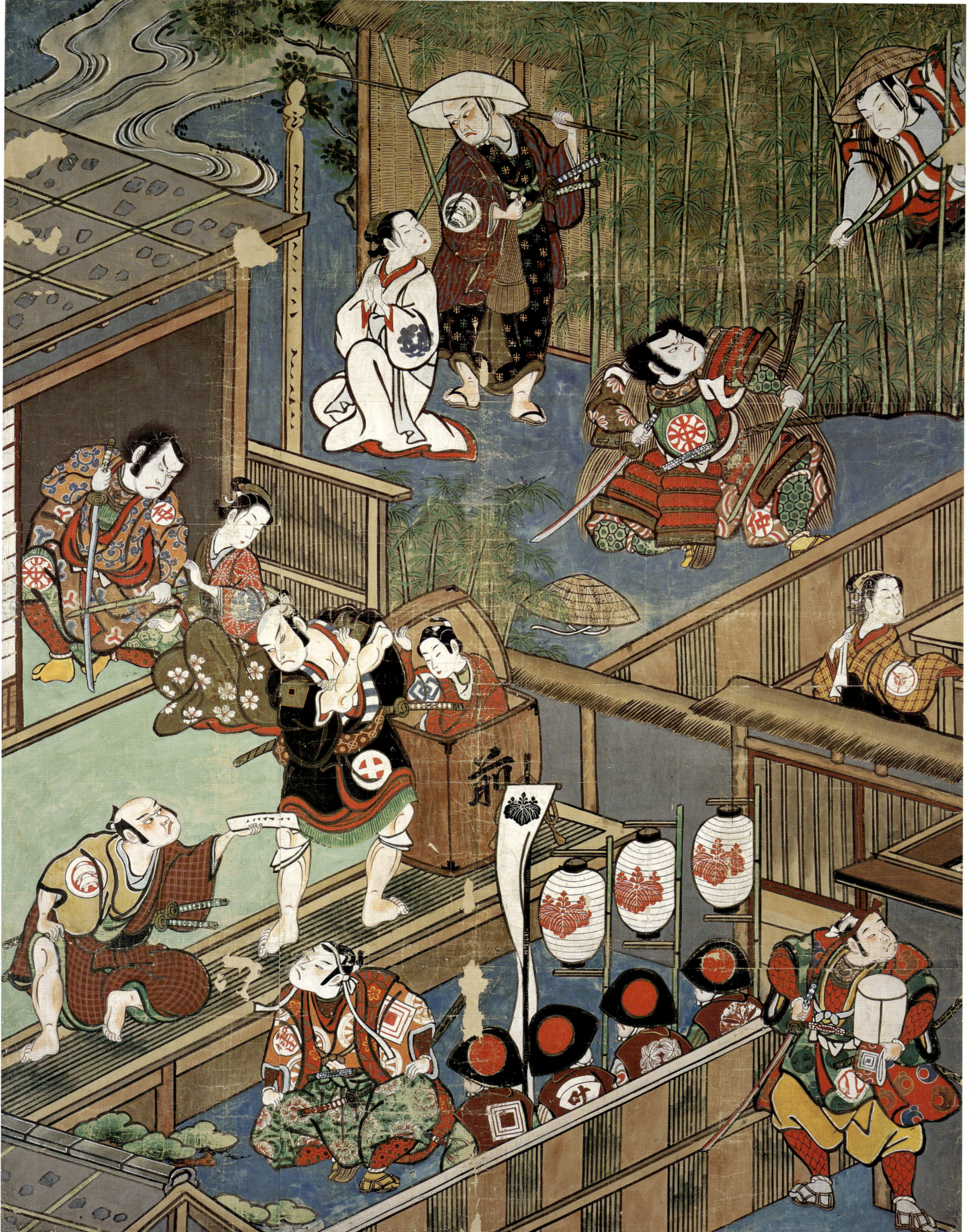

AN AIR OF INNOCENCE, 1765–1780 **SUZUKI HARUNOBU AND HIS CONTEMPORARIES**

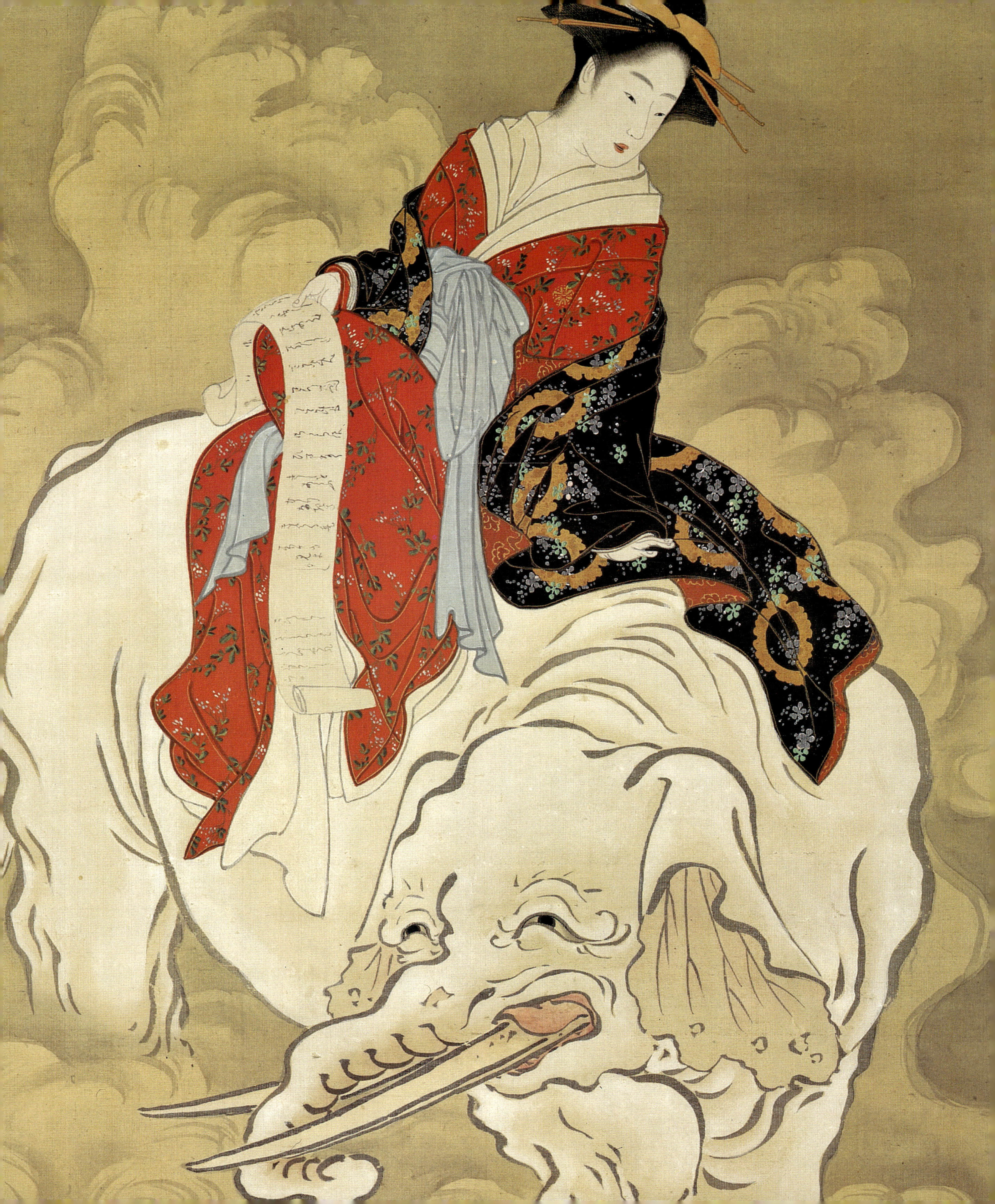

AN AIR OF INNOCENCE, 1765–1780: SUZUKI HARUNOBU AND HIS CONTEMPORARIES

The year 1765 witnessed the birth of the full-color woodblock print. This technological and artistic development transformed ukiyo-e. Prints, which had previously been limited to two or three colors, were no longer dependent exclusively upon expressive linework or hand coloring for their impact. Color printing also had a tremendous influence upon ukiyo-e painting. Even though prints were now created in such a wide variety of colors that they were called brocade pictures (nishiki-e), *paintings became even more refined and elegant, particularly when they were part of extravagant commissions.*

The artist most closely identified with the development of the full-color print is Suzuki Harunobu. By collaborating with a group of witty amateur poets and extremely skilled woodblock carvers and printers, Harunobu was able to create sumptuously printed calendar images (egoyomi). *Harunobu's imagery in these prints, especially his lithe, youthful figures and delicate palette, came to dominate ukiyo-e from 1765 until his death. A prolific artist, Harunobu went on to produce almost one thousand individual print designs. Perhaps because he was so preoccupied with producing the preparatory drawings for these woodblock prints the number of his paintings was extremely limited.*

Full-color printing as well as the master's small, fine-boned figure style were immediately adopted by Harunobu's contemporaries. Isoda Koryūsai, Suzuki Harushige (later known as Shiba Kōkan), and Ippitsusai Bunchō all began their careers working in the Harunobu mode. In fact Harushige would later brag that he was so adept at imitating Harunobu he could pass off forgeries on unsuspecting customers. However, by the 1770s Koryūsai developed his own canon of feminine beauty, which was more naturalistic and voluptuous compared with Harunobu's highly idealized images. After producing hundreds of prints including the popular series Models for Fashion: New Designs as Fresh Young Leaves (Hinagata wakana no hatsu moyō), Koryūsai focused his efforts on painting in the 1780s. His pattern of development, from printmaker in the Harunobu mode in the 1760s, printmaker in a confident, individual style in the 1770s, and then painter in the 1780s, was one shared by Utagawa Toyoharu (1735–1814), Katsukawa Shunshō (1726–1792), and Kitao Shigemasa (1739–1820). In their painted works all of these men depicted contemporary life in Edo in a direct manner, thus effectively conveying the reality of their times. AS

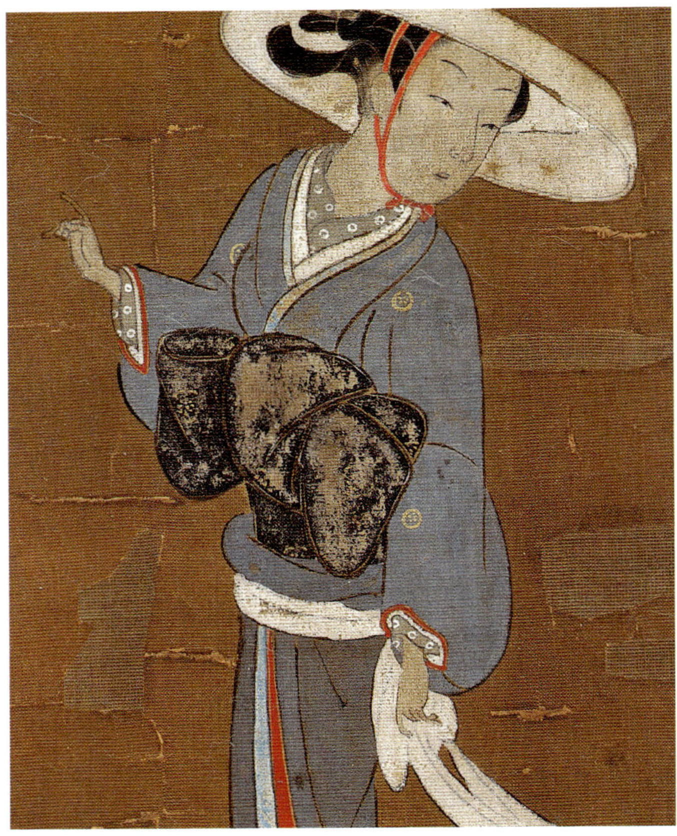

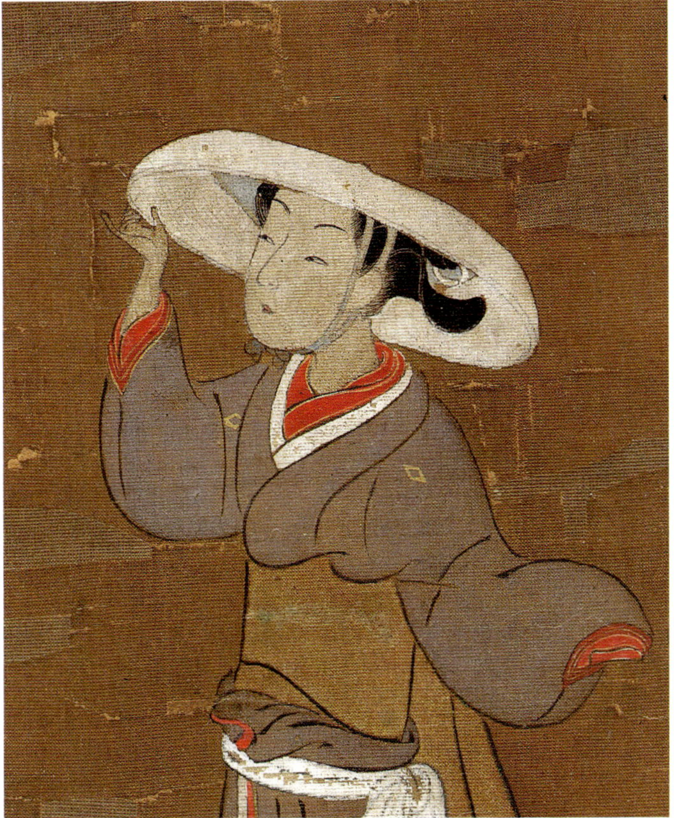

25. **SUZUKI HARUNOBU** (1725–1770)
Spring Outing on the Banks of the Sumida River

Meiwa era (1764–72)
Hanging scroll; ink, color, and gold on silk
32.7 x 54.5 cm (12 ⅞ x 21 7/16 in.)
Signature: Suzuki Harunobu ga (Painting by Suzuki Harunobu)
Seal: Harunobu
William Sturgis Bigelow Collection 11.7355

With the advent of spring, a group of young women and their male companion venture out to stroll along the eastern bank of the Sumida River at the northern edge of Edo. They stoop to pick dandelions, some of the season's earliest flowers, which they gather in their sedge hats. The change in season is underlined by the juxtaposition of their brightly colored outer robes (though still bearing wintry motifs) with the landscape of Matsusaki Inari Shrine across the water in gray ink.

Suzuki Harunobu is celebrated as having been the first Japanese artist to create full-color woodblock prints (*nishiki-e*) in 1765. During his early career he produced designs of actors, but the full-color prints of his later years primarily centered around images of lithe, almost childlike women and their male companions. By the time he died in 1770, Harunobu had designed over one thousand woodblock prints and more than fifteen illustrated books. His production of paintings, however, appears to have been extremely limited; only three can now be attributed to the artist with any certainty.[1]

The artist posed his figures in much the same manner in both his paintings and his prints. For example, the young woman at the extreme left and the youth kneeling to pick the blossoms are similar to those in the print of the third month from the series Popular Versions of Immortal Poets in Four Seasons (Fuzoku shiki kasen), and the central figure with her obi tied in front bears a strong similarity to one in *Plovers at the Tama River* (*Chidori no Tamagawa*) from the series Six Jewel Rivers (Mu Tamagawa). Compared with the woodblock prints, which necessarily incorporated the line quality of the carver and the colors available to the printer, the painting provides an unparalleled insight into Harunobu's individual artistic sensibilities. In addition, the wide piece of silk — more than fifty centimeters — on which the painting was executed allowed for a more expansive composition than that of the twenty-one centimeters of the *chūban*, the size most commonly found among Harunobu prints.

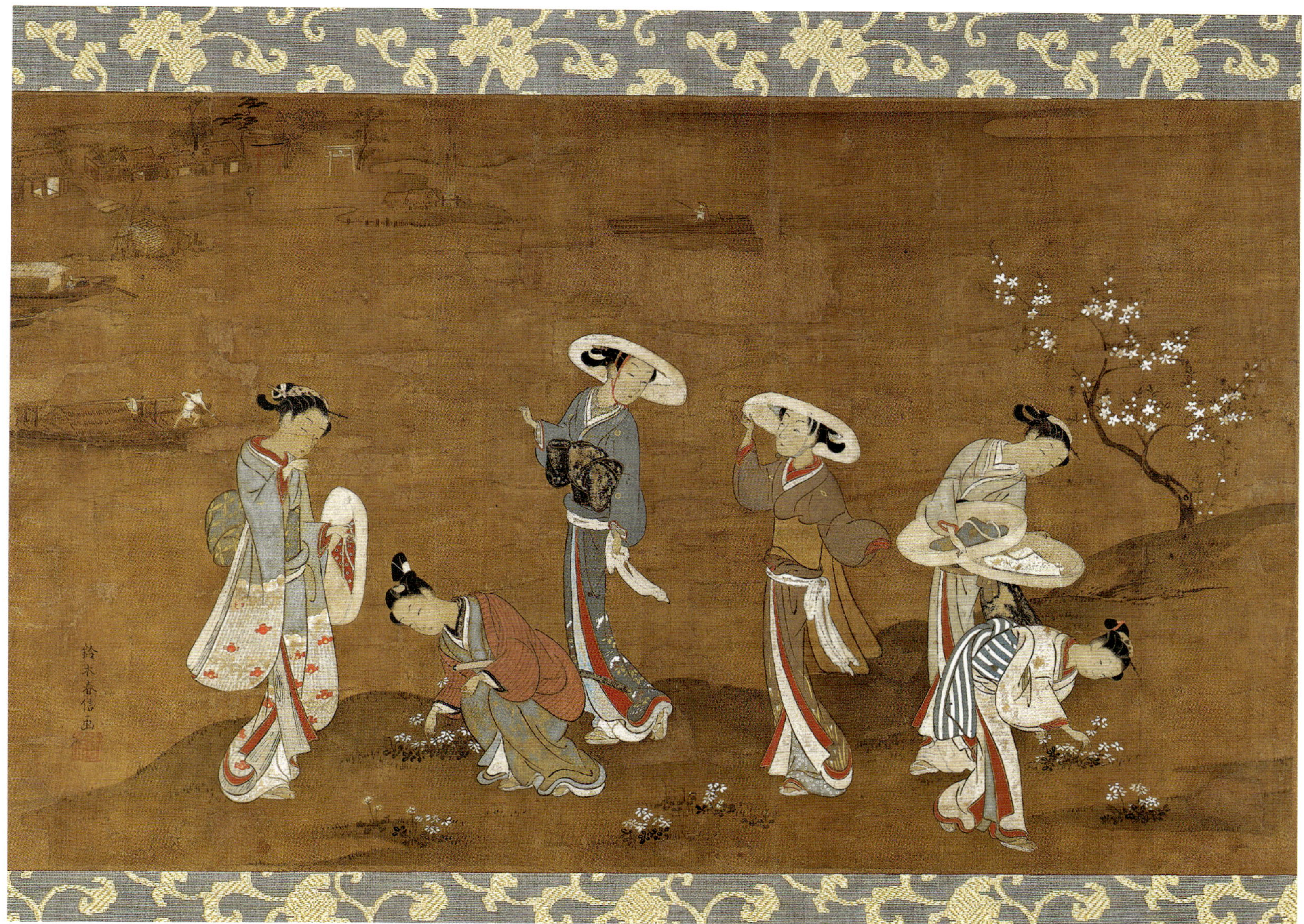

As a result of research conducted before recently remounting this painting, members of the Asian Conservation Studio at the Museum found that *Spring Outing on the Banks of the Sumida River* had been published in an 1893 volume of Japan's leading art journal, *Kokka*, showing that the work had been prized as early as the end of the nineteenth century. A woodblock reproduction that accompanied the article indicated that details had been lost in the intervening century.[2] Thus, the conservators used ultraviolet light to demonstrate that Harunobu had originally included delicate pine needle and stream patterns on the *furisode* of the young woman leaning over to pluck dandelion stems along the right edge of the painting. Unfortunately these motifs are no longer visible to the naked eye. The conservators also used infrared reflectography to determine that the ferryman poling his vessel up the Sumida River on the left-hand side once had ink lines detailing the features of his face. Harunobu's prints are acclaimed for their delicacy, but from this research it appears that the artist showed even more attention to detail in this painting. ANM

1. Aside from the one in the Museum of Fine Arts, Boston, the works widely accepted are the fan paintings *The Evening Glow of the Oil Lamp* and *The Distant Bell of the Clock*, both in the collection of Mitsui Kōyō.
2. "Suzuki Harunobu," *Kokka*, no. 49 (October 1893): 14.

26. **SUZUKI HARUSHIGE** (1747–1818)
Woman Admiring a Snow-Covered Garden

An'ei era (1772–81)
Hanging scroll; ink, color, gold, and silver on silk
88 x 35 cm (34 5/8 x 13 3/4 in.)
Signature: Shōtei Harushige zu
(Drawn by Shōtei Harushige)
Seal: Harunobu
William Sturgis Bigelow Collection 11.7364

Reminiscing about his career, the ever versatile artist Shiba Kōkan (who had previously been known as Suzuki Harushige) declared with bravado in his journal the *Shunparō hikki* that upon the sudden death of the celebrated Suzuki Harunobu he began to produce numerous forgeries of the master's work. He then went on to write:

> But I, of course, knew I was not Harunobu, and my self-respect made me adopt the coloring techniques of such artists as [Qiu Ying] and [Zhou Chen] in painting beautiful Japanese women. I painted *Summer Moon*, depicting a girl dressed in thin robes through which one could see her body, and *Winter Moon* showing a thatched cottage in a bamboo grove and a stone lantern in the garden all covered with snow. Side-lock ornaments used in dressing women's hair were coming into fashion at that time and were bringing about a great change in hair styling. I illustrated the new style, which consequently became exceedingly popular.[1]

The late scholar Calvin French identified *A Young Woman with a Cage of Fireflies,* now in the collection of the Freer/Sackler Gallery in Washington, D.C., as corresponding to *Summer Moon*, and *Woman Admiring a Snow-Covered Garden* as *Winter Moon*.[2] These attributions continue to be accepted by contemporary ukiyo-e specialists.[3]

Woman Admiring a Snow-Covered Garden certainly does conform to the description provided by the *Shunparō hikki*. A diminutive figure huddling under six layers of robes stands inside a snow-covered house and looks out to a wintry bamboo garden executed in thin washes of ink and light color. With her left hand she inserts a silver hairpin into her elaborate *Shimada*-style coiffure. The artist highlighted this hair by using ink reinforced with a lustrous glue. The fragility of the woman is emphasized by her delicate features and the somber purple-gray kimono finely figured with butterflies and dragonflies in silver and gold flitting around rivulets of water — a robe that would seem more appropriate to the warm summer months.

The indebtedness of Harushige (the name that Kōkan adopted during his forging years) to Harunobu is immediately apparent in the handling of the figure. Although the background in *Fujiwara no Nakabumi* from the series Thirty-six Poets (Sanjūrokkasen), a Harunobu woodblock print dating to 1767–68, is completely different, the poses of the women holding hairpins and the disposition of their robes in the two works are very close.[4] However, in the painting Harushige has carefully suggested the weight of the white inner kimono by applying a thin layer of blue pigment to create shadows along the neckline and the folds that form at the feet. This concern for modeling prefigures his obsession with

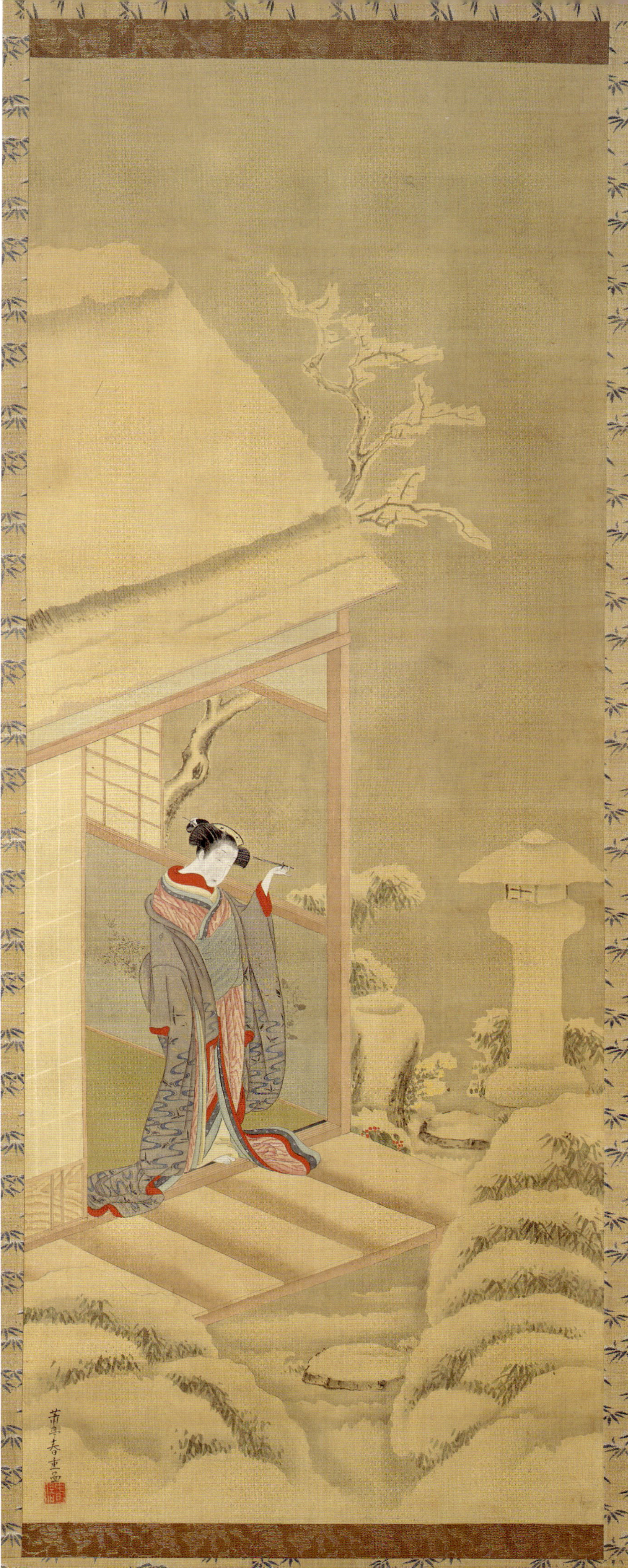

Western chiaroscuro that would dominate his career after 1781, when he discarded the name Harushige and reinvented himself as Shiba Kōkan, the proponent of European naturalism. ANM

1. Translation by Calvin L. French, *Shiba Kōkan: Artist, Innovator, and Pioneer in the Westernization of Japan* (New York and Tokyo: Weatherhill, 1974), 29.
2. French, *Shiba Kōkan*, 37–38.
3. Kobayashi Tadashi, "Sekkei bijin zu," in *Bosuton bijutsukan nikuhitsu ukiyo-e*, vol. 2 (Tokyo: Museum of Fine Arts, Boston, and Kōdansha, 2000), 159.
4. Chiba City Museum of Art, *Suzuki Harunobu: Edo no kararisuto tōjō* (Chiba: Chiba City Museum of Art, 2002), entry 158.

27. **IPPITSUSAI BUNCHŌ** (ACTIVE ABOUT 1755–90)
Courtesans at the Front of an Assignation Teahouse

Meiwa 6–7 (1769–70)
Hanging scroll; ink, color, silver, and brass on silk
100 x 36.5 cm (39 3/8 x 14 3/8 in.)
Signature: Ippitsusai Bunchō ga (Painted by Ippitsusai Bunchō)
Seals: Shushi; Mori uji
William Sturgis Bigelow Collection 11.7324

Ippitsusai Bunchō captures an informal moment in front of an assignation teahouse (*hikitejaya*) in the middle of winter. A high-level courtesan huddled under a thick white robe secured with an ikat-patterned (*kasuri*) sash and a red outer robe decorated with a design of a fence and nandina tends to the embers in the charcoal brazier before her. She pauses to listen to a geisha, who wears the more somber dress of her station and has the black wooden box containing her requisite samisen. Another *tayū*, bedecked in a light blue outer robe ornamented with cranes and stylized pines and a sash figured with wheeling cranes, lingers outside the veranda. Despite the snow-covered ground, she wears no *tabi* socks with her geta—a dress regulation for all courtesans during the Edo period.

The details of Ippitsusai Bunchō's biography are not well established, but he is believed to have received his initial painting training from a relatively obscure Kano-school artist. Best known for his actor prints, he produced a celebrated three-volume set of books entitled *Picture Book of Theatrical Fans* (*Ehon butai-ōgi*, 1770) in collaboration with Katsukawa Shunshō. In his depictions of actors in female roles as well as courtesans, Bunchō was highly influenced by the prints of Suzuki Harunobu. His figures share the slender proportions and lyrical poses of the earlier master, but their expressions are always much more acerbic.

Paintings by Bunchō are thought to be extremely limited in number. However, an examination of these works is critical to understanding the refinement of the artist's sensibilities—a quality not often captured in his mass-produced prints. In this painting Bunchō has paid close attention to the appointments of the *hikitejaya*, where prospective clients of the highest-level courtesans had to await the procession of the women and their entourages from their sometimes-distant quarters. Furthermore, the wintry day is captured by the icicles with their now tarnished silver pigment, which once would have glistened along the eaves. The poem written against the ink-wash sky also highlights the almost randomly applied shell white (*gofun*) that suggests the falling snow. ANM

Awayuki no	Time of frothy snow—
toguru ma sae mo	secret language can't conceal
kokorozeki	passions that run hot
hayaku mo mitashi	and I can't wait to gaze on
Ume-eda no kao.	the lovely face of Plum Branch.

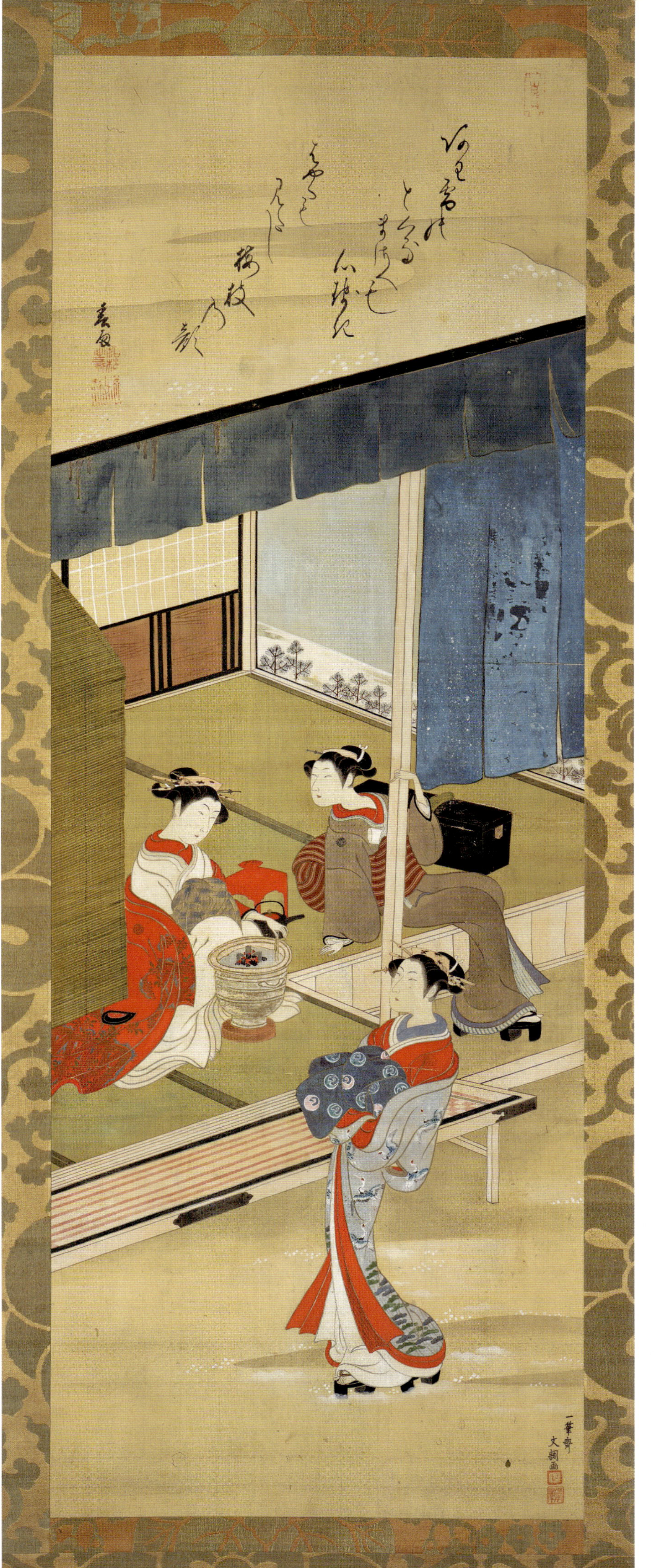

123

AN AIR OF INNOCENCE

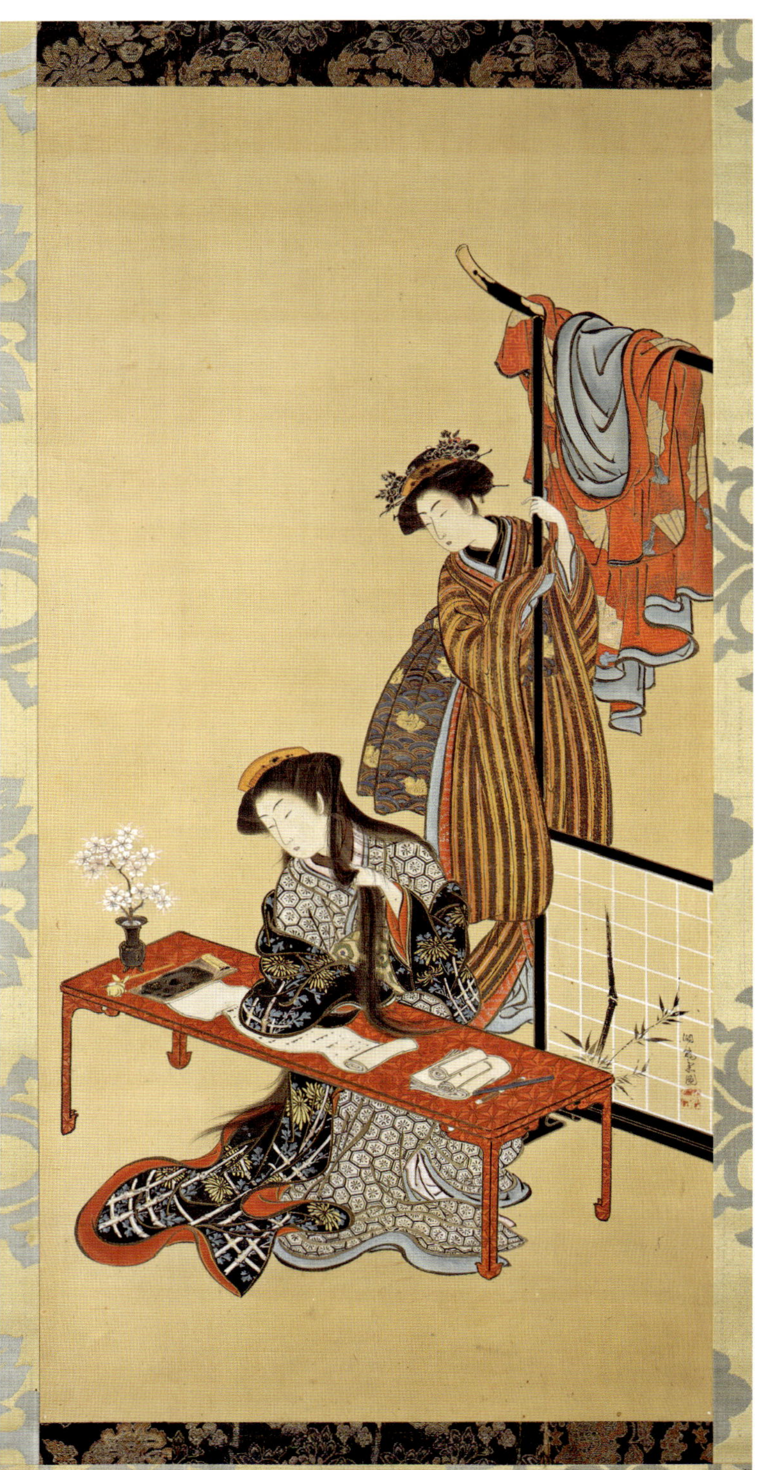

28. **ISODA KORYŪSAI** (ACTIVE ABOUT 1764–1788)

Courtesan at a Writing Desk (Parody of Guan Yu)

Latter half of the An'ei (1772–81) or first half of the Tenmei (1781–89) era
Hanging scroll; ink, color, and gold on silk
75 x 38 cm (29 ½ x 14 15/16 in.)
Signature: Koryūsai zu (Drawn by Koryūsai)
Seal: Isoda
William Sturgis Bigelow Collection 11.7548

This painting provides a sophisticated parody of Guan Yu (Japanese: Kan'u), the legendary Chinese warrior of Shu and hero of the Jin-dynasty (265–420) account *Chronicles of the Three Kingdoms* (*Sanguozhi*), and his retainer. Guan Yu, known for his luxurious beard, was usually depicted seated, with his attendant standing behind him with his halberdlike weapon Green Dragon. Here, Guan Yu is replaced by the seated courtesan writing a letter on a roll of paper. Perhaps she is contemplating a message to a client. Assuming a coquettish pose, she rests her right elbow on her desk and with her left hand twirls her long hair, a substitute for Guan Yu's beard. Guan Yu's attendant has become her attendant: the younger woman in a *furisode* robe standing behind the courtesan clutches the erstwhile Green Dragon (the upright pole of the clothes rack) as she tries hard to catch a glimpse of the letter hidden by the courtesan's sleeve.

The writing implements and the ink painting of bamboo on the panel of the clothes rack behind the courtesan reflect the taste of Chinese literati. Koryūsai adopted the same composition for a print in his celebrated *ōban* series Patterns for New Year Fashions, Fresh as Young Leaves (Hinagata wakana no hatsu moyō), published by Nishimura Eijūdō from about 1776 to 1782.[1] NM

1. *Editor's note:* Koryūsai's series Hinagata wakana no hatsu moyō is the subject of Allen Hockley, *The Prints of Isoda Koryūsai: Floating World Culture and Its Consumers in Eighteenth-Century Japan* (Seattle: University of Washington Press, 2003). A pillar print with a similar composition is in the MFA collection: Isoda Koryūsai, *Mitate-e on Guan Yu and Liu Bei*, woodblock print, ink and color on paper, 71.8 x 13 cm, William S. and John T. Spaulding Collection, 21.8320.

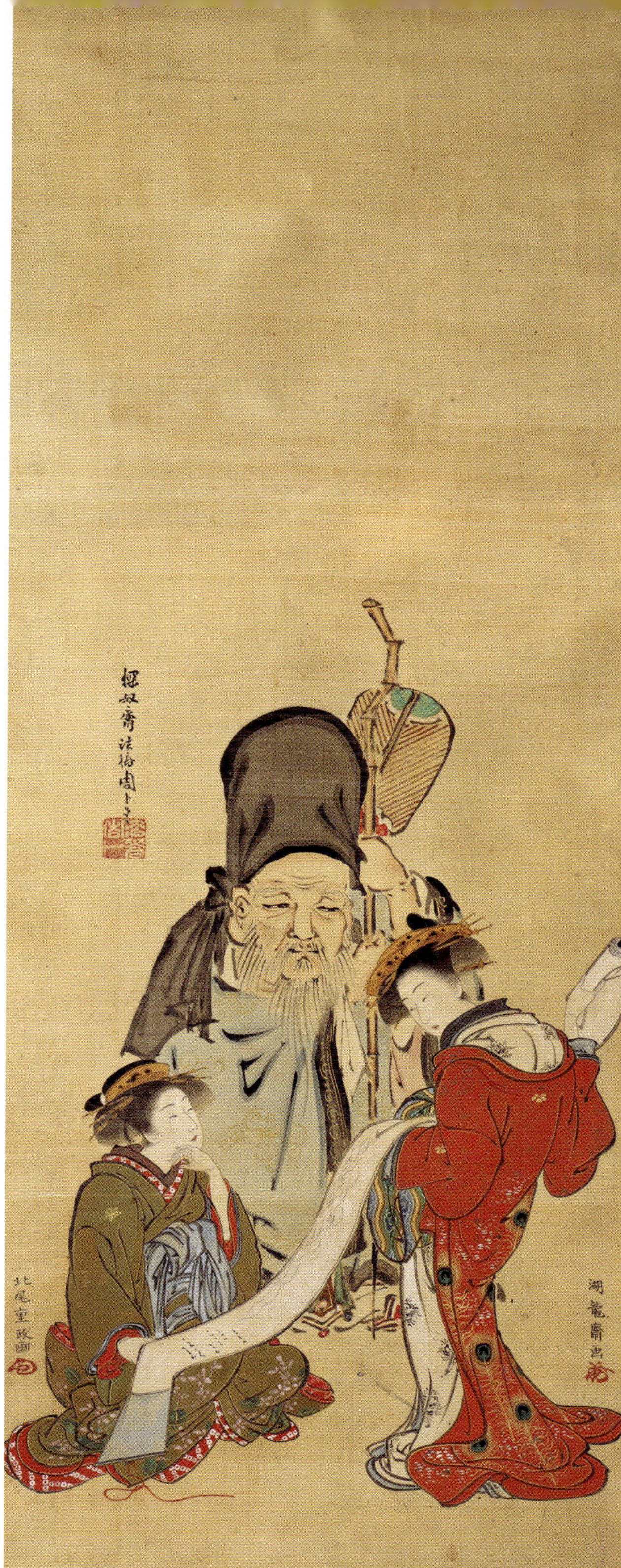

29. **KANO SHŪBOKU** (DATES UNKNOWN)
ISODA KORYŪSAI (ACTIVE ABOUT 1766–1788)
KITAO SHIGEMASA (1739–1820)
Fukurokuju with a Courtesan and a Geisha

About the latter half of the An'ei era (1772–81)
Hanging scroll; ink, color, and gold on silk
81.5 x 32.7 cm (32 1/16 x 12 7/8 in.)
Signatures: Tanshusai hokkyō Shūboku hitsu (Brush of Tanshusai Shūboku of the hokkyō rank); Koryūsai ga (Painted by Koryūsai); Kitao Shigemasa ga (Painted by Kitao Shigemasa)
Seals: Hokkyō Shūboku; cipher; cipher
William Sturgis Bigelow Collection 11.7554

Ukiyo-e artists enjoyed including Buddhist and Shinto deities in parodies (*mitate-e*) and vulgarizing them so that their sacred nature was replaced with more recognizable human traits. In this painting, Fukurokuju, one of the Seven Gods of Good Fortune, is depicted with his characteristic elongated head and beard and the staff he holds in his left hand. He narrows his eyes in a slightly affected expression, leering at a willowy courtesan and a geisha. The two women have seized his handscroll—one of the god's common attributes—and absorb themselves in admiring the elegant ink painting of moon over the waves.

The scroll's playfulness works on an additional level: The three figures were executed by three different artists—Fukurokuju by Shūboku, a member of the Kano school, which was traditionally patronized by the military aristocracy, and the courtesan and geisha by two ukiyo-e painters, Koryūsai and Shigemasa respectively. Ostensibly the theme of the painting belonged to the Kano painter's repertoire, but ironically figures done by the ukiyo-e artists command the viewer's attention.[1]

The faces of both the courtesan, who wears a bright red overrobe with a design of peacock feathers over a background of irregular swastikas on the hem, and of the geisha, who sports a warbler green robe, are consistent with the styles that their creators employed during the An'ei era. NM

---

1. *Editor's note:* Narusawa Katsushige has recently determined that the original theme was that of the ancient Chinese deities the Star of Happiness (Fuxing), the Star of Prosperity (Luxing), and the Star of Longevity (Shouxing). They can be found in a Qing-dynasty painting, artist unknown, *Fulushou and the Three Stars*, hanging scroll, ink and color on silk, 102.5 x 58.1 cm., Kobe City Museum.

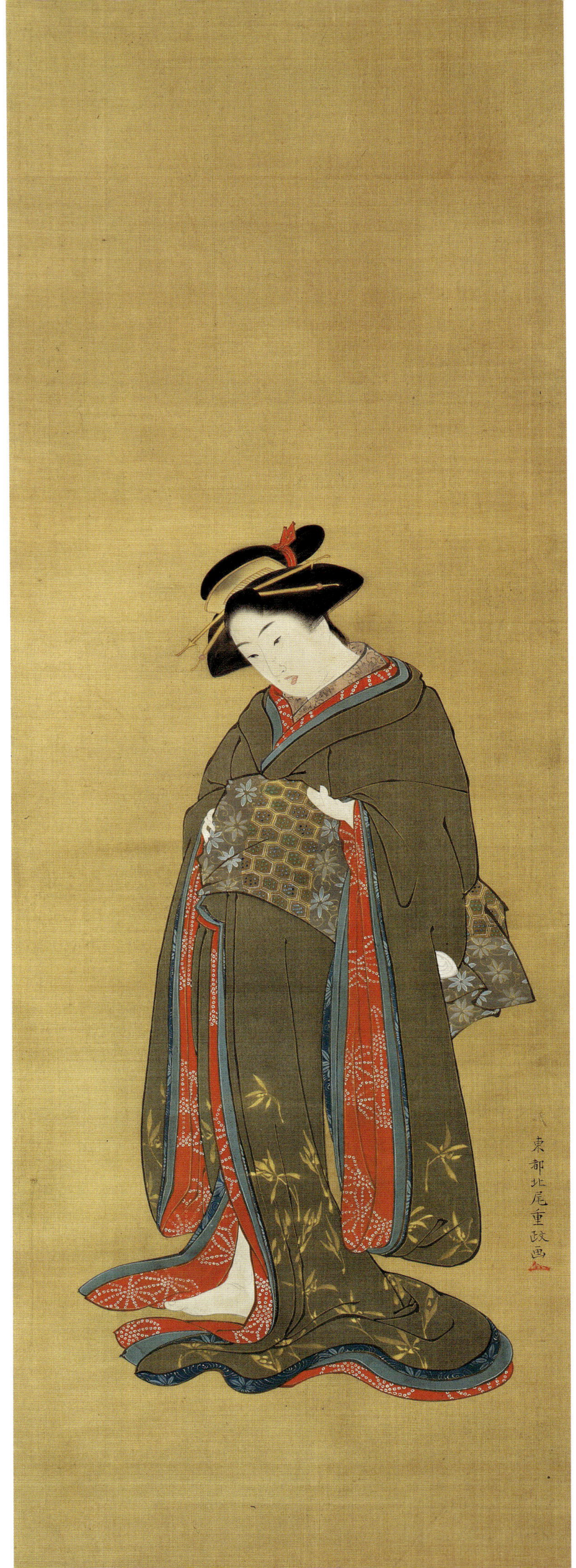
東都北尾重政画

30. **KITAO SHIGEMASA** (1739–1820)

Young Woman Wearing a Kimono with Long, Hanging Sleeves

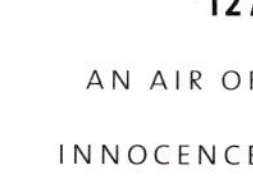

Late An'ei (1772–81) or early Tenmei (1781–89) era
Hanging scroll; ink, color, and gold on silk
86.9 x 31.4 cm (34 3/16 x 12 3/8 in.)
Signature: Tōto Kitao Shigemasa ga (Painted by Kitao Shigemasa of the Eastern Capital)
Seal: cipher
William Sturgis Bigelow Collection 11.7723

A young woman (who is probably a geisha) adjusts her sash; her lower abdomen is slightly thrust forward. She appears to be trying to alter the balance between the wide belt and her pendant-sleeved kimono ornamented with delicate orchid patterns along the hem. Unfortunately, due to her posture, she appears rather heavyset; she is depicted in the style of figure painting popular during the late An'ei through the early Tenmei eras.

The delicate brushwork of the face and robe leaves no doubt as to the exceptional technical skills of Kitao Shigemasa. Founder of the Kitao school, which came to include the artists Kubo Shunman, Kitao Masanobu, and Kitao Masayoshi, Shigemasa was one of the most celebrated artists of *bijin* during the 1770s. This hanging scroll is one of the rare paintings by the artist, who from the 1780s onward devoted himself to providing illustrations for printed books, such as comic yellowbacks (*kibyōshi*). The relative scarcity of works by the self-taught Shigemasa—both painted and printed—may be due to his enormous talents in calligraphy and Edo-school *haikai* poetry, as mentioned in the *Ukiyo-e ruiko*. The few paintings that Shigemasa did produce were of high quality, suggesting that they were made at the request of patrons whom he could not refuse. NM

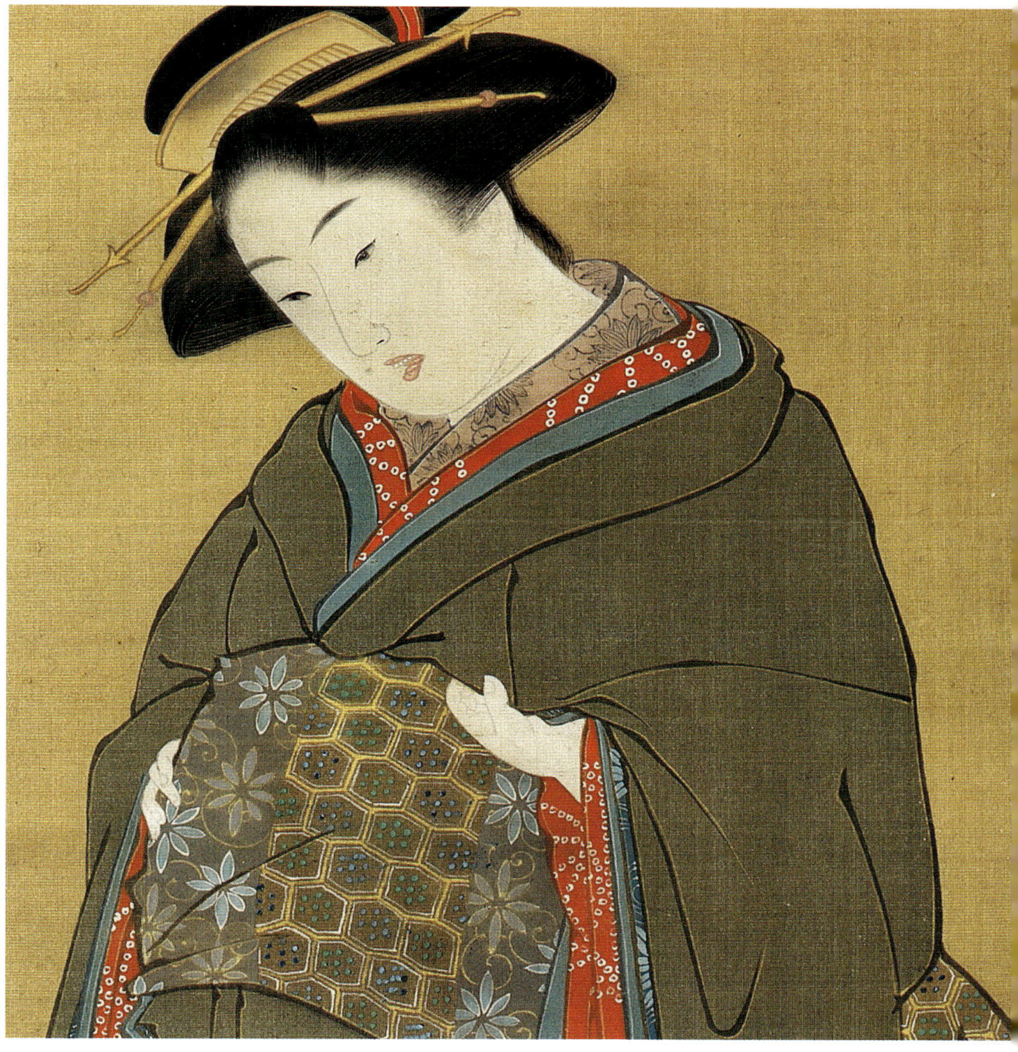

31. **KATSUKAWA SHUNSHŌ** (1726–1792)
Parody of Matsukaze and Murasame

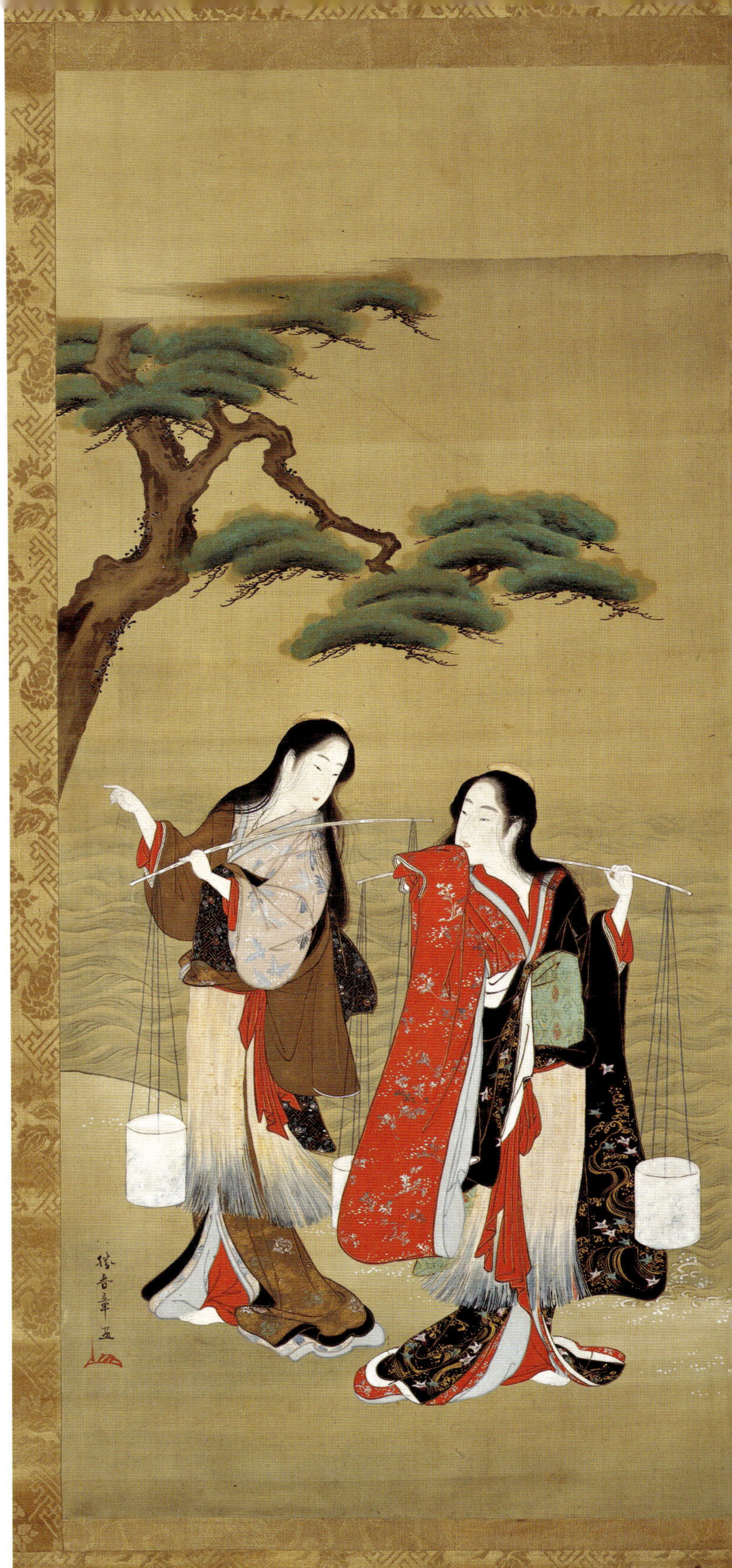

About Tenmei 3–4 (1783–84)
Hanging scroll; ink, color, and gold on silk
92 x 43 cm (36 ¼ x 16 15/16 in.)
Signature: Katsu Shunshō ga (Painted by Katsu[kawa] Shunshō)
Seal: cipher
William Sturgis Bigelow Collection 11.7772

Katsukawa Shunshō here provides the elements of scenery essential to all versions of the Matsukaze story—the sea and the pine tree, the latter of which becomes an emblem of the departed lover Ariwara no Yukihira (see cat. no. 21). In employing ink shading for the tree's trunk and layers of malachite for the pine needles, punctuated by ink lines for the twigs, the artist followed the conventions of academic Kano-school painting. In contrast, he depicted the women, with their graceful, elongated proportions and their finely rendered, flowing hair, in his own distinctive style. One of the figures is garbed in a light pink inner robe decorated with butterflies and an outer robe figured with stylized wave patterns; she turns to the other, who wears a brilliant red inner kimono ornamented with seaweed patterns and a sumptuous black outer robe embroidered with plover and wave motifs.[1] Only the fishermen's skirts, here painted in delicately modeled pink and blue, and the buckets with the brine detailed in swirls of light blue provide an overlay of rusticity to an otherwise thoroughly contemporary depiction of feminine beauty. ANM

1. Although the story itself would suggest that Matsukaze is the sister closer to the tree, Naitō Masato points out that Shunshō may have provided clues to the identity of each sister by borrowing the motifs that were used to ornament the costumes in Kabuki plays about the famed Soga brothers, Jūrō and Gorō. The younger brother, Gorō, characteristically wears underrobes with the butterfly motif. Jūrō is generally designated by the plover motif. See Naitō Masato, "Katsukawa Shunshō mitate Matsukaze Murasame zu," in *Bosuton bijutsukan nikuhitsu ukiyo-e*, vol. 2 (Tokyo: Museum of Fine Arts, Boston, and Kōdansha, 2000), 176.

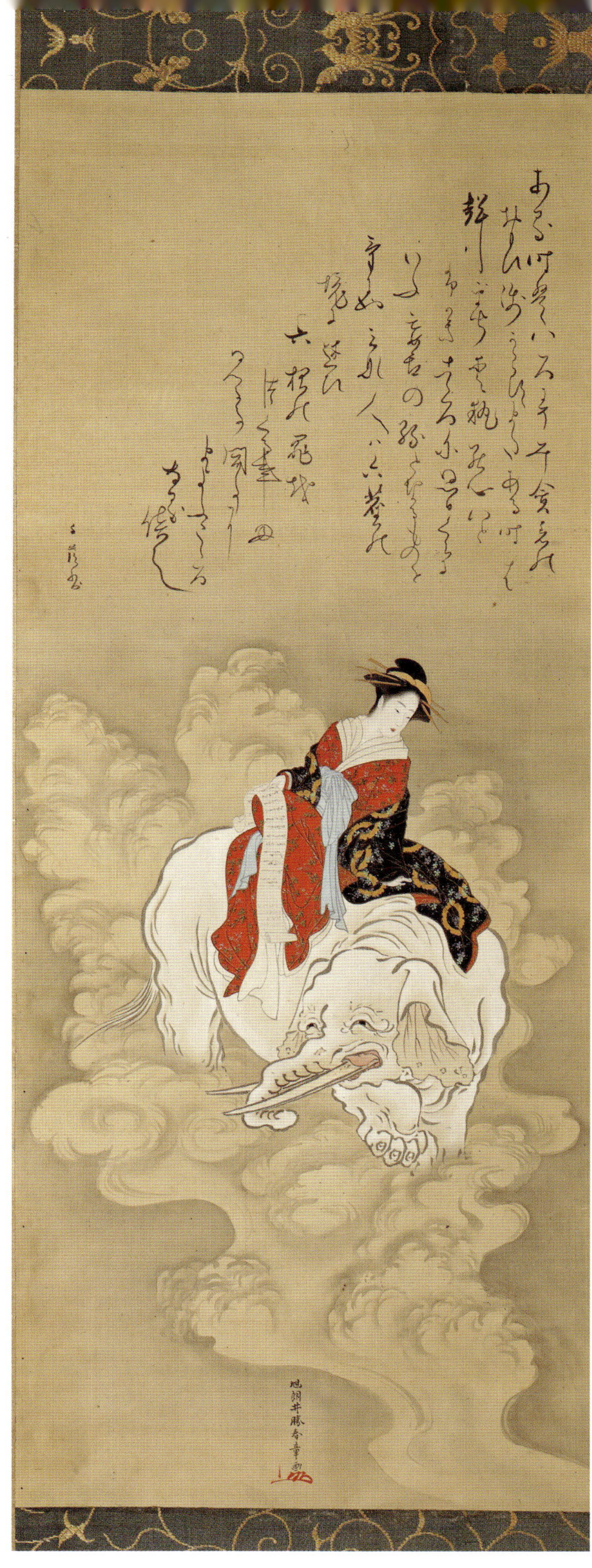

32. **KATSUKAWA SHUNSHŌ** (1726–1792)
Parody of Eguchi no kimi

About Tenmei 5–6 (1785–86)
Hanging scroll; ink, color, and gold on silk
95.8 x 39.2 cm (37 11/16 x 15 7/16 in.)
Signature: Kyokurōsei Katsu Shunshō ga (Painted by Kyokurōsei Katsu[kawa] Shunshō
Seal: cipher
William Sturgis Bigelow Collection 11.7767

In traditional Buddhist paintings Fugen, the Bodhisattva of Universal Virtue, is depicted riding a pure white elephant. Here instead, a courtesan seated on the back of the animal emerges from the imposing cloud that rises from the bottom of the composition. The substitution of the sacred — a Buddha or bodhisattva — with the worldly and vulgar is a common device used in ukiyo-e to parody classical subjects. However, another story, *Eguchi no kimi*, also lies behind this particular painting (see cat. no. 10).[1]

The narrative of *Eguchi no kimi* was first formalized in *Tales of Saigyō* (*Saigyō monogatari*) and then developed further in the later No play *Eguchi*. During the Edo period the story of the twelfth-century poet-monk and the prostitute in the village of Eguchi inspired numerous paintings, both ukiyo-e and non-ukiyo-e.[2] Furthermore, Shunshō himself produced at least three other renditions of the theme. Contemporary patrons must have been eager to have such imagery by one of the leading *bijinga* painters of the day.

Katō Chikage, a scholar of classical Japanese literature, added the following inscription on the painting:

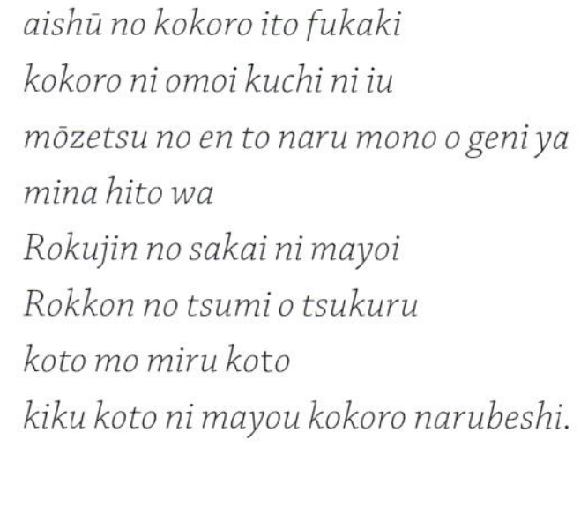

Aru toki wa iro ni somi
tonjaku no omoi asakarazu
mata aru toki wa koe o kiki
aishū no kokoro ito fukaki
kokoro ni omoi kuchi ni iu
mōzetsu no en to naru mono o geni ya
mina hito wa
Rokujin no sakai ni mayoi
Rokkon no tsumi o tsukuru
koto mo miru koto
kiku koto ni mayou kokoro narubeshi.

Lured by the eye
we grow attached to things;
ravished by sweet sounds
we become their thralls.
Such things deceive the mind
and lead the tongue to falseness.

Alas! Man is a wanderer in the world of the Six Dusts
and sins through the Six Organs of Perception,
yet most temptation comes through the eye and the ear.[3] NM

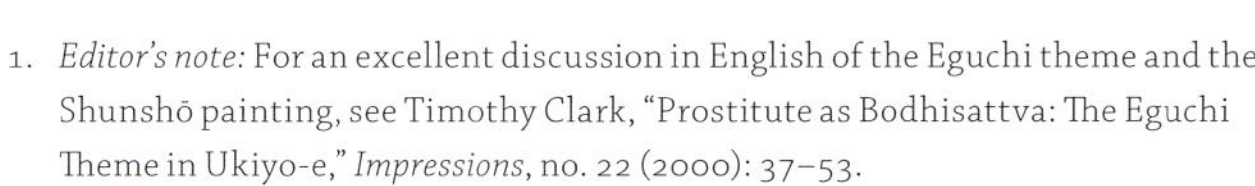

1. *Editor's note:* For an excellent discussion in English of the Eguchi theme and the Shunshō painting, see Timothy Clark, "Prostitute as Bodhisattva: The Eguchi Theme in Ukiyo-e," *Impressions*, no. 22 (2000): 37–53.
2. A well-known work of the latter type is the scroll dated 1794, by the Kyoto artist Maruyama Ōkyo, in the Seikadō Museum of Art, Tokyo, published in *Ōkyo/Goshun*, vol. 22 of *Nihon bijutsu kaiga zenshū* (Tokyo: Shūeisha, 1977), illustration 12.
3. This inscription is quoted directly from the No play. Nippon gakujutsu shinkōkai, *Japanese Noh Drama*, vol. 1 (Tokyo: Nippon gakujutsu shinkōkai, 1955), 123.

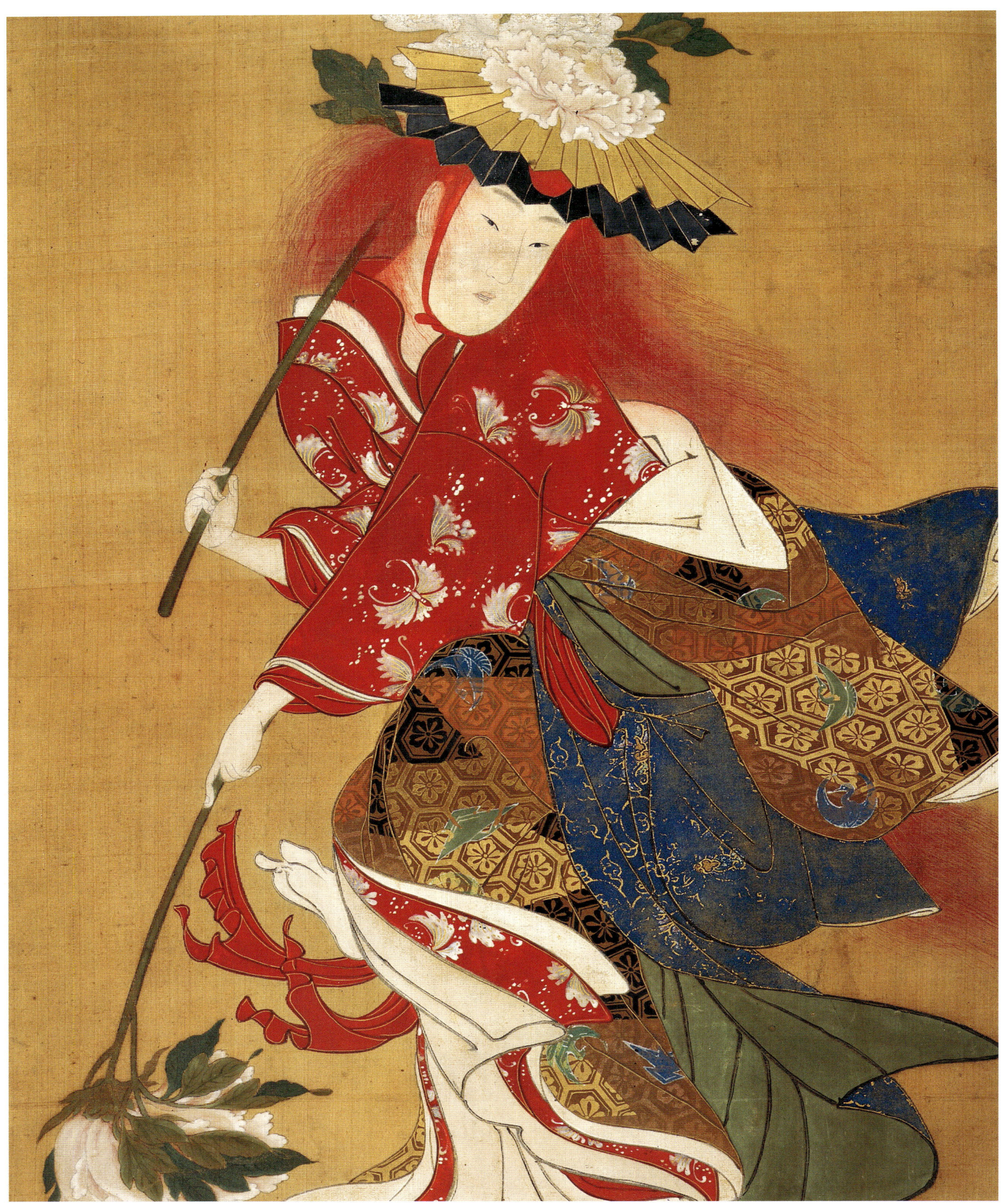

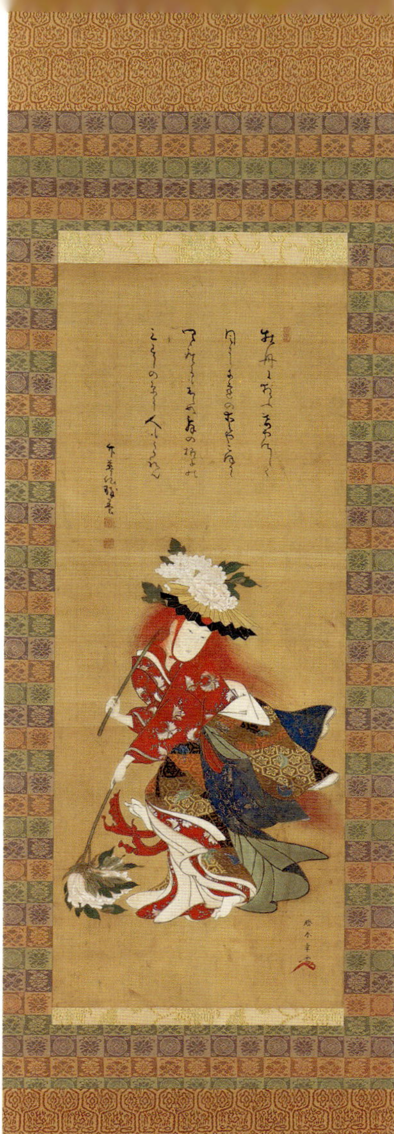

33. **KATSUKAWA SHUNSHŌ** (1726–1792)
Shakkyō, the Lion Dance

Tenmei 7–8 (1787–88)
Hanging scroll; ink, color, and gold on silk
82.5 x 32.5 cm (32 ½ x 12 13/16 in.)
Signature: Katsu Shunshō ga (Painted by Katsu[kawa] Shunshō)
Seal: cipher
William Sturgis Bigelow Collection 11.7762

The woman in this painting wears a red wig and a peony-adorned hat made of fans. She also bears peony branches in her hands. All are identifying attributes of the Shakkyō (Stone Bridge) dance. According to legend, the Heian-period monk Jakushō (lay name: Ōe no Sadamoto) arrived at a natural stone bridge during his travels to Mount Tiantai in China. There he saw a lion (the mount of the Bodhisattva of Wisdom Monju), playing with a peony. This auspicious encounter was first made the subject of a No chant, and then was transformed in the Edo period into an extremely popular Kabuki dance, (see cat. no. 10).

The actor Iwai Hanshirō IV performed the Shakkyō dance at the Kiri Theater in the third month of 1787, around the same time that this painting was created. The work itself displays the highly refined style that Shunshō achieved in the late 1780s, when he was at the peak of his career as a *bijinga* painter. At the top of the composition there is a poem by Nomura Hakujubō (died 1817):

Botan ni kuruu sugata yasashiku
me ni sengin no ai ya koboruru
shiza ni mo shiranu mai no hyōshi no
misuji no ito ni hito mo ukaren.

Intoxicated with the peonies, a graceful figure
Eyes worth a thousand gold pieces, overflowing with love.
Everybody's thrilled about this three-stringed samisen tune
that was quite unknown in the old days of the "Four Theaters."

The verse includes a clever wordplay.[1] "Misuji" (three lines) makes reference to Ichikawa Danjūrō, whose crest took the form of three rice measures. "The 'Four Theaters'" alludes to the Nakamura, Ichimura, Morita, and Yamamura Theaters, which were officially sanctioned by the Tokugawa government in 1670. With the outbreak of a scandal at the Yamamura Theater in 1714, however, this stage was demolished and never rebuilt. NM

1. The last paragraph is the editor's addition.

34. **KATSUKAWA SHUNSHŌ** (1726–1792)

Scenes of Amusement in Spring and Summer

First half of the Kansei era (1789–1801)
Pair of six-panel folding screens;
ink and color on paper
Each 140.9 x 341 cm (55 ½ x 134 ¼ in.)

Signature: Katsu Shunshō zu
(Drawn by Katsu[kawa] Shunshō)
Seal: (only on the right screen) Jūi
William Sturgis Bigelow Collection
11.7774, 11.7775

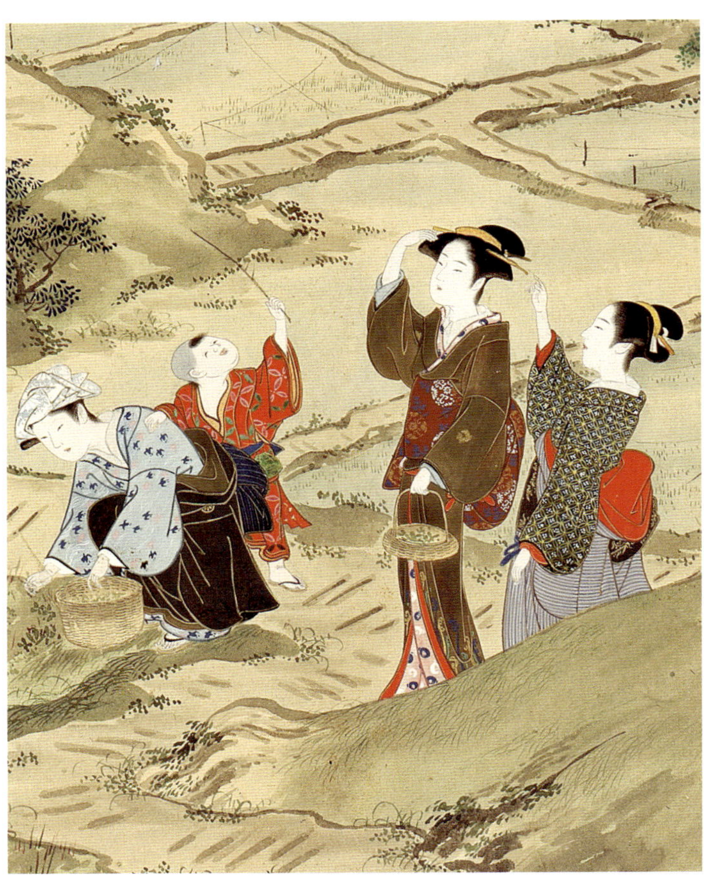

Katsukawa Shunshō conveys a pleasurable sense of the seasons in this superb pair of screens. On the right the artist presents a bird's-eye view of a riverbank on a warm spring day. Blossoming cherry trees punctuate the undulating waterway. Scattered clusters of people enjoy the weather; some admire the flowery canopies, others pick spring herbs. In the lower-right foreground of the right screen, a group stops at a restaurant; a man with rather distinctive features wearing a black head scarf urges his slower companions to hurry up. It is tempting to assume that the scene is set along the Sumida River, but because Shunshō eliminated all landmarks, the location cannot be identified.

Daily life in early summer — suggested by the green willow branches blowing in the breeze — is the subject of the left-hand screen. The garden scene is permeated with the season's languorous air, which is conveyed by the woman lying on her stomach in the building behind bamboo blinds and those smoking their pipes on the veranda. Others fish at the edge of a pond on the right. The setting may be a high-class restaurant or an aristocrat's garden.

Shunshō dedicated the last decade of his life to painting images of beautiful women, rather than making the prints of celebrated Kabuki actors for which he had become so well known. Some of these later works were commissioned by daimyo. Generally ukiyo-e artists produced paintings in small-scale formats, such as hanging scrolls or handscrolls. Only rarely did they try their hand at grander compositions for sliding doors (*fusuma*) or screens. Most likely large-scale works, such as this pair of screens, would have been done at the request of a wealthy client. NM

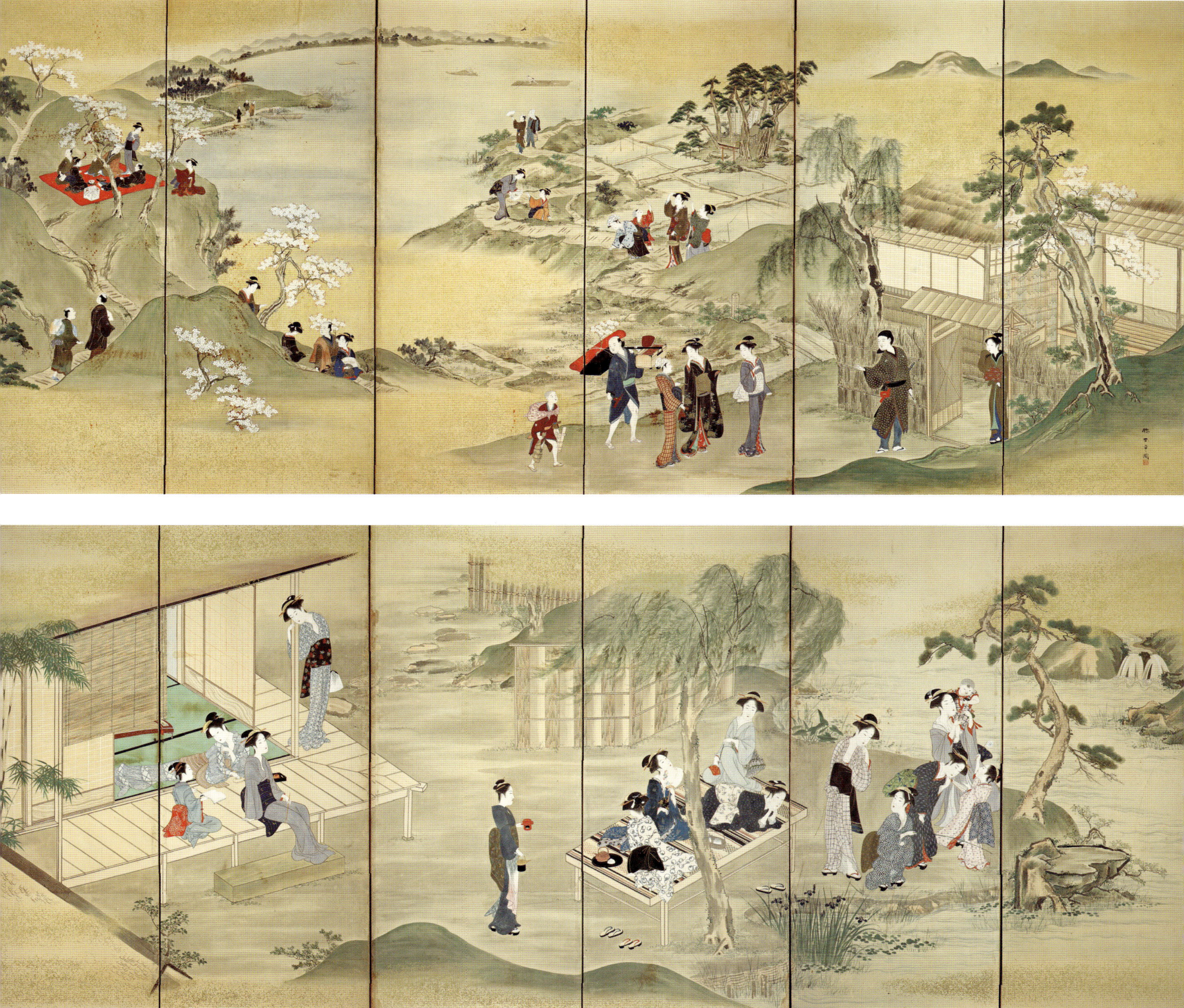

35. **KATSUKAWA SHUNRIN** (ACTIVE ABOUT 1781–1801)
Women Representing the Three Cities

About the Kansei era (1789–1801)
Set of three hanging scrolls; ink, color, gold, and mica on silk
Each 98.5 x 32.3 cm (38 ¾ x 12 ¹¹⁄₁₆ in.)
Signature: Katsukawa Shunrin ga (Painted by Katsukawa Shunrin)
Seal: Shunrin yūga (Superb painting by Shunrin)
William Sturgis Bigelow Collection 11.7757, 11.7758, 11.7759

The effect of these three paintings representing the three major urban centers of the Edo period — Nakagyō (Kyoto), Edo, and Naniwa (Osaka) — with three women dressed in seasonal garb is that of a beauty contest, with the individuals embodying the significant traits of their cities.

The center scroll depicts a woman from Kyoto, Japan's cultural center. She stands under a weeping willow tree in front of a bench; a crescent moon glimmers above her in the night sky. Having just taken a drag on her pipe, she turns her head to exhale the smoke. Generally women from Kyoto were known for their languid elegance, but here she has an air of sophistication that is more often associated with Edo.

To the left, a woman from Osaka, Japan's economic and gastronomic center, stands in front of a window through which one can see a snow-covered nandina tree in the garden. In keeping with the wintry season of the scroll, she wears a kimono decorated with crenellated snow-circle motifs and an overall pattern of mallow leaves. Her casual pose, with her right hand tucked into her sash and her left brought to her mouth, conveys the stinging cold of the winter months.

In the last scroll on the right, Shunrin depicts a *yūjo* from Edo, the political center of the country. The courtesan is caught standing on a veranda on a fine spring day, with the cherry trees in full bloom. She is trying to keep her black outer robe, decorated

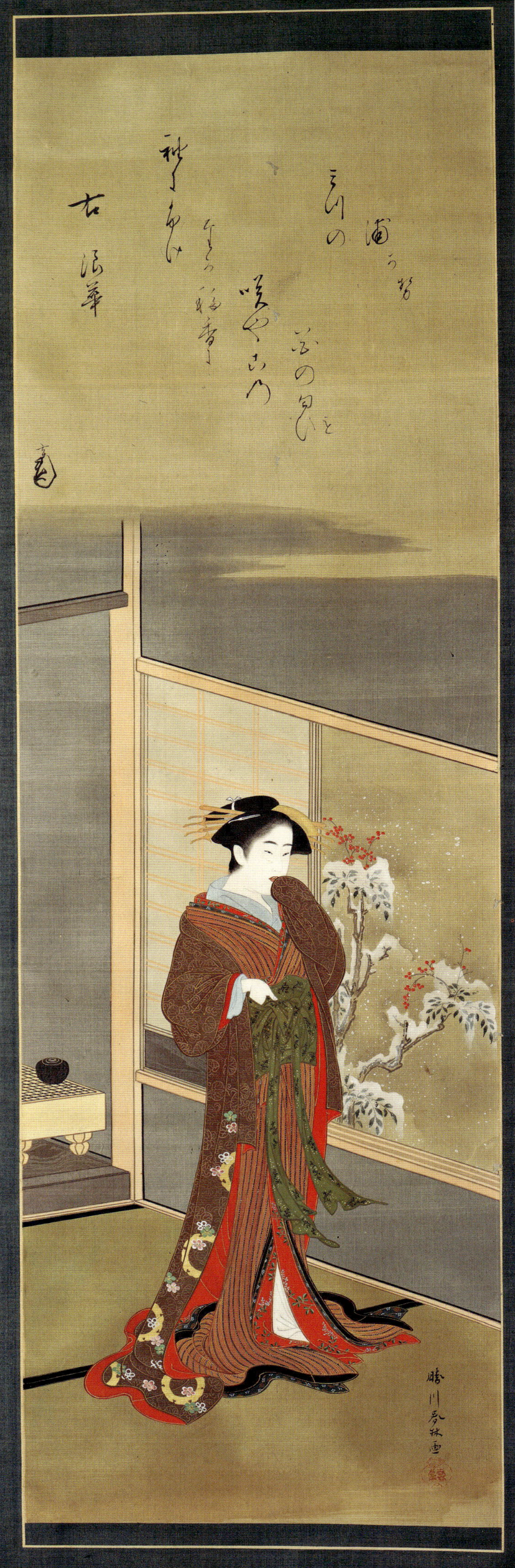

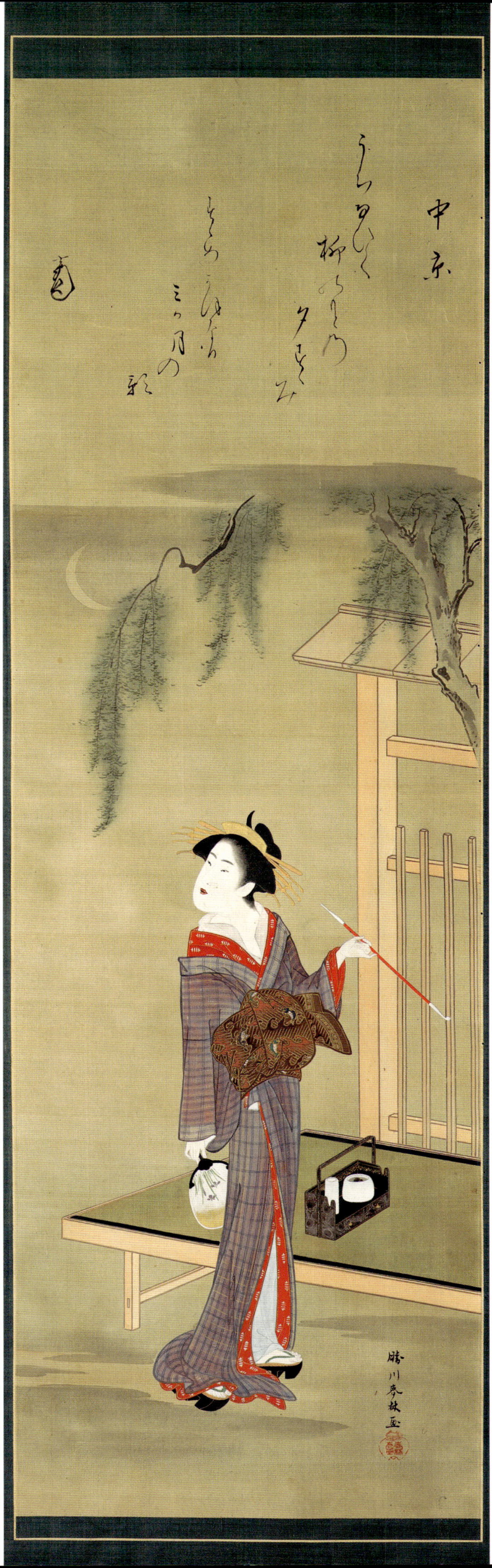

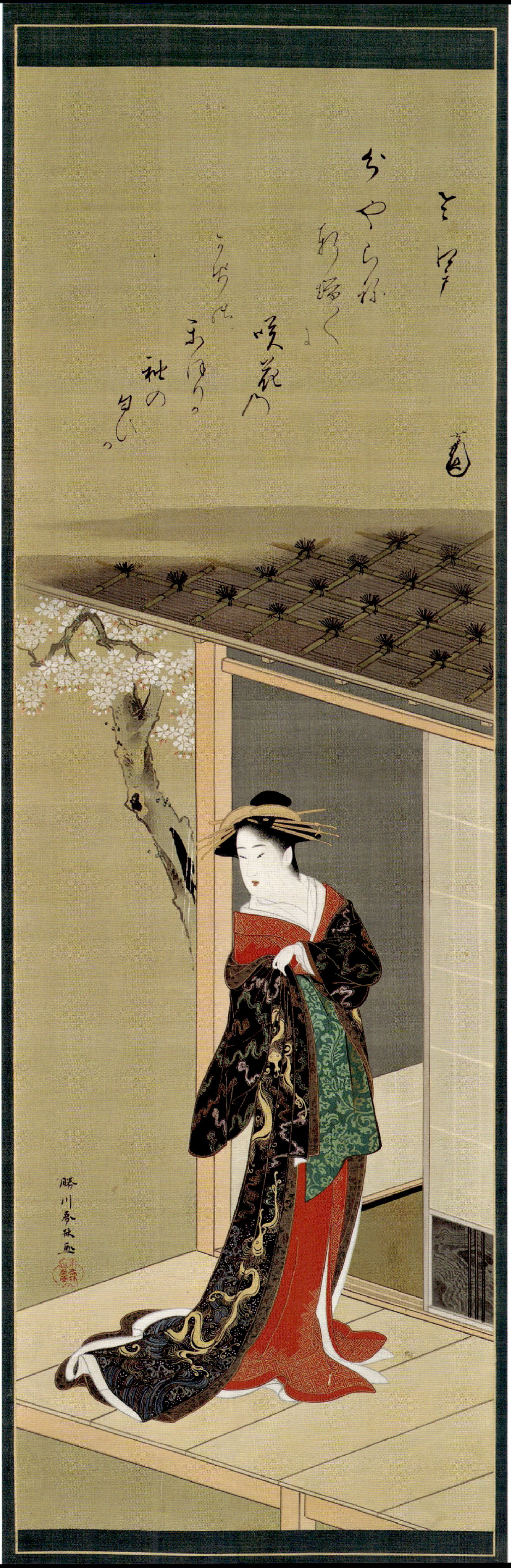

with patterns of waves and dragons among clouds, from slipping off her shoulders.[1]

Unfortunately we do not know who inscribed the paintings with the following verses:

NAKAGYŌ (KYOTO):

Uchi nabiku	Cooling off at dusk
yanagi no moto no	beneath the branches of a
yūsuzumi	waving willow tree
susumegao naru	the crescent moon's alluring
mikazuki no kage.	face casts flirtatious shadows.

NANIWA (OSAKA):

Sode ni fuke	Suffusing my sleeve,
ta ga utsuriga ni	in whose lingering scent does this
saku ya kono	winter flower bloom
hana no nioi mo	as its fragrance drifts to me
mitsu no ura kaze.	on three breezes from the bay?

EDO:

Wakeyaranu	Floating on the wind
nokiba nokiba ni	unbroken, from house to house
sakibana no	the scent of flowers,
kaze no kaori ka	is it the cherry blossoms
sode no nioi ka.	or the perfume of a sleeve?

Shunrin was the disciple of Katsukawa Shunshō during the Kansei era. In these works he adopts the style that his teacher employed in his later years. NM

1. The wave pattern is reminiscent of one found in the mid-seventeenth-century *Beauty on a Veranda* in the Tokyo National Museum, published in *Tokyo kokuritsu hakubutsukan*, vol. 1 of *Nikuhitsu ukiyo-e taikan* (Tokyo: Kōdansha, 1994), entry 4. There may be a hidden reference in this scroll about the journey to Kawachi in the sixty-seventh section of the *Tales of Ise*: "Around the Second Month of a certain year, a man set out with a group of companions on a pleasure jaunt to the province of Izumi. Mount Ikoma in Kawachi, swathed in restless, billowing clouds, slipped in and out of sight as they traveled. After an overcast morning, the sky cleared around noon, and they saw fallen snow, pure and white, blanketing the treetops." Helen Craig McCullough, *Tales of Ise: Lyrical Episodes from Tenth-Century Japan* (Stanford, CA: Stanford University Press, 1968), 114–15.

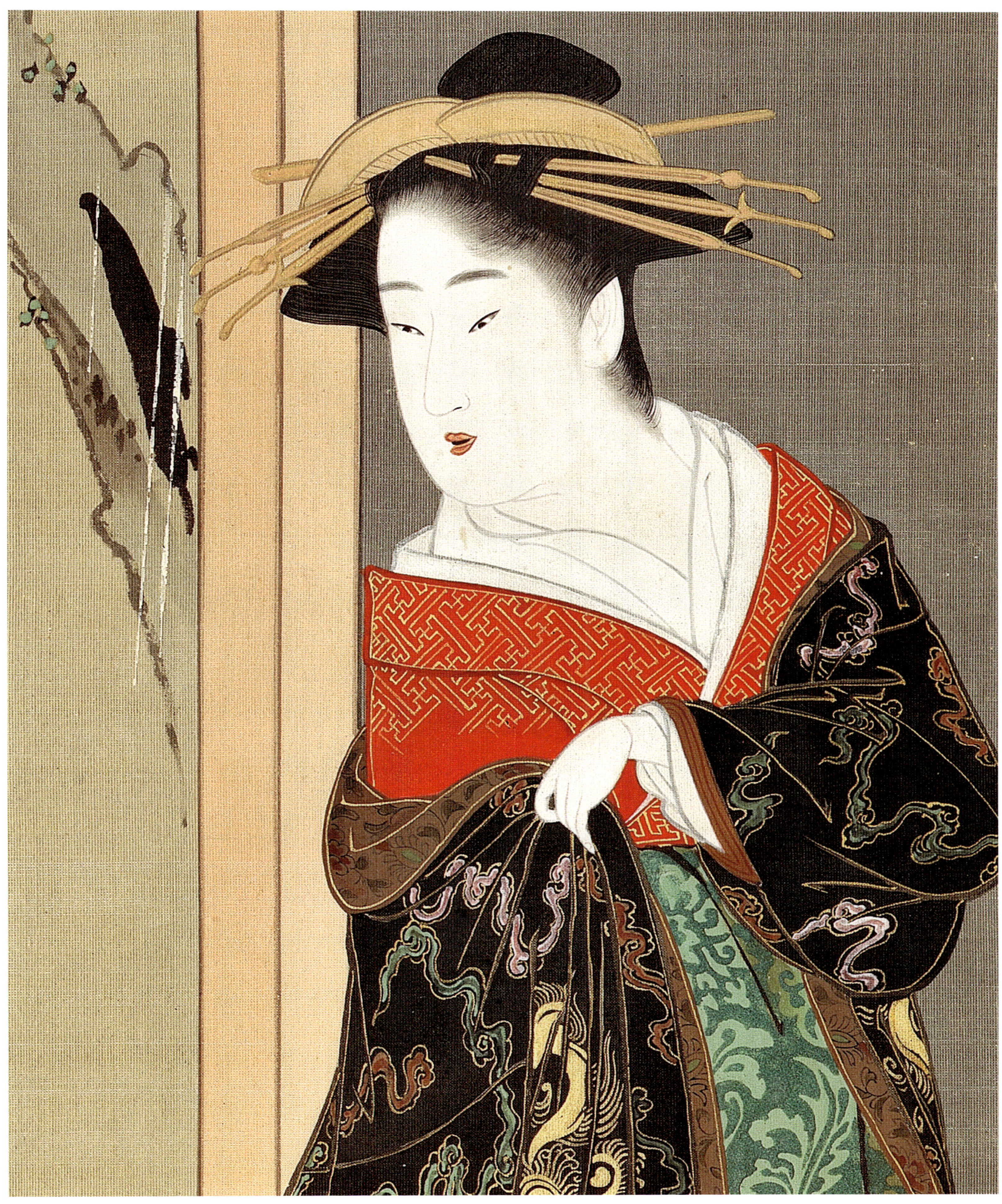

IMAGES OF FEMININE ALLURE, 1780–1805 **TORII KIYONAGA AND KITAGAWA UTAMARO**

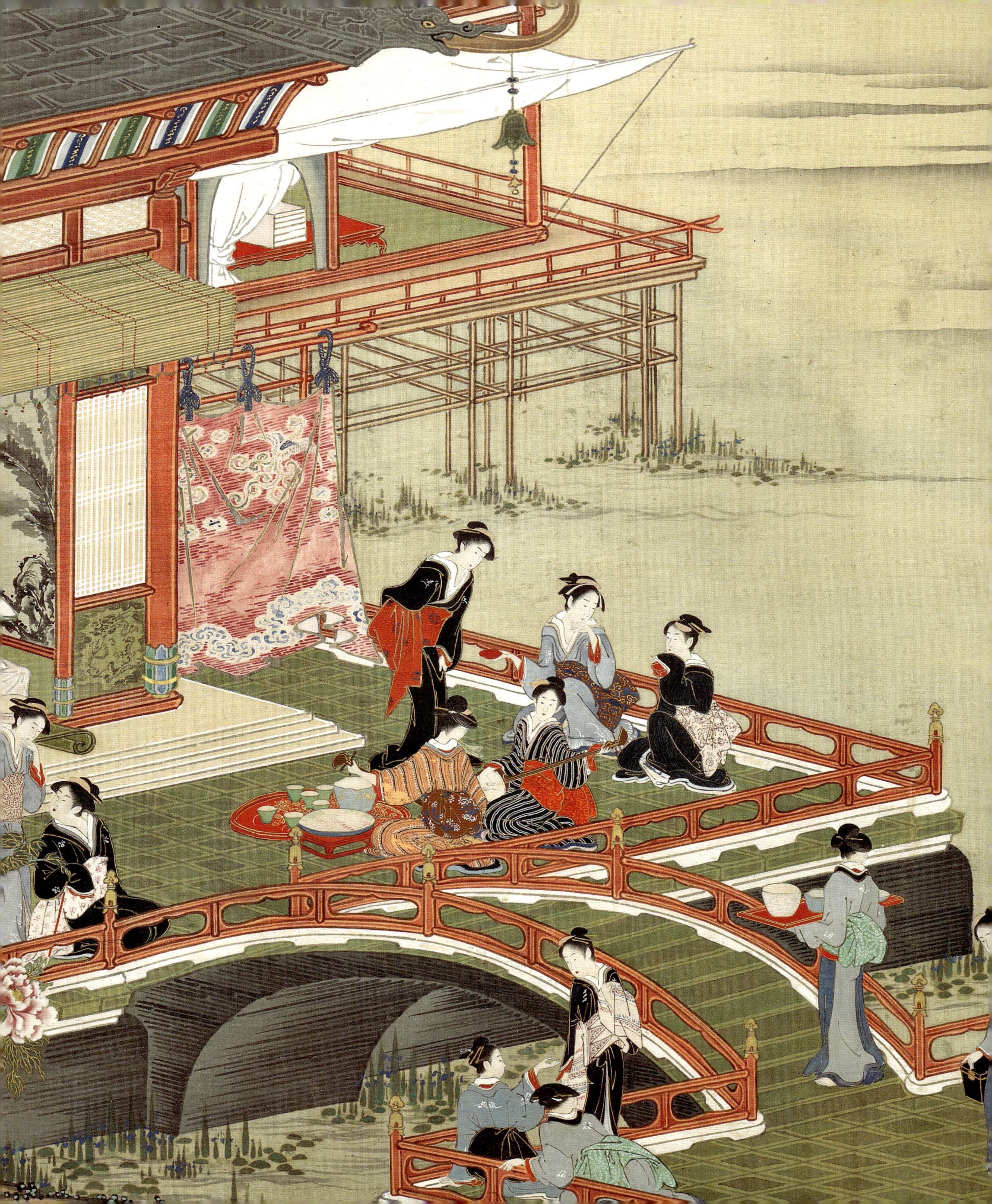

IMAGES OF FEMININE ALLURE, 1780–1805: TORII KIYONAGA AND KITAGAWA UTAMARO

Modern connoisseurs consider prints of beautiful women by Torii Kiyonaga and Kitagawa Utamaro as standing at the pinnacle of ukiyo-e. Kiyonaga's women are informed by a naturalism not found in the works of previous generations. Unlike the almost childlike figures previously favored by Harunobu and his followers, Kiyonaga preferred tall, elongated proportions. This new expression of feminine beauty first appeared in Kiyonaga's prints of the 1780s. Similar qualities can be found in his ukiyo-e paintings, although no more than ten are known to have survived.

Artists from a number of different schools came under Kiyonaga's influence. For example, Katsukawa Shunchō, primarily a print artist who trained under Katsukawa Shunshō, turned to Kiyonaga for inspiration for many of his depictions of beautiful women and for his erotica. Kubo Shunman, a member of the Kitao school active at the beginning of the nineteenth century, similarly followed Kiyonaga's style.

Early in his career Kitagawa Utamaro was Kiyonaga's rival, but by the 1790s he had become the preeminent ukiyo-e artist in Edo. Trained under Toriyama Sekien and initially dependent upon Kiyonaga for his portrayals of women, Utamaro subsequently developed his own distinctive style. His beauties are imbued with a deep sensuousness, often bordering on the erotic. Although Utamaro produced large numbers of woodblock prints and illustrated books, his paintings are few.

*During the late eighteenth century artists hailed from different classes. Whereas Kiyonaga and Utamaro were of townsmen (*chōnin*) heritage, Utamaro's chief competitor, Chōbunsai Eishi, was a samurai of banner-man (*hatamoto*) status who received a hereditary stipend of 500* koku *of rice. Eishi became known for idealized images of beautiful women that were more graceful and serene than those by Utamaro. Also active at this time was the painter Mizuno Rōchō, a banner man who enjoyed a hereditary stipend of 1,450* koku *of rice, which made him somewhat wealthy for the time. Characteristic of the last years of the eighteenth century was the wide support that ukiyo-e enjoyed. Connoisseurs of the genre could be counted among all levels of society, from the emperor and the shogun to the general populace.* AS

36. **TORIYAMA SEKIEN** (1712?–1788)
Night Procession of the Hundred Demons

About the An'ei era (1772–81)
Handscroll; ink, color, and gold on silk
27.8 x 431.5 cm (10 15/16 x 169 7/8 in.)
Signature: Sekien sō Toyofusa hitsu (Brush of Sekien, the old person Toyofusa)
Seal: Kyozai Daigaku no nishi (Residence to the west of Daigaku)
William Sturgis Bigelow Collection 11.7705

One of Toriyama Sekien's important artistic contributions was the publication of illustrated books on monsters and spirits. He published four versions of *Night Procession of a Hundred Monsters and Spirits* (*Hyakki yakō*), each in a three-volume set: *Illustrations of the Night Procession of a Hundred Monsters and Spirits* (*Gazu hyakki yakō*, 1776), *Past and Present Illustrations: More Hundred Monsters and Spirits* (*Konjaku gazu zoku hyakki*, 1779), *Collection of Past and Present Monsters and Spirits* (*Konjaku hyakki shūi*, 1781), and *A Pouch of Musings on Monsters and Spirits* (*Hyakki tsurezure bukuro*, 1784). These proved to be unexpectedly popular in their time. Today some even consider Sekien primarily an artist of the supernatural, but it is unclear whether Sekien himself would have appreciated this characterization.

Unlike the celebrated sixteenth-century handscroll *Night Procession of a Hundred Monsters and Spirits* in the Shinju-an, a subtemple of the Zen monastic complex Daitoku-ji in Kyoto, Sekien's illustrated books on the theme were a type of encyclopedia.[1] Each monster was allotted half a page and properly labeled; in the *Konjaku gazu zoku hyakki*, descriptions were also provided. The MFA's handscroll represents a painted rendition of these encyclopedias. Presumably Sekien made several versions of the scroll upon request, but at present this one is the only known extant example.

The scholar Timothy Clark has pointed out that all the monsters and spirits included in this work correspond to ones illustrated in the 1776 *Gazu hyakki yakō*, except for two, which appeared later in the 1779 *Konjaku gazu zoku hyakki*.[2] In order of appearance they can be identified as:

kodama	Tree spirits represented by an elderly couple
nekomata	Transmogrifying old cat with two tails
nobusama	Flying squirrel (which appears in the *Konjaku gazu zoku hyakki*)
kappa	Amphibious creature with either scales or a shell and a pool of water on its head
kawauso	Otter believed to trick people and pull them underwater
kitsunebi	Will-o'-the-wisp
Uba ga hi	The spirit of an old woman who became a will-o'-the-wisp because she stole oil from votive lamps
tanuki	Raccoon-dog, believed to be a transmogrifier and trickster
tengu	A goblinlike creature living in the mountains with a red face, a beaklike nose, and wings
Yamauba	Mythical hag living deep in the mountains
inugami	Haunted spirits of dogs
ushioni	Bull ogre

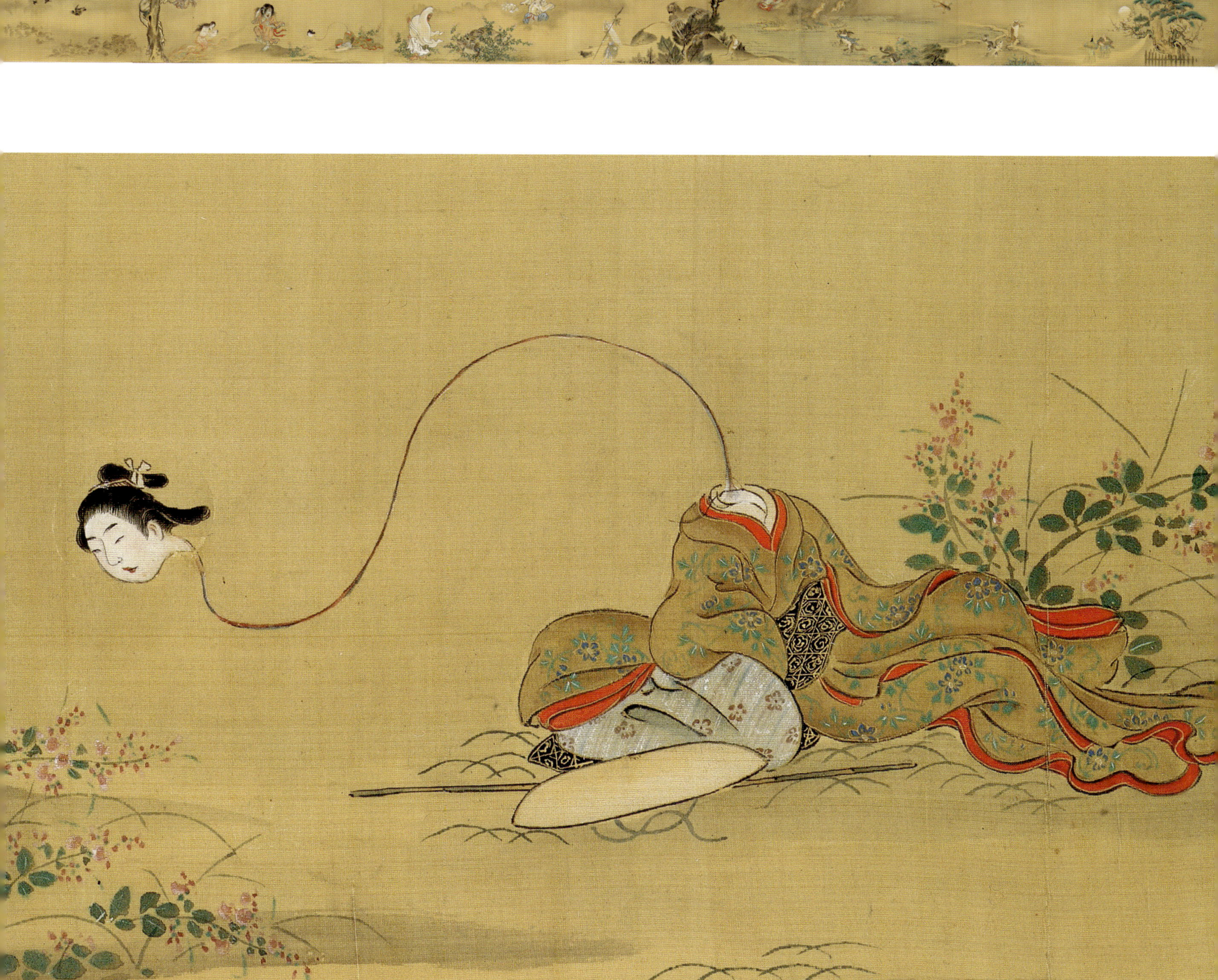

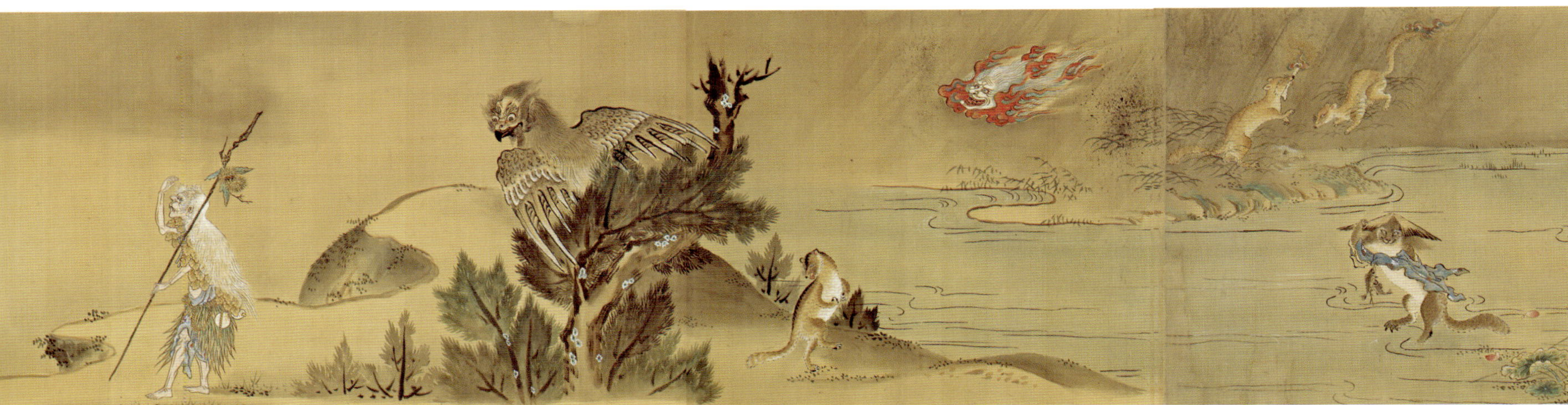

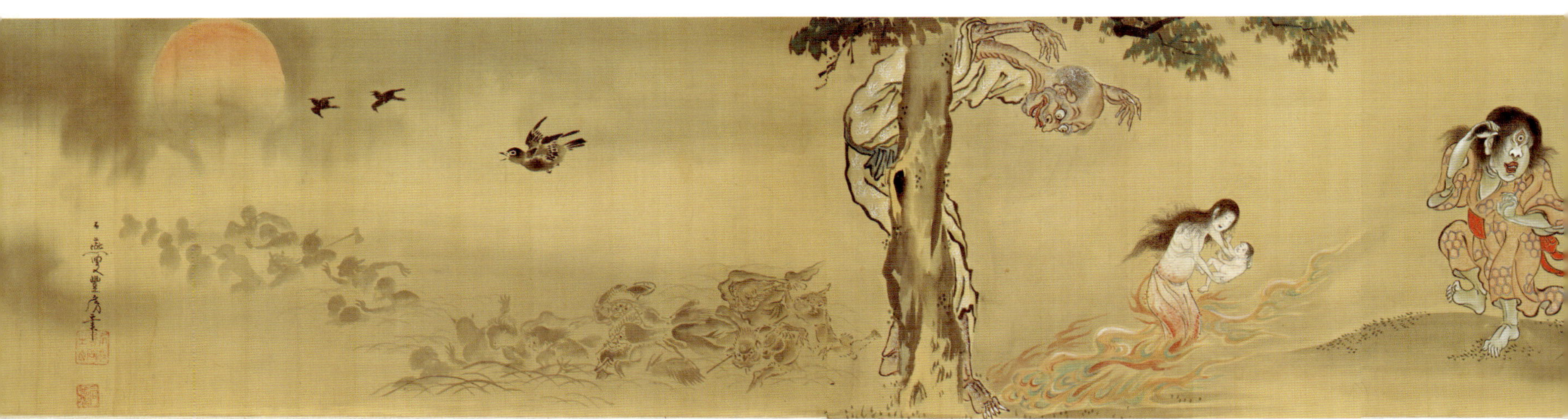

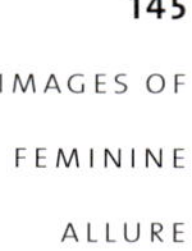

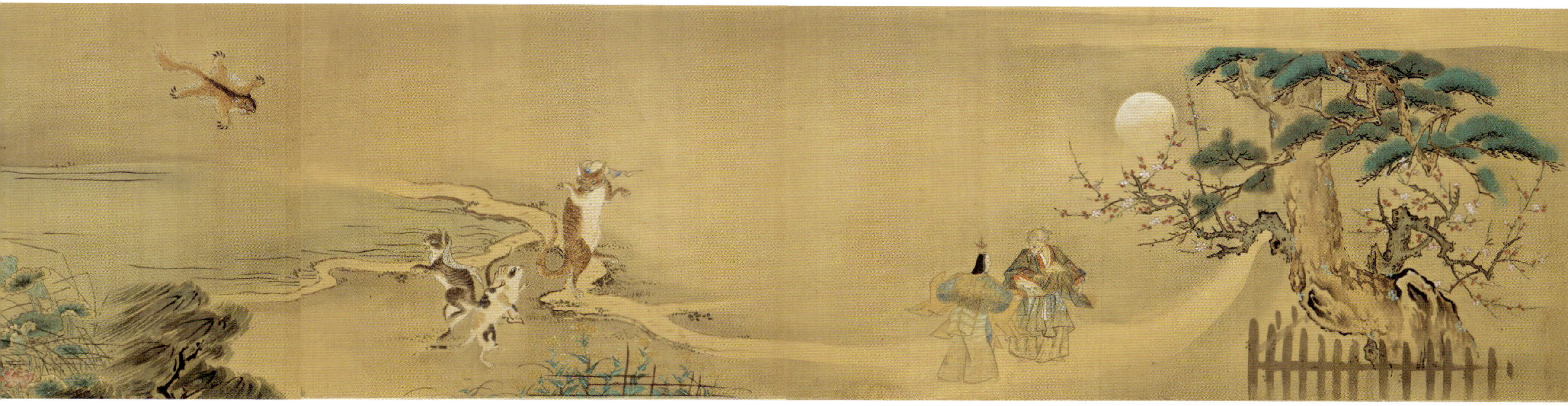

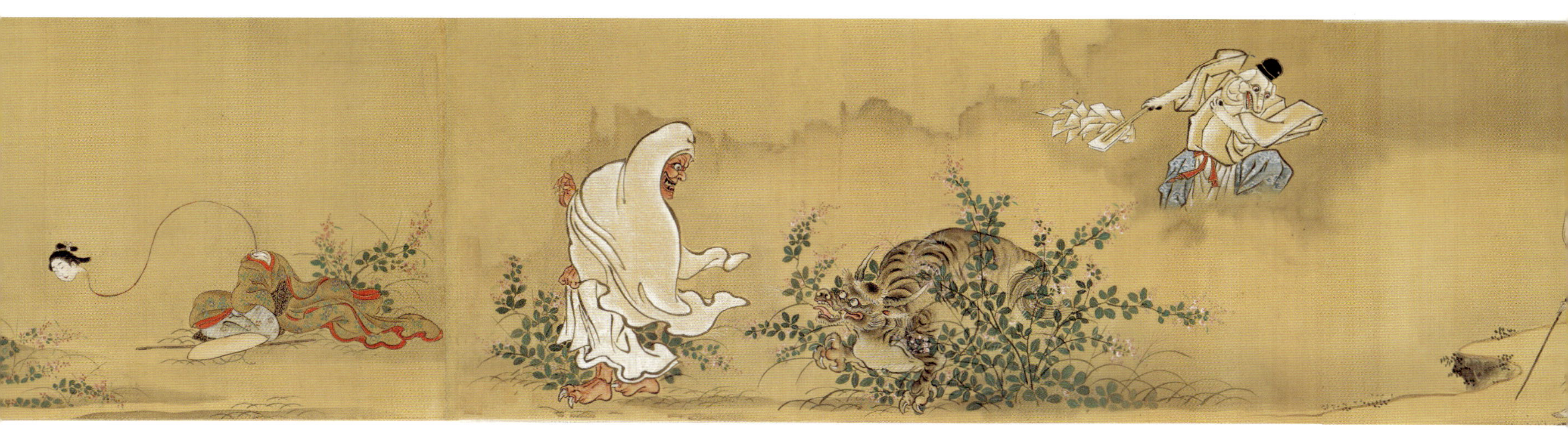

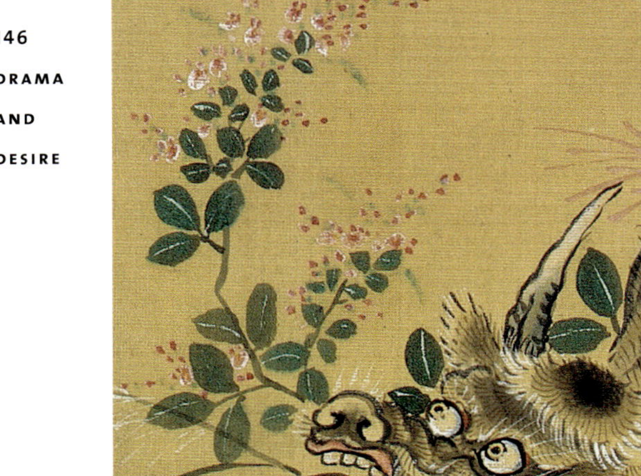

gakoze	(nature unknown)
rokurokubi	Monster with elongated neck
yamawarawa	Also known as *yamawaro*, a creature living in the mountains, or a *kappa* that has retreated to the mountains in winter
ubume	Spirits of women who have died in childbirth and have been transformed into mythical birds
Mikoshi	Also known as Mikoshi nyūdō, a large monster with a long neck that peeks at people from around folding screens.

In addition there are the hundred monsters and spirits running away from the rising sun, an image that can be found in the *Konjaku gazu zoku hyakki*.

According to the preface of the 1776 printed version of *Gazu hyakki yakō*, the project was originally conceived as a six-volume set, which would have included the images in *Konjaku gazu zoku hyakki*. Therefore, the MFA scroll must have been painted sometime after the publication of the 1776 printed three-volume set but before the 1779 *Konjaku gazu zoku hyakki* was issued and the original plan was altered. Sekien's signature and seals appear at the end of the scroll. One of these seals reads "Residence to the west of Daigaku," a reference to his home in Nezu, near Ueno. The only other work known to have the same seal is a set of three hanging scrolls by the artist, entitled *The No Dance-Drama Okina*, in the Mary Griggs Burke Collection, New York.[3] In these works the signature reads, "Painted by Sekien, who is now seventy years old." The seal impression on the *Sanbasō* paintings is much more worn than the one in this scroll, thereby providing additional evidence for the dating of the work. AS

1. *Night Procession of a Hundred Monsters and Spirits* (*Hyakki yakō zu*), first half of the sixteenth century, handscroll, ink and color on paper, published in Tsuji Nobuo, *Nihon bijutsu no rekishi: Jōmon kara manga anime made* (Tokyo: Tōkyō daigaku shuppan, 2005), 239.
2. Timothy Clark, "Hyakki yakō zukan," in *Bosuton bijutsukan nikuhitsu ukiyo-e*, vol. 3 (Tokyo: Museum of Fine Arts, Boston, and Kōdansha, 2000), 160–61.
3. Toriyama Sekien, *The No Dance-Drama Okina*, 1781, set of three hanging scrolls, ink, color, and gold on paper, 87.3 x 27.2 cm, Mary Griggs Burke Collection, New York, published in Miyeko Murase, *Bridge of Dreams: The Mary Griggs Burke Collection of Japanese Art* (New York: Metropolitan Museum of Art, 2000), 363.

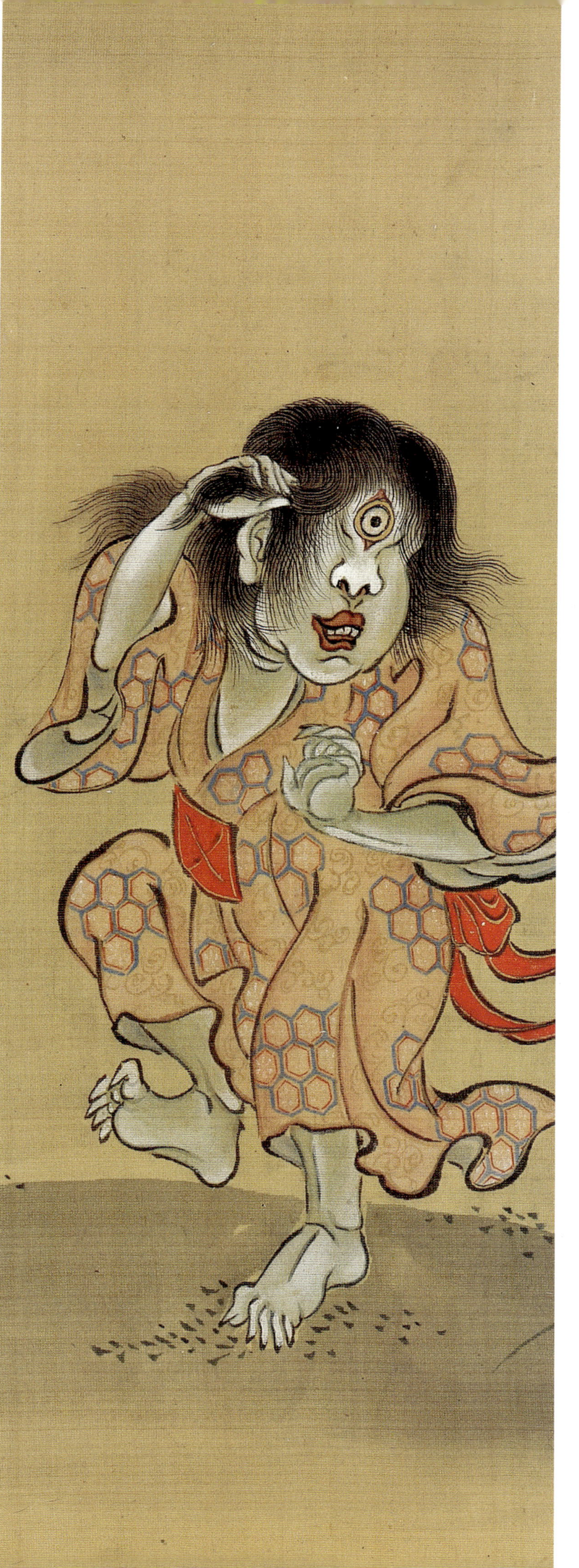

37. **TORII KIYONAGA** (1752–1815)

Two Women beneath a Willow Tree

About Tenmei 4 (1784)
Hanging scroll; ink, color, and gold on silk
87.5 x 34.4 cm (34 7/16 x 13 9/16 in.)
Signature: Seki Kiyonaga ga
(Painted by Seki[guchi] Kiyonaga)
Seal: Seki Kiyonaga
William Sturgis Bigelow Collection 11.7531

On a summer's eve two women — thought to be a mother and daughter — pause under a willow tree on the banks of a stream for a bit of conversation. The older woman, returning from the bath, holds her still loosened chrysanthemum-decorated obi over her left hand; her lightweight black ikat (*kasuri*) kimono falls open to reveal white underrobes. The younger woman leans back to listen; she is dressed in a light pink tie-dyed robe secured with a broad red brocade sash.

In the mid-1780s Torii Kiyonaga created two hanging scrolls of women resting on benches along the waterfront. *Three Women Cooling off at Matsuchiyama,* in the Freer/Sackler Gallery, Washington, D.C., is a monumental composition of a group of friends set against a detailed panorama of the Sumida River.[1] In contrast, this work — considered one of Kiyonaga's masterpieces — reveals how effectively the artist was able to convey the relationship of the women and the ambience of the evening using an economy of forms. The authority of the older woman is clearly established by her statuesque form, which is emphasized by the modeling and layering of the robes — particularly the red underrobe, which is visible through the semitransparent dark ikat material. The fluid calligraphic lines defining the outer kimono of the daughter suggest her more youthful vivaciousness. By positioning the bodies of the two women so that the lines of the heads and right arms create a straight line, and by mirroring the shapes of the daughter's left sleeve and the mother's obi, Kiyonaga communicates the intimacy of the two. The hazy summer evening is evoked by the bands of ink wash across the sky and the stillness of the willow tree that arches over and unifies the figures below.

Although during his early career Kiyonaga produced numerous actor prints under the influence of his mentor Torii Kiyomitsu (about 1735–1785), in the last years of the 1770s he created compositions of fashionable young women. The first of these adopted the petite canon of feminine beauty that had been established by Suzuki Harunobu. However, during the 1780s Kiyonaga developed his own mature style in which he introduced a new naturalism and gave his figures more substantial proportions. This style, which was later termed "classical" by nineteenth- and early twentieth-century art historians, was adopted by most ukiyo-e artists during the late eighteenth century.

Kiyonaga is credited with having produced more than 100 woodblock-print series and 145 woodblock-printed books.[2] His output of paintings was extremely limited by comparison. In her groundbreaking book *Kiyonaga: A Study of His Life and Works* (1939), Chie Hirano, the noted authority on the artist and researcher at the Museum of Fine Arts, Boston, established that just over thirty paintings could be safely attributed to the artist;

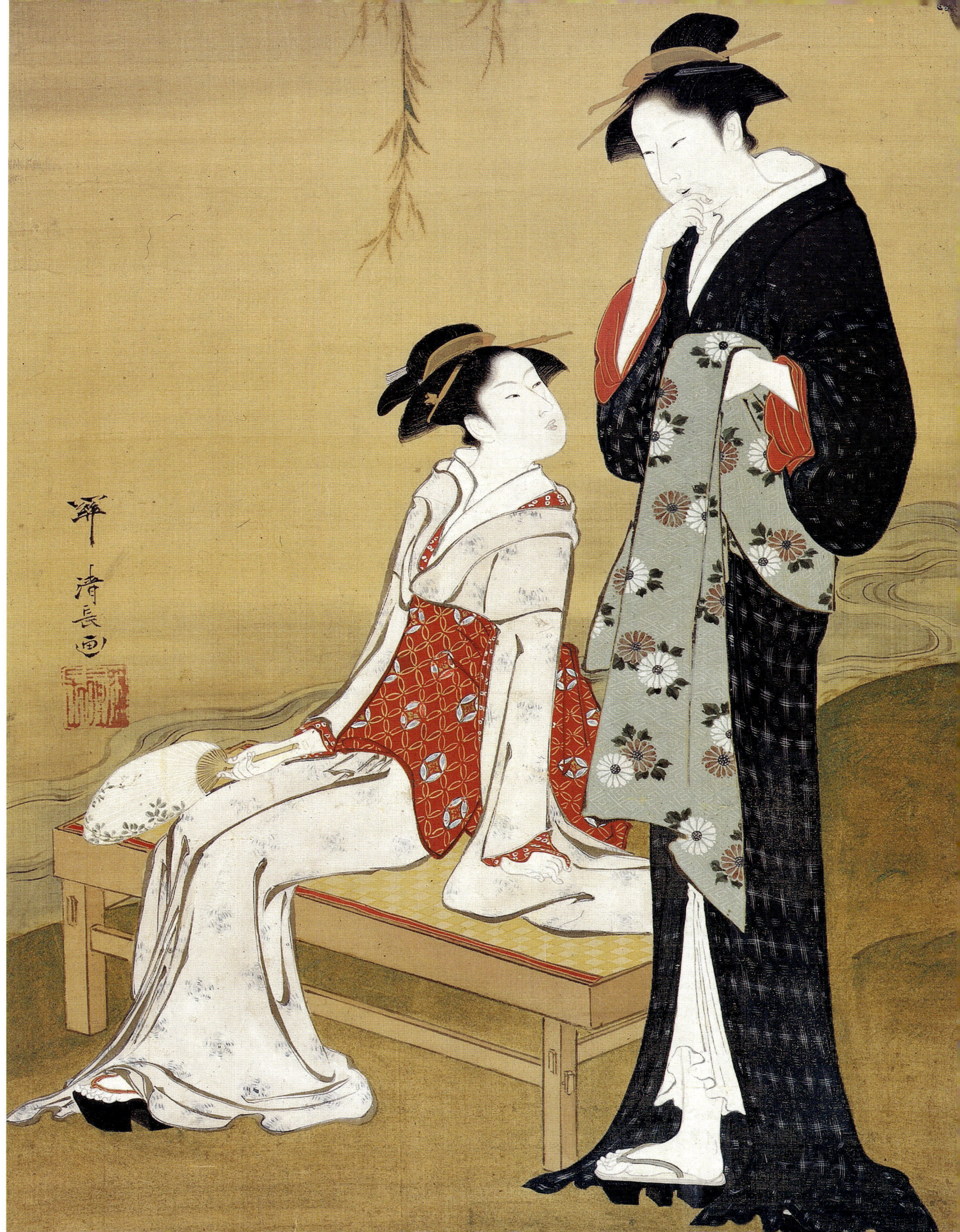
清長画

later scholars, such as Asano Shūgō, have concurred.[3] Hirano noted that Kiyonaga frequently used similar compositional devices in his paintings and prints. However, she remarked that the prints, which were dependent upon the woodblock carver's skill, could never capture the vigor of his brushstrokes.[4] ANM

1. Illustrated in Harold P. Stern, *Ukiyo-e Painting* (Washington, DC: Smithsonian Institution, 1973), 174.
2. Richard Lane, *Images from the Floating World: The Japanese Print* (Seacaucus, NJ: Chartwell Books, 1978), 288–90.
3. Chie Hirano, *Kiyonaga: A Study of His Life and Works* (Cambridge, MA: Harvard University Press, 1939), 475–85; and Asano Shūgō, "Torii Kiyonaga no nikuhitsu ga," in *Azabu bijutsu kōgeikan*, vol. 6 of *Nikuhitsu ukiyo-e taikan* (Tokyo: Kōdansha, 1995), 217–19.
4. Hirano, *Kiyonaga*, 146.

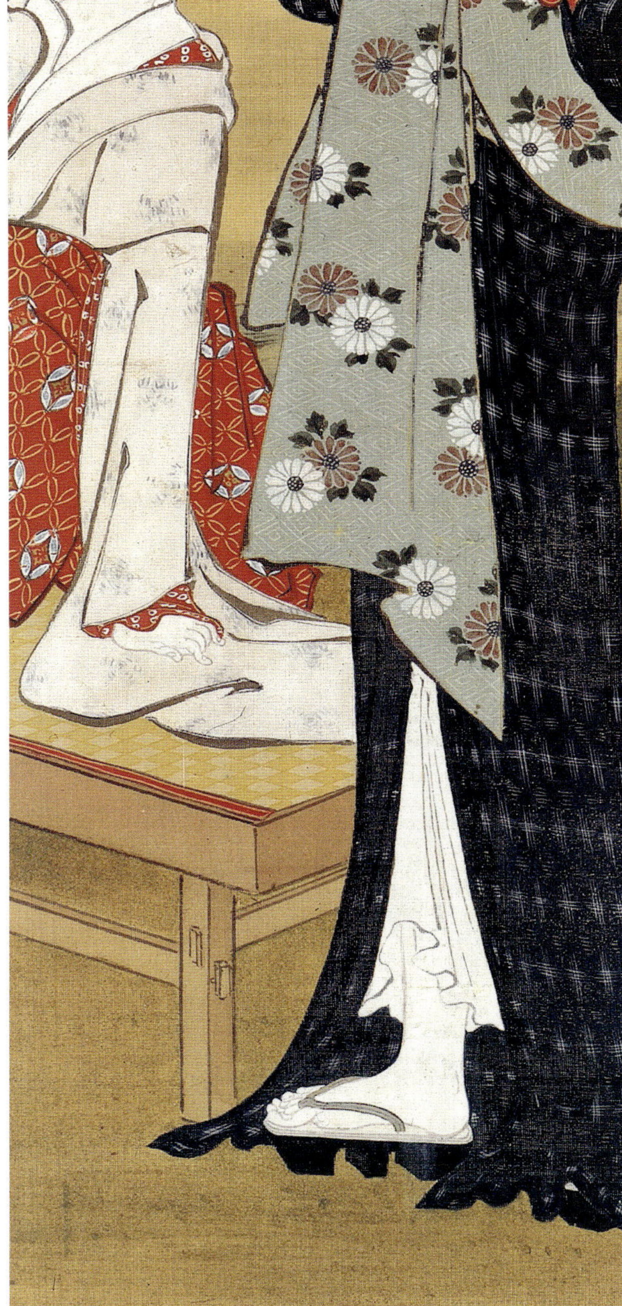

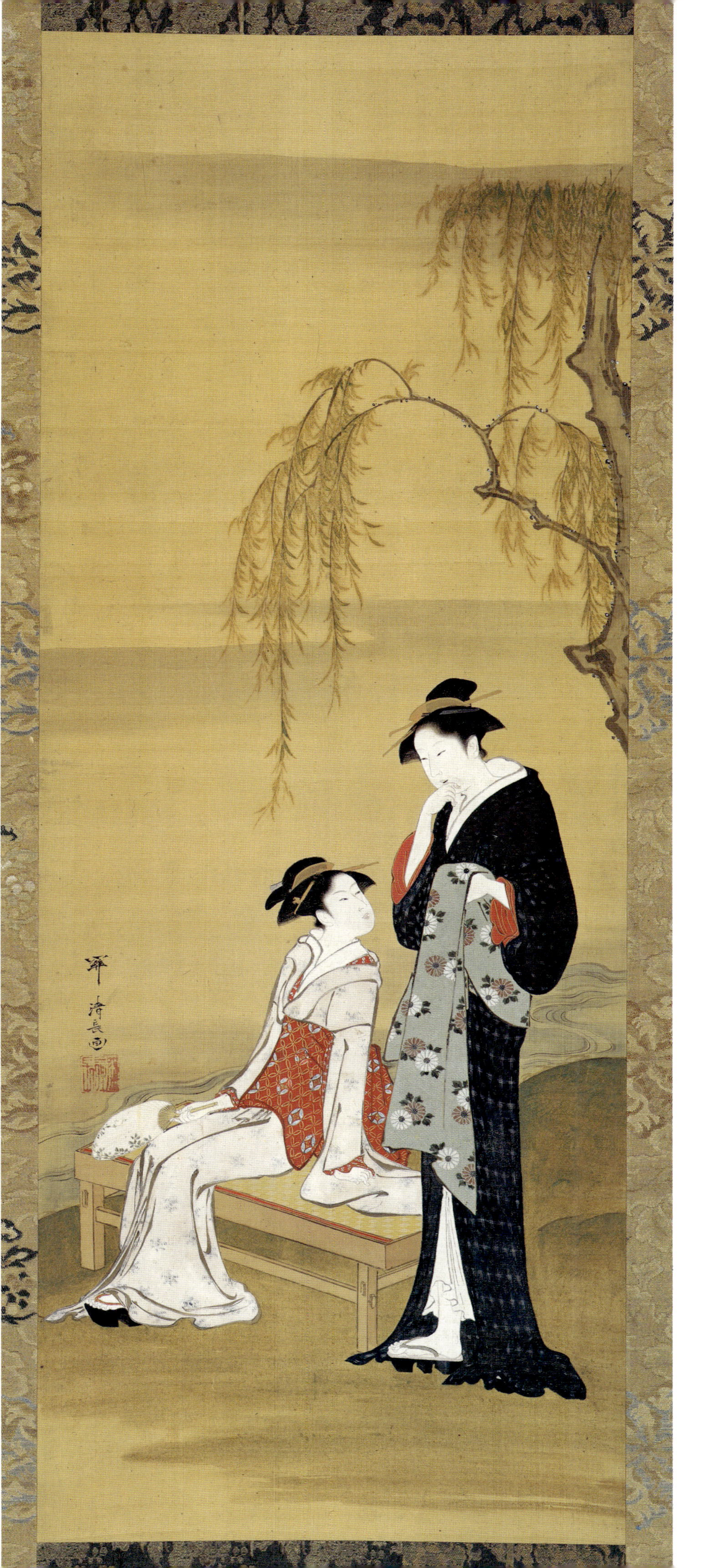

38. **KATSUKAWA SHUNCHŌ** (ACTIVE ABOUT 1781–1801)
Collection of Suggestive Pictures

About the late Tenmei (1781–89) or early Kansei (1789–1801) era
Handscroll; ink, color, gold, and mica on silk
26.9 x 442.1 cm (10 9/16 x 174 3/16 in.)
Signature: Katsu Shunchō sha (Copied by Katsu[kawa] Shunchō)
Seal: cipher
William Sturgis Bigelow Collection Res. 09.239

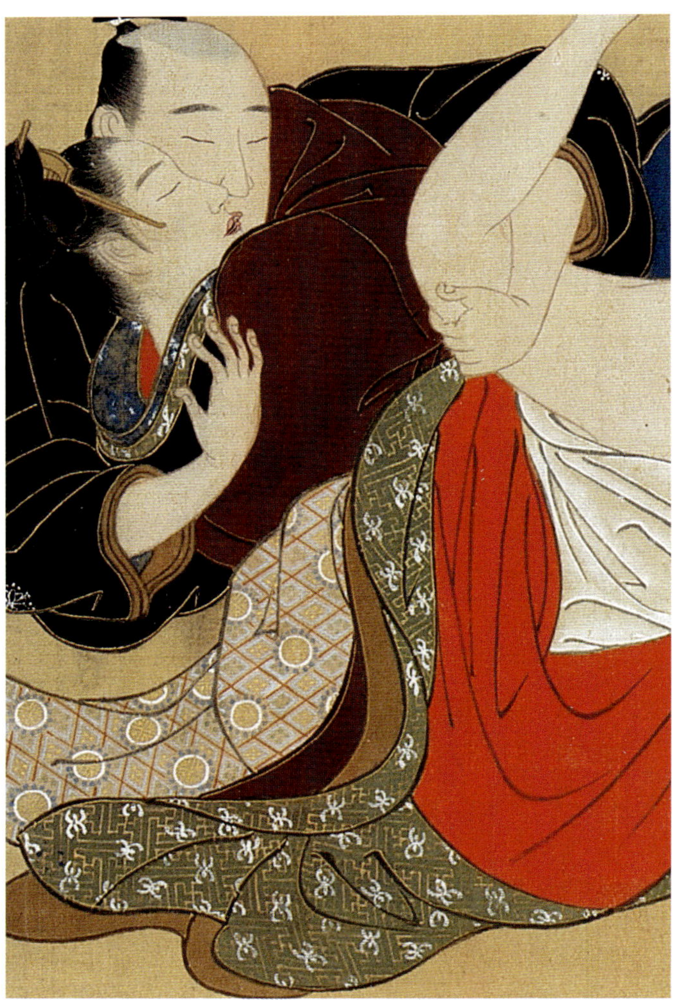

The twelve illustrations of this erotic handscroll capture couples engaged in lovemaking as if the scenes were taking place in a dream. Produced by Katsukawa Shunchō, the leading painter of images of beautiful women (*bijinga*) in the 1780s and 1790s, their style is almost identical to that of his teacher Katsukawa Shunshō, who also produced a great number of *shunga* during the late 1780s and early 1790s.

As an artist, Shunchō was a fascinating individual. In many of his woodblock prints of beautiful women he copied the style of his master's rival Torii Kiyonaga. Eventually, he came to be viewed in ukiyo-e circles as a sort of heir to Kiyonaga after the Torii master retired from *bijinga* production. If this scroll is compared with Shunchō's own woodblock-printed *Collection of Twelve Amorous Illustrations* (*Kōshoku zue jūnikō*), the artist's ability to produce images in both the Shunshō and Kiyonaga styles becomes evident.[1] Here the Katsukawa mode may be seen in the meticulous treatment of the various decorative objects and in how the expression of the lovers was made more interesting by the vibrating lines used to depict their closed eyelids. NM

1. Katsukawa Shunchō, *Kōshoku zue jūnikō*, about 1784–85, set of twelve woodblock prints, ink and color on paper, each 25 x 36 cm, published in Fukuda Kazuhiko, ed., *Hikan Utamaro Kiyonaga Eishi Koryūsai Shunchō* (Tokyo: Haga shoten, 1976), plates 56–63.

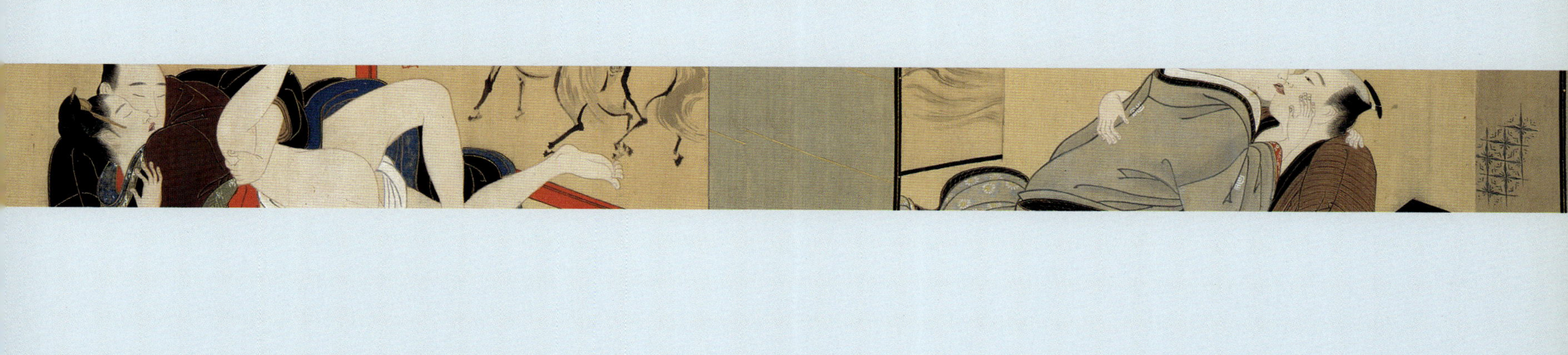

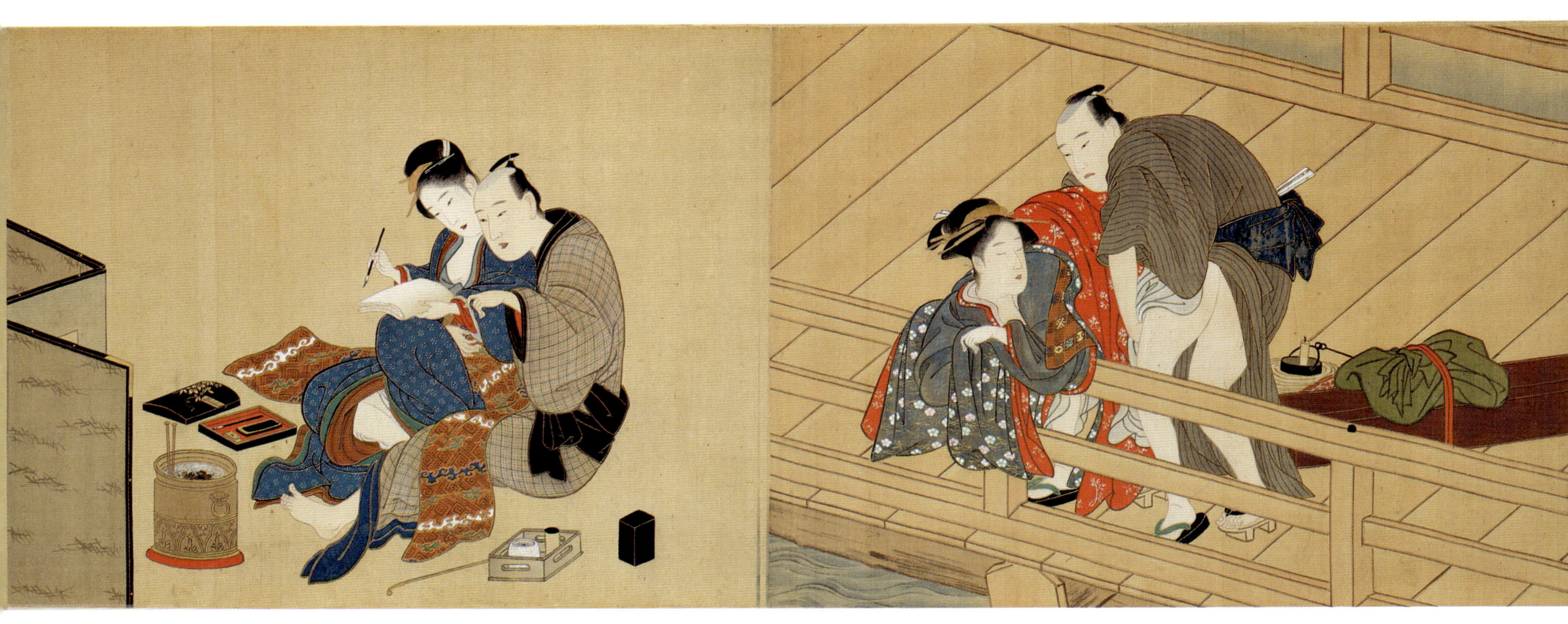

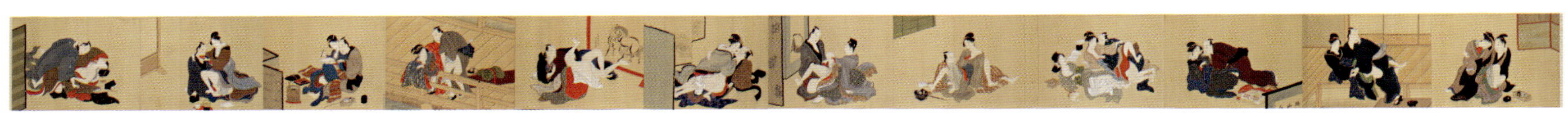

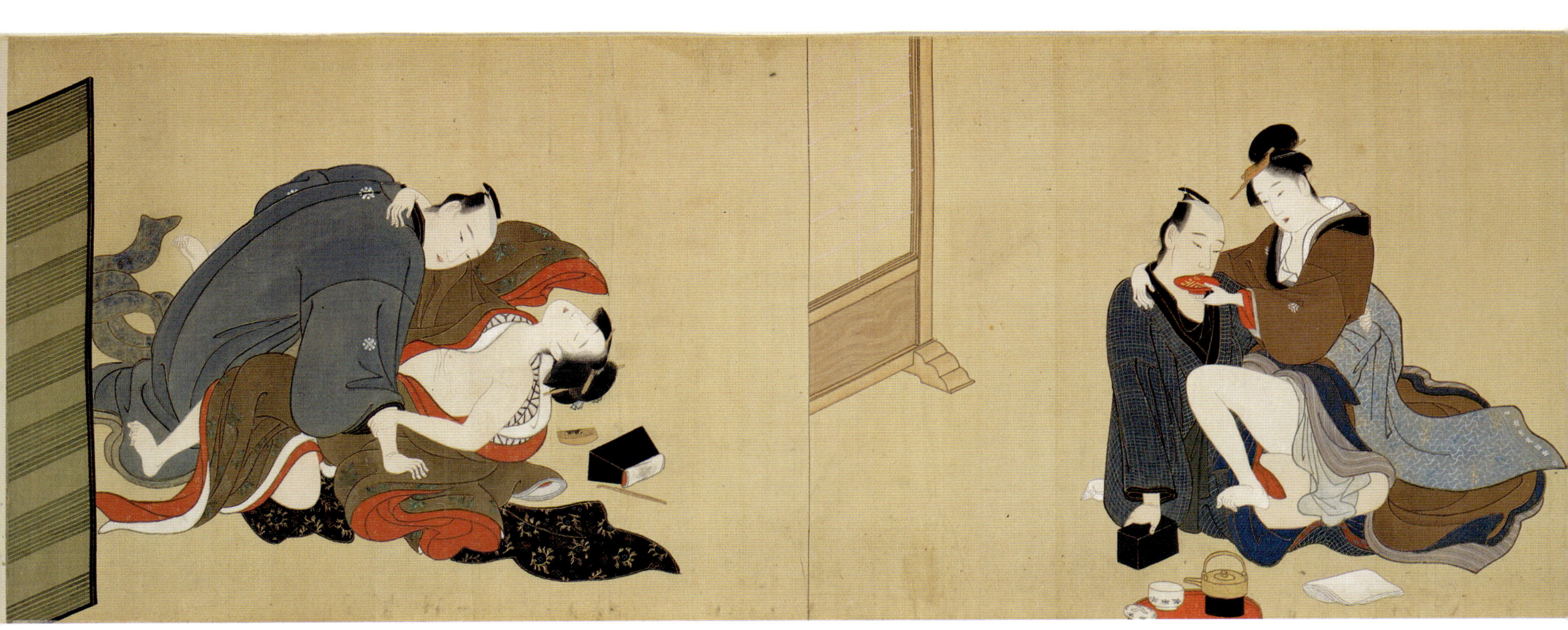

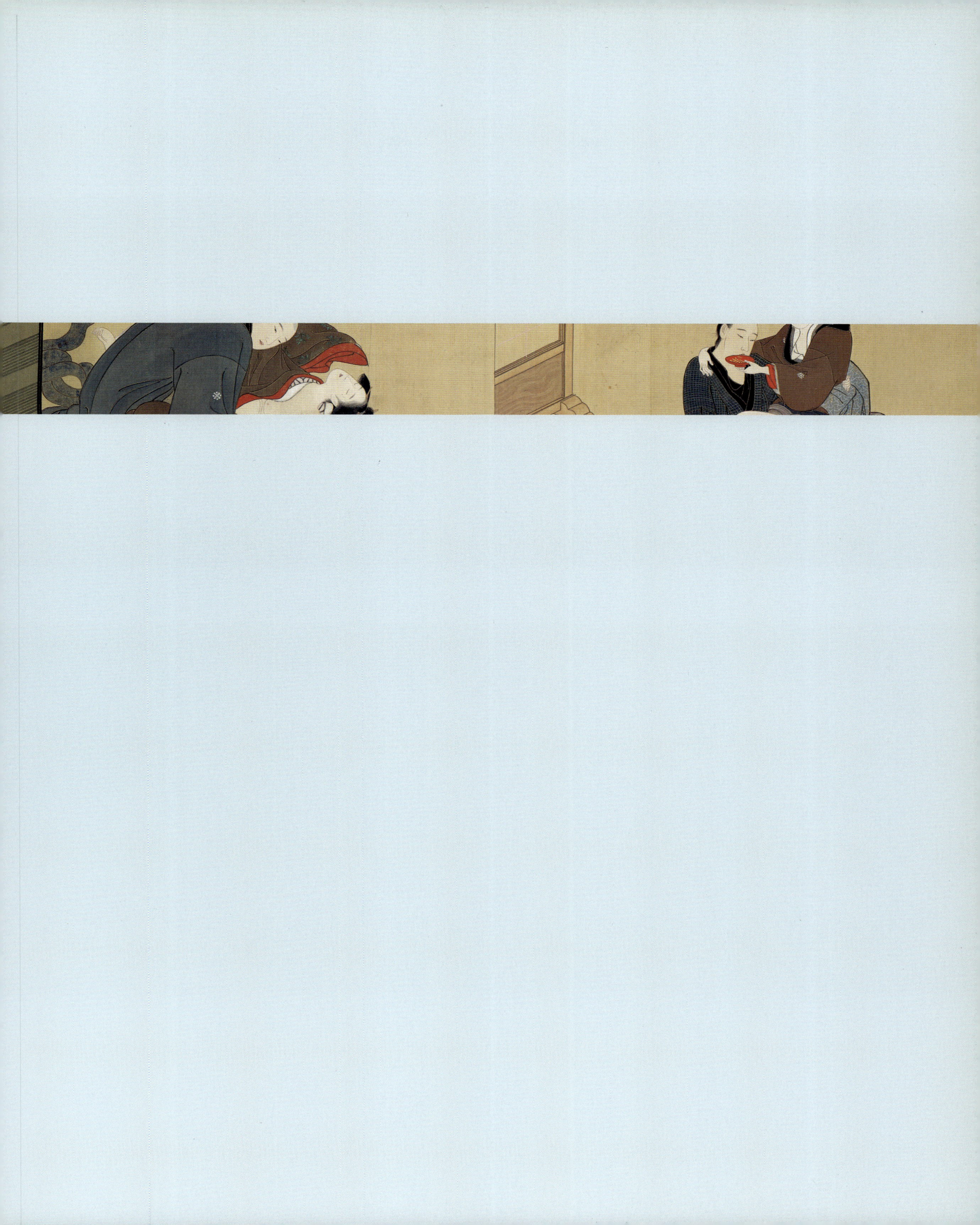

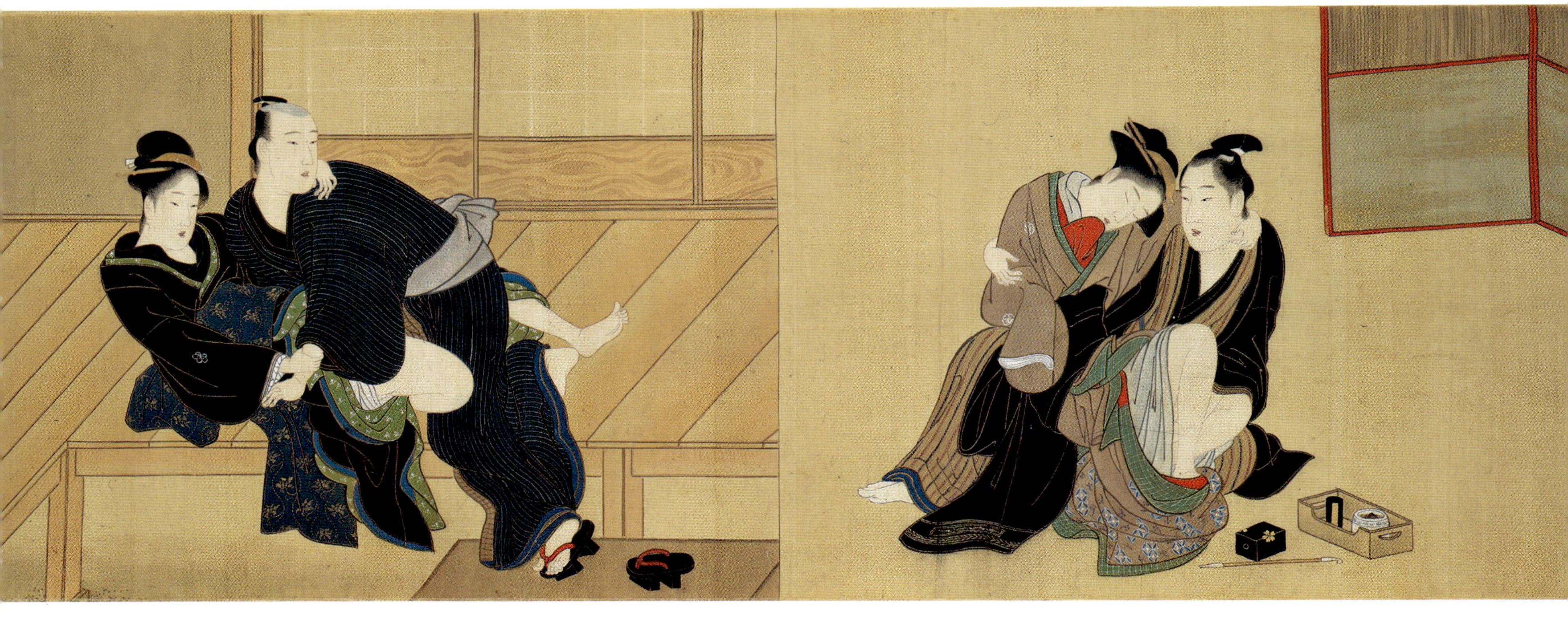

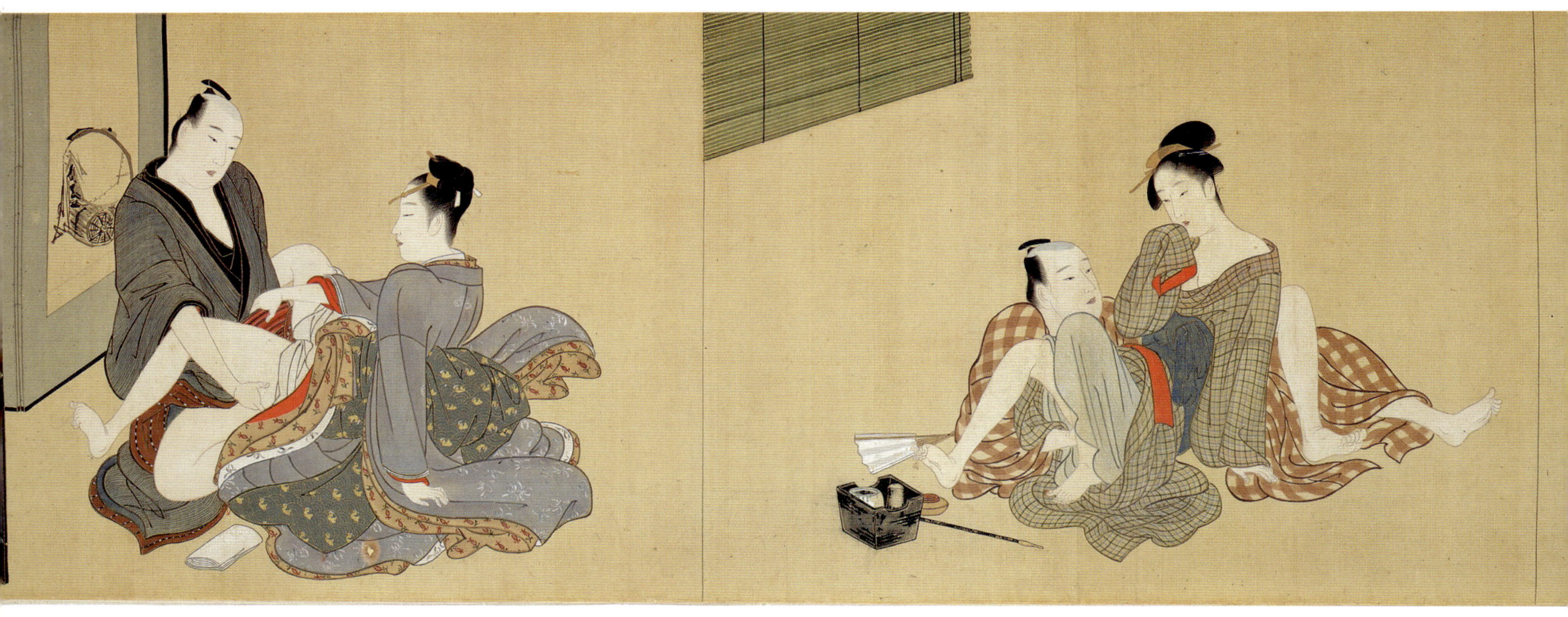

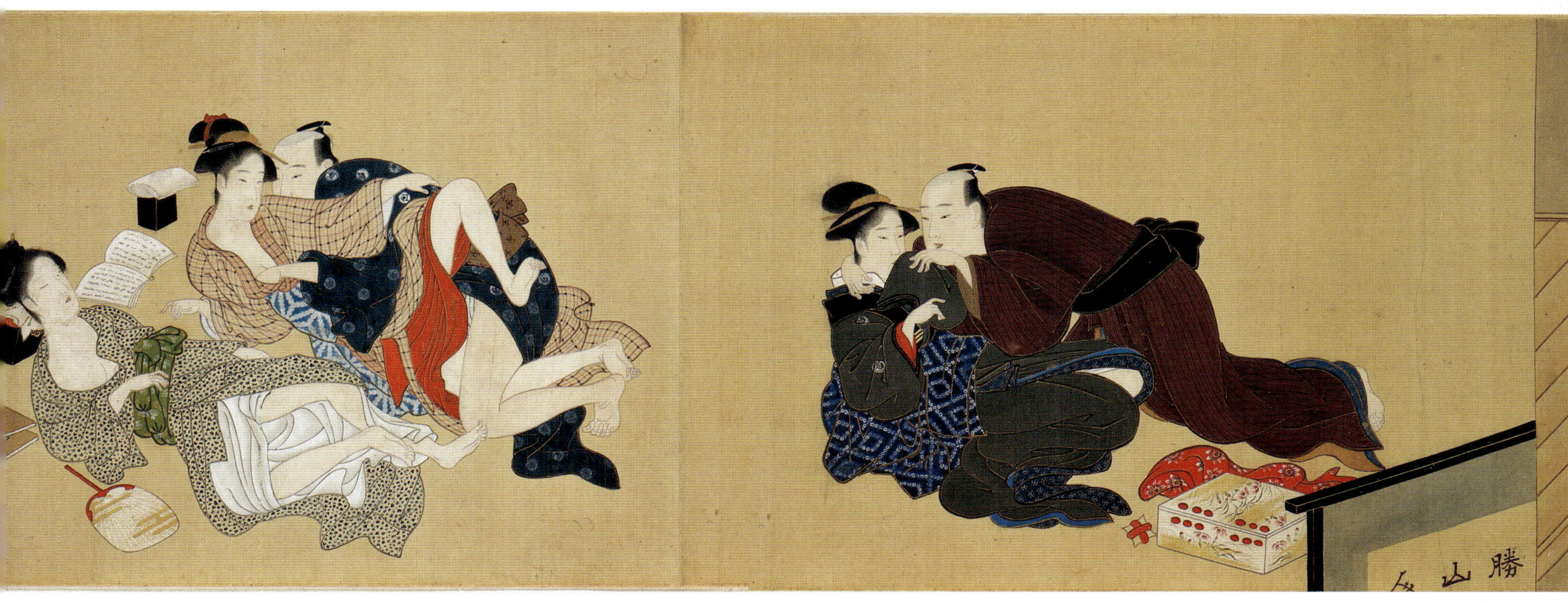
勝山

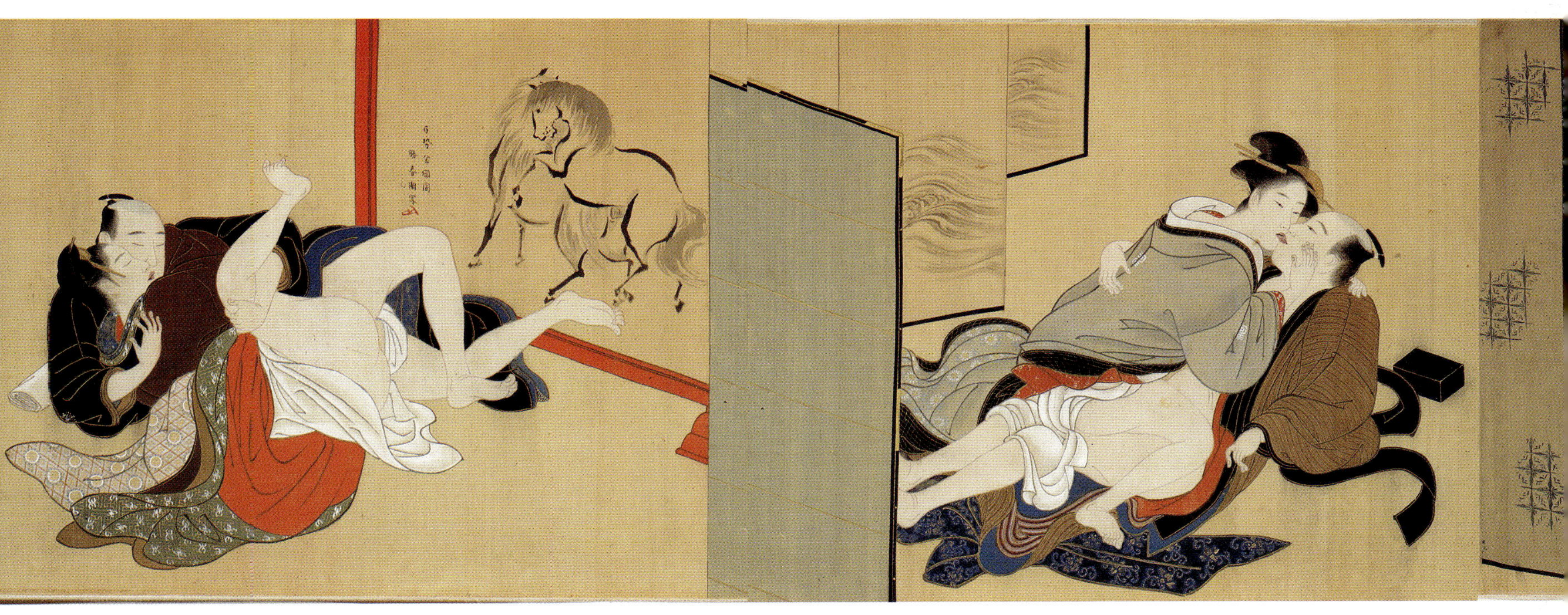

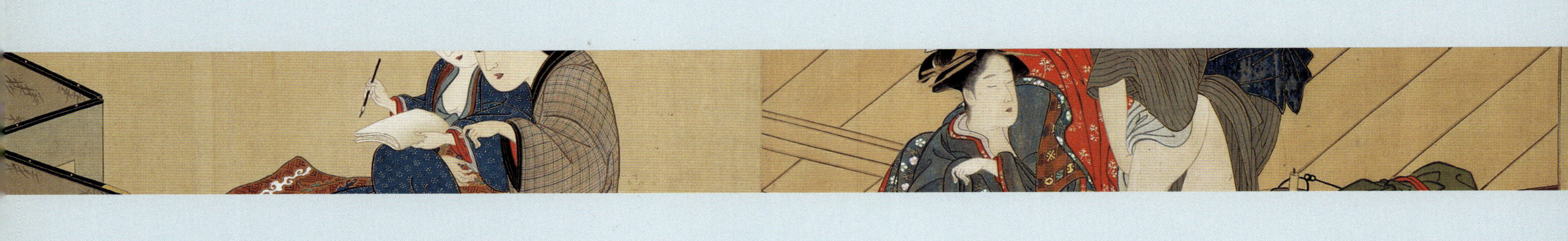

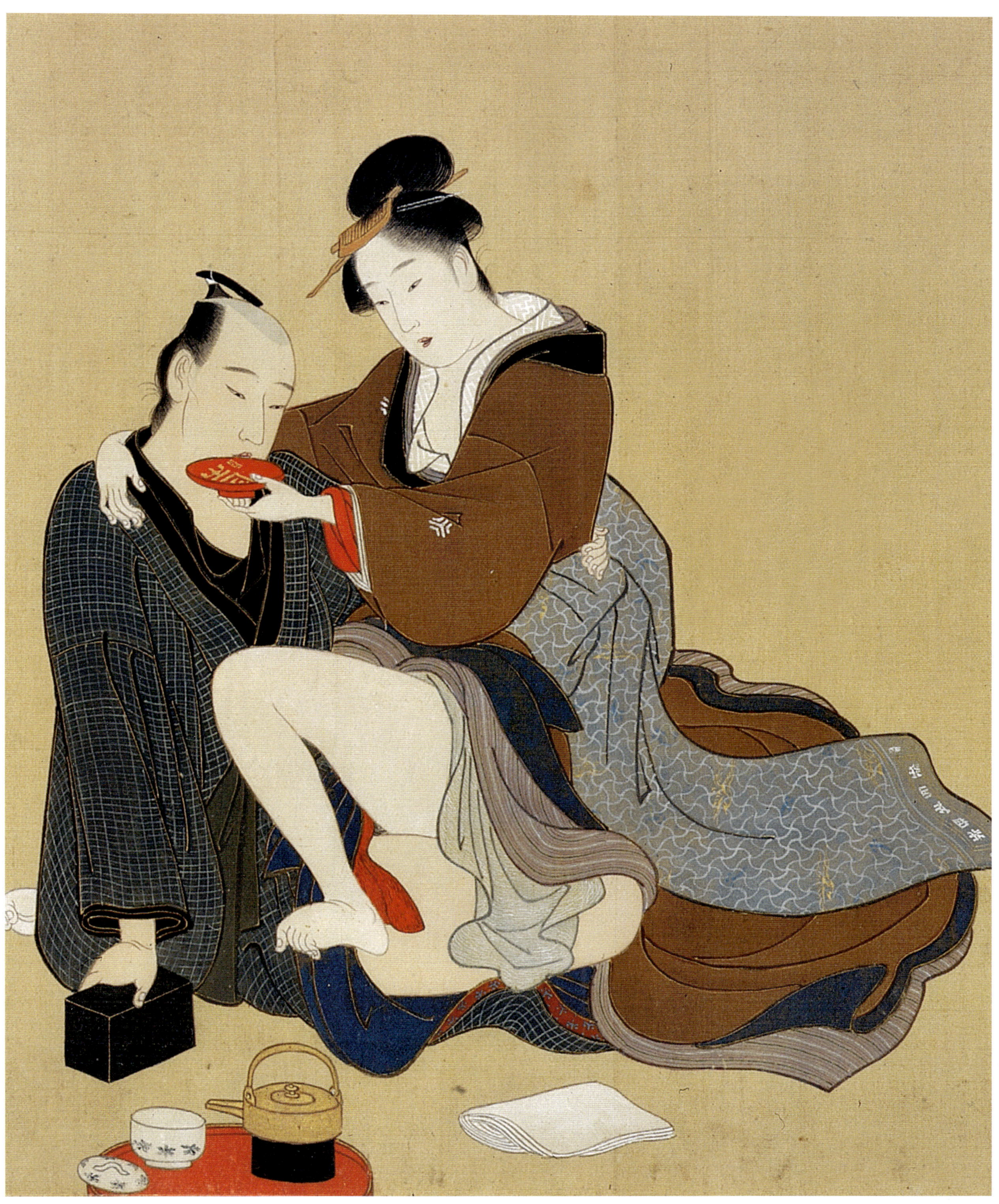

39. **KUBO SHUNMAN** (1757–1820)

Women at a Fulling Block

About the latter half of the Tenmei era (1781–89)
Hanging scroll; ink and light color on silk
76.8 x 30.6 cm (30 1/4 x 12 1/16 in.)
Signature: Kubo Shunman ga
(Painted by Kubo Shunman)
Seal: cipher
William Sturgis Bigelow Collection 11.7753

This painting of a village woman beating cloth underneath an old pine tree by a stream and a young townswoman standing next to her was executed almost exclusively in different tones of ink, with only touches of red and indigo. The technique is known as *sumi saishiki* (literally, "ink coloring"), and this terminology appeared in Kubo Shunman's own advertisements. Isoda Koryūsai is considered to have been the first artist to use *sumi saishiki*, but Shunman was the one who enthusiastically promoted it. He not only created the greatest number of extant paintings in the elegant technique, but also adopted it for his woodblock prints, which were known as *murasaki-e* (literally, "purple pictures") or *benigirai-e* (literally, "disliking red pictures").

The theme of the scroll is the Tama River for Pounding Cloth (Kinuta no Tamagawa) in Mishima, Settsu province, one of the Jewel Rivers (Tamagawa) located throughout Japan that had been individually celebrated in poetry since the eighth century. During the Edo period they were collectively known as the Six Jewel Rivers (Mu Tamagawa). The poem associated with the Tama River for Pounding Cloth is one by the eccentric twelfth-century poet Minamoto no Shunrai, included in the *Anthology of Japanese Poems of a Thousand Years* (*Senzai wakashū*).

Matsukaze no	Even the sound of
oto dani aki wa	breezes blowing through the pines
sabishiki ni	makes autumn lonely—
koromo utsunari	cloth-fullers are still at work
Tamagawa no sato.	in Tamagawa Village.

The iconography of the painting is clearly based on the poem, for it includes the wind, the pine tree, and the townswoman's dress blowing in the breeze. However, the gust does not appear to affect the young village woman or the surrounding undergrowth. The two women look off to the upper right; the moon must be shining beyond their gaze.

The composition of women at a fulling block must have been popular because at least four or five similar works by Shunman remain. Of these the representative work is the scroll in the Chiba City Museum, which was done a little later than the MFA painting, at the end of the Tenmei to the beginning of the Kansei eras. However, the Chiba painting's polychrome composition has been made more orderly, by eliminating the wind in the upper section and the red maple leaves.[1] Thus, the more complicated MFA scroll may be viewed as the prototype for these other paintings featuring women at a fulling block. However, it is not the earliest Shunman work with this theme; another *sumi saishiki* scroll, in which the townswoman lifts her left hand while holding her skirt with her right—now in a private collection—preceded it.[2] Shunman probably slightly revised this earlier work to create the MFA painting. AS

1. Kubo Shunman, *Pounding Cloth*, late Tenmei era (1781–89), hanging scroll, ink and color on silk, 78.9 x 30.2 cm, Chiba City Museum, published in *Chiba-shi bijutsukan*, vol. 10 of *Nikuhitsu ukiyo-e taikan* (Tokyo: Kōdansha, 1994), illustration 26.
2. Kubo Shunman, *Women at a Fulling Block*, hanging scroll, ink and light color on silk, private collection, published in *Bosuton bijutsukan nikuhitsu ukiyo-e*, vol. 2 (Tokyo: Museum of Fine Arts, Boston, and Kōdansha, 2000), 167.

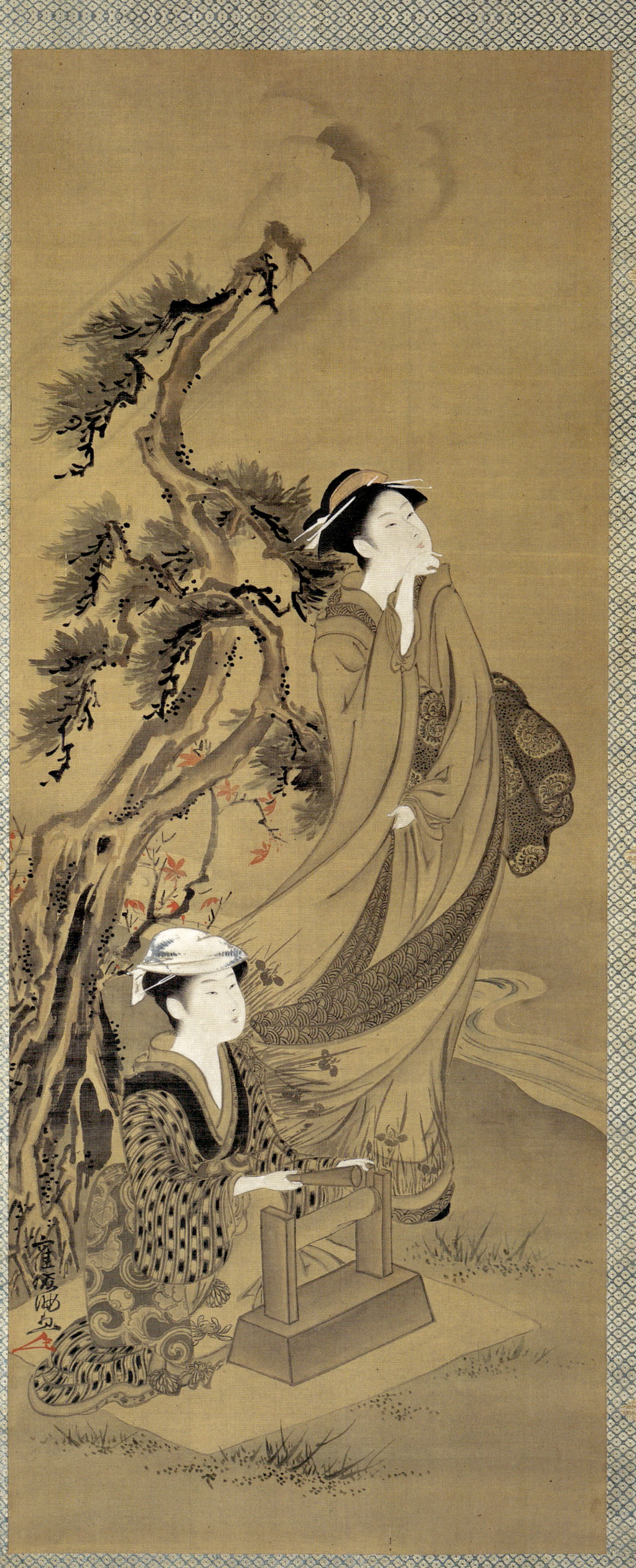

40. **KUBO SHUNMAN** (1757–1820)
Parody of Takasago

About latter half of the Tenmei (1781–89) or first half of the Kansei (1789–1801) era
Hanging scroll; ink and color on silk
79.4 x 29.5 cm (31 1/4 x 11 5/8 in.)
Signature: Kubo Shunman ga (Painted by Kubo Shunman)
Seal: Shunman
William Sturgis Bigelow Collection 11.7749

Takasago (Dune) is a fifteenth-century No play that centers on the legend of the eternal love of a couple, whose spirits came to reside in two pine trees, one on the beach at Takasago on the Inland Sea and the other at the Suminoe Shrine (Sumiyoshi), near Osaka. The legend's continuing popularity has been ensured through the recitation at wedding banquets of lines such as "Takasago! Our light craft under all sail, our light craft under all sail, slips out with the moon, rising, the flood-tide swells."[1] Traditional depictions of the play include figures of the old couple, the woman holding a broom underneath a gnarled pine tree and the man standing with a rake.

In ukiyo-e it was common to present the theme as a parody (*mitate-e* or *yatsushi-e*). Here Shunman replaces the old man, Jō, with a samurai youth, his forelock still unshorn, carrying a small rake more appropriate for a stage dance, and the aged woman, Uba, with a young beauty with a broom at her feet. Earlier representations include Suzuki Harunobu's woodblock diptych *Parody of Jō and Uba*, which he made as calendar prints (*e-goyomi*) for 1765.[2]

All of Shunman's best, most refined work was produced during the late 1780s, when he made this painting. At the time, the artist was perfecting a mode of depicting beautiful, dignified women modeled on those of Torii Kiyonaga. The circular relief seal that Shunman impressed on this painting was one that he began to use in place of his cipher around 1788; it would become his primary seal until the beginning of the nineteenth century. AS

---

1. Royall Tyler, ed. and trans., *Japanese No Dramas* (London: Penguin Books, 1992), 290.
2. Suzuki Harunobu, *Parody of Jō and Uba*, woodblock-print, ink and color on paper, *chūban* diptych, Philadelphia Museum of Art, published in Jack Hillier, *Suzuki Harunobu* (Philadelphia: Philadelphia Museum of Art, 1970), illustration 18.

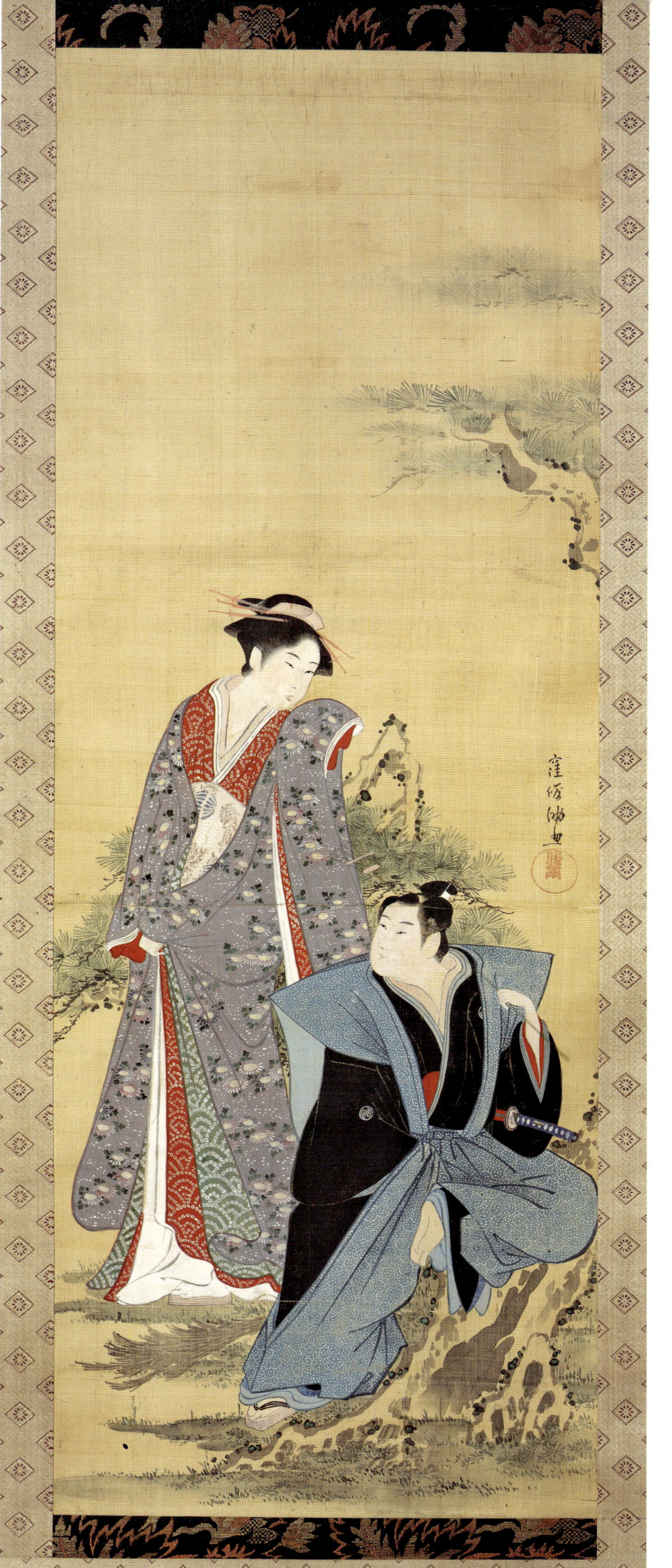
窪俊満画

41. **KUBO SHUNMAN** (1757–1820)

Emperor Xuanzong and Yang Guifei

About the latter half of the Tenmei (1781–89) or first half of the Kansei (1789–1801) era

Hanging scroll; ink, color, and gold on silk

53 x 85.2 cm (20 7/8 x 33 9/16 in.)

Signature: Kubo Shunman ga (Painting by Kubo Shunman)

Seals: Shun; man

William Sturgis Bigelow Collection 11.7754

Yang Guifei (713–56), one of the noted beauties in Chinese history, was believed to have led to the fall of Emperor Xuanzong (reigned 713–56). Once she came to the attention of the emperor and received imperial favor, members of her family were promoted to elevated positions at court. Besotted with her, the emperor neglected his duties in order to enjoy her company. When rebellions eventually broke out and the imperial guard demanded Yang Guifei's death, the emperor was forced to acquiesce.

The story of Xuanzong and Yang Guifei was celebrated even in Japan through the account in the *Song of Everlasting Sorrow* (*Changhenge*) by the Tang poet Bai Juyi (772–846). In ukiyo-e the two intimates were often depicted playing the flute, sometimes side by side; the consort blew into the instrument while both lovers fingered the notes. The lovers were also the subject of parodies in which a contemporary couple replaced their original Tang counterparts and played a samisen or lute.

Shunman has provided a more complex interpretation, with the eighth-century couple holding a samisen. The scene is set in a Chinese-style palace with a plaque under the eaves reading "Drum Sounding Pavilion," but the roof seems to be covered with wooden shingles rather than the stone tiles common to a Chinese structure, and the room in which the couple sits appears to be fronted with a bamboo blind similar to those that hung in the Yoshiwara's houses of assignation. Furthermore, the cityscape in the background blends Chinese and Japanese elements. Finally the women in the foreground appear as contemporary Japanese inhabitants of the Yoshiwara pleasure quarters or servers in restaurants.[1]

The serving women in the scroll are placed on the balustrade in groups of twos and threes. The two at the edge of the platform extending over the water turn back toward the palace and hold a ewer and cup. They resemble figures in works such as Shunman's *Young Woman and Her Chaperone Strolling at Dusk* and *Restaurant at Mukōjima*, with the setting and the individual attributes altered.[2] Furthermore, the waitress behind them holding the samisen box is almost identical to a woman with an umbrella in *Two Beautiful Women amidst Plum Blossoms in Snow*.[3] Thus, it seems that these clusters of female attendants were all adopted from Shunman's earlier hanging scrolls and woodblock prints. The resulting mélange of images of the Chinese palace and the Japanese pleasure quarters represents a product of fantasy in the minds of contemporary Edo sophisticates. AS

---

1. In an insightful study of the artist, the scholar Tanaka Tatsuya points out that as early as 1781, when Shunman published his comic yellowback (*kibyōshi*) novel *Foreign Land: Branch Store of the Yoshiwara* (*Hito no kuni: Demise no Yoshiwara*), he had "created a parody that depicted the palace harem of the first emperor of Qin as the *demise* of the Yoshiwara." Tanaka Tatsuya, "Kubo Shunman no kenkyū (ni)," in *Ukiyo-e geijutsu*, no. 108 (1993): 3–43.
2. Kubo Shunman, *Young Woman and Her Chaperone Strolling at Dusk*, late Tenmei (1781–89)–early Kansei (1789–1801) era, hanging scroll, ink and color on silk, 89 x 34.9 cm, Ōta Memorial Museum, Tokyo, published in *Ōta kinenkan, Hokusai kan, Itabashi kuritsu bijutsukan*, vol. 5 of *Nikuhitsu ukiyo-e taikan* (Tokyo: Kōdansha, 1994), illustration 17; and *Restaurant at Mukōjima*, woodblock print triptych, ink and color on paper, *aiban* size, published in *Sakuhin ni: Kiyonaga–Utamaro*, vol. 7 of *Genshoku ukiyo-e daihyakka jiten* (Tokyo: Taishūkan shoten, 1980), 73.
3. Kubo Shunman, *Two Beautiful Women amidst Plum Blossoms in Snow*, 1786–90, hanging scroll, ink and color on silk, Ōta Memorial Museum, Tokyo, published in Ōta kinen bijutsukan, *Ōta kinen bijutsukan shozō nikuhitsu ukiyo-e meihin zuroku* (Tokyo: Ōta kinen bijutsukan, 1988).

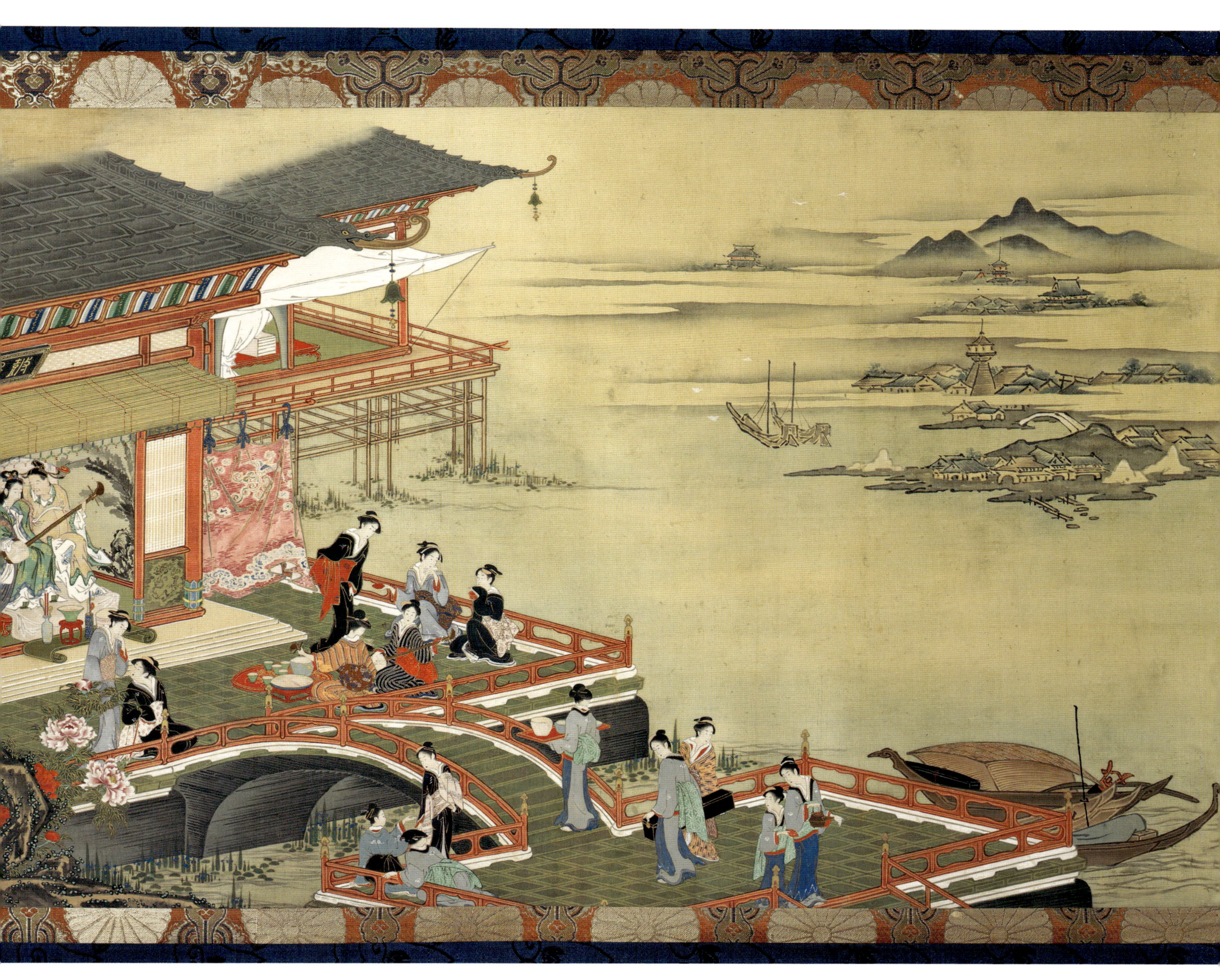

42. **MIZUNO ROCHŌ** (1748–1836)
Picking Young Herbs beneath Cherry Blossoms

About latter half of the Tenmei (1781–89) or first half of the Kansei (1789–1801) era
Hanging scroll; ink, color, gold, and mica on silk
92 × 34.5 cm (36 1/4 x 13 9/16 in.)
Signature: Mizu Rochō giga (Lighthearted painting by Mizu[no] Rochō)
Seals: Seisen; Rochō
William Sturgis Bigelow Collection 11.7693

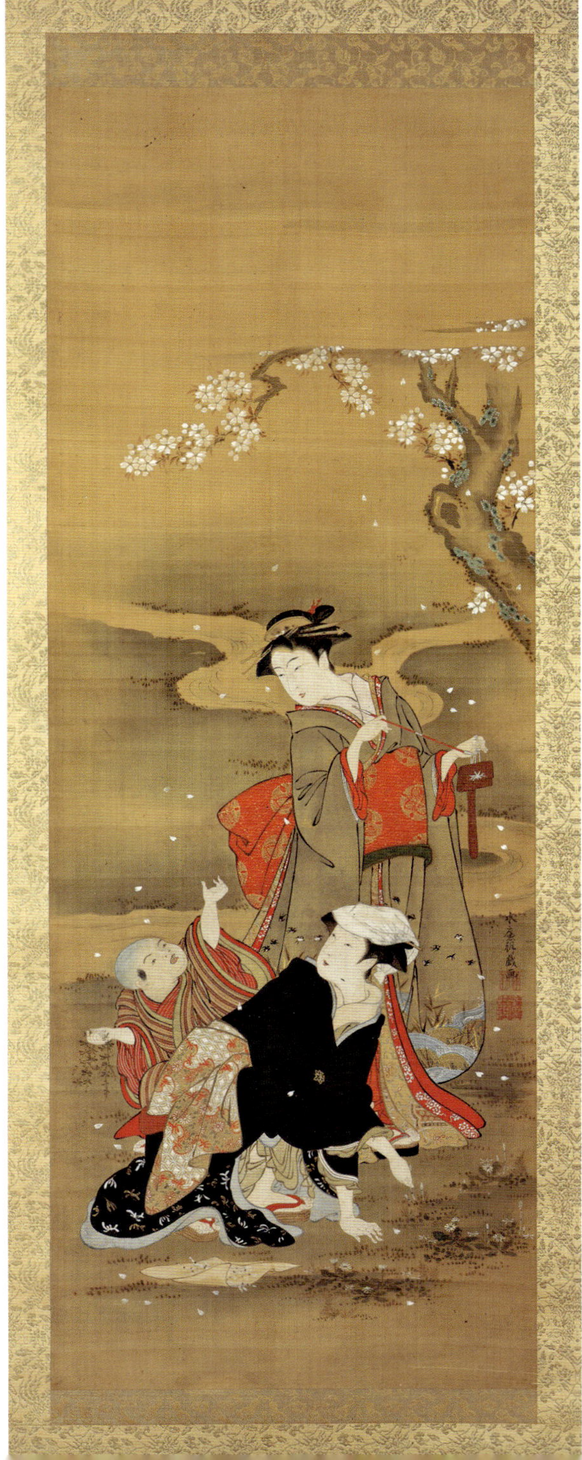

A family ventures on a spring outing to a hill covered with dandelions. A woman (probably the mother) wearing a black short-sleeved robe and a tie-dyed hand towel (*tenugui*) as a head covering picks horsetails; those she has already gathered lie on the white handkerchief beside her. She gazes at the boy, who clutches freshly plucked herbs in his right hand as he shouts with joy at seeing the drifting cherry petals. A younger woman (probably the sister), garbed in a *furisode*, also turns back slightly to look at the youth. In her right hand she holds a thin, long pipe; in her left she carries a tobacco pouch. The paraphernalia indicates that she must already be old enough to smoke.

Although Mizuno Rochō painted images of beautiful women throughout his life, he was a member of the military elite, serving as a lord of the *hatamoto* rank and earning 1,450 bushels of rice (*koku*) a year. It is hard to imagine that he painted to earn his livelihood, but the number and quality of his extant works elevate him to professional artistic status. Rochō created this hanging scroll while he was still perfecting his painting style, and the posture of the younger woman betrays a certain heaviness that is reminiscent of Kitao Shigemasa's figures.[1] However, the entire composition is united by a tone of classy elegance. AS

1. The style of the signature and seals is identical to those found on *Beautiful Woman Changing on a Snowy Night*, formerly in the Kobari Collection. Therefore, the two works must have been painted around the same time.

43. **KITAGAWA UTAMARO** (?–1806)
Courtesan with Child Attendant

First half of the Kansei era (1789–1801)
Hanging scroll; ink, color, gold, and mica on silk
85.4 x 33.5 cm (33 5/8 x 13 3/16 in.)
Signature: Utamaro ga (Painted by Utamaro)
Seals: illegible
William Sturgis Bigelow Collection 11.7920

This painting depicts an *oiran* dressed in formal robes, with her long train trailing onto the floor, and her child attendant (*kamuro*) wearing white toed-socks (*tabi*), suggesting that they are standing indoors. The courtesan's hair is arranged in the "tied *Hyōgo*" (*musubi Hyōgo*) or "tied and standing *Hyōgo*" (*musubi tate Hyōgo*) style, which was a variation of the *Hyōgo* chignon, with the hair twisted at the top like a conch. According to depictions in woodblock prints and printed books, this coiffure was popular among Yoshiwara courtesans from the 1770s to around 1793.

On her outer robe the *oiran* wears a "three-fan" crest, which was the identifying symbol of the Yoshiwara brothel Ōgiya Uemon; a triple "seven-treasure" motif appears on her sash as well as on the shoulders of her *kamuro*'s robe. Timothy Clark has made the observation that since the triple "seven-treasure" motif was the alternate crest used by the courtesan Takigawa at the Ōgiya, she may be the model for this painting.[1] Indeed this crest was used in all of Utamaro's prints of Takigawa produced during the Kansei era (1789–1801). According to the scholar Mukai Nobuo, Takigawa IV made her debut as an *oiran* in the spring of 1783.[2] If this date is correct, then the subject is the courtesan Takigawa V, who was appointed her successor.

The *kyōka* poet Tsuburi no Hikaru (literally, "Glowing Head," 1754–1796), one of the four masters of the school of Yomo no Akara (Ōta Nanpo), inscribed the following verse in the upper section of the scroll.[3]

Itsuzukeba	If I stay over,
ikuyo no mago ni	in what generation might
kaeru ran	I go home at last
momo no koi aru	like an immortal at the
iro no minamoto.	amorous Peach Blossom Spring?

The phrase "stay over" (*itsuzuke*) in the first line is a special term meaning "to spend the night or several days in brothels without returning home." Thus, the poem means that since staying over in the Yoshiwara is so comfortable, in spite of oneself one forgets to return home. The Yoshiwara is the spring of love like the Peach Blossom Spring, the subject of a fifth-century Chinese poem in which a fisherman discovers a mountain retreat where the inhabitants have achieved immortality.

Clark has pointed out the possible relationship of the MFA scroll to another Utamaro work, *Hide and Seek*, in the Ujiie Ukiyo-e Collection in the Kamakura kokuhōkan, which bears the same signature style and seal.[4] However, I would like to propose that these two works might have been part of a triptych, with the MFA painting in the center and *Hide and Seek* to its right. AS

1. Timothy Clark, "Yūjo to kamuro," in *Bosuton bijutsukan nikuhitsu ukiyoe*, vol. 3 (Tokyo: Museum of Fine Arts, Boston, and Kōdansha, 2000), 162–63.
2. Mukai Nobuo, "Utamaro ni egakareta yūjo tachi," *Kikan ukiyo-e*, no. 45 (1971): 77.
3. *Editor's note:* Ōta Nanpo (born 1749), a lower-ranking samurai, threw his energies into creative, artistic "happenings," bringing together wealthy merchants, poets, artists, and courtesans.
4. Clark, "Yūjo to kamuro," 163.

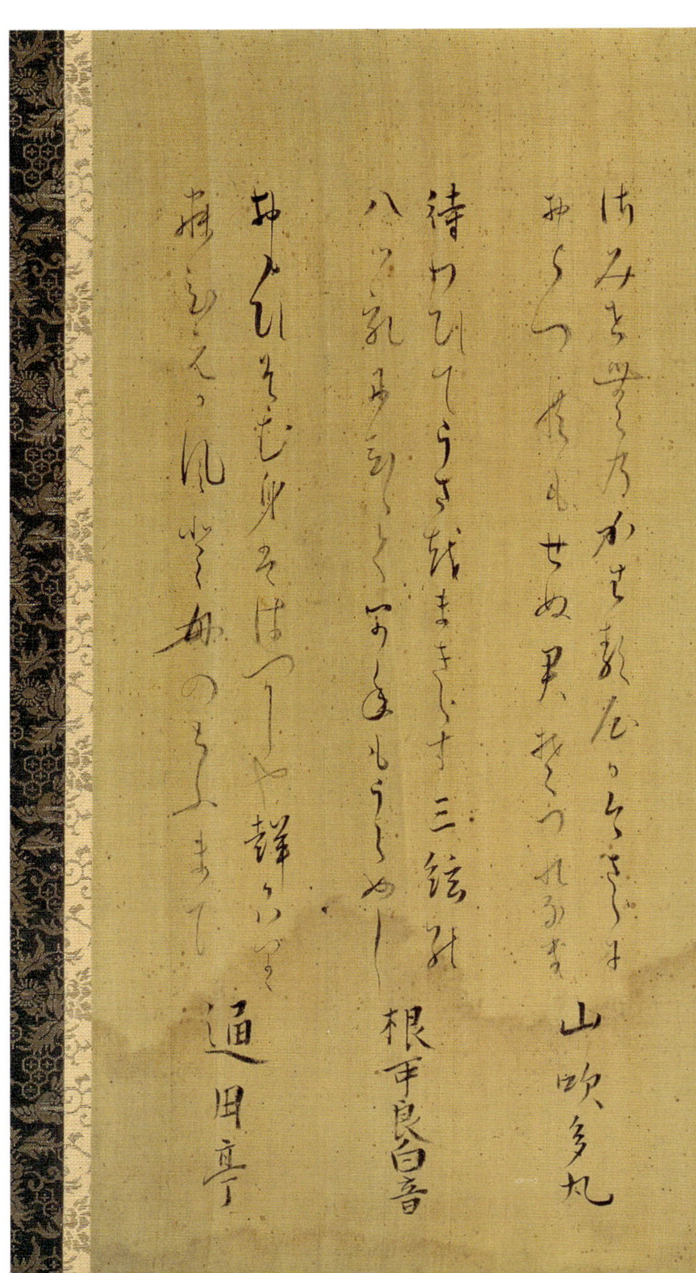

44. **KITAGAWA UTAMARO** (?–1806)
Young Woman Playing the Samisen

About Bunka 1–3 (1804–06)
Hanging scroll; ink, color, and gold on silk
41.5 x 83 cm (16 5/16 x 32 11/16 in.)
Signature: Utamaro hitsu (Brush of Utamaro)
Seal: Utamaro
Fenollosa-Weld Collection 11.4642

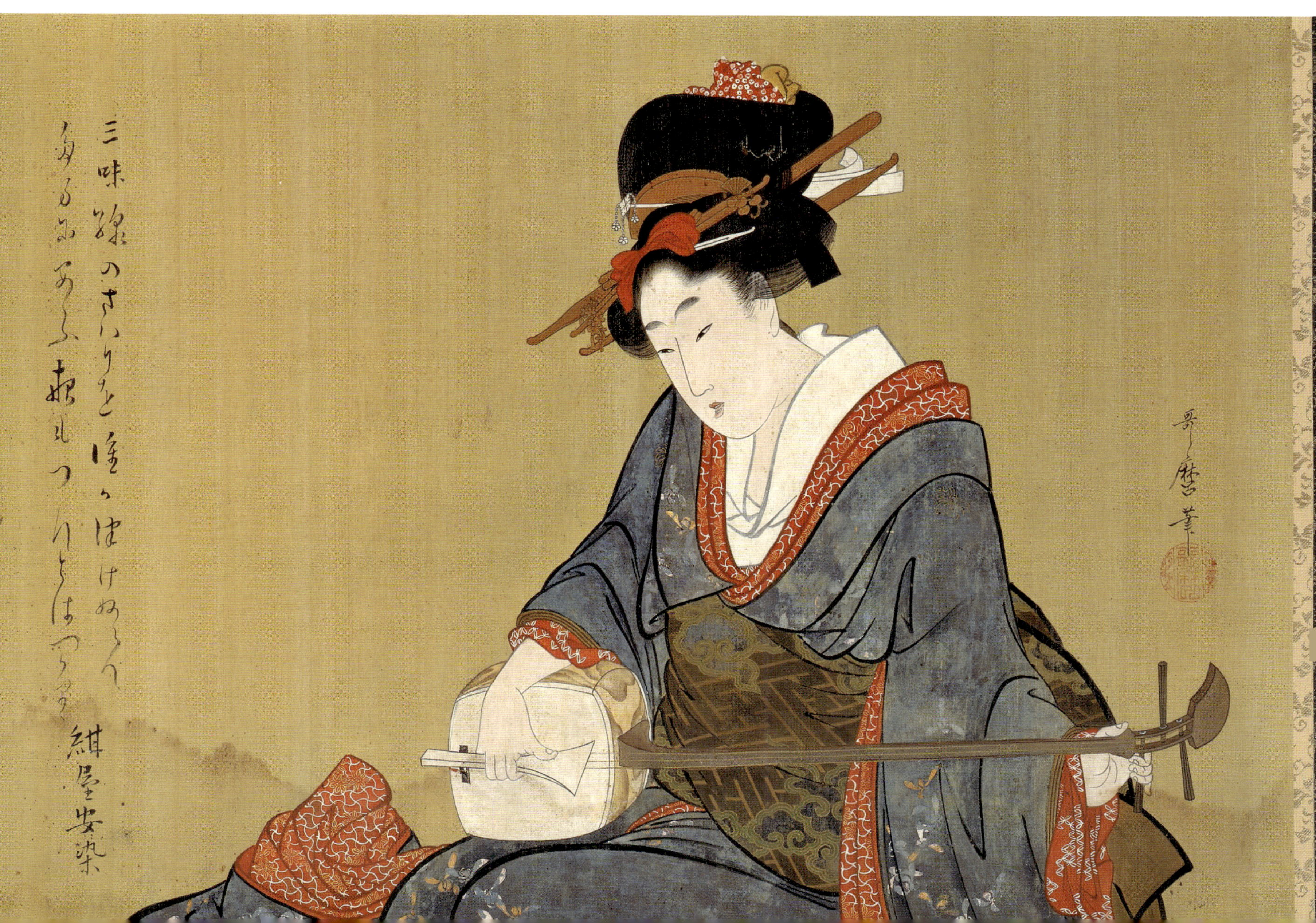

This young woman tunes her samisen, strumming it with the plectrum in her right hand and adjusting the pegs with her left. Her elaborate hair ornaments suggest that she is a geisha or a chanter for the puppet theater (*musume jōruri*), an art that became so popular it was banned in 1805.

Utamaro produced two *ōban*-size print series on the theme of *musume jōruri*: Chanting to Samisen by Young Women of Today (Tōsei musume jōruri) and Flowers of Edo: Young Woman's Jōruri (Edo no hana musume jōruri). This painting, which displays the rich sense of volume in the handling of the figure common to works created in Utamaro's last years, was probably made around the time when *musume jōruri* was banned. On the left side of the scroll there are comic verse (*kyōka*) poems that describe each of the five inscribers' thoughts about love, or rather about his unrequited love toward the woman who is the subject of the painting.[1] The overall balance of the composition clearly reveals that the painting was produced with the inscription of the following poems in mind. AS

Samisen no
sawari o dare ga
tsukenuran
tama ni au yo mo
tsun to bakkari.

Did I hear someone
pluck a sympathetic note
on a samisen?
Even on nights when we meet
it's nothing but cold twanging.

Samisen no
ito komagoma to
kudokedomo
chōshi no awanu
kimi ga kuchisaki.

The delicate sound
of fine samisen strings makes
a fine chat-up line
but, seducer, don't think you
can make sweet music with me!

Samisen no
kawaru kokoro ga
ima sara ni
otozure no senu
kimi zo tsurenaki.

Has your heart changed with
the samisen's fickle tones?
More and more these days
music fades, your visits cease—
ignoring me is cruel!

Machiwabite
usa o magirasu
sangen no
yatsuji ni hibiku
kane mo urameshi.

Waiting forlornly
I tried to calm my feelings
with the samisen
but the closing bell's sad sound
resonated on its skin.

Omoisomu
mi zo hazukashi ya
koegawari
nebie ka kaze to
haha no tou made.

I'm so much in love,
so terribly embarrassed
my voice changes key.
"Have you caught a chill or cold?"
my mother even asks me!

1. Utamaro also combined illustrations and *kyōka* poems in such works as *Picture Book: Selected Insects* (*Ehon mushi erabi*, 1788) and *Myriad Birds: A Kyōka Competition* (*Momochidori kyōka awase*, 1790).

45. **CHŌBUNSAI EISHI** (1756–1829)
Women under Willow, Cherry, and Maple

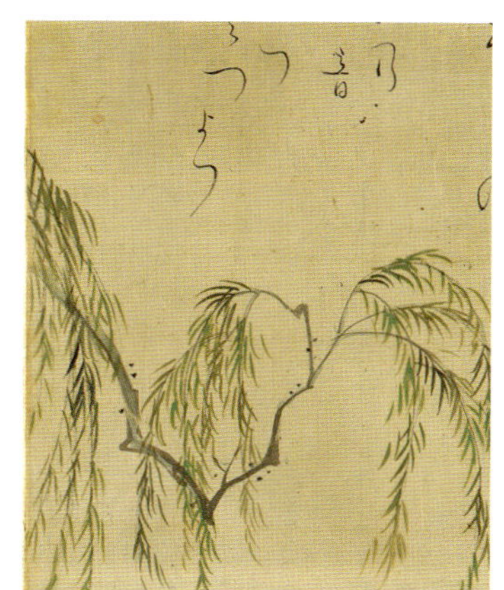
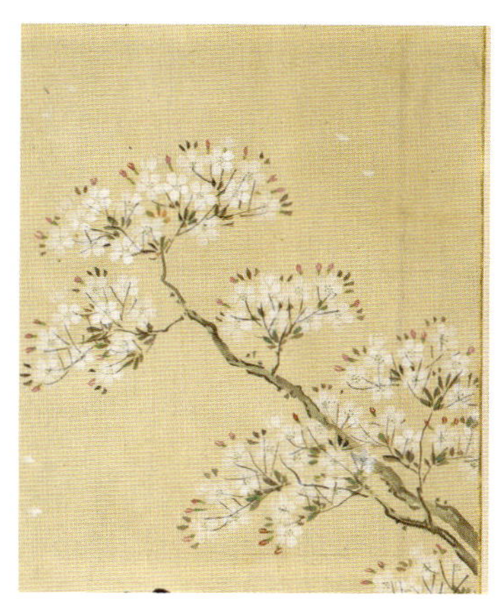
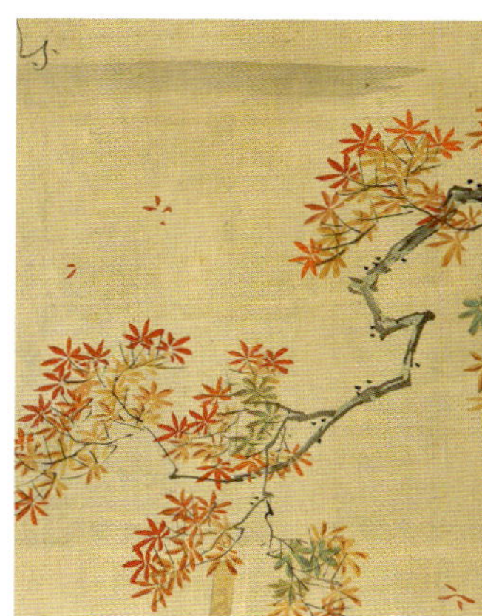

About Kyōwa (1801–04) or first half of the Bunka (1804–18) era
Set of three hanging scrolls; ink, color, gold, and silver on silk
Each 95.3 x 32.8 cm (37 ½ x 12 15/16 in.)
Signature: Chōbunsai Eishi hitsu (Brush of Chōbunsai Eishi)
Seal: Eishi
William Sturgis Bigelow Collection 11.7962, 11.7956, 11.7946

In this set of paintings Chōbunsai Eishi depicts the fashions of women from different classes during three seasons. The center scroll, which by its position is given the greatest prominence, presents an *oiran*, a courtesan of the highest rank, parading down the cherry blossom–lined boulevard of Nakano-chō in the Yoshiwara with her two child attendants in spring. The imposing dignity of the courtesan, showing off her black peacock-decorated outer robe, represents the pride of this government-licensed pleasure quarter. She flashes quite a bit of her purple underrobe, providing a rather impressive effect.

In the left scroll, representing summer, a geisha and her maid on their way to work wait on a pier for a ferryboat, with the willow branches behind them gently swaying in the river breezes. The trees suggest that the site is Yanagibashi (Willow-Tree Bridge), at the mouth of the Kanda River, known for its entertainment district. The geisha, looking out into the distance with a slightly tense expression, seems oblivious to the mischievous wind that has blown open the front of her kimono. The scroll on the right depicts a fine autumn day in Edo when everyone — old and young — gave in to the enjoyment of leaf viewing. Here two convivial sisters stroll among the falling maple leaves. They appear to be chatting about a poem inscribed on an oblong card that had been tied to the maple branch by an earlier visitor.

During the latter half of the Kansei era (1789–1801), Eishi specialized in producing paintings rather than designing prints. A large number of painted works date from that time and later. His depictions of women in the three seasons must have been extremely popular, for there are several extant versions of the theme, including a set now in the collection of the Asian Art Museum of San Francisco (formerly belonging to the MFA), and one with an almost identical composition in the Freer/Sackler Gallery of Art, Washington, D.C.[1] The MFA version bears inscriptions by Ōta Nanpo (born 1749):

(Spring)

Nakano-chō	Seen alongside a
uetaru hana no	glorious blossom parading
katawara ni	down Nakano-chō
miyamagi nado wa	the fine cherry trees in the
ippon mo nashi.	deep mountains count for nothing.

(Summer)

Aoyagi no	Out from the jetty
hashi no tamoto no	underneath the green willows'
sanbashi ni	overhanging fronds
komageta no oto	comes the sound of sturdy clogs —
futatsu mitsu yotsu.	clip-clop! two and three and four!

(Autumn)

Kisaragi no	Russet maple leaves
hana ni mo masaru	more glorious even than
momijiba no	springtime blossoms.
usuki wa imoto	Pale leaves suit the younger girl
koki wa anesama.	and darker leaves the older. NM

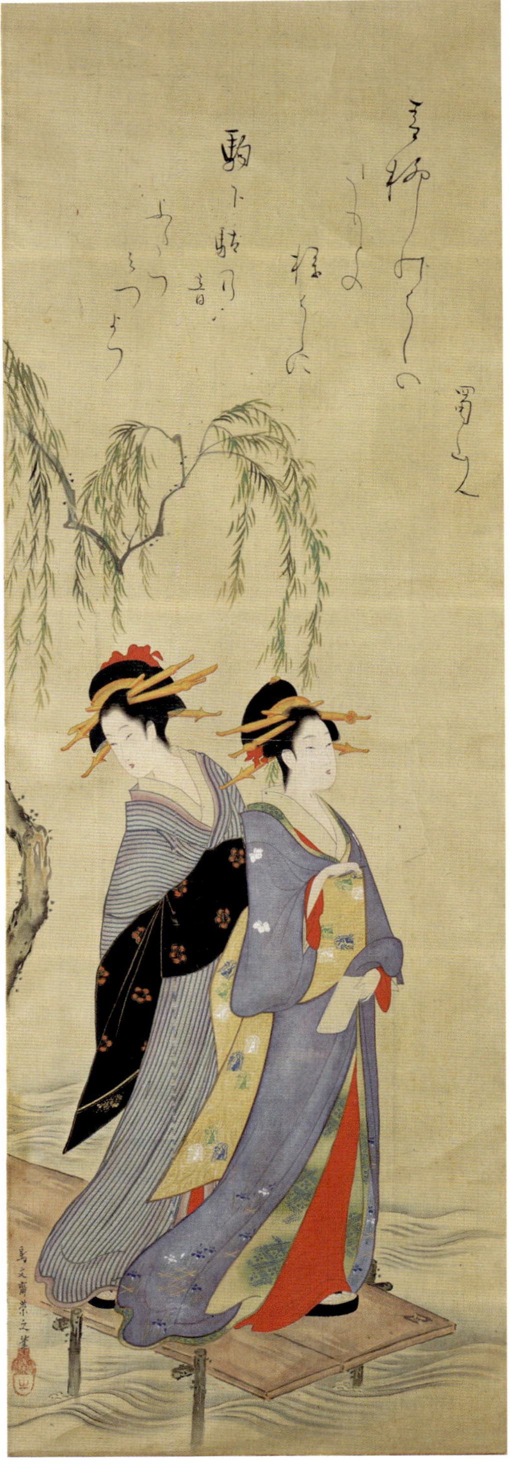

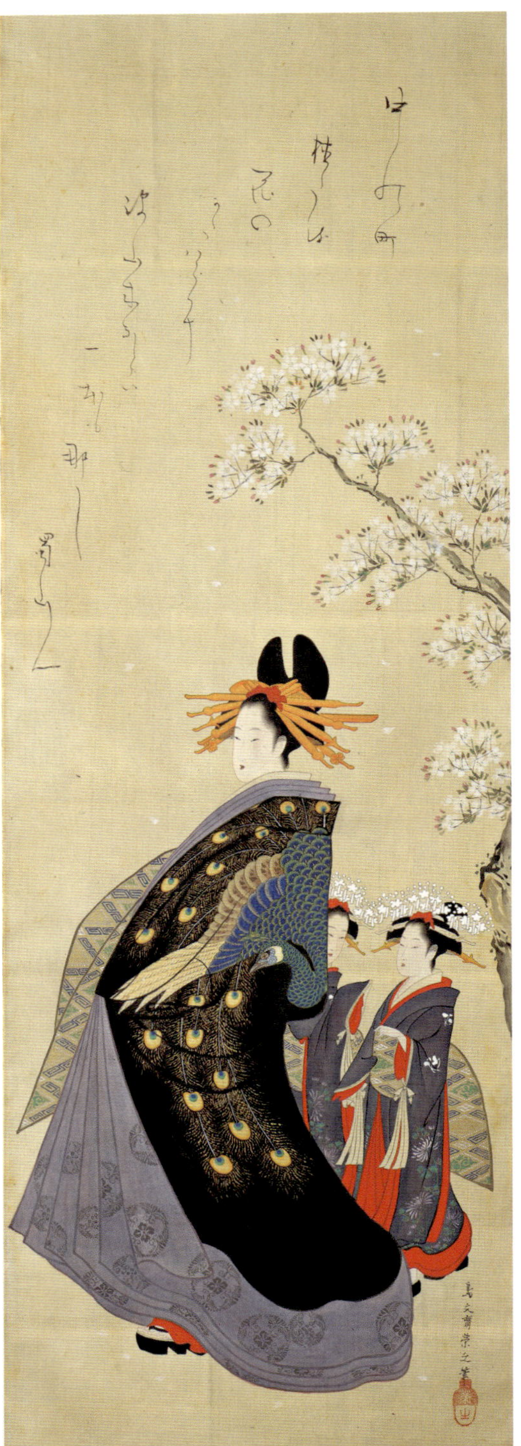

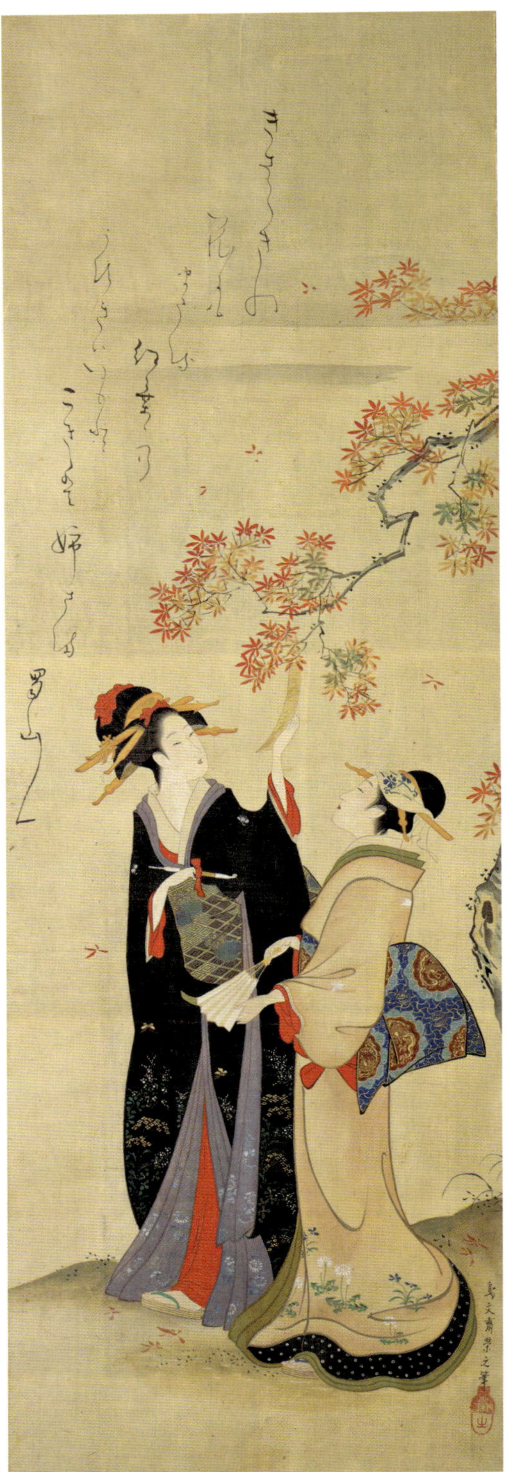

1. Chōbunsai Eishi, *Beauties of Three Seasons*, late Kansei (1789–1801) to Bunka (1804–18) eras, set of three hanging scrolls, ink and color on silk, Asian Art Museum of San Francisco, published in Timothy Clark, *Ukiyo-e Paintings in the British Museum* (London: British Museum Press, 1992), 41; and Chōbunsai Eishi, *Beauties of the Seasons*, set of three hanging scrolls, ink and color on silk, Freer Gallery of Art, Washington, D.C., published in Harold P. Stern, *Ukiyo-e Painting* (Washington, DC: Smithsonian Institution, 1973), 210–15. The Asian Art Museum paintings were deaccessioned from the MFA in 1932.

46. **CHŌBUNSAI EISHI** (1756–1829)
Ferryboat across the Sumida River

About the Bunka era (1804–18)
Hanging scroll; ink, color, and gold on silk
37.5 x 53.4 cm (14 3 ¾ x 21 in.)
Signature: Jibukyō Eishi Fujiwara Tokitomi hitsu
(Brush of Jibukyō Eishi Fujiwara Tokitomi)
Seal: Eishi
William Sturgis Bigelow Collection 11.7955

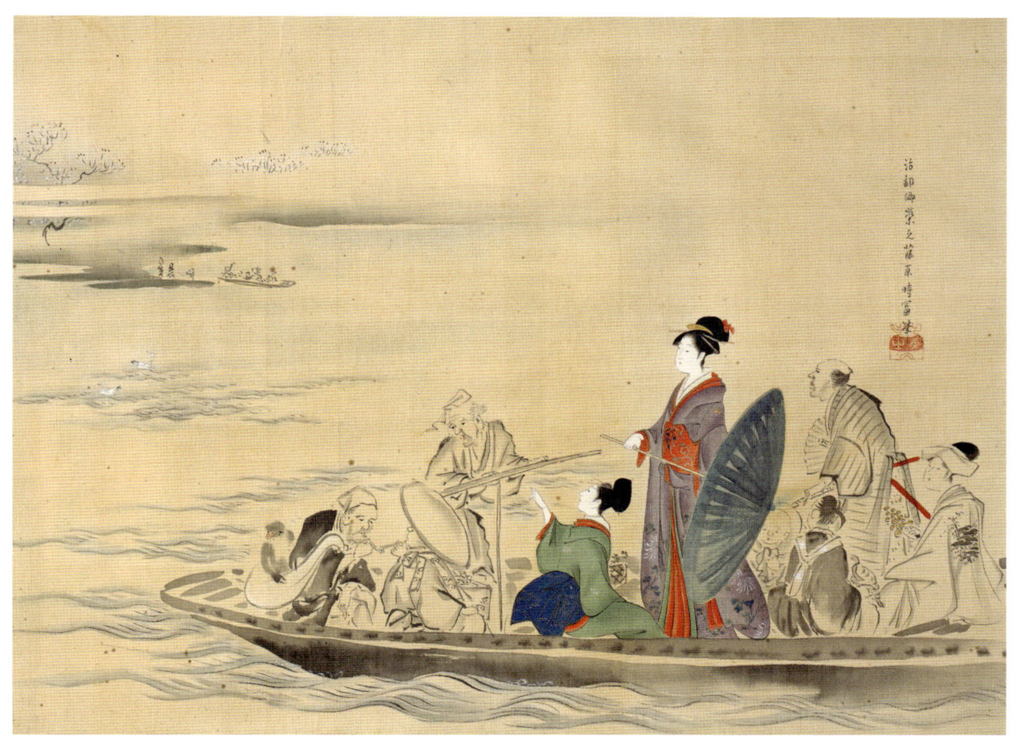

Until the early Edo period, the Sumida River served as the border between the ancient provinces of Musashi (modern-day metropolitan Tokyo and Saitama prefecture) and Shimōsa (Chiba prefecture). Even after the eastern bank of the river became formally part of Musashi, bridges spanning the two shores were relatively limited in number. Thus ferries became the primary means for commuting between the eastern and western banks. Of these, the Hashiba Ferry that docked near Matsusaki Inari Shrine, the Takeya Ferry near Mimeguri Shrine, and the Oumayagashi Ferry near the rice granaries in Asakusa often appeared in ukiyo-e paintings and prints.

The Oumayagashi Ferry is the subject of Eishi's celebrated handscroll *Trip to the Yoshiwara* (*Yoshiwara kayoi*, Idemitsu Museum of Arts, Tokyo), which due to its instant popularity was replicated by the artist in numerous painted copies.[1] Although the boat in the MFA painting has no particularly identifying features, it probably is also the Oumayagashi Ferry, transporting people from various social classes back and forth between the cherry-covered banks. The passengers are oblivious to the white and gray "capital-birds" (*miyakodori*) — known from a poetic reference in the tenth-century *Tales of Ise* — that bob along the waves.[2] Except for the two women in the center of the ferry, those on board are depicted in monochrome — a technique that Eishi also employed in *Trip to the Yoshiwara*. NM

1. Chōbunsai Eishi, *Trip to the Yoshiwara* (*Yoshiwara kayoi*), handscroll, ink and color on silk, 30.8 x 1123.4 cm, Idemitsu Museum of Arts, Tokyo, published in *Idemitsu bijutsukan*, vol. 3 of *Nikuhitsuga ukiyo-e taikan* (Tokyo: Kōdansha, 1994), illustration 55.
2. *Editor's note:* In the ninth chapter of the *Tales of Ise*, a courtier from the Heian capital inquires as to the identity of a bird while he crosses the Sumida River on a ferry. Upon being told that it is a capital-bird, he writes the following verse:

   If you are what your name implies,
   Let me ask you,
   Capital-bird,
   Does all go well
   With my beloved?

   [Translation by Helen Craig McCullough, *Tales of Ise: Lyrical Episodes from Tenth-Century Japan* (Stanford, CA: Stanford University Press, 1968), 76.]

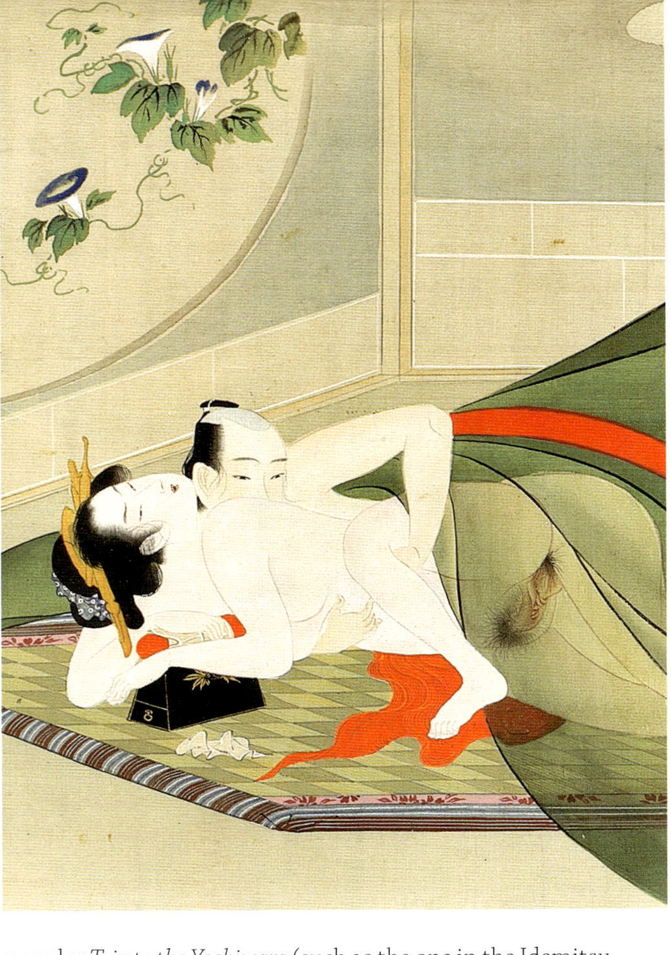

47. **CHŌBUNSAI EISHI** (1756–1829)
The Elephant's Leash (Kisa no tsuna)

Bunka era (1804–18)
Handscroll; ink, color, gold, and mica on silk
30.6 x 536 cm (12 1/16 x 211 in.)
Signature: Chōbunsai Eishi hitsu (Brush of Chōbunsai Eishi)
Seal: Eishi
William Sturgis Bigelow Collection Res.09.232

Composed of twelve scenes, this handscroll captures various types of love and lovemaking between men and women against a backdrop of the four seasons. The title inscribed on the cartouche on the outer frontispiece of the scroll refers to "the leash woven from a woman's hair." According to the Buddhist text *The Sutra on the Discourse of the Five Sufferings* (*Gokushoku-kyō*), a woman's hair captures even a giant elephant, or in other words, any man can easily lose himself in a woman's charms.

Chōbunsai Eishi was a rival to Kitagawa Utamaro (?–1806), the master of compositions of beautiful women. Among the designs included in this scroll are some that resemble Eishi's compositions for nonerotic works; in fact, some are mirror images. For example, the last scene in the MFA scroll bears similarities to the corresponding scene in the earliest versions of Eishi's extremely popular *Trip to the Yoshiwara* (such as the one in the Idemitsu Museum of Arts, Tokyo).

The representations of women in this erotic scroll are not too explicit, and they have an emotional restraint appropriate to a painter from the samurai class, as Eishi was. In addition, the depiction of the trees and paintings within the composition (such as those found on the standing screens and sliding doors) displays strong stylistic traits of the Edo Kano school, which was patronized by the military aristocracy. This more formal style confers a certain degree of dignity to the scenes. The scroll's vivid palette suggests that this lavish erotic work was made under special order. Judging from the color scheme and the painting style, as well as the appearance of the signature, the work may be dated to the Bunka era (1804–18). NM

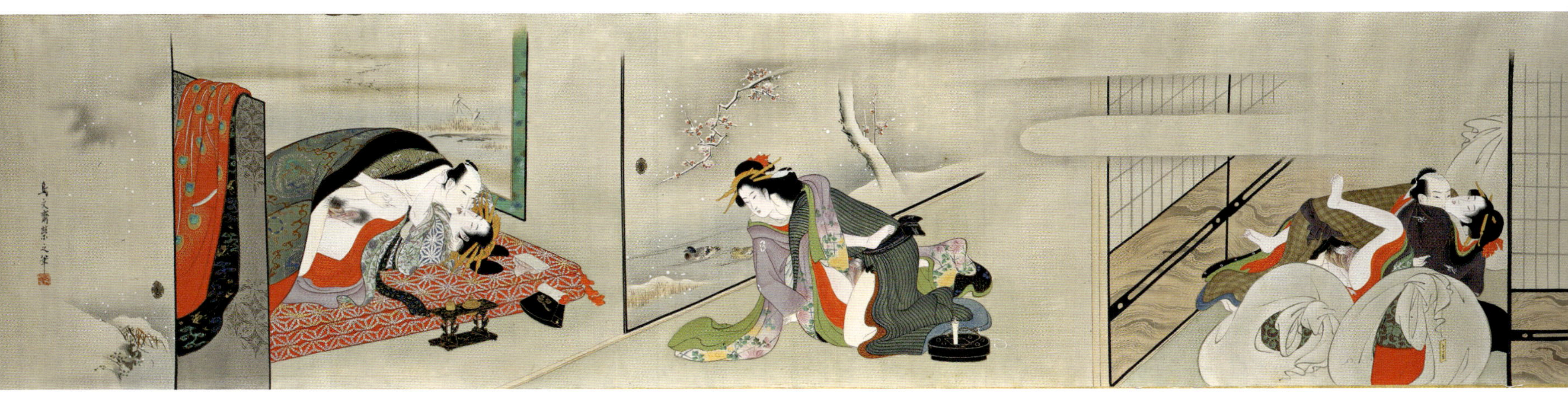

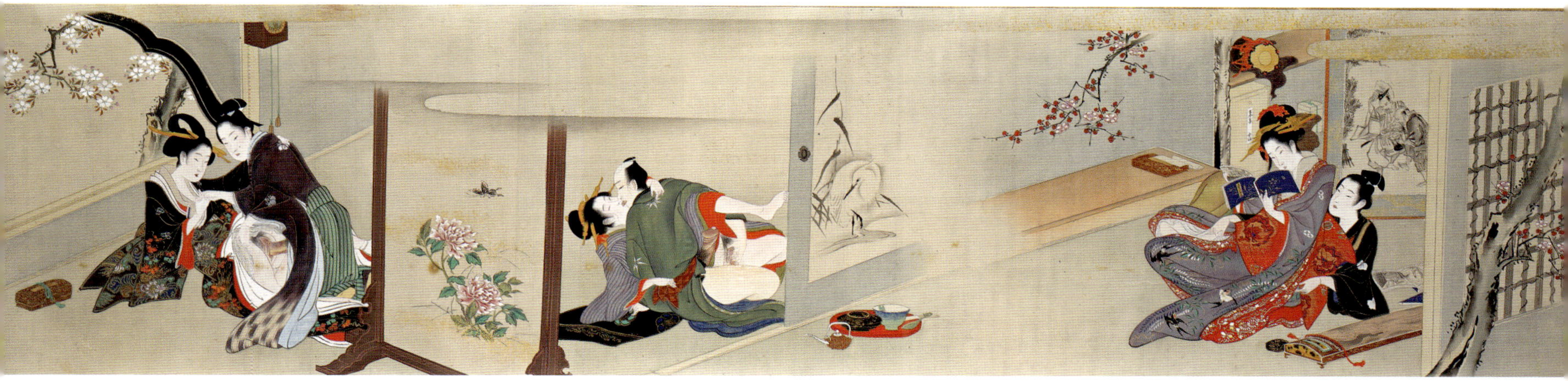

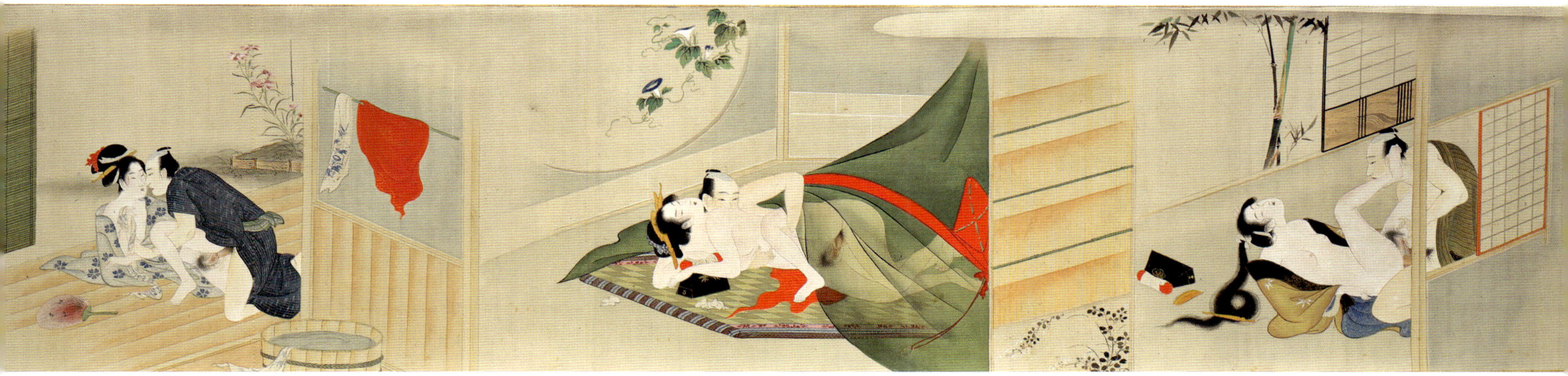

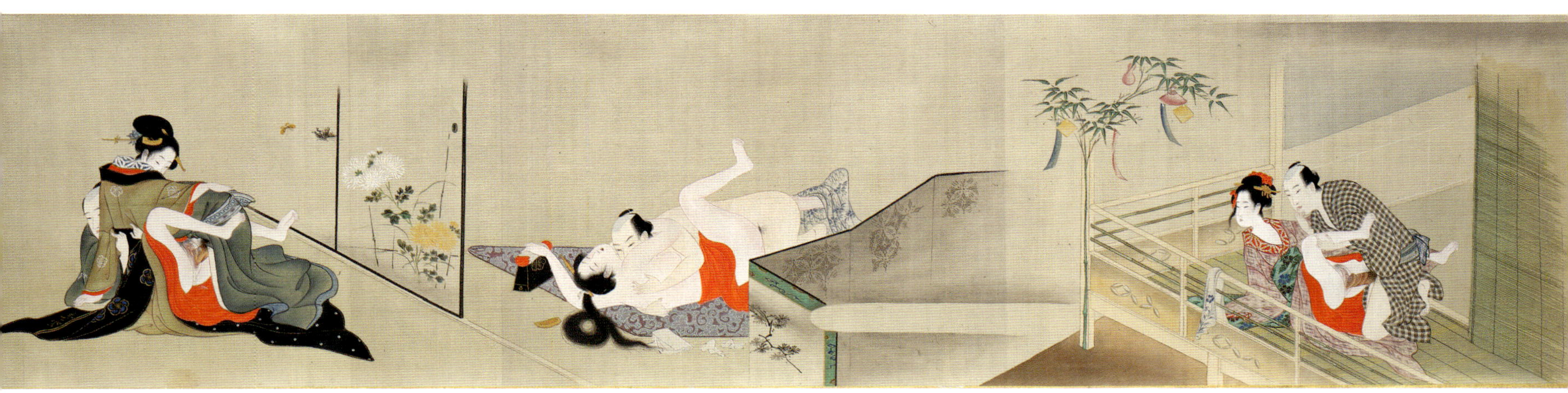

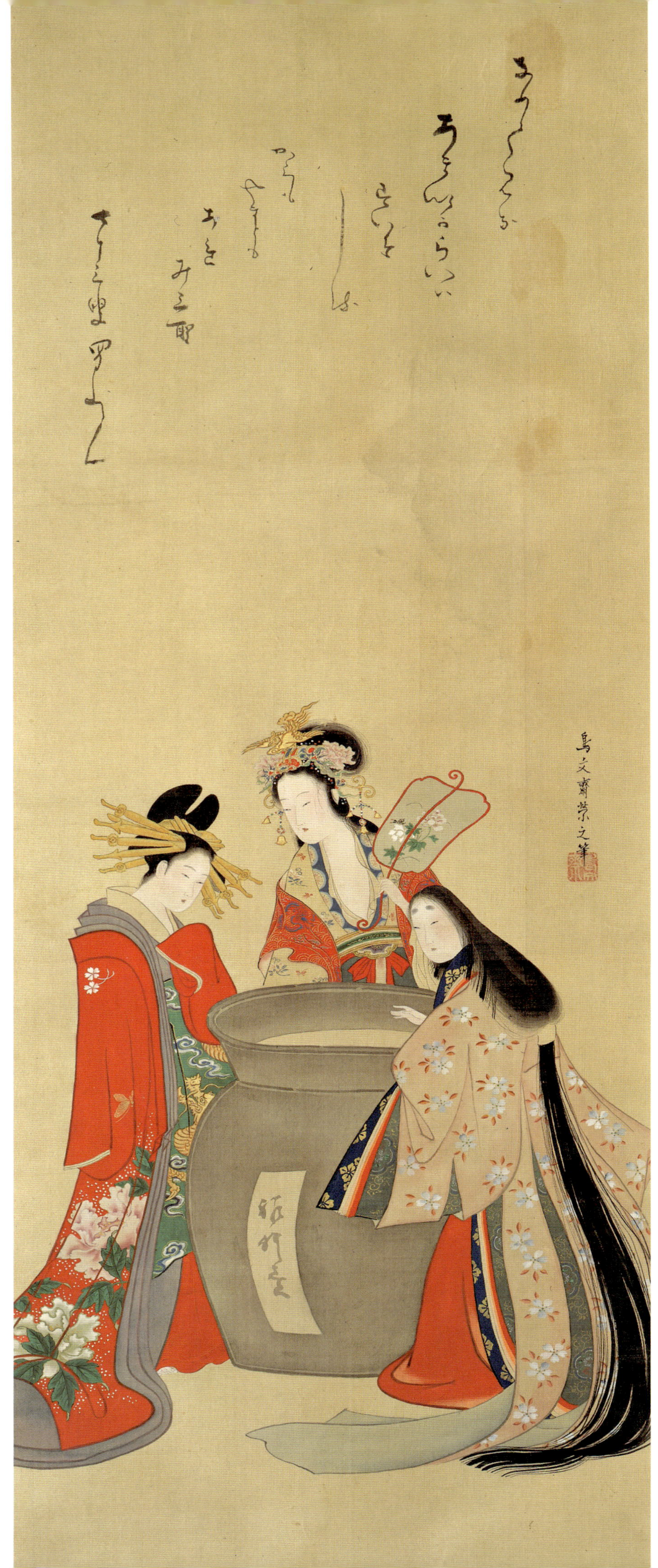
鳥文齋榮之筆

48. **CHŌBUNSAI EISHI** (1756–1829)
Parody of The Three Vinegar Tasters

About Bunsei 4 (1821)
Hanging scroll; ink, color, and gold on silk
97.3 x 40.3 cm (38 5/16 x 15 7/8 in.)
Signature: Chōbunsai Eishi hitsu (Brush of Chōbunsai Eishi)
Seal: Chōbunsai
William Sturgis Bigelow Collection 11.7949

According to legend, the Northern Song poet Su Shi (1039–1112) went with his friend Huang Shangu (1045–1105) to visit the Chan (Japanese: Zen) Buddhist monk Foyin. Expecting to share a large jar of peach wine, the three were surprised to find that the prized liquor had turned into vinegar and simultaneously puckered their mouths at its astringency. This theme is also considered an allusion to the "unity of the three creeds" — Confucianism, Daoism, and Buddhism — and consequently, in some images, the three protagonists are the three founders of the teachings, Confucius, Laozi, and Śakyamuni.[1]

Here Eishi has transformed the traditional theme, which had been popular both in Chinese and Chinese-style Japanese painting, into a type of beauty contest transcending both time and space. He has juxtaposed a contemporary Edo courtesan (on the viewer's left) with celebrated Chinese and Japanese beauties of old, the Tang concubine Yang Guifei (center), and the Heian poet Ono no Komachi (right). The scene has been painted on a larger-than-normal piece of silk and at the top has been inscribed by Ōta Nanpo.[2]

Namete miru	When they try a nip
amai karai wa	the connoisseurs can tell you
sui zo shiru	whether it's sweet or sour.
kara mo yamato mo	Both in China and Japan
aremi sansei.	the Three Sages know.

The verse is followed with a signature that reads, "Seventy-three [year-old] Old Man Shokusanjin."[3] Therefore, we can surmise that the painting must have been done sometime around 1821 and belongs to the last years of Eishi's life; it is a representative work of the first half of the Bunsei era (1818–30). NM

1. *Editor's note:* In their partaking of the vinegar, the sages were forced to recognize the same ultimate reality. For further information about the subject, see John M. Rosenfield, "The Unity of the Three Creeds: A Theme in Japanese Ink Painting of the Fifteenth Century," in *Japan in the Muromachi Age*, ed. John W. Hall and Toyoda Takeshi (Berkeley: University of California Press, 1977), 205–26.
2. Translation of verse by Howard Hibbett.
3. Ōta Nanpo took on many literary names including Yomo no Akara (see cat. 43) and Shokusanjin.

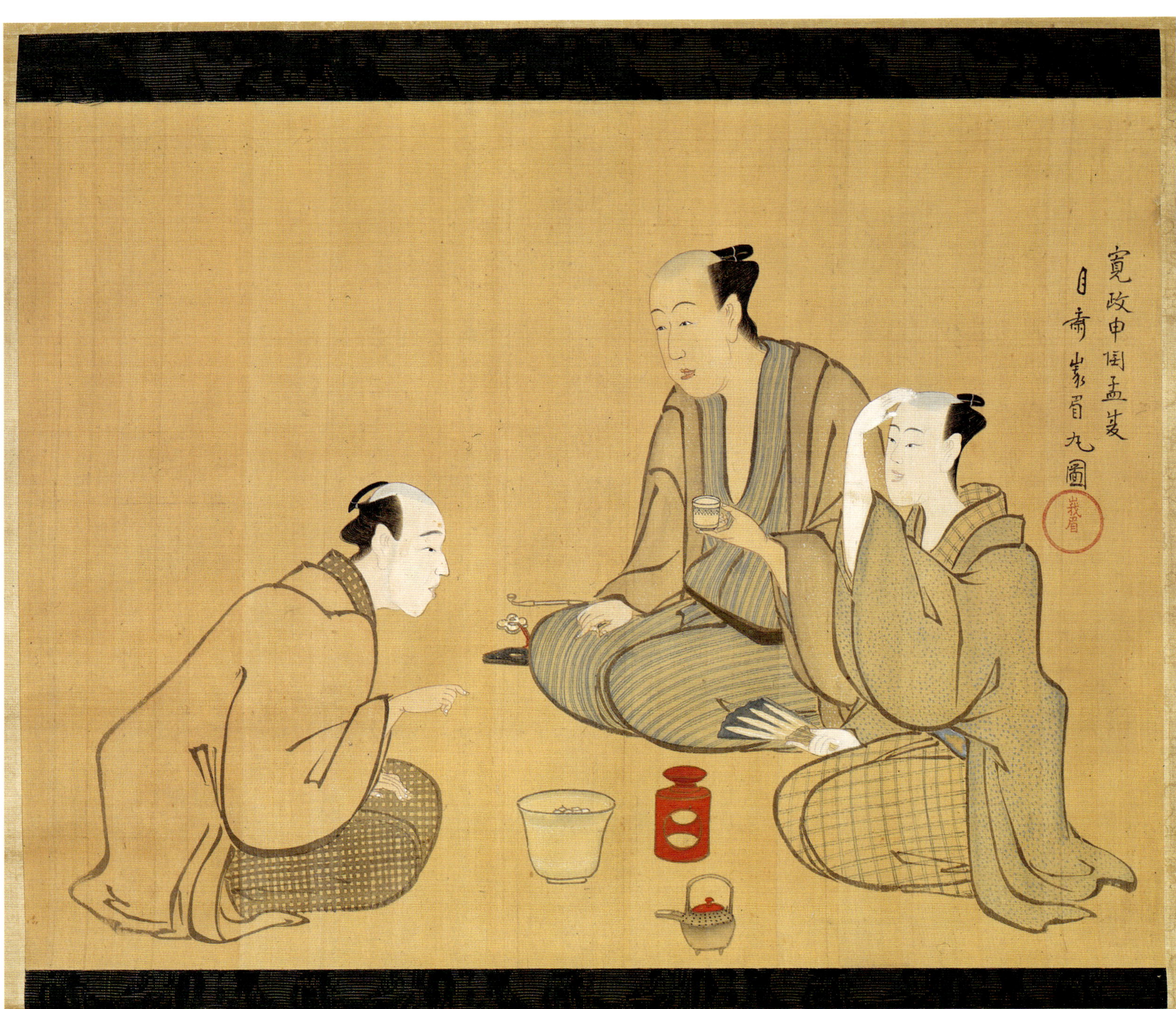
寛政甲寅孟夏
月斎峩眉丸圖
峩眉

49. **GESSAI GABIMARU** (ACTIVE ABOUT 1789–1818)
Party Scene in the Yoshiwara

Kansei 12 (1800)
Hanging scroll; ink and color on silk
39.2 x 51.5 cm (15 7/16 x 20 1/4 in.)
Signature: Kansei saru uru mōka Gessai Gabimaru zu
(Drawn by Gessai Gabimaru, the intercalary month, early summer of the year of the monkey in the Kansei era)
Seal: Gabi
William Sturgis Bigelow Collection 11.7952

This painting captures the witty repartee between two men who may be identified as an entertainer (*hōkan* or *taikōmochi*), on the right and a teahouse owner (or brothel keeper), on the left. Both men are trying to amuse a guest in the center, who seems completely relaxed. The entertainer is depicted with an exaggerated pose that suggests he is waving his fan.

This scroll was created by Gabimaru, who adopted his sobriquet from the term *gabi*, literally meaning "moth eyebrows" but connoting a beautiful woman with eyebrows shaped like a moth's antennae. To the right of the artist's signature the date is inscribed "the intercalary month, early summer of the year of the monkey in the Kansei era," thereby indicating that the work was done in the fourth month (intercalary) of the twelfth year of the Kansei era (1800). The specificity of the date suggests that this painting may document people who were close to the artist. The portraitlike appearance of the three protagonists supports this conclusion. NM

ESTABLISHING A LINEAGE, 1780–1850 **THE UTAGAWA SCHOOL**

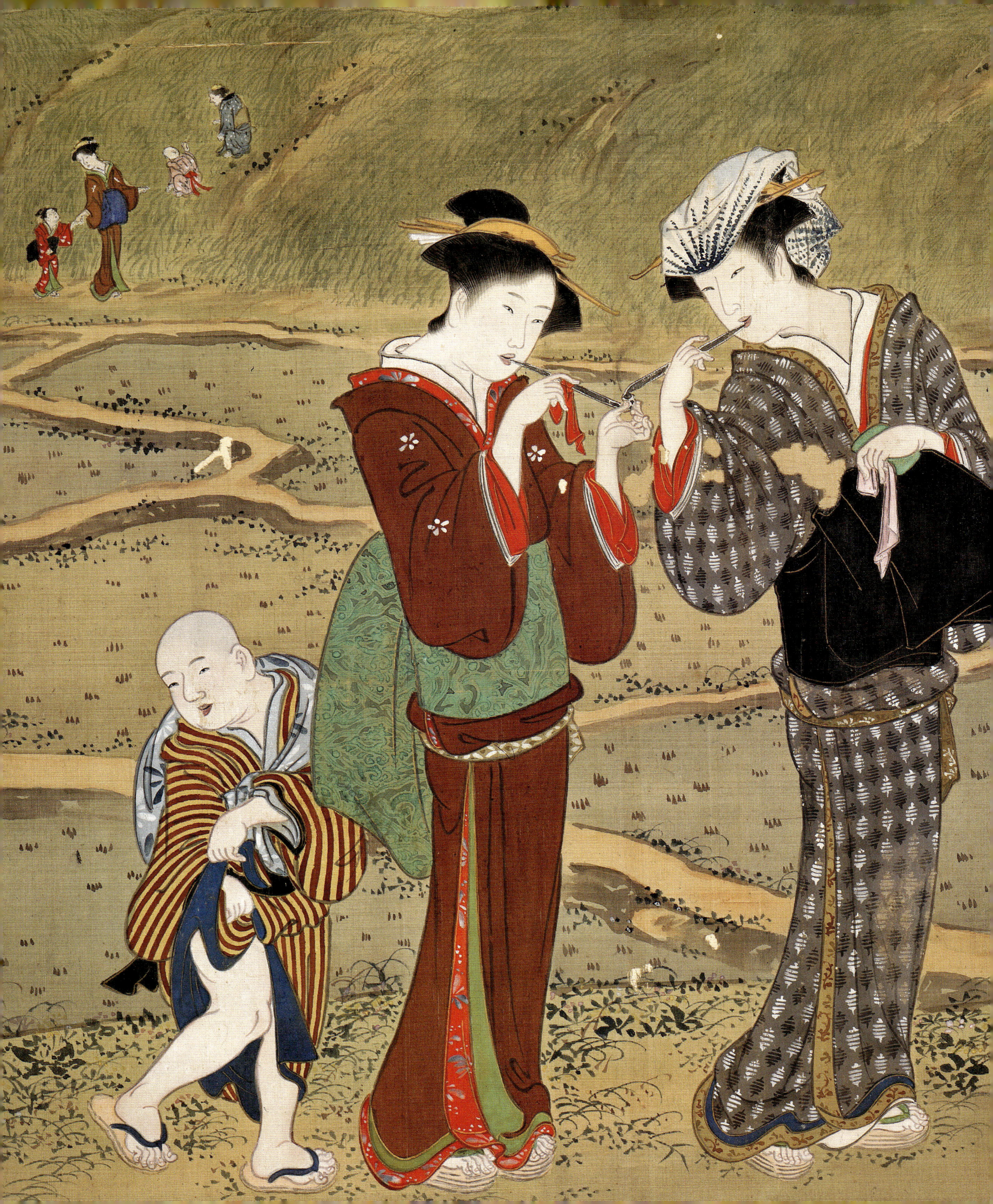

ESTABLISHING A LINEAGE, 1780–1850: THE UTAGAWA SCHOOL

The Utagawa school was founded by Toyoharu (1735–1814), an Edo artist who produced a prodigious number of ukiyo-e paintings from the 1780s through the 1790s. Thought to have been trained by a painter of the Kano school, which is known for its Chinese-style ink painting, Toyoharu subsequently adopted the lithe figure style of Suzuki Harunobu in the 1760s. However, he later established his own distinctive style of female imagery, depicting women with more ample and naturalistic proportions. Toyoharu attained such stature that the artist Sakai Hōitsu, a son of the daimyo who controlled Himeiji Castle, asked to train under him.

Toyoharu's disciple, Utagawa Toyokuni (1769–1825), generally followed the style of his master for paintings of beautiful women. However, he created a dramatic new mode for depicting Kabuki performers that emphasized the actors' individual personalities and by the second half of the 1790s dominated the genre. In the early nineteenth century patrons of well-known actors commissioned Toyokuni to produce several portraits (see cat nos. 55 and 56).

*Toyokuni was assiduous in training his students — artists such as Kunisada (1786–1864) and Kuniyoshi (1797–1861) — and thereby ensured the dominance of the Utagawa lineage at the end of the Edo period. Kunisada was particularly known for producing actor prints that perpetuated the Toyokuni mode, but he added to it a novel, stylized treatment of the figure. He also precipitated a demand for imagery of women with an earthy elegance and during the 1820s to the 1830s created pictures in which he exaggerated the sensuousness of his female subjects. During this latter period Kunisada's popularity was matched only by that of Keisai Eisen (1790–1848), a masterless samurai (*rōnin*) who produced not only landscape prints but also paintings of voluptuous women with elongated faces, prominent noses, and wide-set eyes.*

Perhaps the Utagawa artist best known in the West is Hiroshige. Together with Katsushika Hokusai, Hiroshige is celebrated for having developed landscape and bird-and-flower prints. He studied under the second-generation Utagawa painter Toyohiro, but his own individual style did not become firmly established until the publication of the series Fifty-three Stations of the Tōkaidō (Tōkaidō gojūsan tsugi) in the first half of the 1830s. In these woodblock prints as well as the commission of more than two hundred hanging scrolls of scenic locations by the Tendō domain north of Edo (see cat no. 57), Hiroshige captured the poetic sentiments engendered by the four seasons in Japan. AS

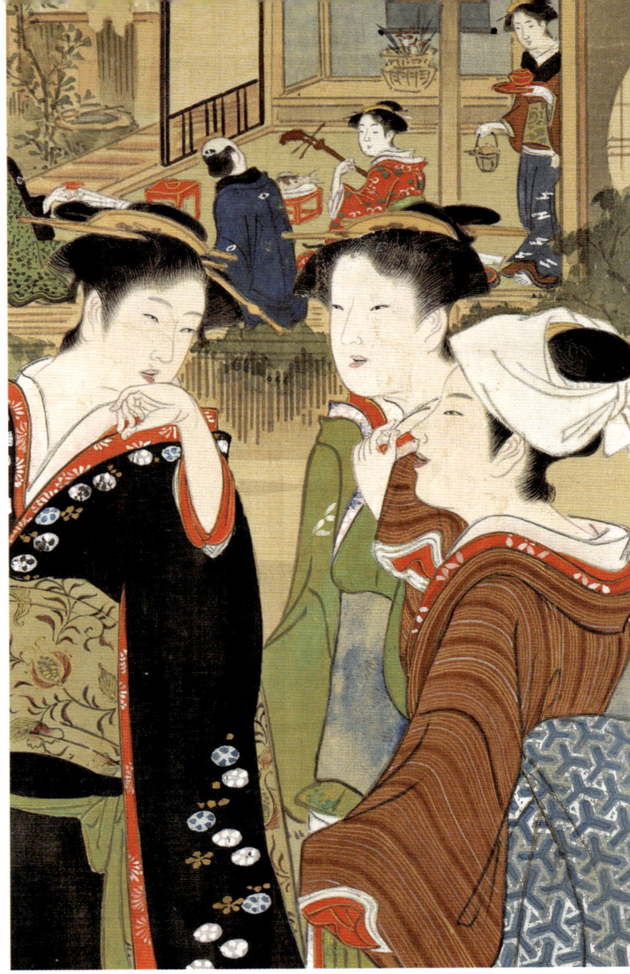

50. UTAGAWA TOYOHARU (1735–1814)

Pleasure Outing at Mukōjima to View Cherry Blossoms

Late Tenmei (1781–89) or early Kansei (1789–1801) era
Hanging scroll; ink, color, gold, and mica on silk
66.4 x 122.1 cm (26 1/16 x 48 1/16 in.)
Signature: Tōtojū Ichiryūsai Utagawa Toyoharu ga (Painted by Ichiryūsai Utagawa Toyoharu, who resides in the Eastern Capital)
Seals: Ichiryūsai; Masaki no in (Seal of Masaki)
Fenollosa-Weld Collection 11.4639

Utagawa Toyoharu provides a panoramic view of the Sumida River embankment at Mukōjima, the historic shogunal hunting grounds that had become a favored destination for pleasure-seeking Edoites in the late eighteenth century. The area was particularly known for its magnificent cherry trees, which had been planted by Tokugawa Yoshimune (1684–1751); ferries conveyed merrymakers there from downriver to a pier near Mimeguri Shrine, where they disembarked so that they could enjoy the sights. In the foreground of this monumental painting, groups of fashionably dressed townspeople — some appear to be a little tipsy — stroll past the Kasai Tarō, one of the area's celebrated eating establishments.[1] A much more staid procession of a daimyo's wife and her entourage slowly makes its way along the embankment. Across the river on the western bank lies the narrow entrance to the San'ya Canal spanned by the Imado Bridge, where habitués of the Yoshiwara would have alighted before proceeding on foot, and the shrine at Matsuchiyama, which was then well known for its image of Shōten (the Esoteric deity that took the form of coupling elephants), nestled behind the trees on the left.

Before becoming a full-time painter in the 1780s, Toyoharu produced a number of highly innovative prints that presented Japanese cityscapes using Western techniques of perspective (*uki-e*). In those prints the artist conveyed distance and depth utilizing compositional lines that converged at a vanishing point on the horizon. In this painting he has been much more subtle in his presentation. Here, eschewing overt use of Western perspective, Toyoharu primarily depends upon the juxtaposition of foreground and background figures and variations in scale and degree of detailing to define the spatial relationship of his forms. He does use some parallel lines in limited areas to suggest depth, such as those in the interior of the restaurant and on the banks of the San'ya Canal.

Toyoharu has used the signature "Painted by Ichiryūsai Utagawa Toyoharu, who resides in the Eastern Capital" for this image. Naitō Masato has suggested that the decision to identify Edo as his residence means that this painting was commissioned by a provincial patron.[2] ANM

1. Several of these figures bear strong resemblances to those in Toyoharu's painting *Viewing Plum Blossoms (Kanbaizu)* in the Ōita Prefectural Art Hall, published in Narazaki Muneshige, ed., *Nikuhitsu ukiyo-e II: Meiwa–Kansei*, no.249 (Tokyo: Shibundō, 1987), illustration 14.
2. Naitō Masato, "Mukōjima kōrakuzu," *Bosuton bijutsukan nikuhitsu ukiyo-e*, vol. 3 (Tokyo: Museum of Fine Arts, Boston, and Kōdansha, 2000).

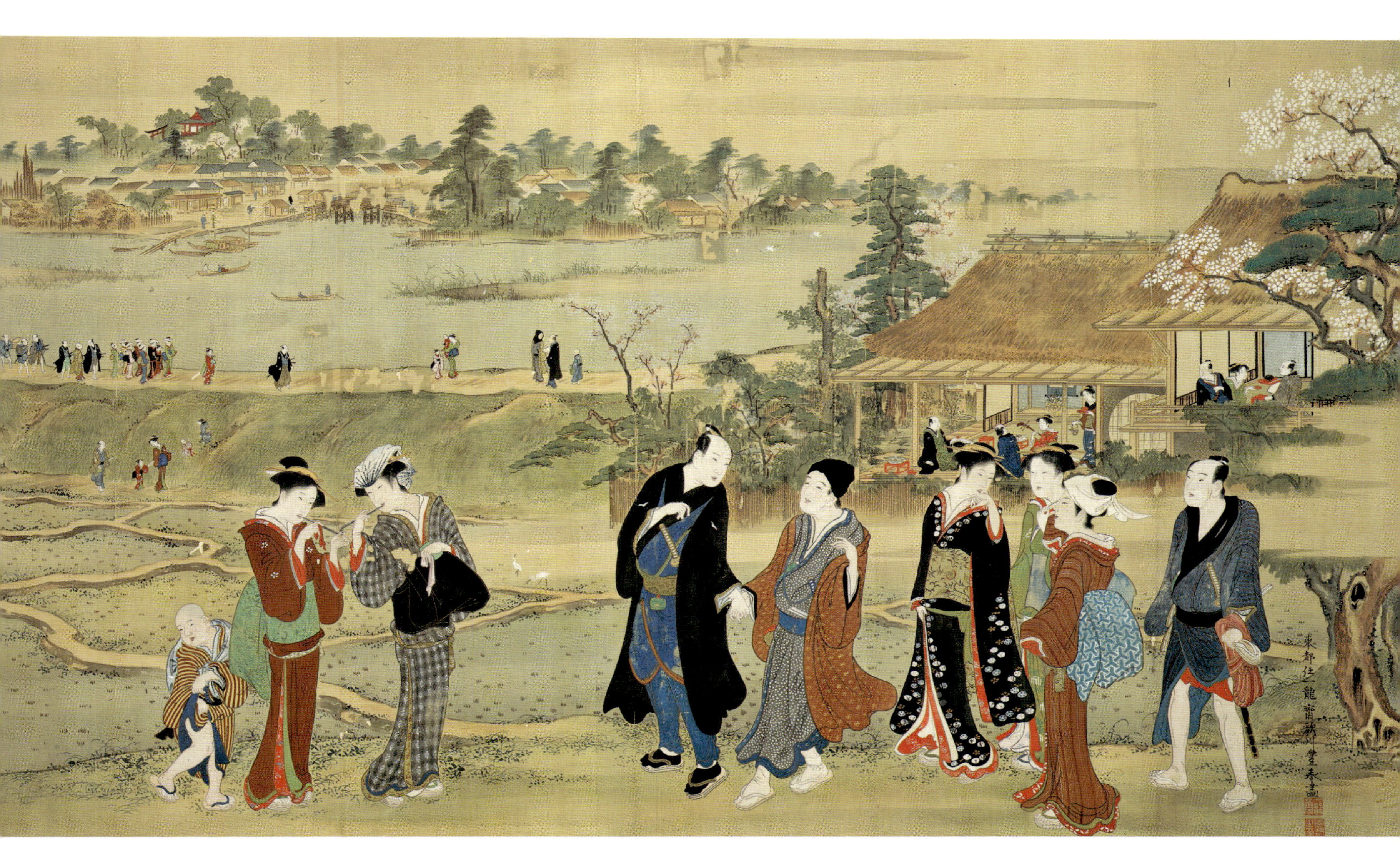

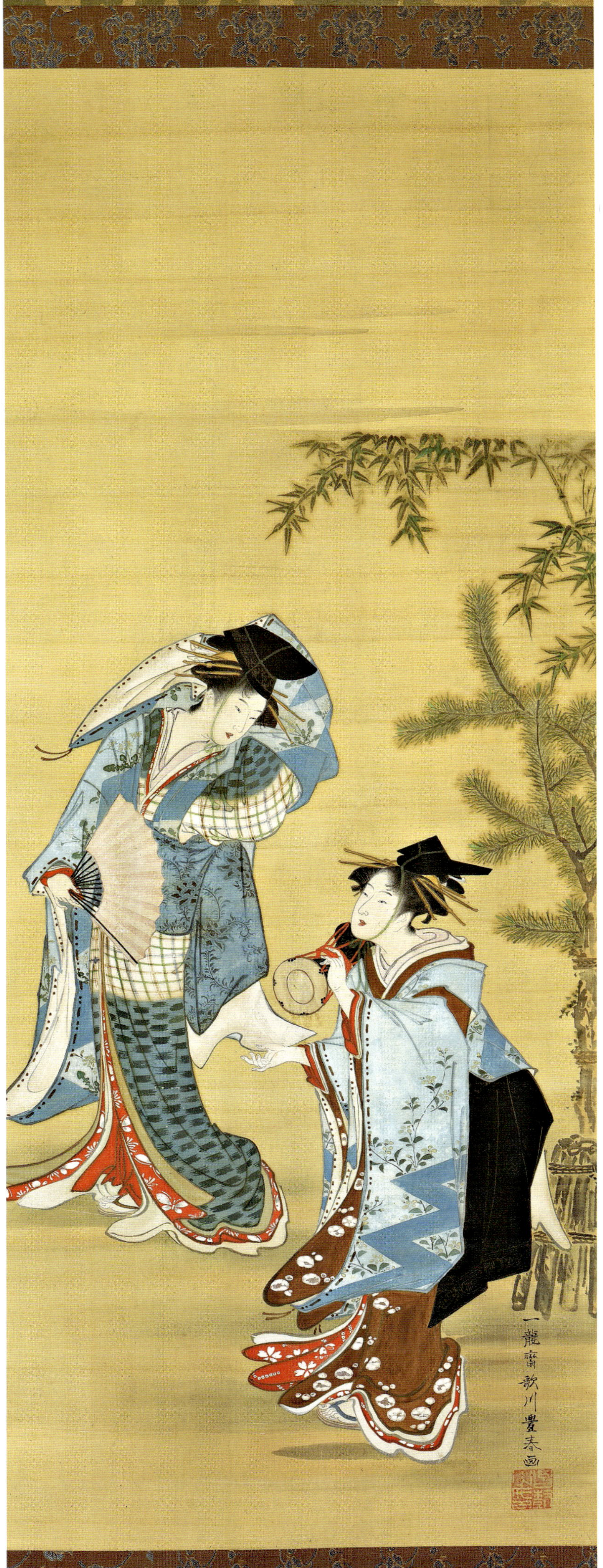

51. **UTAGAWA TOYOHARU** (1735–1814)
Women Performing Manzai

Late Tenmei (1781–89) or Kansei (1789–1801) era
Hanging scroll; ink, color, and mica on silk
98.2 x 43.8 cm (38 11/16 x 17 1/4 in.)
Signature: Ichiryūsai Utagawa Toyoharu ga
(Painted by Ichiryūsai Utagawa Toyoharu)
Seal: Masaki no in (Seal of Masaki)
William Sturgis Bigelow Collection 11.7843

With the advent of the New Year came a spirit of renewal and the decoration of every household's entrance gate with auspicious boughs of pine. A frequent sight in Edo during the holiday was two men's street performance of a comic dance known as Mikawa *manzai*, named after its place of origin (Mikawa province, modern-day Aichi prefecture). The men sang and danced as they made their way from house to house, praying for the prosperity of the residents. In this scroll two women perform what was called "women's *manzai*" (*onna manzai*), based on the male version. Just as in Mikawa *manzai*, the two performers assume the roles of Tayū (left), the primary one who demonstrates the auspicious dance with fan in her hand, and Saizō (right), the accompanist who sings and beats on the drum.

Beginning in the mid-Edo period, paintings of female *manzai* dancers were created time and again for the New Year by artists such as Miyagawa Chōshun and Okumura Masanobu. The popularity of the subject may have been due to the growing preference for the more elegant "women's *manzai*" over the original Mikawa dance. Many painters from the Utagawa school produced almost identical compositions of the subject, and the design may have been one of their signatures. NM

52. **UTAGAWA TOYOHARU** (1735–1814)
Courtesans with Snow, Moon, and Flowers

Kansei era (1789–1801)
Set of three hanging scrolls; ink, color, gold, and mica on silk
Each 117.3 x 34.7 cm (46 3/16 x 13 11/16 in.)
Signature: Ichiryūsai Utagawa Toyoharu ga
(Painted by Ichiryūsai Utagawa Toyoharu)
Seal: Ichiryūsai
William Sturgis Bigelow Collection 11.7834, 11.7835, 11.7836

This set of impressive hanging scrolls juxtaposes women from the different pleasure quarters in Edo with the traditional poetic theme of snow, moon, and flowers. The center scroll (shown here at right) depicts a *yūjo* from the Yoshiwara, also known as the Northern Pleasure Quarters because of its location to the north of Edo Castle. She has her hair arranged in a *Hyōgo* chignon. The hem of her outer robe is decorated with a pattern of peacock feathers set against a black ground and the fan in her left hand is ornamented with a design of cherry blossoms. The left scroll (on page 182) portrays a high-ranking prostitute in the unlicensed brothel district (*okabasho*) of Shinagawa, which was also known as the Southern Station. The flower arrangement of various autumn grasses that has been placed behind her alludes to the moon, which is not shown in the scroll. Shinagawa, which lies to the south of Edo near the bay, was a famous moon-viewing spot.[1] Finally the scroll on the right (page 183) illustrates a geisha belonging to the unlicensed Fukagawa brothels, located to the southeast of the city. The red charcoal in the brazier conveys the cold of winter. A blob of snow is placed on a lacquer tray to the left; later it would probably have been fashioned into the body of a rabbit.[2]

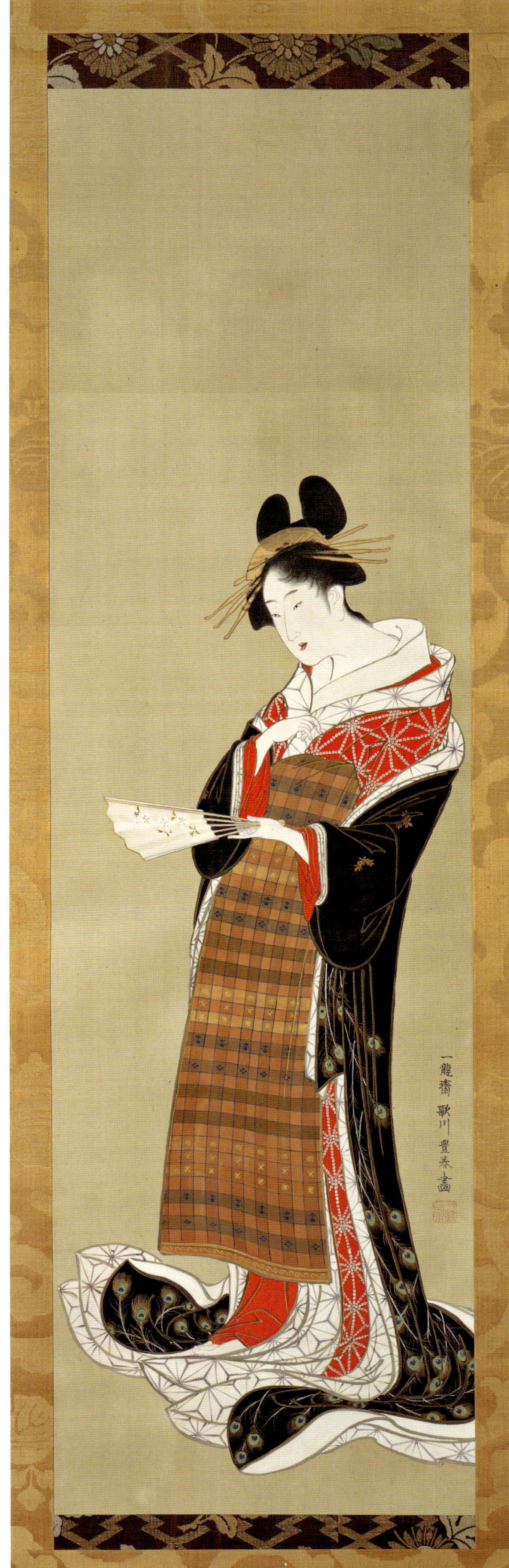

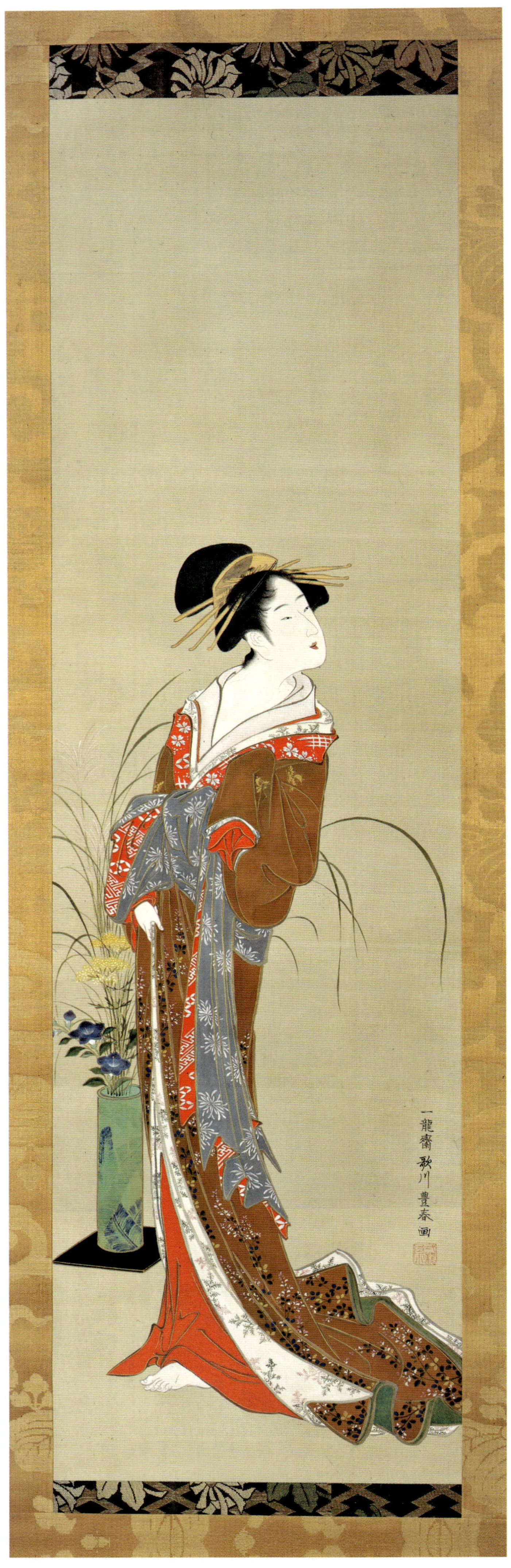

The extreme care with which the lines of the figures are executed and the colors are applied leaves no doubt about the high quality of this set of paintings. It is one of the tours de force of Toyoharu's oeuvre that attest to his mature skills. Judging from the women's hairstyles, these works were probably completed during the Kansei era. NM

---

1. *Editor's note:* The optimum viewing took place on the fourteenth day of the eighth lunar month (known as *yoimachi*, or "waiting for dusk").
2. *Editor's note:* Rabbits were fashioned from snow with leaves and berries attached for the ears and eyes. Such a snow rabbit can be seen at the end of *Genre Scenes in the Four Seasons* by Nishikawa Sukenobu (see cat. no. 18).

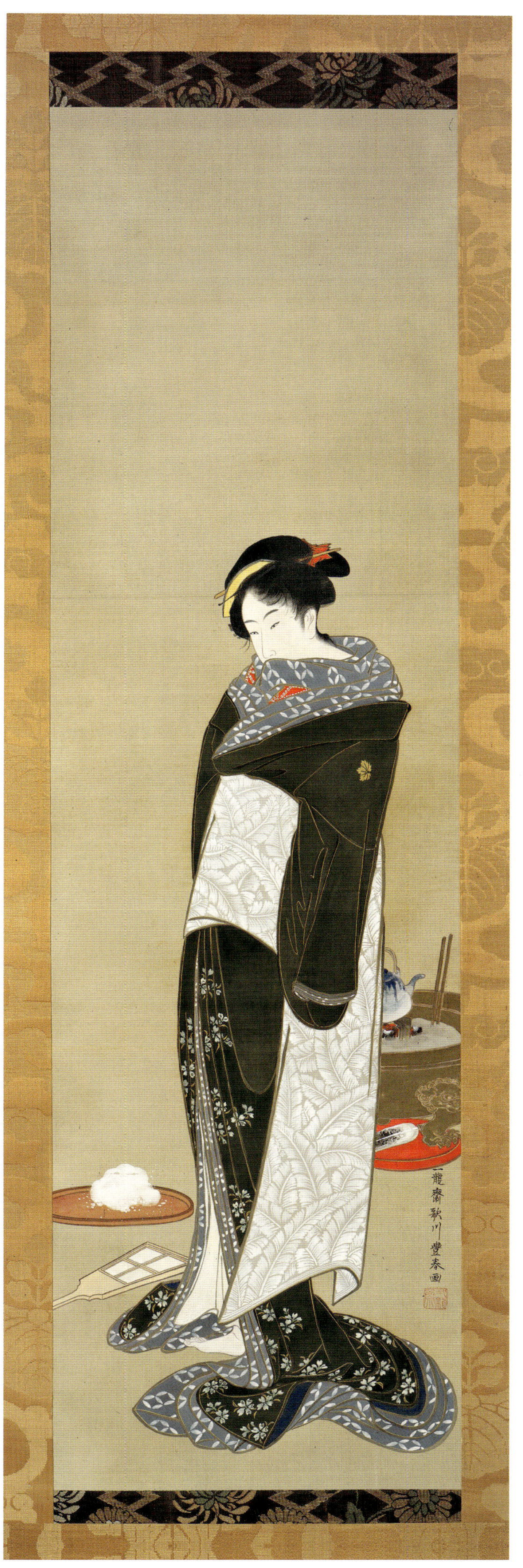
一龍齋歌川豊春画

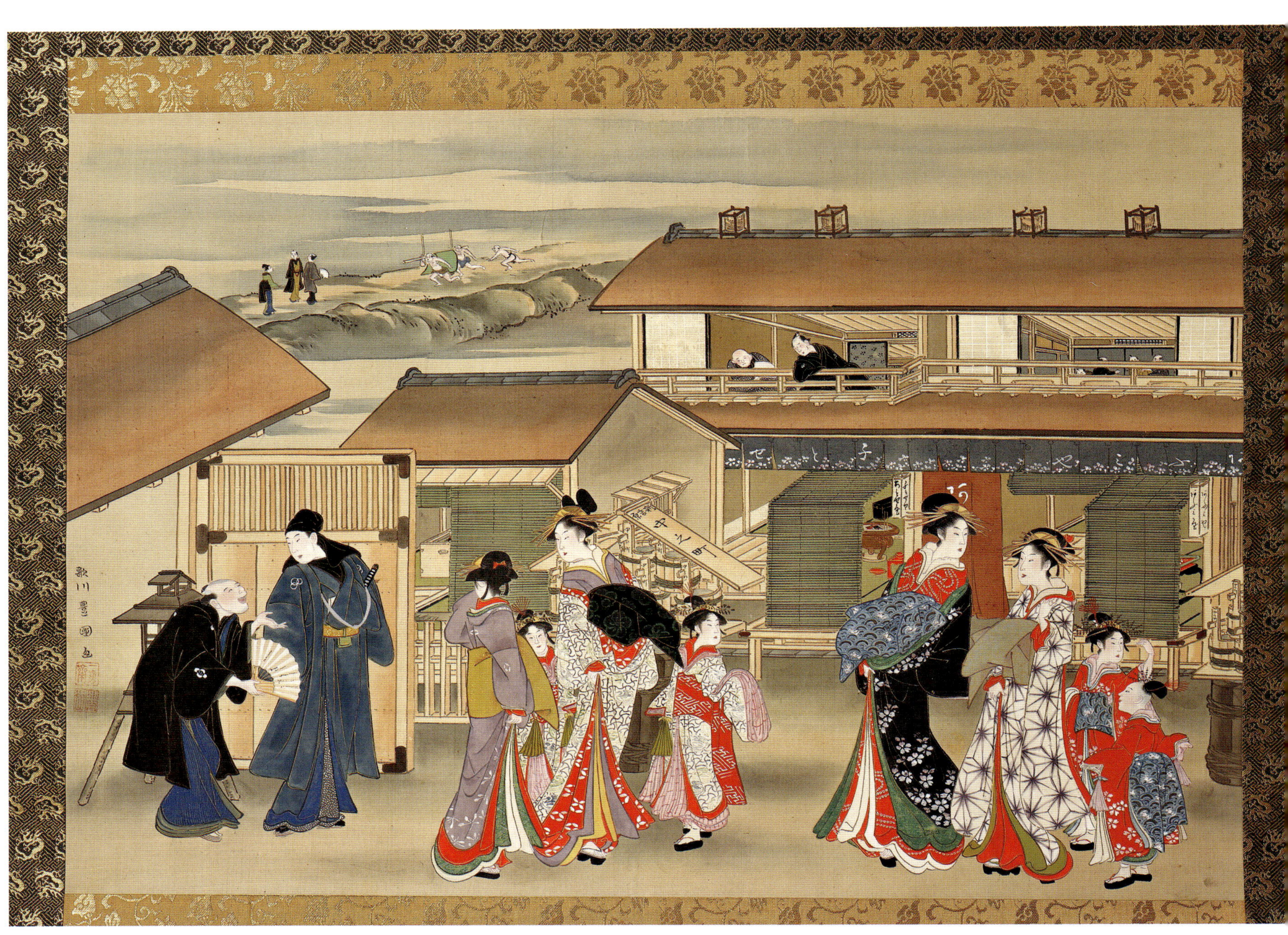
歌川豊國画

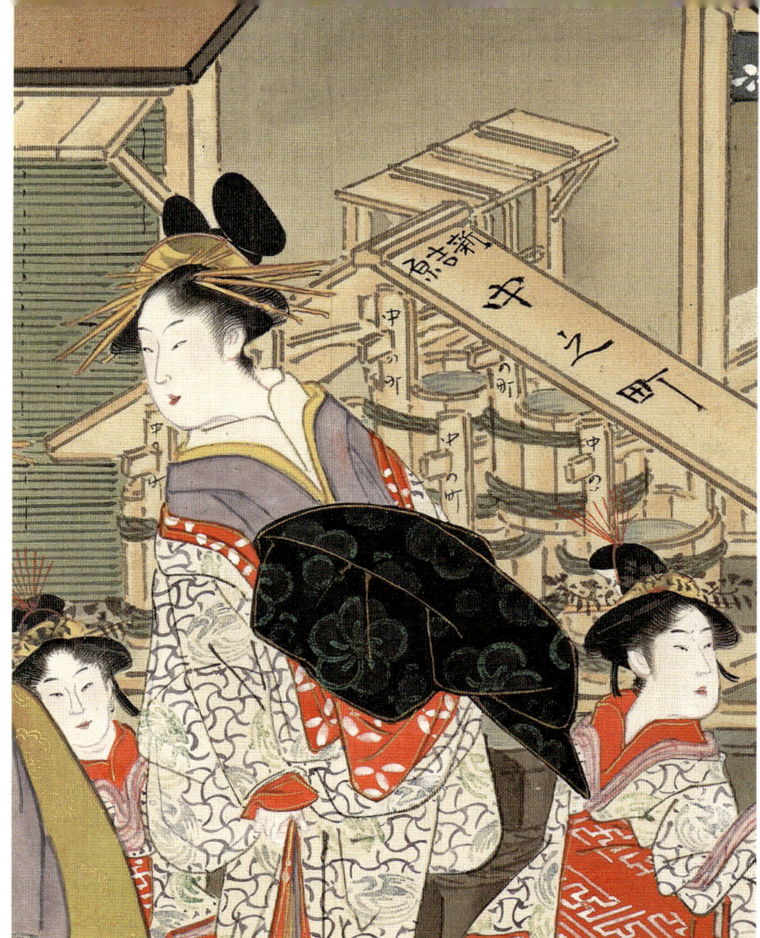

53. **UTAGAWA TOYOKUNI** (1769–1825)
Procession of Courtesans inside the Main Gate of the Yoshiwara

About Kansei 7 (1795)
Hanging scroll; ink, color, gold, and mica on silk
46.1 x 69.1 cm (18 1/8 x 27 3/16 in.)
Signature: Utagawa Toyokuni ga (Painting by Utagawa Toyokuni)
Seals: Ichiyōsai; Toyokuni
William Sturgis Bigelow Collection 11.7869

One of the highly anticipated spectacles in the Yoshiwara was the procession of a high-ranking courtesan and her retinue of attendants down the main boulevard of Nakano-chō, back and forth from her quarters to the teahouse (*hikitejaya*), where her client awaited. Such promenades also were part of greetings at the New Year, as perhaps may be seen in this painting. Set inside the main gate to the pleasure quarters, this work depicts a chic client wearing a long, loose outer robe (*haori*) and a black hat. He is being flattered by a male entertainer (*taikomochi*, literally a "drum holder"), who by contemporary pictorial convention is shown assuming an obsequious, smirking pose. To the right are two groups led by *oiran*, a designation given to prostitutes of the most elevated ranks from the mid-eighteenth century onward. In the one on the left the high-ranking courtesan is accompanied by two child attendants and an older *shinzō*, an assistant courtesan, who wears a short-sleeved (*tomesode*) robe. In the second one on the right the *oiran* is surrounded by her child attendants and a slightly younger *shinzō* garbed in a long, pendant-sleeved (*furisode*) robe.

Utagawa Toyokuni meticulously portrays contemporary life in the Yoshiwara: In the upper left of the composition a palanquin hurries to the pleasure quarters along the Nihontsuzumi (Nihon Embankment), the causeway that led from near the Imado Bridge to the Yoshiwara; some visitors are also leaving. Behind the client in the foreground, inside the main gate, there is the guard post called the *menbansho*, which was under the jurisdiction of the city's police and judiciary headquarters (*machi bugyō*) and was permanently manned by lower-ranking samurai (*dōshin* and *shitayaku*). Their presence ensured that the residents of the quarters did not leave without permission.

Just behind the guard post are lined rows of teahouses with their green bamboo blinds. The names of two of these houses, Chitoseya and Ōmiya, are written on the *noren*, the short paneled curtains along the eaves, and on the lanterns. According to the 1795 spring edition of the *Yoshiwara saiken*, the annual guidebook to the quarters, there were actually three teahouses—Hiranoya Sankurō, Chitoseya Kyūshichi, and Ōmiya Hanshirō—on the left side of the street between the main gate and another portal leading to the side street Fushimi-chō. Although the Hiranoya has not been included here, this painting fairly accurately represents the appearance of the Yoshiwara.

In 1792 or 1793 Toyokuni produced a *yoko ōban*–size woodblock print with a similar composition entitled *Perspective Picture of Night Entertainments in the New Yoshiwara* (*Uki-e Shin Yoshiwara yoasobi no zu*).[1] Since this painting, as can be best determined through the style of the figures and Toyokuni's signature, was created sometime around 1795, it is almost certain that the artist based the painted work on the preexisting print, then reorganized it and enlarged the figures. AS

1. Rikkā bijutsukan, *Uki-e* (Tokyo: Rikkā bijutsukan, 1975), illustration 91.

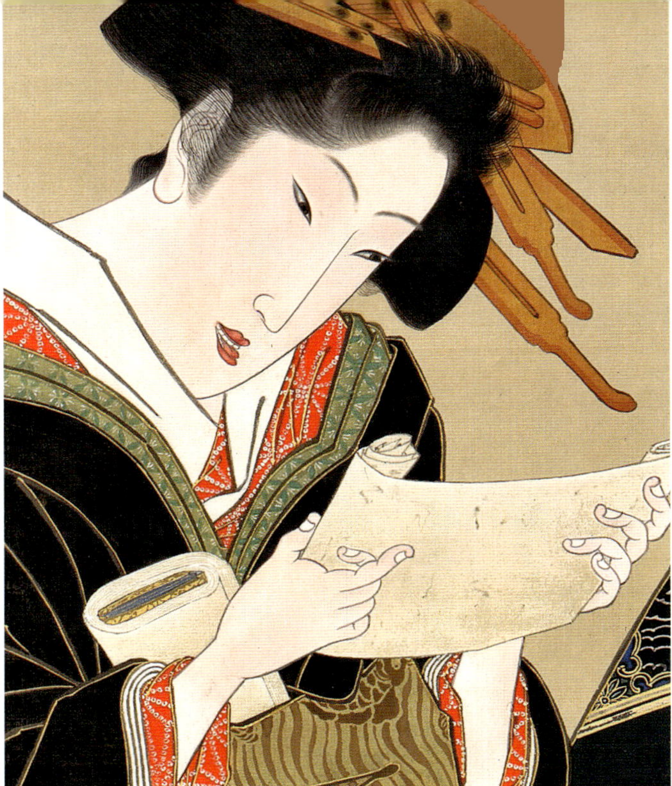

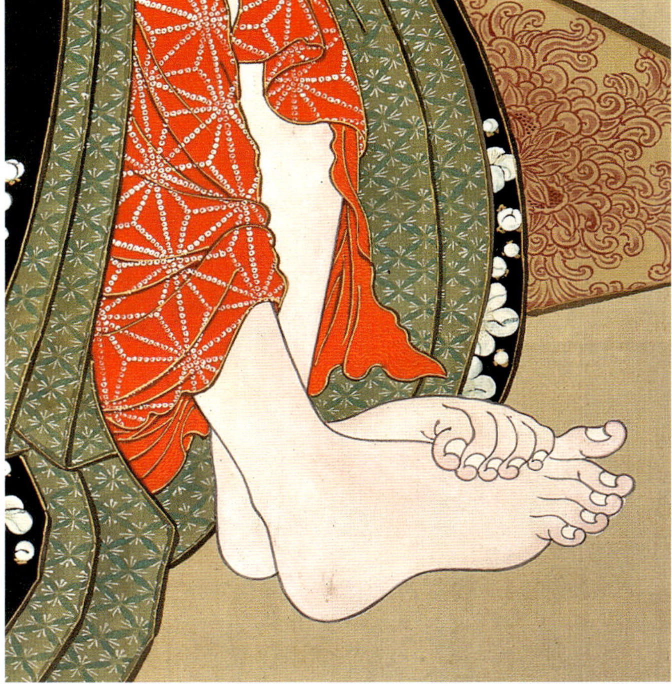

54. **UTAGAWA TOYOKUNI** (1769–1825)

Geisha and Waitress

About latter half of the Bunka era (1804–18)
Hanging scroll; ink, color, gold, silver, and mica on silk
161.9 x 82 cm (63 ¾ x 32 5/16 in.)
Signature: Utagawa Toyokuni ga (Painted by Utagawa Toyokuni)
Seals: Ichiyōsai; Toyokuni
William Sturgis Bigelow Collection 11.7583

Striking a self-conscious pose, a woman (probably a geisha) sits on a *kotatsu* heater in a rather unladylike way, the toes of her left foot curled and held against the top of her right instep in an expression of excitement at reading the content of a love letter. She is dressed in a black short-sleeved (*tomesode*) kimono with the hem decorated with scattered plum blossoms. A passing waitress in the brothel (or the teahouse) pauses to take a look. Conscious of the latest fashions, the artist Utagawa Toyokuni depicted this second woman wearing her hair in what was known as the *mitsuwa* (three-bun chignon), a new style that became popular during the nineteenth century; the center knot was flanked by another bun on either side. Furthermore, the ties that she wears outside her obi had just come into vogue.

The scroll is monumental, with the silk on which it is painted measuring twice the regular width — the scale suggesting that it was commissioned by a special client. Although it is of the largest size for an ukiyo-e painting, the work was executed in an astonishingly meticulous way following Toyokuni's general style for the period. Originally this work was part of a pair of hanging scrolls or one side of a two-panel folding screen; its mate, *The Wife and Daughter of a Townsman*, is now in the collection of the Chiba City Museum of Art.[1] When the MFA and Chiba works are hung side by side, the four women in the compositions are symmetrically arranged; from right to left they are the townsman's daughter, her mother, the waitress, and the geisha. Furthermore, if we consider that the daughter, who holds a ball and wears a *furisode* with a cherry-blossom motif, represents spring, her mother, who has just emerged from the bath and dons a *yukata*, represents summer. The waitress then symbolizes autumn, and the geisha winter.

In 1816 Toyokuni executed a grand work, *One Hundred Modern Fashions* (*Imayō sugata hyakushi zu*), in twenty-six hanging scrolls, formerly in the Manno Museum and now in a private collection.[2] Also a special commission, the groups of women depicted must be somehow related to those in the MFA painting. AS

1. *The Wife and Daughter of a Townsman*, hanging scroll, ink and color on silk, 161.3 x 82 cm, Chiba City Museum of Art, published in *Chiba-shi bijutsukan*, vol. 10 of *Nikuhitsu ukiyo-e taikan* (Tokyo: Kōdansha, 1995), entry 43.
2. *One Hundred Modern Fashions*, set of twenty-six hanging scrolls, ink and color on silk, 40 x 58.5 cm each, published in *Manno bijutsukan*, vol. 7 of *Nikuhitsu ukiyo-e taikan* (Tokyo: Kōdansha, 1996), entry 44.

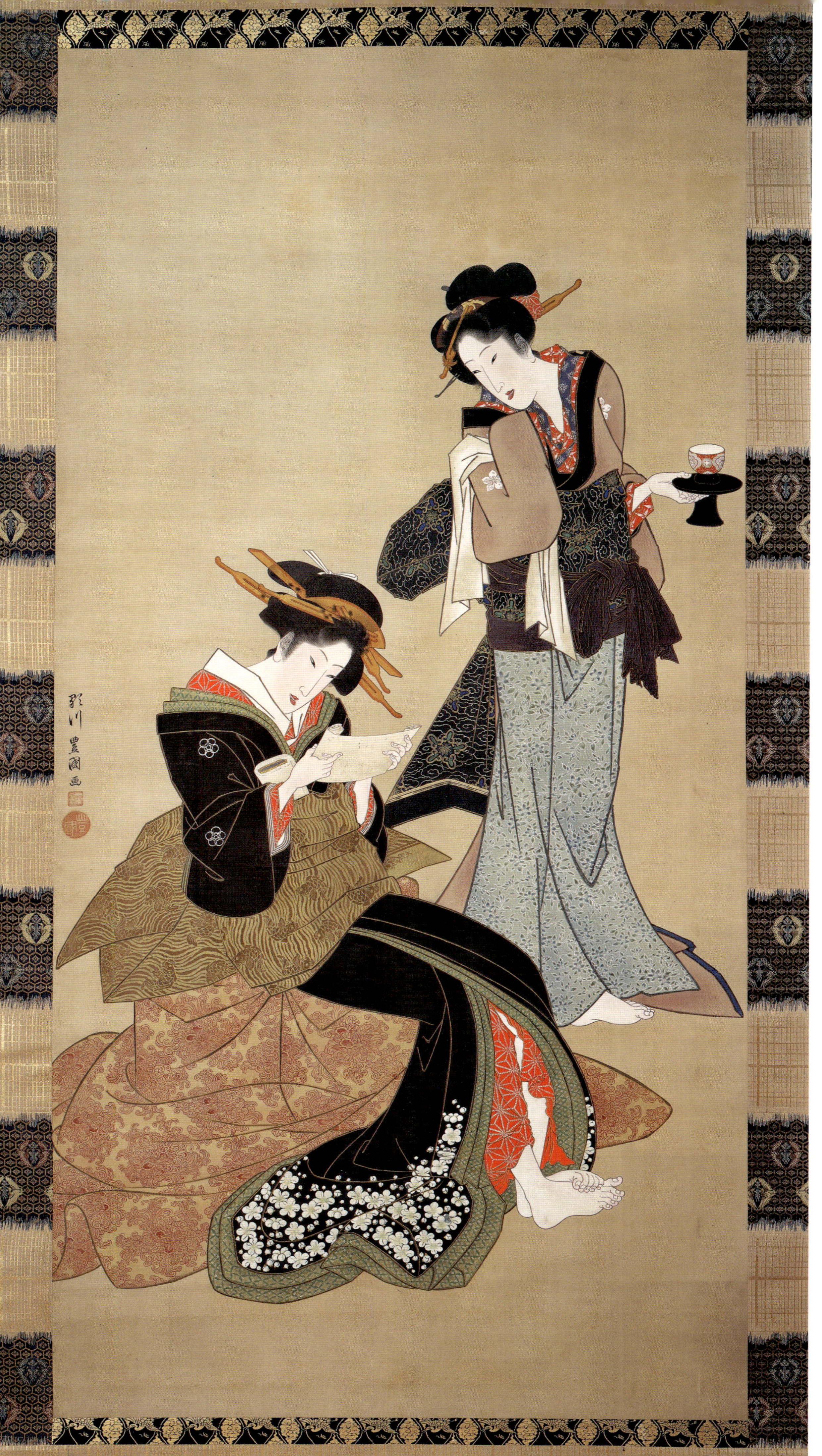
歌川豊國画

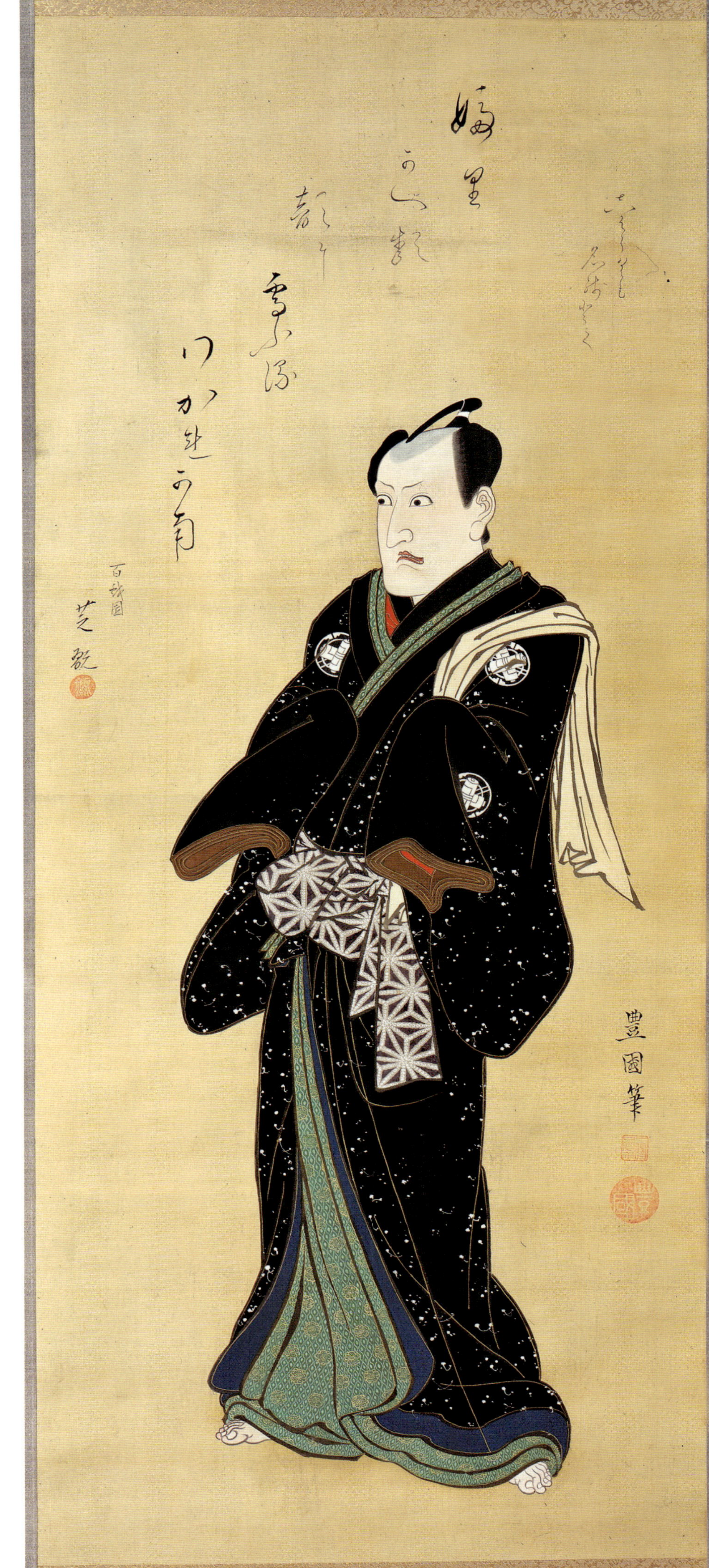
豊國筆

55. **UTAGAWA TOYOKUNI I** (1769–1825)
Nakamura Utaemon III

Bunka 9 (1812)
Hanging scroll; ink, color, and gold on silk
102.7 x 44.6 cm (40 7/16 x 17 9/16 in.)
Signature: Toyokuni hitsu (Brush of Toyokuni)
Seal: Toyokuni
William Sturgis Bigelow Collection 11.7864

During the last decade of the eighteenth century, Utagawa Toyokuni established a new dynamic style of actor prints, which can be seen in his celebrated series Views of Actors on Stage (Yakusha butai no sugata-e). However, aside from a few works such as the 1789 *Soga Brothers' Encounter with Their Enemy*, in the Chiba City Museum of Art, most of his actor paintings date to the nineteenth century.

Like many of Toyokuni's painted portraits of theatrical performers, this scroll is quite large in scale. The subject, Nakamura Utaemon III, can be identified by the distinctive portrayal of his face and his signature Gion charm (Gion *mamori*) crest. He wears a black *habutae* silk robe decorated with a pattern of spring snow (*nagori yuki*). Despite the fact that Utaemon was said to have been short and rather unattractive, the painting is a masterpiece that presents the actor as a dignified presence.

Before Utaemon came to Edo to perform in the Nakamura Theater in 1808, he was already celebrated in Osaka. However, his popularity skyrocketed during the five years that he was on the stage in the Eastern Capital. Utaemon gave his last performance on the seventeenth day of the tenth month of 1812. When he departed for Osaka on the next day, more than two hundred people came to bid him farewell. The number of farewell gifts that he received from his patrons and fellow actors (including Ichikawa Danjūrō VII) was considered exceptional at the time.

This painting must have been commissioned by one of Utaemon's patrons faced with his upcoming departure. The following poem at the top of the portrait was inscribed by the actor himself.

Shibaraku mo	In "Just a Minute!"
nagori tote furikaeru	I made my reputation.
kao ni yuki furu	On my face, as I look back,
wakare kana.	the snow is falling. Is this our parting?

The poem is followed by Utaemon's alternate theatrical name (*gō*), Hyakkeen, and his pen name (*haimei*), Shikan. AS

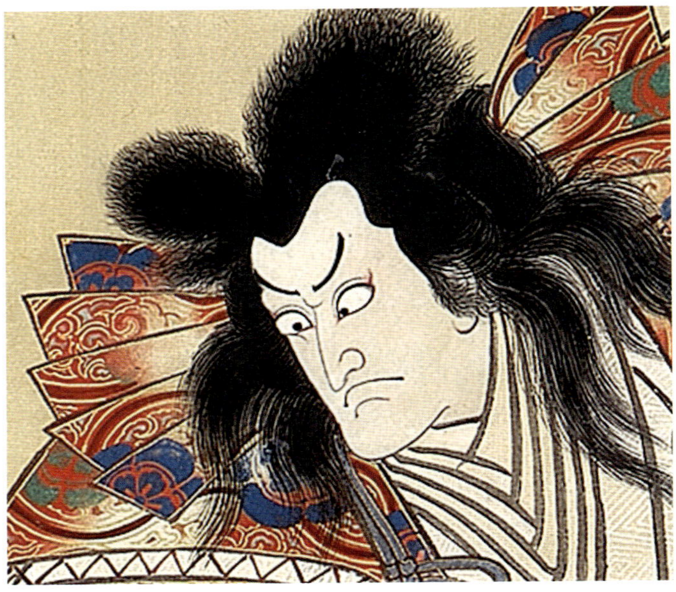

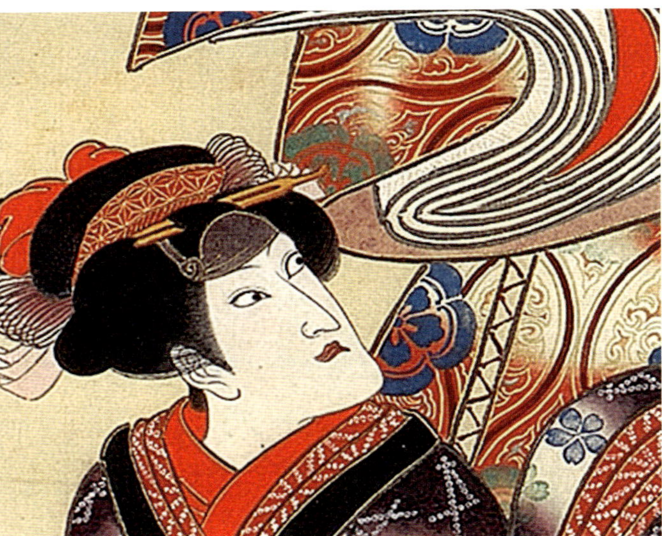

56. **UTAGAWA TOYOKUNI I** (1769–1825)
Nakamura Utaemon III in Seven Roles

Bunka 12 (1815)
Hanging scroll; ink, color, and gold on silk
126 x 58.2 cm (49 5/8 x 22 15/16 in.)
Signature: Utagawa Toyokuni ga (Painted by Utagawa Toyokuni)
Seal: Ichiyōsai; Toyokuni
Fenollosa-Weld Collection 11.4611

After achieving popular acclaim for his performances in Edo from 1808 through 1812 (see cat. no. 55), the Osaka actor Nakamura Utaemon III returned to the Eastern Capital in the fifth month of 1814 before going home again in the tenth month of 1815. From the seventh month of 1815 until his return to Osaka he made appearances at the Nakamura Theater. This painting depicts seven roles that he performed during that short period.

In the upper right, Utaemon is seen in the roles of the villainous Soga no Iruka and the jealous shop owner's daughter Omiwa in the play *Imoseyama onna teikin*. To the left, he dances as Wakatō Sahei in the play *Oriawase tsuzure no nishiki*.[1] In the center, on the right, Utaemon assumes the role of Tsukematsu Kazue from the play *Otokodate iromo Yoshiwara* and to the left that of the fox who disguises himself as the trusted retainer of Minamoto Yoshitsune in the popular *Yoshitsune senbon zakura*. Utaemon's hopping posture and curling fingers reveal his character's real nature. With his fan outstretched, the actor performs as Domo no Matahei, the ever-humiliated court artist, in *Keisei hangonkō*, and finally at the bottom of the scroll as Saitō Taroemon in the play *Ōtō no miya asahi no yoroi*.

The ukiyo-e artist Utagawa Kunisada, one of Toyokuni's most accomplished disciples, designed an *ōban* triptych, *Nakamura Utaemon's Farewell Performance of a Lifetime* (*Nakamura Utaemon isse-ichidai onagori*), now in the collection of the Japanese National Theater. In this print there are images of Utaemon acting in nine roles. However, he did not make appearances in some of these, and thus Kunisada must have made the print before the performances took place. In contrast, the MFA painting depicts roles Utaemon assumed. Despite the somewhat fictitious nature of the print, Kunisada's design is rather powerful and may have affected Toyokuni's own portrayals of the actor.

Nakamura Utaemon had many patrons, and the number of portraits that Toyokuni produced suggests that the artist may also have been a supporter. Included among these are the paintings *Nakamura Shikan and a Geisha in front of Mimeguri Shrine*, in the collection of Keiō University, and *Nakamura Utaemon III in Musume Dōjō-ji*, belonging to Kōsai-ji in Hyōgo prefecture.[2] AS

1. Earlier, during the third month of 1815, Utaemon had performed the role of the servant Yarimochi in the play *Sono kokonoe saishiki zakura*, and there is a possibility that this image refers to that role. However, in the section of the *Kabuki nendaiki zokuhen* for *Oriawase tsuzure no nishiki*, there is a passage stating that Bandō Mitsugorō III, Utaemon's rival, performed as Wakatō Ibe and Utaemon was Wakatō Sahei. Both men received excellent reviews for their acting.
2. I would like to express my appreciation to Shindō Shigeru in the preparation of this entry.

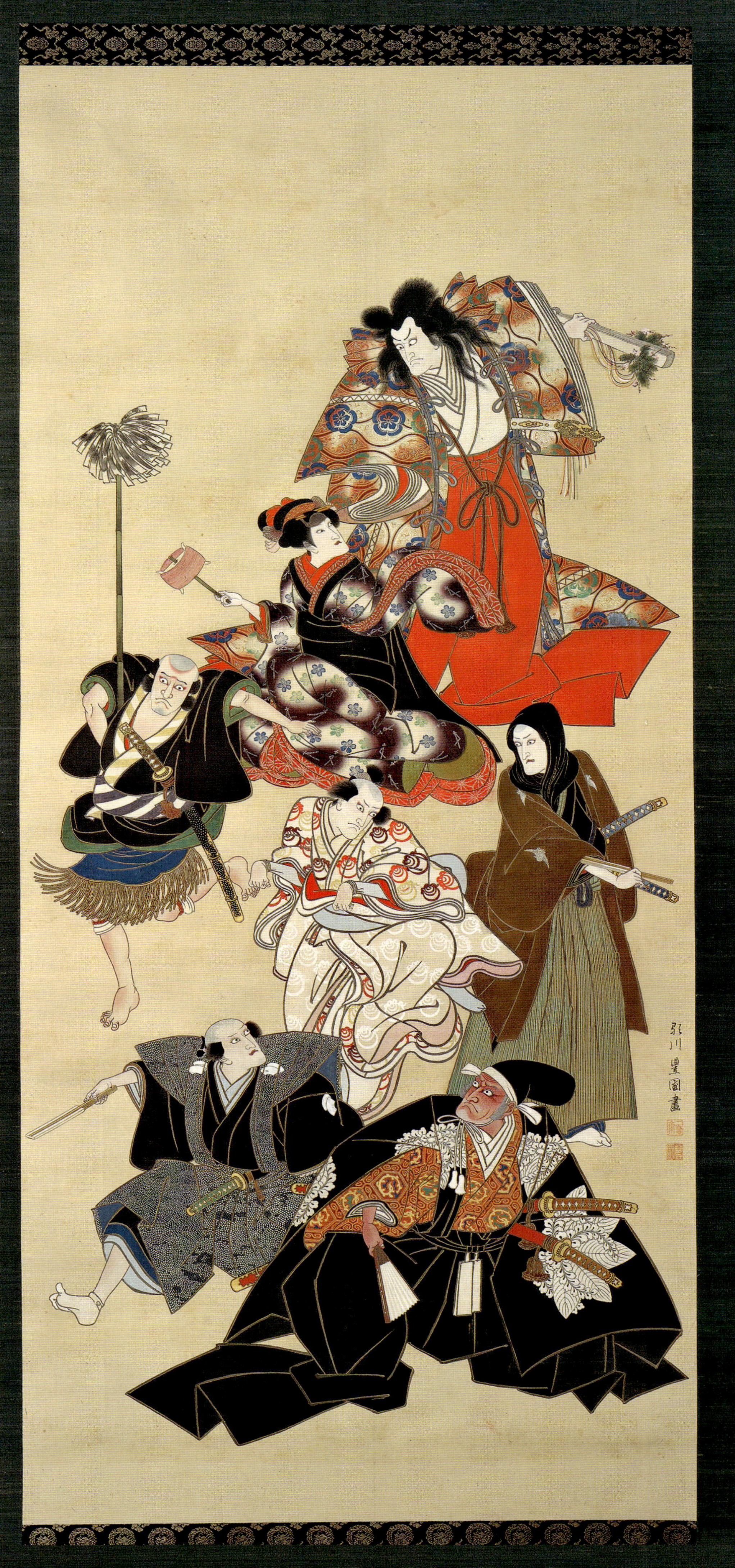
歌川豊國畫

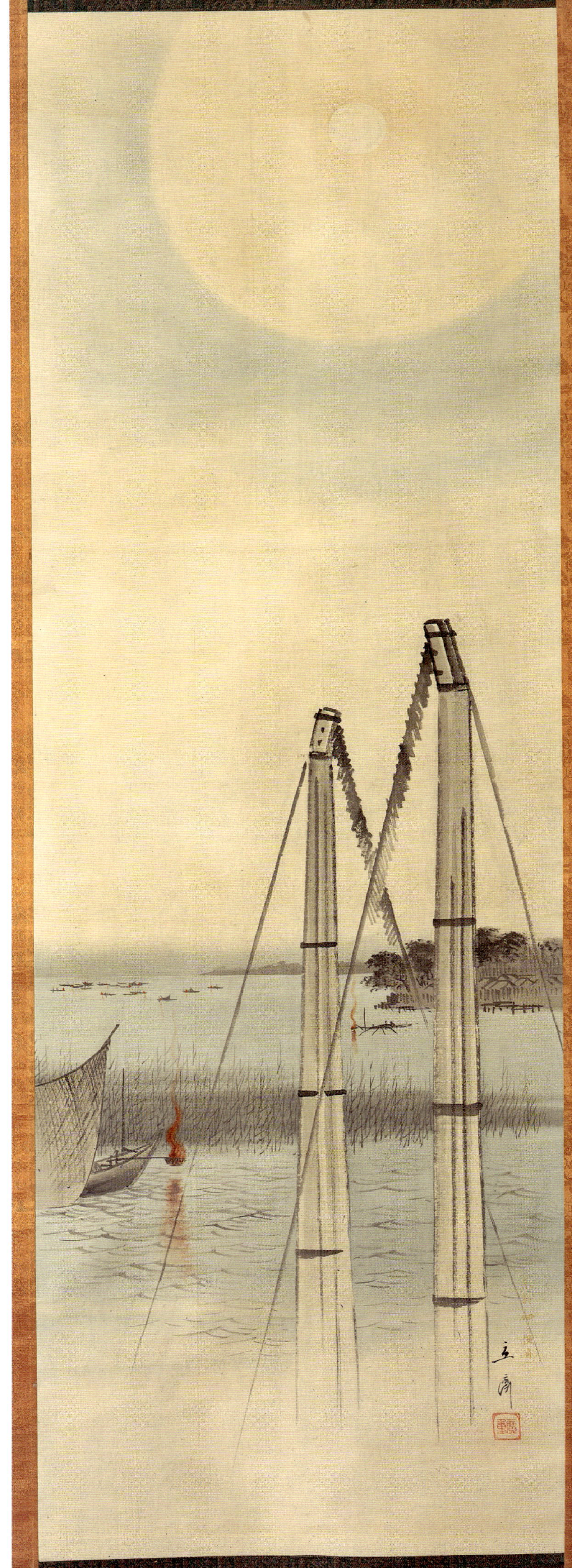

57. **UTAGAWA HIROSHIGE** (1797–1858)
Fishing Boats at Tsukuda Island, Edo

Kaei era (1848–54)
Hanging scroll; ink, color, and gold on silk
91.1 x 31 cm (35 13/16 x 12 3/16 in.)
Signature: Ryūsai
Seal: Hiroshige
William Sturgis Bigelow Collection 11.7371

Two wooden cargo-ship masts executed in ink dominate the foreground of this moonlit composition. Behind them a delicate landscape of reed banks and low-lying islands extends out to the horizon line. Fishing skiffs luring whitebait (*shirauo*) with their metal baskets of burning embers float past in the middle ground; more-distant boats, suggested by abbreviated lines of ink wash and punctuations of red, lie out in the bay. A faint inscription in gold in the lower-right corner identifies the scene as Tsukuda Island, a mudflat at the mouth of the Sumida River that was developed during the seventeenth century as a home for fishermen. Although these men were ostensibly purveyors of whitebait for the military aristocracy, they were also employed as spies on boats coming and going in Edo Bay.

The juxtaposition of the masts against a watery landscape was a compositional device with which Utagawa Hiroshige experimented in two print series entitled Famous Places in the Eastern Capital (Tōto meisho) in 1833 and 1840.[1] After producing this scroll, he would exploit it again to great effect in his woodblock print of Eitaibashi, a bridge that crossed the Sumida River, in the celebrated series One Hundred Views of Edo (Edo meisho hyakkei, 1857). The subdued palette of *Fishing Boats at Tsukuda Island, Edo*, with its thin washes of light blue and ink, and the lyrical handling of landscape elements reveal Hiroshige's indebtedness to contemporary works by the Maruyama-Shijō school in Kyoto.

The inclusion of the title in gold ink next to the artist's signature identifies this painting as belonging to a group of compositions that were often produced in sets of two or three hanging scrolls at the order of the Tendō fief of Dewa province in northwestern Japan. Deeply in debt, the lords of Tendō attempted to defer repayment of the loans made by the area's wealthy merchants and farmers by presenting them with Hiroshige's scrolls.[2] All of the works were depictions of famous sites — many in Edo and Kyoto — but they were not necessarily recognizable to their provincial owners; hence, Hiroshige felt it prudent to inscribe the place-names. ANM

1. Asano Shūgō, "Tōto Tsukuda no gyoshū," in *Bosuton bijutsukan nikuhitsu ukiyo-e*, vol. 3 (Tokyo: Museum of Fine Arts, Boston, and Kōdansha, 2000), 183–84.
2. For an extensive discussion of the commission, see Kobayashi Tadashi, "The Rediscovery of the Tendō Hiroshiges," trans. Henry Smith, *Impressions*, no. 22 (2000): 17–35.

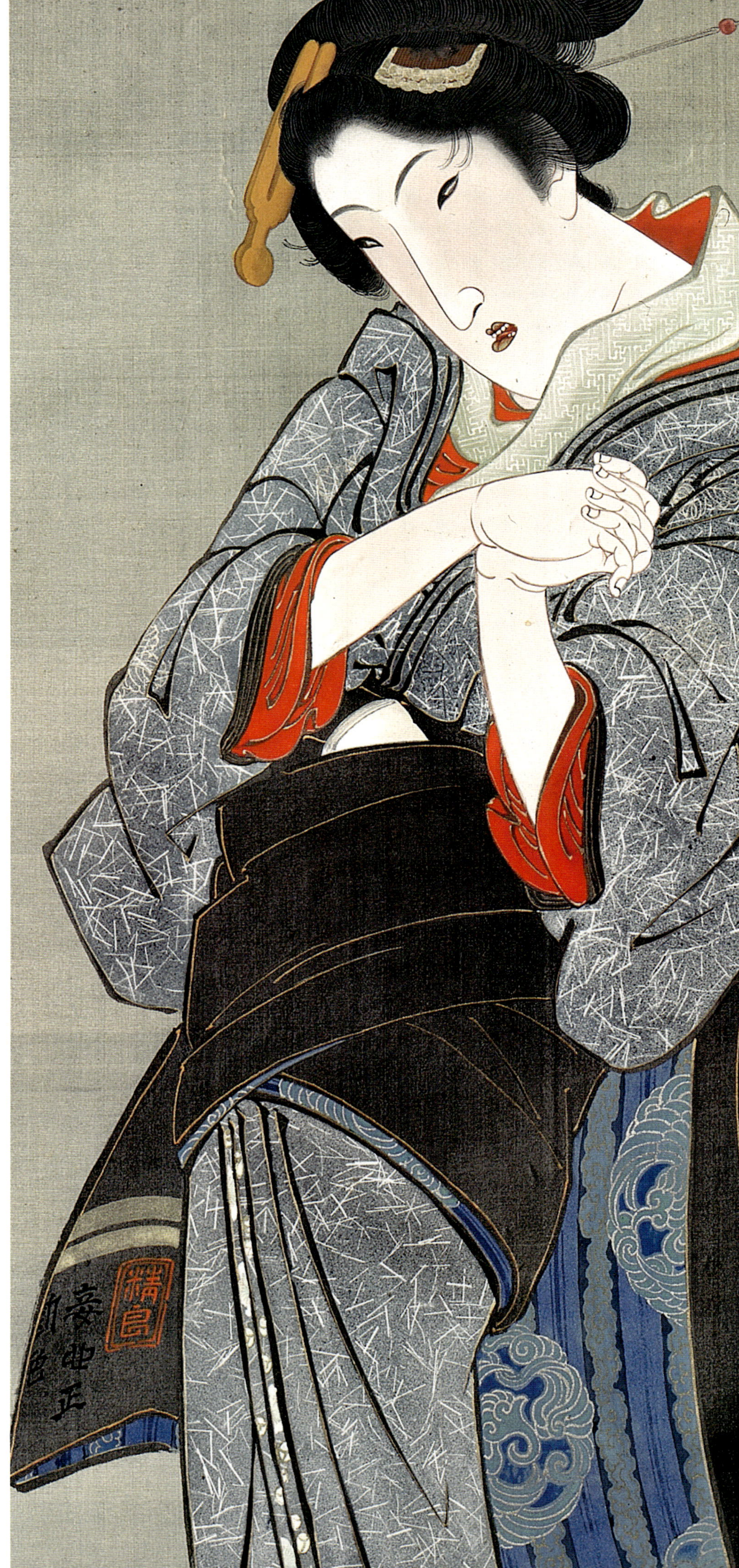

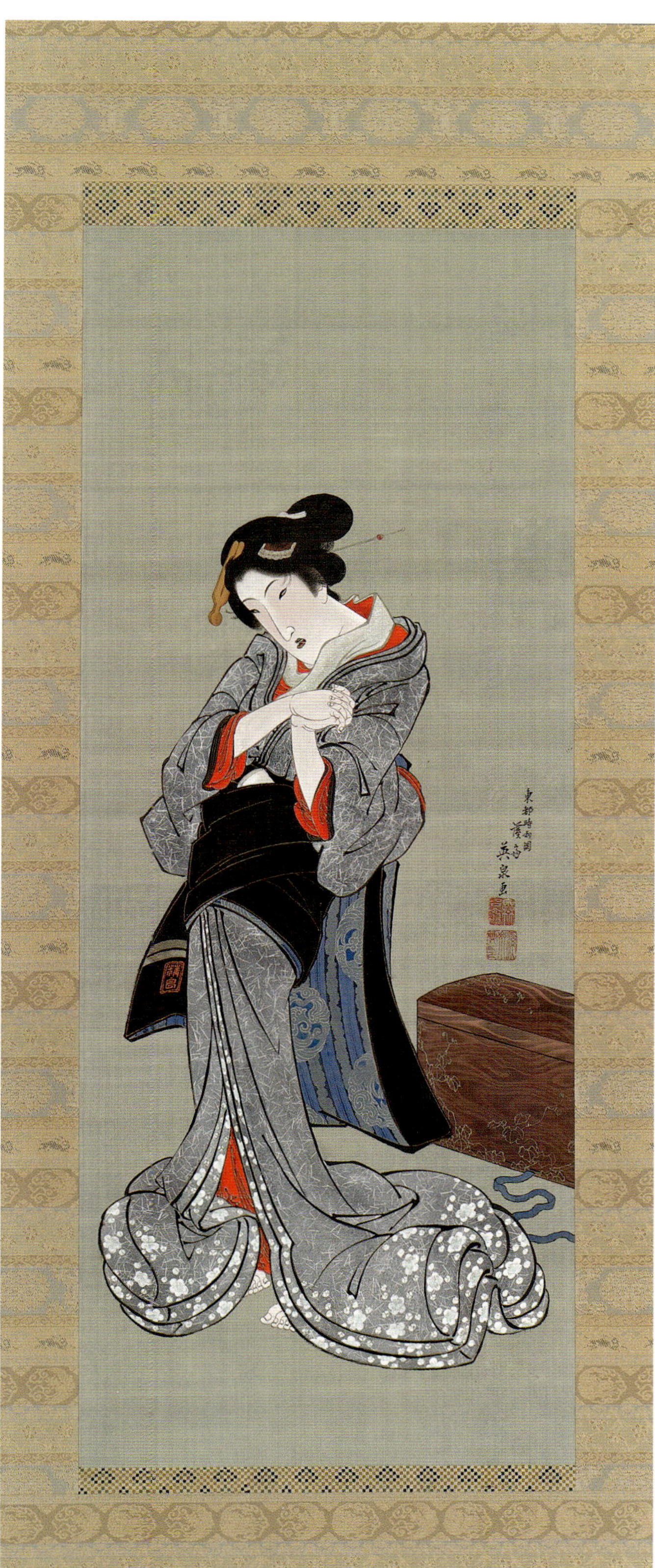

58. **KEISAI EISEN** (1790–1848)
Geisha

About Tenpō 3–5 (1832–34)
Hanging scroll; ink, color, and gold on silk
103.7 x 41.2 cm (40 13/16 x 16 1/4 in.)
Signature: Tōto Shigurenooka Keisai Eisen ga (Painted by Keisai Eisen, Shigurenooka in the Eastern Capital)
Seals: Mumeiō; Keisai ga in (Seal of a painting by Keisai)
Fenollosa-Weld Collection 11.4662

During the 1830s Keisai Eisen's images of beautiful women took the form of depraved older women beckoning one from the depths of hell. In this painting a geisha stands next to a samisen box pondering something at night.[1] Her expression displays a characteristic Eisenesque venomousness with a deep seductive glow. On the bottom left of her sash appear some suggestive phrases: two characters in red read "excellent," and five characters in black read "my heart is truly made new with desire."

Eisen's signature is preceded by the notation "Shigurenooka in the Eastern Capital," indicating that the scroll was painted between 1832 and 1834, when Eisen was living in Negishi, in northeastern Edo. During this period he authored *Essays by a Nameless Old Man* (*Mumeiō zuihitsu*, 1833), a critical essay on ukiyo-e. Therefore, the seal "Mumeiō" (Nameless Old Man) must also relate to his studio name from that time. Considering that few of Eisen's painted works can be dated, the significance of this work can hardly be overstated. AS

1. While recently remounting this scroll, the Asian Conservation Studio at the MFA discovered that the darkened background was created by a dark blue lining paper applied to the back of the silk.

"THE MAN MAD ABOUT PAINTING," 1760–1849 **KATSUSHIKA HOKUSAI**

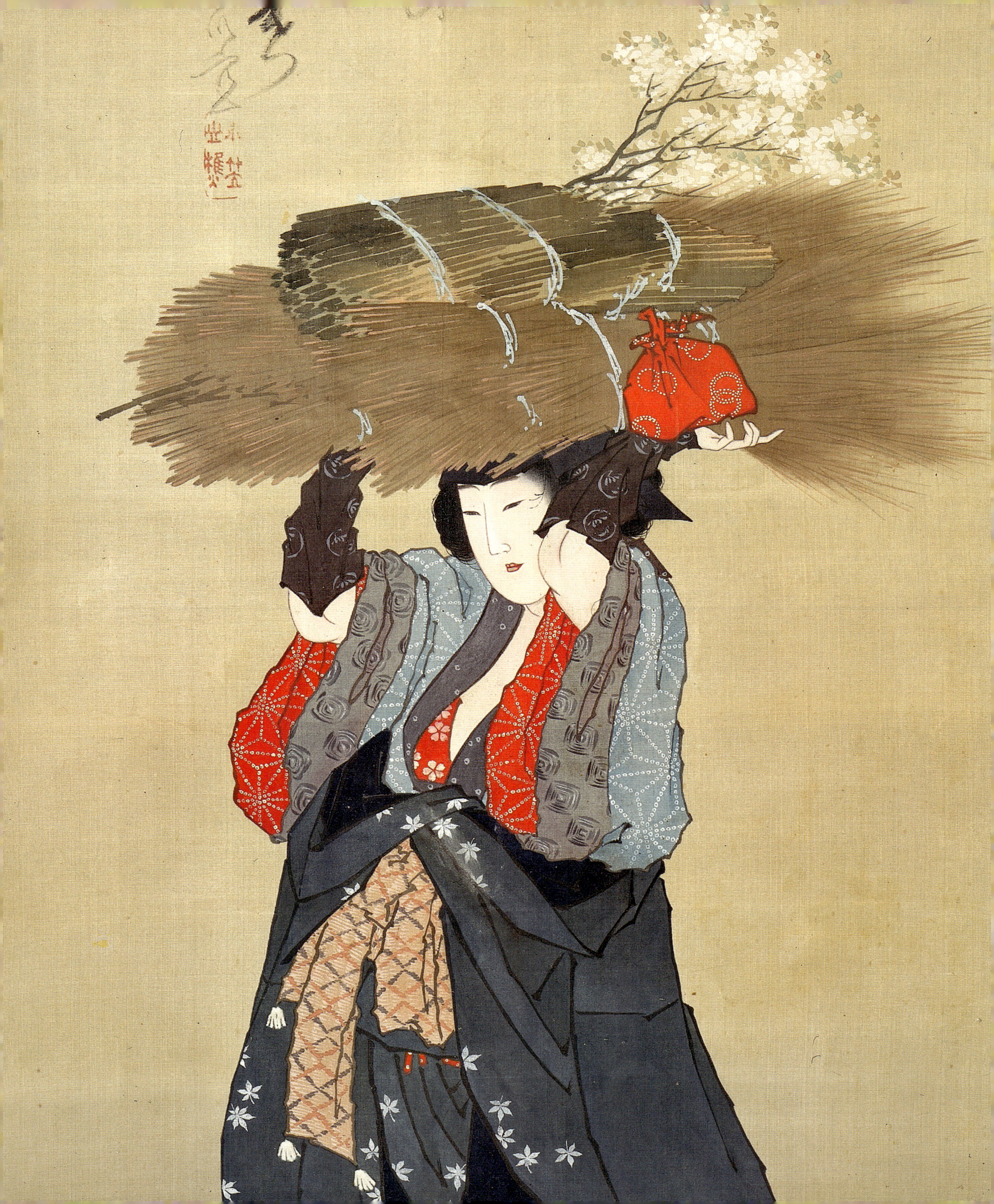

"THE MAN MAD ABOUT PAINTING," 1760–1849: KATSUSHIKA HOKUSAI

Katsushika Hokusai was a giant in the world of ukiyo-e. During his career of more than seventy years (the longest of any ukiyo-e artist), he constantly experimented and established new styles. Today he is celebrated for his landscape prints, in particular the series Thirty-six Views of Mount Fuji (Fugaku sanjūrokkei), which was published in the first half of the 1830s. However, he produced a range of other incomparable images, including privately commissioned deluxe prints (surimono)*, illustrated books, and paintings, in addition to commercially published prints.*

Hokusai studied under Katsukawa Shunshō, who, during the 1780s, specialized in hanging scrolls and screens of beautiful women, but the young artist did not realize his talents as a painter until after Shunshō died in 1792. From the 1790s until his own death, Hokusai produced numerous paintings. During the first two decades of the nineteenth century he dedicated himself primarily to experimenting with the female form (cat. nos. 59 and 62). His style of painting beautiful women turned during the 1810s from subdued, elongated images to highly sensual figures with garments described in agitated lines. Gradually he explored bird-and-flower, landscape, theatrical, and Chinese themes as well.

Not only did Hokusai produce compositions in the standard hanging scroll, handscroll, and screen formats; he also decorated everyday articles such as banners, lanterns, textiles, and festival floats. During the last years of his life his paintings centered on fantasy and supernaturalism, subjects that resonated with an awareness of his impending mortality and a desire to connect with the divine.

Although Hokusai had about two hundred pupils (including amateur artists), the only one with whom he had a close relationship was his daughter, Katsushika Ōi (cat. no. 69). His followers were not as tightly organized as the Utagawa artists, but they included such talented men as Hishikawa Sōri (cat. no. 67 and 68), Totoya Hokkei, Ryūryūkyo Shinsai, Teisai Hokuba, Hōtei Gosei, Suzuki Hokusai (Hokusai II), and Tōenrō Hokusen (Taito II). AS

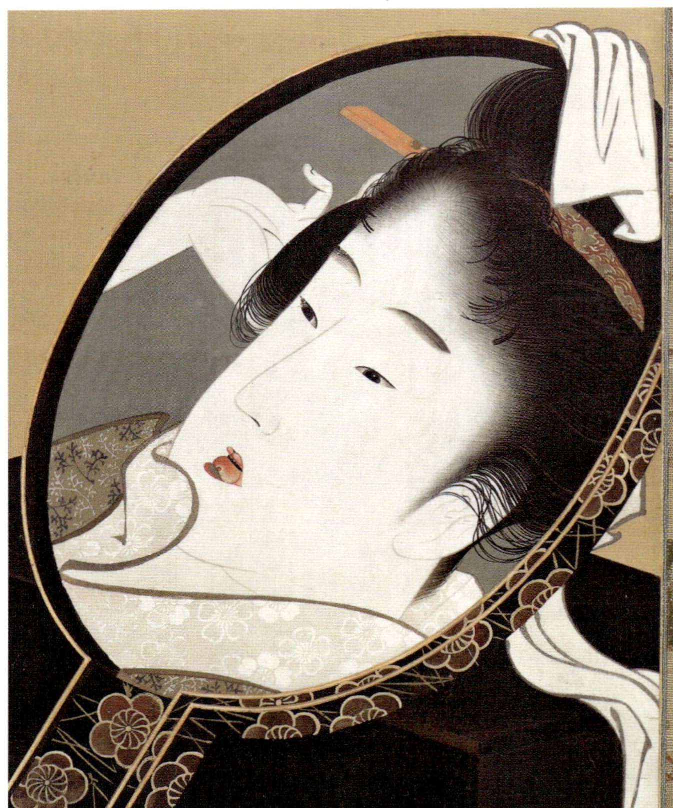

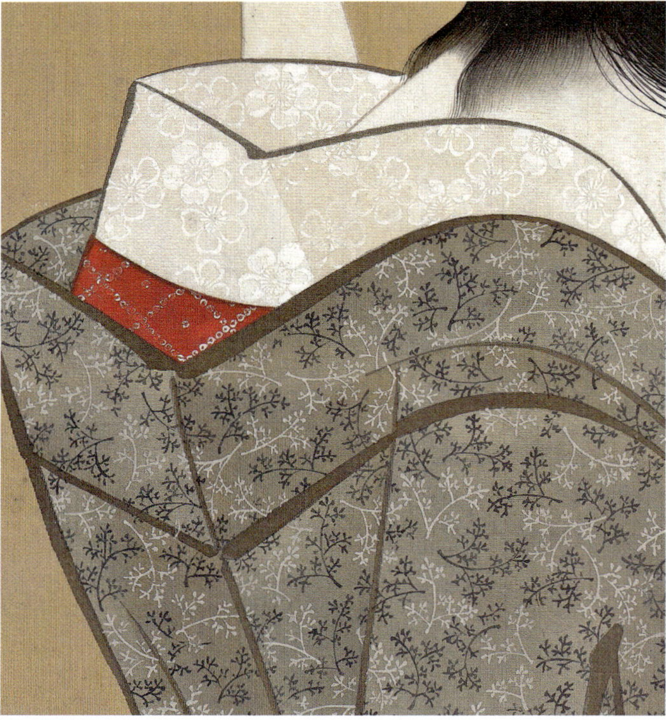

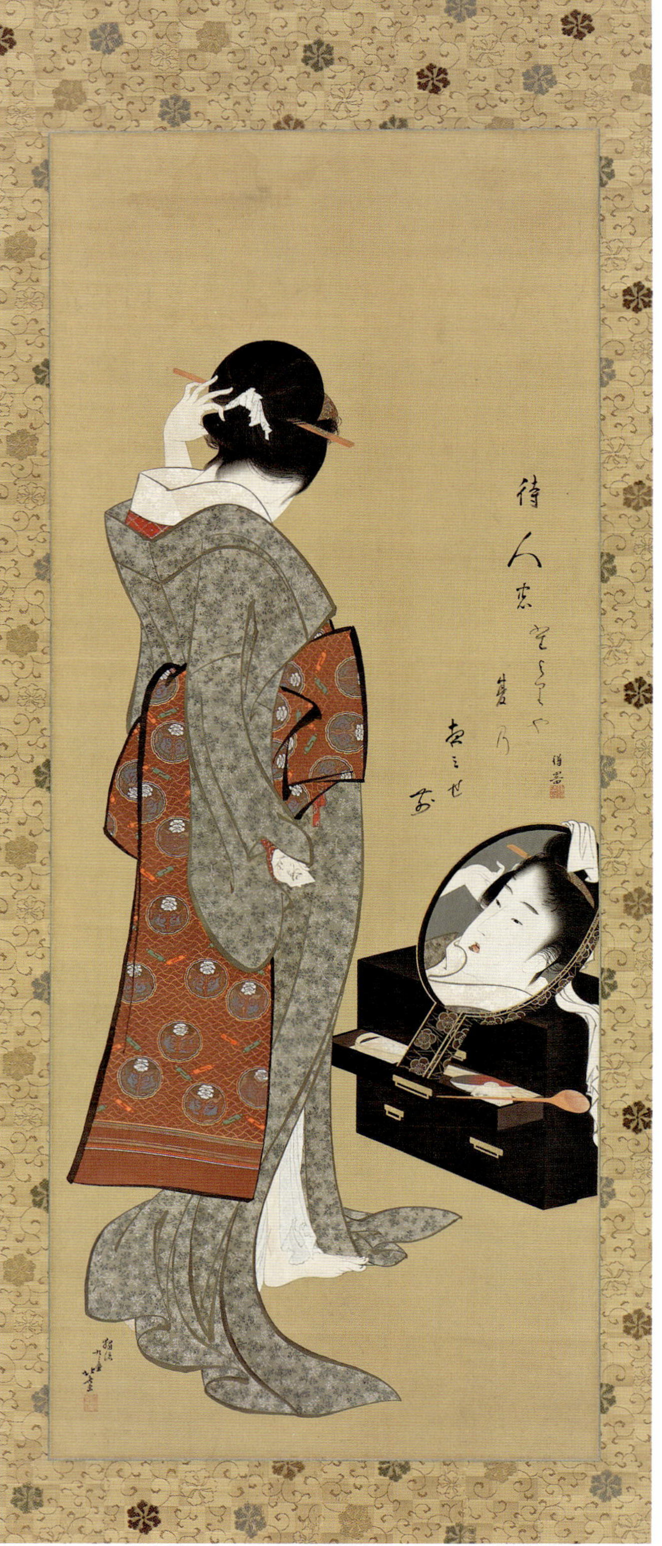

59. **KATSUSHIKA HOKUSAI** (1760–1849)
Woman Looking at Herself in a Mirror

About Bunka 2 (1805)
Hanging scroll; ink color, gold, and mica on silk
138.7 x 57.5 cm (54 5/8 x 22 5/8 in.)
Signature: Dokuryū Kukushin Hokusai ga (Painted by Kukushin Hokusai of the Independent Lineage)
Seal: Kimō dasoku (Hair on the turtle, legs on the snake)
William Sturgis Bigelow Collection 11.7424

A commanding woman, absorbed in her toilette, dominates this composition. Seen from behind, she adjusts her coiffure with her left hand, much concerned about achieving the proper shape. Her so-called Fuji-shaped face — after the name and shape of the mountain, an emblem of her beauty — is dramatically reflected in the mirror resting on her cosmetic chest. Between her blackened teeth she holds a ground-cherry (*hōzuki*). The crimson flesh of this fruit was traditionally used as a medicine to control hysteria; however, here the woman bites it in a seductive gesture.

The iconography of a beautiful woman seen from behind originates in the well-known *Woman Looking over Her Shoulder*, in the Tokyo National Museum, by the pioneer ukiyo-e artist Hishikawa Moronobu. Other, later examples of the type include several works by Hokusai's teacher Katsukawa Shunshō as well as a number by Kitagawa Utamaro. Hokusai himself included the imagery in other scrolls, but this painting certainly surpasses those in scale and quality.[1]

When examined closely, the handling of the woman's body appears a bit awkward in some places. For example, the right hand holding a letter is weak, and the positioning of the right foot is unclear. However, the distortion of the figure reflects a stylistic preference of Hokusai's during the mid-1790s to early 1810s, when he was signing his works with the names Sōri and Hokusai.[2] Attempting to move from the sensitive style of his mentor Shunshō, who had depicted somewhat implacid women with pure white skin in shell pigments, Hokusai wanted to create images of greater imagination. The fact that he went out of his way to include the words "independent lineage" in the signature on this painting indicates his own pride at having surpassed his teacher.

At the top of the composition is a poem inscribed by Shima Tokki, a master of *haikai* who lived in Otamagaike in the Kanda district of Edo at the time. It reads:

Matsu hito no	Does that letter from
tayori ya natsu no	the man she waits for promise
yomise mae.	a summer's night out?

NM

1. Katsushika Hokusai, *Courtesan Viewing Herself in a Mirror*, hanging scroll, ink and color on silk, 86 x 32.4 cm, private collection, Japan.
2. In this painting Hokusai uses a second alternate name, Kukushin, in addition to his more commonly known appellation; thus, we are able to date the work to around 1805 (Bunka 2).

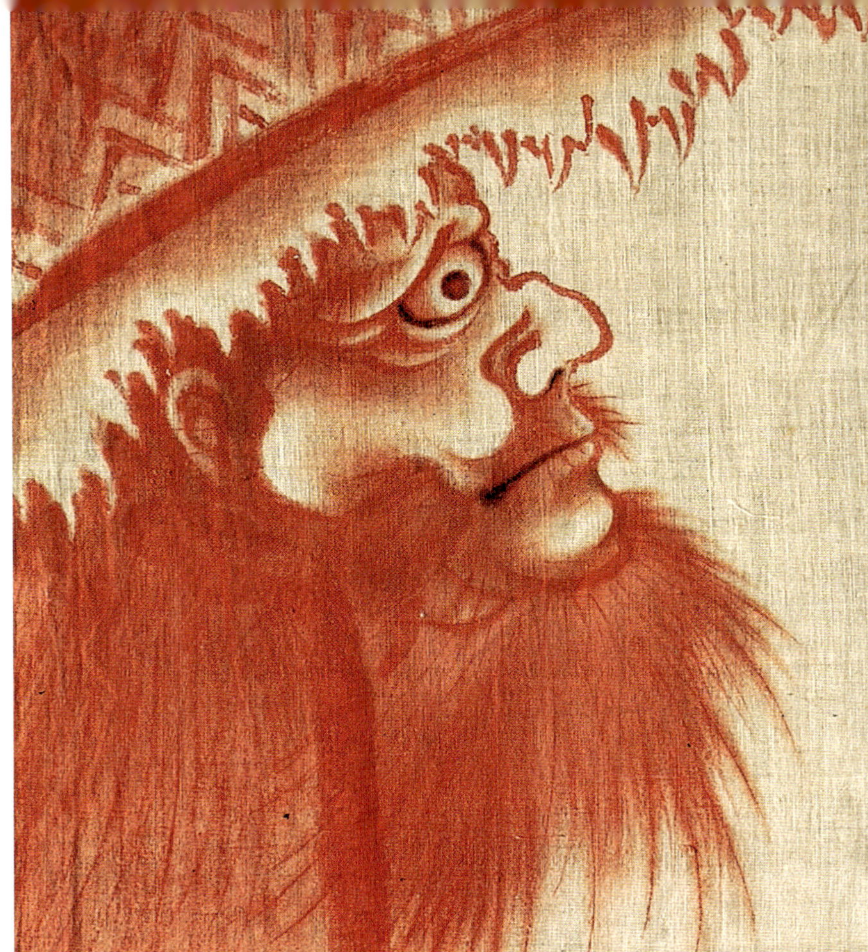

60. **KATSUSHIKA HOKUSAI** (1760–1849)
Zhong Kui, the Demon Queller

About Bunka 2 (1805)
Banner; color with ink on cotton
236 x 94 cm (92 18/19 x 37 in.)
Signature: Kukushin Hokusai ga (Painted by Kukushin Hokusai)
Seal: Hokusai no in (Seal of Hokusai)
William Sturgis Bigelow Collection 11.9240

Banners emblazoned with images of Zhong Kui (Japanese: Shōki), the Demon Queller, were traditionally flown aloft in Japan on Boys' Day, the fifth day of the fifth month.[1] The legendary Chinese figure — readily identified by his bulging eyes, sharpened sword, and heavy boots — was said to have been unfairly passed over for civil service after taking the state examinations. In response, Zhong Kui committed suicide by dashing his head against the palace steps, but his honor was eventually restored by Gaozu, founding emperor of the Tang dynasty. Later Zhong Kui appeared as an apparition to the ninth-century emperor Xuanzong and declared that in gratitude for his posthumous recognition he would protect the nation from demons and disease. In China, woodblock prints of Zhong Kui were displayed in houses at the time of the Dragon Boat Festival, which was also celebrated on the fifth day of the fifth month.

During the Edo period, images of the Demon Queller were produced primarily in ink or cinnabar, the latter of which was said to provide protection against smallpox. Hokusai created numerous representations of Zhong Kui in both colors. Most of these renditions postdate the banner in the Museum of Fine Arts, which by its signature can be dated to the early years of the first decade of the nineteenth century.[2] In a vermilion rendition in hanging-scroll format dating to Bunka 8 (1811), also in the MFA, and in his ink rendition dating to around 1826, now in the Kumamoto Prefectural Museum of Art, the artist provided a much more staid figure with his feet planted on the ground. In both of these later works, Hokusai primarily suggested Zhong Kui's power by emphasizing his massive form under highly modeled drapery.[3] Here too Hokusai has masterfully exploited his medium with assertive calligraphic outlines and subtle washes of red that give substance to his forms; only slight touches of black ink are added to the bulging eyes, nostrils, and grimacing mouth. However, the pose of the figure in the MFA banner, captured in full stride with his robes flying forward, must have imbued Zhong Kui with a particular immediacy, especially as the painting fluttered in the breeze. ANM

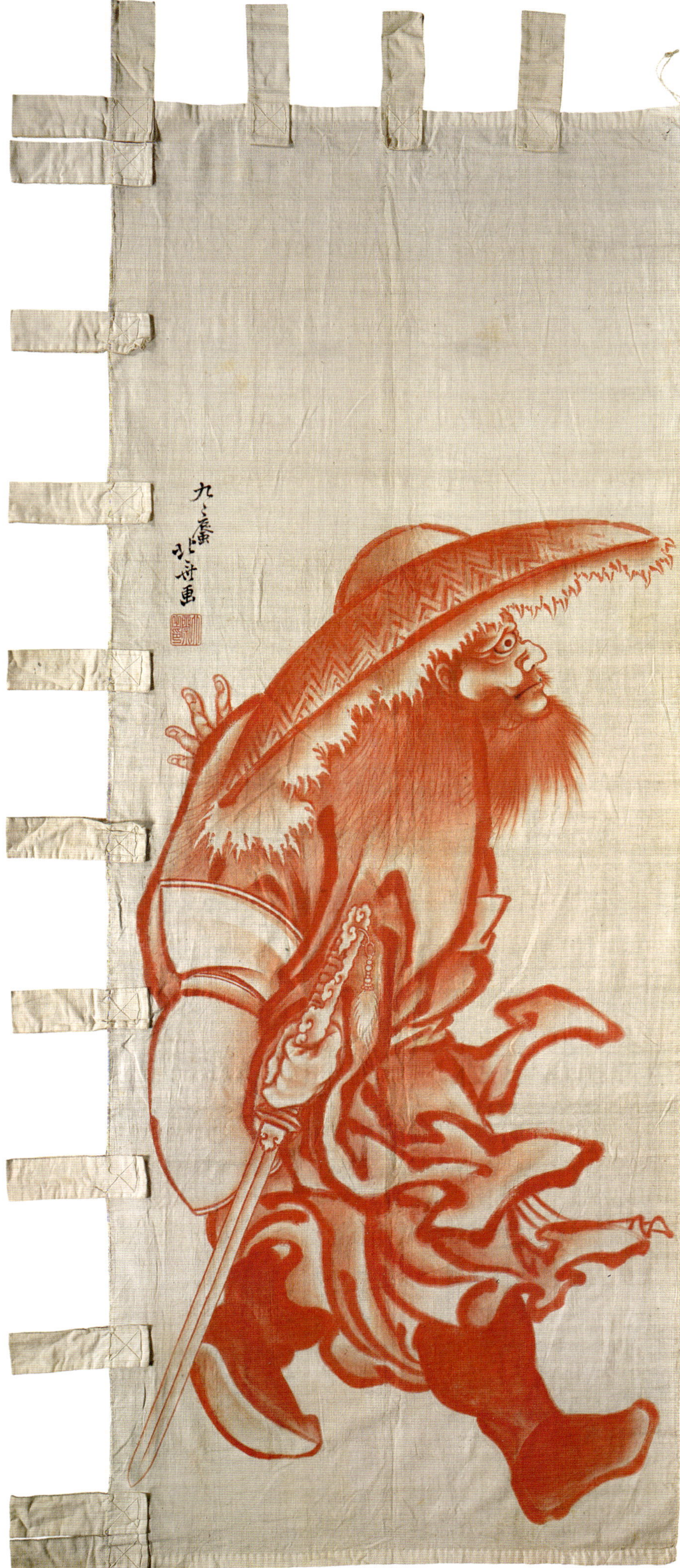

1. For an illustration by the Hokusai school depicting a banner flown on Boys' Day, see *Two Women*, ink and color on Dutch paper, 40 x 27.5 cm, about 1826, Rijksmuseum voor Volkenkunde, Leiden, published in Matthi Forrer, *Hokusai* (New York: Rizzoli, 1988), illustration 329.
2. Predating the MFA banner is the 1793–94 *Shōki, the Demon Queller*, hanging scroll, ink and color on silk, 53.6 x 26 cm, in the Hokusai Museum of Art, published in *Hokusai* (Tokyo: Nihon keizai shinbunsha, 2005), illustration 46. This painting dates from Hokusai's earliest period of artistic activity, when he was signing his works "Katsukawa Shunrō ga" (Painted by Katsukawa Shunrō).
3. Katsushika Hokusai, *Zhong Kui* (*Shōki, the Demon Queller*), 1811, hanging scroll, red ink on paper, 122.5 x 50.9 cm, Museum of Fine Arts, Boston, published in *Bosuton bijutsukan nikuhitsu ukiyo-e*, vol. 3 (Tokyo: Museum of Fine Arts, Boston, and Kōdansha, 2000), illustration 63, and *Shōki, the Demon Queller*, about 1826, hanging scroll, ink and color on silk, 102.2 x 30.4 cm, Kumamoto Prefectural Museum of Art, published in *Hokusai* (Tokyo: Nihon keizai shinbunsha, 2005), illustration 432.

61. **KATSUSHIKA HOKUSAI** (1760–1849)
Dragon and Tiger
Dragon and Snake
About the Bunka era (1804–18)
Lantern paintings; ink and light color on paper
Tiger: H. 40.6 cm, Diam. 30.5 cm (H. 16 in., Diam. 12 in.)
Snake: H. 50.8 cm, Diam. 30.5 cm (H. 30 in., Diam. 12 in.)
William Sturgis Bigelow Collection 11.9100, 11.9113

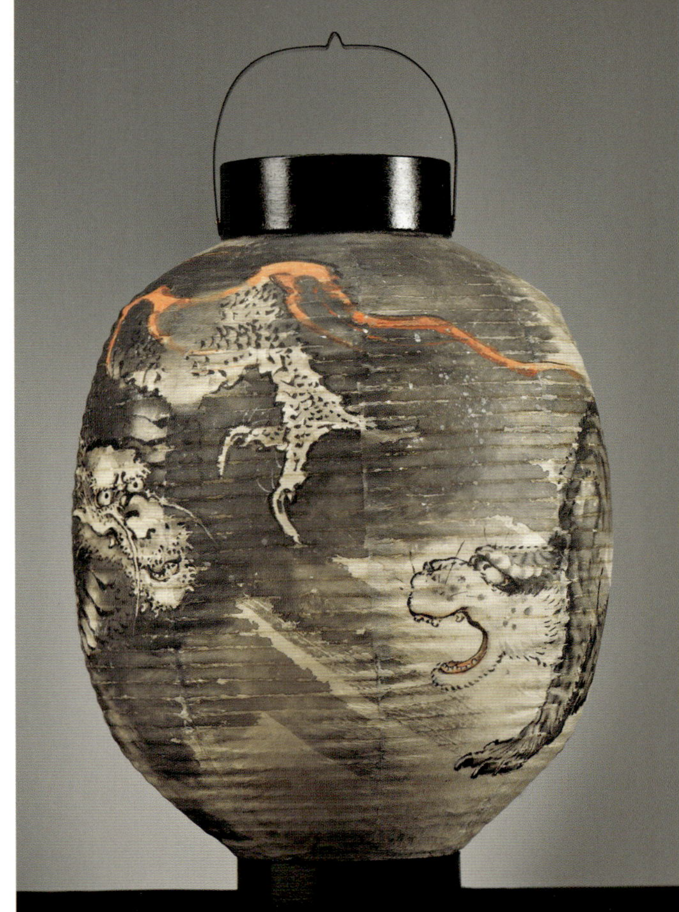

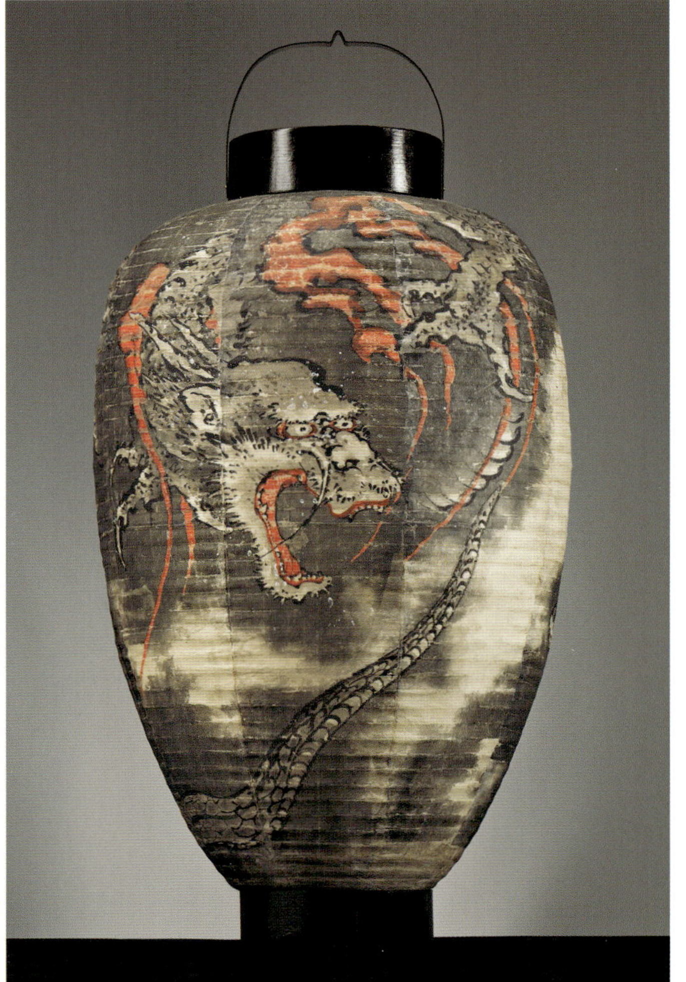

During his lifetime Hokusai was recognized for his fantastic lanterns, made to line the grounds of local shrines and the quarters of the Yoshiwara during annual festivals. The scholar Yasumura Toshinobu has noted that *Records of the Kansei Era* discusses those made in 1799 for a particularly extravagant display of "sacred treasures" (*kaichō*) at Mimeguri Shrine along the banks of the Sumida River in Edo. The silk lanterns were described as having been decorated with ukiyo-e scenes.[1] The *Katsushika Hokusai den* (1893), by Iijima Kyoshin, also confirms that banners and lanterns were part of the artist's production.[2]

The confrontations of the dragon with a tiger and a serpent represent the complementary forces of yin and yang. According to traditional Chinese cosmology, the dragon represents the male principle; the tiger and the snake, the female principle. The rounded forms of the lanterns, which by their very nature have no beginning or end, provide particularly effective frameworks for the presentation of the eternal opposition and yet interdependence of the two principles. Neither of these works bears a signature or seal, but the treatment of the roaring dragons, snarling tiger, and coiling serpent has strong corollaries with other established works by Hokusai, both in paintings and printed books.

During the nineteenth century these lanterns were dismantled, flattened, and then mounted in two handscrolls in order to better preserve their designs. Consigned to the "study collection" when they were first acquired by the MFA, they

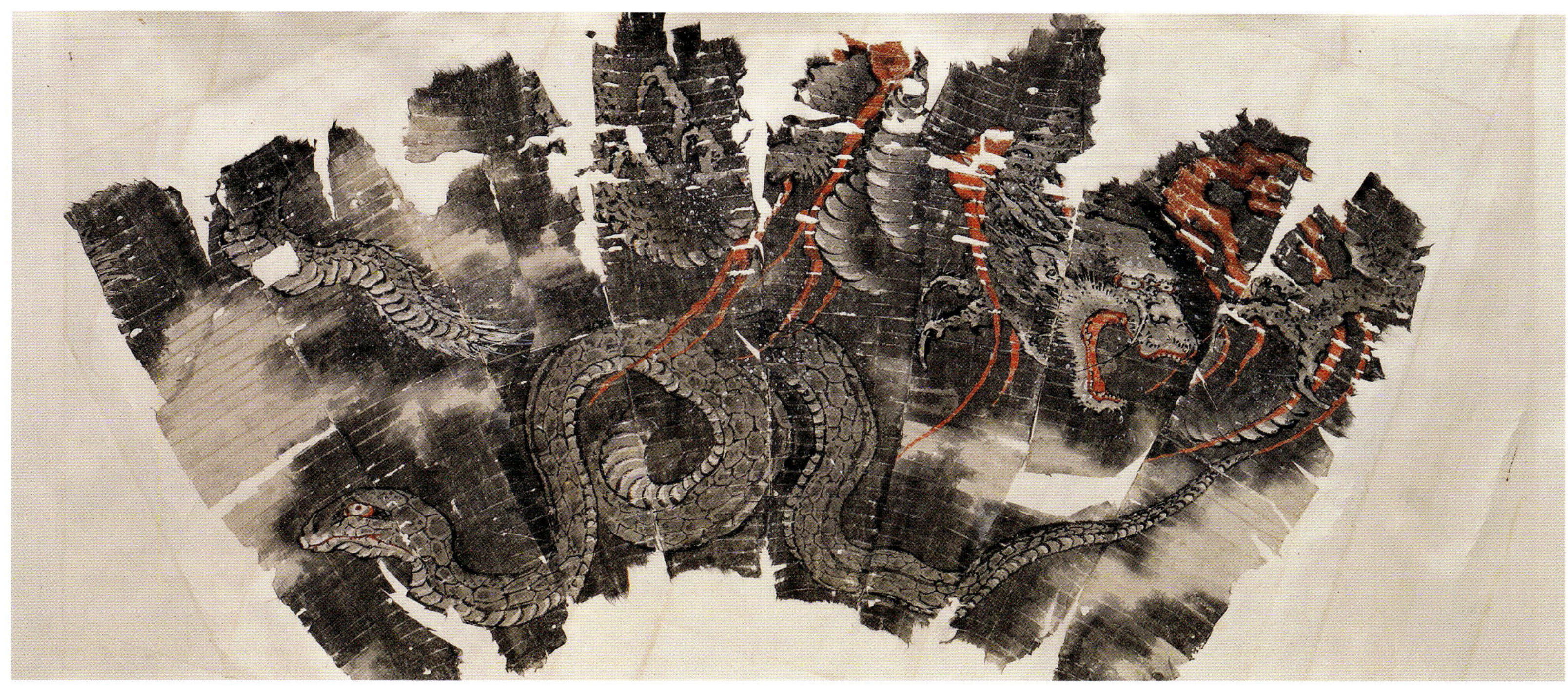

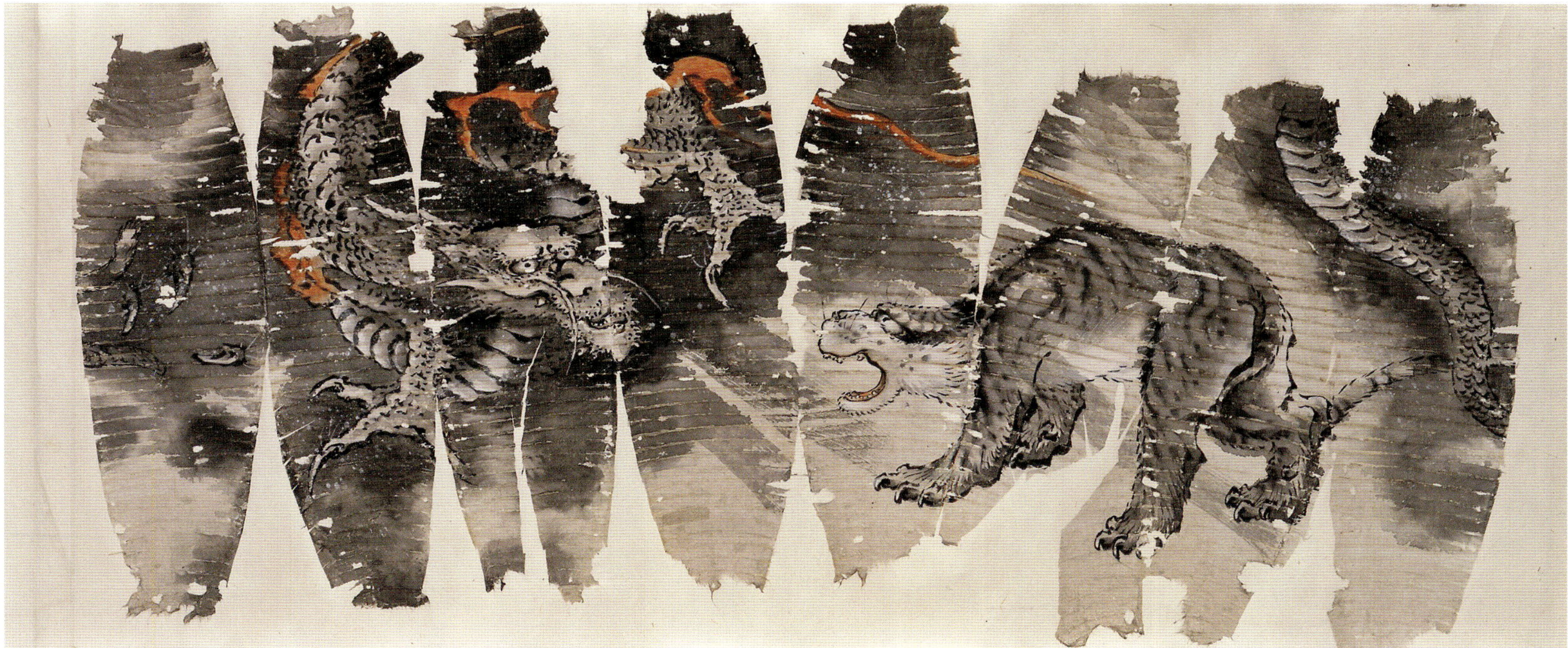

received little attention from Hokusai connoisseurs until 1997, when a team of scholars sponsored by the Kajima Foundation for the Arts reexamined the Museum's ukiyo-e holdings (among its other Japanese collections). Within the last year, in preparation for the current exhibition, the Asian Conservation Studio at the Museum undertook the restoration of the lanterns to a three-dimensional format. Although the new ethafoam base, which supports the individual paper-backed panels, does not permit the re-creation of the original internal lighting, the rounded form makes it possible to fully appreciate the dynamic composition of intertwined cosmological forces. ANM

1. Yasumura Toshinobu, "Decorating Spaces in Late Edo Japan," in *Kazari: Decoration and Display in Japan, 15th–19th Centuries*, ed. Nicole Coolidge Rousmaniere (London: British Museum Press, 2002), 62.
2. Tsuji Nobuo, "Mukan (Katsushika Hokusai) chōchin-e ryūko," in *Bosuton bijutsukan nikuhitsu ukiyo-e*, vol. 3 (Tokyo: Museum of Fine Arts, Boston, and Kōdansha, 2000), 190.

62. **KATSUSHIKA HOKUSAI** (1760–1849)

Woman from Ohara Carrying Bundles of Firewood

Late Bunka (1804–18) or early Bunsei (1818–30) era
Hanging scroll; ink and color on silk
92.8 x 33.7 cm (36 9/16 x 13 1/4 in.)
Signature: Hokusai aratame Taito hitsu (From the brush of Hokusai, now known as Taito)
Seal: Fumoto no sato (Village at the foot of the mountain)
William Sturgis Bigelow Collection 11.7432

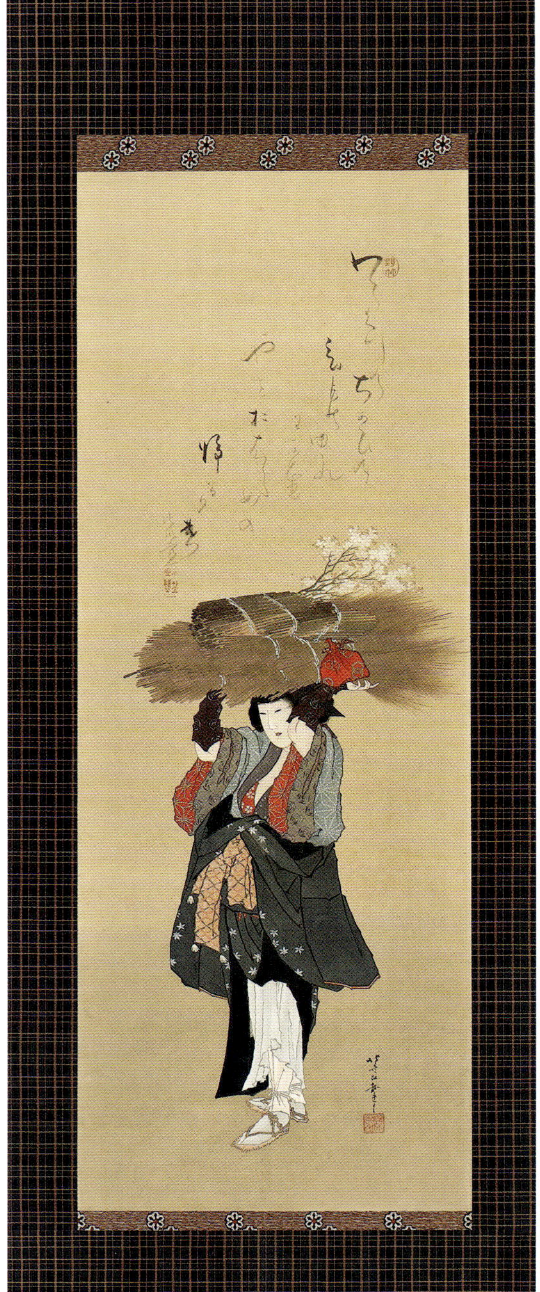

Women from the village of Ohara, north of Kyoto, came to sell goods in the streets of the ancient capital. Carrying their merchandise on top of their heads or sometimes on the backs of oxen, they were considered one of the famous sights of the city. These women were immortalized in poetry and also often appeared in Kabuki. Readily identifiable with their ikat kimono, cloth leggings, fingerless gloves, and offerings — firewood, charcoal, or flowers — they had long appeared in genre paintings of people of various occupations (*shokunin zukushi*) before becoming subjects of ukiyo-e as well.

In this painting one can see a dramatic shift in Hokusai's approach to images of beautiful women from that taken when he was at the height of his popularity. From 1810 to about 1814, when Hokusai was signing his works Taito, one of his alternate studio names, his figures assumed an even more impressive voluptuousness particularly evident in his erotic works. Here the artist rendered the woman's body in flesh tones instead of shell white, and he used a trembling outline for her robes.

Underneath the signature a single seal reads, "Village at the foot of the mountain." It is carved in a style that imitates "thread seals," with the individual characters in the phonetic *hiragana* syllabary.[1] This particular seal was one that Hokusai used only during his Taito period; after that time he gave it to Tatsujo, who is thought to be his daughter.

In the upper section of the scroll, there is the following poem:

Waragutsu no
chigai no himo no
yukiwakare
Yase Oharame no
kaeru yūgure.

Girl from Ohara —
Crossed laces on your sandals
pointing different ways
mean that you and I must part
when you walk home this evening.

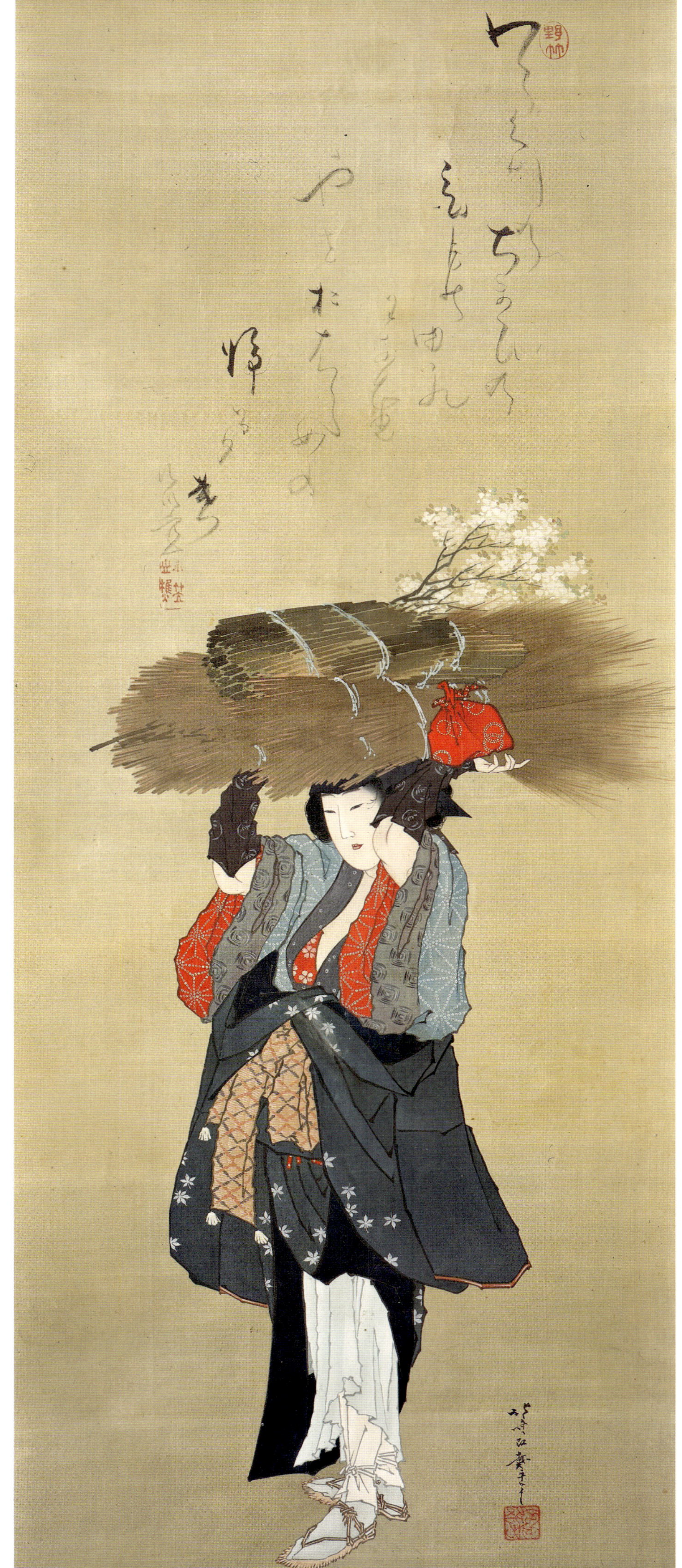

The inscriber has not been conclusively identified, but the lines bear a seal reading Ogasa Sanshō. It may be possible to attribute the poem to Nakai Tōdō, a calligrapher and author of poems in Chinese, who is known to have used that name. If Nakai, who was also a prolific writer of popular fiction and comic verse (*kyōka*), indeed inscribed this work, then the lines were added sometime prior to his death in 1821. Such a dating would be consistent with the style of the painting. NM

1. Thread seals were used in China from the Song period onward as official seals.

63. **KATSUSHIKA HOKUSAI** (1760–1849)
Wild Boar in the Moonlight

Bunsei era (1818–30)
Hanging scroll; ink and light color on paper
138.2 x 59 cm (54 7/16 x 23 1/4 in.)
Signature: Zen Hokusai Iitsu hitsu (Brush of Iitsu, previously known as Hokusai)
Seal: Katsushika (?)
William Sturgis Bigelow Collection 11.7430

The incongruities of this boar's abnormally long back leg, which has been extended to maintain its footing as it searches for food on a steep mountain cliff, and its severely shortened body may lead us to doubt that this work is by the master draftsman Hokusai. However, the signature is undoubtedly his, and the seal, though illegible, can be identified as one frequently used by the artist.

From the traces of the seams of a tatami mat visible in sections of the painting, we can speculate that the work was a *sekiga*, a "party painting" executed in an impromptu fashion in front of others. Perhaps this was the inevitable consequence of some party guest insisting that Hokusai tackle the challenging subject of a boar descending a steep slope in a vertical composition. Yet the painting, which is executed entirely in medium tones of ink, naturally expresses the atmosphere of a moonlit mountain, imbuing it with a mysterious appeal. The face of the boar is also quite charming; one can almost see Hokusai himself in its smiling eyes.

Hokusai frequently depicted the twelve animals of the Chinese zodiac, particularly the animal that corresponded to the current year. Since Hokusai used the seal found on this painting during the Bunsei era (1818–30), when he was in his sixties, it is possible that the MFA scroll was done in 1827, the year of the boar. TN

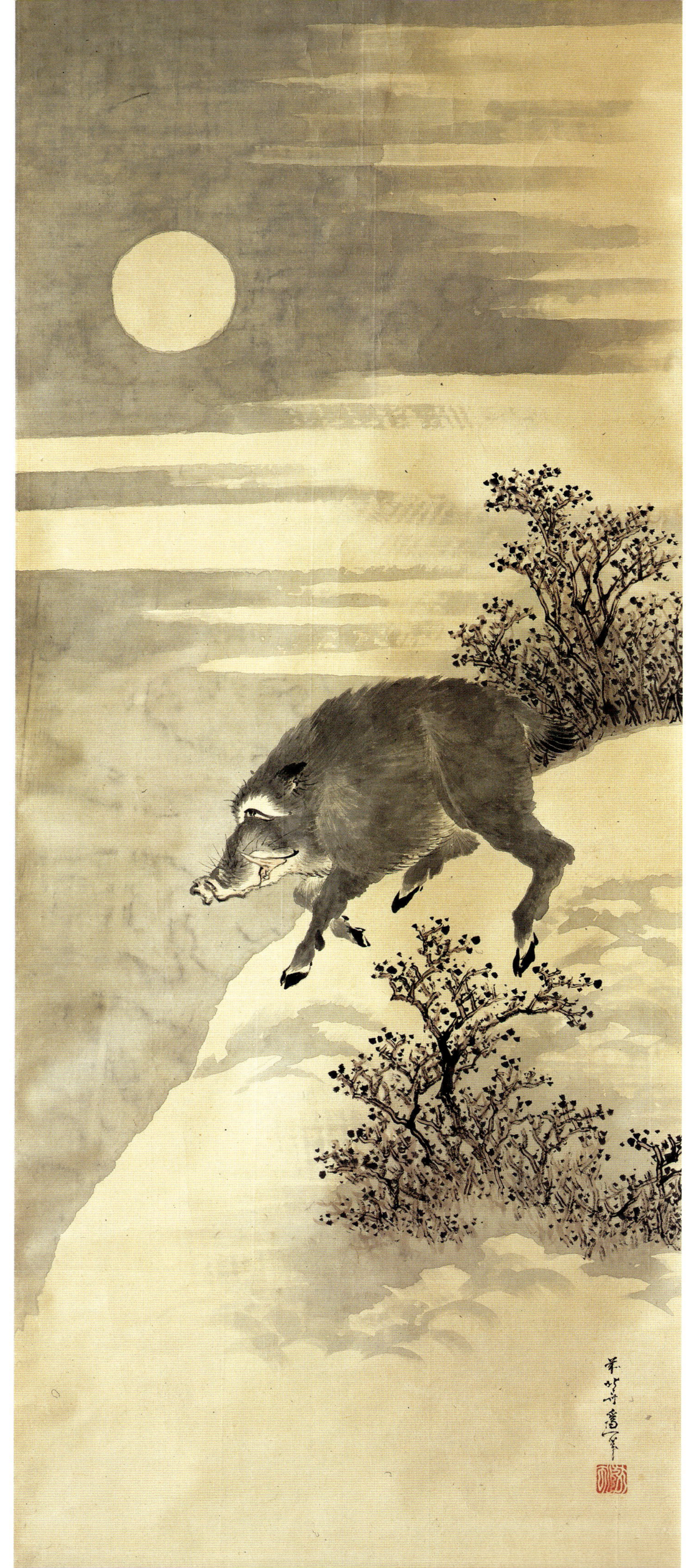

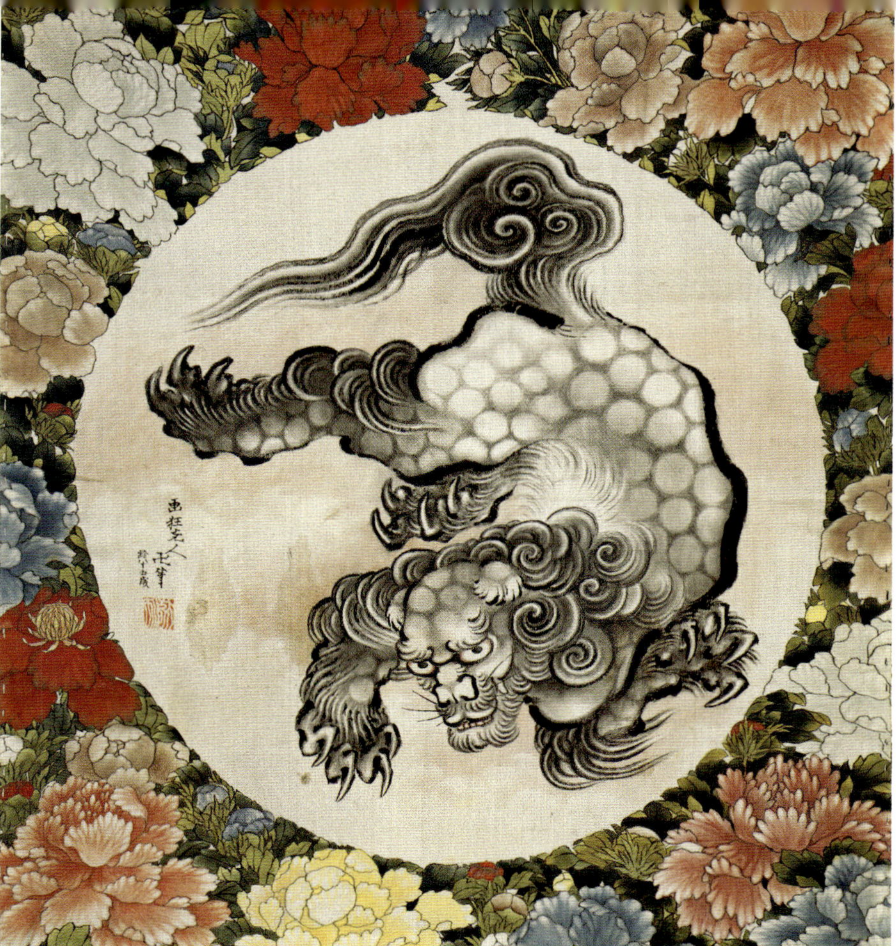

64. **KATSUSHIKA HOKUSAI** (1760–1849)
Mythological Chinese Lion

Kōka 1 (1844)
Fukusa; silk plain weave with color
66.6 x 71.6 cm (26 ¼ x 28 3/16 in.)
Signature: Gakyō rōjin Manji hitsu, yowai hachijūgosai (Brush of Manji, the Old Man Mad about Painting, aged eighty-five)
Seal: Katsushika (?)
William Sturgis Bigelow Collection 22.398

Since the late eighteenth century, *fukusa*, lined silk squares, have been integral to the formal presentation of gifts in Japan; they provide elegant coverings for offerings placed on trays. Many are embellished with elaborate embroidery, but this particular example was handpainted by Hokusai and members of his school. Connoisseurs of Hokusai's works attribute the central motif of the whirling Chinese lion, executed in ink with only tinges of color for the eyes and mouth, to the master.[1] An unnamed disciple (possibly his daughter Ōi) is thought to be responsible for the carefully modeled peonies, the three-dimensionality of which has been heightened by the textured surface of the crêpe silk. The finished composition makes reference to the well-known fifteenth-century No play *The Stone Bridge* (*Shakkyō*). According to the plot, Jakushō, an early eleventh-century monk, attempts to make the perilous crossing over a slippery stone bridge that spans a cavernous ravine near Mount Tiantai. A woodsman advises him that no one can successfully pass over without the aid of the Buddha. Shortly thereafter, a lion bearing red and white peonies — the traditional attendant of Monju, the Bodhisattva of Wisdom — appears. During the Edo period this play became the basis for a popular Kabuki dance (see cat. nos. 10 and 33).

The scholar John Carpenter has pointed out the formal similarities of the central lion to the numerous ink sketches of the mythical animal produced by Hokusai from 1842 to 1844 as talismans to ensure his longevity.[2] Entitled *Daily Exorcisms* (*Nisshin joma*) by the artist, indeed the group contains one lion dated to the tenth month, eleventh day, that is almost identical in pose to the one found on the *fukusa*.[3] ANM

1. Tsuji Nobuo,"Karajishi zu," in *Bosuton bijutsukan nikuhitsu ukiyo-e*, vol. 3 (Tokyo: Museum of Fine Arts, Boston, and Kōdansha, 2000), 190.
2. John T. Carpenter, "Mythological Chinese Lion," in *Kazari: Decoration and Display in Japan, 15th–19th Centuries*, ed. Nicole Coolidge Rousmaniere (London: British Museum Press, 2002), 236.
3. Illustrated in Gian Carlo Calza, *Hokusai* (London: Phaidon Press, 2003), 390.

65. **KATSUSHIKA HOKUSAI** (1760–1849)
Phoenix

Tenpō 6 (1835)
Eight-panel folding screen; ink, color, cut gold leaf, and sprinkled gold on paper
35.8 x 233.2 cm (14 1/8 x 91 13/16 in.)
Signature: Yowai toshi shichijūrokusai Zen Hokusai Iitsu aratame Gakyō rōjin Manji hitsu
(Age, seventy-six years old; brush of Hokusai Iitsu, now known as Manji, the Old Man Mad about Painting)
Seal: shape of Mount Fuji
William Sturgis Bigelow Collection 11.7433

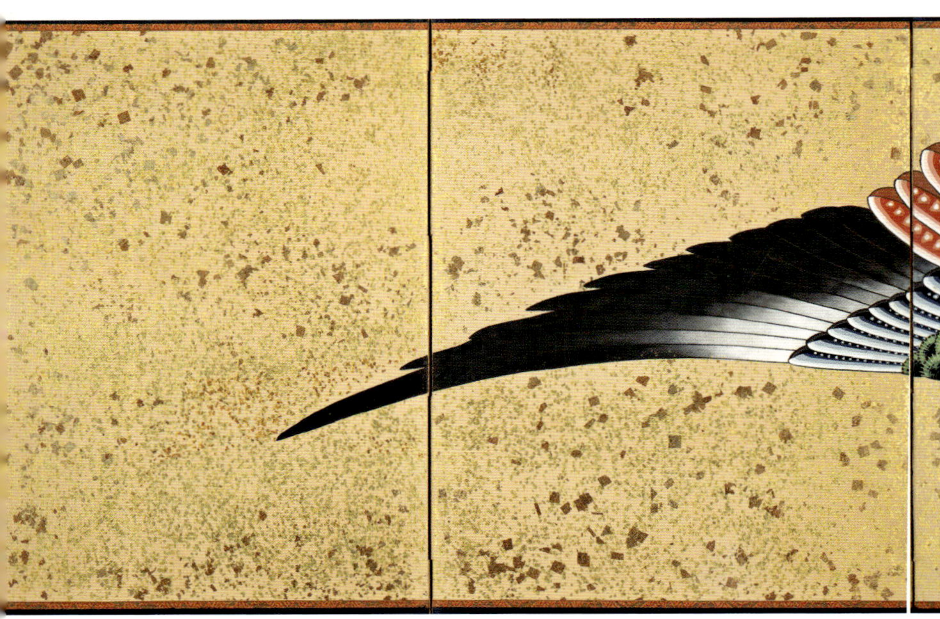
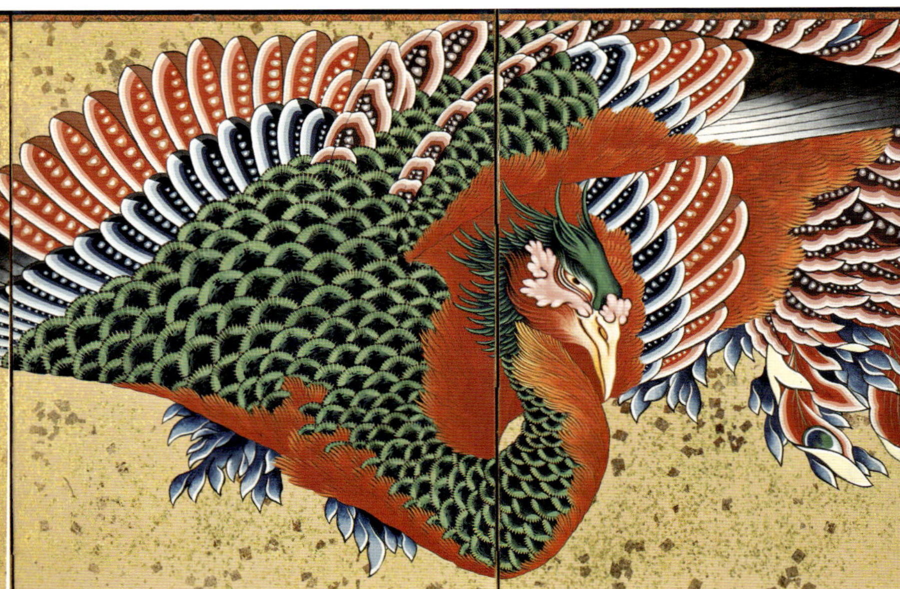

A phoenix in flight extends across this magnificent eight-panel screen, which is not quite thirty-six centimeters in height. Known as a pillow screen (*makura byōbu*), this type of work was placed around a pillow to shield the sleeper from drafts. It may have been made as a wedding gift or as an adornment for a chamber in the pleasure quarters during ceremonies of a sexual nature. Whatever its use, it has a suggestive glow.

The phoenix is an imaginary bird, but even so, Hokusai took quite a number of liberties with its form. Apart from its naturalistic head with its piercing eyes, it has a body divided into several strange patterns, each appearing to float freely within

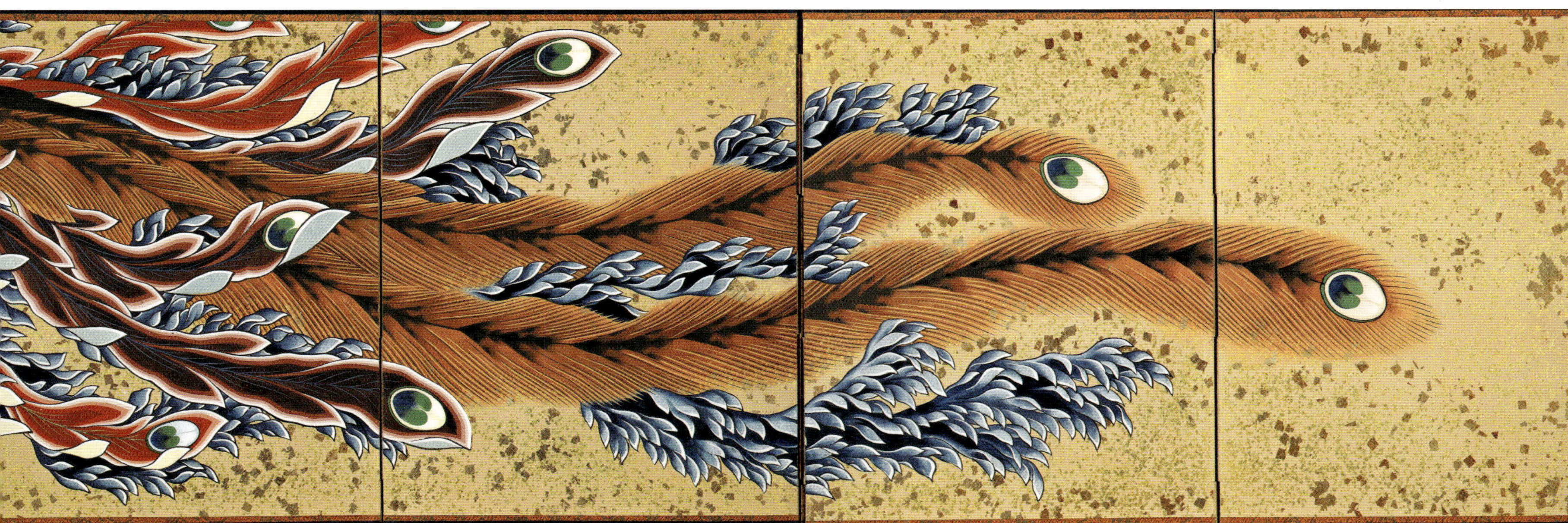

the composition. Thus, it is impossible to determine where the bird's extended right wing ends and its torso begins. The left wing is tucked into the body, and the peculiarly shaped tail, in its customary outstretched position, fans out. Long, brown fuzzy feathers and short reddish purple, kelplike forms appear to make up the tail, but it is impossible to determine whether these tangled, undulating feathers emanate from the tail or extend from the torso.

A silk cartouche is now affixed to the bottom-left corner of the frame. It contains a signature in rather rigid characters, "Age, seventy-six years old; brush of Hokusai Iitsu, now known as

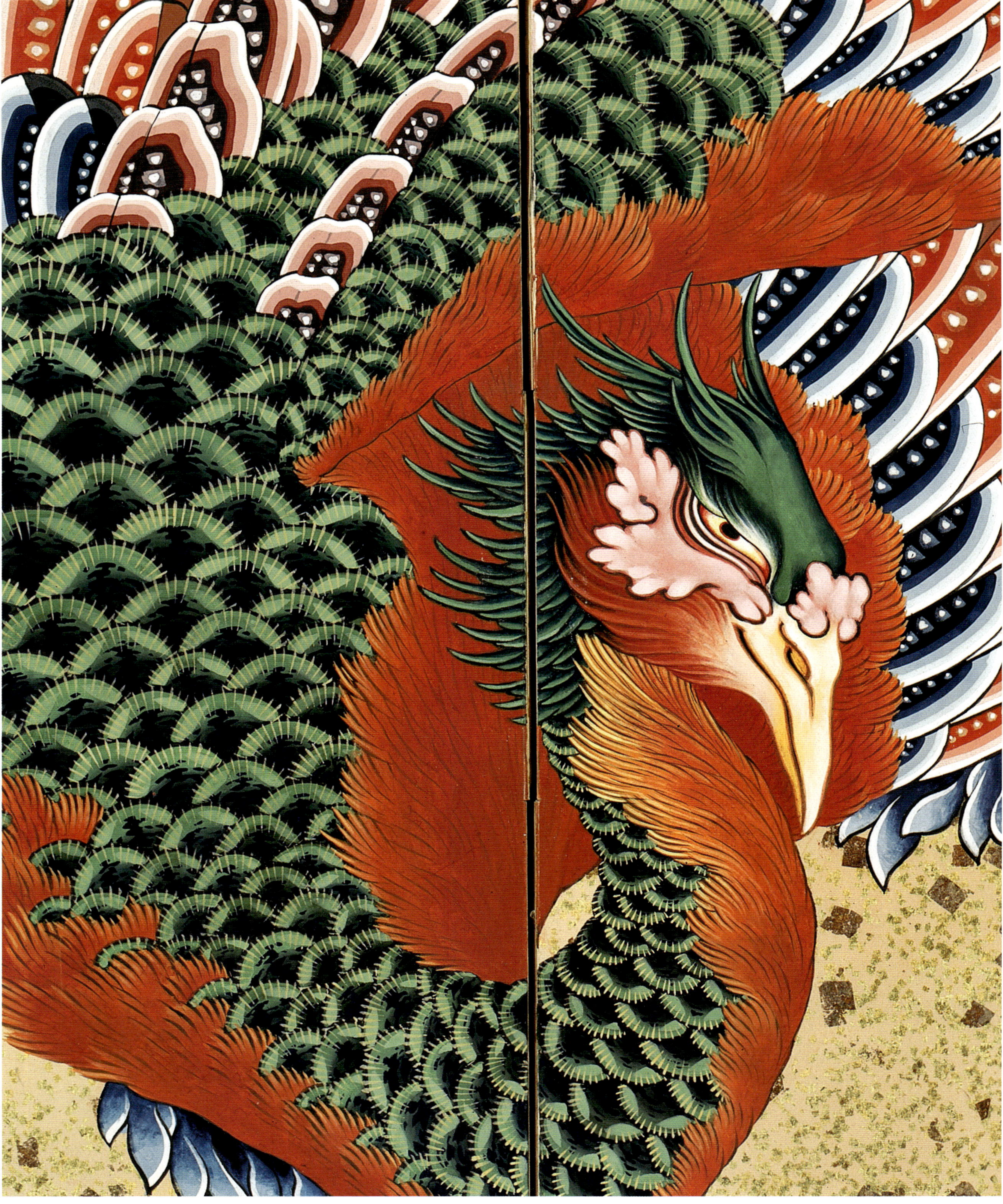

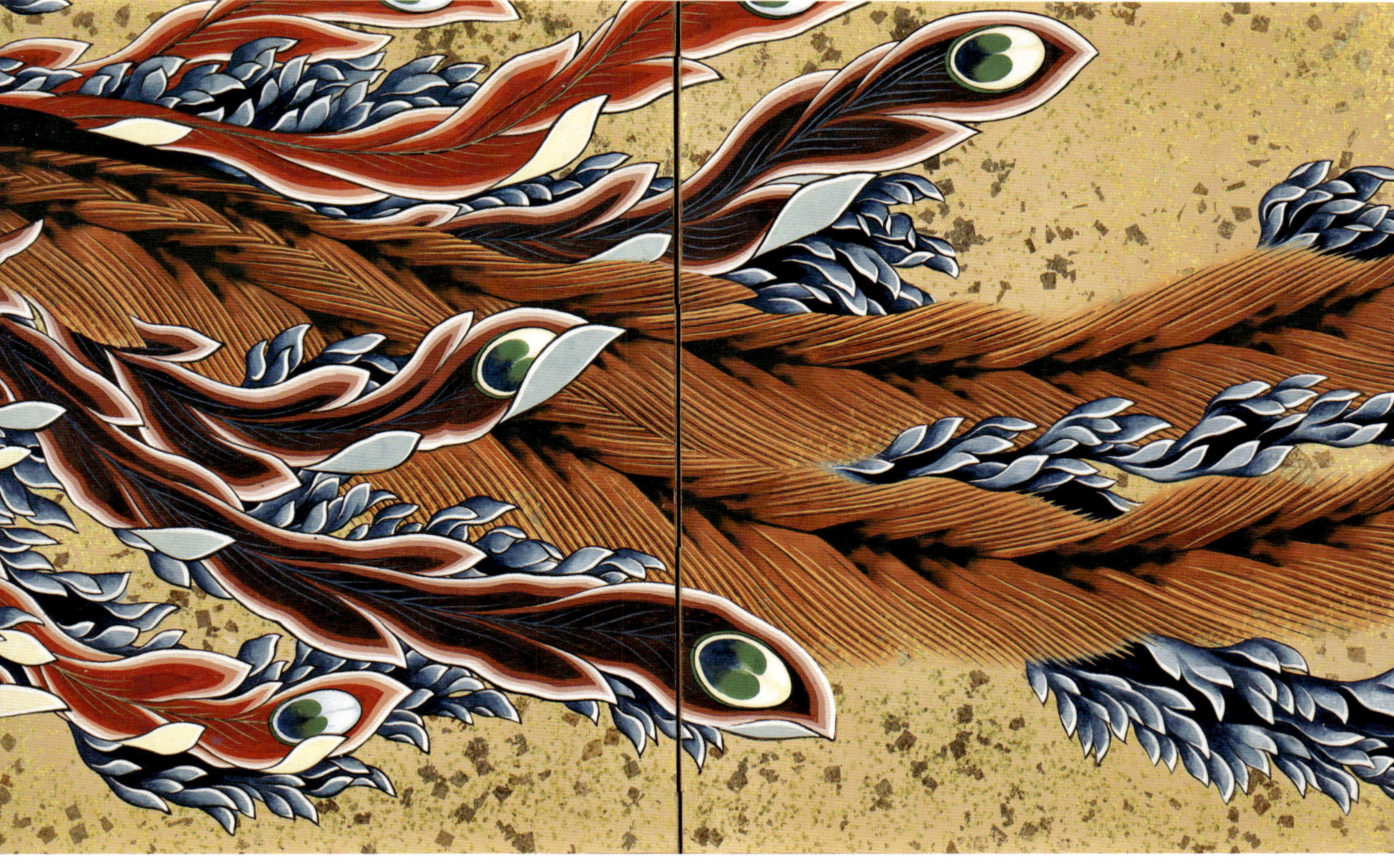

Manji, the Old Man Mad about Painting," and a seal in the shape of Mount Fuji. These are unmistakably the signature and seal of Hokusai, and they indicate that this work was painted in 1835 (Tenpō 6). Nine years later, Hokusai traveled to Obuse, in modern-day Nagano prefecture, where he reconfigured the same peculiar phoenix for the square ceiling decoration of a festival float.[1] TN

1. This work was brought to scholarly attention only recently by Gian Carlo Calza, "Hokusai's 'Phoenix Screen' in the Boston Museum of Fine Arts," in *La modernizzazione in Asia e in Africa; Problemi di storia e problemi di metodo: Studi offerti a Giorgio Borsa* (Pavia: Universitá di Pavia, 1989), 8; and Money L. Hickman, "Hokusai and *Hō-ō*: The 'Phoenix Screen' in the Museum of Fine Arts, Boston," in *Hokusai Paintings: Selected Essays*, ed. Gian Carlo Calza, with the assistance of John T. Carpenter (Venice: International Hokusai Research Centre, University of Venice, 1994), 217–35.

66. KATSUSHIKA HOKUSAI (1760–1849)

Li Bai Admiring a Waterfall

Kaei 2 (1849)
Hanging scroll; ink and color on silk
93.4 x 30 cm (36 3/4 x 11 13/16 in.)
Signature: Yowai kyūjūsai Gakyō rōjin Manji hitsu (Brush of Manji, the Old Man Mad about Painting, aged ninety)
Seal: Hyaku (One Hundred)
William Sturgis Bigelow Collection 11.7452

Painted during the last year of his life — when the artist was suffering from many infirmities — this work presents the well-known theme of the Chinese Tang-dynasty poet Li Bai contemplating the sheer face of a waterfall on Mount Lu. Although there is no inscription on the scroll, the poem that Li Bai is said to have composed on the occasion was well known.

The sun shines on Mount Xianglu,
picking out its purple haze.
From afar the waterfall
seems like a hanging river.

Three thousand feet of water
flying headlong to the base
almost as if the Milky
Way had fallen from the skies.[1]

Waterfalls themselves had been the subject of many Hokusai compositions; some of the most celebrated are the series of eight woodblock prints that the artist composed entitled Going the Round of the Waterfalls in All Provinces (Shokoku taki meguri), dating from around 1832. About the same time Hokusai specifically created an image of the Chinese poet gazing at the waterfall in his series Images of Poets (Shika shashinyō). However, in all of these earlier images the figures actively engage the landscape. Here the poet — a small figure with a child clutching his side — stands in awe of the almost completely abstract torrents of water that dominate the composition. The surrounding cliffs are confined to the right margin and are merely suggested by washes of ink punctuated by irregular rectangular forms.[2]

Hokusai declared his ambition to continue to create until the end of his life:

> Although from around the half-century mark, my prints and illustrations were regularly published, prior to my seventieth year nothing I drew was of particular note. At the age of seventy-three I could somewhat understand the structure of animals, insects, and fish, and the vital nature of plants and trees. Thus, at eighty my art will have greatly improved, at ninety will have attained real depth, and at one hundred will be divinely inspired. At one hundred and ten my every dot and every stroke will come to life. I only ask that those of you gentlemen who enjoy long life judge if my words hold true.[3]

The seal "Hyaku" (One Hundred) that is impressed on the painting provides further testimony of the artist's hope to reach the age of "divine inspiration." Although the artist died at the age of eighty-nine (ninety by traditional Japanese reckoning), this composition speaks to the force of his last works. ANM

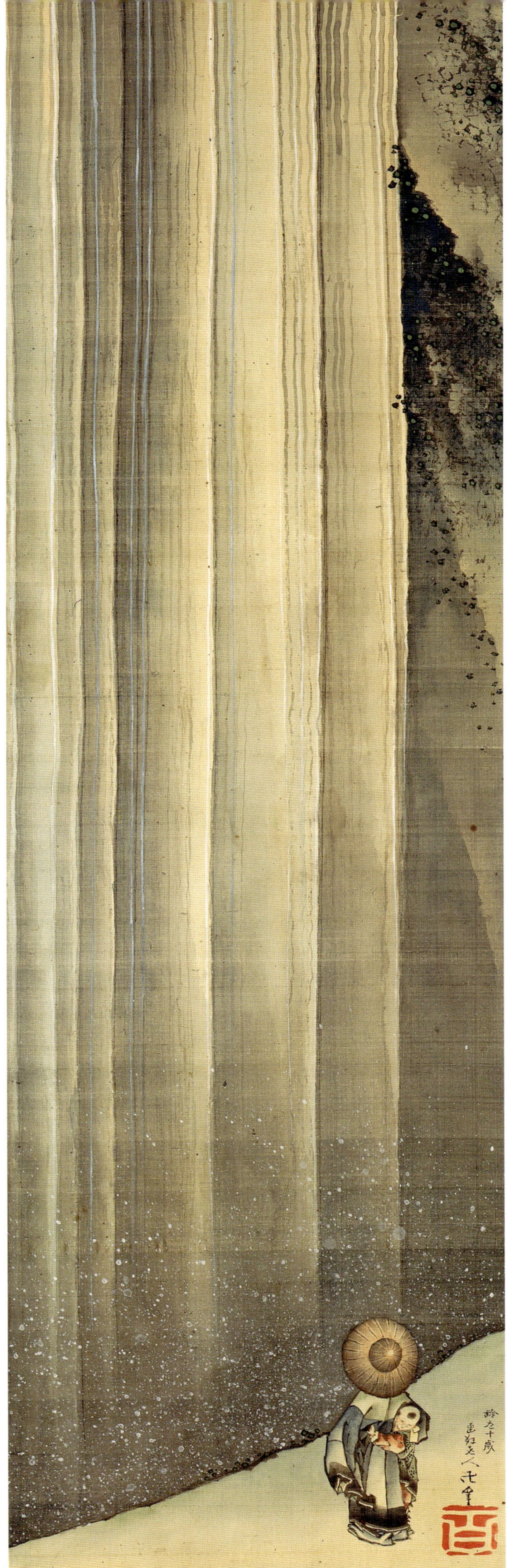

1. Translation by Joe Earle. According to Earle, Xianglu was a peak in the Lushan range in Jiangxi Province, celebrated for its resemblance to an incense burner.
2. An examination by the Asian Conservation Studio at the MFA suggests that the artist dipped the blunt edge of an object at hand to create the facets of the rock face.
3. This translation is cited in Narazaki Muneshige, "Paintings of Hokusai's Final Years," in *Hokusai Paintings: Selected Essays*, ed. Gian Carlo Calza, with the assistance of John T. Carpenter (Venice: International Hokusai Research Centre, University of Venice, 1994), 261.

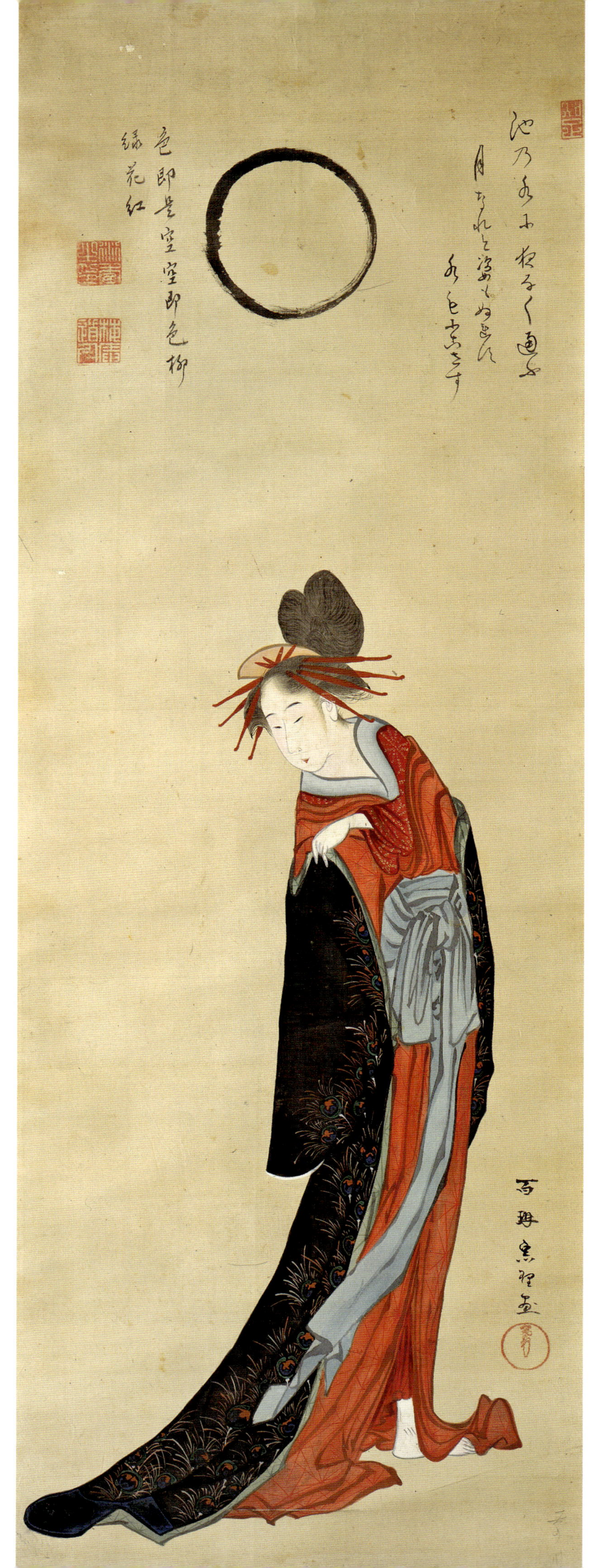
色即是空空即色
柳緑花紅
百琳宗理画

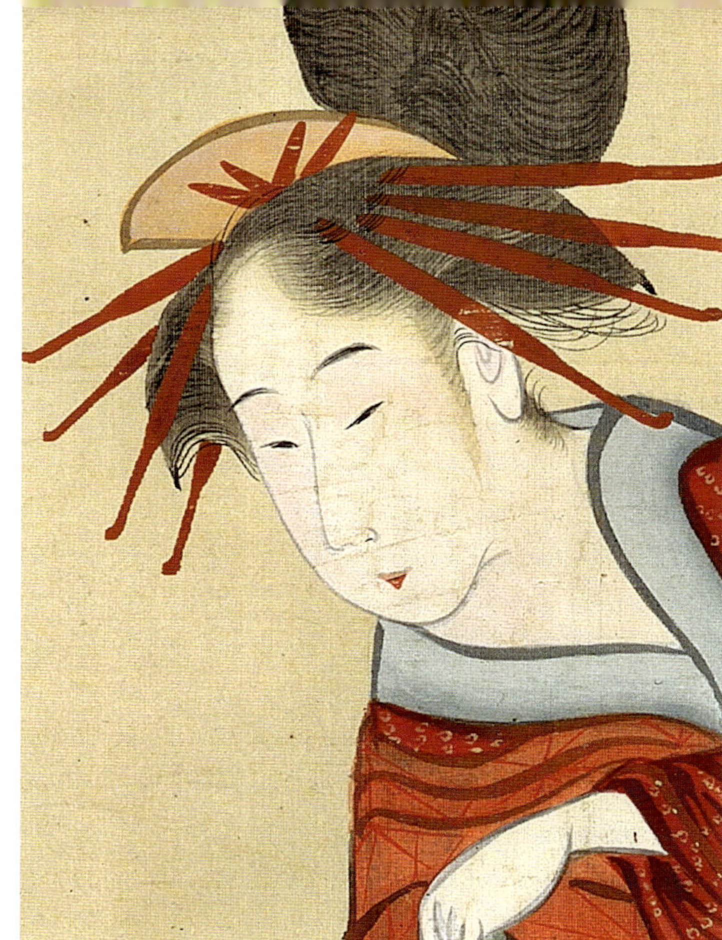

67. **HISHIKAWA SŌRI** (ACTIVE ABOUT 1789–1818)
Courtesan

Kansei 10 (1798) to mid-Bunka era (1804–18)
Hanging scroll; ink, color, and gold on silk
98.7 x 36 cm (38 7/8 x 14 3/16 in.)
Signature: Hyakurin Sōri ga
(Painting by Hyakurin Sōri)
Seal: Genchi
William Sturgis Bigelow Collection 11.7444

This distinctive treatment of a beautiful woman with long, slender limbs can be found in the early works of Katsushika Hokusai, who also called himself Sōri before adopting the sobriquet Hokusai in 1798. However, the woman's narrow, slanted eyes are executed in a style quite different from that of Hokusai's. In fact, this scroll is by Hishikawa Sōri, the disciple to whom Hokusai passed on the Sōri name. Several paintings by the artist remain today — all thought to have been produced in the late Kansei (1789–1801) to the mid-Bunka (1804–18) eras. Sōri's career, though, was relatively short, and he was never able to fully develop his own style.

The courtesan's hair is arranged in a *Hyōgo*-style chignon, and she lightly touches her black outer robe (*uchikake*), decorated with a design of peacock feathers, with her left hand. At the top of the composition is a circle (*ensō*) in ink and an inscription by the Zen monk Baian, first in Japanese,

Ike no mizu ni	Although it passes
yoru na yoru na kayou	nightly, nightly across the
tsuki naredo	surface of the pond
sugata mo nurezu	the moon's pure face is not soaked
mizu ni gosazu.	the water is undisturbed.

and then in Chinese:

Form is emptiness, and emptiness is form.
Willows are green and flowers are red [things are indeed what they seem].

Zen Buddhists profess to disdain words as insufficient to describe the nature of enlightenment. Thus, symbols such as the circle became an expedient means for explaining the Buddha nature as something that is true emptiness and formlessness, without beginning or end.

Buddhism was often introduced into ukiyo-e through parody (*mitate*). For example, in playful essays the courtesan's hellish contract with the brothel owners was often described as exceeding the nine years that Bodhidharma, the first patriarch of the Zen sect, spent facing a wall in meditation before achieving enlightenment. Even so, the verse here is a bit forced as an inscription on a painting of a courtesan. NM

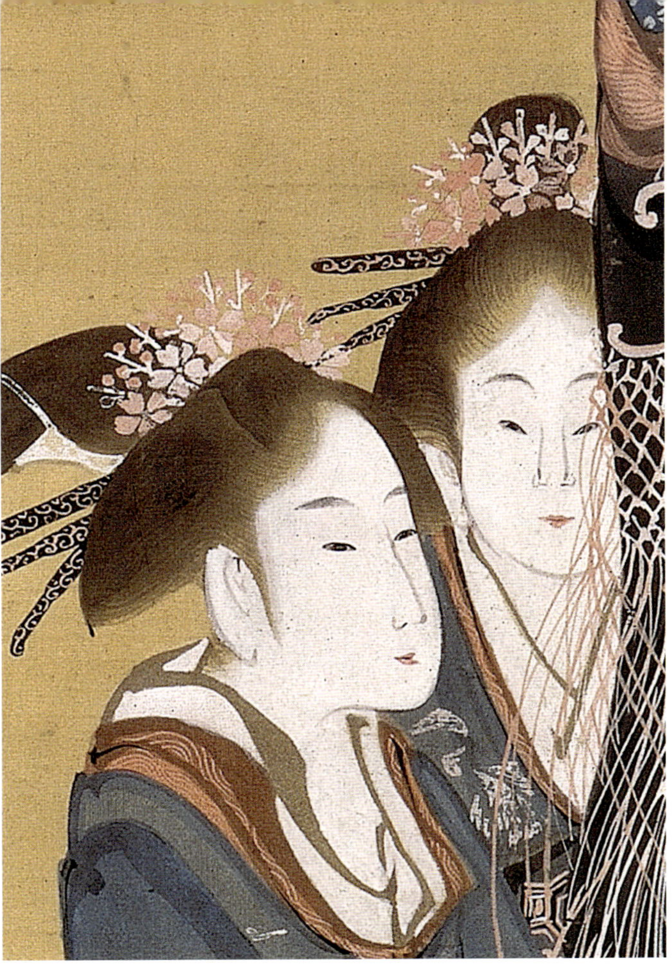

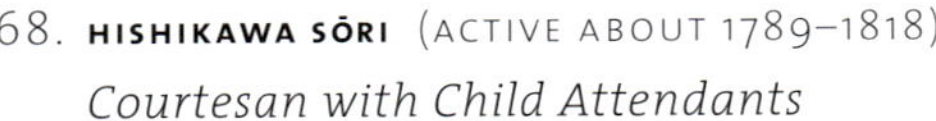

68. **HISHIKAWA SŌRI** (ACTIVE ABOUT 1789–1818)

Courtesan with Child Attendants

Kansei 10 (1798) to mid-Bunka era (1804–18)
Hanging scroll; ink and color on silk
85.5 x 33.2 cm (33 11/16 x 13 1/16 in.)
Signature: Sōri ga (Painted by Sōri)
Seal: Genchi
William Sturgis Bigelow Collection 11.7445

Arresting in its subdued color scheme, this composition depicts a courtesan dressed in a luxurious overrobe (*uchikake*) decorated with a design of a cloak. This motif makes reference to the feather robe of the heavenly maiden, stolen by a fisherman in the No play *Hagoromo*. As the courtesan walks, she raises her sash, which is decorated with an allover design of a zither. Her attending *kamuro*, who almost appear to be twins, wear kimonos that are coordinated with that of their "elder sister." Their robes are embellished with motifs of auspicious pines and cranes on a blue background. The poem inscribed above them reads:

Isa o mote	The tidy fortune
tsukurishi kura no	hidden in the storehouse you
kogane o mo	built with might and main
kono hagoromo ya	will all be rubbed away by
nadetsukusuran.	this beautiful feathered robe.[1]

The oval shape of the courtesan's face and the frontal depiction of the attendant in the center are reminiscent of Hokusai's handling of forms in his paintings of beautiful women, and therefore evidence that this artist was one of Hokusai's pupils. However, although the profile of the attendant on the far left does resemble the faces found in the master's works, the other figures are finished in a somewhat different mode. As in *Courtesan* (cat. no. 67), here we can see traces of the frustration of a painter who has not been quite able to establish his own style. NM

1. *Editor's note:* This poem alludes to a passage in *Hagoromo*, which has been translated by Arthur Waley as:

   May our Lord's life
   last long as a great rock rubbed
   only by the rare trailing
   of an angel's feather-skirt.

   See Arthur Waley, *The No Plays of Japan* (London: George Allen and Unwin, 1921), 224.

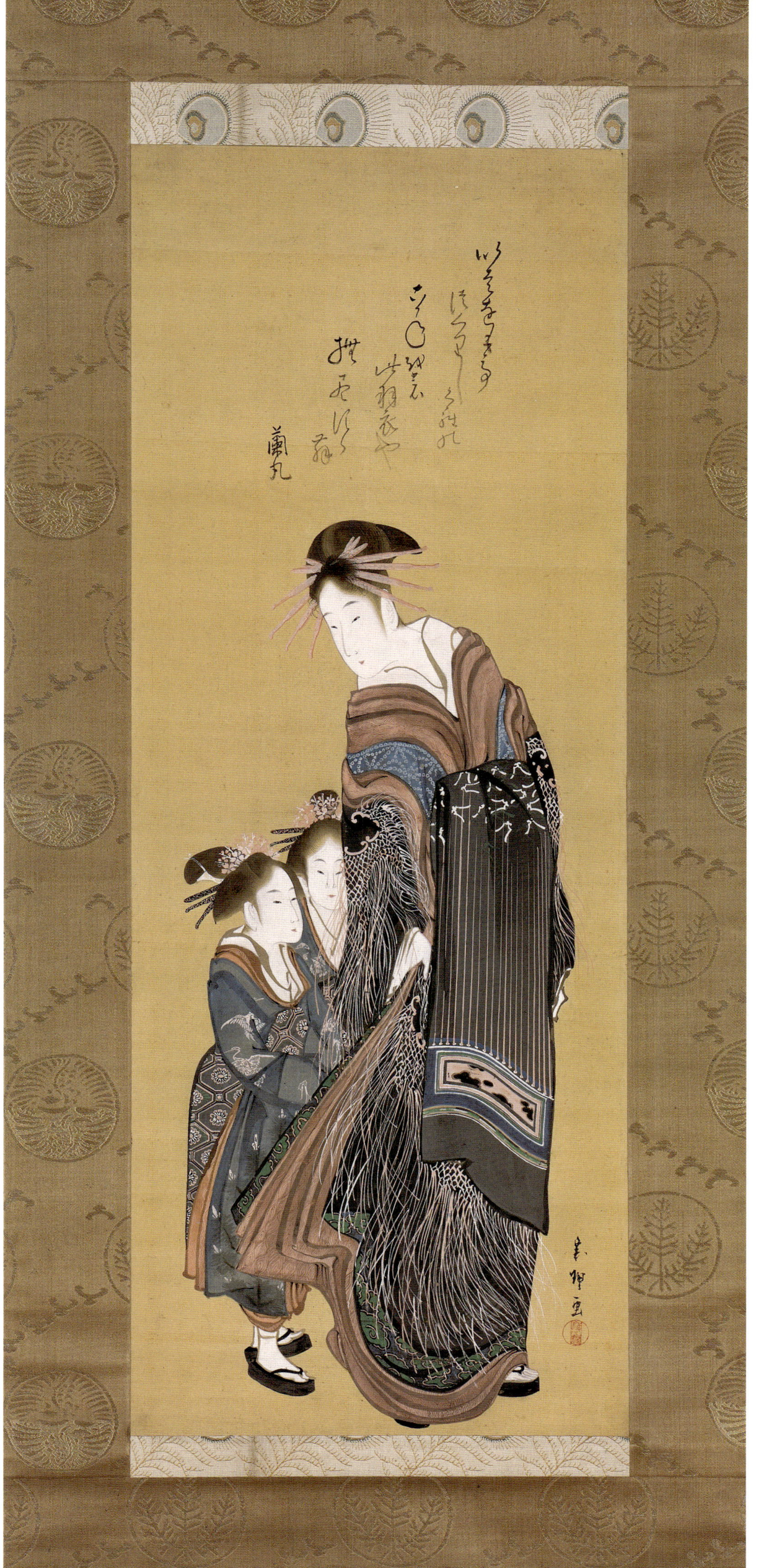

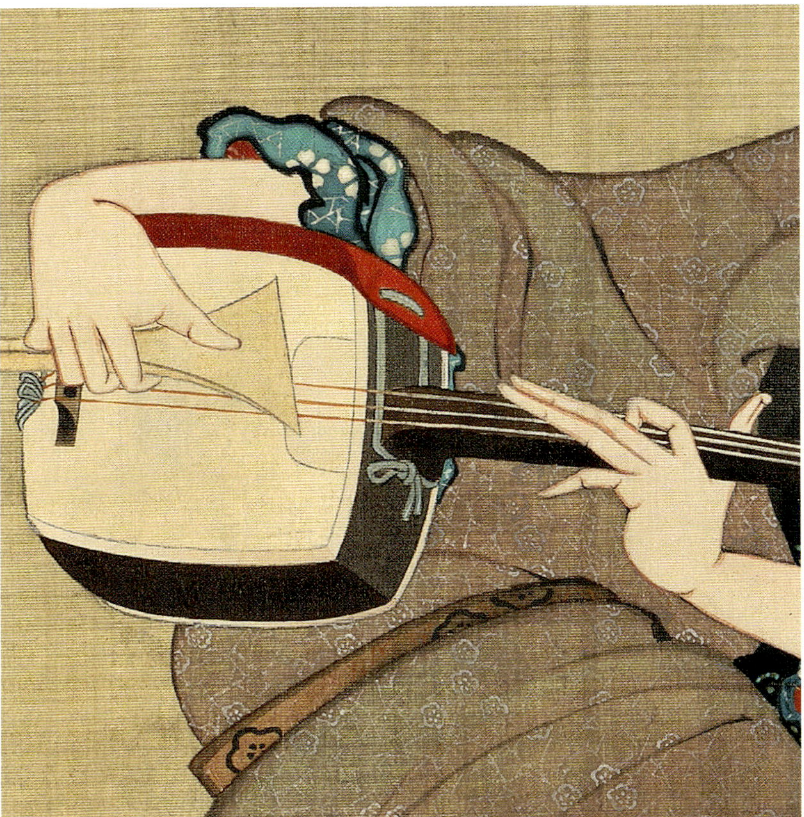

69. **KATSUSHIKA ŌI** (ACTIVE ABOUT 1818–AFTER 1854)
Three Women Playing Musical Instruments

About the Bunsei (1818–30) or Tenpō (1830–44) era
Hanging scroll; ink and color on silk
46.7 x 67.4 cm (18 5/16 x 26 9/16 in.)
Signature: Ōi suijo hitsu
(Brush of Ōi, the drunken woman)
Seal: Ō
William Sturgis Bigelow Collection 11.7689

Gathered together in a tight circle, three women — a geisha, a teenage courtesan (*furisode shinzō*), and a young townswoman — engage in a traditional trio of samisen, koto, and *kokyū* music, known as *sankyoku*. As Kobayashi Tadashi has pointed out, the status of each woman is indicated by her dress and coiffure.[1] To the right the geisha, with her more somber purple-gray robe figured with plum blossoms, strums the three-stringed samisen with an ivory plectrum. In the center, with her back to the viewer, the *furisode shinzō*, an attendant to a high-ranking courtesan, artfully plucks at the zitherlike koto. Perhaps in a subtle commentary on the short-lived future of the young woman, her black, long-sleeved robe (*furisode*) is ornamented with butterflies flitting across dew-covered grasses; her red underrobe is decorated with butterflies drawn to spiderwebs. Dressed in plaid layered over tie-dyed underrobes, the townswoman draws a bow across a *kokyū*, a folk instrument that became popular in Edo during the mid-eighteenth century.

Always at her father's beck and call, Katsushika Ōi, Hokusai's daughter, took the name by which we know her today from the somewhat vulgar expression "come here [*ōi*]." However, as this painting attests, she was an accomplished artist in her own right. Few printed works by Ōi are known; to date, scholars have been able to identify only two illustrated books — *The Illustrated Handbook for Daily Life for Women* (*E-iri nichiyō onna chōhoki*) and *A Concise Dictionary of* Sencha (*Sencha tebiki no tane*) — that include her compositions.[2] The number of paintings that can undeniably be attributed to her is similarly limited, yet Hokusai is quoted as saying, "When it comes to paintings of beauties, I can't compare with her — she's quite talented and expert in the technical aspects of painting."[3]

Ōi's indebtedness to her father is evident in this painting in the pose of the central figure, who has her torso elegantly twisted to the side; the handling of the woman is very close to one found in Hokusai's celebrated illustrated books, the *Hokusai Manga*.[4] However, the sense of three-dimensional form found in this work, particularly in the folds of the women's weighty robes, is Ōi's own contribution. This prefigures her preoccupation with chiaroscuro, evident in her later works such as *Night Scene in the Yoshiwara*, in the Ōta Memorial Museum, Tokyo, and *Operating on Guan Yu's Arm*, in the Cleveland Museum of Art. Here Ōi heightens the illusion of depth by combining layers of thick mineral pigments with thinner, almost translucent applications of vegetable pigments, such as the gamboge used for the central sash. ANM

1. Kobayashi Tadashi, "The Floating World in Light and Shadow: Ukiyo-e Paintings by Hokusai's Daughter Ōi," translated and adapted by Julie Nelson Davis in *Hokusai and His Age*, ed. John T. Carpenter (Leiden: Hotei Publishing, 2005), 100.
2. Kobayashi, "Floating World," 95.
3. Iijima Kyoshin, *Katsushika Hokusai den*, vol. 2 (Tokyo: Kobayashi Bunshichi and Hōsukaku, 1893), 62b, as quoted by Kobayashi, "Floating World," 93.
4. Kikuchi Sadao, *Bosuton bijutsukan shozō Nihon kaiga meihin ten* (Tokyo: Tokyo National Museum of Art, 1983), entry 77.

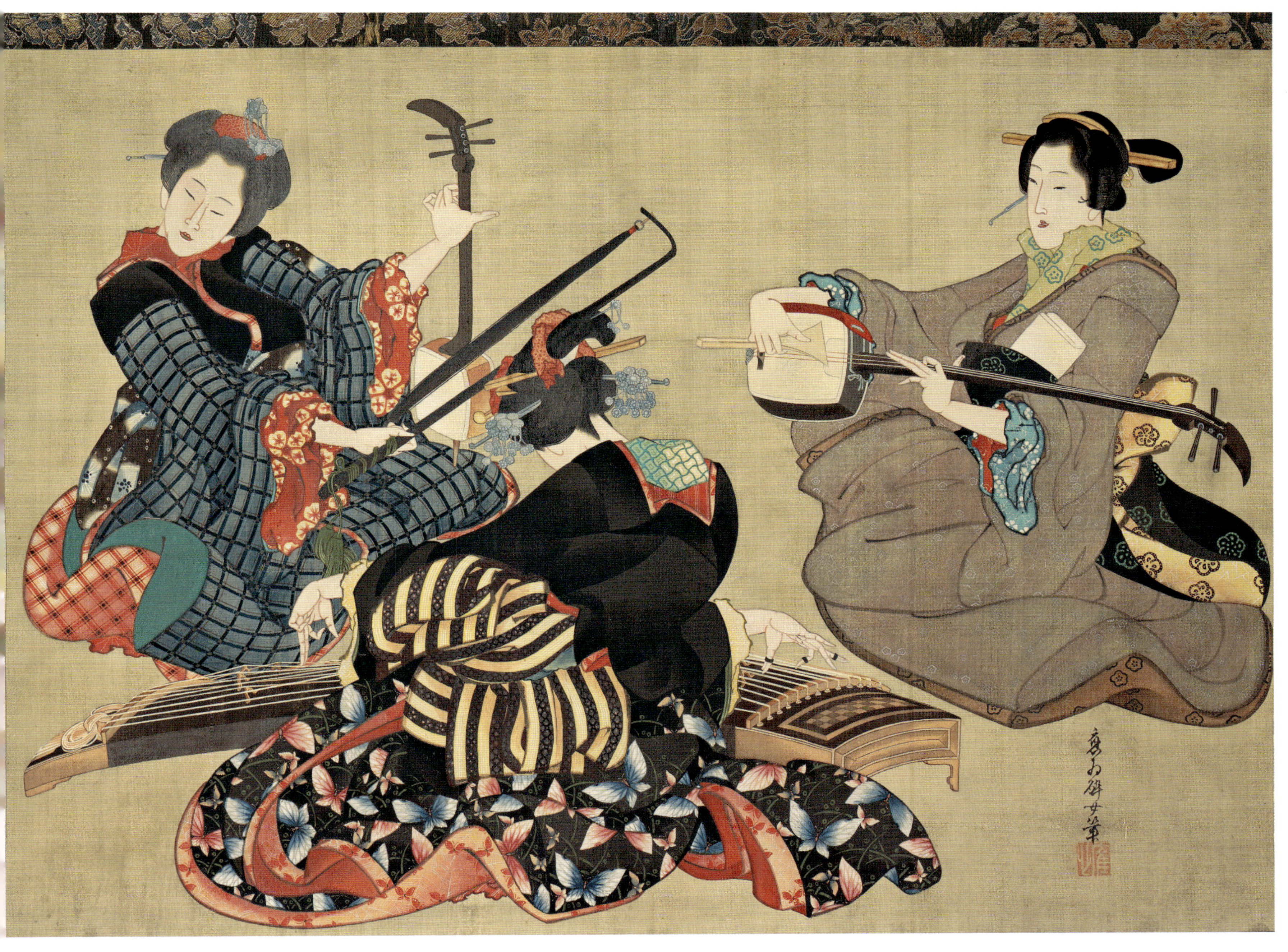

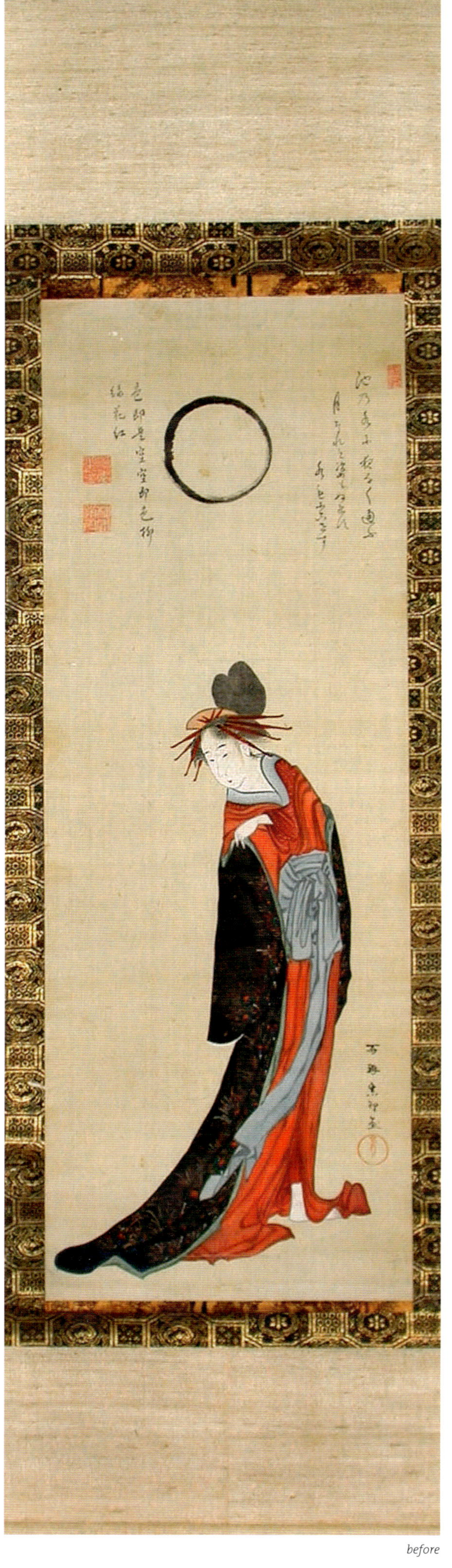

before

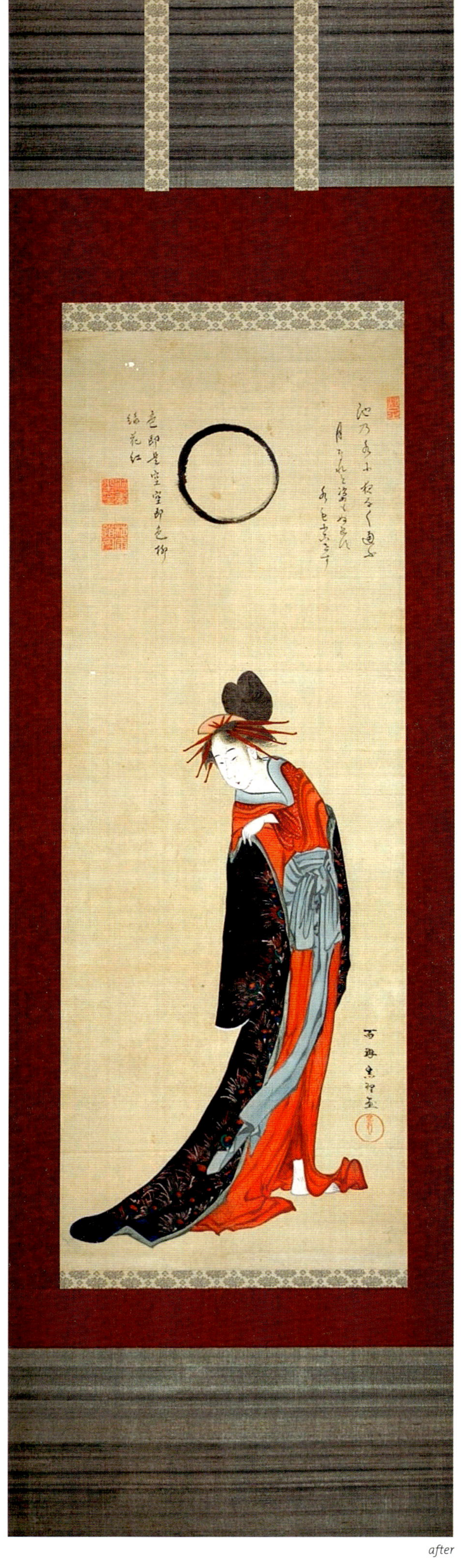

after

APPENDIX MOUNTINGS AND PAINTING TECHNIQUES OF UKIYO-E HANGING SCROLLS *Philip Meredith and Tanya Uyeda*

At first glance, Japanese paintings look dramatically different from Western paintings. Unlike oil paintings executed on heavy canvas fixed to a wooden stretcher, traditional Japanese paintings are created on much thinner and more fragile materials, usually paper or fine silk. While Western paintings are fitted with rigid frames for their protection and display, more flexible mounting formats serve the same purposes in the Asian art tradition. In Japan, the most common mounting format is the hanging scroll.

A hanging scroll is composed of various textiles or papers attached in specific proportions around a painting, and may be hung on a wall for viewing or rolled up for storage. Traditional Japanese artists typically do not make scroll mountings for their own work; instead they pass their completed paintings to a scroll mounter (*hyōgushi*). Collectors, whether individuals (such as a tea master or art dealer) or institutions (such as temples), similarly turn to the mounter for treatment of works among their holdings. Now as in the past, mounting studios may specialize in certain genres or establish exclusive relationships with particular clients.

Despite its advantages of compactness and flexibility as well as its decorative qualities, the scroll's kinetic format and fragile materials require that it undergo a regular cycle of maintenance. Storage conditions, repeated handling, and structural weaknesses in the scroll materials (whether original or from subsequent repairs) can all cause a scroll to deteriorate, eventually to the point where it can no longer support and protect the artwork. The modern conservator of Japanese art takes a cautious approach, placing the highest priority on careful evaluation of a painting's condition, and replacing the mounting completely only if the degree of deterioration warrants it. If any part of the old mounting is considered to be appropriate to the art and in good condition, the conservator often will reuse it.

If the work of art is to be remounted, all the old linings — layers of papers pasted to the back of the painting and mounting silks — first must be removed. The conservator takes new materials and then lines, trims, and pastes them to the outer edge of the painting before giving the overall structure a final lining of its own. All of the paper linings provide support to the painting and the border silks, and help to keep them stable over time. After drying flat under tension, the mounting can be fitted with a wooden hanging stave and braid at the top, and a roller with decorative knobs at the bottom. In this way, the painting and the mounting become a single object, with the aesthetics of one part affecting the other (fig. 23).

Artists, connoisseurs, curators, and conservators in modern times might have strong opinions as to what type of mount is right or wrong for a particular painting, but fundamentally, the choice is a matter of taste and tradition. Guidelines for dimensions, formats, and materials appropriate for various subject matter, historical periods, and sizes of paintings are handed down from master scroll mounters to apprentices in a strong and long-established system of hands-on training in private (usually family-run) conservation studios. Modern-day studios keep meticulous records, but documentation from the past is usually sparse, consisting of not much more than the name of the work of art and the owner; likewise, old inscriptions on mountings that indicate when or by whom a particular painting was treated are rare. Moreover, the historical cycles of scroll conservation have resulted in the survival of few truly original period mountings on ukiyo-e or any other type of Japanese painting. The Edo-period paintings included in this book were likely remounted at least two or three times since they were created, and there is almost no way to know now how they appeared when they were first made into scrolls.

In Western museums today, decisions about fabrics, papers, and the degree or method of treatment (such as how much in-painting should be done) are usually made collaboratively among conservators and curators. During conservation treatment for this exhibition, we remounted eighteen hanging

fig. 23
Hishikawa Sōri
(active about 1789–1818)
Courtesan
Kansei 10 (1798) to mid Bunka era (1804–18)

before

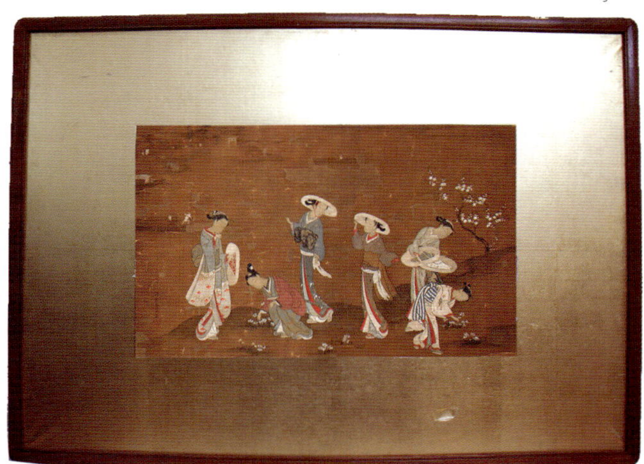

after

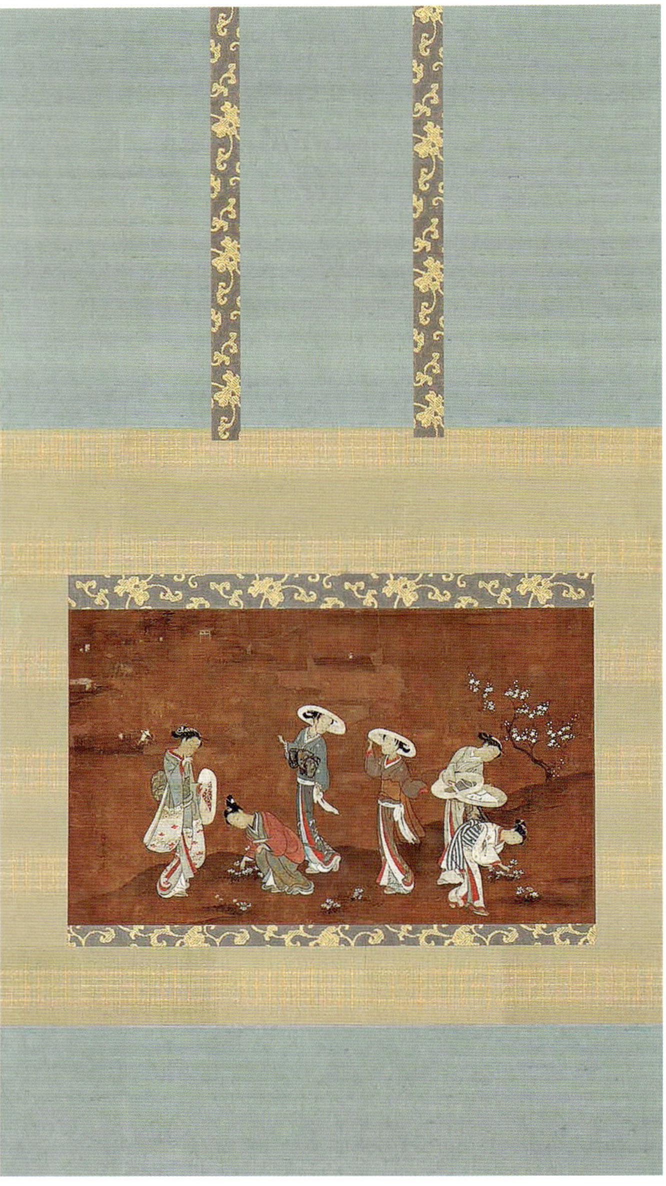

scrolls from the MFA's ukiyo-e collection, a process that took three years to complete. The treatments provided an opportunity to explore the relationship between the works of art and their mountings, and to examine ukiyo-e artists' painting techniques.

Scroll mounting choices

Most of the hanging scroll paintings included in this book are part of the William Sturgis Bigelow collection accessioned by the MFA in 1911. Our examination of the paintings has led us to believe that many were remounted prior to export from Japan, perhaps as a condition of sale. The mounting fabrics reflect the taste in textiles and patterns common among collectors toward the end of the nineteenth century. In addition, we have observed that many scrolls in the Bigelow collection share similar features — the same textiles, unusually generous dimensions, and the same type of large end-knobs and rollers, for example — which may indicate that they were mounted by the same person or studio.

One notable exception is Suzuki Harunobu's *Spring Outing on the Banks of the Sumida River* (see cat. no. 25), which entered the MFA as a framed panel with a gold-leaf border (fig. 24, left). This painting was most likely put onto the panel in Japan, perhaps as a condition of sale because of its degraded condition, and as a part of a growing trend for such mountings at that time. An article published in the Japanese art-historical journal Kokka in 1893 confirmed our suspicion that the Harunobu painting was originally a hanging scroll, and therefore in consultation with the curator, we decided to return it to that format.

For the new mount (fig. 24, right), we chose a finely woven antique gold brocade on a light green ground for the window-like border around the painting. Because of the heavy damage sustained by this rare and valuable work, a pristine, brightly colored new fabric would have created too great a contrast and detracted from its subtle beauty. To make the mounting as elegant and refined as the painting, for the innermost border we chose a gauze silk with a gold pattern based on an antique design. For color and depth, we dyed the silk a pale blue and

fig. 24
Suzuki Harunobu
(1725–1770)
Spring Outing on the Banks of the Sumida River
Meiwa era (1764–72)

before

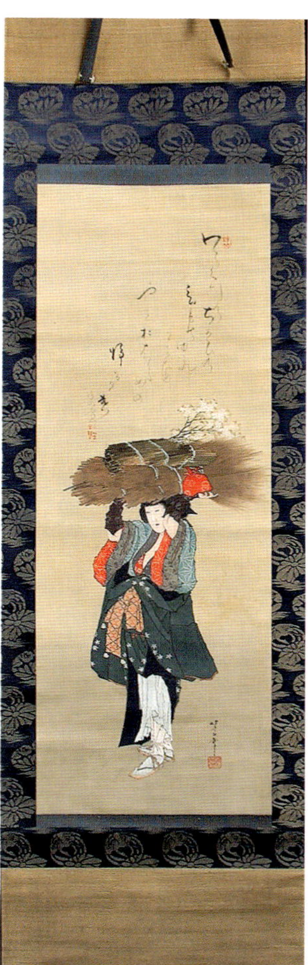

after

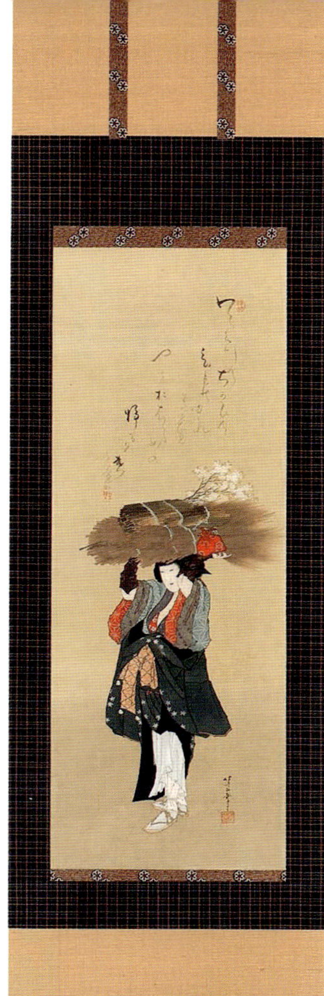

lined it with an indigo blue paper that shows through the open weave of the textile. At the outermost borders, monochrome blue-toned glossy silk without pattern completes the mounting. Our choices of textures and coloration were intended to complement not only the age and condition of the painting, but also the subject, young women gathering flowers on a spring day by the river.

Use of kimono fabrics in ukiyo-e mountings

Many ukiyo-e hanging scroll paintings have mountings that incorporate distinctive kimono or obi fabrics, especially for the central window-like border. Because many of these mountings appear to date back to the mid- or late-Edo period, conservators in Japan today accept this style as a "legitimate" one for ukiyo-e paintings. However, the use of garments in scroll mountings is not unique to the Edo period or to ukiyo-e. An earlier example is the fourteenth- to fifteenth-century practice of using a Buddhist priest's stole (*kesa*) to mount one of his works of calligraphy before passing it on to his disciples.

Some conservators and textile specialists have speculated that the use of garment fabrics in Edo-period ukiyo-e mountings reflected not only an abundance of such material, but a growing sense of fashion among clients and *hyōgushi* alike. Echoing and complementing garments depicted in ukiyo-e images, kimono fabrics knitted together a painting, its mounting, and the floating world of the rising urban middle class.

We took this into consideration for the mounting of *Woman from Ohara* by Katsushika Hokusai (see cat no. 62). Not only were the previous mounting silks badly deteriorated, but we determined that they were aesthetically ill-matched to the painting (fig. 25, left). To highlight the figure's rustic beauty, we strove to harmonize the new mounting (fig. 25, right) with the simple working-class garments the woman is wearing. We chose an indigo-dyed remnant from an antique silk kimono with a simple plaid design for the inner window-like section, and an unusual cotton chintz remnant for the narrow horizontal borders above and below the painting. Sections closest to the work of art are more commonly made of gold brocade, but we have observed cotton chintz used for this section on many ukiyo-e painting scrolls. As a working-class fabric, cotton seemed particularly appropriate for *Woman from Ohara*. Finally, we completed the rustic appearance of the scroll with a roughly textured, unpatterned monochrome silk for the large top and bottom sections. Glossy red-lacquered end knobs were chosen to accent the vivid red under-kimono of the figure.

Artists' Techniques Observed in Ukiyo-e Paintings

In treating the eighteen hanging scrolls for the exhibition, we were able to observe artist's techniques that were otherwise hidden from view under the lining papers. For example, the back of Hokusai's *Woman Looking at Herself in a Mirror* (see cat. no. 59) revealed some interesting variations on an ancient technique. The artist painted the silk from the back as well as the front, filling out the weave of the silk with color from both sides to achieve extra depth and opacity. Some of the earliest Japanese Buddhist paintings on silk have revealed this same technique, usually with some correspondence or similarity of colors and paint applied in solid areas, but the cosmetic box at the lower right of Hokusai's painting is unusual because it has

fig. 25
Katsushika Hokusai (1760–1849)
Woman from Ohara Carrying Bundles of Firewood
Late Bunka (1804–18) or early Bunsei (1818–30) era

been painted with black from the front and a rich brown pigment, red iron oxide, from the back (fig. 26). A close examination of the front, moreover, revealed that Hokusai used a variety of black washes on that side; some heavy and dense and others thinner and more transparent. This innovative application allows the brown pigment on the back of the silk to show subtly through in places, much in the same manner that black lacquer has transparent depths due to the layers of contrasting ground color applied during the lacquering process.

front

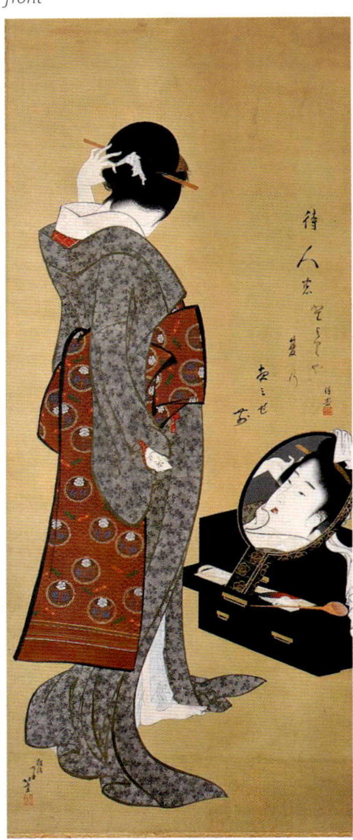

back

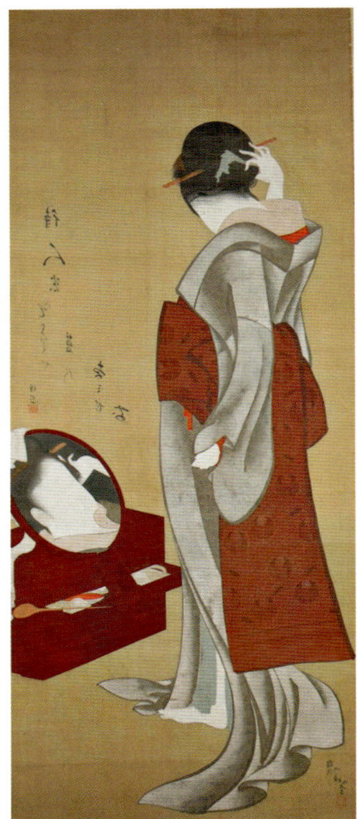

fig. 26
Katsushika Hokusai (1760–1849)
Woman Looking at Herself in a Mirror
About Bunka 2 (1805)

The manner in which other areas of the painting have been treated on the reverse provides evidence of Hokusai's interest in pictorial three-dimensionality. Other ukiyo-e artists of this time commonly applied color in flat layers when depicting clothing, a technique that results in a two-dimensional quality. Hokusai, by contrast, rendered the back of the figure's kimono with opaque grey pigment that he modulated in thickness, a technique that may be compared to the gradation in woodblock printing called *bokashi* (fig. 27). Here it creates a suggestion of volume in the folds and creases of the robe when seen through the painting silk from the front.

Our study of the MFA's collection revealed that Hokusai and other ukiyo-e painters combined the use of organic pigments (derived from plant and animal dyes) and mineral colors (derived from colored earths or pulverized stone), the former more transparent than the latter. Traditionally, mineral pigments were more frequently employed for Japanese painting, while organic colors were more common in the production of woodblock prints. The thinner organic pigments printed well onto absorbent paper and combined easily into various color mixtures. They also cost less than their mineral counterparts, and their sensitivity to light was not considered a problem when creating what were regarded during the Edo period as ephemera.

Harunobu drew our interest in investigating the palette of ukiyo-e artists, not only because he is closely associated with the development of full-color woodblock printing (*nishiki-e*), but also because *Spring Outing on the Banks of the Sumida River* is one of only three extant paintings known to be from his hand. From the front of the painting, the only organic pigment we could detect was indigo blue in the sashes and kimonos of some of the figures, and small touches of a transparent purple used for the violets on the bank. After we removed the lining papers from the back of the painting, however, we could see evidence of organic color that had faded from exposure to light from the front. At the center of the cherry blossoms are touches of pink (probably carmine or crimson lake, made with cochineal, an organic purple dyestuff derived from dried coccus cacti insects). The flowers on the banks also revealed touches of organic yellow and red visible from the back but not from the front. Although the small surface area of the colors in the flowers and their contamination with other age-degraded materials in the painting made it impossible to determine

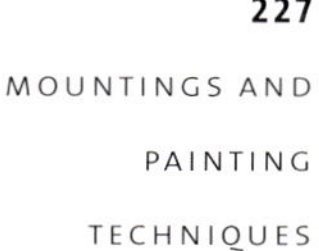

their composition with certainty, we could be sure that Harunobu had used a number of organic colors in his painted work.

Printing techniques adapted for paintings

Any ukiyo-e painter who also designed woodblock prints would have been aware of the materials and techniques of print production, even if publishers and printers produced the final products. Aside from Harunobu, Hokusai was another artist whose painted work reveals that he adapted printing techniques for use in the other medium. In the upper right of his *Li Bai Admiring a Waterfall* (see cat no. 66, fig. 28), for example, the rough texture of the rocky patch by the waterfall has been rendered with a monoprint technique: the artist repeatedly impressed the silk with a rectangular stamp dipped in black ink. At the bottom of the image, the spray from the waterfall is suggested by spattered white pigment, perhaps applied by rubbing a stiff brush over a wire mesh. In order to keep the bank and figures in front of the falls free of the spattered white color, Hokusai must have masked these areas, most likely with a cut-paper stencil. In printmaking, the technique of using stencils, known as *kappazuri*, dates back to at least the first half of the eighteenth century.

Keisai Eisen also used a spray and stencil technique for the kimono in his painting of a geisha (see cat. no. 58, fig. 29). The kimono was first painted a uniform white. This was then masked off with a stencil, probably cut from paper, to cover all other areas of the painting. Following this, the exposed area was scattered with chopped fibers about half an inch long, and sprayed or spattered with a fine mist of indigo color. When dry, the stencil and fibers were removed, leaving the traces of the fibers as a resist pattern in the sprayed indigo. Finally, Eisen completed the design of the kimono by adding painted plum blossoms around the hem of the garment.

There is still much technical research to be carried out in the field of ukiyo-e paintings and the history of their mounting. Treating scroll paintings provides us with a unique opportunity to examine these works in a manner not otherwise possible, and to learn more about their makers' sometimes unorthodox and experimental techniques. Future examination and treatment surely will add to our growing body of knowledge of the methods of ukiyo-e painters and the mounting of their works in the hanging scroll format.

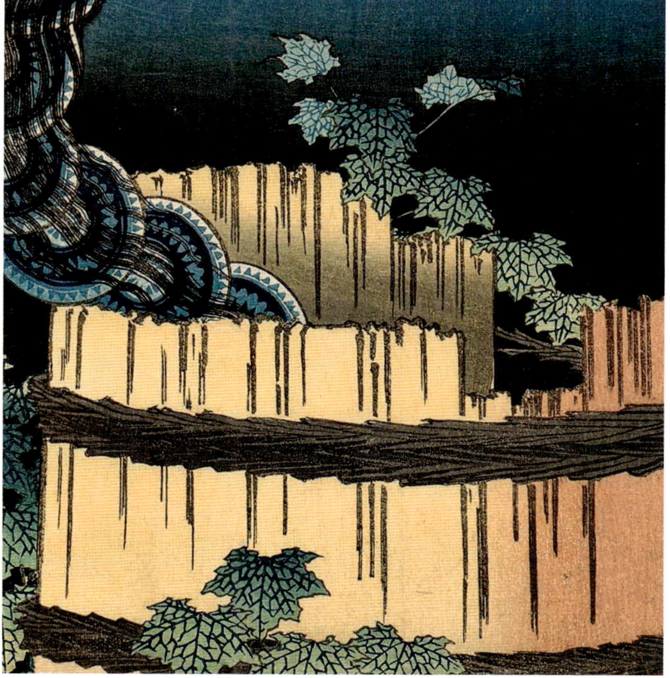

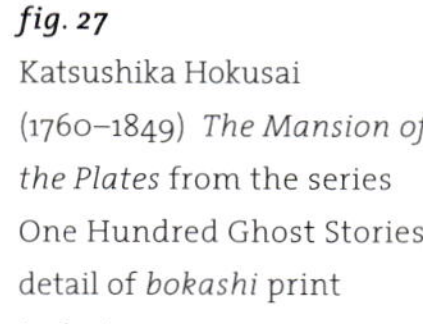

fig. 27
Katsushika Hokusai (1760–1849) *The Mansion of the Plates* from the series One Hundred Ghost Stories; detail of *bokashi* print technique

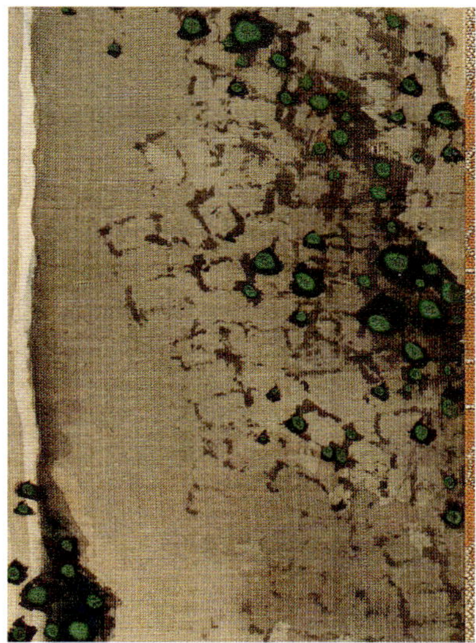

fig. 28
Katsushika Hokusai (1760–1849); *Li Bai Admiring a Waterfall* (Kaei 2) 1849; detail of stamping technique

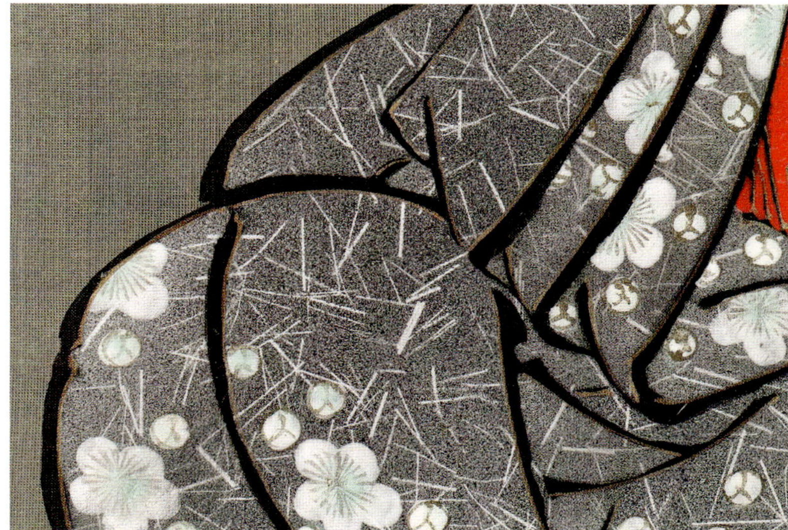

fig. 29
Keisai Eisen (1790–1848) *Geisha;* about Tenpō 3–5 (1832–34); detail of stencil and spray technique

GLOSSARY

ageya A seventeenth- and early eighteenth-century house of assignation where high-level courtesans met their clients.

bijin A "beautiful person." The term was adopted during the Meiji era to refer generically to attractive women and occasionally to young men.

bijinga Pictures that take *bijin* as their subjects.

chōnin "Townspeople." The merchant and craftsman classes in Edo-period Japan. In Edo itself they shaped the core of the city's culture, aesthetics, style, and attitudes.

chūban "Medium format." Prints that measure approximately 26 x 19 cm. This print size was favored by artists working from the mid-1760s to the mid-nineteenth century.

dōchū The stately procession of a high-level courtesan and her entourage from the brothel where she resided to the house of assignation (*ageya*).

Edokko "Child of Edo." Refers to those born and raised in Edo, particularly those who espouse Edo styles and attitudes. The appellation is still somewhat in use today for Tokyoites who can trace a lineage of family members born and raised in Tokyo for over three generations.

ehon Traditional Japanese-style book that includes pictures. Often used to refer specifically to books illustrated with woodblock prints.

furisode *Kosode* with long, pendant sleeves; generally worn by entertainers and young women who had not officially attained adulthood.

fūzokuga Genre painting; a term used since the Meiji era to refer to works of art that take the lives and customs of contemporary people as their subject.

haikai A poetic form of linked verse. The introductory verse follows a pattern of 5-7-5 syllables. It was originally called a *hokku* during the Edo period but is commonly called haiku today.

harimise The practice of displaying lower-ranking courtesans in latticed rooms so that they could be considered by prospective clients.

hashira-e "Pillar print." Woodblock print measuring between 69 and 75 cm in height by 12 to 17 cm in width.

hatamoto "Banner man." Direct samurai retainer to the shogun. Traditionally the shogun's chief commanders, men of this rank held similar positions of authority within the governmental hierarchy during the sustained peace of the Edo period.

hikitejaya A teahouse of the late eighteenth century and onward from which a patron could summon a high-level courtesan. From there she escorted him back to her quarters in the brothel.

hosoban "Narrow ." Woodblock print that generally measures 33 x 15 cm.

jōruri Chanting accompanied by samisen music that provides the text of puppet plays.

Kabuki Flamboyant dramatic form that began in 1603 with dance performances by Okuni and her female company on the banks of the Kamo River in Kyoto. In 1629 women were banned from the stage by the Tokugawa government. After 1652 youths were similarly prohibited from appearing.

Kano school Founded by Kano Masanobu in the early fifteenth century, a hereditary school of painters who enjoyed the status of official artists to the military aristocracy. Primarily known for compositions informed by Chinese Song-, Yuan-, and Ming-dynasty subjects and styles but tempered by the indigenous painting tradition. Three branches of the school were based in Edo and were widely influential in instructing aspiring artists, although they might eventually work in a variety of styles.

kibyōshi "Yellowback." Sophisticated, illustrated novels with yellow covers bound in the traditional Japanese manner. Particularly popular from the late eighteenth through the early nineteenth centuries.

kosode "Small sleeves." Precursor of the contemporary kimono; a robe worn by both men and women. Distinguished from the *ōsode* ("large sleeves") by the small opening for the wrists.

Kyōgen Comic theatrical form that provides interludes to the more staid No theater. It was highly influential in the development of Kabuki during the mid-seventeenth century.

mitate-e Parody pictures in which an earlier scene, usually one with a historical or legendary theme, is reenacted by contemporary figures.

nikuhitsuga A term created in the Meiji era for ukiyo-e painting in order to distinguish it from woodblock prints.

nishiki-e "Brocade picture." Full-color woodblock print that was first developed about 1764–65.

No A dramatic form that developed during the fourteenth century from popular religious festival entertainments into performances of almost mystical beauty. Its subject matter deals with the tragedies of historical and legendary figures. Plays are performed on a stark wooden stage by masked actors who follow stylized and controlled movements.

ōban "Large format." Woodblock print measuring 46 x 33 cm. or 39 x 27 cm.

oiran From the mid-eighteenth century onward, a term designating courtesans of the highest ranks.

samisen Also *shamisen*. Popular three-stringed instrument introduced to Japan in the mid-sixteenth century from the Ryūkyū Islands.

shunga "Spring picture." An erotic print or painting.

tayū A term used from the seventeenth through the mid-eighteenth centuries to designate courtesans of the highest rank.

tokonoma Recessed alcove in a traditional Japanese room with a raised floor, used for the display of hanging scrolls and small objects.

Tosa school. Founded by Tosa Mitsunobu in the fourteenth century, this hereditary school of professional artists traditionally provided the official painters to the imperial court. Known for compositions inspired by classical Japanese literature and informed by Heian-period (794–1185) painting styles.

uchikake. Unbelted outer robe worn over the *kosode* during the winter months. Often styled with a heavily padded hem beginning in the eighteenth century.

wakashu. Young, sexually attractive man, often wearing feminine attire.

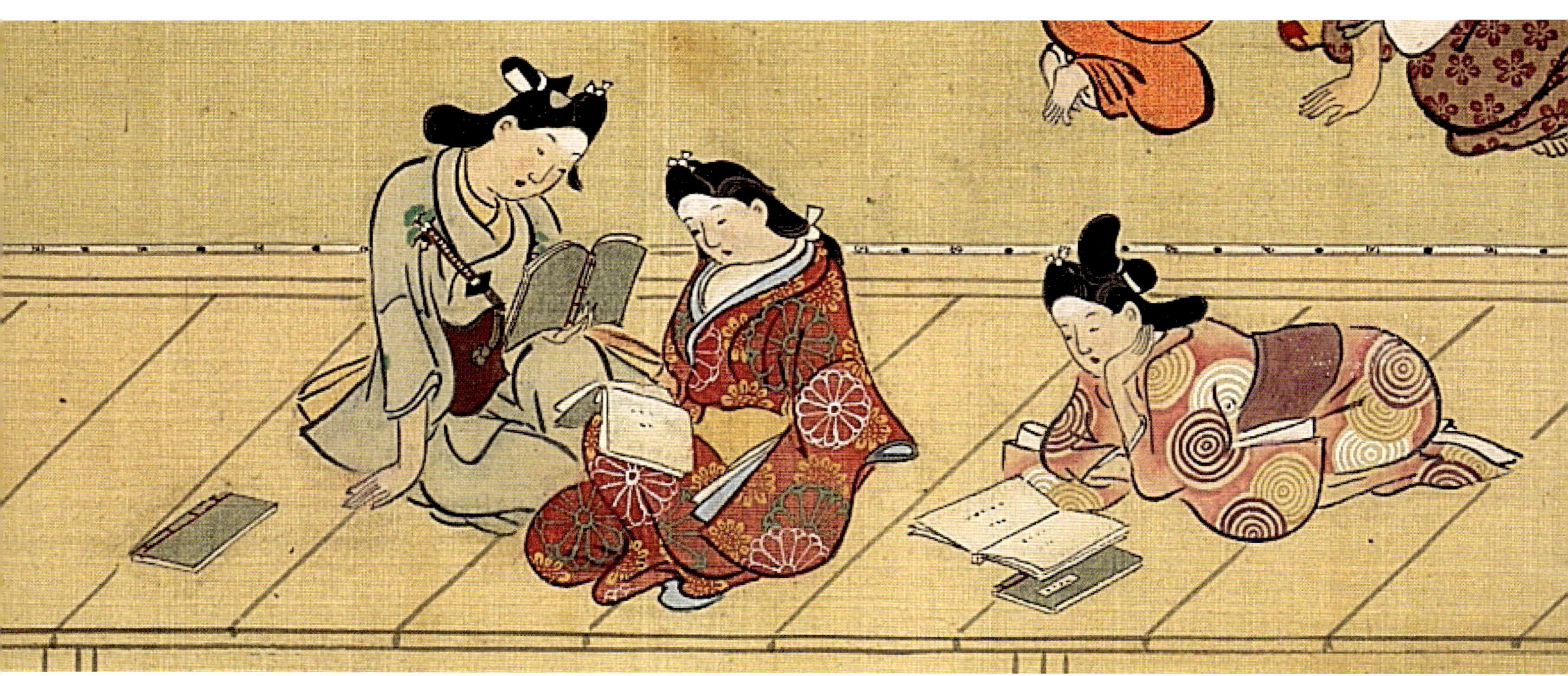

SUGGESTED READING (WESTERN LANGUAGES)

Asano Shūgō. "Concerning the Seals on Hokusai's Paintings." Translated by Timothy Clark in *Hokusai and His Age: Ukiyo-e Painting, Printmaking and Book Illustration in Late Edo Japan*, edited by John T. Carpenter, 105–133. Amsterdam: Hotei Publishing, 2005.

Asano Shūgō and Timothy Clark. *The Passionate Art of Kitagawa Utamaro*. 2. vols. Tokyo and London: Asahi Shimbun and the British Museum Press, 1995.

Avitabile, Gunhild. *Early Masters: Ukiyo-e Prints and Paintings from 1680 to 1750*. New York: Japan Society, 1992.

Brea, Luigi Bernabo, and Kondo Eiko. *Ukiyo-e Prints and Paintings from the Early Masters to Shunshō: Edoardo Chiossone Civic Museum of Oriental Art, Genoa.* Genoa: Sagep Editrice, 1980.

Calza, Gian Carlo, with the assistance of John T. Carpenter. *Hokusai's Paintings: Selected Essays*. Venice: International Hokusai Research Centre, University of Venice, 1994.

Carpenter, John T., ed. *Hokusai and His Age: Ukiyo-e Painting, Printmaking and Book Illustration in Late Edo Japan*. Amsterdam: Hotei Publishing, 2005.

Clark, Timothy. *Ukiyo-e Paintings in the British Museum*. London: British Museum Press, 1992.

———."Frilly Undergarments: Some Paintings by Hokusai's Pupils." In *Hokusai and His Age: Ukiyo-e Painting, Printmaking, and Book Illustration in Late Edo Japan*, edited by John T. Carpenter, 77–91. Amsterdam: Hotei Publishing, 2005.

———. "Prostitute as Bodhisattva: The Eguchi Theme in Ukiyo-e." *Impressions*, no. 22 (2000): 37–53.

Clark, Timothy, Anne Nishimura Morse, and Louise E. Virgin, with Allen Hockley. *The Dawn of the Floating World, 1650–1765: Early Ukiyo-e Treasures from the Museum of Fine Arts, Boston*. London: Royal Academy of Arts, 2001.

Fenollosa, Ernest Francisco. *Hokusai and His School, Special Exhibitions of the Pictorial Art of Japan and China*, no. 1. Boston: Museum of Fine Arts, Boston, 1893.

Galeries nationales du Grand Palais, Paris. *Images du Monde flottant*. Paris: Galeries nationales du Grand Palais, Paris, 2004.

Gerstle, C. Andrew. *18th Century Japan: Culture and Society*. Sydney, Australia: Allen & Unwin, 1989.

Gluckman, Dale Carolyn, and Sharon Sadako Takeda. *When Art Became Fashion: Kosode in Edo-Period Japan*. Los Angeles: Los Angeles County Museum of Art, 1992.

Hibbett, Howard. *The Chrysanthemum and the Fish: Japanese Humor since the Age of the Shoguns*. Tokyo, London, and New York: Kodansha International, 2002.

———. *The Floating World in Japanese Fiction*. Rutland, VT, and Tokyo: Charles E. Tuttle, 1975.

Hickman, Money L. "Hokusai and Hō-ō: The 'Phoenix Screen' in the Museum of Fine Arts, Boston." In *Hokusai's Paintings: Selected Essays*, edited by Gian Carlo Calza, with the assistance of John T. Carpenter, 217–35. Venice: International Hokusai Research Centre, University of Venice, 1994.

———."Views of the Floating World." *Bulletin of the Museum of Fine Arts, Boston*, no. 76 (1978): 4–33.

Hillier, Jack. *Catalogue of the Japanese Paintings and Prints in the Collection of Mr. and Mrs. Richard P. Gale*. 2 vols. London: Routledge & Kegan Paul, 1970.

———. *The Harari Collection of Japanese Paintings and Prints*. 3 vols. London: Lund Humphries, 1970–73.

———. *Hokusai: Paintings, Drawings, and Woodcuts*. London: Phaidon, 1955.

Hirano Chie. *Kiyonaga: A Study of His Life and Works*. 2 vols. Cambridge, MA: Harvard University Press, 1939.

Izzard, Sebastian. *The Floating World in the Eighteenth Century*. New York: Sebastian Izzard, 2006.

———. *Kunisada's World*. New York: Japan Society, in collaboration with the Ukiyo-e Society of America, 1993.

———. *Masterpieces of Ukiyo-e: Paintings from the Manno Art Museum*. New York: Sebastian Izzard, 2003.

Jenkins, Donald. *The Floating World Revisited*. Portland: Portland Art Museum and University of Hawai'i Press, 1993.

———. *Ukiyo-e Prints and Paintings: The Primitive Period, 1680–1745*. Chicago: Art Institute of Chicago, 1971.

Jones, Sumie. *Imaging/Reading Eros*. Bloomington: East Asian Studies Center, Indiana University, 1996.

Keyes, Roger. "The Dragon and the Goddess: Using Prints to Date, Identify, and Illuminate Hokusai's Early Paintings." In *Hokusai and His Age: Ukiyo-e Painting, Printmaking, and Book Illustration in Late Edo Japan*, edited by John T. Carpenter, 17–31. Amsterdam: Hotei Publishing, 2005.

Kobayashi Tadashi. "The Floating World in Light and Shadow: Ukiyo-e Paintings by Hokusai's Daughter Ōi." Translated and adapted by Julie Nelson Davis in *Hokusai and His Age: Ukiyo-e Painting, Printmaking, and Book Illustration in Late Edo Japan*, edited by John T. Carpenter, 93–103. Amsterdam: Hotei Publishing, 2005.

———. "The Rediscovery of the 'Tendō Hiroshiges.'" Translated by Henry Smith. *Impressions*, no. 22 (2000): 17–35.

Lane, Richard. "Appendix: In the Shadow of Hokusai: A Note on Sōri III." In *Hokusai's Paintings: Selected Essays*, edited by Gian Carlo Calza, with the assistance of John T. Carpenter, 59–65. Venice: International Hokusai Research Centre, University of Venice, 1994.

———. *Images of the Floating World*. Secaucus, NJ: Chartwell Books, 1978.

———. *Kaigetsudō*. Vol. 13 of the Kodansha Library of Japanese Art. Tokyo and Rutland, VT: Charles E. Tuttle, 1959.

Maruyama Nobuhiko. "Fashion and the Floating World: The Kosode in Art." In *When Art Became Fashion: Kosode in Edo-Period Japan*, edited by Dale Carolyn Gluckman and Sharon Sadako Takeda, 211–35. Los Angeles: Los Angeles County Museum of Art, 1992.

Narazaki Muneshige. *Masterworks of Ukiyo-e: Early Paintings*. Tokyo: Kodansha International, 1968.

Okamoto Hiromi. "Variations on the Theme of 'Two Courtesans': *Bijin* Paintings by Hokusai and His Pupils." Translated by John T. Carpenter in *Hokusai's Paintings: Selected Essays*, edited by Gian Carlo Calza, with the assistance of John T. Carpenter, 117–25. Venice: International Hokusai Research Centre, University of Venice, 1994.

Peabody-Essex Museum. *Geisha: Beyond the Painted Smile*. Salem, MA: Peabody-Essex Museum and George Braziller, 2004.

Screech, Timon. *Sex and the Floating World: Erotic Images in Japan, 1700–1820*. Honolulu: University of Hawai'i Press, 1999.

Seigle, Cecilia Segawa. *Yoshiwara: The Glittering World of the Japanese Courtesan*. Honolulu: University of Hawai'i Press, 1993.

Stern, Harold P. "Ukiyo-e Painting: Selected Problems." Ph.D. diss., University of Michigan, 1958.

———. *Ukiyo-e Painting*. Washington, DC: Smithsonian Institution, 1973.

Swinton, Elizabeth de Sabato. *The Women of the Pleasure Quarter: Japanese Paintings and Prints of the Floating World*. Worcester, MA: Worcester Art Museum, 1996.

Tsuji Nobuo. "Hokusai Studio Works and Problems of Attribution." Translated by John T. Carpenter in *Hokusai's Paintings: Selected Essays*, edited by Gian Carlo Calza with the assistance of John T. Carpenter. Venice: International Hokusai Research Centre, University of Venice, 1994.

Yonemura, Ann, ed. *Hokusai*. 2 vols. Washington, D.C.: Freer Gallery of Art and Arthur M. Sackler, Smithsonion Institution, 2006.

Young, Martie W., and Robert J. Smith. *Japanese Painters of the Floating World*. Ithaca, NY: Andrew Dickson White Museum of Art, Cornell University, 1966.

SUGGESTED READING (JAPANESE), FEATURING MFA PAINTINGS

Asahi shinbunsha: *Bosuton bijutsukan shozō nikuhitsu ukiyo-e ten* [The Allure of Edo: Ukiyo-e Painting from the Museum of Fine Arts, Boston]. Osaka: Asahi shinbunsha, 2006.

Asano Shūgō. "Katsushika Hokusai hitsu Shu Shōki zushi" [Shōki, the Demon Queller by Katsushika Hokusai]. *Kokka*, no. 1261 (December 2000): 38–40.

Chiba City Museum of Art. *Hishikawa Moronobu ten* [Exhibition of Hishikawa Moronobu]. Chiba: Chiba City Museum of Art, 2000.

Clark, Timothy. "Utagawa Toyokuni hitsu Yoshiwara Ōmon uchi oiran dōchū zu" [Entrance to the Yoshiwara Pleasure District by Utagawa Toyokuni]. *Kokka*, no. 1261 (December 2000): 35–36.

Kobayashi Tadashi. "Suzuki Harunobu no nikuhitsu" [The Ukiyo-e Paintings of Suzuki Harunobu]. *Kokka*, no. 1261 (December 2000): 24–30.

Morse, Anne Nishimura. "Uiriamu Sutaajisu Bigerō: Nihon aikoka ni shite Nihon shugisha" [William Sturgis Bigelow: Japanonist and Japanophile], In *Edo no yūwaku: Bosuton bijutsukan shozō nikuhitsu ukiyo-e ten* [The Allure of Edo: Ukiyo-e Painting from the Museum of Fine Arts, Boston]. Osaka: Asahi shinbunsha, 2006), 159–69.

———. "Miyagawa Chōshun hitsu Yoshiwara fūzoku byobū" [Scenes in the Yoshiwara Pleasure Quarter by Miyagawa Chōshun]. *Kokka*, no. 1261 (December 2000): 19–23.

Morse, Anne Nishimura, and Tsuji Nobuo. *Bosuton bijutsukan Nihon bijutsu chōsa zuroku: Dai niji chōsa Edo jidai Kano ha/Tosa Sumiyoshi fukko Yamato-e ha/nikuhitsu ukiyo-e/Soga Shōhaku Itō Jakuchū/Kindai* [Japanese Art in the Museum of Fine Arts, Boston: Edo Kano; Tosa, Sumiyoshi, and Yamato-e Revival; Ukiyo-e Painting; Soga Shōhaku, Itō Jakuchū; and Modern]. 2 vols. Tokyo: Museum of Fine Arts, Boston, and Kōdansha, 2003.

Naitō Masato. "Chōbunsai Eishi hitsu Mitate sansanzu" [Parody of the Three Vinegar Tasters by Chōbunsai Eishi]. *Kokka*, no. 1261 (December, 2000): 37–38.

———. "Katsuskawa Shunshō no nikuhitsu bijinga ni tsuite." [Paintings of Beautiful Women by Katsukawa Shunshō] *Bijutsushi*, no. 125 (March, 1989): 57–81.

———. *Ukiyo-e saihakken: daimyōtachi ga medeta ippin zeppin* [Rediscovery of Ukiyo-e: Masterpieces and Rarities Appreciated by the Daimyō]. Tokyo: Shōgakkan, 2005.

Nakamura Tanio. "Bosuton bijutsukan zō Bigerō-shi kizō no nikuhitsu ukiyo-e bijinga gun" [A Selection of Paintings of Beautiful Women in the William Sturgis Bigelow Collection at the Museum of Fine Arts, Boston]. *Kobijutsu* 66 (April 1983): 4–22.

Narazaki Muneshige, ed. *Nikuhitsu ukiyo-e*. [Ukiyo-e Paintings]. 10 vols. Tokyo: Shūeisha, 1980–82.

———. *Nikuhitsu ukiyo-e*. [Ukiyo-e Paintings] Vol. 3 of *Zaigai hihō* [Masterpieces Abroad]. Tokyo: Gakken, 1969.

———. *Nikuhitsu ukiyo-e I: Kanbun–Hōreki* [Ukiyo-e Painting I: Kanbun–Hōreki Eras], no. 248 Tokyo: Shibundō, 1987.

———. *Nikuhitsu ukiyo-e II: Meiwa–Kansei* [Ukiyo-e Painting II: Meiwa–Kansei Eras], no. 249. Tokyo: Shibundō, 1987.

———. *Nikuhitsu ukiyo-e III: Bunsei–Meiji* [Ukiyo-e Painting III: Bunsei–Meiji Eras], no. 250. Tokyo: Shibundō, 1987.

———. *Hizō ukiyo-e taikan* [Overview of Ukiyo-e Treasures], 13 vols. Tokyo: Kōdansha, 1987–90.

Nihon keizai shinbunsha. *Hokusai*. Tokyo: Nihon keizai shinbunsha, 2005.

Tokyo National Museum. *Bosuton bijutsukan shozō Nihon kaiga meihin ten* [Exhibition of Masterpieces of Japanese Painting in the Museum of Fine Arts, Boston]. Tokyo: Tokyo National Museum, 1983.

Tsuji Nobuo. "Shibaichō yūri zu byobū" [Scenes of the Nakamura Theater and the Yoshiwara Pleasure District]. *Kokka*, no. 1261 (December 2000): 31–33.

———. "Moronobu oyobi Hishikawa ha no henka gakan (Bosuton bijutsukan zō" [Fantastical Scenes by Moronobu and the Hishikawa School in the Museum of Fine Arts, Boston]. *Kokka*, no. 1280 (June 2002): 16–19.

———, ed. *Bosuton bijutsukan nikuhitsu ukiyo-e* [Ukiyo-e Painting in the Museum of Fine Arts, Boston]. 4 vols. Tokyo: Museum of Fine Arts, Boston, and Kōdansha, 2000.

LIST OF FIGURE ILLUSTRATIONS

fig. 14, page 42
HISHIKAWA MORONOBU (died 1694)
left: *Scenes from the Yoshiwara Pleasure Quarter* (detail from panel 4)
Jōkyō (1684–88) or Genroku (1688–1704) era
Six-panel folding screen;
ink, color, and gold on paper
139.8 x 355.2 cm (55 1/16 x 139 13/16 in.)
Gift of Oliver Peabody 79.469

right: *Scenes from the Yoshiwara Pleasure Quarter* (detail from panel 2)
Jōkyō (1684–88) or Genroku (1688–1704) era
Six-panel folding screen;
ink, color, and gold on paper
139.8 x 355.2 cm (55 1/16 x 139 13/16 in.)
Gift of Oliver Peabody 79.469

fig. 15, page 43
left: *Scenes from the Yoshiwara Pleasure Quarter* (detail from panels 5–6)
Jōkyō (1684–88) or Genroku (1688–1704) era
Six-panel folding screen;
ink, color, and gold on paper
139.8 x 355.2 cm (55 1/16 x 139 13/16 in.)
Gift of Oliver Peabody 79.469

right: *Scenes from the Yoshiwara Pleasure Quarter* (detail of panels 3–4)
Jōkyō (1684–88) or Genroku (1688–1704) era
Six-panel folding screen;
ink, color, and gold on paper
139.8 x 355.2 cm (55 1/16 x 139 13/16 in.)
Gift of Oliver Peabody 79.469

fig. 16, page 44
Scenes from the Yoshiwara Pleasure Quarter (detail of panel 6)
Jōkyō (1684–88) or Genroku (1688–1704) era
Six-panel folding screens;
ink, color, and gold on paper
139.8 x 355.2 cm (55 1/16 x 139 13/16 in.)
Gift of Oliver Peabody 79.469

fig. 17, page 44
MIYAGAWA CHŌSHUN (1682–1752?)
Scenes in the Yoshiwara Pleasure Quarter (detail of panel 5)
About Hōei (1704–11) to
Early Kyōhō (1716–36) eras
Six-panel folding screen;
ink, color, gold, and silver on paper
83.2 x 266.6 cm (32 3/4 x 104 15 1/6 in.)
Fenollosa-Weld Collection 11.4624

fig. 18, page 45
UTAGAWA TOYOKUNI (1769–1825)
Procession of Courtesans inside the Main Gate of the Yoshiwara (detail)
About Kansei 7 (1795)
Hanging scroll; ink, color, gold,
and mica on silk
46.1 x 69.1 cm (18 1/8 x 27 3/16 in.)
William Sturgis Bigelow Collection 11.7869

fig. 19, page 46
Scenes from the Yoshiwara Pleasure Quarter (detail of panel 2)
Jōkyō (1684–88) or Genroku (1688–1704) era
Six-panel folding screen;
ink, color, and gold on paper
Each 139.8 x 355.2 cm (55 1/16 x 139 13/16 in.)
Gift of Oliver Peabody 79.469

fig. 20, page 47
ISODA KORYŪSAI (active about 1766–1788)
Geisha and Male Prostitute
Meiwa (1764–72) or Early An'ei (1772–81) era
Pair of hanging scrolls;
ink, color, and gold on paper
Each 102.4 x 26.7 cm (40 5/16 x 10 1/2 in.)
William Sturgis Bigelow Collection
11.7547, 11.7555

fig. 21, page 49
KITAO SHIGEMASA (1739–1820)
The Tucking Up of Garments by Eastern Men (*Ehon Azuma karage*), vol. 1, 1797 edition
Woodblock-printed book; ink on paper
22.4 x 15.8 cm (8 13/16 x 6 1/4 in.) 2006.1340.1

fig. 22, page 101
NISHIKAWA SUKENOBU (1671–1750), ARTIST
Morita Shōtarō (dates unknown), PUBLISHER
Fujimura Zen'eimon (dates unknown), ENGRAVER
Murakami Gen'eimon, ENGRAVER
The Picture Book of Evergreens (Ehon tokiwagusa), vol. 2, 1731
Woodblock printed book; ink on paper
27.1 x 18.8 cm (10 11/16 x 7 3/8 in.)
Gift of Mrs. Jared K. Morse in memory of Charles J. Morse 2006.1343.2

FIGURE ILLUSTRATIONS FROM APPENDIX *MOUNTINGS AND PAINTING TECHNIQUES*

fig. 23, page 222

HISHIKAWA SŌRI (active about 1789–1818)
Courtesan
Kansei 10 (1798) to mid-Bunka era (1804–18)
Hanging scroll: ink, color and gold on silk
98.7 x 36 cm (38 7/8 x 14 3/16 in.)
William Sturgis Bigelow Collection 11.7444
before and after treatment

fig. 24, page 224

SUZUKI HARUNOBU (1725–1770)
Spring Outing on the Banks of the Sumida River
Meiwa era (1764–72)
Hanging scroll; ink, color, and gold on silk
32.7 x 54.5 cm (12 7/8 x 21 7/16 in.)
William Sturgis Bigelow Collection 11.7355
before and after treatment

fig. 25, page 225

KATSUSHIKA HOKUSAI (1760–1849)
Woman from Ohara Carrying Bundles of Firewood
Late Bunka (1804–18)
or early Bunsei (1818–30) era
Hanging scroll; ink and color on silk
92.8 x 33.7 cm (36 9/16 x 13 1/4 in.)
William Sturgis Bigelow Collection 11.7432
before and after treatment

fig. 26, page 226

KATSUSHIKA HOKUSAI (1760–1849)
Woman Looking at Herself in a Mirror
About Bunka 2 (1805)
Hanging scroll; ink, color, gold, and mica on silk
138.7 x 57.5 cm (54 5/8 x 22 5/8 in.)
William Sturgis Bigelow Collection 11.7424
front and back

fig. 27, page 227

KATSUSHIKA HOKUSAI (1760–1849), ARTIST
Tsuruya Kiemon (Senkakudō, dates unknown), PUBLISHER
The Mansion of the Plates (Sara yashiki)
from the series One Hundred Ghost Stories (Hyaku monogatari)
About Tenpō 2-3 (1831–2)
Woodblock print *(nishiki-e)*; ink and color on paper; Vertical *chūban*
William Sturgis Bigelow Collection 11.20441
example of *bokashi* print technique

fig. 28, page 227

KATSUSHIKA HOKUSAI (1760–1849)
Li Bai Admiring a Waterfall
Kaei 2 (1849)
Hanging scroll; ink and color on silk
93.4 x 30 cm (36 3/4 x 11 13/16 in.)
William Sturgis Bigelow Collection 11.7452
detail of stamping technique

fig. 29, page 227

KEISAI EISEN (1790–1848)
Geisha
About Tenpō 3–5 (1832–34)
Hanging scroll; ink, color, and gold on silk
103.7 x 41.2 cm (40 13/16 x 16 1/4 in.)
Fenollosa-Weld Collection 11.4662
detail of stencil and spray technique

endpapers, front and back

Map of Edo
Genroku 8 (1695)
Woodblock printed map; ink on paper with handcoloring
22.1 x 14.9 cm (8 11/16 x 5 7/8 in., folded)
Source unidentified 2006.1342

INDEX